A Gorgon's Mask

Psychoanalysis and Culture

12

A Gorgon's Mask

The Mother in Thomas Mann's Fiction

Lewis A. Lawson

Amsterdam - New York, NY 2005

PT 2625
.A44
Z 73297
2005x

0 59008437

The paper on which this book is printed meets the requirements of "ISO 9706:1994, Information and documentation - Paper for documents - Requirements for permanence".

ISBN: 90-420-1745-7
©Editions Rodopi B.V., Amsterdam – New York, NY 2005
Printed in The Netherlands

Table of Contents

Acknowledgements

Throughout the years the years spent on this project, I was buoyed, as always, by the love of my wife Barbara, our son John, and our daughter Rachel, her husband Don, their son Pat. My writing style has been considerably improved by the timely arrival of Pat, whose recent Lego constructions have taught me a thing or two about putting things together and taking them apart. My colleague Roberta Maguire sacrificed hours that she did not have to spare from her own work to be the only reader of this project-in-gestation. My colleague Charles Caramello, Chair of the Department of English, University of Maryland, College Park, generously contributed to its prenatal care. My colleague Shawn Saremi was essential to its delivery.

Permission to reprint Thomas Mann's sketch *"Mvtter Natvr"* has been very kindly granted by Dr. Brigitte Weyl, for Verlagswerte GmbH, Kreuzlingen/TG, Switzerland. The sketch originally appeared in Viktor Mann's *Wir waren Fünf,* © Südverlag GmbH, Konstanz, Germany, 1949.

I

Introduction

This study proposes that the infant Thomas Mann experienced such frustration, both physiological and psychological, at the breast that he became ridden with anxiety about his mother's love.[1] Thus was born the experience that developed into his lifelong experience of *Sehnsucht,* 'inconsolable yearning'.[2] This fundamental sense of alienation was repressed into Mann's unconscious, so that he experienced infantile amnesia regarding his thwarted instincts of nutrition and of sexuality and his thwarted need for maternal love. There is evidence that although his alienation was repressed from consciousness it manifested itself in his earliest attempts at imaginative creation. Such attempts would necessarily involve symbolization, for, according to D. W. Winnicott, the first symbol the infant creates is the hallucination of the lost breast.[3] Thus Mann's fiction throughout his career reflected his ambivalence about the lost breast. At the age of twenty Mann experienced "the return of the repressed", an outbreak of his infantile frustration now accompanied by psychoneurotic symptoms. The clamorous images escaping from his unconscious stimulated him to create "Little Herr Friedemann" (1897). To defend himself from the image of the mother still so enticing that it threatened to drive every other thought out of his mind, he expelled her into his story displaying her physical beauty for all to see, but he endowed her with a spiritual ugliness that would be apparent to those who could see beneath the surface. At the same time, he candidly included himself in his story as a deformed young man driven to self-destruction by the beautiful but malignant figure. With justification T. J. Reed terms "Friedemann" and Mann's other early stories as "grotesque", translating Mann's own definition: "The grotesque is properly something more than the truth[...], something real in the extreme[...] , not something arbitrary, false, absurd, and contrary to reality" (1996: 33-36).[4]

After "Herr Friedemann", Mann's fiction progressively reveals a process which culminates with the inner Gargoyle nature of the still beautiful mother figure becoming bounteous and the deformed inner nature of the son fiigure becoming supremely attractive to women. The process culminates in *The Confessions of Felix Krull: Confidence Man*, published, with the appendage "The Early Years", in 1954. In it the mother figure, Diane Houpflé, invites the son figure into her bed, in which he is so virile that she likens him to the mythological Hermes, who in his earliest representation was "a vegetation-god fertilizing mother earth" (Rank 1932: 342). At the end, though, the mother figure reappears as Maria Pia da Cruz-Kuckuck, who apparently invites the son figure into her bed but in reality invites him to join the shades. An empiric could see a connection between its publication and Mann's death the next year—it was the end of the story. Such a process of the transformation of a fearsome object into a benevolent object Annie Reich describes in "The Structure of the Grotesque-Comic Sublimation" (1973: 99-120).[5] But while the sublimation of his mother problem enabled Mann to draw upon his sexual energy for artistic creativity, it insured that throughout his career he would incorporate the by-products of the mother problem— day-dreams of returning to the original connection with mother, of homoerotic and incestuous behavior, and of royal/exceptional birth— in his fiction.

Paul Thomas Mann was born in Lübeck on 6 June 1875, the second child of Thomas Johann Heinrich Mann and Julia da Silva Bruhns—a son, Luiz Heinrich, had been born four years earlier. There would be three more siblings, two sisters and a brother. To date, English-language biographers of Thomas Mann (N. Hamilton [1979], Winston [1981], Hayman [1995], Prater [1995], and Heilbut [1996]) have had very little to say about his infancy. The first four biographers accept, either explicitly or implicitly, Mann's statements that "[m]y childhood was sheltered and happy" (qtd. in Winston 1981: 13) and that "[o]f the five children, it was I, I think, who was closest to my mother" (qtd. in N. Hamilton 1979: 23). Heilbut includes the first quotation above (1996: 14) and an even stronger version of the second—"I, her second child, was dearest to her heart'"(qtd. in 1996: 10).

Opening his discussion of infantile sexuality, Freud observes:

> writers who concern themselves with explaining the characteristics and reactions of the adult have devoted much more attention to the primaeval period which is comprised in the life of

the individual's ancestors—have, that is, ascribed much more influence to heredity—than to the other primaeval period, which falls within the lifetime of the individual himself—that is, to childhood. (*Three* 173).

The five biographers cited above are described by Freud's generalization: following traditional methods of research, they rely upon testimony written or spoken. Since no one left testimony describing Mann's frustration at the breast—including Mann himself, under the seal of infantile amnesia—the biographers emphasize Mann's ancestry, mention of his infancy only his recollection that he was early told that he was born under a favorable "planetary aspect", with a horoscope promising him "a long and happy life and a gentle death" (qtd. in Winston 1981: 12-13). Mann's frustration at the breast must, therefore, be inferred from his childhood physical behavior (in psychoanalytic parlance, "acting-out") observed and related by himself or others and from the fictional world that he created in response to the imperatives of his unconscious. The reconstruction of Mann's frustration at the breast will be deferred at this point, to be dealt with in discussions of his fiction from "A Vision" to *The Confessions of Felix Krull*, for their fictional world contains the breast scene as Mann's unconscious wanted it presented. What will be considered here is aspects of Mann's childhood and adolescent behavior that, it can be argued, reveal Mann's unconscious reaction to the source of his first frustration. These vivid fictional constructs reveal the vicissitudes that would necessarily characterize such a painful experience over time.

In the welter of Mann's memories of his early life can be discerned those in which his unconscious had attempted to communicate to him, even though his recall of them indicates no awareness of their special significance. Perhaps the earliest experience that he remembered was that of his rocking-horse. While he must have been two, maybe even three years old before he could mount his rocking-horse, still his experience of it would have awakened the earlier experience of being rocked to sleep, an experience almost inseparable from that of satiation at the breast, and, in Freud's judgment, another early source of sexual excitement (*Three* 201-202). In Nigel Hamilton's words:

> The old stuffed rocking-horse, with saddle and stirrups, glass eyes and pony fur, was given to little Thomas. He threw his arms about its neck, christened it Achilles, and loved it "not as a

> knight his horse, but out of sympathy for the creature, its furry
> coat, its hooves and nostrils"[...]. It was the Trojan horse of later
> Homer reading, a tangible image for distant myths of Greece and
> beyond. (qtd. in 1979: 20)

This memory, as Nigel Hamilton sees it, may indicate the early origin
of Mann's fascination for myth, but rather than associating the mythic
Achilles with his adult military experiences, why not associate him
with his baby experiences as the lucky child, the survivor whose
mother Thetis, a sea goddess, had thrown each of her seven earlier
newborns into the fire (Rose 1959: 26)?

The furriness of the rocking-horse must also be caressed for
meaning. In *The Skin Ego* the French psychoanalyst and dermatologist
Didier Anzieu, accepting the theory that the infant mentality creates
fantasy (Freud's "primary process") before developing the capacity to
think (Freud's "secondary process"), acknowledges that the impetus for
his study was provided by a myth:

> a myth develops by means of a double process of encoding—of
> external reality on the one hand (botanical, cosmological,
> socio-political, toponymic, religious, etc.) and inner psychical
> reality on the other. In that process, inner psychical reality is
> brought into correspondence with the encoded elements of
> external reality. In my view, the myth of Marsyas is an encoding
> of the particular psychical reality I call the Skin Ego. (1989: 47)[6]

Surely one of the first fantasies is that of the skin ego, in
which the infant hallucinates that he and his mother are inseparable
within the same skin (Kirshner 1990: 543).[7] When, however, the
infant loses the breast and begins to notice that his needs for psychic
interaction, nutrition, and cleanliness are not immediately met, he
experiences separation, which gives rise to the fantasy that his skin
ego is shredded. In response to the new experience of alienation, he
has a choice, to grow a tough skin that will protect him (Anzieu's
"narcissistic variant") or to accept a future in which his thin skin will
always get bruised, scratched, rended, flayed, castrated (Anzieu's
"masochistic variant"). According to Anzieu, "phantasies, dreams, everyday
speech, posture and disturbances of thought" will betray the variant response
that an individual has chosen (1989: 4). The "sympathy for the creature, its
furry coat, its hooves and nostrils" that Mann felt must have resulted from
his identification with it. When Mann remembers that he had
christened the rocking-horse "Achilles"—probably his first literary
creation—he must have felt at once that the creature Achilles, like

himself, had a vulnerable skin, a defect caused by its mother. That Mann later pictured himself as having chosen the "masochistic variant" of the skin fantasy is confirmed by Anzieu:

> In masochistic phantasy, fur ([as in] Sacher-Masoch's *Venus in Furs* [a novel which describes the author's obsession for sexual activity accompanied by beatings and whippings with studded quirts]) represents figuratively the return of a contact of skin with skin—velvety, voluptuous and odorous (nothing smells so strongly as a new fur)--and to that physical embrace which is one of the attendant pleasures of genital *jouissance*. That Sacher-Masoch's flagellating Venus, in life as in the novel, is naked beneath a fur confirms the primary value of the fur-skin as an object of attachment before it acquires a value as denotative of the sexual object. (1989: 42)

Little Thomas's attachment to the fur reveals his desire to be reattached to his mother under a common skin. The etymology of *fur, 'a sheath or lining'*, reinforces Anzieu's interpretation of the fur fantasy. Thus, while the young Thomas Mann projected a tough-skinned, narcissistic impassivity (a "reaction formation" in psychoanalytic parlance), his early unconscious behavior and later his fiction reveal that he thought of himself as thin-skinned.

Several of the biographers mentioned above cite Mann's memories of his mother's reading to and singing and playing the piano for her children. Especially vivid was Mann's recollection that his mother read from her own childhood book of classical mythology:

> A specially sharp impression was made on me by the "sickle which cut as sharply as a diamond" and was wielded by Zeus in the battle against Typhon. I kept repeating this passage to myself. And I was as much at home outside Troy, on Ithaca and on Olympus as my young contemporaries were in the land of the leatherstockings. And what I absorbed so greedily, I also performed. I hopped through the room as Hermes with paper shoes that were wings. As Helios I balanced a shiny gold helmet of rays on my head. As Achilles I inexorably pursued my sister, who for better or worse was standing in for Hector, three times around the walls of Troy. (qtd. in Hayman 1990: 90)

Notice that the narrator speaks of his thin-skinned "paper shoes" to distinguish himself from his thick-skinned "contemporaries[...] in the land of the leatherstockings". If the child Thomas feared that he would not get out of his predicament with a whole skin, then surely the word *sickle* would activate his "Marsyas complex", a term coined by Anzieu, recalling the silenus who was flayed by Apollo. Moreover, the sentence containing *"sickle"*—emphasized by a pun, an "especially sharp impression", and by Mann's admission that he employed ritual repetition to defend himself—should remind us of Freud's observation that in "the phase of the Oedipus complex" a boy in love with his mother fears that he will be castrated by his father (*New* 86). After all, Zeus would make a mighty potent father figure. Then Mann tells us that he was stirred to various physical activities—hopping, balancing, pursuing— which, we may infer, were prompted by the need to prove to himself that he had the agility to escape the paternal sickle. All of the activities consititute exhibitionism, about which Freud comments, "The compulsion to exhibit[...]is[...]closely dependent upon the castration complex: it is a means of constantly insisting upon the integrity of the subject's own (male) genitals[...]" (*Three* 157fn2; parenthesis in orig.).

By the time he was eight years old Thomas Mann, with his sexual drive now in latency, eagerly looked forward to the family's one month summer vacation at Travemünde, a seaside resort not far from Lübeck. As an adult he recalled his delight at the daily afternoon band concert at the pavilion: "I crouched on the steps in the summery scent of the beech tree, insatiably sucking music—my first orchestral music—into my soul" (qtd. in Hayman 1995: 94). Thus he associates the receiving of music with the receiving of the breast. Then he continues more generally, describing "the holiday paradise, where I have indubitably spent the happiest days of my life, the days and weeks of deep satisfaction—of wishing for nothing at all— were not surpassed or pushed into oblivion by anything in my later life" (qtd. in Hayman 1995: 94). What he describes here is the bliss resulting from nursing satiation, the forerunner of what Freud, in *Civilization and its Discontents*, called the "oceanic feeling" (59), an ecstatic conviction that no barrier exists between self and universe.[8]

Out of Mann's experience as a spectator at his mother's readings and recitals came his early fascination with a puppet theater: like many another artistically inclined person he soon realized that the theater with which he played could be used to represent the theater of his mind. As early as his fourteenth year Thomas Mann committed himself to a literary career; he began to write and present plays for his parents and aunts, using his sisters as his fellow performers.[9] In his first extant letter, 14 October 1889, to his one-time nanny, he quoted from one of his plays, *Aischa,* signing his name "Th. Mann. Lyric-dramatist" (N. Hamilton 1979: 34).[10] After Christmas that year he wrote the nanny, Frieda Hartenstein, of a cherished gift, "Schiller's works" (Winston 1971: 4). He was especially taken with Schiller's play *Don*

Carlos, later recalling, "how shall I ever forget the first passion for language kindled in me by its glorious verse when I was a boy of fifteen?" ("On Schiller" 28). Schiller's dramas apparently inspired several early plays, which he later described as "stupid little pieces, one I remember with the title 'You Can't Poison Me!'" (qtd. in Prater 1995: 5). This title can be subjected to Freud's scrutiny: "[t]he fear of being poisoned is also probably connected with the withdrawal of the breast. Poison is nourishment that makes one ill. Perhaps children trace back their early illnesses too to this frustration" (*New* 122). Mann's recollection of the plot of "You Can't Poison Me"—"a crafty inn-keeper perhaps, who plans to poison and rob his guest, a young knight, but he is hindered by his otherwise compliant daughter, who loves the knight, etc" (*On Myself* 28)--supports an Oedipal interpretation.[11]

At about the same time he began to experience puberty, in which his reawakening sexual excitement focused upon a male classmate, Armin Martens, as its object.[12] With the conception of Hermes as the dancer already in his mind, Mann must have idealized the real when he saw Armin in a dancing class they both attended. His infatuation lasted two years (Heilbut 1996: 15), but must have been dashed abruptly when he tried to express it to an unprepared Armin (Feuerlicht 1982: 89). When he wrote "Tonio Kröger" in 1903, Mann recreated his infatuation for Armin in fourteen-year-old Tonio's love for his classmate Hans Hansen.

Mann's turn toward homoeroticism was necessarily connected with his repressed realization that his reawakening desire for his mother was futile. If he could not celebrate his attainment of the object, he could certainly celebrate his loss. When he was fourteen Mann discovered that the Lübeck opera house held both the fantasy of the restored breast and the hopeless longing that laments the breast's absence. It offered, first of all, music—that medium that he had long equated with mother's milk. The very edifice itself contributed to his experience:

> My passion for the Wagnerian enchantment began with me so soon as I knew of it, and began to make it my own and penetrate it with my understanding. All that I owe to him, of enjoyment and instruction, I can never forget: the hours of deep and single bliss in the midst of the theatre crowds, hours of nervous and intellectual transport and rapture, of insights of great and moving import such as only this art vouchsafes. My zeal is never weary, I am never satiated, with watching, listening, admiring[...]. (" Sufferings" 314)

Although he stresses that listening to music is a "deep and single bliss", yet he acknowledges his placement "in the midst of the theatre crowds" and describes the experience in terms that would well describe the oceanic feeling.

On 13 October 1891, at the age of fifty-one, Thomas Mann's father died. Because of the stipulations of his will Frau Mann was forced to move into a smaller house with her children. Twenty-year-old Heinrich returned to Berlin, where he was working. Even though the new house would have accommodated four children, sixteen-year-old Thomas was sent to live in a boarding house maintained by Dr. Hupe, a school master (Hayman 1995: 101). In March 1893, Mann's forty-one-year-old mother, taking her three younger children, left Lübeck to establish a new life in Munich. Thomas was left to board for his final school year, first with Dr. Hupe, then with Professor Timpe. Cut off from his mother, Mann there experienced an infatuation for the son of the house, Willri, to be memorialized in *The Magic Mountain* as Hans Castorp's schoolboy crush on Pribislav Hippe (Heilbut 1996: 56). Mann's mother had him move yet again, to the boarding house of a Herr Hempel (Hayman 1995: 101). No reason for Mother Mann's decision is known, but it may be inferred that the move was necessary because of Mann's infatuation. Prater concludes that there was "less heartache" in Mann's second infatuation (1995: 15), but it may have been sufficient to inspire Mann to sense its infantile origins. Thus it may have created the mood out of which grew his first published prose.

"A Vision"

In May 1893 Mann and some of his classmates founded *Frühlingssturm*, a monthly publication for art, literature, and philosophy. In the June/July issue there appeared "A Vision", written by Mann under the pseudonym "Paul Thomas". While several years had elapsed between Mann's efforts at drama and "A Vision", there is a direct thematic link. Since this work is not widely available in translation, it is presented here in its entirety:

> As I MECHANICALLY ROLL another cigarette and the speckles of brown dust tumble onto the yellow-white blotting paper of my writing folder, I find it hard to believe that I am still awake. And as the warm damp evening air, flowing in through the open window beside me, shapes the clouds of smoke so strangely,

wafting them out of the light of the green-shaded lamp into matte black darkness, I am convinced I am dreaming.

How wild it is! My notion is snapping its reins on fantasy's back. Behind me the chair-back creaks, secretly nattering, sending a sudden shudder through all my nerve ends. It annoys me and disturbs my deep study of the bizarre shapes of smoke drifting around me, through which I had already resolved to draw a connecting thread.

Now the silence has gone to the dogs. Jangling movement flows through all my senses. Feverish, nervous, crazed. Every sound a stab! And tangled up in all this, forgotten things rise up. Things long ago imprinted on my sense of sight now strangely renew themselves, along with their old forgotten feelings.

With interest I notice that my awareness expands hungrily, embracing that area in the darkness in which the bright forms of smoke stand out with increasing clarity. I notice how my glance engulfs these things, only imaginings, yet full of bliss. And my sight takes in more and more, it lets itself go more and more, creates more and more, conjures more and more, more...and...more.

Now the creation, the artwork of chance, emerges, clear, just like in the past, looming from things forgotten, re-created, formed, painted by fantasy, that magically talented artist.

Not large: small. And not really a whole, but perfect, as it had been back then. And yet infinitely blurring into darkness in all directions. A world. A universe. In it light trembles, and a powerful mood, but no sound. Nothing of the laughing noises around it can penetrate: the laughing noises not of now, but of then.

Right at the base, dazzling damask. Across it, woven flowers zigzag and curve and wind. Translucently pressed upon it and rising up slender a crystalline goblet, half-filled with pallid gold. Before it, dreaming, a hand stretches out, the fingers draped loosely around the goblet's base. Clinging to one finger is a matte silver ring upon which a ruby bleeds.

Where the vision strives to form an arm above the delicate wrist, in a crescendo of shapes, it blurs into the whole. A sweet enigma. The girl's hand lies dreamy and still. Only where a light-blue vein snakes its way over its pearly whiteness does life pulse and passion pound, slowly and violently. And as it feels my glance it becomes swifter and swifter, wilder and wilder, till it turns into a pleading flutter: stop, don't...

But my glance is heavy and cruelly sensual, as it was then. It weighs upon the quaking hand in which, in the fight with love, love's victory pulsates...like then...like then.

Slowly, from the bottom of the goblet, a pearl detaches itself and floats upward. As it moves into the ruby's orbit of light it flames up blood red, and then on the surface is suddenly

> quenched. The disturbance threatens to dissipate everything, and
> my eyes struggle to rekindle the vision's soft contours.
>   Now it is gone, faded into darkness. I breathe, breathe
> deeply, for I notice that I had forgotten now, as I had back
> then... I lean back, fatigued, and pain flares up. But I know now
> as surely as I did then: You *did* love me... Which is why I can
> cry now. ("A Vision" 23-27; ellipses, cap., and ital. in orig.)

Five of Mann's recent biographers mention "A Vision".
Winston notes that the sketch is dedicated to Hermann Bahr, who
"formulated and exemplified the ideals of literary Impressionism" (1981: 48), but
rather dismisses the sketch itself: "[t]he parts are superior to the whole; there
are phrases and bits of observation that would do credit to any mature writer. The
tone is that of a school exercise by an unusually gifted pupil". Winston, having
given a ten-line paraphrase of the sketch, is pained by the phrase "pain
twitches" (his translation of the phrase rendered above as "pain flares up"):
"Even two or three years later Thomas Mann would not have permitted himself that
kind of false note. Now, however, he capped it by the banality of his ending: 'But I
know it now as surely as I did then: You loved me after all... And that is why I can
weep now'" (1981: 47). Prater characterizes the sketch as written "in true
fin de siècle style" (1995: 10). Hayman also notes that the sketch is
dedicated to Bahr, "who, in 1891, had published *Die Überwindung des
Naturalismus (The Defeat of Naturalism),* an essay calling for Naturalism to
be replaced by a 'Literatur der Nerven'". The latter phrase leads into
Hayman's judgment: "The narrative ends in lame sentimentality [...]" (1995:
102). Heilbut, risking a charge of reading under the influence, pans "A
Vision", dismissing it as "a facile sketch about the joys of smoking" (1996:
58), in which "the moderately stoned smoker hallucinates a girl's disembodied
hand arranging one perfect red flower—shades of Dorothy Parker—in an exquisite
vase" (1996: 67). Kurzke declares that "A Vision"

> concerns the sadistic conquest of a lover, basically a rape fantasy.
> The narrating first person imagines himself in the role of one who
> coldly observes the budding desire of his female opposite, her
> throbbing and beseeching convulsive movements, and
> simultaneously satisfies her and kills her with a look[...]. Now,
> we must not assume that Thomas Mann did such a thing to a
> woman. It is much more plausible to see him in the role of the
> woman. The sketch then becomes an expression of his fear of
> being raped. (2002: 47)

"A Vision" lends itself to a psychoanalytic reading, using
Bertram D. Lewin's formulation of the "dream screen".[13] Basing his
formulation on dreams reported by his patients in therapy, Lewin

believes that when the infant at breast nurses to satiation, he drops off to sleep with his last visual impression being the breast. Since he is so physically close to it, the breast appears flat, covering his entire visual field. In sleep the infant retains his vision of the breast, dreams of a blank screen, as if he were a moviegoer watching the movie screen before any film images are projected on it. "Notably the screen equivalent in such dreams is of badly defined thickness and consistency; it is thick or fluid, dark or whitish or milky, out of focus[...]" (Lewin 1953: 183). As he ages, the infant, though he retains his visualization of the blank screen when he goes to sleep, is not satiated, so that he begins to hallucinate, to have dreams of manifest content that are superimposed on the blank screen. (Ironically, in "A Vision" the manifest content of the dream projected onto the breast/dream screen is a symbolic representation of the lost breast.) Although many people do not recall the dream screen when they report the manifest content of a dream, some do awaken with the experience of seeing the dream screen—from which the manifest dream has already faded—receding, losing its flat appearance, assuming a smaller, curved shape surrounded by a vacant field. Clinical experience confirms that dreamers with deep oral fixations are more likely to report seeing the dream screen. Rycroft adds: "Dreams showing the dream screen are likely to occur when patients with narcissistic fixations are attempting to re-establish emotional contact with the external world" (1951: 183).

The reference to "the warm damp evening air" suggests that Mann was inspired to write the sketch in March, very soon after his mother left him alone in Lübeck. As he rolls a cigarette, the narrator drowsily experiences a regressive state, in which touch and taste sense modes once again assume the predominance they had in infancy. As he fingers the cigarette paper that contains the "fixin's", then licks the edge of the cigarette paper to seal it, he imagines other cylinders that his fingers have grasped or would like to grasp and that his tongue has touched or would like to touch. (Since "the speckles of brown dust tumble onto the yellow-white blotting paper of [his] writing folder", the narrator is confessing that cigarette "speckles" and "pencil shavings" [the latter in *The Magic Mountain*], both associated with cylindrical objects, will always fall upon his writing. Indeed, "find[ing] it hard to believe that [he is] still awake" indicates that he dimly understands that "the yellow-white blotting paper" is the externalization of his "dream screen" on which he will project the manifest content of his dream.) As the narrator inhales, then exhales the tobacco smoke, it begins to spread over the "matte

black darkness" (recall Lewin's description of the texture and hue of the
dream screen), "convinc[ing him that he is] dreaming".

In the second paragraph the narrator reveals that he is .
descending into primary process thinking.[14] Although the creaking of
his chair "annoys [him] and disturbs [his] deep study of the bizarre shapes of
smoke", he resolves "to draw a connecting thread" through them. The entire
sketch is to be, in other words, an account of consciously organizing
the material that rises from the unconscious during creative regression.

In the third paragraph, the narrator blames the external noise
for his increasing tension. But, even as he says this, he implies that
tension caused by an internal source might be causing him to
exaggerate the volume of the noise, for he confesses that he is
experiencing what Freud would call "the return of the repressed": "And
tangled up in all this forgotten things rise up. Things long ago imprinted on my sense
of sight now strangely renew themselves, along with their old forgotten feelings".

In the fourth paragraph, as the narrator sees an object fade in
on the dream screen, he "hungrily" anticipates gustatory "bliss": "And my
sight takes in more and more, it lets itself go more and more, creates more and more,
conjures more and more, more...and...more". The salivating frenzy conveyed
by the previous sentence is explained by Freud's comment: "the child's
avidity for its earliest nourishment is altogether insatiable, [so] that it never gets over
the pain of losing the mother's breast" (*New* 122).

In paragraphs five and six the dream of manifest content,
inspired by past frustration, begins to be superimposed on the dream
screen. The narrator has the intimation that he views "[a] world. A
universe", anticipating Joyce McDougall's concept of the "breast
universe—food, warmth, tenderness, liveliness, and so on" (1985: 184).[15]

In paragraphs seven and eight the dream of manifest content
fully appears on the dream screen, which resembles a table cloth, then,
with a shift of perspective, perhaps a pillow case. "Translucently pressed
upon it and rising up slender a crystalline goblet, half-filled with pallid gold". This
goblet, the manifest dream content, must be examined closely: "Freud
(1933) called the manifest dream a 'compromise formation,' by which he meant that
its various elements could be thought of as compromises between the opposing forces
of the latent dream content, on the one hand, and those of the defenses of the ego, on
the other" (Brenner 1974: 162). The latent dream content is an
unconscious wish for the breast, but the defense of the ego, repression,
refuses to allow that wish to be nakedly visualized. Hence the dream
work provides the manifest dream a symbol: the goblet represents the
breast in that it, too, has the essential function of dispensing a
delicious, nourishing fluid. Thus the fingers that are "draped loosely

around the goblet's base" are the maternal fingers that support the breast during nursing.

In paragraph eight, since the dream scene dates from early infancy, it presents a part-object (Brenner 1974: 100), the breast supported by the hand. Having "pulse and passion", the hand has sentience, becoming aware of the dreamer's/infant's importunity, then pleading, "stop, don't...." It is possible to interpret the manifest dream as being a scene between a timid girl and her ardent lover, but it is more likely the earlier scene between a mother—reluctant for whatever reason—and her demanding nursling. In paragraph nine, the dreamer implies that he is aware that the present scene represents the original, nursing scene. He also implies that he is aware that his infantile desire for the breast was driven by both hunger and sexual excitement—a combined desire that Felix Krull explicitly remembers (*Confessions* 46).

In paragraph ten, a pearl, actually a bubble of air, rises to the surface, jarred loose by the "glance"? Is it the memory of the original scene reaching the surface of consciousness? If so, its very eruption would cause its disappearance, despite the dreaming narrator's effort "to rekindle the vision's soft contours" of the breast.

In paragraph eleven, the narrator is aware that he has lost both the manifest dream and the dream screen.

In paragraph twelve, he experiences the original scene, when as an infant he had lain back in fatigue, not in victorious satiation but in defeated pain, a pain of hunger now exacerbated by the pain of loss. But he asserts his conviction that he *had been* loved by his mother even though she had taken her breast away. With that conviction he can bear to mourn his loss. Rycroft's comment above should be recalled: "Dreams showing the dream screen are likely to occur when patients with narcissistic fixations are attempting to re-establish emotional contact with the external world" (1951: 183).[16] That is to say, "A Vision" reveals the narrator attempting to transcend his attachment to the fantasy breast, an internal object, by telling himself that his mother, an external, if now absent object, loves him even as she did then. Perhaps Thomas Mann was still in some such mood when, on 16 March 1894, he left Lübeck to dwell in his mother's home in Munich.

Notes to Introduction

[1]When Thomas Mann's mother, Julia da Silva Bruhns, was five years of age, her Portuguese-Brazilian Creole-German mother died in childbirth. Within a

year, Ludwig Bruhns, her German father, took her and her four siblings from their plantation home near Rio de Janeiro to Lübeck, his native city. The three elder children were to be cared for by their grandmother, while Julia and her younger sibling were to be cared for by a French woman, Thérèse Bousset, who helped her mother maintain a modest boarding school. With these arrangements made, Herr Bruhns returned to Brazil, taking with him Anna, the children's black nurse who had accompanied them on the voyage (Hayman 1995: 86-87, Heilbut 1996: 8-10, Winston 1981: 10-12). Certainly the factors that form a personality are so many and so different in kind and so often hidden or disguised that most attempts to locate the keystone factor end in futility or superficiality, usually in controversy. Even so, searching for the keystone is a common activity, for the need for narrative is a universal trait. The toddler has already intuited that actions must contain cause-and-effect sequence to be regarded as meaningful; in time, it is to be hoped, the post-toddler realizes that a cause-and-effect sequence constructed to explain a mental—as opposed to a physical—phenomenon should be regarded as provisionally and problematically meaningful. Due caution thus piously expressed, an argument will be offered that the circumstances of inadequate mothering that beset Julia Bruhns—certainly from her fifth year and probably earlier—indelibly marked her personality. Such a female personality often becomes, in her turn, a mother "incapable of meeting abnormally strong affectional demands" from her children (Booth 1978: 25).

Nor were the early circumstances the only ones to deny Julia's need for contact. While being schooled in the impoverished Bousset house, she could visit her grandmother's house only on Sunday (Hayman 1995: 87). Although her father had remarried in Brazil, he retained strict control over his children in Lübeck, denying sixteen-year-old Julia's wish to marry a Latvian businessman (Heilbut 1996: 8). After her sister's marriage, Julia became obsessed with her vulnerability: "I mustn't stay single, I mustn't be an old maid" (qtd. in Winston 1981: 11). All the while she was a flirt, who encouraged suitors, then rejected them, then felt "dreadfully ashamed" (qtd. in Winston 1981: 11). The ultimate phase of this pattern suggests that Julia knew that each suitor was a stand-in for the man who controlled her life. When she was nearly eighteen, she accepted the proposal of Heinrich Mann, a wealthy businessman, perhaps because she was confident that her father would approve of such a marriage, as indeed he did (Winston 1981: 11-12). This sequence of events lends weight to Heilbut's conclusion that Julia's marriage "does not seem to have been a love match" (1996: 10). Given the circumstances, it is easy to draw conclusions from sketches of his mother that Thomas Mann's elder brother Heinrich made in his seventies. Hayman speaks of details: "One of them shows Julia in her boudoir, making up in front of the mirror on her dressing table; another, dated 1875, shows her in the garden, leaning flirtatiously back in a rocking chair and fanning herself, while her other arm is stretched out across a table toward the officer sitting well forward in his chair, gazing at her intently. The young Heinrich [then four-years-old] is lying on the grass not far away from them, and the baby, Thomas, is in his cot" (1995: 88). Heilbut generalizes: "In his sketches Heinrich depicts Julia as ramrod straight, with deep, emotive eyes and imposing cheekbones. He presents an imperious temperament in a steel-lined corset, with the unforgiving gaze of a nineteenth-century Joan Crawford" (1996: 10).

[2]In 1942 Mann declared: "A work must have roots deep in my life, secret threads must lead back from it to the dreams of earliest childhood, if I am to consider myself entitled to it, if I am to believe in the legitimacy of what I am doing" (qtd. in Kaufmann 1973:137). As early as 1904 Mann, in a letter to his fiancee Katja

Pringsheim confessed his worship of *Sehnsucht*: "You don't know how I love that word. It is my favorite word, my holy word, my magic formula, my key to the mystery of the world" (qtd. in Stock 1994: 4).

[3]Throughout this entire study I depend primarily upon the theories of Sigmund Freud regarding infantile sexuality, infantile anxiety/primal repression, and sublimation, found in *Three Essays on the Theory of Sexuality* (1905), "Leonardo da Vinci and a Memory of his Childhood" (1910), and *An Outline of Psycho-Analysis* (1940). But I also use a theory about the origin of the capacity for symbolization found in the work of object-relations psychoanalysts, many of whom accept the contention that the first symbol is the hallucination of the breast that was lost because of weaning. Following D. W. Winnicott, Susan Deri traces out the significance of this "protosymbol":

> It is at this point of mental development, at the earliest move toward symbolization, that Winnicott conceives the origin of what he calls the intermediate or transitional space, transitional between dream and reality, between inside and outside, between person and environment. It is par excellence the dimension of connectedness or, even better, of mutual immanence. This is the space for creative symbol formation, since it is the function of symbols to bridge between opposites. This transitional space, this space for connectedness, accounts for an order in the world based on *inner relatedness* instead of the Cartesian principle of dividedness. (1985: 252; ital. in orig.)

[4]Reed's interest in the grotesque is not psychoanalytic but stylistic:

> In so far as Mann's apparent savagery of portrayal is a matter of stylistic facility and the tendency of language towards self-sufficient complexity and over-elaboration, its analogies are not with realism or social satire, but with other modern exponents of the Grotesque whose creations are generated by language itself— Christian Morgenstern, for example. (1996: 36)

[5]Mrs. Reich first offers a psychoanalytic definition of sublimation:

> In sublimation the original sexual aim of an instinct is given up and a new desexualized one is assumed. This new aim is genetically related to the original one but is regarded as socially and culturally more valuable. Simultaneously with this desexualization the renunciation of the original incestuous object takes place. (1973: 99)

She does not assume that all "diverted sexual instincts" are transformed "into creative achievements" (1973: 99). The success of such a transformation depends upon the natural endowment called "talent": "without this precondition of talent the same conflicts may lead to neurotic symptoms or character deficiencies" (1973: 99). The term describing the precondition for creativity, "talent", applies to all cases, but "talent" in each case depends upon a unique set of circumstances.

Mrs. Reich then focuses on "one very special kind of sublimation[...], the grotesque-comic" (1973: 100). After offering a fragment of her case history of Catherine, who "has an outstanding talent for grotesque-comic acting" (1973: 100), she summarizes:

> The grotesque comic is characterized by a special form of disguise, that is, by particular disfigurement and deformation of the object. To understand the specific mechanism that is going on here and at the same time the particular difficulty of achievement and the great probability of failure of these endeavors to produce comic pleasure, it seems to be necessary to consider the particular instincts involved. In our case we find exhibition of devaluated parts of the body, of defects, which serves, via projection, at the same time to unmask the rivals. Confession and self-punishment are combined with aggression against others. This combination of aggression and exhibitionism turned simultaneously toward the actor's own body and against a hated rival are, I assume, typical for all cases of grotesque-comic art whether theatrical or graphic. The synthesis of these contrasting components seems to be the most effective method of weakening and disguising the infantile instincts. The combination of gratifications and punishment seems to be ego-syntonic. (1973: 111-112)

We are warned that the grotesque-comic process is particularly "labile" (1973: 100), subject to rapid, abrupt transformations.

The context in which Mrs. Reich uses "graphic" argues that she defines it as "written", but she makes no references to a literary work in her article, preferring examples of the grotesque-comic taken from "theatrical" experience, e.g., child behavior, primitive custom, vaudeville, circuses, and carnival—"acting-out", in the psychoanalytic sense of the term. These examples are used only to illustrate her analysis of Catherine, not to propose an aesthetic generalization. For these reasons the significance that her article holds for literary analysis must be inferred.

Following Ernst Kris, Mrs. Reich does offer one very useful generalization for the study of literature: "What today impresses us as comic was terrifying yesterday. The triumph resulting from mastering the past anxiety helps by repeating the victory and overcoming half-assimilated fear. Thus the function of the comic is to overcome anxiety while at the same time it is based on already mastered anxiety. From this essential peculiarity of the comic arises the double-edged [labile] character: the ease with which it passes from pleasurable success to unpleasurable" (1973: 111). My purpose in this study is to show that in Thomas Mann's early work the grotesque-comic reveals his reawakened infantile anxieties and that in his later work the comic prevails as he developed a defense against them.

[6]Anzieu relies on the version of the myth that Sir James Frazer provides in *The Golden Bough*, hence Frazer's summary will be cited here:

> [Marsyas] was said to be a Phrygian satyr or Silenus, according to others a shepherd or herdsman, who played sweetly on the flute. A friend of Cybele, he roamed the country with the disconsolate

goddess to soothe her grief for the death of Attis. The composition of the Mother's Air, a tune played on the flute in honour of the Great Mother Goddess, was attributed to him by the people of Celaenae in Phrygia. Vain of his skill, he challenged Apollo to a musical contest, he to play on the flute and Apollo on the lyre. Being vanquished, Marsyas was tied up to a pine-tree and flayed or cut limb from limb either by the victorious Apollo or by a Scythian slave. His skin was shown at Celaenae in historical times. (1958 : 411)

[7]In his lengthy review, Kirshner summarizes Anzieu's conception of the skin ego:

The term appears to refer to at least four related, but by no means identical constructs. (1) The skin ego is a structure of the mind, "preprogrammed" at birth (p. 5) in potential form (p. 102), a precursor to the ego (p. 115) or "the ego in its original state" (p. 84), deriving as Freud noted from the body surface as a projection of that surface (pp. 136, 153); thus a contribution to ego psychology and the early development of the emerging structure, "ego." (2) It is a mental representation (p. 101) of maternal holding. "The skin ego is part of the mother" (p. 98), that is, a chronologically intermediate structure between fusion with the mother and differentiation (p. 4), "a system of double feedback as an envelope of mother-child" (p. 57) related conceptually to the transitional object of Winnicott (pp. 26, 37). (3) In addition, the skin ego belongs in Lacanian terms to the realm of the imaginary, i.e., a "phantasy" (p. 59), "a mental image' (p. 40) of which the ego of the child makes use to satisfy its need for a narcissistic envelope and container. (4) Finally and perhaps most descriptively telling, it is "a metaphor of very broad scope" (p. 6), which the author hopes will generate "a set of operational concepts susceptible of factual or theoretical refutation" (p. 38). (1990: 543)

[8]On the final page of her study, Ezergailis notes that in his essay "Süsser Schlaf" Mann links his love of sleep with his love of the ocean, then adds: "The ocean is an image of the relaxation of individuation. In this, it is related to the female principle. Use of the ocean in this way suggests Freud's similar connection of the sea and diffusion of identity in the conception of the 'oceanic feeling'" (1975: 188). My thesis grounds the "oceanic feeling" in the experience of satiation after nursing, the absence or presence of which fundamentally affects the attitude toward the "female principle" that the infant, male or female, develops.

[9]In *The Basic Neurosis*, Edmund Bergler argues *"that there is only one basic neurosis and that neurosis is oral in genesis"* (1949: 38; all ital. in quotations from Bergler are orig.). Following Freud and Ferenczi, Bergler assumes that the infant soon "lives for some time in the fantasy of magic omnipotence", convinced that he "produces everything out of himself" (1949: 2). But there comes a time in the first few months when his cry for the breast is not immediately answered: a "deep

narcissistic wound is inflicted—unavoidably inflicted—to the child" (1949: 3). The repetition of these inflictions, highlighted by "the 'tragedy'—once more unavoidable—of weaning", causes the "collapse" of the child's fantasy that he is self-sufficient. Then he realizes that he is helpless, and he becomes furious because he concludes that his mother (or her substitute) has refused to help him. But his expression of his fury invites a "triad of retribution": "*punishment, moral reproach, guilt*". Some children quickly learn to adapt to this great change in their relationship with mother, but others still cling to their "original aims and subjects with the unavoidable external, later internal punishment in the form of guilt".

The "latter group of children becomes the material for '*psychic masochism*'. The term describes in *two words a life technique* of people who—despite conscious ignorance of so doing—are *unconsciously lovers of humiliation, defeat, refusal*". *Those* children who persist in their aggression toward mother, even though they suffer the inevitable retribution, are apparently confronted by an irresolvable problem. But, Bergler believes, the problem is solved "in an amazing way: pain, depression, punishment, guilt are changed into pleasure. *The only pleasure one can derive from displeasure is to make out of displeasure pleasure*[...]. A psychic masochist is in the making." (1949: 4).

Psychic masochism must be understood from two aspects: "The genetic picture comprises the sequence of early infancy: offense to megalomania incurred by a libidinous frustration, fury, motor helplessness, external, later internal, inhibition of aggression—boomeranging of aggression—libidinization of guilt" (1949 : 4). "The clinical picture is based on the fact that the inner conscience (superego) objects to this peculiar type of infantile pleasure. The result is that the unconscious ego creates new secondary defenses. These secondary defenses comprise the '*triad of the mechanism of orality*'" (1949: 4):

> (1)   I shall repeat the masochistic wish of being deprived by my mother, by creating or misusing situations in which some substitute of my pre-oedipal mother-image shall refuse my wishes.
> (2)   I shall not be conscious of my wish to be refused and initial provocation of refusal, and shall see only that I am justified in self-defense, righteous indignation and pseudo-aggression because of the refusal.
> (3)   Afterwards I shall pity myself because such an injustice "can happen only to me," and enjoy once more psychic masochistic pleasure. (1949: 5)

This lengthy summary of Bergler's "basic neurosis" will serve as the introduction to his theory of the psychology of the creative writer. Before "psychoanalytic studies by Freud, Rank, Sachs, Reik, Brill" (1949: 186) there was "the rather naive preanalytic assumption that the artist expresses his *conscious* wishes in a camouflaged form", but "analysis proved that *unconscious* wishes and fantasies were presented" (1949: 186). The first four analysts above think that the wishes and fantasies develop in the oedipal stage; Brill alone traces them back to the oral stage. Following Brill, Bergler traces literary creativity to fantasies in the oral stage as he has defined it above:

1.　　　I came to the conclusion that the writer does *not,* in his work, *express his unconscious wishes and fantasies*, as had been assumed previously; but rather that, under pressure of his unconscious guilt feelings, he gives expression to his unconscious *defense against these wishes and fantasies.*

2.　　　My clinical experience taught me that the writer does *not* suffer from a "shameless urge to reveal himself," that is, from the *exhibitory* impulse which, since Rank, has been asserted by every psychoanalytic biographer. On the contrary, I could prove that every writer, on the deepest level of his being, is a *voyeur* who utilizes his exhibitionistic tendencies as a defense against these scopophiliac impulses.

3.　　　The basic unconscious difficulty in writers is an *oral-masochistic conflict* with a *specific defense twist* in his unique "solution". However, according to my conception, the writer's type of neurotic orality is not greediness or a wish "to receive" in repetition of the child-mother situation, but rather a spiteful desire for *oral* independence. By this, the artist *identifies* himself with the "giving" mother **out** of defensive pseudo-aggression toward her and thus eliminates her. He achieves oral pleasure for himself through "beautiful" words and ideas. In its deepest sense, it is a desire to refute the "bad" pre-oedipal mother and the masochistic "disappointments" experienced through her, by establishing an "autarchy," *acting a magic gesture.* The peculiar solution of the writer (and every real artist) is the fact that he—and he *only*—acts in his productivity *both roles (mother—child) on himself.* No other neurotic or normal "solution" is known in which a person makes out of the *duality* (mother—child) a *unity*: every neurotic and normal person needs for the acting out of infantile fantasies *two* people. The writer (and artist) condenses this duality into— one person. He thus makes of the typical neurotic duality—a "***one person show***". (1949: 187; boldface in orig.)

Bergler's remarkable study strengthens statements that I have already made and that I will make, both in the interpretation of Mann's texts and in the analysis of his motives and behavior. As to the latter, analysis of motives and behavior, I am convinced that Mann's "basis neurosis" accounts for his early exhibitionism, his subsequent voyeurism, his obsession with incest as a return to unity, and his characteristic practice of producing his daily wordage, then feeding it to his family audience, a practice that began when he was writing *Buddenbrooks*, "the almost nonsensical scribbling of a somewhat unconventional twenty-year-old youngster, which I read to my family amidst roars of laughter" (Mann "Address" 705). As to the former, interpretation of texts, each citation of Bergler that I use for the interpretation of a text builds on the present note.

[10]In *The Incest Theme in Literature and Legend* (1912), Otto Rank, having frequently acknowledged Freud's pioneering effort both as psychoanalyst and as exegete, draws his conclusion: "we do not claim that literary talent derives exclusively from powerful incest impulses fixated in childhood. We claim simply to have recognized that the psychic energy (affects) resulting from the repression of

these impulses constitutes one of the major driving forces in literary production" (1992: 570; parenthesis in orig.). Rank believes that the pre-eminence of "this general human theme" (1992: 35) in Western literature remains constant, but that because of "the increasing degree of sexual repression in the human psyche" the presentation of "this typical theme" has changed over time. Analyzing Sophocles' *Oedipus the King*, Shakespeare's *Hamlet*, and Schiller's *Don Carlos*, he traces the evolution of the theme through three manifestations:

> The incest fantasy is realized in *Oedipus*, and the son lovingly embraces the mother (though he does not know it). In *Hamlet*, owing to greater repression, only the reverse side of love for the mother appears—jealous hatred. In *Don Carlos* the rejection of the incest wish has gone so far that it is no longer even the actual mother the son desires, but rather the stepmother—a woman who only bears the name Mother; she is no blood relative, but is nevertheless the father's wife. (1992: 36)

In his chapter on "The Incest Theme in Modern Literature" Rank does not mention Thomas Mann's work, but cites Heinrich Mann's *Die Schauspielerin* (1906) as portraying "with great psychological sensitivity a man's psychic impotence and a woman's frigidity arising from failure to transcend the incest complex" (1992: 551). Heinrich admitted that before he fell in love with Ines Schmied in the spring of 1905 tthe only woman in his life had been his sister Carla (N. Hamilton 1979: 106). Perhaps his new erotic focus allowed him to see his relationship with Carla for what it was? Wysling notes that Heinrich and his sister Clara were the respective models for the man and the woman in *Schauspielern* and that Thomas later acknowledged to Heinrich that that work had anticipated his use of the incest theme in "Blood of the Walsungs" (1998: 16).

[11]It is likely that, as Mann made his first efforts to write in a literary genre, he also began the life-long practice of keeping a very candid diary. Heilbut notes that the diaries "have been read as documents of a supreme egotist, obsessively self-regarding" (1996: 312). That description does not go far enough, if it is reasonable to assume that, in Mann's case, the urge to create a diary sprang from the same source as the urge to create literary works, the grotesque-comic sublimation. For Mrs. Reich argues that "the grotesque-comic play" is not only "a more or less disguised breaking through of instincts" but also "has the meaning of confession, self-humiliation and self-punishment" (1973: 109). The former serves the id; the latter, the superego. It is no wonder that in 1896 Mann burned all the diary entries up to that time (Hayman 1995: 118).

[12]Freud offers an account of "the psychical genesis of homosexuality" ("Leonardo" 98-99)--of the type of homosexual that includes Thomas Mann:

> In all the cases we have examined we have established the fact that the future inverts, in the earliest years of their childhood, pass through a phase of very intense but short-lived fixation to a woman (usually their mother), and that, after leaving this behind, they identify themselves with a woman and take *themselves* as their sexual object. That is to say, they proceed from a narcissistic basis, and look for a young man who resembles themselves and

whom *they* may love as their mothers loved *them*. Moreover, we
have frequently found that alleged inverts have been by no means
insusceptible to the charms of women, but have continually
transposed the excitation aroused by women on to a male object.
They have thus repeated all through their lives the mechanism by
which their inversion arose. Their compulsive longing for men
has turned out to be determined by their ceaseless flight from
women. (*Three* 144-45; ital. in orig.)

Freud acknowledges that the "trait of inversion may either date back to the very
beginning, as far back as the subject's memory reaches, or it may not have become
noticeable till some particular time before or after puberty" *(Three* 137). For the type
of inversion that Thomas Mann experienced, a very early date of origin seems likely.
When the little boy performed before his mother as Hermes, he must have identified
with his mother, seen himself, as it were, through her eyes, laying the foundation for
his later quest for the Hermes figure in the external world and for his autobiographical
characters' quest in his fictional world. In *Confessions of Felix Krull* he finally
rewards himself by creating himself as the Hermes figure who excites the admiration
of two mother figures, Madame Houpflé and, later, Senhora Kuckuck. Perhaps his
wife Katja's apparent imperturbability at his boy-watching resulted from her intuition
that he did it with a mother's eye.

[13]Lewin developed the "dream screen" in "Sleep, the Mouth, and the Dream
Screen", *The Psychoanalytic Quarterly* 15 (1946): 419-34; in "Inferences from the
Dream Screen", *International Journal of Psycho-Analysis* 29(1948): 224-30; and in
"Reconsideration of the Dream Screen", *The Psychoanalytic Quarterly* 22(1953):
174-99. Psychoanalysts who have published elaborations of the "dream screen"
include Charles Rycroft, Joseph Kepecs, Gert Heilbrunn, Mark Kanzer, Angel Garma,
L. Bryce Boyer, Carel van der Heide, and David R. Edelstein. As Share points out,
the

> data offered in the Isakower, Lewin, and Spitz phenomena
> provide some evidence that earliest memories can be recorded,
> retained, and possibly reconstructed. On the other hand, it is not
> clear if these are actually specific, discrete *memories* of
> experience or are composites (or general schemas) that create
> templates for a class of experiences associated with breast-
> feeding. (1994: 84)

She then adds that more recent research "indicates that infants are capable of storing
and retaining discrete memories of very distinct phenomena and experiences from
earliest time" (1994: 84).

[14]For an explanation of primary process, see the chapter "Dreams", pp. 149-
70, in Charles Brenner's *An Elementary Textbook of Psychoanalysis* (Garden City,
NY: Anchor, 1974).

[15]In the first sentence of "Tonio Kröger" Mann creates the "breast
universe"—"The winter sun, poor ghost of itself, hung milky and wan behind layers
of cloud above the huddled roofs of the town"—only, as the first sentence anticipates,
the second sentence reveals that it is the "lost breast universe"—In the gabled streets

it was wet and windy and there came in gusts a sort of soft hail, not ice, not snow" (85).

[16]The following summary by Brenner supports the thesis that has been followed in Chapter 1:

> Freud outlined a series of *typical* situations which may be expected to occur in sequence in the child's life. The first of these, chronologically, is separation from a person who is important to the child as a source of gratification. This is often referred to in the psychoanalytic literature as "loss of the object," or as "loss of the loved object," although at the age when this is *first* perceived as a danger the child is still much too young for us to attribute to it such a complex emotion as love. The next typical danger situation for the child is the loss of love of a person of its environment on whom it must depend for gratification. In other words, even though the person is present, the child may fear the loss of its love. This is referred to as the "loss of the object's love." The next, typical danger situation is different for the two sexes. In the case of the little boy the danger is the loss of his penis, which is referred to as castration in the psychoanalytic literature. In the case of the little girl the danger is some analogous genital injury. The last danger situation is that of guilt, or disapproval and punishment by the superego. (1974: 77; ital. in orig.)

II

Early Works

In Munich Thomas was once again in the same dwelling with his mother, sisters, younger brother, and even his older brother Heinrich, who had lived apart from the family for the past five years. Heinrich had just had a novel, *In einer Familie*, privately published, thanks to his mother's subvention (N. Hamilton 1979: 41). Although Thomas and Heinrich had often been at odds with one another when they were younger, Thomas now enjoyed Heinrich's company, even though the elder brother appeared successful in both his literary ambitions and his romantic pursuits (Winston 1981: 57).

Mrs. Mann was having her successes, as well. She could afford an eight-room apartment which, being on the ground floor, boasted a verandah and a garden (N. Hamilton 1979: 45). Still attractive at forty-three, she quickly became a popular hostess. In her quiet moments she was trying her hand at writing children's stories and short stories (N. Hamilton 1979: 46).

She must have decided that two writers in the family were quiet enough, for she informed Thomas that she would not support his desire to be a writer. She saw to it that within a month of his arrival, Thomas was working as an unpaid apprentice in the South German Fire Insurance Company. Apparently he was casually supervised, for he spent his time writing a short story, *"Gefallen"*, which appeared in October 1894 in *Die Gesellschaft*, the same journal that published a poem of his in October 1893 (Hayman 1995: 103). Strengthened by success, he renewed his plea to his mother, who relented, provided that he audited courses at the Technical High School that would prepare him for a career in journalism (N. Hamilton 1979: 47).

Mann now had the time for his writing, even though much of the time it may have been impossible for him to concentrate. He was still living in his mother's apartment; although he received six hundred marks each quarter from his father's estate, he was obliged to

pay over half of it to his mother for his room and board (Hayman
1995: 107). In a letter to Heinrich on 8 January 1904, responding to
his brother's criticism of his "egoistic indifference toward Mama", Thomas
protested, "*I had already grieved and brooded myself sick over Mama, and all the
while you were looking at pictures in Italy, when I myself* was much more terribly
obsessed than I am now" (Wysling 1998: 61; ital. in orig.). Heinrich had
left Munich in January 1895 for his second stay in Italy (N. Hamilton
1979: 48). An indirect confirmation of Thomas's difficulties with his
mother is to be found in his December 1895 answers to questions
posed in a friend's album. "His 'idea of happiness' was 'to live independently
on terms of understanding with myself,' while his idea of unhappiness was to be
'without means and therefore dependent'[...]. The qualities he most valued in women
were 'beauty and virtue,' and in men intellect and spirituality" (qtd. in Hayman
1995: 117). Of all the fictional characters whom he knew, he thought
himself most like Hamlet—without offering any points of analogy.

        Just before his twenty-first birthday, 6 June 1896, Thomas
Mann was working on a short story published as "Der kleine Herr
Friedemann" ("Little Herr Friedemann"). Winston speculates that
Mann was revising a story called "The Little Professor" which had
been rejected by an editor in 1894. If so, the revision of the title from
identification by profession to identification by name suggests that a
shift from the objective to the subjective also occurred. That the story
is autobiographical is strongly suggested by a comment that Golo
Mann makes about his father's creation of a fictional person:

> It is well known that he usually did not invent his characters, but
> discovered them and drew them from life[...]. If he was more
> familiar with his model he was frequently unable to give up the
> name even, that is to say he invented names which were like those
> of the people he was using because it seemed to him that person
> and name were inwardly connected. (1965: 8)

Hence, Thomas Mann becomes "Friedemann", the man who yearns
for peace. A letter of 23 May 1896 to his friend Otto Grautoff reveals
Mann's   assessment   of   his   manuscript-in-progress: "completely
psychopathic" (qtd. in Hayman 1995: 117, 622 ch2n9).

        The period during which Mann worked on "Little Herr
Friedemann" was a time of great stress, a period that he later described
as "a late and violent outbreak of sexuality (I am speaking of my twentieth year)"
(qtd. in Heilbut 1996: 33). By 17 February 1896, he had burned "all his
diaries and some of his stories". Writing to his friend Grautoff, Mann
became rhetorical about his action:

Why? Because they were burdensome to me...bulky, and besides...You think it is a pity? But where should I leave them if, for example, I went away for a long time?...It would be painful and awkward for me to have such a mass of secret—very secret— papers lying around....You would be well advised to make a similar purge. It has done me a lot of good. One is literally liberated from the past to live light-heartedly and harmlessly in the present and the future. (qtd. in Hayman 1995: 118; ellipsis in orig.)

That he burned some of his stories, as well as his diary, argues that he was already drawn to his past for material, an act that he would never abandon.

Only a month after he claimed to be "liberated from the past to live light-heartedly and harmlessly in the present and the future", he was railing to Grautoff about Munich: "Is it not the *unliterary* city par excellence? Banal women and healthy men—God knows what a lot of contempt I load into the word 'healthy'" (Hayman 1995: 118; ital. in orig.). It could be that—rather than the community at large—it was a certain resident who aroused his disgust, a widow whose dwelling attracted "uncles" (Hayman 1995: 106, Heilbut 1996: 36). His contempt for "healthy men" might have been fueled by his feeling that, though it was not apparent, he was "unhealthy".

In June 1896 Mann spent three weeks in Vienna, made possible by a small bequest for which he was eligible upon reaching his majority. Of his recent biographers, only Winston is curious about the visit. He doubts that Mann went looking for romance, notes that Mann spoke only of staying at the Hotel Klomser and seeing a "semioriental deputation" that was to be received by the Emperor (qtd. in Winston 198: 96). Winston concludes: "But what else he did there in the security of his 'deepest youthful incognito'[...]we do not know" . Mann's comments above and following suggest that he was suffering from a psychological condition then known as hysteria—as common in Europe then as depression now is in the United States. Mann later revealed nothing else about his trip to Vienna, perhaps because he was at the time in an amnesiac flight from reality, a fugue state, often presented in the psychoanalytic literature as an unconscious search for home, for the paradise—one comes to realize—that has been lost. The two associated data that he did recall—the building connoting a refuge for the wayfarer and the people from the "semioriental" area in which the idea of paradise as an enclosed garden originated—offer a key to the unconscious motive of his visit.

On 27 September, Mann wrote Grautoff, "My last few weeks, since I returned from Austria, have passed very quietly: too quietly, for my nerves demand a change. I am glad that my Munich days are numbered" (qtd. in Winston 1981: 95). In the same letter he wrote that he had "eine längere Novelle >>Der kleine Herr Friedemann<< geschrieben, die Geschichte eines Buckligen; ich weiss noch nicht, wohin ich sie schicken werde" (De Mendelssohn 1974: 78). The fact that Mann did not try to place "Little Herr Friedemann" before he left on his trip allows speculation that he might have revised the story in response to his Italian experience.

After spending three weeks in Venice and two days in Rome, Mann arrived in Naples on 4 November 1896. His month-long stay was to bring his crisis to a head. Heilbut notes that "[y]ears later, he characterized this period as haunted by a 'psychological susceptibility, a power of vision, a melancholy, which even today I hardly understand, but under which I had to suffer indescribably'" (1996: 75). Winston, Heilbut, and Hayman have focused on the confession of suffering that Mann made in Naples, but there are inferences yet to be drawn about his "psychological susceptibility" to the sights of Naples and the "power of vision" that he gained from them.

It is necessary, before Mann's stay in Naples is discussed, to sketch his "psychological susceptibility" at the time. Mann must have felt relieved to be away from Munich, away from the physical presence of his mother, for his ancient ambivalence toward her seems to have contributed to the late awakening of his desire for sexual contact. He felt that he had been prematurely deprived of her breast—this evidence is already obvious in "A Vision". At the same time he felt that his deprivation resulted from her deliberate coldness. Responding to both maternal influences, Mann remained caught in the oral phase in early adolescence, not yet tortured by the shift of sensuous intensity from the mouth to the genital. At the same time, reacting to his mother's remoteness, he associated the experience of emotional yearning with distance and restraint, worship from afar. At fourteen he was first overwhelmed with an infatuation, for a classmate, Armin Martens, the first of many unconsummated passions of the mouth and eye that Mann was to experience during a lifetime of male-watching. In a diary entry on 25 April 1934, Mann offers himself a thorough analysis of desire as he experienced it:

> At noon I took a walk by myself by way of Johannisburg. Passing the plant nursery I was pleasurably smitten by the sight of a young fellow working there, a brown-haired type with a small cap on his head, very handsome, and bare to the waist. The rapture I

felt at the sight of such common, everyday, and natural "beauty," the contours of his chest, the swell of his biceps, made me reflect afterward on the unreal, illusionary, and aesthetic nature of such an inclination, the goal of which, it would appear, is realized in gazing and "admiring." Although erotic, it requires no fulfillment at all, neither intellectually nor physically. This is likely thanks to the influence of the reality principle on the imagination; it allows the rapture, but limits it to just looking. (Kesten 1984: 207)

The particular environment of this occasion, a garden-like "plant nursery", the locus of the mother, would have intensified his attraction.

By 1934 Mann had, of course, participated in a sexual union of twenty-nine years with his wife Katja Pringsheim which had produced six children. Marriage seems to have represented the reality principle—with Mann's sexual drive thus conventionally exercised, he could indulge himself in the rapture of homoerotic gazing. But in 1896 Mann was still viewing his problem in absolutes, abstinence versus sexual activity (with male? with female? with both?).

By postcard, on 6 November, Mann informed a friend in Munich that he was "staying at Via S. Lucia 28^{II}—too expensive, but with a very fine view of the sea and Vesuvius" (Wysling 1998: 7). Mann mainly wanted writing and publishing gossip, but he did add, "Here I feel very much at ease. Only now do I feel that I am really in the southland; that's because of the audible note of the Orient that forms part of the medley. It is very amusing". Mann apparently agreed with the assertion quoted in a contemporary guidebook:

> The shrieks and howls that denote fresh vegetables, oranges, boiled shell-fish and roasted chestnuts are varied, it is true, but equally unendurable[...]. The tongues of the Neapolitans are the most active part about them, and they consider an hour lost during which they are silent. (Murray 1892: 26)

But Mann's professed jauntiness is suspect. He may have thought himself distant from the cause of his ancient problem, mother, but the cause of his present problem, his genital, was undeniably near, and his long letter to Grautoff, on 8 November, slowly approaches that problem.

In the second paragraph Mann thanks Grautoff for sending one of his poems, commenting, "Es ist dieselbe Stimmung, die den Grundton meiner Novelle 'Der kleine Herr Friedemann' ausmacht, die Sehnsucht nach neutralem Nirwana, Frieden und der Untergang im Geschlechtlichen" (qtd. in Parkes-Perret 1996: 290). In the third paragraph Mann reports on his own movements. He came to Naples, he says, to get away from

"Germanism, German ideas, and German *Kultur*, to the 'remotest, most alien South'"
(Winston 1981: 96)--though, again, he may not be entirely
forthcoming about what he is trying to escape. Then he avers:

> I was not disappointed. The oriental note sounds audibly here—
> although that almost excludes the proud aristocratic distinction
> that is characteristic of Rome, that majestic city par excellence.
> Naples is more plebeian, but with a naive, lovable, gracious, and
> amusing vulgarity. It does not have the bold and imperial
> Caesarean profile of Rome; its physiognomy has a somewhat
> turned-up nose and puffy lips, but very beautiful dark eyes.[...] I
> have been closely studying this physiognomy for four days; its
> sensual, sweet southern beauty grips me more and more.

About the preceding paragraph, Winston wisely notes: "These are
suspiciously equivocal terms for the description of a city, especially when we learn
that the young letter writer is 'a little weary from loneliness'" (1981: 96).

Perhaps fearing to engage in any more introspection, Mann
tries in the next paragraph of the letter to be an ordinary tourist:

> Die Via Santa Lucia, an der ich wohne, hat vielleicht das
> urwüchsigste und ungenierteste Volksleben. Das ist nicht mehr
> Europa,--endlich nicht mehr Europa!....Jenseits der Bucht beginnt,
> während ich schreibe, der Vesuv zu erglühen.
> (De Mendelsson 1974: 80; ellipsis in orig.)

But then Mann cannot bottle his feelings any longer:

> I think of my suffering, of the problem of my suffering. What am
> I suffering from? From knowledge—is it going to destroy me?
> What am I suffering from? From sexuality—is it going to destroy
> me?--How I hate it, this knowledge which forces even art to join
> it! How I hate it, this sensuality, which claims that everything fine
> and good is its consequence and effect. Alas, it is the *poison* that
> lurks in everything fine and good!--How am I to free myself of
> knowledge? By religion? How am I to free myself of sexuality?
> By eating rice? (Winston 1981: 97)

Given the context in which Mann uses the word *poison*, Freud's
comment about that substance should be recalled.

At this point Mann breaks off the letter, perhaps hopeful that
nourishment of a different sort will restore his spirits. Later, supplying
a new heading–"Abends"—he resumes the letter: "Ich habe diniert und in der
Galleria Umberto den Kaffee getrunken" (De Mendelssohn 1974: 80). Again
he attempts a tourist's sketch, but soon reverts to his problem:

Here and there, among a thousand other peddlers, are slyly hissing dealers who urge you to come along with them to allegedly "very beautiful" girls, and not only to girls. They keep at it, walk alongside, praising their wares until you answer roughly. They don't know that you have almost resolved to eat nothing but rice just to escape from sexuality! (Winston 1981: 97)

Mann attempts to regain his composure by closing the letter with a few comments about practical concerns.

It is very unlikely that Mann spent all of his time in his lodgings, venturing out to the fashionable arcades of the Galleria Umberto only for his dinner. Since he loved music, he may have attended performances at the Teatro San Carlo, which faces the Galleria. Ambitious to be a world-renowned writer, he must have sought inspiration at the legendary tomb of Virgil on the hill of Posilipo (Hutton 1958: 102). He must have inspected the excavations at Pompeii and at the smaller Herculaneum and visited the various castles and museums, especially the National Archeological Museum of Naples, the repository for so much of the cultural treasures found in the excavations.

It was in the National Archeological Museum that he found the art pieces that would serve him as objectifications of the two related aspects of his suffering, his ambivalence toward the mother figure—imagining her simultaneously as the zenith of beauty and as the nadir of ugliness—and his fascination for the male figure. With respect to the male figure, when Mann first glimpsed the bronze statue of the nude Hermes found at Herculaneum he must have experienced a shock of recognition. While all the art critics admire it as the best expression of "Hermes as the celestial messenger" (Johnson 1968: 180), Mann may simply have regarded it as the idealization of youthful male beauty. He was predisposed to be mindful of Hermes, for as a child at home he had "hopped about as Hermes with paper wingéd sandals" ("On Myself" 138). Such pandemonium probably took place in the Manns' drawing room, whose walls featured "Olympians gamboling on the [...] wallpaper" (Heilbut 1996: 11). Indeed, perhaps his childhood memories sent him looking for that "most celebrated work of art in Naples" (Hutton 1958: 84). The wingéd sandals of the Herculaneum Hermes may have been the feature that caught Mann's attention—or perhaps it was the statue's erect pencil-thin penis, unseen in most of its photographs because of a discreet camera angle. Did Mann already intuit the connection between tumescence and nursing that his Hermes character Felix Krull gives body to (*Confessions* 46)?

Whatever the source of his attraction to the Herculaneum Hermes, Mann never lost it. In 1934, in a letter to Karl Kerényi, he wrote:

> In my youth it would have been out of the question to take pleasure in such a scene as the one you mention—Jacob's dream of Anubis—and in something like the answer of the jackal-headed boy: "I shall one day be rid of my head too"[...]. This is almost a private joke, which most readers would pass over. But what is involved is the career of a god. For this Anubis, now still half beast and satyr-like, is the future Hermes-Psychopompos[...]. Have you noticed that I placed him on his rock exactly in the pose of the Hermes of Lysippos in Naples? I am very much in love with this statue, of which there is a fine copy in the Alte Museum in Berlin, and this passage is a secret expression of homage. (Kerényi 1975: 37)

In 1941 he recorded in his diary: "Conny K. [his secretary Konrad Katzenellenbogen (later Kellen)] nebst etwas armseligen Briefen, brachte Mythologie-Bücher englisch, französisch und deutsch. Über Hermes exzerpiert, entzückt wieder von dem Bilde der Lysippos-Statue, die ich über alles liebe" (De Mendelssohn 1974: 256-57). The reclining Herculaneum Hermes may have also received "a secret expression of homage" in Ludwig von Hofmann's oil painting *Die Quelle* ("The Spring"), which pictures two reclining nude young men observing another nude young man drinking from a falling spring. Heilbut notes that this painting "graced Mann's various studies from 1914 until his death. It inspired the Arcadian scene in the chapter 'Snow'[in *The Magic Mountain*], and may have stimulated Mann as he wrote about a series of Hermeses, from Joseph to Felix Krull" (1996: 419; caption under photograph of the painting; 1996: 419). Scholars have found a wealth of meanings attributed to Hermes in his development as a very significant mythic figure, and no doubt Mann attached some of those meanings to his Hermes characters as he increasingly employed mythic material in his fiction. But first and always foremost, Hermes represented for Mann a contradictory figure, the temptation of dreams of sexual bliss at the breast versus the temptation of homosexual sensuousness whose actualization would be fatal.

Hofmann's painting has another meaning. The homoerotic element is made prominent by one youth, erect but bent forward with his weight resting upon his left knee, gazing fixedly at the drinking youth's buttocks. But an object-relations element is announced by the second observant youth, reclining on an elbow so that his plumbingless pubes are revealed, who directs his gaze toward the youth's mouth as he drinks the quenching water. Gutheil notes that often in dreams a lactating breast is symbolized as a spring (1951: 153). Mann must have intuited that the painting revealed the origin of both his homoerotic gazing and of his desire to create: frustration at the breast.

With respect to his ambivalence toward the mother figure, since he was in flight from the fascinating aspect of that figure, Mann may have anticipated that in Naples he would discover a defense against her, an objectification of the mother as demon. In his two letters from Naples there are hints he felt that discovery was near: both letters speak of "the audible note of the Orient", while the second letter also registers the "physiognomy" out of which the sound issues: "a somewhat turned-up nose and puffy lips, but very beautiful eyes[...]. I have been closely studying this physiognomy for four days; its sensual, sweet southern beauty grips me more and more". The concluding sentence indicates that he is still captivated by the beautiful maternal mask, which could awaken his loneliness for his mother, a "southern beauty". Mann had yet to glimpse the Gorgon visage that is revealed if the mask is ripped off.

Mann always and frequently credited his introduction to mythology to the edition of Friedrich Nösselt's *Lehrbuch der griechischen und römischen Mythology* read by his mother as a child and passed on to her children (Kerényi 1975: 191, 192-93n1). It is to be expected, then, that his "mythological thinking" would always be related to his "psychological thinking" (with the understanding that, for Mann, the foundation of "psychological thinking" lay in his experience of maternal alienation). Mann recalled, too, that Nösselt's book had a "Pallas Athena on the cover" (Kerényi 1975: 191, "On Myself" 138). A rendering of Pallas Athena would undoubtedly include the Gorgoneion, specifically the head of Medusa, on the goddess's breastplate or on her shield or her *aegis,* depending upon which version of the myth the illustrator was following. The Gorgoneion recalls the daring feat of Perseus, 'the Cutter' (Feldman 1965: 492), who decapitated Medusa and presented the fruit of his act to his patroness Athena. Perseus' patron was Hermes, who was thus an enemy of Medusa: knowledge of that patronage may have increased Mann's attraction to the wingéd-sandaled one.

As Mann learned the myths of Pallas Athena and Medusa that he found in Nösselt's *Lehrbuch* he might have intuited a distinction between the two females that Edelman emphasizes: Pallas Athena possesses the qualities of the Great Mother (1998: 51), while Medusa is related to the Terrible Mother (1998: 63). But their relationship did not begin with Medusa DOA at Athena's temple: the best known version of the Perseus story is that Medusa had so infuriated Athena by using her temple as a trysting place with Poseidon that she transformed the beautiful mortal face into a monster's visage. Afterwards Athena sent Perseus to separate the face from its body (Edelman 1998: 59); perhaps Athena had heard by the Olympian grapevine that Medusa was pregnant by Poseidon, prompting her to decide that, really, some things just could not be allowed. If so, she was foiled, for even headless—in fact because headless, Medusa gave birth to Pegasos, the wingéd horse, and to Chrysaor, 'he of the golden sword', who dutifully perpetuated his mother's monster notoriety (Barnes 1974: 4). Thus, though they are mythically so different, Athena and Medusa are, psychologically speaking, very closely related, in that each embodies an extreme "mother face"—Athena the "good face", Medusa the "bad face"—a distinction that most two-year-olds can discourse on at length.

Despite the richness of the Medusa-as-Gorgon myth, it was, if Jane Harrison is correct, a myth created to substantiate a pre-existing ritual object. In her interpretation of the Gorgon,

> the primitive Greek knew that there was in his ritual a horrid thing called a Gorgoneion, a grinning mask with glaring eyes and protruding beast-like tusks and a pendent tongue. How did this Gorgoneion come to be? A hero had slain a beast called the Gorgon, and this was its head[...].The ritual object comes first; then the monster is begotten to account for it; then the hero is supplied to account for the slaying of the monster. (1959: 187)

The Gorgoneion is thus one kind of the many apotropaic ritual masks that human beings early developed for hiding behind when confronting their enemies. In a pinch many a six-year-old instinctively uses his face as such a mask, by pulling down the lower eyelids with index finger and pinkie of one hand while pushing up the nose with one or two fingers of the other hand. As is well known among the six-year-old cohort, the potency of the ritual is greatly increased by crossing the eyes and sticking out the tongue. Arguing from the etymology of the name *Gorgo*—the Sanskrit root denotes a "*gurg*ling, guttural sound, sometimes human, sometimes animal, perhaps closest to the *grrr* of a growling beast"--Feldman asserts that the sound associated with the Gorgoneion was as terrifying as its appearance (1965: 487). Of

Medusa's origins Feldman says: "She began as a menacing, shaggy, feline head, an animaloid outcry, and a devastating look which came more and more to have the power to turn men to stone, to castrate, in effect" (1965: 492). Thus the two essential qualities of the Gorgoneion, utterance and physiognomy, are the two distinctive features that Mann discerned in the Neopolitan environment.

Naples originated as Parthenope ('maiden face' [Graves 1957: vol. 2, 408]), named by the founding Greek colonists for the Siren of that name, whose corpse was said to have washed up there after she threw herself into the sea out of love for Ulysses (Evans 1981: 836). Later those early arrivers renamed their town *Palæoplis* ('the old city') to distinguish it from the nearby town called *Neapolis* ('the new city') established by pushy parvenus. Colonists arrived as early as the eighth century B.C.E., and "until the fall of the [Roman] Republic [in 31 B.C.E.], Naples was a prosperous provincial and municipal town still largely Greek in its culture, institutions, and population" (Hutton 1958: 11). Thus there were still many Gorgoneions in Naples and environs to catch Mann's attention, in the Archeological Museum (De Caro 1994: 39) and at Pompeii (Brion: 199). At some point Mann must have unconsciously connected the Gorgoneions that he was seeing with the visage of the frowning or impassive maternal face so memorable from his childhood. It is possible, too, that Mann identified his mother with Medusa because of the effect that her stare had upon him. When he was thirty-four (Heilbut 1996: 21), he wrote an essay in praise of "Sleep, Sweet Sleep". Mann's description of sleep utilizes many of the infantile and pastoral images that he attributes to the consciousness of his surrogate characters:

> [E]ach day has its goal[...] a green twilight, a murmuring spring, a grove awaits us, where soft moss consoles our feet, our brows are cooled with blissful airs of home and peace; and with arms outstretched, head dropping backward, with opening lips, with eyes grown blessedly dim, we enter within its priceless shades. (269-70)

The locale of sleep receives its just due:

> what high rank in the hierarchy of our household goods is held by the bed, metaphysical chattel that it is, wherein are celebrated the mysteries of birth and death? It is a sweet-odoured linen shrine, where we lie unconscious, our knees drawn up as once in the darkness of the womb, attached anew, as it were, to nature's umbilical cord and by mysterious ways drawing in nourishment

and renewal; it is a magic cockle-shell, standing covered and unheeded by day in its corner, wherein by night we rock out upon a sea of forgetfulness and infinity. (272)

Mann immediately emphasizes the connection between the figurative and the actual: "Infinity...the sea...Old as my love of sleep is my love of the sea, whose vast simplicity I have always preferred to the exacting many-sidedness of mountain scenery" (273; ellipsis in orig.). Is it any wonder that he offers this memory:

> You will smile to hear that I preserve a clear and grateful memory of every bed I ever slept in for any length of time: every single one, from the earliest little railed, green-curtained cot to the majestic mahogany resting-place in which, in fact, I first saw the light, and which for many years stood in my bachelor quarters. (272)

Each night thus offers a regression to original union with mother: "They tell me that I was a quiet child, that I did not cry and break the peace [*Friede*], but was given to sleep and dreams, to a degree most comfortable to my nurses" (270). Probably Mann was not being ironic when he mentioned "nurses", not mother. The day came when his peacefulness was violated:

> I remember loving sleep and forgetfulness at a time when I had hardly anything to forget; and well I know what it was the made the indelible impression upon my mind and fanned my latent fondness to a conscious love. It was the tale of the man who did not sleep; who was so abandonedly committed to time and affairs that he invoked a curse on sleep, and an angel granted him the awful boon of sleeplessness, breathing on his eyes till they became like grey stones in their sockets, and their lids never closed again. How this man came to rue his wish; what he had to bear as a sleepless solitary among men, dragging out his doomed and tragic life, until at last death released him, and night, that had stood inaccessible before his stony eyeballs, took him to and into herself; such details I have forgotten, and only know that I could scarcely wait for the evening of that day to be left alone in my bed, to throw myself upon the bosom of slumber. And never had I slept more profoundly than in the night after I heard that story. (270)

Sleep is the Good Mother, the mother who, swallowed, causes the eyes to grow "blessedly dim"; sleeplessness is the Bad Mother, the swallowing mother whose stare turns the "eyes like grey stones in their sockets". When the child Mann discovered Medusa, he found a name for the mother whose look of disapproval could deprive him of easy sleep.

Bilderbuch für artige Kinder

Mann soon used the Gorgoneion to express himself. When he rejoined his brother Heinrich in Rome at the end of November, they collaborated on *Bilderbuch für artige Kinder,* a "Picture Book for Well-Behaved Children". Their hand-lettered text, accompanied by their hand-colored drawings, was to be a present for their sister Carla, who was to receive the sacrament of confirmation in the spring of 1897 (Winston 198: 99). The book disappeared in 1933, so it is impossible to say anything definitive about the text. The "sixteen works of poetic art" and incidental illustrations and prose seem to have been dedicated to burlesque and satire. Perhaps they were harmless enough, their barbs aimed outside the house at "Kaiser, pope, beggar, and worker" (Heilbut 1996: 73), but some of the drawings which survive suggest that Thomas Mann, at least, may have had an ulterior motive. Hayman describes the *Bilderbuch*: "Bound in cardboard and linen, it had an ink drawing by Thomas on the cover—a head sticking out a marshy pond and looking mournfully out at a moonlit landscape" (1955: 124). Since Thomas had submitted "Little Herr Friedemann" for publication when he returned to Rome (Hayman 1995: 14), it seems very likely that the cover scene refers to the final scene of that story.

"Little Herr Friedemann"

According to the author himself, "Little Herr Friedemann" conveys this meaning:

> This melancholy story of the little hunchback represents a milestone in my personal history too, in so far as it strikes for the first time a basic motif, which in the combined work plays a role similar to the leitmotif in the individual work. The chief figure is a man whom nature has treated like a stepmother, but he finds himself able to come to terms with his fate in a wisely gentle peaceful philosophic way, and he has attuned his life entirely to repose, contemplation, and peace. The appearance of a remarkably beautiful and yet cold and cruel woman means the invasion of passion into this guarded life, which upsets the whole structure and annihilates the quiet hero himself. ("On Myself" 141)

The tale itself is not so unequivocal as the teller's interpretation. Before a discussion of the tale, though, one feature of the interpretation should be teased for meaning, "nature" as the "stepmother", a figure who is, legendarily, cruelty personified, the very opposite of the benevolent mother figure. In the interpretation Mann links "stepmother" with "nature" by simile; in the *Bilderbuch* sketch he fuses them pictorially as *"Mvtter Natvr"*. The drawing is reproduced in Viktor Mann's *Wir waren fünf* (1964: plate following 56) and described by Karl Kerényi as "a smiling hag with a porcine face, dressed in a slip and corset" (1975: 23n32). Winston describes the figure as "an obese, lewd female with tousled hair and porcine features, grinning sadistically and licking her lips" (1981: 99). Hayman pictures the figure as "fat, old, and obscene, with disheveled hair, piglike features, and a malicious grin" (1995: 125), while Heilbut is content to call her "a lewd lip-smacking Mother Nature" (1996: 89). Winston notes that

> [s]o deeply embedded in Thomas Mann's mind was this drawing in his youth that he alluded to it half a century later in *Doctor Faustus* where the devil, explaining his involuntary changes of appearance, speaks of "the mummery and hocus-pocus of Mother Nature, who always has her tongue in the corner of her mouth". (1981: 99)

Winston adds a footnote: "H. T. Lowe-Porter, unfortunately unaware of the picture Thomas Mann had in mind, translated this [lolling tongue] as 'tongue in her cheek' [i.e., 'speaking insincerely']" (1981: 99fn; my interpolations). Mann's emphasis in *Doctor Faustus* on Mother Nature's tongue as the Devil discusses changes of appearance argues that the Gorgon was his model in the *Bilderbuch*. Certainly a brutal conception of mother, but fitting for a young man who was suffering brutally from the return to consciousness of material repressed since early childhood, according to Freud's formula: "Early trauma—defense—latency—outbreak of neurotic illness—partial return of the repressed" (*Moses* 80). Mann's fictional mothers may be "remarkably beautiful" on the surface, but when they are "cold and cruel" they show that in their depths they are Gorgons. In a sense, Mann's creation of *"Mvtter Natvr"*--or Mother's nature--in the artwork of his twentieth year, is his lifting of the Gorgon mask to defend himself against the "remarkably beautiful" but "cold and cruel" mother who always lurked in his memory. What could be more "cold and cruel" to a person attempting to reconstruct his past than the denial of the maternal breast, whether actual or only imagined? The "remarkably beautiful" mother will continue to force her way into his fiction, but his ironic treatment of her will always indicate that he is still holding up the Gorgoneion against her hidden Gorgon nature. The observation of this defense is crucial to an understanding of Mann's work from "Little Herr Friedemann" on.

Rejoining his brother Heinrich in Rome on 3 December 1896 Mann submitted "Little Herr Friedemann" to the *Neue Deutsche Rundschau* before the year was out (Hayman 1995: 14). Receiving an enthusiastic acceptance by the editor, Oscar Bei, it was published in the May 1897 issue (Heilbut 1996: 78).

The story opens with a remarkable paragraph:

> IT WAS THE NURSE'S FAULT. When the first suspicion arose, what good did it do for Frau Consul Friedemann to urge her earnestly to suppress such a vice? What good did it do for Frau Friedemann to let her have a daily glass of red wine as well as the nourishing beer? It suddenly turned out that this girl sank so low as to drink the fuel meant for the alcohol burner. But before she could be dismissed, before a replacement for her arrived, the accident occurred. One day, when the mother and her three adolescent daughters came home, little Johannes, who was about a month old, had fallen from the nursery table. He lay on the floor, emitting a dreadfully faint whimper, while the nurse stood next to him in a daze. (Neugroschel 1998: 23)

For a variety of reasons the critics have not paid sufficient attention to the precision of Mann's language. Even though he concludes that "Mann's great theme" is "the Oedipus quest in modern dress", Neider (1968: 357) ignores the cause of Friedemann's hunchbacked condition, hurrying on to say that the physical deformity symbolizes "the artist's spiritual deformity, his irregularity" (1968: 334). In his "Themes and Methods in the Early Stories of Thomas Mann", Nemerov ignores any human responsibility for Friedemann's condition with the comment that he was "[d]eformed by an accident in infancy" (1963: 289). Hayman considers the opening as a parody, "which pokes fun at Naturalism by attributing the deformity"—the infant is permanently afflicted by his fall with a hunchback and a pigeon breast—"to the negligence of a drunken nurse" (1965: 120). Heilbut also imputes an ideological intention to the paragraph: "The shock of this opening section is its apparent callousness, deformity as anecdote. It also exhibits Mann's usual treatment of the working classes as sources of comic relief, folk wisdom, and vulgar prejudice" (1996: 78).

An early psychological critic, Hirschbach notes that it is significant that Friedemann is "injured by a woman", adding,

> While he cannot be expected to have been conscious of the sex of
> his nurse at the age of one month, it is possible that a realization
> of it lives in his subconscious mind, and besides he knows, of
> course, the circumstances of his injury. (1955: 6)

Following Hirschbach, Beharriell, although purporting to study
"Psychology in the Early Works of Thomas Mann", simply blames the
nurse: "her injuring the baby, rather than any hereditary handicap, is the source of
the hero's later difficulties" (1962: 155). Despite (or perhaps because of)
the Freudian focus of his study of Mann's fiction, McWilliams
emphasizes that Friedemann adopts repression (as a defense), but fails
to mention the memory of being injured (both physically and
psychologically) that was repressed (1983: 60-61). A very recent
critic, Parkes-Perret, argues that Mann included the nurse in the story
for literary reasons:

> Mann appears to have borrowed a secondary, ironic motif, that of
> the unreliable nurse, from Euripides' drama, giving his story a
> uniquely ironic twist as well. In *Hippolytos*, the nurse causes,
> first, Phaidra's suicide and, then, the ensuing unfolding of the
> entire tragedy by running to tell chaste Hippolytos of his
> stepmother's passionate love for him. It is a fatal miscalculation
> on the nurse's part for she had hoped to bring about an
> assignation between the two. However, although it seems as
> though the nurse were to blame for everything, she is merely
> doing what Aphrodite wants her to do.
>   Mann's novella begins with the pronouncedly terse
> statement: "Die Amme hatte die Schuld" (VIII 77). The nurse
> appears only in the first paragraph of the novella and thus there is
> a certain incongruence to her presence. Her appearance is, I
> believe, Mann's way of acknowledging Euripides' drama in his
> own story. Supposedly, everything is the nurse's fault. Because of
> her drinking, she let the baby Friedemann fall from the dressing
> table which resulted in his bodily infirmity. But, of course, it was
> not the nurse's fault. The babe's mother was quite aware of the
> nurse's drinking problem and did nothing to rectify the matter.
> (1996: 289)

The reading offered here reponds to the arguments offered by
Hirschbach, Beharriell, McWilliams, and Parkes-Perret. The key
words in the opening paragraph are "nurse" and "nourishing". The "nurse"
is a wet nurse, as the German word *Amme* indicates; she was hired
because she was already nursing an infant of her own, thus capable of
relieving Frau Consul Friedemann of the responsibility of breast-
feeding Johannes. The translator of the first American publication of

the story, Herman George Scheffauer, bluntly begins, "It was the fault of the wet-nurse" (1928: 203). Although Mrs. Lowe-Porter translates *Amme* simply as "nurse", she knew the meaning the word conveyed, for she supplied a reason for the daily beer-ration, "the beer which was needed for the milk" (*Stories* 3), the German text making no reference to milk. The nurse was provided "a daily glass of red wine" because "the nourishing beer" already provided did not stimulate sufficient additional breast milk.[8] The wine could also have been a bribe to the lower-class nurse so that the middle-class mother, who had declined to breast-feed her baby, could spend a leisurely afternoon away from home with her three adolescent daughters. Whether she could not or would not suckle her baby is, of course, immaterial to the baby who only knows that something is missing that would have made all the difference.

Additional information is provided:

> Before the birth of the child, the poor woman had had to suffer the loss of her husband, the Netherlandish consul, who had been snatched away by a sudden violent illness, and she was still so broken up that she was incapable of hoping that little Johannes might survive for her. (Neugroschel 1998: 23)

Apparently sympathetic to the mother, the sentence could have been inspired by the ironic temperament so often attributed to its author. Like Friedemann's father, Mann's father had been the Netherlandish consul (Hayman 1995: 84): in either case the father's early death left his son helpless before a mother whose bland appearance masked a lack of genuine maternal concern. The last clause could mean that Frau Friedemann does not care whether her baby lives or dies, and it is likely that the twenty-year-old Mann—in the midst of his sexual dilemma—attributed the same indifference to his mother.

It should be remembered that dreaming, a form of unconscious mentation, often uses a "nurse" to symbolize "mother" (Gutheil 1951: 133). In Johannes' case, the first object, the mother, enters his unconscious as the alienating object. Freud writes:

> A child's first erotic object is the mother's breast that nourishes it; love has its origin in attachment to the satisfied need for nourishment[...]. And for however long it is fed at its mother's breast, it will always be left with a conviction after it has been weaned that its feeding was too short and too little. (*Outline* 188-89).

If Freud's statement is valid, then Thomas Mann had a profound understanding of the nursing experience, displayed not only in this story but also in a 1932 book review, *"Die Einheit des Menschengeistes"* (reprinted in *GW*, X, 751-756), a portion of which is translated below:

> The mother is called Ninmah, "almighty mistress." But by what other name is she called, at least in certain intimate moments? "Mama," "Mami"—thus one addresses her. Early mankind [babbles] at her feet, at her breast, as we all have [babbled], as they will [babble] on this earth forever. A touching symbol of the unity of all that is human, this primitive sound of innocence that is timeless and at home in East and West.
>
> But there is a [babbling] more sensual than that of the toothless infant, and this too bears witness to the fascination that the mother-goddess exercises on humanity and to the universal function of this goddess. "Nana"—so too is the Beloved Lady called. One wonders whether Emile Zola was impelled by memories of the history of religion when he gave this enticing name to his symbolic heroine, that Astarte of the Second Empire. (Ezergailis 1975: 22)[2]

The etymology of "Mama" reveals that the infant associates the mother with her nipples. The translation above is verbatim, except that in the four brackets Ezergailis's choice of the English *stammer* for the German *lallen* has been replaced by *babble*, a translation better suited to emphasize the desire for the breast that is present in both the infant and the infant-in-the-adult.

It is possible that Johannes was abruptly weaned after the fiasco—or, if not, that there was a delay before a new wet nurse could be found. Thus the deformity that Mann treats in his story is not merely Johannes' deformity of body but more importantly the deformity of psyche that was in the making long before his body betrayed its untreatable injury. Johannes learns to bear the physical restrictions that his infirmity places upon him; he also decides to defend himself from his psychological trauma by repressing all memory of its cause. His early summers are spent in a small garden behind the Friedemann house, he cracking walnuts while observing his mother and three now-adult sisters through a vulviform tent opening, they apparently sharing the secrets of their sex. The garden is, of course, universally evocative of the feminine (Cirlot 1962: 110), but Mann also had a personal susceptibility to garden nostalgia. In his seventies Mann's brother Heinrich recaptured scenes of his early life in drawings; one of them, dated 1875, shows their mother

> in the garden, leaning flirtatiously back in a rocking chair and fanning herself, while her other arm is stretched out across a table toward the officer sitting well forward in his chair, gazing at her intently. The young Heinrich is lying on the grass not far away from them, and the baby, Thomas, is in his cot. (Hayman 1995: 88)

The supernumerary three adult sisters provide the first hint of the Gorgon nature of the mother, since they personify the "threeness" inherent in that legend. Further, Anton Ehrenzweig reminds us that "Freud recognized that three sisters always stand for a powerful mother figure" (1967: 250).

Johannes' nut-cracking activity suggests that, because of his disabilities, physical and psychological, he will be unable to respond to the phallic challenge when it comes. Inside the house, he spends much of his time gazing out the window, preparing, as it were, for lifetime spectatorship, replacing the desire to touch with the desire to look (Wurmser 1981: 154). What is left unsaid is that a bedrock of shame in his unconscious was laid down by his conclusion that he was not worthy of the breast and that daily the stare of others increases the amount of his petrifaction.

At sixteen Herr Friedemann is struck by an infatuation for a "cheerful blond creature" (Neugroschel 1998: 25) of the same age, the sister of a classmate. But he does not declare his feeling to her: "[h]e felt a strange anxiety in her presence, and he was deeply saddened by the self-conscious and artificial courtesy with which she, too, treated him" (Neugroschel 1998: 26). While on a solitary walk, he inadvertently spies the girl necking with "a tall, redheaded boy", a phallic fellow. As he steals away, "a sharp, urgent pain shot from his chest into his throat"—the adolescent pain of the heart reawakens the infantile pain of the unsatisfied throat. He concludes: "Fine,[...] it's over. I will never again concern myself with any of that. It brings others joy and happiness, but for me it can only mean grief and sorrow. I'm done with it. Never again".

At seventeen Herr Friedemann leaves school to begin a career in business. The supreme ambition of his life is now to reach the goal of peacefulness—his surname indicates his self-conception (and it recalls the 1896 letters of a Mann seeking peace). Thus Friedemann practices ingratiation and industry. The death of his mother, when he is twenty-one, does not really affect him, either with sadness or with jubilation, for he had, by repressing the memory of his trauma, always defended himself against the physical presence which had caused it. The fact that her death causes him to remember "a thousand childhood memories" merely indicates that they pictured "screen memories", memories that retain the insignificant aspects but omit the disturbing aspects of an event (Freud *Moses* 303-23). He continues his program of being an "epicurean" of all happinesses—except "the greatest happiness that life can offer us" (Neugroschel 1998: 27). He can even enjoy *"yearnings"*, as long as he remembers, like the man in "Disillusionment", that their fulfillment would inevitably disappoint him.

Little Herr Friedemann is essentially a creature of shame, as Wurmser defines the experience, "the characteristic and specific pattern of anxiety and defense against scopophilia and exhibitionism" (1981: 156). But, seeing "[s]exual scopophilia and exhibitionism" as "narrower versions of[...] broadly conceived partial drives", Wurmser will "coin two broader terms: *theatophilia* and *delophilia*":

> *Theatophilia* can be defined as the desire to watch and observe, to admire and to be fascinated, to merge and master through attentive looking, operating as a basic inborn drive from earliest infancy.
>   *Delophilia* is defined as the desire to express oneself and to fascinate others by one's self-exposure, to show and to impress, to merge with the other through communication. Again, it would originate in archaic times. (1981: 158)

Instances of Friedemann's *"theatophilia"*, his obsessive observation in house, garden, schoolyard, and countryside, have already been noted. His *"delophilia"* develops as his self-esteem is nurtured by his business success: "With his comical self-importance, this unfortunate cripple strutted along in a light-colored overcoat and a shiny top hat (he was, strangely, a bit vain)[...]" (parenthesis in orig.).

Having become a successful independent businessman, Friedemann, at thirty, is seen "sitting after lunch in the gray garden tent[...]; he had a good cigar in his mouth and a good book in his hand":

> Once, when he lowered the book on his lap and blinked up at the blue, sunny sky, he said to himself: Now, that's thirty years. Another ten or even twenty may still come, God knows. They will come along quietly and soundless and flow by like the ones that have already passed, and I look forward to them with peace in my heart. (Neugroschel 1998: 29)

He has apparently vanquished his three Gorgon sisters. Now diminished to the *Graiai*, probably with one eye and one tooth between them (Rose 1959: 29), they are cooped up within the house, while he sits in the vulviform tent. There he enjoys that renowned substitute for the "good breast", the "good cigar". As Hans Castorp might say, his life is "hermetic".

But the day comes when Friedemann sees Gerda von Rinnlingen, the wife of the new district commander. Friedemann is indulging his *"delophilia"*:

> He was strolling, tiny and self-important, alongside Wholesaler Stephens, an unusually big and burly man with rounded sideburns and dreadfully bushy eyebrows. Both men wore top hats and had unbuttoned their overcoats because of the heat. They were talking politics while tapping their canes on the sidewalk in a regular cadence[...]. (Neugroschel 1998: 31)

In this scene, when contrasted with Wholesaler Stephens, Herr Friedemann is indeed *"Der Kleine"*, "tiny and self-important", but he is not worried about *"Der Kleine"*, an affectionate name for "the genital", as Freud observes in *The Interpretation of Dreams* (357, 362). After all, is not Herr Friedeman, like Wholesaler Stephens, accoutered with invincible masculine talismans, a top hat and a walking stick (Freud *Interpretation* 360, 354)? And since he is paired with "an unusually big and burly man with rounded sideburns and dreadfully bushy eyebrows", a regular bear of a man, perhaps Friedemann feels fused under the fur.

Then suddenly Stephens spies a singular scene: "God damn it if that isn't the Rinnlingen woman driving this way" (Neugroschel 1998: 31). Frau Hagenström, the lawyer's wife, had already expressed to Herr Friedemann's sister Henriette, the view of the law-abiding townswomen:

> She smokes, she goes horseback riding—all well and good! But her behavior is not only free and easy, it's tomboyish, and even that's not the right word[...]. Look, she's not ugly by any means; you might even find her pretty. And yet she's devoid of any feminine charm, and her eyes, her laughter, her movements, lack everything that men love. She's no flirt, and goodness knows I'd be the last person not to find that praiseworthy. But should such a young woman—she's only twenty-four—be so thoroughly lacking in natural grace? My dear, I'm not good at expressing myself, but I do know what I mean. Our gentlemen are still dumbstruck for now. But you'll see, within a few weeks they'll turn away from her in disgust.

There is more:

> You ought to see it! You will see it! I am the first to insist that a
> married woman should have a certain degree of aloofness toward
> the opposite sex. But how does she behave toward her own
> husband? She has a way of giving him an icy look and saying
> "Dear friend" to him with a pitying stress that I find outrageous!
> You should see *him* at such times—correct, stalwart, chivalrous,
> forty years old and splendidly preserved, a brilliant officer!
> They've been married for four years. My dear... (Neugroschel
> 1998: 30; concluding ellipsis in orig.)

Frau von Rinnlingen's appearance in the street-scene arouses Herr
Friedemann's *"theatophilia"*:

> She wore a very light-colored wide jacket, and her skirt was also
> of a light hue. From under a small, round straw hat with a leather
> band, her reddish-blond hair, which was combed over her ears,
> welled out and fell deep down the nape of her neck, into a thick
> knot. Her oval face was a matte white, and bluish shadows lurked
> in the corners of her brown eyes, which were unusually close-set.
> Her short but quite finely shaped nose had a small ridge of
> freckles, which suited her nicely; but one could not tell whether
> her mouth was beautiful, for her lower lip kept incessantly sliding
> out and then in, chafing the upper lip.
>   When the cart reached them, Wholesaler Stephens
> greeted her with extraordinary deference, and little Herr
> Friedemann likewise doffed his hat, while looking at Frau von
> Rinnlingen with large, attentive eyes. She lowered her whip,
> nodded slightly, and drove slowly past, viewing the houses and
> shop windows to the right and the left. (Neugroschel 1998: 31)[3]

When Wholesaler Stephens comments, "She's gone for a spin, and now she's
driving home," Friedemann asks, "What did you say?" Like the other men of
the town, he, too, has been "dumbstruck".
       In his reading of the story Parkes-Perret argues "that [Mann] uses
the Greek goddess Aphrodite as a 'mask' for Gerda von Rinnlingen, the lame Greek
god Hephaestus as a 'mask' for Mr. Friedemann, a hunchback, and Ares for the
commandant, Gerda von Rinnlingen's husband[...]" (1996: 277-78). It is more
likely, though, that the only character animated by a mythic archetype
is Gerda, whose mannerisms are reminiscent of Medusa, who, though
mythic, was mortal. The matte surface of her face suggests that she
wears "an apotropaic mask—a sort of talisman which both killed and redeemed"
(Dumoulié 1995: 779), the function of the very ancient Medusa-head
mask, which was widely known before myths were ever attached to

her person (Rose 1959: 29-30). Probably some intuition of the power of Gerda's mask elicits Frau Hagenström's conclusion: "Our gentlemen are still dumbstruck for now. But you'll see, within a few weeks they'll turn away from her in disgust." This is not to say, however, that Gerda is simply Medusa modernized, for she gives no evidence that *she* sees herself as Medusa. If she displays mannerisms that evoke Medusa, those same mannerisms can also be interpreted as revealing, instead, that she is simply a young woman who feels deprived of physical and psychic satisfaction. Herr Friedemann, given the particularities of his development, sees her first as the beautiful goddess, only to discover at the end that her mask hides the lolly-tongued Gorgon.

Others may be quick to note details that set Gerda apart, such as Frau Hagenström, although she admits that she fumbles for the words to express her intuitions. It is appropriate that she first mentions Gerda's horseback riding, for "the earliest stratum [of the Medusa myth] connects her with the horse" (Baring 1993: 342). Of course, her horseback riding and smoking reveal her rejection of the *gute Hausfrau* conventions of the time. She is "tomboyish" and without a baby after four years of marriage! She puts the notorious Medusa stare even on her husband, has struck the men of the town dumb, even as she affects Friedemann, who is all eyes, when he first sees her on the street. Although Frau Hagenström acknowledges that she is "pretty"— as later mythic representations pictured Medusa (Dumoulié 1995: 780)--Gerda betrays by a mannerism her Gorgon origin. Loyal to his identification of Gerda as Aphrodite, Parkes-Perret asserts that her "lipchafing" "can be easily misinterpreted as an indication of pouting, a coquettish signal" (1996: 295), insisting, rather, that it "is an obvious indication of her desire to keep herself under control" (1996: 286). Quoting a 1909 letter in which Mann insists, "'Frau von Rinnlingen' ist keine Kokette", Parkes-Perret adds:

> Mann wants to make sure that his readers do not misconstrue Gerda von Rinnlingen as being coquette. He could, of course, have simply removed the passages treating Gerda's lipchafing from the novel, but then Friedemann would not have had this important sign to misinterpret. (1996: 295n60)

The present reader will trust the tale, not the exegete. It could be a coquettish signal, lubricating labia hints at lubricated labia. But if Gerda has been enthused by Medusa, then her slipsliding lips arouse an unwary viewer's amorous attention, just before parting to reveal

the "dentate vagina" (Dumoulié 1995: 783) that could put an end to the
viewer's protruberance in the nether parts, according to Freud
("Medusa's" 273). Perhaps Heilbut is wise merely to interpret the lip
movement as a "slight tic"—but then he speculates that it and the "blue
shadows around her close-set eyes" contribute to her personification of
"damaged, moribund beauty" (1996: 79).

When Friedemann had looked upon Gerda in the street, he
then "looked down at the sidewalk" (Neugroschel 1998: 32), as if aware of
the threat that her face projected. In consequence, when Gerda and her
husband visit the Friedemann house three days later, Herr Friedemann
avoids facing her by not showing his face. At lunch after their visitors
leave, the three Friedemann sisters excitedly tell him whom he missed.
Then they invite him to go with them to reciprocate the visit on
Sunday: "Herr Friedemann hadn't registered the question, and he ate his soup with a
silent and anxious mien. It was as if he were listening for something, for some
uncanny noise" (Neugroschel 1998: 33).[4] Friedemann's anxiety recalls
Wurmser's definition of shame, here extended: "Shame as a specific form
of anxiety is a motive of defense directed mainly against exhibitionism and
scopophilia and is rooted in a primitive, physiological reflex pattern". Wurmser
quotes Fenichel: "'I feel ashamed' means 'I do not want to be seen'". Then
Wurmser adds, "It leads not only to hiding but also to a refusal to look[...]"
(1981: 150). In his study of shame Wurmser several times cites the
psychoanalytic literature on Medusa (1981: 149-50, 173). Still
dumbstruck, Friedemann is unconsciously fearful that his repressed
mother is just about to return.

Although sensitive to the threat that Gerda poses, Friedemann
is still prey to his *"delophilia"*and his*"theatophilia"*, for the evening after
the von Rinnlingen visit he attends a presentation of *Lohengrin* at the
City Theater. The setting emphasizes the autobiography that
permeates the story, for Winston writes that the adolescent Mann went
"almost nightly" to the Lübeck City Theater, especially to hear Wagner's
operas, particularly *Lohengrin,* which he heard "so many times that for the
rest of his life he knew it virtually by heart" (1981: 38-39).

Friedemann is dressed "in an impeccable black tuxedo with a dazzling
white, sharply protruding shirtfront" (Neugroschel 1998: 33)--grandiosity
trying to hide shame caused by physical and psychic traumata.
Friedemann starts to enter his box, upon which all eyes are focused,
for, unknown to him, the von Rinnlingens are already seated there,
making their first appearance at the theater. When he sees Gerda, he
raises his hand "toward his forehead, and for an instant his nostrils dilated

convulsively", the former action as if to hide his eyes and the latter, as if to be guided by scent toward the breast, the two actions in concert revealing his ambivalence.

When Friedemann seats himself, he is aware that Gerda is staring at him, "pushing her lower lip out" (Neugroschel 1998: 34). She is the "only woman there with a slight décolletage", which is enough, for she has a "full bosom".[5] She strips the glove from her left arm, "and he had no choice, he was forced to keep seeing this rounded, matte-white arm, which, like the unbejeweled hand, was traversed by utterly pale-blue veins". His vision destorted by desire, Friedemann sees the utterly pale-blue-veined arm udderwise. As the violins sing and the trumpets blare, the evil Telramund is slain, with Friedemann sitting, "one forefinger on his mouth and the other hand in his jacket lapel", that is, sucking his finger and caressing the only breast available—like a child with his banky.

When the von Rinnlingens return from intermission, Gerda again stares at Friedemann:

> without wanting to do so, he lifted his head toward her. Their eyes met, and she did not avert her gaze; instead she continued, peering at him without a trace of abashedness, until he himself, subdued and humiliated, lowered his eyes. He turned even paler, and a strange, sweetly pungent anger mounted in him. (Neugroschel 1998: 35)

When Gerda drops her fan, both she and Friedemann bend to retrieve it, but she reaches it, saying with "a mocking smile", "Thank you". "Their heads had been very close together, and for an instant he had been forced to inhale the warm fragrance of her bosom". This is more than he can stand; standing, he leaves before the conclusion. For when Gerda drops her fan, her social masking-device, Herr Friedemann can see her not as Gerda but as the "beautiful face" lost so long ago. But in leaving he reveals to Gerda his fascination for her. Apparently Friedemann misses the part of the opera when Lohengrin is compelled by Elsa, his new wife, to reveal his identity. The revelation requires that he forswear her. According to Ehrenzweig, Elsa's insatiable curiosity marks her as a representative of oral sadism—Lohengrin's admission requires that he return to "the secret all-male society of the Holy Grail" (1967: 237-38). Had Friedemann stuck it out until Lohengrin's dove-pulled boat went around the bend, he might have noted a resemblance between Gerda's and Elsa's oral actions and between his and Lohengrin's acknowledgements of identity.

Appropriately, Main Street, on which he had first seen Gerda, is the route home, to which he is going, literally and figuratively. The narrator reveals Friedeman's musings:

> The way she had looked at him! What? She had forced him to lower his eyes? She had humbled him with her gaze? Wasn't she a woman and he a man? And hadn't her strange brown eyes actually trembled with joy?
> He again felt that powerless, voluptuous hatred rising inside him, but then he relived that moment when her head had grazed his, when he had inhaled the fragrance of her body[...].
> (Neugroschel 1998: 36)

When he gets home, he tries to block out his memories by concentrating on the sight and scent of a "big yellow rose that someone had placed in a tumbler for him", but he shoves the tumbler aside: "What should he care about such a fragrance? What should he care about all the things that had made up his 'happiness' until now?" (Neugroschel 1998: 37). Gerda's stare has forced him to experience the "return of the repressed". Imagining that he hears the *Lohengrin* music, he falls "into a heavy, fever-dulled sleep" with the vision of "Frau Rinnlingen's figure in front of him, her white arm on the red velvet". Since he has been confronted by Mother-Medusa, his sleep-peace is, predictably, disturbed:

> Often he was on the verge of awakening, but he was afraid to do so, and each time he lapsed back into unconsciousness. When it grew light, however, he opened his eyes and looked around with a large, painful gaze. Everything was clear in front of his soul; it was as if his suffering had been completely uninterrupted by sleep[...]. His head was numb, and his eyes were burning [...].
> (Neugroschel 1998: 37)

He awakens to what others would regard as "a beautiful Sunday morning", the day that he and his sisters are to visit the von Rinnlingens. Hoping that he has beaten back the attack of "the repressed", he tells his sisters that he will not accompany them. After breakfasting, he lights a cigar and sits by the window: "Breakfast had done him good, and he felt happy and hopeful. He took a book, read, smoked, and squinted into the sun" (Neugroschel 1998: 38). By sheer will power he will return to the peacefulness of small pleasures and symbolic substitutes!

Within an hour, though, "straining his muscles as he quelled all the anxious warnings inside him", he decides to visit Gerda. Watching the maid climb the red-carpeted stairs to announce his presence, Friedemann puts down his stick, is shaking so badly that he nearly drops his top hat. Climbing the stairs without his stick he is not the *alter Steiger* that Freud speaks of (*Inter.* 355fn2). Rather he probably remembers the arm that was a breast lying on the red velvet of the opera box. Gerda approaches him, invitingly everting her lower labium as usual. He glances up at her, "for he only reached up to her bosom" (Neugroschel 1998: 40), babbles his excuses for his behavior and the pun describing it:

> He could think of absolutely nothing else to say, but she stood and gazed at him relentlessly, as if trying to force him to keep speaking. The blood suddenly shot to his head. She wants to torture me and ridicule me! he thought. And she sees through me! How her eyes glitter!

Continuing to stare at him, Gerda asks about his health, brushes aside his answer to complain, "I get sick a lot too,[...] but nobody notices. I'm nervous, and I experience the most bizarre fits."

Gerda apparently belongs to the hysterics, a sect so prominent in Europe at the time. Dr. Freud would have suspected that Lieutenant Colonel von Rinnlingen is stiff, but maybe not in all the right places. Gerda tries another stratagem: "She fell silent, dropping her chin to her bosom, and looked up at him expectantly". But, having renounced touch in infancy, he can only look. Gerda fits yet another arrow in her bow. In response to Friedemann's information that he plays the violin, Gerda

> looked vacantly past him, lost in thought. "Well, then we can play duets together now and again," she suddenly said. "I can accompany somewhat. It would be nice to find someone here[...]. Will you come?" (Neugroschel 1998: 41)

It is possible that Gerda is practicing *double-entendre* here. If so, she gets no rise out of Friedemann, which gets a rise out of her: "Abruptly her expression changed. He saw her face twist into barely perceptible cruel scorn, saw her eyes focus on him with that sinister glitter, rest on him firmly and quizzically, as twice before".

Blushing, he casts his eyes carpetward. For the moment she is apparently convinced that he is impotent, not worth looking at, even as she looks past her husband, who now enters the room (Neugroschel 1998: 42). Taking his leave, Friedemann walks along the path where years ago he had observed the titillating teenage twosome and renounced all claim to such pleasure. He thought that he had convinced himself that he would be content with peace and quiet:

> Now that woman had come, she had had to come, it was his fate, she herself was his fate, she alone! She had come, and even though he had tried to defend his peace, she had aroused everything he had suppressed since youth for fear of torture and ruin, and now it had all seized hold of him with terrible, irresistible violence and was destroying him! (Neugroschel 1998: 44).

Before he had left the villa, Friedemann had accepted an invitation to a party the next Sunday. Once there he drinks too much and moons over Gerda, who finally calls to him, "I've been waiting in vain for you these past few days, for you and your violin" (Neugroschel 1998: 45). Mumbling, Friedemann ducks his head. After dinner, with his coffee and cigar, he positions himself so that he can watch Gerda: "She was slowly smoking a cigarette, whereby she exhaled the smoke through her nose while pushing out her lower lip" (Neugroschel 1998: 46). Then she approaches: "Would you care to escort me into the garden, Herr Friedemann?" (Neugroschel 1998: 47). Through a glass-paneled door, then down some steps she leads him, as if from the real to the desired.

Outside, Gerda leads him down the central garden path, whose entrance is "blanked by two low squat obelisks", perhaps *Hermæ*, often used as garden ornaments (Evans 1981: 548): "At the end of the very straight, chestnut-lined path they saw the river, shimmering greenish in the moonlight" This is the landscape of memory—he cracking walnuts, mother in the tent—but it is also the landscape of the unconscious, the vaginal passage that leads to the amniotic sac. "By the river", she says, "there's a lovely spot, where I often sit. We could chat there for a moment or two".

The spot is invitingly deserted, so they sit on a bench. Gerda speaks to Friedemann in a tone so "soft, wistful, and gentle" that it registers not only as a vocable but also as a caress: "How long have you had your handicap, Herr Friedemann?[...] Were you born with it?" (Neugroschel 1998: 48) As he replies to her questions, Friedemann must dare to think that, since Gerda is speaking like a solicitous mother, she will recognize the infantile appeal for maternal love contained in his factual response. But when she says, "I know a thing or two about unhappiness, [...] Such summer nights by the water are the best remedy" (Neugroschel 1998: 48), she could be encouraging his romantic attentiveness to her own needs.

In the throes of regression Friedemann

> suddenly quivered on his seat, straightened up, sobbed, emitted a sound, a wail that was also a cry of relief, and he sank slowly to the ground in front of her. He touched her hand, which had been

> resting next to him, and while he clutched it, while he also took
> hold of the other, while this little, utterly deformed man knelt
> before her, trembling and twitching, and buried his face in her lap,
> he stammered in an inhuman, gasping voice: 'You do know... Let
> me... I can't anymore... My God... My God...'. (Neugroschel
> 1998: 49, ellipses in orig.)

Admittedly, Friedemann's actions here are equivocal. As expected, my interpretation accords with my thesis. Sinking to the position of an infant, Friedemann clutches Gerda's hands because their dependent fingers appear as the nipples for which he has long yearned (even as, in *The Magic Mountain*, Hans Castorp is very aware—at first sight—of Clavdia Chauchat's stubby fingers). Kneeling at Gerda's feet, crying, "My God . . . My God", as he had the night he abruptly left the opera (Neugroschel 1998: 35, 36), Friedemann enacts the infant's response to the mother-goddess that Mann described in the 1932 review (*"Die Einheit..."*) previously cited. By burying his face in Gerda's lap, Friedemann betrays his wish to return to the womb or at least to the breast. What is unequivocal is the fact that he makes no attempt to join his genitals to hers.

Friedemann's speech is similarly ambiguous. My interpretation would thus replace the ellipses: "You do know [that I seek you as a mother figure]. Let me [offer oral love to you]. I can't anymore [function as a man]". Gerda's response is just as opaque:

> She did not resist, nor did she bend down toward him. She sat,
> high and erect, leaning back slightly, and her small, close-set
> eyes, which seemed to reflect the liquid shimmer of the water,
> stared tensely straight ahead, over him, into the distance.
> And then suddenly, with a jerk, with a brief, proud,
> scornful laugh, she had wrested her hands from his hot fingers,
> had grabbed his arm, had hurled him sideways and sent him
> sprawling on the ground, had leaped up and vanished along the
> wooded path.

First of all, she does not bend forward to offer maternal comfort. Her slight tilt backward might suggest an initial receptivity to what she assumed was to be a mature male sexual advance. (It might also imitate his mother's posture that Heinrich caught in his drawing of the 1875 garden.) Perhaps Gerda's earlier verbal recognition of his "handicap" indicated that she was willing to overlook it because of the fervency of his ardor. But now, when she looks "straight ahead, over him, into the distance", could she not be denying his existence because of his impotence?

Mann then writes, "Er lag da, das Gesicht im Grase, betäubt, ausser sich, und ein Zucken lief jeden Augenblick durch seinen Körper" (*GW* 8: 105). Neugroschel translates, "He lay there, his face in the grass, numb, beside himself, his body twitching incessantly" (1998: 49). Lesér notes that in "the German text, *zittern* indicates all of Friedemann's tremors except those in his first and last appearances, where *zucken* is used" (1989: 249n31). In Friedemann's first appearance, as the dropped baby, Neugroschel translated "zuckenden" (*GW* 8: 77) as "convulsing" (23). Lesér does not realize the significance of her observation, nor does Neugroschel recognize the significance of the repeated word, for he does not give *zucken* the same translation in the first and last scene. By returning to the use of *zucken* in the final scene, Mann intends to show that Friedemann is reliving the first abandonment in the second. As if to confirm that Friedemann is traumatized by the denied breast the narrator then writes, in the Lowe-Porter translation,

> What were his sensations at this moment? Perhaps he was feeling that same luxury of hate which he had felt before when she had humiliated him with her glance, degenerated now, when he lay before her on the ground and she had treated him like a dog, into an insane rage which must at all costs find expression even against himself—a disgust, perhaps of himself, which filled him with a thirst to destroy himself, to tear himself to pieces, to blot himself utterly out. (*Stories* 22)[6]

The first reference to "she" is vague enough to be directed at his mother, who first put the Medusa gaze on him. Then to say that Friedemann experiences an all-consuming "thirst to destroy himself, to tear himself to pieces, to blot himself utterly out" is tantamount to saying that it was his original unquenched thirst that was his fate, death in the maternal water.[7]

That "Little Herr Friedemann" had its origin in autobiography is demonstrated by an event which occurred shortly before Mann's death at the age of eighty. In May, 1955, he returned to his hometown of Lübeck for a week's visit. He was presented with honorary citizenship at the town hall and invited to give a reading from his work at the City Theater. Accepting the invitation, "he requested that the prelude to *Lohengrin*, which he had listened to with such great enthusiasm as a boy in this very place, be played before the reading" (K. Mann 1975: 151). It would be a pleasure to report that he read "Little Herr Friedemann" to his

audience, but, alas, he did not (Heilbut 1996: 591). Perhaps that would
have been getting too close to home.

Little Herr Friedemann: Novellas

Thomas Mann always maintained that "Little Herr
Friedemann" represented his artistic breakthrough. Within six months
of its publication he had written enough new stories and revised
unpublished stories for a collection. Published in May 1898, it
consisted of "Little Herr Friedemann", "The Will to Happiness",
"Death", "Disillusionment", "Tobias Mindernickel", and "The
Dilettante" (also known as "The Joker" or "The Clown") (Prater
1995: 22). "Little Herr Friedemann" having been earlier considered,
the latter five stories will be touched upon here only insofar as they
reveal the motif of early childhood alienation.

"The Will to Happiness"

"The Will to Happiness" (orig. publication, 22 and 29 Aug.
and 5 Sept. 1896, *Simplicissimus* [Mann *Six* 74]) has its origin in a
matrix of self-referentiality—to Thomas Mann, not to the unnamed
narrator. Paolo ('Paul') Hofmann is the child of a German father who
"had made his fortune as a plantation owner in South America", who "had married a
local woman of good family, and moved back to his native north Germany soon
after". Paolo "was the image of his mother", had been "cosseted at home", and
was therefore very unhappy when he experienced the separation
caused by school attendance (Mann *Six* 75). The narrator probably
hints at a homoerotic desire for Paolo when he writes that "[w]e[...] took
dancing lessons together—I think we were sixteen—and as a result we both fell in
love for the first time". Remaining silent about the object of his attraction,
the narrator describes Paolo's object as a "little girl, a blond, cheerful
creature who had smitten his heart, with a melancholy ardor that was remarkable for
his age, and which sometimes seemed to me almost uncanny" (Mann *Six* 76).
(The narrator admits that he has always kept "a quick charcoal sketch of a
face much like that girl's, signed 'You are like a flower! Paolo Hofmann fecit'"
[Mann *Six* 77]; how he came by it and why he kept it he does not say.)
The source of his sense of uncanniness is implied when the narrator
reveals that at one dancing lesson Paolo, after the "blond, cheerful
creature" danced twice with another boy, had fainted. His fainting was
diagnosed as a sign of a defect of his heart—thus linking an organic
condition with an emotional state, a grotesque—that is to say,
rationally inexplicable—linkage that provokes the experience of the

uncanny. A psychoanalytic interpretation would add that Paolo's ardor seems uncanny because its apparent object is really a surrogate for the original object.

When Paolo's family moved to Karlsruhe, he was left to board with a tutor while he finished his last school year, but he was sent packing when the teacher in religion class discovered under his Old Testament "a buxom female figure, fully sketched except for her left foot, exposing herself to view with no sense of shame" (Mann *Six* 77), perhaps a Baubo of the type to be referred to in *The Magic Mountain*. (Perhaps this plot incident has its origin in Mann's last school term in Lübeck?)

Five years have passed when the narrator next sees Paolo in Munich: "I saw someone coming down the steps of the Academy, who from a distance looked almost like an Italian figurine. When I came nearer, it really was he" (Mann *Six* 78).[9] Since the narrator cannot be reminded of Baubo, perhaps he is reminded of Hermes? Graduated from the Academy, Paolo is in failing health because of his irreparable heart condition. He also has the other kind of heart trouble; he is in love with Ada, known Biblically and locally as a Hebrew beauty, the nineteen-year-old daughter of Baron von Stein, of the "cash nobility" (Mann *Six* 79). And she loves Paolo—but Papa resists Paolo's plea because of his palpitations.

Another five years pass before the narrator once again meets Paola in Rome. In time Paolo receives a letter from Baron von Stein rescinding his ban of the banns. Paolo dies "the morning after the wedding night—almost during the wedding night" (Mann *Six* 96). Thus the demise of Paolo the painter, whose surname should have been *Fried*hofmann. Various conclusions have been drawn by interpreters of the story, but none—at least those I have read—notices the writer who survives to narrate the story. Arguably in love with Paolo, he has apparently decided to forgo *his* will to happiness in deference to his will to vocation. Given what can be inferred about Mann's emotional state during the period in which "The Will to Happiness" was written, it could be argued that the character of the narrator also reflects considerable self-referentiality, hence affects any conclusion about the story.

"Death"

Since "Death" (first published 16 Jan. 1897, *Simplicissimus*) was submitted for a contest for stories "in which sexual love plays no part" (Mann *Six* 100), aspects of childhood alienation are negligible.

"Disillusionment"

Not quite five pages long, "Disillusionment" (composed Nov. 1896 [Hayman 1995 14]) is the narration of a young German who meets an older fellow countryman on the Piazza di San Marco, Venice. After a concert by a military band all others in the audience depart, save these two. The older man describes a life of boredom brought on by an initial disillusionment, his childhood discovery that no event in reality, even the total conflagration of his parents' house, ever fulfilled his prior imagination of it. Thus he has lived in the penult. Even the pain of losing the woman he loved to another did not match his expectation of pain. The exemplary experience of disappointment that he offers: "Often I have thought of the day when I gazed for the first time at the sea. The sea is vast, the sea is wide, my eyes roved far and wide and longed to be free. But there was the horizon. Why a horizon, when I wanted the infinite from life" (*Stories of Three Decades* 346; hereafter cited as *Stories* 26). (This kind of boredom will be treated at length when "The Dilettante" is discussed.) What the man desires is Romain Rolland's "oceanic feeling", the sense of infantile fusion. In that respect he anticipates Hanno Buddenbrook and Hans Castorp, both of whom view the sea in anticipation; in that respect he reflects his sea-loving creator, who provided his character on Piazza di San Marco with the mood music that he had heard from the pavillion at Travemünde. Mann reported to Grautoff on 6 April 1897:

> Since "Little Herr Friedemann" I am suddenly able to find the discreet forms and masks in which I can walk abroad among people with my experiences. Whereas formerly, if all I wanted to do was communicate from myself to myself, I needed a secret diary. (Winston 1981: 100)

"Disillusionment" indicates that even before "Little Herr Friedemann" Mann had learned to use "discreet forms and masks".

"Tobias Mindernickel"

Anzieu's psychoanalysis of fur offers an *aperçu* into "Tobias Mindernickel" (1897). In the first paragraph the domicile of Tobias is described: while on the first and second floors both the right and the left apartments are occupied, on the third floor the apartment opposite his solitary appartment is vacant. Tobias is, therefore, not "twinned". In the second paragraph Tobias' facial features are described:

> His scrawny neck seemed longer because it rose out of a low turn-down collar. His hair had gone grey and he wore it brushed down smooth on the temples. His wide hat-brim shaded a smooth-shaven sallow face with sunken cheeks, red-rimmed eyes which were usually directed at the floor, and two deep, fretful furrows running from the nose to the drooping corners of the mouth. (*Stories* 51)

His appearance is an introduction to his demeanor, which is that of a hound dog that has been beaten.

A recluse, Tobias rarely leaves his apartment, for when he does he is mocked by old and young alike. All realize that the object of their scorn is one of the world's weaklings, who cannot even hold his head up as he walks. On one occasion Tobias helps one of his ten-year-old tormentors who had injured himself. By extending sympathy to the malefactor, Tobias experiences a sense of connection and holds his head high. All are so surprised that for a while they cease to persecute him, but in time lapse back into their old behavior.

On a walk Tobias sees a hound pup for sale and buys it, though the price strains his purse. Honoring the behavior of the apocryphal Tobias whose name he bears (Lesér 1989: 56), he must have a pet dog. When he gets home, he walks through the jeering crowd carrying it in his arms. Once in his room, he names the dog "Esau", relying upon the Bible to furnish him a good "twin" name. Additionally, "Esau"—'hairy' (Gen. 25.25)--is a good "doggy" name. Up to this point, Tobias' behavior conforms to a popular practice: people often get a pet because they are lonely. But his naming of the dog hints that because the dog is a creature of fur, it has awakened in Tobias the fantasy of the shared skin. The dog is thus the substitute for an unattainable object.

While he feeds the dog well and lavishes love on it, Tobias beats the dog when it, following its own nature, fails to follow his instructions. Once the dog is in such doggy spirits that it gets loose down the stairs to the street, "where [it] at once [begins] to chase a cat, to eat dung in the road, and jump up at the children frantic with joy" (*Stories* 56). Tobias beats it.

When Tobias accidentally cuts the dog with the bread knife, he ministers to it. Feeling that the dog is now experiencing the pain of life that he feels, Tobias is happily "twinned". But, in time, the dog regains its health and high spirits. When Tobias tries to take the dog in his hands, the dog snaps at him. Enraged, Tobias swipes the dog's shoulder with his knife.

Once again he ministers to dog, anticipating the joyous experience of mutual suffering that he had felt on the previous occasion. But Esau dies. Tobias is as motionless as the dog: "He had laid his face against Esau's body and he wept bitter tears" (*Stories* 57). His fantasy of the shared skin had led Tobias to expect a fusion of ego: like many another absolutist "lover" he kills what he cannot control. But his act also kills the fantasy that gave him a reason for living.

"The Dilettante"

There is general agreement among the critics that the life pattern of the twenty-seven-year-old unnamed narrator of "The Dilettante" (1897), as the story is called in *Stories of Three Decades*, closely resembles that of its twenty-two-year-old author. He is born in a town like Lübeck to a family proud of its four generations of "well-to-do, respected business men" (*Stories* 28). The narrator's memory of the interior of his home accords with Mann's memory. There is an especially vivid recollection of the drawing-room, the locus of his mother:

> I would sit on the massive, straight-backed mahogany sofa listening, and watching my mother as she played [the piano]. She was small and fragile and wore as a rule a soft, pale-grey gown. Her narrow face was not beautiful, it was more like that of a quiet, gentle, dreamy child, beneath the parted, slightly waved, indefinitely blond hair. Sitting at the piano, her head a little on one side, she looked like one of those touching little angels who sit in old pictures at the Madonna's feet and play on their guitars.
>
> When I was little she often used to tell me, in her low, deprecatory voice, such fairy-tales as nobody else knew; or she would simply put her hands on my head as it lay in my lap and sit there motionless, not saying a word. Those, I think, were the happiest, peacefullest days of my life.—Her hair did not grey, she became no older; only her figure grew more fragile with the years and her face thinner, stiller, and more dreaming. (*Stories* 29)

When he had to attend school, the narrator remembers, he had quickly demonstrated that he could not attend to his teachers or to his lessons. Dreamy like his mother, he spent his time acting as if he were attentive, while casually versifying or planning the evening

performance of his puppet theater, the latter his "favourite occupation" up
to his "thirteenth or fourteenth year" (*Stories* 31). By then his practical-
minded papa was beginning to think that academic training was lost
on his son. His mother, on the other hand, thought that he was "gifted"
(*Stories* 32), that he had artistic potentiality. To strengthen his tie with
his mother, he tried to demonstrate giftedness at the piano, but six
months of lessons demonstrated that he lacked "manual dexterity" and a
"sense of rhythm" (*Stories* 32).

At eighteen he left school before completing the last grade,
accepted an apprenticeship that his father arranged for him at a
wholesale lumber business. He was no more diligent as a clerk than he
had been as a student, preoccupied by the book that he was reading or
by the theatrical attraction that he was to attend. When he was twenty
his father died, and six months later his mother also. He was an heir to
"some hundred thousand marks" (*Stories* 35).

He promptly began a three-year tour that took him through
Switzerland, Italy, Sicily, the African coast, Spain, and France—at a
cost of twenty thousand marks. Returning to Germany, he took up
residence in a town somewhat like Munich, there to live, on interest
income, a life of dabbling. A pleasant enough town, especially when
"the band is playing on a summer afternoon" (*Stories* 37). But in time he had
to confess to himself that he was living a life of "boredom" (*Stories* 38).

The text—being written by the narrator as a contribution to
"the literature of unhappy love" (*Stories* 48)--has just announced the
subtext, a psychoanalysis of boredom, not of the occasional but of the
unremitting variety. Since psychoanalytic theory regards present
neurosis as a symptom of a past cause, a generalization is warranted:

> The psychoanalysis of individuals suffering from pathological
> boredom reveals a higher than normal ambivalence toward the
> primary object-mother and reflects the excessive influence of the
> depressive constellation. (Anthony and Benedek 1975: xxx)

There has been enough confession by the narrator to entertain the
possibility that he contracted boredom with his head on his mother's
lap, that, like Mann, he is haunted by the band playing in the pavillion.
In her state of boredom, his mother is static, sees nothing wrong in her
son's adoption of her behavior. Thus the narrator in his late twenties
(like Mann in his early twenties) remains an adolescent:

> Adolescents are particularly prone to feeling bored. Maturation
> prods them on to leave their intimate family. Unconsciously,

however, they continue to long for it. Pushed by their heightened
sexuality they have to disconnect their attention from daydreams,
impulses, and masturbatory fantasies lest these become focused
on familiar attachment figures, and from the fears and guilt
feelings this would evoke. (Wangh 1975: 521)

The narrator confesses that there is no remedy for his boredom. But he
also confesses that he, "a man of seven-and-twenty", hangs onto a slender
thread of hope:

> A span of blue sky, the twitter of a bird, some half-vanished
> dream of the night before—everything has power to suffuse his
> heart with undefined hopes and fill it with the solemn expectation
> of some great and nameless joy.—I dawdled from one day to the
> next—aimless, dreamy, occupied with this or that little thing to
> look forward to, even if it were only the date of a forthcoming
> publication, with the lively conviction that I was certainly very
> happy even though now and again weary of my solitude. (*Stories*
> 39)

Adam Phillips has analyzed the kind of boredom that the
narrator experiences. To initiate his discussion he quotes and
paraphrases Christopher Bollas' concept of the "transformational object":
Initially the mother, [the transformational object] is "an object that is
experientially identified by the infant with the process of the alteration of self
experience." This earliest relationship becomes the precursor of, the
paradigm for, "the person's search for an object (a person, place, event, ideology)
that promises to transform the self." At the first stage

> the mother is not yet identified as an object but is experienced as
> a process of transformation, and this feature remains in the trace
> of this object-seeking in adult life, where I believe the object is
> sought for its function as signifier of the process of transformation
> of being. Thus, in adult life, the quest is not to possess the object;
> it is sought in order to surrender to it as a process that alters the
> self. (1993: 76-77)

The narrator has admitted to both his boredom and his "solemn
expectation of some great and nameless joy". Phillips argues that, rather than
the two states being opposed, the former serves the latter:

> Boredom, I think, protects the individual, makes tolerable for him
> the impossible experience of waiting for something without
> knowing what it could be. So the paradox of the waiting that goes
> on in boredom is that the individual does not know what he was

> waiting for until he finds it, and that often he does not know that
> he is waiting.[...]With his set of approximations the bored
> individual is clueless and mildly resentful, involved in a
> halfhearted, despondent search for something to do that will make
> a difference. (1993: 77-78)

The narrator bears out Phillips' analysis by confessing that he is
consumed by resentments, of the fact that he is unhappy even though
meeting his own criteria for happiness, of the people who are perfectly
happy with the world as it is, and of the people who are perfectly
unhappy with the world as it is.

One day in October, buoyed up by a change of weather, the
narrator is excited: "I [...] got up before nine, in a bright and joyful mood,
possessed by vague hopes of change, of unexpected and happy events" (*Stories*
42). He expresses his elation by ascending the long ridge that
overlooks the city, there to happen upon a young woman,
accompanied by an older man, driving a two-horse cart. The narrator
is instantly overwhelmed: "I felt pleasure and admiration, but at the same time a
strange and poignant pain—was it envy, love, self-contempt? I did not dare to think"
(*Stories* 43). A week later, at the opera, he notices the young woman,
again accompanied by the man, her father. If he did dare to think, he
might realize the source of his attraction:

> This innocent little face, quite devoid of coquetry, the detached
> and merrily roving glance, the delicate white throat, confined only
> by a ribbon the colour of her blouse, the gesture with which she
> called the old gentleman's attention to something in the stalls, on
> the stage, or in a box—all this gave the impression of an
> unspeakably refined and charming child, though it had nothing
> touching about it and did not arouse any of those emotions of pity
> which we sometimes feel for children. It was childlike in an
> elevated, tempered, and superior way that rested upon a security
> born of physical well-being and good breeding. (*Stories* 44)

In short, the narrator is unconsciously reminded of his "childlike"
mother by the childlike young woman (*Stories* 34).

The theater, ever for Mann a romantic place, becomes the
theater of the mind, for as the narrator continues to watch the young
woman, he sees a young man enter her box. Suited with signs of
success, the young man is obviously a welcome suitor. The narrator
follows the father and daughter home, learning from the door plate
that the father is a justice.

Anticipating that the young woman will participate in a
charity bazaar announced in the newspaper, the narrator goes there

determined to speak to her. There he finds her, surrounded by her suitor and other admirers, dispensing potables—the very activity that his fantasy expects of her. Just the sight of her arouses "old mingled feelings of envy, yearning, chagrin, and bitter exasperation" (*Stories* 47). He controls himself enough to request a glass of wine, but not enough to engage her in conversation. If Phillips (following Bollas) is correct, the narrator does not desire to capture the object, but rather to surrender to it, thereby to be transformed. She, not he, must act. But, as in the original—Oedipal—love affair, the intrusion of the third party dooms the narrator's quest—she does not speak, he can only retreat in silence. A few days later the narrator reads of the young woman's engagement to "Herr Dr. Alfred Witznagel" (*Stories* 48).

His bizarre behavior at the bazaar strips him of the hope that he might find a transformative object. But he is haunted by the mystery of why he had focused on the young woman in the first place:

> Was I—if I might ask the question—was I in love with this girl? Possibly.... But how—and why? Such love, if it existed. was a monstrosity born of a vanity which had long since become irritable and morbid, rasped into torment at sight of an unattainable prize. Love was the mere pretext, escape, and hope of salvation for my feelings of envy, hatred, and self-contempt.
>
> Yes, it was all superficial. And had not my father once called me a dilettante? (*Stories* 48l; ellipsis in orig.)

The narrator senses that his instantaneous attraction to the young woman was in consequence of some earlier event, but he is unable to release his memory of that event into consciousness. He senses, too, that he had not sought romantic reciprocation, but rather a restoration of the sense of worth that he once had. But again, he is unable to call up the picture of his mother, with whom had shared "the happiest, peacefullest days of [his] life" (*Stories* 29). The only clue that his unconscious offers him is the memory of his father, whose intrusion into his mother-world had destroyed his feeling of vital self-worth. But the clue of the father, pointing directly at the mother, goes unheeded. The narrator thus concludes his story: "Good God, who would have thought, who could have thought, that such is the doom which overtakes the man born a dilettante!" (*Stories* 50). What *he* cannot think is that a dilettante is the product of nurture, not nature.

It is a commonplace in Mann criticism that his early stories are highly biographical. But what has not been sufficiently appreciated is that they are intensely psychobiographical, revealing the

extraordinary effort of Thomas Mann to probe his past, thus to use the
energy resulting from its stresses for a lifetime of writing.

Buddenbrooks

When *Little Herr Friedemann: Novellas* was accepted by
Samuel Fischer in May 1897, he asked Mann to undertake a novel.
Published in 1901, *Buddenbrooks* was intended by Mann to be a
realistic novel tracing the decline of a Lübeck merchant family over
four generations. The story of the first two generations, based on the
stories of the Mann family, particularly the Mann men, achieves the
objectivity that Mann desired. But when the third-generation male,
Thomas Buddenbrook, based on Mann's father (G. Mann 1965: 17),
becomes the focus, Mann's treatment, though still primarily
sociological, becomes more psychological, especially when Thomas
reaches mating age.

Thomas's secret first love is Anna, who tends a flower shop:
"She was wonderfully pretty. Delicately built as a fawn, she had an almost mongol
type of face, somewhat prominent cheek-bones, narrow black eyes full of a soft
gleam, and a pale yellow skin the like of which is rare anywhere" (138). Her
name, features, and environment evoke the vision of Edenic bliss so
easily regained. But while she lives in a bower, the lass, alas, has no
dower. Sincerely professing his love for her, Thomas bids her adieu,
having accepted his father's decision that he should work in
Amsterdam "for a long, long time" (127). His loyalty to his father and the
family firm represses his desire, endangers his psychological and
physical health (144), charts the path that his life will follow (128).

In time, Thomas returns to Lübeck, to become, upon the death
of his father, the head of the firm. Ten years after his first visit,
Thomas returns to Amsterdam, where he is presented to a woman with
whom he had been acquainted when they were children. He is smitten
by her looks, her accomplishments (she plays her Stradivarius very
well), and her father's wealth. He successfully woos her, capturing her
heart and her "three-hundred-thousand-mark dowery" (241). Her money will
invigorate the firm; her maidenhead will be sacrificed for its future
head.

When Thomas Buddenbrook's betrothed first appears in
Lübeck, the "gallants" term her "[t]ip-top",

> [b]ut among the solid, respectable citizens there was much head-
> shaking. "Something queer about her," they said. "Her hair, her

> face, the way she dresses—a little too unusual." Sorenson
> expressed it: "She has a certain something about her!" He made a
> face as if he were on the Bourse and somebody had made him a
> doubtful proposition. (242)

Having viewed the beautiful mask of the Gorgon without
comprehension, hence unable to identify the object which causes his
disquiet, Sorenson instinctively makes a ugly face against the hidden
ugly face. In a scene reminiscent of "Little Herr Friedemann", the
broker (and *littérateur*) Gosch first gazes upon her in the street.
Inspired by his fascination, he declares, "Ah! [. . .] what a woman! Hera and
Aphrodite, Brunhilda and Melusina all in one!" (243). The fourth of his
appellations hints at her Medusan qualities, for Melusina "was
condemned to become every Saturday a serpent from her waist downward" (Evans
1981: 727). It should come as no surprise that Thomas's betrothed is
also named Gerda. Golo Mann writes that Mann was characteristically
so dependent upon the connection between a character he was creating
and the person who inspired it that he chose a name for the former that
preserved the "rhythm and sound" of the name of the latter (1965 : 8):
Gerda = Julia. Gosch's evocation of a mythological subtext is later
supplemented by an incident involving Johann, the son born to
Thomas and Gerda. Drawing upon his own childhood experience,
Mann pictures Johann, delighted with a Christmas gift that "he had
wished for, a mythology, in a red binding with a gold Pallas Athen[a]
on the cover" (435). Apparently the child Johann is under the
protection of the goddess who wore Medusa's head as an accessory,
although he nearly dies at birth (326) and is sickly as an infant (346),
as if one of those children menaced by Lilith.

    Despite her pregnant introduction, Gerda Buddenbrook goes
virtually unmentioned until she is delivered of her pregnancy. In short,
as long as she is fruitless she as a wife is of no consequence to a
merchant dynasty like the Buddenbrooks. Thomas does admit that "she
can sometimes be a little cold" (249), but apparently she sufficiently warms
to his attentions, for, after three years, he sires a son, christened with
the patronymics "Justus, Johann, Kaspar" (328), nicknamed "Hanno"
by his mother (346). It is almost as if he is cursed by his mother's
diminutive, for he reveals weakness both in spirit and in body. He
inherits the Buddenbrook nose, but his other facial features reflect his
mother's (347). He also inherits the weak Buddenbrook teeth (not
enough milk in infancy?), in contrast to his mother's strong white
teeth.

Hanno senses that his mother is an unattainable object. Thus he must seek a "transition object", as the object-relations psychoanalysts call it, the substitute object that begins with the thumb. For eight-year-old Hanno, as for Thomas Mann, it was the summer seaside at Travemünde:

> best of all was to go back to the beach and sit in the twilight on the end of the breakwater, with your face turned to the open horizon. Great ships passed by, and you signaled them with your handkerchief; and you listened to the little waves slapping softly against the stones; and the whole space about you was filled with a soft and mighty sighing.... How calm his heart felt, how evenly it beat, after a visit to the sea. Then he had his supper in his room—for his mother ate later, down in the glass verandah—and drank milk or porter, tasting strongly of malt, and lay down in his little bed, between the soft old linen sheets, and almost at once sleep overcame him, and he slept, to the subdued rhythm of the evening concert and the regular pulsations of his quiet heart. (qtd. in Winston 1981: 20-21; translation by Lowe-Porter amended by Winston)

Hanno experiences the "oceanic feeling" in the oceanic environment. He has inherited the symbolic values of the ocean from his creator, who early learned that his mother had come from across the sea and who regarded her as a goddess. So Hanno sits on the end of the breakwater waving his handkerchief, anticipating the return of the "Good Mother", ready to communicate with her. Still with hope that her coming may someday happen, he is fortified to return to his room, to a real mother who does not share his meal. He drinks his milk or porter—as will Hans Castorp—then seeks the sleep of forgetfulness, which some call repression.

Also by the time Hanno is eight-years-of-age (412), his father realizes that his son has inherited more from his mother than just her features:

> Gerda's violin-playing had always added to her strange eyes, which he loved, to her heavy, dark-red hair and her whole exotic appearance, one charm the more. But now that he saw how her passion for music, strange to his own nature, utterly, even at this early age, possessed the child, he felt in it a hostile force that came between him and his son, of whom his hopes would make a Buddenbrook—a strong and practical-minded man, with definite impulses after power and conquest. (415)

Thomas begins a campaign to woo his son away from the world of music to the world of merchants and markets. Hanno willingly accompanies his father on his proprietorial rounds:

> But the little boy saw more than he should have seen; the shy, gold-brown, blue-shadowy eyes observed too well. He saw not only the unerring charm which his father exercised upon everybody: he saw as well, with strange and anguished penetration, how cruelly hard it was upon him. He saw how his father, paler and more silent after each visit, would lean back in his corner of the carriage with closed eyes and reddened eyelids; he realized with a sort of horror that on the threshold of the next house a mask would glide over his face, a galvanized activity take hold of the weary frame. (505)

While Hanno loves his father, he is appalled at the thought of following in his father's footsteps. Confronted with such a prospect, Hanno is not invigorated in mind or body; defeated in his project to pass on his values to his son, Thomas soon loses his remaining vigor.

Gerda, however, though apparently remaining deferential to the Buddenbrook ethos, becomes forceful through her unchangeableness. The author characterizes Gerda eighteen years into her marriage, now forty-five-years-of-age:

> Gerda had scarcely altered[...]. She seemed to be, as it were, conserved in the nervous coldness which was the essence of her being. Her lovely dark red hair had kept its colour, the white skin its smooth texture, the figure its lofty aristocratic slimness. In the corners of her rather too small and close-set eyes were the same blue shadows. You could not trust those eyes. Their look was strange, and what was written in it impossible to decipher. This woman's personality was so cool, so reserved, so repressed, so distant, she showed so little human warmth for anything but her music—how could one help feeling a vague mistrust. (517-18)

Her immobilizing eyes, her cold-bloodedness, and her slimness betray the Medusa who is her true nature and behind that mortal-goddess the snake from which she descended.

To account for the feeling of uncanniness that Gerda inspires in them, the townspeople seize upon her relationship with a young army officer, Renée Maria von Throta, like Gerda devoted only to music (518). Musically gifted, he often visits Gerda's salon to play duets with the "impassioned Wagnerite" (407). Soon enough the conventional wisdom has it that Gerda is doing her husband wrong right over his first-story office. Thomas rejects the gossip that their meetings constitute a union of bodies, even as he wishes they only were. Not that he would acknowledge them as such and thus subject the family name to scandal. He thinks that the meetings constitute a communion of souls under the godhead of music, that they indicate just how separated from and indifferent to Buddenbrook values Gerda is and will remain. That Gerda has already left his bed (525-26), suggests that because of her coldness Thomas "gat no heat", as Scripture puts it (1 K 1:1). Small wonder that, although only forty-eight-years-of-age, Thomas feels "that his days [are] numbered" (522).

Thomas begins to neglect his business to sit in the garden. But he finds no "splendor in the grass", for in his garden a snake has been the instrument of knowledge: he must die. He is temporarily consoled by Schopenhauer's "message" (525), but soon resigns himself to the will of God. He who has always struggled to "to keep his body artificially erect and well-preserved" (529) before the public is felled by a fatal stroke on Fishers' Lane, which separates his mansion from the flower shop where his first love, now Frau Iwersen, is producing a bountiful crop (544, 550).

Thomas's stroke was preceded by the botched extraction of a tooth (543-44). Mann's inclusion of this seemingly trivial detail reveals the close attention that he gives to narrative technique. For as long as humans have interpreted dreams, they have regarded a dream of tooth difficulty as an omen of death (Gutheil 1951: 216), so that the extraction scene is a foreshadowing. The infected tooth also recalls the Buddenbrook constitution, which has grown weaker with each generation. Overcome by tooth difficulty, Thomas cannot bite, hence is defenseless against that strong biter, Gerda.

After a funeral befitting Thomas's station in the community, Gerda discovers the real state of his finances. His will states that the firm must be liquidated and the estate settled within a year (558). The liquidation is so botched that his widow soon realizes that she must dispose of his real estate in order to survive. Symbolically, Gerda buys a small villa outside the Castle Gate, distancing herself from Lübeck. Then she dismisses Mamsell Jungmann, the Buddenbrook housekeeper for forty years (560). For Hanno, Mamsell had first been his nanny, then the virgin protectress of youth, so that he is now fatally vulnerable.

The rigors of school press upon him as always (Part 11, Chapter II). His only respite is music. But the prominence which is given to a performance of *Lohengrin,* to which he is taken one Sunday evening (562), suggests that his yearning for music is but a screen for his yearning for his mother's love—as that opera so often announces the mother-motif in Mann's work. When Hanno comes home from school on a particular day, the interaction between mother and son may be regarded as typical. After early dinner, at his mother's instigation, he, at the piano, and she, with her Stradivarius, begin to play "Sonata Opus 24 of Beethoven" (595), ostensibly an activity involving mutual respect and shared emotions. Perhaps Hanno even pictures himself as the replacement for Lieutenant von Throta. But his mother finds her instrument out of tune, plays no more, goes "up to rest". Remaining "in the salon", Hanno goes over to look through "the glass door that [leads] out on the small verandah[...]into the drenched garden". His registering mind sees the garden not directly, but through the medium of a glass panel that would also reflect his seeing self, thus his consciousness could see himself haunted by his yearning for the original Garden. So he suddenly steps back, jerks the curtain across the door, in other words defensively intuits that the repressed fantasy of existence-before-alienation threatens to return to full awareness. Then he improvises on the piano such a piece of yearning, desire, and "ultimate faith and renunciation" (597) that Mann takes nearly three pages to analyze it. Hanno the composer is attempting to subdue his emotions to form, to transform that which is pathological to that which is creative, thus restoring health, even as Mann is confessing that his writing proceeds from the same motivation.

After supper, Hanno and his mother play a game of chess to stalemate. Hanno cannot succeed in gaining his mother's unconditional love; his mother cannot throw off the constitutional coldness that prevents her from giving love to her son. Hanno goes to his room, improvises at his harmonium, "but [plays] in thought only, for he must make no noise". Again Hanno reveals the repression to silence that controls his life, the repression that he inherited from his father. The chapter ends with disarming understatement: "This was one day in the life of little Johann" (597, Part 11, Chapter II).

The following Chapter III is a nearly three-page description of the course of typhoid fever to a fatal conclusion (598-600). Not until Chapter IV is it revealed that the case described is that of Hanno Buddenbrook. In a letter to Theodor Adorno, Mann confesses that his description of typhoid fever was "unabashedly lifted from an encyclopedia article and then 'versified'" (Winston 1971: 494-95). What is significant to my argument is that Mann's letter is a plea that Adorno provide him with "a few significant, suggestive *specific* details" (Winston 1971: 500) about music and musicology that he can use in his novel-in-progress (*Doctor Faustus* [1948]) to convince his readers that he knows whereof he speaks. Mann's apparently coincidental linkage of Hanno's death from typhoid fever and music (which is Hanno's substitute for mother-love) argues, first, that Mann felt that, to reverse the order, the deprivation of mother's love revealed in Hanno's behavior in Chapter II leads to Hanno's death in Chapter III, and, second, that Mann's choice of Hanno's fatal disease is not coincidental.

While Mann does not discuss the source of typhoid fever in Chapter III, in Chapter I he carefully records an incident that could account for Hanno's contact with the source, the bacterium *salmonella typhosa*:

> When Frau Permaneder [née Antonia "Tony" Buddenbrook, Thomas's sister] visited her sister-in-law, she would draw her nephew to her and tell him of the Buddenbrook family past, and of that future for which, next to the mercy of God, they would have to thank little Johann. The more depressing the present appeared, the more she strove to depict the elegance of the life that went on in the houses of her parents and grand-parents; and she would tell Hanno how his great-grandfather had driven all over the country with his carriage and four horses. One day she had a severe attack of cramps in the stomach because Friederike, Henriette, and Pfiffi [her Buddenbrook cousins] had asserted that the Hagenströms were the crème de la crème of town society. (561)

"The source of infection [of typhoid fever] is the feces of a person who has the disease or is a symptomless carrier of the causative bacteria" (Clayman 1989: vol. II 1017). If Aunt Tony is the infectious source for Hanno, she must be a symptomless carrier, for there is no revelation before or after this incident that she has the disease. If she is a symptomless carrier, she may "harbor typhoid bacilli in the gallbladder and shed them in the feces for many years" (Clayman 1989: vol. II 1017). It is possible that Aunt Tony's "stomach cramps" is a sly way of acknowledging a bout of diarrhea, a condition heightening her contagiousness.

The context clearly provides an alternative explanation of Aunt Tony's distress: she cannot stomach what she is hearing. All her life she has been stretched between two poles, pride and shame, continually overwhelmed by the one state or the other. In the incident described she first experiences pride as she exaggerates the glories of the Buddenbrook past, then drops into shame when her cousins assert that her ancient enemies—the Hagenströms—have supplanted the Buddenbrooks in public esteem. Tony may be one of those people who, as toddlers, form "an immutable link between excretion and shame" (Nathanson 1992: 176), hence when she experiences shame, she attempts to expel it bodily. Hence the alternative explanation of her illness coincides with the first explantion: she infects Hanno with illness both of the flesh and the spirit. Despite his claim that his description of typhoid fever is based on an encyclopedia article, Mann concludes it by venturing far beyond medical materialism:

> When the fever is at its height, life calls to the patient: calls out to him as he wanders in his distant dream, and summons him in no uncertain voice. The harsh, imperious call reaches the spirit on that remote path that leads into the shadows, the coolness and peace. He hears the call of life, the clear, fresh, mocking summons to return to that distant scene which he had already left so far behind him, and already forgotten. And there may well up in him something like a feeling of shame for a neglected duty; a sense of renewed energy, courage, and hope; he may recognize a bond existing still between him and that stirring, colourful, callous existence which he thought he had left so far behind him. Then, however far he may have wandered on his distant path, he will turn back—and live. But if he shudders when he hears life's voice, if the memory of that vanished scene and the sound of that lusty summons make him shake his head, make him put out his hand to ward off as he flies forward in the way of escape that has opened to him—then it is clear that the patient will die. (600)

If Hanno had felt shame for neglecting his duty to struggle for life, he would have gained the strength to live. But, shortly after his christening, Hanno suffered an attack of cholera-infantum (346), acute diarrhea caused by the bacterium *vibrio cholerae* (Clayman 1989: vol. I 274); thus weakened by one strain of bacteria he is the potential victim of another. Having experienced the existential shame of being exposed as a shitty baby before his cold mother, he lives in fear that he will thus be exposed again. When it happens, dying is a welcome escape. After Hanno's death, as Aunt Tony prates of family glory to the circle of manless Buddenbrooks, Gerda, having destroyed the family line, leaves Lübeck forever. At this point as always, Mann is silent about her thoughts, brilliantly allowing her to return to her Gorgon origin, forever terrifying to the human mind.

"The Wardrobe"

During the years that Thomas Mann devoted himself to the principal task of writing *Buddenbrooks,* he continued to experience an erotic desire ambivalent about its object. After his third visit to Italy, 1897-1898, he soon moved out of his mother's apartment, into a bachelor apartment, at 82 Theresienstrasse, "very pleasant" accommodations, he wrote Grautoff. But within weeks he moved to 69 Barerstrasse, then, by October, to 5 Marktstrasse, close enough to his mother's that he could take his meals there (Winston 1981: 114). The Marktstrasse apartment was unfurnished, so he took his mother's unneeded furniture, including "the massive mahogany bed in which he had been born" (Winston 1981: 115). Lacking chairs, he bought some, spending "whole days" painting them with red enamel (Mann *Sketch* 15). Esther Lesér notes that when Mrs. Mann, accompanied by her youngest son, came to see the apartment, Thomas showed her that the wardrobe supplied by the landlady had only a burlap screen as its back panel (1989: 256n35).

By the end of November he had written, in seven days' time (Winston 1981: 116), the story called in English "The Wardrobe". Mrs. Lesér's observation that "The Wardrobe" is reminiscent of "A Vision" (1989: 64) gains significance from the possibilities that Mann's removal—even though voluntary—from his mother's dwelling had once again awakened his earlier yearning, that sleeping in the bed in which he was born had influenced his dreaming, and that dream material inspired a quickened creative process.

As the story opens, Albrecht van der Qualen—whose surname places him among the 'sufferings' family (Lesér 1989: 256n38)--is asleep on the Berlin-Rome express bound for Florence, "although Berlin had not been the beginning of his journey" (*Stories* 72). When the train stops at some station in Germany its noises and movements disturb van der Qualen sufficiently to awaken him, but instead he begins to dream.[1] (Thus he illustrates Freud's belief that the function of dreaming is to prevent a sleeper from waking because of a disturbance, external or internal [*Interpretation* 678-81]). The last paragraph of the story all but confirms that everything preceding it has been a dream, incorporating such surreal features as condensation, distortion, and symbolism.

It might be thought that the introductory material about railway travel, while it appeases our desire for realistic detail, is inessential to the theme of the story. But if the story is to be interpreted psychoanalytically, close attention must be given to that early material. Freud notes:

> It is a puzzling fact that boys take such an exraordinarily intense interest in things connected with railways, and, at the age at which the production of phantasies is most active (shortly before puberty), use those things as the nucleus of a symbolism that is peculiarly sexual. A compulsive link of this kind between railway-travel and sexuality is clearly derived from the pleasurable character of the sensations of movement. In the event of repression, which turns so many childish preferences into their opposite, these same individuals, when they are adolescents or adults, will react to rocking or swinging with a feeling of nausea, will be terribly exhausted by a railway journey, or will be subject to attacks of anxiety on the journey and will protect themselves against a repetition of the painful experience by a dread of railway-travel. (*Three* 202)

Van der Qualen has unconsciously enjoyed the sexual pleasure stimulated by the train's movements, so much so that "the cessation of rhythmic motion" (*Stories* 71) threatens to awaken him to the "sufferings" he feels about his sexual desire. Thus he begins a dream of wish-fulfillment: looking out the window he sees a "tall, stout woman in a long raincoat, with a face expressive of nothing but worry, [...] dragging a hundred-pound suitcase". Here Gutheil's *Handbook of Dream Analysis* would support Mann's creative intuition: "Luggage may represent a burden, pangs of conscience" (1951: 252fn1). Denying that the dream "window" is a mirror reflecting his image, van der Qualen pities the woman for her heavy burden of worry, while insisting to himself that he is "carefree" (*Stories* 71), even though several physicians have told him that he has but a short time to live (*Stories* 72). To avoid "all upsetting knowledge", he sleeps, sometimes for twenty-four or more hours, and keeps himself ignorant of the hour, the day, even the month—idiosyncrasies symptomatic of the repression to which he subjects himself.[10]

Without motive, van der Qualen leaves the train. Ostentatiously, he carries "neither stick nor umbrella" (*Stories* 72), but does light up a cigar: let those who observe him know that he is not genital but oral. Denying that he should be associated with men, he ignores a hackney coachman's inquiry, "*Hotel zum braven Mann*"? Crossing a bridge, he goes beyond "*the* river. It is nice to think that I call it that because I do not know its name" (ital. in orig.). Well might he deny knowing its name; for him the river represents the amniotic fluid to which he wishes to return. Beyond the river he consistently veers left,

recalling Stekel's judgment that in dreams "left" represents
"homosexuality, incest or perversion" (Freud *Interpretation* 358).

Eventually he stands before the door of a house on which a
sign says: "In this house on the third floor there are rooms to let" (*Stories* 73). If
Freud's belief is valid that in "every dream an instinctual wish has to be
represented as fulfilled" (*New* 18-19), Van der Qualen's search for a room
represents his instinctual wish to return to the womb. But the mother
figure who answers the door is no Madonna, instead "a lady, tall, lean,
and old. She wore a cap with a large pale-lilac bow and an old-fashioned, faded black
gown. She had a sunken birdlike face and on her brow there was an eruption, a sort of
fungus growth. It was rather repulsive".[11] Undeterred, van der Qualen asks
about the rooms; the woman "nod[s] and smile[s] slowly, without a word,
understandingly, and with her beautiful long white hand ma[kes] a slow, languid, and
elegant gesture towards the next, the left-hand door". Having entered the first
room, van der Qualen looks into the second room:

> This room was pathetically bare, with staring white walls, against
> which three straw chairs, painted pink, stood out like strawberries
> from whipped cream. A wardrobe, a washing-stand with a
> mirror.... The bed, a mammoth mahogany piece, stood free in the
> middle of the room. (ellipsis in orig.)

Those strawberries on whipped cream—their symbolism as the long-
sought breast disguised by their preponderance—encourage him once
again to focus on her "lovely long, white hand", even though it passes
"lightly over the fungus growth on her forehead" (*Stories* 74). The hand he
sees, like the one seen in "A Vision", is the hand that he remembers
supporting the breast when, as an infant, he was brought to it. By
focusing on that hand, he is able to ignore the repulsiveness of the
mother figure to whom it belongs. Since he denies the passage of time,
he blinds himself to its ravages. Renting the apartment, he returns to
the city, for, aroused by those strawberries, he must have a meal for
nourishment, then a cigar for oral satisfaction.

Returning to his apartment, he sips cognac as he finishes his
cigar. Then, undressing for bed, he prepares to hang his clothes in the
backless wardrobe. (It is curious that Mann neglects to emphasize the
makeshift burlap back, so like the texture and color of the "dream
screen", as Lewin describes it). As van der Qualen turns to hang his
clothes, he is aware of the bedroom's "four white walls, from which the three
pink chairs stood out like strawberries from whipped cream". His mental state is
overwhelmed by his oral fantasy. But then he looks into the wardrobe:

> Somebody was standing in it, a creature so lovely that Albrecht
> van der Qualen's heart stood still a moment and then in long,
> deep, quiet throbs resumed its beating. She was quite nude and
> one of her slender arms reached up to crook a forefinger round
> one of the hooks in the ceiling of the wardrobe.[12]

Thus the figure--the manifest dream--assumes the pose of Botticelli's Venus.

Van der Qualen notices "that down in the right corner the sacking was loosened from the back of the wardrobe" (*Stories* 76), thus allowing the beautiful young female to enter it without being observed. That is to say, Van der Qualen's "censor of dreams" (Freud *Interpretation* 506) has failed to keep the developing distraction of genital sexuality repressed, despite his insistence that he is impervious to the passage of time, that is, the coming of sexual maturity. The fulfillment of his wish to return to the mother-image has been accomplished by van der Qualen's dream, but the effort has so weakened his dream mechanism that a new element displays itself:

> The condition of rest free from stimulus, which the state of sleep
> wishes to establish, is threatened from three directions: in a
> relatively accidental manner by external stimuli during sleep, and
> by interests of the previous day which cannot be broken off, and
> in an unavoidable manner by unsated repressed instinctual
> impulses which are on the watch for an opportunity of finding
> expression. In consequence of the diminishing of repressions at
> night there would be a risk that the rest afforded by sleep would
> be interrupted whenever an instigation from outside or from
> inside succeeded in linking up with an unconscious instinctual
> source. The process of dreaming allows the product of a
> collaboration of this kind to find an outlet in a harmless
> hallucinatory experience and in that way assures a continuation of
> sleep. The fact that a dream occasionally awakens the sleeper, to
> the accompaniment of a generation of anxiety, is no contradiction
> of this function but rather, perhaps, a signal that the watchman
> regards the situation as too dangerous and no longer feels able to
> control it. And very often then, while we are still asleep, a
> consolation occurs to us which seeks to prevent our waking up:
> "But after all it's only a dream!" (Freud *New* 17)

Van der Qualen is again in danger of waking up, thus of being overwhelmed by anxiety. Hence the dream female suddenly asks, "Shall I tell you a story?" (*Stories* 76), reassuring van der Qualen that, after all, a story is all a dream is. Van der Qualen eagerly accepts her proposal. The story tells of a heterosexual romance: "But it ended badly; a sad ending: the two holding each other indissolubly embraced, and while their lips rest on each other, one stabbing the other above the waist with a broad knife—and not without good cause. So it ended" (*Stories* 77). By ending with fatal betrayal, the dream-story reveals the false promise of indissoluble embracement offered by heterosexuality, reassuring van der Qualen that his fear of heterosexuality is well grounded.

Van der Qualen listens to the nude girl's stories every evening. Each is, no doubt, a variation on the theme of the original story. Although they proscribe heterosexuality, they arouse genital excitement: "Often he forg[gets] himself.—His blood swell[s] up in him, he stretche[s] out his hands to her, and she d[oes] not resist him" (*Stories* 77; dashes in orig.). These instances must be the "masturbation fantasies" that Hayman sees in the story (1995: 141). After van der Qualen experiences an instance of orgastic relief, the female does not appear in the wardrobe for several evenings, and when she does, she does not resume her story-telling for several evenings, but when she does there comes a time when—"he again forg[ets] himself" (*Stories* 77). Thus twenty-three-year-old Thomas Mann confesses one aspect of his sexual confusion in the fall of 1898.

"The Wardrobe" apparently predicts Mann's sexual dilemma and strategy for handling it during the next two years. Then he reverted to the homoerotic fantasizing that he had displayed in early adolescence. Although Mann met Paul Ehrenberg in the fall of 1898, the earliest evidence suggesting that he was infatuated with him is a letter to Ehrenberg, dated 29 June 1900 (Winston 1971: 13-16), which, though containing no direct statements of affection, is marked by the stylistic mannerisms of flirtation. In a letter to his brother Heinrich, dated 7 March 1901, Mann described his relationship with Ehrenberg:

> What is involved is not a love affair, at least not in the ordinary sense, but a friendship, a friendship—how amazing!--understood, reciprocated, and rewarded—which (I candidly admit) at certain times, especially in hours of depression and loneliness, takes on a character of somewhat excessive suffering. According to Grautoff, I am simply going through an adolescent infatuation; but that is putting it in his own terms. My nervous constitution and philosophical inclination has incredibly complicated the affair; it has a hundred aspects from the plainest to the spiritually wildest. But on the whole, the dominant feeling is one of profoundly joyful astonishment over a responsiveness no longer to be expected in this life. (Wysling 1998:48)

Despite the ardor that he felt for Paul, Thomas left Munich in April, to visit with Heinrich at his pension in Florence. There he intended to gather material on Girolamo Savonarola, long an interest of his (Wysling 1998: 37). While waiting for Heinrich to return from Naples, where he was gathering material (Wysling 1998: 50-51), Thomas met two English girls, the sisters Edith and Mary Smith. Since they knew Heinrich, they were immediately friendly with Thomas, who was soon infatuated with the younger, Mary, who reminded him of a Botticelli blonde (Hayman 1995: 162). Mann acknowledged that there was even "talk of marriage" (qtd. in N. Hamilton 1979: 74), but nothing came of it. It must have been a vacation romance—like champagne, quick to exhilarate, quick to evaporate. Years later Mann listed "certain misgivings" that cooled the romance, youth and difference in nationality (N. Hamilton 1979:75). But just as likely the romance was doomed by the recurrence of his dream of the girl in the wardrobe.

"Gladius Dei"

When Mann returned to Munich in June, he began a short story, *"Gladius Dei",* that grew out of his interest in Savonarola. In modern-day Munich, Hieronymus, who garbs himself in monk's attire, is drawn by a crowd to observe an art-shop window:

> The large red-brown photograph in the choice old-gold frame stood on an easel in the centre. It was a Madonna, but an utterly unconventional one, a work of entirely modern feeling. The figure of the Holy Mother was revealed as enchantingly feminine and beautiful. Her great smouldering eyes were rimmed with darkness, and her delicate and strangely smiling lips were half-parted. Her slender fingers held in a somewhat nervous grasp the hips of the Child, a nude boy of pronounced, almost primitive leanness. He was playing with her breast and glancing aside at the beholder with a wise look in his eyes. (*Stories* 185)

This is the original object-relationship, as seen not by a pious painter but by Dr. Freud, a good many mothers, and all fortunate infants. Absent is the Child's traditional chubbiness, replaced by an undeniable evolutionary sign. Hieronymus—Hayman notes that the name is a variant on Girolamo (1995: 164)--is a modern-day Savonarola, who immediately demands that the art-shop owner burn the photograph—and, indeed, all his other wares that depend upon a "stupid and shameless exploitation of the animal instincts" (*Stories* 191)--"these statues and busts,[...]these vases and ornaments, these shameless revivals of paganism, these elegantly bound volumes of erotic verse[...]" (*Stories* 192). The story ends with his hallucination that he is Savonarola glimpsing the fiery sword in Florence: *"Gladius Dei super terram ... cito et velociter!"* (*Stories* 193; ellipsis in orig.).

The story has been read as an allegory of puritanism attempting to censor artistic freedom. Such a reified reading, though, does not consider the psychological nuances that Mann sketches into both positions. In much of the early portion of the story the narrator satirizes the individual who appreciates an artwork only insofar as it titillates his prurient interest, the two "[h]umanistically educated people" ogling the Madonna and gossiping about the the model for the Madonna, the master's mistress (*Stories* 185), the "man in a yellow suit, with a black goat's-beard, looking at a portfolio of French drawings, over which he now and then emitted a bleating laugh" (*Stories* 187), the "leisurely Englishman" fondling "the dainty figure of a nude young girl, immature and delicately articulated, her hands crossed in coquettish innocence upon her breast" (*Stories* 187). Some artists and admirers betray artistic freedom by indulging in pornographic license.

Similarly, in introducing Hieronymus, the narrator immediately probes beneath the professional garb to present the person:

> No one in that tolerant and variety-loving town would have taken offence at his wearing no hat; but why need the hood of his ample black cloak have been drawn over his head, shadowing his low, prominent, and peaked forehead, covering his ears and framing his haggard cheeks? What pangs of conscience, what scruples and self-tortures had so availed to hollow out these cheeks? It is frightful, on such a sunny day, to see care sitting in the hollows of the human face. His dark brows thickened at the narrow base of his hooked and prominent nose. His lips were unpleasantly full, his eyes brown and close-lying. When he lifted them, diagonal folds appeared on the peaked brow. His gaze expressed knowledge, limitation, and suffering. (*Stories* 183-84)

After making his devotions in Ludwigskirche, Hieronymus continues to Odeonsplatz, where the art-shop is located:

> Holding his mantle closely together with both hands from inside, he moved his hood-covered head in short turns from one thing to the next, gazing at each awhile with a dull, inimical, and remotely surprised air, lifting the dark brows which grew so thick at the base of the nose. (*Stories* 185)[13]

He studies the picture of the Madonna for a quarter of an hour:

> his cheeks, half-shrouded in the black hood, seemed more sunken than ever and his thick lips had gone pale. Slowly his head dropped lower and lower, so that finally his eyes stared upwards at the work of art, while the nostrils of his great nose dilated.

After being obsessed by the picture for three days, Hieronymus hears a command "to intercede and lift his voice against the frivolity, blasphemy, and arrogance of beauty" (*Stories* 186). Returning to the art-shop, he proclaims that the picture is not only sensual but even leads people "astray upon the doctrine of the Immaculate Conception" (*Stories* 190). In concluding his condemnation he points toward the window containing the picture

> with a hand that shook as though palsied. And in this commanding attitude he paused. His great hooked nose seemed to jut more than ever, his dark brows were gathered so thick and high that folds crowded upon the peaked forehead shaded by the hood; a hectic flush mantled his hollow cheeks. (*Stories* 192)

Herr Blüthenzweig, the art-shop owner, having had enough, orders Krauthuber, his German lifter, to escort Hieronymus from the premises. Like a child, Hieronymus is carried to the doorsill by the "gigantic son of the people" (*Stories* 192). From that vantage point, Hieronymus hallucinates all the "vanities" piled up to be burned: "'*Gladius Die super terram...*' his thick lips whispered; and drawing himself still higher in his hooded cloak while the hand hanging down inside it twitched convulsively, he murmured, quaking: '*cito et velociter!*'" (*Stories* 193; ellipsis in orig.).

The persistent attention paid to Hieronymus' "hood"—'cowl' is another word for it—and to his facial features argue that his desire to destroy the picture of the Madonna is fundamentally inspired by an unconscious motive. When Hieronymus is first described, the narrator offers an interpretation: "His gaze expressed knowledge, limitation, and suffering" (*Stories* 184). As Hieronymus looks at the picture he focuses finally on "the Child": "He was playing with her breast and glancing aside at the beholder with a wise look in his eyes" (*Stories* 185). Presumably the Child's wisdom resides in his knowledge that he enjoys free access to the breast. Presumably Hieronymus's suffering resides in his knowledge of the limitation that he had experienced at the breast. His thick lips suggest his orality; his "peaked brow" and "haggard cheeks" suggest a malnourishment that began in infancy. Even though he lost the breast, Hieronymus must retain his love for his mother, explaining to himself that he deserved to lose the breast. Convinced of his sinfulness, he turns to religion for redemption, specifically the Roman Catholic Church, which proclaimed the dogma of Mary's Immaculate Conception, 8 December 1854. When he "took the cowl" he was seeking to be reborn as the infant with a caul—legendarily a lucky child. He worships the canonized sexlessness of Mary, even as he struggles with his own sexuality, which convulses his hand so often that he keeps it hidden under his cloak. Mann's story is a case history of a man suffering from the return of the repressed.[14]

For *"Gladius Dei"* Mann provided a dedication, in English: "To M. S. in remembrance of our days in Florence" (qtd. in Winston 1981: 145). His English-language biographers record the dedication but see no significant linkage between Hieronymus's suffering and Mann's failed romance with Mary Smith. Perhaps the dedication was meant only to celebrate their summer romance in Florence—or maybe Mann thought that "clever" Mary would perceive that Hieronymus's unconscious behavior explained his creator's romantic waxing, then waning. He had written to Heinrich even while the romance was still going on:

> Miss Mary, whose birthday was day before yesterday and whom I presented with a little basket of candied fruit, has been a source of much pleasure. But now I think I'm becoming too melancholy for her. *She is so very clever* [italicized clause in English in the orig.], and I'm always dumb enough always to love the ones who are clever, even though I can't keep up over the long run. (Wysling 1998: 52)

Typically, the melancholy stage of a romance occurs when the lover cannot ignore a discovery of disparity between the new real object and the long-cherished ideal object. Then the pretense and discontent begin. Back in Munich, having slightly strayed, Mann told his true love Paul that the parting scene between Mary and himself was "worthy of a play" (Prater 1995: 37).[15]

"Tristan"

In February 1901, before his romance with Mary in Florence, Mann wrote Heinrich that he had begun work on a "burlesque" story, that he would probably call "Tristan" (Wysling 1998: 47). On 18

November 1901 he gave a public reading of the story to the *Akademisch Dramatischer Verein* (Lesér 1989: 102). Since "Tristan" and *"Gladius Dei"* were composed almost at the same time, it is not surprising that they have similar themes. The most obvious similarity is between the role of the principal female in each story. In *"Gladius Dei"* the female is the picture of the Madonna, whose image awakens Hieronymus's hitherto repressed mother-longing. In "Tristan" the female is Frau Gabriele Klöterjahn, née Eckhof, whose Madonna-aspect is suggested by her given name: she is named for the angel who announces to the Virgin Mary that she is to bear a son (Luke 1: 31). When Gabriele first appears at Einfried, Dr. Leander's sanatorium, her husband fondly calls her his "angel" (*Stories* 135, 136),[16] and the other patients soon agree with his description.

When the story opens Detlev Spinell, a writer who has a single published novel,[17] has been staying at the sanatorium for some weeks (*Stories* 138). As he later tells Gabriele, he is not sick; he comes to Einfried whenever his temperament demands the Empire style of furniture:

> Obviously, people feel one way among furniture that is soft and comfortable and voluptuous, and quite another among the straight lines of these tables, chairs, and draperies. This brightness and hardness, this cold, austere simplicity and reserved strength, madame—it has upon me the ultimate effect of an inward purification and rebirth. Beyond a doubt, it is morally elevating. (*Stories* 141)

Although Detlev may love décor, he loves words more, and one word, *Empire*, denoting an entity completely unified under one ruler, describes his unconscious attraction to Einfried, a place of "oneness" that fosters a feeling of "peace". It is not "rebirth" that he seeks, but "re-babyhood". At Einfried he usually keeps to himself, as if he were its only occupant. If he is overtaken by an occasional aesthetic enthusiasm, he is transported:

> "How beautiful!" he would say, with his head on one side, his shoulders raised, his hands spread out, his lips and nostrils curled and distended. "My God! look, how beautiful!" And in such moments of ardour he was quite capable of flinging his arms blindly round the neck of anybody, high or low, male or female, that happened to be near. (*Stories* 138-39)

Such performances of gesture and posture betray his pregenital mentality.

Detlev is "a dark man at the beginning of the thirties, impressively tall, with hair already distinctly grey at the temples, and a round, white, slightly bloated face, without a vestige of beard". His skin is nearly hairless, his eyes are "doe-like", his feet are large, and his teeth are "carious", the last condition suggesting that he failed to receive proper nourishment when he was an infant. Given his appearance, he has been nicknamed "the dissipated baby" by another resident. Although the narrator says the nickname is "not very apt" (*Stories* 138), the etymology of "dissipated", 'thrown apart', makes the word quite apt, for Detlev suffers so deeply from a sense of fragmentation that he yearns for the sense of unity that he experienced as a baby.

Enter Frau Klöterjahn, brought "from the shores of the Baltic" (*Stories* 135), by Herr Klöterjahn, whose family name suggests the Low German word for the testicles (Hayman 1995: 166). "[O]f medium height, broad, stout, and short-legged[,] his face full and red, with watery blue eyes shaded by very fair lashes[,] with wide nostrils and humid lips", Klöterjahn has lived up to the family name, for he has sired "Anton Klöterjahn, junior, a magnificent specimen of a baby" (*Stories* 137), now ten months old. The proud father is a successful businessman who loves good food and drink and, when the opportunity arises, a bad chambermaid.

When Herr Klöterjahn soon returns to his Baltic business, Detlev begins to hover around Gabriele whenever possible. Since Detlev's unconscious motive is to return to Eden, he haunts the Einfried garden. As he tramps through the snow, covered in fur right down to his toes, she, "bundled in wraps and furs", watches him from the terrace. Bare winterish though it may be, the garden engenders the skin-ego complex in this Alpine Adam and Eve: the next step would be he and she on or under the furs, a swoon in the Mann canon not to be taken until "The Blood of the Walsungs".

As she had observed him, so he had observed her. Approaching her on the terrace, he proclaims aesthetically: "Today on my morning walk I saw a beautiful woman—good Lord! how beautiful she was". Then he characteristically tilts his head and flutters his hands. When Gabriele asks for a description, he replies that he never looks directly at a beautiful woman, that he is not "avid of actuality" (*Stories* 143), preferring that his visual image be influenced by his pre-existing ideal. Gabriele says, in effect, that he is getting too deep for her. Detlev reaches the peak of his excitement:

"I know only one face," he said suddenly, with a strange lift in his voice, carrying his closed hands to his shoulders as he spoke and showing his carious teeth in an almost hysterical smile, "I know only one face of such lofty nobility that the mere thought of enhancing it through my imagination would be blasphemous; at which I could wish to look, on which I could wish to dwell, not minutes and not hours, but my whole life long; losing myself utterly therein, forgotten to every earthly thought...." (*Stories* 143-44; ellipsis in orig.)

Standing there, looking at the vein on her brow that had caught his attention on the day of her arrival (*Stories* 135), Detlev has been consciously paying court to Gabriele, but, unconsciously, to his mother, whose face he sees in Gabriele's features. Those carious teeth he received from the deprivation of her breast, from which vantage point he must have studied the fatal blue vein on her brow.[18]

Just as baby Klöterjahn had depleted Gabriele's physical energy, so now baby Spinell begins to deplete her spiritual energy (*Stories* 144). In a way, then, the babies are "brothers", perhaps even "twins", a portent of coming characters in Mann's fiction. Like a conventional lover, Detlev wishes to plumb Gabriele's past, thus to reveal it as a part of his future. First off, he wants to know her maiden name, for he has hated the word *Klöterjahn* since he first heard it. His ire must be fueled by his knowledge of its Low German meaning. When she replies that she was born of the family Eckhof, he immediately admires the name because there was "a great actor named Eckhof" (*Stories* 145). Literally, though, "Eckhof" (corner garden), should appeal to his unconscious. Later it is revealed that the many letters that Detlev writes (few are answered) are on stationery "in whose upper left-hand corner was a curious involved drawing of a landscape and the name Detlev Spinell in the very latest thing in lettering" (*Stories* 158): Freud's interpretation of "landscape" as a symbol of mother's genitals should be recalled.

When Gabriele says that she was born in Bremen, Detlev claims that he was there once, for an evening, sighing as if it had been a moment in paradise. When, in response to his prompting, she acknowledges that her merchant family has lived there for generations, he then implies that he is the scion of just such a family (*Stories* 146). And when she says that she and her father were especially close because of their shared love of music, he a master violinist and she a merely competent pianist, Detlev is nearly ecstatic, for he can imagine daughter and father each active, both thrilled by their mutual activity, a relationship denied him by circumstance.

He does become ecstatic when she describes the garden of her youth, the *place* of the goddess: "In the middle was a fountain with a wide border of sword-lilies. In summer I spent long hours there with my friends. We all sat round the fountain on little camp-stools".[19] Flinging up his shoulders, he exclaims, "How beautiful!" He is now aesthetic enough to expect the operatic: "You sat there and sang"? "No, we mostly crocheted". "But still[....]" "Yes, we crocheted and chattered, my six friends and I[....]" He rhapsodizes: "How beautiful! Good Lord! think of it, *how beautiful!*" "Now, what is it you find so particularly beautiful about that, Herr Spinell?" "Oh, there being six of them besides you, and your being not one of the six, but a queen among them...set apart from your six friends" (*Stories* 146; ital. and ellipsis in orig.). Detlev is thrilled that there were six friends, for he associates them with "the six spotless virgins who tended the sacred fire brought by Æneas from Troy, and preserved by the state in a sanctuary in the Forum at Rome" (Evans 1981: 1163).

A voyeur, motivated by oral nostalgia (Wurmser 1981:147), Detlev speaks of standing unseen in that garden, able to see the crown that Queen Vesta wears. Gabriele replies that it was not he but Klöterjahn who parted the bushes and that they were engaged three days later, even though her father was opposed: "He would rather I had stopped with him, and he had doubts in other ways too" (*Stories* 147). In her translation of Gabriele's recollection of her desire to marry, Lesér emphasizes the insistence that she shows by relying upon variations of the word *will*, arguing that Gabriele had been driven by Schopenhauer's "will to live" (1989: 91). Detlev is subdued by such a frank confession of the sexual drive, and prefers to think that Eckhof and Klöterjahn "clave" unto one another (*Stories* 147), rather than that the corner enclosure was intimately entered, just as Klöterjahn had parted the garden bushes to come to the fountain in the middle.

There comes a day when there is to be a "sleighing party" in the mountains. Gabriele announces that she will not go; true to the prediction of those who call Detlev the "dissipated baby", he also declines to go, saying that he has work to do (*Stories* 149). In time Detlev finds Gabriele and Frau Spatz in the salon. In time he asks Gabriele to play the piano. Although she tells him that she has been forbidden to play by Dr. Leander, Detlev easily induces her to play. By the time she has played three Chopin nocturnes, she has completely given over to the forces of darkness. She looks for more music, and Detlev produces the score of *Tristan and Isolde* (that he has probably planted). She plays the Prelude, seeming to intuit the fatal choice offered by the *Sehnsuchtsmotiv*: "Here two forces, two beings, strove towards each other, in transports of joy and pain; here they embraced and became one in delirious yearning after eternity and the absolute ..." (*Stories* 153; ellipsis in orig.). With Frau Spatz's departure, Gabriele plays the Second Act, from Isolde standing in her garden awaiting Tristan to their consummation in love and in worship of the night.

All at once there is a burst of light from the doorway, revealing Frau Pastor Höhlenrauch, who, hollow-headed from fourteen pregnancies, is now a witless witness to the ravages of the "will to life". Gabriele understands the choice Frau Pastor presents; unheedingly, she plays "the finale,[...]Isolde's song of love and death" (*Stories* 155), then the *Sehnsuchtsmotiv* (*Stories* 156). Then silence—until the sleigh bells of the returning party are heard.

Two days later Gabriele is a hopeless case. Sent for, Herr Klöterjahn comes, bringing pudgy baby Klöterjahn and the source of his pudginess, his "full-figured" nannie. Again the voyeur Detlev watches their arrival with "a peculiar gaze, both veiled and piercing". Detlev's reaction to Gabriele's condition perfectly expresses his orality: he secludes himself to write a long letter to Klöterjahn. His looking at himself in a mirror "of many little panes set in lead" (*Stories* 157) reveals the narcissistic anxiety of a "dissipated baby". His long letter condemning Klöterjahn and all that he stands for is stamped and mailed, from Einfried to Einfried. Receiving the letter, Klöterjahn seeks out Detlev, whom he finds "sitting on the sofa reading his own novel with the appalling cover-design" (*Stories* 161). Klöterjahn launches a furious rebuttal, and would be yelling yet, had he not been interrupted by news that his wife has taken a turn for the worse. Frau Spatz tells him:

> It is so frightfully sad.... She has brought up so much blood, such a horrible lot of blood.... She was sitting up quite quietly in bed and humming a little snatch of music... there it came...my God... such a quantity you never saw.... (*Stories* 64; ellipsis in orig.)

After studying himself in the mirror, Detlev drinks a cognac, then attempts to nap. But his mind is filled with the indignities that Klöterjahn had hurled at him, so he decides to take a walk. The sun in descent reminds him of his virginal vision of garden Gabriele with her six vestals, prompting him to hum the *Sehnsuchtmotiv* (*Stories* 165). But the reality that the sun reveals is that of "an exuberant figure, all arranged in red and gold and plaid", pushing little Klöterjahn sitting up in his perambulator:

> He had a bone teething-ring in one hand and a tin rattle in the other; and these two objects he flung aloft with shoutings, shook them to and fro, and clashed them together in the air, as though purposely to frighten Herr Spinell.

That teething-ring reveals that Spinnell's "twin" Anton has strong teeth, an indication that Anton has nursed to contentment, will escape the oral regression that has plagued Spinnell's life. Knowing well the implications of the scene, the narrator is fully justified in drawing his conclusion about Spinnell: "Pursued by the youthful Klöterjahn's joyous screams, he went away across the gravel, walking stiffly, yet not without grace; his gait was the hesitating gait of one who would disguise the fact that, inwardly, he is running away" (*Stories* 166).

The biographers cited above agree that, in creating Detlev Spinell, Mann borrowed traits from both Arthur Holitscher, his friend at the time, and Heinrich, his brother. They also agree that, primarily, he gave Detlev his own physical features, mannerisms, contemporary circumstances. He did more than that: he gave his creation his own state of mind. The last sentence of the story—abruptly introducing brutal moralism—reveals just how harshly he judged himself when he wrote it.

"Tonio Kröger"

In both "*Gladius Dei*" and "Tristan" Mann creates an adult male protagonist who is unconscious of the fact that his behavior is an outgrowth of his infantile response to his mother. Mann's nearly simultaneous creation of a coherent and meaningful narrative for each of these stories reveals just how vigorously his unconscious was struggling to make his mother problem known to him. Accordingly, the next story that Mann wrote—"Tonio Kröger"—treats a young writer who has reached a crucial point in his mental life. (While Detlev Spinell is also a writer, he is so oblivious to his mother problem that he has, so far, escaped the crisis that confronts Tonio Kröger.) Like the protagonists of "*Gladius Dei*" and "Tristan", Tonio Kröger has repressed his experience of being alienated in infancy, but unlike them he has become so plagued by his sense of alienation that he endeavors to find its source in his past. As many commentators have noted, "Tonio Kröger" is highly autobiographical.

As late as May 1940 Mann said "Tonio Kröger" was "the story which perhaps still today is closest to my heart" ("On Myself" 44). Perhaps his fondness for the story resulted from his belief that he had accurately revealed the cause and depth of Tonio's suffering and that he had made credible Tonio's belief that he could transform private agony into art. Thus, if Mann had succeeded in those projects, he had used form to make coherent his existential situation and artistic project.

In order to deal with Tonio's condition, past and present, Mann had to depict two levels of memory, conscious and unconscious. Conscious memory is revealed by what Tonio thinks and by what he writes to Lisabeta Ivanovna and by what he says, primarily to Lisabeta. Repressed memory is revealed by the phenomena Tonio's vision registers, but which his mind does not find significant. The story opens with a description of the weather: "The winter sun, poor ghost of itself, hung milky and wan behind layers of cloud above the huddled roofs of the town. In the gabled streets it was wet and windy and there came in gusts a sort of soft hail, not ice, not snow" (*Stories* 85).

Apparently a rather conventional opening for a story, the description is Tonio's conscious memory of a winter scene in his hometown on the Baltic. He then sees himself, at fourteen, in that scene. But the reader sees, in retrospect, that the description conveys symbolically the state of alienation in Tonio's unconscious. Tonio is no more than human to believe in his heart of hearts that he once existed in the warm, lush, bright "good place", Eden. Then he becomes aware that at some point he had fallen into the cold, viscid, wan "bad place". How to account for his "fall"? By using symbolic language, Tonio's unconscious makes an effort to tell him that his agonized need for love was born when the sun became a "ghost", still appearing "milky" only because of "layers of cloud".

After the introductory paragraph comes Tonio's conscious memory of his infatuation for Hans Hansen when they were schoolmates. By then Tonio was physically, socially, and scholastically unimpressive, introspective, intense, self-conscious, and Latin, fatally formed to have a crush on Hans, who was handsome, well-built, popular, confident, academically successful if totally unreflective, and Nordic. The bulk of the memory is of a walk they took one day after school, but interspersed in it is his state of mind in adolescence. He took pride in his family line and loved his parents. He felt that his father's "annoyance" at him was justified; he felt that his mother loved him, but showed a "blithe indifference" toward him (*Stories* 88). Because he has subjected himself to repression, the mature Tonio is unable to conceive of a "pre-history" for his alienation, which he thinks originated in adolescence. He would scoff at the idea that he loved Hans because he thought Hans had all the qualities his parents would have loved.

The depth of Tonio's repression is indicated by his admiration of Schiller's *Don Carlos,* which he strenuously urges that Hans read (*Stories* 89). Tonio must unconsciously feel that if Hans understands the fundamental plot of that play he will understand the source of the love that is being offered him. In the play Don Carlos has so repressed his fantasy of incest with his mother that even his step-mother falls under taboo. Suffering from equally severe repression, Tonio transfers his desire to Hans.[20] Then Tonio remembers his infatuation for Ingeborg Holm when they were sixteen years old. The bulk of this memory is of a dancing class that both he and Ingeborg attended:

> He had seen her a thousand times; then one evening he saw her again; saw her in a certain light, talking with a friend in a certain saucy way, laughing and tossing her head; saw her lift her arm and smooth her back hair with her schoolgirl hand, that was by no means particularly fine or slender, in such a way that the thin white sleeve slipped down from her elbow; heard her speak a word or two, a quite indifferent phrase, but with a certain intonation, with a warm ring in her voice; and his heart throbbed with ecstasy, far stronger than that he had once felt when he looked at Hans Hansen long ago, when he was still a little, stupid boy. (*Stories* 92-93)

Precipitated by his longing into an intense self-consciousness whenever he is in Nordic Ingeborg's presence, Tonio is inept when he is in her set in dancing class. Belittled by the dancing master, Herr Knaak, Tonio is the butt of laughter for all assembled, except for Magdalena Vermehren, his "twin" in personality, who adores him, but, alas, frequently falls face flat. Tonio tells himself that he will get over his unrequited love for Ingeborg, just as he has gotten over Hans. But his memories—which are no doubt recurrent—are proof that he has not gotten over the shame of having felt love for uncomprehending objects.

Tonio next remembers the dissolution of his family. With the death of his father, the family firm and home had been sold. After a year, Tonio's mother had married an Italian musician and left with him for "remote blue distances". Tonio thinks that her behavior had been "a little irregular", but so strong is his repression of his unconscious that it will not allow himself to give vent to his real feelings. His unconscious offers him symbols by which he could understand his situation: "And so he left his native town and its tortuous, gabled streets with the damp wind whistling through them; left the fountain in the garden and the ancient walnut tree, familiar friends of his youth; left the sea too, that he loved so much, and felt no pain to go" (*Stories* 98). But he is prevented by repression from comprehending the Edenic imagery of garden and tree and the "oceanic feeling" aroused by the sea.

There follows a thirteen-year interval:

> He lived in large cities and in the south, promising himself a luxuriant ripening of his art by southern suns; perhaps it was the blood of his mother's race that drew him thither. But his heart being dead and loveless, he fell into adventures of the flesh, descended into the depths of lust and searing sin, and suffered unspeakably thereby. It might have been his father in him, that tall, thoughtful, fastidiously dressed man with the wild flower in his buttonhole, that made him suffer so down there in the south; now and again he would feel a faint, yearning memory of a certain joy that was of the soul; once it had been his own, but now, in all his joys, he could not find it again. (*Stories* 111)

Vacillating between the opposed life styles learned from his father and mother, Tonio is fulfilled by neither. Thus he is all the more driven to express himself in writing: "as his health suffered from these excesses, so his artistry was sharpened" (*Stories* 99).

Now "slightly past thirty", Tonio lives in Munich. Presumably, his memories of Hans and Ingeborg have come to him as he is writing one morning (*Stories* 101). Then he goes to see his painter friend, Lisabeta Ivanovna, whom he treats as a sounding board.[21] It is spring, and his "blood tickles" him. While he cannot escape being a writer, any more than he could escape a curse, he is "sick to death of depicting humanity without having any part or lot in it" (*Stories* 103). Why is it that the price of being of the party of the spirit is that the artist must be a castrato (*Stories* 104)? After having told Lisabeta his troubles all summer long, Tonio informs her that he is going to visit Denmark, by way of Lübeck, because he "wants to see the Baltic again" (*Stories* 110).

Like most people on their first homecoming after a long absence, Tonio finds Lübeck "tiny and close" (*Stories* 111), vaguely wonders why he is still intrigued by it. His visit ends in farce when a policeman suspects that he is "wanted by the Munich police for various shady transactions" (*Stories* 117). Since his visit is a regression to find the transformative object, what better way to convey the sense of guilt that he feels?

Tonio does the sights in Copenhagen, steadily more depressed that all the buildings seem haunted, but all the citizens seem

unhaunted—a contrast often noted by introspective persons. Soon
restless, he takes a ferry up the coast to Helsingör (*Stories* 122).
Although he had told Lisabeta that he wanted "to stand on the terrace at
Kronberg, where the ghost appeared to Hamlet" (*Stories* 110), he rushes
directly through the town, out to the "bath-hotel" (*Stories* 122) at
Aalsgaard. If questioned, he might attribute his omission to simple
forgetfulness, but it would appear to be an act of defensive repression:
refusing to put himself in Hamlet's place, he is refusing to
acknowledge the mother incest fantasy that he shares with Hamlet.

Since Tonio's story from the very first sentence has been
about the hold of the past on the present, his choice of final destination
represents his attempt to return to the *Kurhaus* at Travemünde, where
he (and his creator) had experienced the "oceanic feeling" when he was
very young. When Tonio sailed from Lübeck to Copenhagen he had
been aware when the ship soon passed Travemünde (*Stories* 119), but
he does not allow himself to think about its significance. At Aalsgaard
Tonio spends his time alone, in or near the sea, revelling, like Little
Herr Friedemann, "in the peace and quiet" (*Stories* 123). But the day
comes when there is to be a "family reunion" (*Stories* 124) at the bath-
hotel. (And a "family reunion" is, of course, what Tonio's story is all
about.) Immediately anticipating that the party visitors will be of the
party of life, Tonio hallucinates a vision of those who had represented
that party in his youth, Hans and Ingeborg, entering one door "hand-in-
hand" and exiting by another (*Stories* 125).

All day long he waits, gladly anticipating their reappearance
at the party. When he sees each of them through the glass door that
separates him from the party, he realizes that he is only seeing
someone who reminds him of the original. Now some of the party of
life see him, resenting his gaze. Then a dancing couple stumbles and
falls. Tonio had previously observed that the female partner was one
of the introspectives and understands the shame that she feels. He
remembers that Ingeborg and Hans had laughed at him when he fell
and, despite that, even he had not been sympathetic to Magdalena
Vermehren, "who always fell down in the dance" (*Stories* 97). Now he enters
life, lifting the Danish girl up. Gratefully, she thanks him: *"Tak, O,
mange tak!"* (*Stories* 130). Then he leaves.

Back in his room, he writes Lisabeta:

> My father, you know, had the temperament of the north: solid,
> reflective, puritanically correct, with a tendency to melancholia.
> My mother, of indeterminate foreign blood, was beautiful,

> sensuous, naïve, passionate, and careless at once, and, I think, irregular by instinct. (*Stories* 132)

Tonio (speaking for Mann) thinks that this clash of temperaments is responsible for his alienation from both the party of life and the party of spirit. While he is of the party of spirit, he is not one of "those proud, cold beings who adventure upon the paths of great and dæmonic beauty and despise 'mankind'":

> For if anything is capable of making a poet of a literary man, it is my *bourgeois* love of the human, the living and usual. It is the source of all warmth, goodness, and humour; I even almost think it is itself that love of which it stands written that one may speak with the tongues of men and of angels and yet having it not is as sounding brass and tinkling cymbals.

By indirect reference to 1 Cor. 13.1, he asserts that it is St. Paul's "charity", brotherly love, that makes "a poet of a literary man". He will continue, in his writing, to avow his love for "the blond and blue-eyed, the fair and living, the happy, lovely, and commonplace". Lisabeta had earlier called him "a bourgeois on the wrong path, a bourgeois *manqué*" (*Stories* 110), so he feels that he must justify his love for the bourgeois temperament: "it is good and fruitful. There is longing in it, and a gentle envy; a touch of contempt and no little innocent bliss" (*Stories* 132).

Mann's earlier stories had had their origin in his sense of alienation resulting from the disquiet of his childhood, showing adult protagonists driven to action by unconscious impulses. "Tonio Kröger" is transitional, in that while Tonio also acts upon unconscious impulses, he consciously attributes his sense of alienation to the isolation from the bourgeois that his role as observing artist demands of him. Unconsciously, though, he may sense that his continued attachment to the mother figure, his oral nostalgia, inhibits him from being anything other than an observer. His sense of isolation must have been intensified by his frustrated infatuation for Paul Ehrenberg.

"The Hungry"

The next few stories treat rather abstractly the isolation that the self-conscious person feels when he watches the happy unself-conscious. Even before he was able to bring "Tonio Kröger" to a conclusion, he wrote "The Hungry", a sketch of Detlef, who attends a "fête" in a theater with "Lily and the little painter", who, according to Heilbut (1996:133), are based on Lily Teufel and Paul Erhenberg, her future husband. The sketch, then, is Mann's confession that he has lost Paul. When Detlef is "struck by the sense of his own superfluity" (*Stories* 167), he leaves the couple, but observes them from a distance. The theater becomes a *theatrum mundum*, as Detlef views Lily and the little painter as representatives of the carefree party of life. In despair, Detlef reaches the exit, glimpsing on the sidewalk "a red-bearded, hollow-cheeked, lawless face, with horribly inflamed, red-rimmed eyes that stared with sardonic despair and a certain greedy curiosity into his own" (*Stories* 171). Detlef is too caught up in his own isolation to respond to the need of the other; instead he merely considers him a symbol of all those others cut off from the carefree existence. Hence Detlef foolishly thinks of himself and the tramp as *"brothers"*—since each is "hungry". Back in his comfortable home, "among his books and pictures, and the busts ranged along the wall" (*Stories* 172, ital.in orig.), Detlef thinks of the New Commandment given by Jesus, "that you love one another, even as I have loved you" (John 13: 34). Perhaps Detlef thinks that he can give his "brothers" "release through the Word" (*Stories* 172), but the red-bearded "brother's" immediate hunger is for bread. Is it possible that Mann is satirizing Detlef, apparently a writer like himself, for comparing his self-imposed and self-pitying "hunger" with the actual hunger from which so many suffer?

"A Gleam"

In the summer of 1903 Mann visited his friend Kurt Martens, who, on one of their walks, told Mann a story from his days in the cavalry (Lesér 1989: 130). Martens recalled an occasion when the garrison officers hosted a dance for the Swallows, a troupial of female singers, who probably swallowed off-stage, as well, if not better. Those officers who were married decided to bring their wives, to show the local bourgeoisie that, as aristocrats, they set their own standards. In October Mann wrote the story in eight days (Wysling 1998: 53), spotlighting the leading light of the officers, the frivolous Baron Harry the hirsute, and his sensitive wife Baroness Anna. The pain suffered by Baroness Anna as she observes her husband's boisterous behavior with the Swallow Emmy repeats the condition of the narrator in "The Hungry". Indeed, as "The Hungry" ends with the narrator's experience of brotherhood with the lower class man in the street, an experience which may be spurious and is certainly not reciprocated, so in "A Gleam" Baroness Anna gains a moment of sisterhood when Emmy, "a little chit of a strolling chorus-girl", returns to her the wedding band that Baron Harry had taken from his finger and placed on hers, then kisses her hand, adding one request, "Forgive" (*Stories* 282).

Winston notes that Mann, carefully implying that he is the narrator, begins by positioning the story between two works-in-progress, *Fiorenza* and *Royal Highness* (1981: 175). Implicitly Mann is preparing his loyal readers for a story not quite up to his usual standard—he wrote his brother Heinrich that the story was written "on commission for the money" (Wysling 1998: 60). Even if of dubious merit, though, "A Gleam" does reveal that Mann was still focused on the wistful spectator.

"The Infant Prodigy"

A month after writing "A Gleam", Mann wrote "The Infant Prodigy", another study of the cleavage that exists between the unreflective majority and the artist. Mann reveals the mental processes of Bibi Saccellaphylaccas, an eight-year-old pianist (*Stories* 173), as he performs in a concert, and of various members of the audience—a teacher, or a critic, for example. In this story there is again no obvious "mother problem". There is, though, a clear personal reference, which occurs at the conclusion of the story when the audience is departing the concert hall. One group consists of "an elegant young lady who was being arrayed in her evening cloak and fur shoes by her two brothers, two lieutenants. She was exquisitely beautiful, with her steel-blue eyes and her clean cut, well-bred face. A really noble dame" (*Stories* 179). Yet she is modest, reminding one of her brothers not to spend so much time primping before a mirror. A "girl with untidy hair and swinging arms, accompanied by a gloomy-faced youth, came out just behind them". Envious of the adulation that the audience had showered upon Bibi, the girl with the untidy hair muses aloud, "We are all infant prodigies, we artists", and her escort gloomily nods his head in agreement: "Then they were silent and the untidy-haired girl gazed after the brothers and sister. She rather despised them, but she looked after them until they had turned the corner" (*Stories* 180). Although he is silent, the "gloomy-faced youth" (Mann) obviously shares the ambivalent attitude of his companion toward those who, though they are not artists, are rich and well content with the world as it is.

Heilbut (1996: 171) is convincing when he asserts that the models for the "elegant young lady" and "her brothers, two lieutenants" were Katja Pringsheim and two of her four brothers, children of a rich Jewish professor. Mann thought he was fourteen when he first saw the likeness of Katja Pringsheim reproduced in a magazine, but actually

he was seventeen (Heilbut 1996: 36). Unidentified, she and her
brothers had posed as clowns for an 1892 painting by Friedrich
August von Kaulbach, "Kinder Karneval", that was widely
reproduced. While Katja's costume marks her gender, she shares her
brothers' looks, especially those of the youngest brother, with whom
she shares twinship. The subliminal message, sibling play, especially
between twins, would have had erotic overtones for the young Mann.
He kept a clipping of the illustration above his desk for a time. Eleven
years later in Munich, he saw Katja, probably on a tram (K. Mann
1975: 15), but he did not connect her image with the little girl in
"Kinder Karneval". After that first sighting he had often used his
opera glasses to observe her and her four brothers at concerts
(Winston 1971: 34). Only after he had been invited to the Pringsheim
home, where he saw the original painting (K. Mann 1975: 11-12), did
he realize that fantasy sometimes anticipates reality.

"At the Prophet's"

        "The Hungry", "A Gleam", and "The Infant Prodigy" have
their source not in Mann's distant past but in his near past. "At the
Prophet's", Mann's next story, continues that pattern, for it is based
on an event that happened only a month or so before he wrote about it.
Again, Mann presents a study of the relationship between one who
performs, a prophet named Daniel[22], and those who observe. Daniel
has invited a group of people to his rooms on Good Friday evening to
hear his "Proclamations" read aloud:

> There were the Polish artist and the slender girl who lived with
> him; a lyric poet; a tall, black-bearded Semite with his heavy, pale
> wife, who dressed in long, flowing robes; a personage with an
> aspect soldierly yet somewhat sickly withal, who was a retired
> cavalry captain and professed spiritualist; a young philosopher
> who looked like a kangaroo. Finally a novelist, a man with a stiff
> hat and a trim moustache. He knew nobody. He belonged to quite
> another sphere and was present by the merest chance, being on
> good terms with life and having written a book which was read in
> middle-class circles. (*Stories* 283)

The invitees are received by a mute boy, then greeted by Daniel's
sister Maria Josepha. Then others arrive:

> a designer, a fantastic creature with a wizened childish face; a
> lame woman, who was in the habit of introducing herself as a

priestess of Eros; an unmarried young mother whose aristocratic family had cast her out, and who was admitted into the circle solely on the ground of her motherhood, since intellectual pretensions she had none; an elderly authoress and a deformed musician—in all some twelve persons.

The narrator's purpose in presenting such a   congregation of caricatures quickly becomes apparent, for it serves as a foil to an new guest:

> a rich woman who out of sheer amateurishness had a habit of frequenting such gatherings as this. She came from the city in her satin-lined coupé, from her splendid house with the tapestries on the walls and the giallo-antico door-jambs; she had come all the way up the stairs and in at the door, sweet-scented, luxurious, lovely, in a blue cloth frock with yellow embroidery, a Paris hat on her red-brown hair, and a smile in her Titian eyes. She came out of curiosity, out of boredom, out of craving for something different, out of amiable extravagance, out of pure universal goodwill, which is rare enough in this world.

She seats herself near the novelist, "who had entrée at her house": "The novelist was slightly overcome; how thankful he was that he had on presentable clothes! 'How beautiful she is!' thought he. 'Actually she is worthy of being her daughter's mother'" (*Stories* 286).

Then we are given their *tête-à-tête*:

> "And Fräulein Sonia?" he asked over her shoulder. "You have not brought Fräulcin Sonia with you?" Sonia was the rich woman's daughter; in the novelist's eyes altogether too good to be true, a marvellous creature, a consummate cultural product, an achieved ideal. He said her name twice because it gave him an indescribable pleasure to pronounce it.
>
> "Sonia is a little ailing," said the rich woman. "Yes, imagine, she has a bad foot. Oh, nothing—a swelling, something like a little inflammation or gathering. It has been lanced. The lancing may not have been necessary but she wanted it done."
>
> "She wanted it done," repeated the novelist in an enraptured whisper. "How characteristic! But how may I express my sympathy for the affliction?"
>
> "Of course, I will give her your greetings," said the rich woman. And as he was silent: "Is not that enough for you?"
>
> "No, that is not enough for me," said he, quite low; and as she had a certain respect for his writing she replied with a smile:
>
> "Then send her a few flowers."

"Oh, thanks!" said he. "Thanks, I will." And inwardly
he thought: "A few flowers! A whole flower-shopful! Tomorrow,
before breakfast. I'll go in a droshky." And he felt that life and he
were on very good terms. (*Stories* 287)

Mann did encounter Katja's mother, Hedwig Pringsheim, at
the reading at Derleth's apartment on Good Friday, 1 April 1904
(Prater 1995: 57-58, Winston 1981: 188). He had been wooing Katja
through her mother for the past six weeks (Wysling 1998: 64-66), so
"the novelist's" flattery of "the rich woman" is probably close to what he
actually said at the reading. But "the novelist's" surprise at Katja's illness
is fictional, for he had written Heinrich on 27 March: "In the moment,
Katja is sick in the Surgical Clinic, whither I sent her a couple of beautiful flowers
this morning, with the permision of the beautiful Lenbach Mama, who always smiles
encouragingly when I refer simply to 'Katja' in her presence" (Wysling 1998:
67). After writing the story in April, Mann showed it to "Frau Professor
P" (Winston 1971: 37), thus recycling his flattery. She had no
objections to its publication.

No doubt Mann's conscious motives for writing the sketch
were to publicize his suit for Katja's hand and to insure her mother's
sympathy for it by his profuse description of her "Titian" beauty (K.
Mann 1975: 26). His admiration was not feigned, for he wrote
Heinrich that she was "a Lenbach beauty" (Wysling 1998: 65)--he may
have changed his comparison from Titian to a popular painter of the
time in view of Heinrich's tastes or prejudices. Unconsciously, Mann
was announcing that he was once again under the full sway of the
incestuous mother fantasy, which often manifests itself in an
infatuation for an older married woman, before being displaced onto
her daughter (Rank 1992: 73).

"Fiorenza"

Just as Mann's antipathy for loose Latin behavior had its
origin in his 1896 stay in Naples, so too, probably, did his sympathy
for Girolamo Savonarola (1452-1498), the priest who suppressed such
behavior in Florence from 1494 to 1498. Mann soon began making
notes for a play that would climax in the confrontation between
Savonarola and Lorenzo de' Medici (1449-1492) over whether
Florence would be a theocratic or a secular state. Mann visited
Florence in 1898 to do library research and to gain visual impressions.
In 1900, during his brief stay in the army, he wrote Heinrich from the

garrison infirmary, "I am even studying my Savonarola as if I were at home" (Wysling 1998: 37). In the summer of 1903, as he worked on his play, Mann recorded in his notebook, "Not for nothing is Savonarola my hero.... I hate those most who, through the feelings they arouse in me, draw attention to my weaknesses" (qtd. in Prater 1995: 49; ellipsis in orig.).

For all his research, though, by the time that Mann finally finished the play in January 1905, his characterization of Savonarola had become highly autobiographical. The time is 8 April 1492; the setting is the Villa Medicea, near Florence. The duration of the action is that of real time. From the very first scene all talk among the ailing Lorenzo's two sons and numerous retainers concerns the threat to the power of the Medicis posed by the preaching of Savonarola. The priest himself does not appear until scene six of act three, but by then many witnesses have given their impression of him.

The most telling impression is related to Lorenzo by Fiore, his mistress, just before Savonarola makes his long-deferred appearance, as if to reveal to her lover the origin of the implacable hostility that he is about to witness. She had, as a child, lived in Ferrara. Nearby lived "a citizen named Niccolo, learned, wealthy, and of ancient lineage, in favour at court. He lived there with his Monna Helena, and two daughters and four sons" (254). The second oldest, Girolamo, about eighteen, was, in Fiore's words,

> small, weak, ugly as darkness. When all Ferrara streamed out of doors to the public festivals, he buried himself in his books, played mournful melodies upon his lute, and wrote what no one was allowed to read.[...]Between us two [Fiore was then thirteen], things stood very strangely. He seemed to flee the sight of me with fear and loathing, yet to be condemned to meet me forever, indoors and out and everywhere I went. Then he seemed to play the coward and avoid me, yet he would force himself, pressing his thick lips together as he came towards me, passed and greeted me, blushing red and bending on me a sour and injured gaze. In this wise I came to understand that he was in love with me, and I rejoiced in the power I had over his gloomy arrogance. I played with him and led him on, I gave him hope and dashed it with a look. It thrilled me to know that my eyes could control the flow of his blood. He grew more lean and silent still, he began a fast that hollowed out the caverns of his eyes; one saw him sitting long hours in church, bruising his brow against the altar step. But one day, out of curiosity, I brought it about that he was alone with me in a room at twilight. I sat silent and waited. Then he groaned and was as though pulled towards me, and whispered and confessed. I made as though astonished and repulsed him; he seemed then to rave, almost like an animal, begging me with gasps and panting with parched lips to yield me to him. With horror and disgust I

> thrust him from me—it may even be that I struck at him, since he
> would not leave his avid clinging. And when I did so, he tore
> himself away and stood up with a shriek, inarticulate and hoarse,
> and rushed off, his fists before his eyes. (*Stories* 254-55)

     Savonarola's secretiveness about his writing is reminiscent of
Mann's diary-keeping (and diary-destroying) at the same age, just
when he was beset by the return of the repressed. Judged by the agony
manifested by Savonarola's actions, he suffers from the same
condition. Although nothing is told of Savonarola's mother except her
name, Helena, it is enough to suggest her lovable character, for the
name denotes the "type of lovely woman, patient and hopeful, strong in feeling,
and sustained through trials by her enduring and heroic faith" (Evans 1981: 542).
Perhaps the popularity of this denotation is to be traced to St. Helena
(c. 250-c. 330), who is credited with having discovered the true cross
in the Holy Land.

     Like Johannes Friedemann, Girolamo hopes to return to the
Good Mother by way of another woman. But, like Gerda von
Rinnlingen, Fiore immediately repulses Girolamo. Unlike Johannes,
Girolamo, upon rebuff, does not commit suicide, instead enters a
"cloister of Dominicans" (*Stories* 255). Many men have been thus teased,
but most of them have not reacted with such vehemence. Girolamo's
immediate entrance into mother church and dedication of himself to
the Madonna—signified by his seal, the Madonna with "the letters *FH* on
either side" (*Stories* 226)--are visible manifestations of the mother
fantasy that drives him. *FH*: FioreHelena?

     In the meantime, Fiore becomes the mistress of the master of
Fiorenza. She is so suffused with erotic femininity that every man
addresses her as the goddess of love with the salutation that he
prefers.[23] Leone claims that she is the foam-born (*Stories* 219),
Aphrodite. Piero de' Medici salutes her as "Ravishing Anadyomene"
(*Stories* 233), Aphrodite of the Divine Derrière. Close to his end,
Lorenzo calls her "Venus Genetrix", the life giver, and "Venus
Fiorenza", Venus of Florence or of the flowers (*Stories* 270).

     Invited to bring his mission to Fiorenza, Savonarola quickly
selects Fiore as the personification of its licentiousness, the Bad
Mother. Undaunted by his attack, Fiore deliberately provokes him by
boldly attending his services (*Stories* 203), in which he hides his
personal animosity, even from himself, by using the Book of
Revelation against her: "Behold![...] turn ye and behold. She comes, she is here,

the harlot with whom kings have dallied on earth, the mother of abominations, the woman on the beast, the great Babylon" (*Stories* 207).

It is only a matter of time before Fiore brings Savonarola and Lorenzo face to face. Knowing that Lorenzo wants to confess, Fiore invites Savonarola to visit her master. She visits Lorenzo first, though, to reveal the origin of Savonarola's rage for reform. When Savonarola enters, he finds Fiore sitting at Lorenzo's feet, ready to provoke him by referring to his youthful passion. Now that his passion is to reform the world, he once again addresses her as the temptress: "I call you the bait of Satan, the poison of the spirit, the sword of souls, wolf's milk for him who drinks it, occasion of destruction, nymph, witch, Diana I call you" (*Stories* 263).[24] Having accomplished her purpose, Fiore withdraws.

Early in their debate Lorenzo sympathically observes that Savonarola is exhausted, "By God, you should spare yourself—you ought to rest". Scornfully, Savonarola replies, "I know no rest. Rest the many know who have no mission. For them it is easy. But an inward fire burns in my limbs and urges me to the pulpit". (Earlier Savonarole had told Fiore, "You lashed me with opprobrium. You drove me up—up to my pulpit" [*Stories* 263].) Lorenzo replies,

> An inward fire—I know—I know, I know! I know this fire. I have called it dæmon, will, frenzy—but it has no name. It is the madness of him who offers himself up to an unknown god. He despises the base, cautious, home-keeping folk and lets them stare amazed at one for choosing a wild, brief, burning life instead of their long, wretched, frightened one. (*Stories* 264)

Lorenzo concludes that since both he and his opponent are driven by an all-consuming ambition, they are brothers (*Stories* 265).

Savonarola rejects any relationship with Lorenzo, but in his rejection, implies that the source of his ambition is longing (*Stories* 267). Since Lorenzo has also always experienced this sense of *Sehnsucht,* he intensifies his conclusion that they are brothers, saying that they are "warring brothers" (*Stories* 268).[25] Again Savonarola rejects the likeness that Lorenzo has drawn.

Continuing their argument, each admits to being contemptuous of those whom they lead, both being interested only in playing, as Savonarola puts it, "one's own tune" (Stories 270). As he feels himself sinking, Lorenzo asks to know the "conditions of grace"— which are three, stipulates Savonarola. Lorenzo accepts the first two conditions, repentance for his actions and return of all illegally acquired property to the state. The third condition is that Lorenzo give up power in Florence, the result being, as Lorenzo immediately realizes, that Savonarola, not Christ, will reign. Lorenzo refuses, even as he dies.

As Savonarola stands over him triumphant, Fiore enters to admonish him: "Descend! The fire you have fanned will consume you, you yourself, to purify you and the world of you. Shudder before it—and descend. Cease to will, instead of willing nothingness. Void the power! Renounce! Be a monk!" (*Stories* 272). Prophetically, she envisions his great Bonfire of the Vanities, in 1497, and the next year his *auto-da-fé*, after being "excommunicated [for heresy] by the Church, deserted by the fickle populace, and condemned by a new, hostile administration" (Fuller 1945: II 10). Exiting, Savonarola says, "I love the fire", knowing that he cannot extinguish the "inward fire" that has burned in his heart since it was reignited by Fiore.

"A Weary Hour"

On 11 February 1905 Mann and Katja Pringsheim were married. Given the Mann family neurosis their response to the marriage was predictable. A month before the wedding, Mama Mann wrote Heinrich,

> here are plenty of other girls, nice, sweet and less spoilt, who would have loved him more deeply and more faithfully, and looked after him better.... I am sorry to make so much fuss, but if only Tommy were free again (I mean his heart!) I think it would relieve me of a great burden. (qtd. in Hayman 1995: 207; ellipsis in orig.)

Mann had been staying with his mother before the wedding; Nigel Hamilton writes that Julia cried at breakfast before Mann left to be married and that she could not attend the ceremony because Katja had insisted on a civil union (1979: 104). Mama did attend the post-ceremony reception, but wept silently (Heilbut 1996: 183). Heinrich and sister Carla chose not to return to Munich for the wedding.

The newlyweds honeymooned for two weeks in a luxury hotel in Zurich. Despite the fact that her gynecologist had advised Katja to defer pregnancy for three or four years, she conceived before the honeymoon was over (Hayman 1995: 209), for Mann was in haste to be a father. Her pregnancy was suspected soon after they returned to Munich, for Mann wrote a friend, "the marriage-bed waits. It's not certain whether the prince is already on the way, one must stir oneself" (qtd. in Prater 1995: 65). Mann was determined that the child be male. When he and the pregnant Katja were guests in the Berlin home of her "grandmother Dohm, the advocate of women's rights", the grandmother asked, "Well, Tommy, what do you want, a boy or a girl?" He replied, "A boy, of course. After all, a girl is not to be taken seriously" (K. Mann 1975: 22). Alas, it was a lass, named Erika, born 9 November. Mann wrote Heinrich, 20 November,

> So it is a girl: a disappointment for me, I'll admit between us, for I had very much wanted a son and haven't stopped wanting one. Why? It's difficult to say. I feel that a son is more poetic, more of a continuation, a new beginning of myself under new conditions. Or so. Well, he needn't be done without. And perhaps the daughter will offer me a closer relation to the "other" sex, of which I still, though now a husband, actually know nothing. (Wysling 1998: 73)

Mann's statement "a new beginning of myself under new conditions" becomes highly significant in light of an observation by Rank on

> the great psychological events in a man's life brought about by marriage: the replacement of the unattainable and forbidden mother ideal by the wife, esteemed in the full compass of sexual life, and a second, perhaps even more meaningful event— becoming a father after having held on so long and so intensely to the role of son. (1992: 76)

Mann's reference above to the "prince" whom he wants his wife to bear indicates that he still harbors a childhood fantasy of being of royal blood.[26] Only a year before, 1904, he had alluded to its early origin:

> Sitting in a little basket-carriage, in which my nurse carried me around over the garden paths or in the entrance hall, I for some reason pulled my mouth downwards as far as possible, so that my upper lip lengthened, and slowly blinked my eyes, which reddened and filled with tears, partly because of the irritation and partly because of my inward excitement. I sat silently in the little carriage, impressed by my greatness and dignity, but my nurse was obliged to tell everyone who approached about the situation. "I'm taking the Kaiser for a walk here," she announced, pressing her flat hand authoritatively against her temple, and everyone bowed to me. (qtd. in Hayman 1995: 90-91)[27]

Many years later he offered a recollection of a subsequent event in which he was conscious of the fantasy:

> I awoke one morning[...]with the resolution to be for the day an eighteen year old prince by the name of Karl. I clothed myself in a certainly kindly majesty, carried on an animated conversation with a governor or adjutant, whom I had appointed in my imagination, and walked about proud and happy in the secret of my dignity. One could have lessons, be taken for a walk, hear stories read aloud, without its being necessary to interrupt the game for a moment,--and that was the practical part of it. ("On Myself" 26-27)

It was as much the force of this royalty fantasy as of the mother incest fantasy that caused him to identify himself on a 1895 questionnaire as Hamlet-like (Hayman 1995: 117). Indeed, it may have been his identification with Hamlet that caused him to link incest with royalty, since both are properties whose source is an obsession with bloodlines. Throughout history royalty had enjoyed the prerogative of incestuous relations. In September 1904, in an ardent letter to Katja, he all but confessed his feeling that their consummation would be incestuous:

> Do you know why we suit each other so well? Because you belong to neither the bourgeois nor the Junker class; because you, in your way, are something extraordinary—because you are, as I understand the word, *a princess*. And I—you may laugh now, but you must understand me—I have always seen myself as a kind of prince, and in you I have found, with absolute certainty, my predestined bride and companion. (Winston 1971: 45; ital. in orig.)

In accord with the incestuous mother fantasy sequence sketched by Rank, Mann has fallen silent about the older woman, shifting his desire to her daughter, whom he thinks of as sister-wife.

When Mann returned to his desk after the honeymoon, he accepted an invitation from the journal *Simplicissimus* to contribute a piece to an issue honoring Schiller on the hundredth anniversary of his death (Winston 1981: 204). Schiller had personified the *littérateur* for Mann ever since one of his Lübeck teachers had praised his ballads: "This is not just *any* reading you are having; it is the very best reading you could have!" ("Sketch" 7). Mann's decision to imagine "A Weary Hour" in Schiller's life, rather than to offer a critical analysis or an encomium, indicates the empathy that he felt for his literary forebear. "A Weary Hour" captures the self-doubt and creative difficulty that assailed Schiller as he attempted to complete one of his plays. Late at night Schiller finds himself unable to subdue his thoughts to writing, thus unable to escape his sense of self through engrossment in his work. Schiller thinks of "another person, who lived over in Weimar and for whom he felt a love which was a mixture of hostility and yearning" (*Stories* 291). That man, Goethe, is his opposite: a "radiant being, so sense-endowed, so divinely unconscious, that man over there in Weimar, whom he loved and hated" (*Stories* 294). That man looks outward and writes what he sees, while he, Schiller, looks inward and struggles to know. Schiller knows that his life's theme is to proclaim the quest for "freedom" (*Stories* 295), but like many others obsessed with freedom he has no answer to the question, what is it that he is denied the freedom to do. Schiller's agitated steps have taken him to the bed of his young wife, whom he loves, but for whom he will not abandon his "mission" (*Stories* 296). Deciding that his steadfastness to his duty is the core of his existence, he returns to his writing desk.

In treating "A Weary Hour" Mann's recent biographers have considered his fictional account of Schiller's concerns as a veiled statement of his own concerns at the time. Primarily Winston finds in the subtext an account of "the subtle adjustment of roles that follows the formation of a newly married pair" (1981: 207). Prater sees "Schiller's apparent failure to find the dramatic form that he seeks" as "a reflection of Mann's own efforts to finish *Fiorenza*" (1995: 67); Hayman also cites *Fiorenza*, then cites Schiller's dedication to the primacy of work as the example that Mann means to follow (1995: 210). Heilbut thinks that the Schiller/Mann critique of relatively painless creativity is "a possible knock at the voluble Heinrich [Mann]" (1996: 189); he implies, too, that Mann shares the "gloomy perception" that he imputes to Schiller:

> Here was the despairing truth: the years of need and nothingness, which he had thought of as the painful testing time, turned out to have been the rich and fruitful ones, and now that a little happiness had fallen to his lot, now that he had ceased to be an intellectual freeloader and occupied a position of civic depth, with office and honors, wife and children—he was exhausted, worn out. (1996: 188-89)

Heilbut comments, "At this moment, Mann predicts his large family and his hallowed reputation with something approaching terror" (1996: 189). It is the thesis of this study that the private meaning hidden in Schiller's return to his writing desk reveals Mann's intuition that, like Schiller, only by writing can he stave off the threat of regression to orality.

"The Blood of the Walsungs"

There is no doubt that Mann felt a close affinity with Schiller the man, for nearly a year later (17 January 1906) he wrote Heinrich,

> I have returned very strongly to Schiller, have studied him intensely. He is ultimately *nothing* but artist and therefore not at all objective, at least not so in his innermost self, just as little as Wagner was, who also indulged the pretense of all kinds of objectivity, while, however, being nothing but a great artist—and whom Schiller's need anticipated in the most astounding way. (Wysling 1998: 78; ital. in orig.)

In other words, Mann located the source and force of artistry in the need of the unconscious to make itself heard. The comparison of Wagner with Schiller probably has its origin in Mann's inspiration by both men's "innermost self" in the story that he had recently completed, "The Blood of the Walsungs". In the same letter Mann added, "[m]y reading[...]for a long time now has consisted not of belles lettres but of biographies, memoirs, correspondences[...]" (qtd. in Wysling 1998: 79). Although consciousness of his motive was repressed, Mann had been reading to fathom Schiller's unconscious: "In the gratified spectator of a work of art, who thus 'likes' the work, the same psychic impulses that drove its creator to artistic production are gratified much as in the experience of the creative artist himself" (Rank 1992: 119).

From his earliest literary creations Mann's material had been selected by the demand of his incest fantasy. Those works already treated in this study have featured a protagonist victimized by his mother problem, which stipulates that he desire a woman possessed by another man (Rank 1992: 71) or a male surrogate. Those works still to be treated deal with the protagonist's mother problem, but, additionally, with his sibling incest complex when it displaces his mother incest complex. In *The Incest Theme in Literature and Legend* Otto Rank offers an extensive analysis of the writers Mann mentioned in the letter above, Schiller and Wagner, in fact devoting two lengthy chapters to Schiller, the first on his mother complex and the second on his sibling complex. The account given below of Mann's work beginning with "The Blood of the Walsungs" depends on Rank's insights.

The setting of "The Blood of the Walsungs" is the section of Berlin known as the Tiergarten, after the famous zoo located there.

Although Mann studiously avoids the words "Jew" or "Jewish" in the story, at the time Tiergarten contained the houses of many wealthy Jewish families, in one of which Mann had been a guest[28]. Shortly after twelve noon, Herr von Beckerath, "a government official[...]of a good family" (*Stories* 298), joins the family of Villa Aarenhold for lunch. At age thirty-five, Beckerath cuts a strikingly dull figure, but he has been accepted as the betrothed of nineteen-year-old Sieglinde Aarenhold because of his social qualifications: being Protestant, possessed of a "von", and connected, however marginally, with the civil service. But while the members of the Aarenhold family have acquiesced to the betrothal, they seethe with outraged family and racial pride. Unlike Beckerath, they are rich, quick-witted, and cosmopolitan, yet because they are of the Jewish minority among the Gentile majority, they realize the advantage of adding a German to the family, even though it means the violation of their strongly endogamous tradition (Patterson 1963: 625).

When the apologetic Beckerath offers an excuse for his tardiness, "it is so far from the Ministry to the Zoo", he is expressive far beyond his intention. Quoting Lévi-Strauss, Nike Wagner writes, "The incest prohibition is 'the fundamental step thanks to which, through which, and, above all, in which the transition from nature to culture is performed'" (1998: 62). Close to the zoo, nature's domain, is the Aarenhold house, culture's domain. But Mann intends to reveal that culture is as often controlled by nature as is consciousness by the unconscious. Even earlier he describes the sound of the gong announcing the meal as a "cannibalistic summons" (*Stories* 297)[29]: if the Aarenholds violate one taboo, why would they scruple at another?

Pater Aarenhold is introduced first, but since he plays no active part in the incest fantasy that dominates the story, he is of little interest. The mater is another matter:

> She was small, ugly, prematurely aged, and shrivelled as though by tropic suns. A necklace of brilliants rested upon her shrunken breast. She wore her hair in complicated twists and knots to form a lofty pile, in which, somewhere on one side, sat a great jewelled brooch, adorned in its turn with a bunch of white aigrettes. (*Stories* 297)

Schneider writes: "This unfavorable portrait of Frau Aarenhold, a composite of a Jewish mother, is one of the ugliest images Thomas Mann ever painted of a woman. Is Frau Aarenhold an indirect attempt by Mann to criticize the mother of incestuous offspring, to brand her rather than her attractive children?" (1995: 22). I would counter that Mann has three reasons, two conscious, one unconscious, for the portrait. First, since he had consciously presented Katja's mother in all her beauty in "At the Prophet's" (283), he could deny any charge that Frau Pringsheim was the model for Frau Aarenhold. Second, the now married Mann and soon to be sire defiantly identifies his mother, who was born under "tropic suns", to declare independence from her influence, then mocks her mammae and crowns her with a Medusa mop. This "uglification" announces that this story will concern not the incestuous mother fantasy, but rather its frequent sequel, the incestuous sibling fantasy.

The mother problem quickly surfaces. Mann tells us that the elder brother, Kunz (*Kunst*?), "always felt annoyed with his mother" when "von Beckerath was present" (*Stories* 301), for she is the reason that he is not the Aryan he appears to be: "[...]in a braided uniform, a stunning tanned creature with curling lips and a killing scar. He was doing six weeks' service with his regiment of hussars" (*Stories* 297-98). In Kunz there lingers a slight residuum of incest fixation, now directed toward his younger sister, but, just as he hides his Jewish identity behind his looks and manner, so does he hide his mother-influenced homosexuality behind his hussar uniform. On the other hand, the younger son, Siegmund flaunts his similarly-influenced homoeroticism by mannerism and dress, although privately acting out his "need for purification" by continual bathing (*Stories* 305). This "need for purification" has been aroused not only by acts committed but also by an act pondered.

Enter the Aarenhold children: Kunz, Märit, Siegmund and Sieglinde. Kunz and Märit—first- and second-born, respectively, but equals in arrogance—are also tangential to the plot. Not so with Siegmund and Sieglinde, who "came last, hand in hand, from the second floor. They were twins, graceful as young fawns, and with immature figures despite their nineteen years" (*Stories* 298). Their constant handholding—is each paddling the other's palm?--proclaims their inseparability: they consider themselves a zygote. His gift to her, a "large pearl", "[hangs] down upon her brow" like a drop of sperm; her gift to him, a "heavy gold chain" enclosing "one of his boyish wrists", provides the generative circle (*Stories* 298). Their description "as young fawns" foreshadows the role that Anzieu's "fur fantasy" will have in the story (cf. ch1n7).

During the meal, the comments of the parents Aarenhold and their two elder children make it clear that they early developed the kind of skin-ego that Anzieu defines as "narcissistic"; they are tough-skinned analists. Kunz betrays "curling lips", while Marit offers "a bitter contemptuous mouth". But the silent twins Siegmund and Sieglind have the "masochistic" skin-ego; both have "full lips lying softly together" (*Stories* 298), displaying their potentiality for sensuality. As Freud would predict, they will kiss each other because they cannot kiss themselves (*Three* 182), thus confessing their fixation at the oral level. Despite displaying some tough-skinnedness at the family table, they are ultimately thin-skinned: "neither Siegmund nor Sieglinde displayed any interest. They held each other's narrow hands between their chairs. Sometimes their gaze sought each other's, melting together in an understanding from which everybody else was shut out" (*Stories* 301).[30]

Toward the end of the meal Siegmund initiates his plan by addressing "von Beckerath" (*Stories* 304). He wonders if the bridegroom would permit Sieglinde and himself to attend *Die Walküre* that evening. Kunz immediately reveals that he intuits Siegmund's plan by drumming "the Hunding motif" on the tablecloth: in Wagner's opera Siegmund has already entered Hunding's house and encountered Hunding's wife Sieglinde, so that their mutual arousal to (incestuous) desire exists before "the Hunding motif" announces the entrance of His Shagginess. Densely Beckerath acccdes, saying that he, too, is free to go: "All the Aarenholds", Wagnerians all, "bowed over their plates to hide their laughter". With exquisite malice, Siegmund explains that he and the girl want to enjoy *Walküre* "alone together" (*Stories* 304; ital. in original). The gull agrees. Playing to his sniggering fellow plotters, Siegmund suggestively says that he had reserved the "box" "long ago".

In his room Siegmund glances over at the Tiergarten, then closes the drapes, as if aware of its symbolism. Then he switches on the circle of electric bulbs that "filled the room wih soft milky light" (*Stories* 305). As Siegmund readies himself for the opera, he manifests the concerns that dominate his self-image (*Stories* 305). If he is to go out in the evening, he must make his second shave of the day: his desire for a baby-smooth skin is another manifestation of his fur fantasy, for at the same moment he is wearing a house-jacket "with revers of grey fur". Perhaps *Venus in Furs* is one of the books that he has actually read. Standing on a "white bearskin" (*Stories* 307) rug as he begins to dress, he luxuriates in the feel of its "long soft hair" (*Stories* 308) and in the scent of the toilet water he had just sprinkled on himself so lavishly.[31] He appreciates the linen dress shirt that "glides" over his shaggy-haired torso. Similarly all of his other garments are either silk or silky, so that his ego is dominated by the illusion that he is all skin. Standing on the bearskin, he anticipates the opera and *après opéra*.

When Sieglinde joins Siegmund in his bedroom, they display a panoply of skin-ego behaviors:

> She looked at him admiringly, proudly, adoringly, with a world of tenderness in her dark, shining eyes. He kissed the lips lying so softly on each other. They spent another minute on the chaise-longue in mutual caresses.
>
> "Quite, quite soft you are again," said she, stroking his shaven cheeks.
>
> "Your little arm feels like satin," said he, running his hand down her tender forearm. He breathed in the violet odour of her hair.
>
> She kissed him on his closed eyelids; he kissed her on the throat where the pendant hung. They kissed one another's hands. They loved one another sweetly, sensually, for sheer mutual delight in their own well-groomed, pampered, expensive smell. They played together like puppies, biting each other with their lips. (*Stories* 308-09)

In her chapter "Incest in *The Ring*" Nike Wagner, Richard's great-granddaughter, must have this scene in mind when she speaks of "Thomas Mann's sibling caprice" (1998: 67). No matter if "caprice" turns puppy-play into goat-play.

Fittingly both Sieglinde and Siegmund are "fur-mantled" for the trip to the opera (*Stories* 315), made in a "warm little-silken-lined retreat" (*Stories* 316), a closed coupé drawn by a pair of "glossy thoroughbreds" (*Stories* 315). In the throes of their mutual fantasy they fashion an amniotic enclosure. Mann closely describes the action of Act 1: Siegmund, his breast covered with a "pelt" (*Stories* 313) and his "sturdy legs wrapped round with hide and thongs" (*Stories* 310), enters the house, collapsing from exhaustion on a "bearskin rug"; Sieglinde, her ample "alabaster bosom" mantled by deerskin, enters the room; he takes the drinking-horn that she offers; mutually smitten they prepare to put the horns on the hulking Hunding, just entering. After discovering that his guest is his enemy, Hunding honors the tradition of "guest-right", giving a fugitive sanctuary for the night, but promising to kill him first-thing in the morning. Then he orders Sieglinde to spice his "night-drink" and to hop into his bed.

At this point, apparently influenced by her anticipation of what is to come, Sieglinde Aarenhold offers her "Gigi" her "mother-of-pearl" box containing maraschino cherries, one of which he takes. Reassuring Siegmund, she tells him what he certainly knows, "She will come back to him again at once" (*Stories* 312). Thus she speaks not only of Ms Walsung's future action but also of her own.

Sieglinde Walsung apparently spices her husband's drink with a soporific, for he can be heard snoring off-stage as she, undressed for bed, returns to the bearskin. She sings the full story of all the misery that has befallen her. In response, Siegmund presses her cheek against his pelt, then sings of how "their brother-and-sister love should be their revenge!" (*Stories* 313). "Crouching on the bearskin" they compare likenesses and contrast differences, coming to the realization that they, with one notable *différence*, are really and truly twins. After various Wagnerian vernal phenomena occur out the door, Sigmund unsheathes the sword, pointed out by Siglinde, by pulling it out of the ash tree, then he and she singe the bearskin as the curtain falls.

Siegmund Aarenhold is hot and bothered as he starts to leave the box. And so is his sister: "She lingered a moment, with her elbows on the ledge, still gazing at the stage. He looked at her as she rose and took up her silver scarf. Her soft, full lips were quivering". As above, so below. Walking "downstairs and up again, sometimes holding each other by the hand", they share "cherries" (*Stories* 314).

After the opera, the twins return to Villa Aarenhold, to find it obligingly vacant of family. A light meal has been prepared, but Siegmund becomes petulant, curtly bidding his sister "Good night", yet knowing that she will come to his room (*Stories* 317). McWilliams notes that Siegmund's behavior at this point is that of a son toward his mother (1983: 125-26), an observation which supports Rank's theory that the sibling incest fantasy is a sequel to the maternal incest fantasy. Sigmund's squirming inability to find a comfortable physical position betrays his conflicted mental condition. Finally he studies himself in the mirror, which reveals "each mark of his race"—he is inescapably a Jew, jealous of the Gentile who will violate Jewish blood, but even before that racial identification, he is a brother (and son) jealous of any rival. Accepting Sieglind's violation as an inevitability, he decides to carry through the pre-emptive act that he had contemplated:

> In the mirror he saw the bearskin lying behind him, spreading out its claws beside the bed. He turned round, and there was tragic meaning in the dragging step that bore him towards it—until after a moment more of hesitation he lay down all its length and buried his head in his arm. (*Stories* 318)

Having assumed one Walsung's position, Siegmund knows that Sieglinde will assume the other Walsung's position. Soon enough, lovely in lace, Sieglinde joins him on the bearskin; it is too late for symbolism, so she does not carry her mother-of-pearl box. After they compare likenesses and contrast differences, Siegmund speaks of what he will do: "it is a revenge, Sieglinde" (*Stories* 319). For once, we are given access to Sieglinde's unconscious:

> She did not blush at his half-spoken, turbid, wild imaginings; his words enveloped her senses like a mist, they drew her down whence they had come, to the borders of a kingdom she had never entered, though sometimes, since her betrothal, she had been carried thither in expectant dreams. (*Stories* 319)

Faced with marriage, the relationship essential to the origin of culture, Sieglinde has dreamed of a prelude in nature's neighborhood. Twice, when she faces Beckerath, Singlinde's eyes betray her desire to do like the animals (*Stories* 302, 307).

Closing their eyes, kissing "each other's hands", they forget "themselves in caresses, which [take] the upper hand". This pun, as well as the post-climactic one to follow, hints that Mann's notorious irony pervades the scene: "She sat there on the bearskin, with parted lips, supporting herself with one hand, and brushed the hair out of her eyes". Earlier those lips had been described as "lying so softly on each other" (*Stories* 308), then "quivering" (*Stories* 314). Regarding her "parted lips", as above, so below; nor is it likely that she will ever get the heir out of her eyes.

In confusion, Sieglinde asks Siegmund, "Beckerath, Gigi...what about him, now?" "'Oh, he said—and for a second the marks of his race stood out strong upon his face—"we have begoniffed ['tricked'] him—the goy!'" (qtd. in Heilbut 1996: 195; ellipsis in orig.).[32] This response emphasizes Seigmund's calculated revenge upon Beckerath, not the twins' joint submission to the sibling incest fantasy. Such a "realistic" interpretation of Sigmund's words certainly aroused Katja's father's fury, so that Mann had to demand that the publisher withdraw the issue of the journal containing it before it was distributed. The only conclusion to be drawn about Mann's use of the offensive sentence is that he was blinded to any possible meaning for the story's interpretation other than the one he had intended, the psychological, in which, unconsciously, he had so much invested. In the story Mann splits his self-image, endowing Beckerath with certain of his traits and Sigmund with others. In Beckerath he confesses a fear that his newly acquired in-laws might think him a creature unworthy of their daughter; in

Siegmund Aarenhold he reveals part of his subjective motive that they cannot see, the sister incest fantasy in which Katja has a very prominent role. Sigmund Aarenhold admits to himself that he has no real experience and cannot create, even though he has incestuous passion, the stimulus of creation (*Stories* 314), thus he is driven to spend his passion on his sister, thus acknowledging, according to Bergler, that he is creatively blocked. But Sigmund-Mann, whom they certainly cannot see, has not only experience and incestuous passion but the artistry to bend experience and passion to creativity, like Schiller or Wagner. The very fact that he could write such a story is proof to himself that his defense against oral regression is holding firm. While Siegmund Aarenhold says, "We have begoniffed him—the goy", Sigmund-Mann is saying, "The goy has begoniffed you!"

Royal Highness

As early as 1903 Mann was thinking of a story whose protagonist would be a prince (Hayman 1995: 184). Since the idea of living the life of a prince had haunted his consciousness from early childhood, Mann intended to bestow his self-representation upon the consciousness of the prince whom he would depict (Wysling 1998: 56). Since he also thought obsessively of himself as an artist, he intended to present the role of a prince as a metaphor for the role of the artist: "The artist invariably finds direct personal intimacy and communicativeness unsatisfying and trivial because he habitually represents his life in symbols (works of art). He leads a symbolic, representative life—like the prince!" (qtd. in Hayman 1995: 185). Since the story, entitled *Royal Highness* from the very beginning (Wysling 1998: 55), was to be so personal, Mann may have thought that it could be quickly written, but he did not complete it until 13 February 1909 (Prater 1995: 80).

Fulfilling Heinrich's prediction "that the title would distinguish itself well in the shop window" (Wysling 1998: 55), *Royal Highness* was an immediate popular success, for it sold about twenty-five thousand copies by the end of 1910 (Hayman 1995: 234). But, for a variety of reasons, most of the critics who reviewed it were disappointed in it as the successor to *Buddenbrooks*. Hermann Bahr offered the best approach to the novel when he likened it to a fairy story, but he regarded "prince Klaus Heinrich and the rich Fräulein Spoelmann" only as "figures of their economic situation" (qtd. in Hayman 1995: 236), a "Marxist fairy story" Hayman calls it.

It is very unlikely that twenty-five thousand people bought the book because it was a "Marxist fairy story". Probably most buyers were attracted to *Royal Highness* because it contained the kind of "fairy story" that Freud had described in "Creative Writers and Day-Dreaming", published in the March 1908 *Neue Revue*, a "newly established Berlin literary periodical" (*SE* vol. 9, 142). Since Mann indicated in February 1908 that he read the *Neue Revue* (Wysling 1998: 91), it is very likely that he read Freud's article as he was struggling to finish his novel, though he would not have been pleased with all that he read.[33]

Freud quickly provides his theory of the origin of "imaginative activity": "Might we not say that every child at play behaves like a creative writer, in that he creates a world of his own, or, rather, re-arranges the things of his world in a new way which pleases him?" (143-44). Mann, recently confessing that he was once the toddler prince, could hardly disagree. The reverse is true: "The creative writer does the same as the child at play. He creates a world of phantasy which he takes very seriously—that is, which he invests with large amounts of emotion—while separating it sharply from reality". To support the link that he has forged, Freud observes: "Language has preserved this relationship between children's play and poetic creation. It gives [in German] the name of '*Spiel*' ['play'] to those forms of imaginative writing which require to be linked to tangible objects and which are capable of representation" (144; interpolations in orig.). He then discusses the derivatives, *Lustspiel* and *Trauerspiel*, 'comedy' and 'tragedy', respectively. It could be that in choosing the family name of Spoelmann, Mann comes within a vowel of acknowledging that Katja Pringsheim is a tangible object—*Spielmann*. In Mann's mind she *is* a princess (Wysling 1998: 66; Winston 1971: 45). Indeed, Mann's selection of "Imma" ("I'm a"?) over "Emma" stirs up so much attention that it has to be explained away in the text (168).

Freud acknowledges that maturity usually forces people to give up pretend-play with objects and the pleasure that it brought them. But they do not renounce play; they just renounce play with real objects. They begin to construct phantasies, engage in day-dreams ("Creative" 146). Freud insists that only unsatisfied people engage in day-dreams, phantasies of obtaining those experiences absent in their lives. These day-dreams are of two types, wish-fulfillments of success, public or pubic. Arousing the dander of female generations yet unborn, he thinks that women day-dream almost exclusively about the erotic, "for their ambition is as a rule absorbed by erotic trends" ("Creative" 147)--that is, barred from highly remunerative work they can only wish for support by a successful male—but that in men erotic wishes often cohabit with "egoistic and ambitious wishes" ("Creative" 147). In either case the transparent meaning of day-dreams is concealed from others to defend the ego, just as the latent meaning of night-dreams is concealed from consciousness to defend that same entity ("Creative" 148-49).

Having examined phantasies Freud turns to "the creative writer" ("Creative" 149). First, he makes an "initial distinction". "We must separate writers who, like the ancient authors of epics and tragedies, take over their material ready-made, from writers who seem to originate their own material". If he read the article, Mann must have quickly, indeed proudly, recognized himself as a native of the second province. Then Freud divides the second type:

> We will keep to the latter kind, and, for the purposes of our comparison, we will choose not the writers most highly esteemed by the critics, but the less pretentious authors of novels, romances and short stories, who nevertheless have the widest and most eager circle of readers of both sexes.

Again, if he read the article, Mann must have been getting just a little apprehensive, especially if his eye had moved on to the next sentence, for Freud could be predicting the form of *Royal Highness* and its fate as a "less pretentious" work:

> One feature above all cannot fail to strike us about the creations of these story-writers: each of them has a hero who is the centre of interest, for whom the writer tries to win our sympathy by every possible means and whom he seems to place under the protection of a special Providence.

When we discover the "revealing characteristic of invulnerability we can immediately recognize His Majesty the Ego, the hero alike of every day-dream and of every story" ("Creative" 150).

Freud calls the kind of literature that he is studying "egocentric stories" in which "only one person--[...] the hero—is described from within". But he is perceptive enough to detect some sub-types. One sub-type he calls "eccentric" stories ("Creative" 151), in which the "person who is introduced as the hero plays only a very small active part; he sees the actions and sufferings of other people pass before him like a spectator". And, too, Freud was aware that many novelists of the latter half of the nineteenth century manifested a fragmented self: "The psychological novel in general no doubt owes its special nature to the inclination of the modern writer to split up his ego, by self-observation, into many part-egos, and, in consequence, to personify the conflicting currents of his own mental life in several heroes".

> She was at first surprisingly small and weak, but she soon grew
> like [Klaus], caught him up, and the two became inseparable.
> They shared each other's life, each other's views, feelings, and
> ideas: they communicated to each other their impressions of the
> world outside them. (39)

The introduction of the sibling incest theme serves, in turn, to
introduce the sibling rivalry theme. Albrecht, the Royal Highness, is
described: "He seemed to be extremely stand-offish, cold from embarrassment, and
proud from lack of graciousness" (41). Just to make sure that everyone
knows he is talking about his brother Heinrich, Mann adds: "He lisped a
little and then blushed at doing so, because he was always criticizing himself".
     With the dynamics of the sibling relationship in place, Mann
returns to the parents, as perceived by the child Klaus Heinrich.
Regarding his father:

> He saw the dull haughtiness of his blue eyes, the furrows which,
> proudly and morosely, ran from nostril down to his beard, and
> were often deepened or accentuated by weariness and boredom....
> Nobody dared to address him or to go freely up to him and speak
> to him unasked—not even the children. (45; ellipsis in orig.)

Regarding his mother:

> Did she love anyone—himself, Klaus Heinrich, for instance, for
> all his likeness to her? Why, of course she did, when she had time
> to, even when she coldly reminded him of his hand. But it seemed
> as if she reserved any expression or sign of her tender feelings for
> occasions when lookers-on were present who were likely to be
> edified by them. (47-48)[36]

Unlike Albrecht and Ditlinde, who resemble their Teutonic father,
Klaus Heinrich resembles his Slavic mother (46), Mann's adaptation
of his mixed German and Brazilian parentage.
     When Klaus Heinrich celebrates his eighteenth birthday, he is
the subject of a brilliant court ceremony recognizing his majority (90).
He is "declared to be of age and fit and entitled to wear the crown, should necessity
require it" (95). All eyes are upon him, even though Albrecht stands
beside him, for the Heir Apparent has been sickly since early
childhood and, like Heinrich Mann, spends most of his time in Italy.
Soon enough Grand Duke Johann Albrecht dies of gangrene, of the
soul as much as of the body. His dying complaint is that he is "dead sick
of the whole thing" (106). Even before the Duke's death, his wife had

begun to lose her beauty and her mind (113-14). After her husband's death, she becomes a recluse.

It is as if the parents must give over their space on the stage so that Klaus Heinrich will not be cramped. So, too, must his siblings. At twenty, Ditlinde marries an older man, who, if only a nominal prince, is a phenomenal businessman (114-15). Having tea with Klaus Heinrich, she describes her decision to marry down as an abdication, but regrets it not one whit (123), describing herself as "the little mermaid in the fairy-tale[...]who married a mortal and got legs instead of her fish's tale". When Albrecht joins them, he immediately—speaking with his lisp (125)-- begins to complain of all his Grand Ducal duties, sounding just like his father when he summarizes his life: "I'm sick of it" (127). After the tea, following up on his complaints, he privately asks Klaus Heinrich to represent him at all public functions. Albrecht acknowledges that he cannot formally abdicate (138), but he has letters published informing the country that Klaus Heinrich is now the Royal Highness (140). Sparing his brother Heinrich's feelings, Thomas Mann is announcing that he has superseded him as the son responsible for reviving the Mann magnificence.

The stage is set for the "fairy-tale comedy love-affair" between Klaus Heinrich and Imma Spoelmann. (Further indication of Imma Spoelmann's indebtedness to Katja Pringsheim is seen in Mann's description of the latter as his "fairy bride"—twenty-five years after the wedding ["Sketch" 35].) She comes to the duchy with her father Samuel N. Spoelmann, an Uncle-Sam millionaire whose legend has come before him. Fräulein von Isenschnibbe, invited by Mann to blab at the above-cited *tête-à-thé,* calls him a "colossus" (132), a "Leviathan, a Crœsus" (133). All the superlatives are applicable, in the case of "colossus" probably painfully so, for Spoelmann comes to the duchy to take the waters, especially of lithium-laced Ditlinde spring, hoping that they will dissolve a large kidney stone. Fräulein adds that His Plutocracy "has appropriated the Prince's suite in the Spa Hotel[...]as provisional lodgings" (134). Further interrogated, Fräulein delightedly adds that Spoelmann is accompanied by his daughter: "She's a wonderful girl from all I've read about her. He himself is a bit of a mixture, for his father married a wife from the South—creole blood, the daughter of a German father and a native mother" (135). When Ditlinde jokes that the daughter is "a creature of many colours", her punning allusion to the Hebrew Joseph has a significance beyond her ken: like Joseph, Imma will preserve life (for the duchy).

Klaus Heinrich is asked his impressions of the visitors, but, looking "past [Fräulein's] head at the bright window", he stammers a deflective reply. Perhaps he is addled by his memory of the first act of *Die Walküre* when the front door bursts open, releasing moonlight on Sieglinde and Siegmund, so that Spring and Love are joined (Fellner 1958: 227). He falls in love with Imma, sight unseen, for the fact that she, like her father and his mother, is of mixed blood. He can now trade in his mother incest complex for a sibling incest complex.

Having appropriated the Prince's suite at the Spa Hotel, Spoelmann in time appropriates Grand Ducal Schloss Delphinenort, which, after renovation, is to be his permanent residence (171). As a "railway king" (134), he has the wherewithal to appropriate the entire duchy if he wants. Klaus Heinrich has seen the railway princess "often at the theatre, in the street, and in the town park" (178), but when he and Imma finally meet, they "meet cute", Hollywood's romantic comedy term for the unexpected encounter (186). Her attire is calculated to raise high his fur fantasy: "The coat, toque, and muff which she was wearing today were made of the costliest sable, and her muff was suspended on a golden chain set with coloured stones. Her black hair showed a tendency to fall in smooth locks over her forehead". Quite an eye-catching muff. Appropriately, they meet at Dorothea Children's Hospital, named after Klaus Heinrich's mother, in the "milk-kitchen[...]where the milk is cooked for the children", thus giving off an odor guaranteed to inspire a mammary memory and to awaken mammary desire. Resembling Sieglinde Aarenhold, Imma proves to share her sharp tongue, housed in a *muffig* mouth. When a hospital sister explains the function of the milk-kitchen, Imma replies, "So one would have supposed" (186). When Klaus Heinrich, trying to spread princely pablum, asks, "So you are paying a visit to the hospital, Miss Spoelmann", she replies: "Nobody can deny that everything points in that direction" (187). Thus the first meeting between Klaus Heinrich and Imma is apparently, appropriately unpromising. But, having viewed the maid in the milk kitchen, Klaus Heinrich must envision her as the one who could nourish the duchy's dismal dental condition.

The Royal Highness continues to pay court at Delphinenort. The day comes when Imma speaks of her mixed blood (234), explaining that it is regarded as an ineradicable blot in the United States. Afterward he realizes that he has discovered the source of the bitterness that she and her father share: shame. Recalling the time that he had gotten drunk and thus introduced to shame, he senses their likeness, thinking of her as "Little Sister!" (236).

Imma offers no encouragement of Klaus Heinrich's suit until his twenty-seventh birthday (251). Then she calls attention to his stunted left arm, "asking softly": "Were you born with that?" (252) Her question is almost exactly that of Frau von Rinnlingen to Herr Friedemann. His response is almost exactly that of Herr Friedmann: "with a cry, which rang like a cry of redemption, he sank down before her, and clasped her wondrous form in both his arms. There he lay, in his white trousers and his blue and red coat with the major's shoulder-straps". Then he cries, "Little sister,[...] little sister—". She admonishes him that he must "[t]hink of appearances", as his mother had admonished him (47). But she does not reject him, as Frau von Rinnlingen had rejected Herr Friedemann; instead she takes up his left hand to kiss it, understanding and accepting the reason that he had called her "Little sister".

Having surmounted his congenital impediment, our hero will surmount all future obstacles. With the rapidity of a dream, the fairy-tale reveals the "plighting of troth", with his salutation, "Little sister,[...]Little bride" (298). It is left to lisping Albrecht to confirm Freud's literary criticism in "Creative Writers" by saluting Klaus Heinrich: "You're a Sunday child. Everything turns out trumps for you.[...]I wish you luck" (307; ellipsis in orig.). And Klaus and his spouse live happily ever after.

"The Confessions of Felix Krull: Childhood"

Although Georges Manolescu's *A Prince of Thieves* had been published in a German translation in 1905, Mann may have learned of it from a review of the book published in the March 1906 *Neue Rundschau* (Hayman 1995: 219). Given his obsession with princes, he would have been attracted by the very title, and when he read the book he found the subject matter captivating: "the memoirs of a Rumanian adventurer" ("Preface" vii). That same year he made a note about a story which would feature a character who would impersonate a member of nobility:

> The confidence trickster meets a young count who is having an affair and his family, wanting to extricate him from it, have arranged for him to travel round the world. They send him a large sum of money for it and demand letters from the places he stays at. Felix proposes that they should change places. He is given the money, together they write letters out of Baedeker and Felix travels as the count, posting the letters at the various places while the real count stays with his sweetheart. (qtd. in Hayman 1995: 220)

In June 1909, after he had finally completed *Royal Highness*, he began
to write the story, retaining for the main character the name given him
in the note. In an interview in September 1909 he described the story
as "a kind of psychological supplement to my novel about court life" (qtd. in
Heilbut 1996: 225). But Mann experienced great difficulty in
advancing the story. On 10 January 1910 he analyzed the source of his
difficulties in a letter to Heinrich:

> I'm gathering, noting, and studying for the confessions of the
> confidence man, which will probably become my strangest work.
> Working on it surprises me sometimes at the things I'm finding in
> myself. But it is unhealthy work and not good for the nerves.
> Perhaps that is why Kerr really has succeeded now in enervating
> me and disturbing my work. In the *Tag* he'd already spit a couple
> of times in my direction. Now, in an essay about Shaw, he's
> smuggled the following sentence into the [*Neue*] *Rundschau:* "He
> does not boast like your *middling novel-makers. Any eccentrically
> neurasthenic clerk or old sanatorium patient who one day takes to
> writing novels is going to depict himself in a high social position
> and cover up his Achilles['] tendon in fiction."* (qtd. in Wysling
> 1998: 102; ital. and interpolation in Wysling)

At forty-three, Alfred Kerr was Berlin's most authoritative theater
critic. His hostility to Mann probably was caused by social, racial,
professional, and personal factors: he was a Berliner, not a Lübecker,
a Jew (born "Kempner" [Wysling 1998: 341]), a critic, not a fictionist,
and an unsuccessful suitor of Katja Pringsheim (K. Mann 1975: 11).

Certainly Mann's work had always relied on personal
circumstances, but he had selected the biographical details to be
released and, with his craft, made them serve his creative purposes.
Now, though, it was another story. Kerr had taken two aspects of his
suffering as a creative writer, isolating those activities as an
"eccentrically neurasthenic clerk" and as an "old sanatorium patient", thus
causing him to feel shame, the feeling of inferiority that pride tries to
mask. Mann must have felt that, stripped from his life-context, those
acts revealed him in his nakedness. Kerr certainly understood the
connection between shame and pride, for he pointed directly at
Mann's likening himself to a prince as evidence of defensive pride.
And by referring to boasting "middling novel-makers", Kerr could be
indicating that he had read Freud's linkage between "egocentric" novels
and day-dreaming. If he came to Freud's idea on his own, it is all the
same. He was disparaging Mann's motives and techniques in *Royal*

Highness—and the same motives and techniques that Mann had planned to use in the story of Felix Krull.

Yet—impelled to write "a psychological supplement", not to the narrative of *Royal Highness* but to his lifelong day-dream—Mann had no choice but to forge ahead. Felix's first words—"As I take up my pen at leisure and in complete retirement[...]" (3)[37]--inform us that what he is to write is a recapitulation of his active life. He soon describes his "extraordinary gift and passion for sleep, a characteristic[...]from infancy" (8), then adds:

> it is only now, when I have turned forty and have become old and weary, when I no longer feel the old irrepressible urge toward the society of men, but live in complete retirement, it is only now that my capacity for sleep is impaired so that I am in a sense a stranger to it, my slumbers being short and light and fleeting; whereas even in prison—where there was plenty of opportunity— I slept better than in the soft beds of the Palace Hotel. (9)

We must bear in mind that Krull's selection and interpretation of formative incidents in his life are subject to his controlling day-dream. And we must also bear in mind Freud's stipulation that "a happy person never phantasies, only an unhappy one". Thus the pride Felix exhibits over his "successes" really masks the underlying shame that he feels.

Felix tells us that he was born in the Rhine Valley, the son of Engelbert Krull, the maker of a champagne so disreputable that only its bottle could sell it: "silver wires and gilt cords fastened with purplish-red sealing wax;[...]an impressive round seal—such as one sees on ecclesiastical bulls and old state documents—suspended from a gold cord;[...]gleaming silver foil" and a label bearing "a number of coats of arms and stars, [the] father's monogram, the brand name, *Loreley extra cuvée*, all in gold letters, and a female figure arrayed only in bangles and necklaces, sitting with legs crossed on top of a rock, her arm raised in the act of combing her flowing hair. (5-6). (This *Loreley* is certainly a siren who lures Rhine boatmen to their death.) Is Engelbert's son warning us that his father's gaudy product is a fit metaphor for the book that he is offering?

Felix describes his mother as an absence, rather than a presence, in his early life. Indeed he indicates that he "made no attempt to aid [his] mother's efforts" to give birth to him (8), indicating that he now thinks his alienation was prenatal. At birth he was passed off to an "excellent wet-nurse" [sic], upon whose breast he thrived, unlike little Johannes Friedemann. There he did more than satisfy the cravings of his stomach, for he soon tells us: "I have it from an excellent authority (whom I shall shortly identify) that even at my nurse's breast I displayed the most unambiguous evidence of sensual pleasure",[38] thus supporting Freud's 1905 statement in *Three Essays*, "No one who has seen a baby sinking back satiated from the breast and falling asleep with flushed cheeks and a blissful smile can escape the reflection that this picture persists as a prototype of the expression of sexual satisfaction in later life" (182). That he emphasizes his enthusiastic reactions to "the breast of [his] excellent wet-nurse", without accounting for the absent breast of his mother, suggests that the nursing situation decisively forms his *Sehnsucht* for the maternal, even if he will not admit it.

Felix says that he was born "in the merry month of May—a Sunday to be exact" (8) and assumes that because he was "a Sunday child" (9) his parents gave him such an auspicious name. Accepting the significance of the name, Felix, like Mann himself, quickly begins to daydream of invulnerability, pretending that he is the Kaiser (9) and, later, "an eighteen-year-old prince named Karl" (10). This recollection by the "retired" Krull indicates the origin of his self-identity as an "impostor". Describing the type "Impostor" as one of the "twenty-seven clinical pictures of oral regression" (cf. ch1n10), Bergler lists "social climbing" as one of its "specific *descriptive* characteristics":

> In German the word "Hochstapler" expresses exactly that social-climbing: "hoch" means "high," and the old "stapfen" means "to walk"; in other words, "a crook pretending to be of higher social circles" (Meyer). What the phrase basically refers to is the swindling of money or of social acknowledgment or both through the pretense of being "somebody" by someone whom—to quote an impostor—the "snobbish outerworld" would consider a "nobody". (1949: 266-67)

This comment, among others by Bergler about the "impostor", gives us a more precise picture of Mann's intention in *Die Bekenntnisse des Hochstaplers Felix Krull.*

Young Krull is left alone to his daydreams, while his father chases after family maids, first "a Fräulein from Vevey" (3) and undoubtedly others, and while his mother—if she is not the Madonna, then she must be the whore—chases any workman who enters the house. At a very early age Krull's sister Olympia, several years his senior (11) becomes her mother's concupiscent competitor (15). For diversion his parents hold "social affairs", actually spouse swapping sessions, that scandalize the town they live in (16).

At age eight, Felix is given the opportunity to pretend to play a violin in a resort orchestra (17-18), again displaying his facility as an impostor. In time he becomes his godfather's model; that painter, Schimmelpreester, is, *soi-disant,* the "high priest of mould" (20); thus Felix is able to dress up "in all sorts of costumes", each of which prompts its own daydream. Although Schimmelpreester had been run out of Cologne for an undisclosed reason and although he poses the late-teen (23) Felix in the nude for "a large picture out of Greek mythology" (20-21), Felix offers no hint that he understands the lubricity of such a pose in a Greek context, only saying, "indeed I was a little like a young god, slender, graceful, yet powerful in build, with a golden skin and flawless proportions" (21). In time he will come to identify himself with the young god Hermes.

Like Mann, Felix finds formal education a bore, so he works up a repertoire of signs that convince even the family doctor that he is too ill to attend school (33-34). Thus he displays what Bergler calls the impostor's "pseudo-identification-mimicry":

> The impostor plays the role he has designated for himself with utmost confidence, as if he really *were* the person he would personify. His identification is that of an actor. On the other hand, he is always aware of his faking, inwardly making fun of the disguise and the people who are taken in by it. (1949: 268; ital. in original).

On other occasions, Felix simply cuts school, then forges an excuse from his father (31-32), a skill that he perfects for future use. On a rare occasion when he does go to school, he learns that at the noon hour a certain delicatessen is unattended:

> I stood enchanted, straining my ears and breathing in the delightful atmosphere and the mixed fragrance of chocolate and smoked fish and earthy truffles. My mind was filled with memories of fairytale kingdoms, of underground treasure chambers where Sunday children might fill their pockets and boots with precious stones. It was indeed either a fairytale or a dream. (42)[39]

Krull shoplifts the deli daily, learning the valuable lesson that he is an expert thief (44). He begins to think that the whole world is vulnerable to his fingers.[40]

Similarly, having learned to forge a signature, he generalizes to the observation that any act of writing can be used for deception. When he takes his "fluent pen" (45) in his fingers, it becomes their extension, useful for theft or titillation (of course, he forswears such use). There is the suggestion that he learned early to use his fingers on himself, accompanying his activity with appropriate day-dreams, discovering his private pleasure principle, which he calls "The Best of All" or "The Great Joy" (46).

Enter the "excellent authority" (46) whom he had promised to identify. When Felix is sixteen he begins an affair of several years' duration with the family housemaid Genovefa, who had been with the family "from a tender age" and is now in her "early thirties". Depressed to be in his own clothes again, after a night of dress-up with Schimmelpreester's costumes, he meets Genovefa on his way to bed. She seduces him, because, he suspects, she has become heated by the salient evidence of his maturity. He is willing, he says, because his "only possible consolation" for his depression "lay in Genovefa's arms", for such skin-to-skin contact would arouse renewed day-dreams, especially that one originating in the skin-ego. What he emphasizes about their coupling is significant: "the soul-satisfying, unimaginable delights I experienced on Genovefa's white, well-nourished breast" (47). It must have been in the post-coital pillow-talk that she told him about his frisky nursing, having been present at the erection of his sensuality. Given her age, she could be his mother. Perhaps he does not realize it, but Felix is telling us that he has fulfilled his fantasy of maternal incest. He does know that his fancy language tells us he is a stud:

> my desire was not of a selfish nature, for characteristically I was truly inflamed only by the joy Genovefa evinced. Of course, every possibility of comparison is out of the question; I can neither demonstrate nor disprove, but I was then and am now convinced that with me the satisfaction of love is twice as sweet and twice as penetrating as with the average man. (47-48)

Felix does not conclude the story of his introduction to copulation by referring to the sweet sleep that follows climax. Rather he becomes intellectual, discussing his discovery that sexual performance has an instrumental value:

> it would be unjust to conclude that because of my extraordinary endowment I became a libertine and lady-killer. My difficult and dangerous life made great demands on my powers of concentration—I had to be careful not to exhaust myself. I have observed that with some the act of love is a trifling matter, which they discharge perfunctorily, going their way as though nothing had happened. As for me, the tribute I brought was so great as to

leave me for a time quite empty and deprived of the power to act. True, I have often indulged in excesses, for the flesh is weak and I found the world all too ready to satisfy my amorous requirements. But in the end and on the whole I was of too manly and serious a temper not to return from sensual relaxation to a necessary and healthful austerity. Moreover, is not purely animal satisfaction the grosser part of what as a child I had instinctively called "The Great Joy"? It enervates us by satisfying us too completely; it makes us bad lovers of the world because on the one hand it robs life of its bloom and enchantment while on the other hand it impoverishes our own capacity to charm, since only he who desires is amiable and not he who is satiated. For my part, I know many kinds of satisfaction finer and more subtle than this crude act which is after all but a limited and illusory satisfaction of appetite. (48)

Here Felix speaks for the true impostor, for in Bergler's dictum, "Gential sex plays a relatively unimportant role in the make-up of impostors. This fact has been repeatedly observed and described by various authors" (276). It is most useful when it enhances the "capacity to charm", "inspiring", in Bergler's words, "confidence by firmness and self-assurance and winning everyone's friendship" (267). In Felix's case, lurking behind every sexual partner who must be charmed is the mother.

Then Mann once again relies upon his family's history. Chapter IX records the decline and bankruptcy of the Loreley Sparkling Wine Company (unlike Senator Mann, Engelbert Krull commits suicide). But, in July 1911, Mann discontinued work on the book, turning to a new project, "Death in Venice" (Bade 1978: 272). Since that story is not concerned with the incest theme, I will suggest only that perhaps Mann, unconsciously realizing that his mother problem sponsored both the homoerotic and the incest themes in his fiction, was driven to return to the former theme, which he had recently ignored. That return was sparked by his reaction to the Polish boy he had watched on vacation in Venice.[41]

After finishing "Death in Venice" Mann returned in the autumn of 1912 (Hayman 1995: 21) to the story of Felix Krull, writing Chapters I-VI of Book Two. The son's first task as man of the house is to get his poor father a Church funeral. Since his father had committed suicide, Felix realizes that he will have to use the controlling characteristic of the impostor, "charming, disarming behavior" (Bergler 1949: 267), easily persuading the town priest to accept the fiction that the pistol discharged accidentally. Spiritual Counsellor Chateau quickly betrays his susceptibility, telling Felix:

> your personality makes a pleasing impression and I should like to
> praise you in particular for the agreeable quality of your voice. I
> should be much surprised if Fortuna did not prove gracious to
> you. I make it my business at all times to recognize those with
> bright prospects, such as have found favour in the eyes of God.
> (60)

The priest recognizes that Felix, like St. Paul, manifests the charisma
of "tongues" (Bévenot 1953: 791-92). Perhaps that is why Felix gets
Biblical in his narrative, claiming that his success depends upon "the
immaterial yet nevertheless corporeal emanation of a child of fortune, a Sunday
child" (62). Felix is so impressed by the priest's prophecy that he
begins to think of himself not as a product of heredity, but as an
Original (64-65).

     Having buried the father, the family survivors leave town.
Perhaps in memory of her father's product, Olympia undulates down
the Rhine, perhaps hoping to be a Loreley. Felix and his mother move
to Frankfurt, she to set up a boarding house, "Pension Loreley" (73),
and he to wait upon his army physical examination and upon an
opportunity to take up a probationary position in a Paris hotel. He puts
his time to good purpose, at night haunting the better section to watch
the wealthy and the things their wealth obtains, then sleeping "almost to
excess" in the daytime (75). Felix is ecstatic as he describes "all the
treasures of fairyland" that he sees (78). Earlier he had mentioned the state
of his skin-ego:

> It must further be observed that the texture of my skin was of an
> extraordinary delicacy, and so very sensitive that, even when I
> had no money, I was obliged to provide myself with soft, fine
> soaps, for if I used the common, cheap varieties, even for a short
> time, they chafed it raw. (63)

It is not surprising, then, that prominent among the "treasures of fairyland"
are satin, silk, and leather garments, the skin-like textures that his skin
desires (77). Krull is one of the thin-skinned narcissists described by
Anzieu (1989: 42).

     Thus Felix is ready to experience the ultimate day-dream of
the skin-ego, sighted on "an open balcony of the *bel étage* of the great Hotel
Zum Frankfurter Hof" (79):

> Onto it stepped one afternoon[...]two young people, as young as
> myself, obviously a brother and sister, possibly twins—they
> looked very much alike—a young man and a young woman
> moving out together into the wintry weather. They did so out of

> pure high spirits, hatless, without protection of any kind. Slightly
> foreign in appearance, dark-haired, they might have been Spanish,
> Portuguese, South American, Argentinian, Brazilian—I am
> simply guessing—but perhaps, on the other hand, they were
> Jews—I could not swear they were not and I would not on that
> account be shaken in my enthusiasm, for gently reared children of
> that race can be most attractive. Both were pretty as pictures—the
> youth not a whit less than the girl. In evening dress, both of them,
> the youth with a pearl in his shirt front, the girl wearing one
> diamond clip in her rich, dark, attractively dressed hair and
> another at her breast, where the flesh coloured silk of her princess
> gown met the transparent lace of the yoke and sleeves. (79-80)

Felix's two speculations introduce the incest motif. The young man
and woman, possibly twins, possibly Jewish (pointing back to "The
Blood of the Walsungs"), hint at sibling incest, while the possibility
that they are South American, even Brazilian, like Mann's mother,
hints at maternal incest; together the speculations imply the
inseparability of the two incest fantasies in Mann's mind. Since it is
cold and snowing, the "twins" exaggerate the effect of the weather on
their skins, then go inside, enticing Krull to imagine what they will do
to get warm. He admits that he dreams of them for many nights
afterward.

In retrospect, Krull now understands the singular impact of
the scene:

> Dreams of love, dreams of delight and a longing for union—I
> cannot name them otherwise, though they concerned not a single
> image but a double creature, a pair fleetingly but profoundly
> glimpsed, a brother and sister—a representative of my own sex
> and of the other, the fair one. But the beauty here lay in the
> duality, in the charming doubleness, and if it seems more than
> doubtful that the appearance of the youth alone on the balcony
> would have inflamed me in the slightest, apart perhaps from the
> pearl in his shirt, I am almost equally sure that the image of the
> girl alone, without her fraternal complement, would never have
> lapped my spirit in such sweet dreams. Dreams of love, dreams
> that I loved precisely because—I firmly believe—they were of
> primal indivisibility and indeterminateness, double; which really
> means that only then is there a significant whole blessedly
> embracing what is beguilingly human in both sexes. (80-81)[42]

Twins, aware they were once simultaneously enveloped in the same
skin, seem, to Mann's way of thinking, naturally susceptible to sibling
desire.

Felix is not the first person to be fascinated by the "double creature". Undoubtedly, the poet Aristophanes, in Plato's *Symposium,* offers the most charming explanation of its origin. In the beginning, he says, the human creature consisted of two conjoined bodies, each body with a head, two arms, and two legs. In some of the conjoined creatures one body was female and the other body was male; in other creatures both bodies were of the same sex, either female or male. Zeus, fearing these creatures as a threat, divided their bodies to weaken them. Ever after, female and male human beings have been lonely, seeking to be reunited with their severed twin, female or male.

Aristophanes' explanation of desire does not convince science or the other major religions, but neither has it been supplanted by their offerings. In the present instance, it reveals that Krull's (and Mann's) fascination for the "double creature" is a manifestation of a universal drive, desire, albeit acknowledgment of the source of the drive is all but universally repressed. Yet avowals of heterosexual desire abound with expressions that announce the lover's sense of incompleteness, for example, "better half" and "soulmate". But because of cultural proscription, only the poet can reveal, albeit unconsciously, that homosexual and incestuous behavior is caused by the same drive, desire, to seek the same goal, reunion.

Felix then faces a danger that has traumatized many a thin-skinned narcissist: he must stand naked before a military induction medical board. He admits that "the blood left [his] face" (90)--as above, so below—leaving his skin in peril, for he had realized "that nakedness, the condition in which Nature brought us forth, is levelling and that no sort of injustice or order of precedence can obtain between naked creatures". But he immediately rejects that realization by suppressing the involuntary response of blanching. So successful an actor is he that he evades military service by faking a seizure that convinces the medical board that he is epileptic. Once again his action confirms Bergler's descriptive characteristic, "pseudo-identification-mimicry" (1949: 268). Then he returns to his life on the street. There he soon realizes just how desirable he is to both females and males—indeed, so charming that one night he is picked up by a prostitute who is feeling charitable. She displays several Mannian attractions: she is "long-legged after the fashion of a filly" (112), she displays a hand whose veins are prominent, and she lubricates her upper lip with her lower. Once in the cab, she twines a leg over his, in effect creating the "double creature". Her room is replete with "soft, furry hides" (114) and "a great abundance of mirrors, even in places where one does not ordinarily expect them".

Currently without a pimp, Rozsa—as she calls herself—has decided to take Felix for a test drive. Finding pleasure in her work, she is thrilled to discover that Felix, although untutored, has enormous natural ability. He remains in service to her for six months, delighted to meet her every need. Discussing his meeting her need, Felix observes, "Somewhere in these pages I have already remarked that because of the extraordinary demands life imposed on my energies it was not permissible for me to squander myself in enervating passion" (117). During his time with Rozsa he squandered himself upon request. But, he implies, he had learned that he is unlike other men in that he can "benerve" himself, will himself to rise to the occasion, just as he had, as a boy, learned to contract or expand the pupils of his eyes (11). Admitting that he is proud of his invention of the word "benerved" and, doubtless, of the condition it describes, he expands on its meaning: "it is the enervating that benerves us— if certain vital prerequisites are met—and makes us capable of performances and enjoyments in the world that are beyond the compass of the un-benerved" (117). His sexual prowess is another display of his "pseudo-identification-mimicry". In closing the episode, he credits Rozsa with bringing out the best in him: "I know from the very bottom of my being that I could never have borne myself with so much subtlety and elegance in the many vicissitudes of my life if I had not passed through Rozsa's naughty school of love".

At this point, Mann put aside the manuscript, in order to begin writing the story that eventually became *The Magic Mountain*. Or was it that, having written a climactic episode, he found himself in a state of innervation, then discovered that he could not "benerve" himself to continue writing that story?

Notes to Early Works

[1]Since his concern is for stylistics rather than for object-relations, Reed ignores the essential function of baby Friedemann's nurse, discussing instead the intrusive ironic narrator: "this is not the point at which we expect to be reminded that beer is nutritious. It is not at all sure this adjective figured in the Frau Konsul's speeches; the narrator is providing information we do not need and thus asserting a right to detach himself from the proceedings and pay attention, rather incongruously, to a trivial general truth" (1996: 12).

[2]In "The Sufferings and Greatness of Richard Wagner" (1933), Mann silently borrows from "Die Einheit":

> Who can fail to see in Zola's epic the tendency to symbol and myth that gives his characters their over-life-size air? That Second Empire Astarte, Nana, is she not symbol and myth? Where does she get her name? It sounds like the babbling of

primitive man. Nana was a cognomen of the Babylonian Ishtar:
did Zola know that? ("Sufferings" 17)

Here the translator, Mrs. Lowe-Porter, also prefers "babbling".

[3] In *Ars amandi: The Erotic of Extremes in Thomas Mann and Marguerite Duras*, Ursula W. Schneider studies the work of the two writers for representations of narcissism, voyeurism, incest, fetishism, sado-masochism, homosexuality, and lesbianism, "the so-called darker sides of love" (1995: 5). She sees "Little Herr Friedemann" as a story that can be analyzed by referring to "Sacher-Masoch's theory of male masochism, which he explores in *Venus in Furs*". Thus she likens Gerda von Rinnlingen to Wanda von Dunajew, Sacher-Masoch's sadist female (1995: 10). The "sado-masochistic relationship that develops between Gerda von Rinnlingen and her admirer" is suggested at their first meeting when Gerda tips her horsewhip to Friedemann (Schneider 1995: 139). (If Mann is alluding to *Venus in Furs* at this point, he is content to leave it pretty much at that, for Gerda never appears befurred but bare to Friedemann. Perhaps at the conclusion, when Friedemann buries his face in Gerda's lap, there is a bow to Severin von Kusiemski, who is often so situated with Wanda von Dunajew.) During their subsequent meetings, Gerda "becomes in Johannes Friedemann's eyes a sort of archaic, whip-carrying mother figure who punishes at will and with mocking cruelty" (Schneider 1995: 152). When she finally rebuffs him, Friedemann turns the "sensual hate and anger" that Gerda's "poisonous looks" have aroused in him "masochistically against himself" (Schneider 1995: 137). *Ars amandi* can be read with profit, though the organization leaves much to be desired.

[4] Freud notes "that an uncanny experience occurs either when infantile complexes which have been repressed are once more revived by some impression, or when primitive beliefs which have been surmounted seem once more to be confirmed" ("Uncanny" 249). In this instance Little Herr Friedemann is experiencing the return of the repressed. In each instance that Mann uses the word "uncanny" (*'unheimlich'*) Freud's psychoanalysis of the uncanny experience should be recalled.

[5] Just how overcome Herr Friedemann is by Gerda's torso may be sensed by Mann's comment, over fifty years later, about women's dress in his youth: "The body was something to be covered, excepting only the deep necklines of ladies' evening dresses, in aristocratic and hence also in bourgeois society" ("Years" 254). He confesses his erotic excitement when he read Tolstoy's description of bared breasts and shoulders in *Anna Karenina*.

[6] Asserting that Mann was influenced by mythology as early as "Little Herr Friedemann" Reed says:

> Not only is the work built on the contrast of anxious control and
> helpless surrender to passion which can be called Apolline and
> Dionysiac; at the close, the humiliated Friedemann feels a "thirst
> to tear himself in pieces" ([*GW*] viii. 105), which is hardly apt to
> the realistic context—he commits suicide by drowning—but
> matches the inner theme. For it transposes into psychological
> impulse the fate which, in the Dionysus legend, befell those who
> resisted the god's power. (1996: 404; parenthesis in orig.).

Reed's "realistic context" apparently does not include the past; a "psychoanalytically realistic context" would find Friedemann's experience of traumatic "thirst" quite "realistic". Since it was at the moment of forced weaning that baby Friedemann felt that he was torn from the maternal object, it was at that moment that he experienced the Marsyas complex, the shredded skin ego. Hence his reawakened "thirst" is "to tear himself to pieces".

[7]Opposing my object-relations reading is Izenberg's view:

> Reading backward from a knowledge of Mann's homosexual preference, the prominence of the trope of the yearning man and the coldly rejecting woman can seem puzzling, unless in the interests of disguising that preference the female figures are stand-ins for men, the more traditionally feminine ones for Mann himself, the more "masculine" ones (like Gerda von Rinnlingen) for the unavailable homosexual object. (2000: 108)

Izenberg does acknowledge that "Gerda von Rinnlingen and Amra Jacoby [in "Little Lizzy"] share striking traits wih Mann's mother, Julia, and along with other of his female portraits raise the suspicion that she—or a fantasy-distorted version of her—may have been their model". This acknowledgement, written by a psychoanalyst (2000: v), contains a curious distinction, for what is anyone's conception of another person but "a fantasy-distorted version"?

[8]In "The Will to Happiness" Mann's references to Italy depend on his first visit to that country with his brother Heinrich just before he wrote it. He finished "Little Herr Friedemann" during his second visit.

[9]Perhaps the unidentified city is Munich, for although its landmarks recall Lübeck (Hayman 1995: 140), the furniture of the room that van der Qualen rents recalls the apartment in which Mann wrote the story.

[10]Noting van der Qualen's desire for sleep and his disregard of time's markers, Mann provides an analysis with which Freud would concur, for he finds "the wish to sleep and intentional turning away from the external world" among "the most striking and peculiar features of dreams" (*New*: 19).

[11]Heilbut (1996: 89) senses a resemblance between the sketch of *"Mvtter Natvr"* that Thomas had drawn for *Bilderbuch für artige Kinder*, a "Picture Book for Well-Behaved Children", and the fungous landlady, but does not pursue it.

[12]Heilbut believes that the wardrobe dream girl resembles Mann's "youngest [sic] sister, Carla" (1996: 89). If so, "The Wardrobe" lightly touches a theme—sibling incest—soon to become prominent in Mann's fiction. Heilbut's belief gains some support by the fact that Mann dedicated the story to Carla (Prater 1995: 28).

[13]Mann may include himself among the art-shop's patrons, for there is a walk-on character who enters, buys a bust of "young Piero de' Medici, son of Lorenzo", exits (*Stories* 188). His purchase probably proclaims partisanship: Piero was forced into exile by Savonarola in 1494.

[14]Hayman writes that "Hieronymus's *saeva indignatio* derives partly from sexual frustration" (1995: 165) but offers no support for his statement.

[15]Mann must have sensed another resemblance between Savonarola and himself, a resemblance intimately related to their shared mother-fixation, for he wrote Grautoff, "Fra Girolamo too had a friend who admired him and whom he loved" (qtd.

in Prater 1995: 41). This resemblance would offer another justification for Mann's abandonment of Mary for Paul.

[16]Kirchberger acknowledges that it could be an "accident when Gabriele Eckhof's Christian name is the feminine form of that of an archangel", but argues that Klöterjahn's subsequent use of "mein Engle" proves that Mann's intention is to parody E. T. A. Hoffman's use of "angelic" names for his feminine characters (1960: 291).

[17]Detlev Spinell suffers from "writer's block", if Bergler's analysis of that condition is valid. Bergler begins his analysis with a categorical statement:

> Before the writer is technically capable of writing, he must develop a "plot". A plot presupposes "imagination"; and the basis of the latter is sublimated voyeurism. Normally, in the process of writing, *voyeurism is changed into exhibitionism,* simply because by writing down his story, the author exhibits before publisher and reader. Hence, the transformation of voyeurism into exhibitionism, is essential. (1949: 188-89; ital. in orig.)

Now "at the beginning of the thirties" (138), Spinell has one published novel to his credit:

> On his table, for anyone to see who entered his room, there always lay the book he had written. It was a novel of medium length, with a perfectly bewildering drawing on the jacket, printed on a sort of filter-paper. Each letter of the type looked like a Gothic cathedral. Fräulein von Osterloh had read it once, in a spare quarter-hour, and found it "very cultured"—which was her circumlocution for inhumanly boresome. Its scenes were laid in fashionable salons, in luxurious boudoirs full of choice *objets d'art,* old furniture, gobelins, rare porcelains, priceless stuffs, and art treasures of all sorts and kinds. On the description of these things was expended the most loving care; as you read you constantly saw Herr Spinell, with distended nostrils, saying: "How beautiful! My God! look, how beautiful!" After all, it was strange he had not written more than this one book; he so obviously adored writing. He spent the greater part of the day doing it, in his room, and sent an extraordinary number of letters to the post, two or three nearly every day—and that made it more striking, even almost funny, that he very seldom received one in return. (*Stories* 138-39)

The existence of the novel proves that during its composition Spinell's voyeurism had been replaced by exhibitionism, which, indeed, is the subject of the novel and Spinell's salient behavioral trait. Try though he may, Spinell has lost the ability to "convince his inner conscience that he is *not interested in his original wish, but only in the defense",* as Bergler puts it (1949: 189). That is to say, Spinell acts as if he were still a confident exhibitionist, but his conscience knows that he is a voyeur, accusing "the writer of infantile sexual connotation (of being an infantile Peeping-Tom)" (Bergler 1949: 189). "The moment the alibi is not accepted, sterility sets in"

(Bergler 1949: 189). So Spinell writes letters that are rarely answered, all the while pleading with his conscience. As he tells Gabriele Klöterjahn, the woman who represents for him the return of the repressed:

> The conscience, madame, is a bad business. I, and other people like me, work hard all our lives to swindle our consciences into feeling pleased and satisfied. We are feckless creatures, and aside from a few good hours we go around weighted down, sick and sore with the knowledge of our own futility. We hate the useful; we know it is vulgar and unlovely, and we defend this position, as a man defends something that is absolutely necessary to his existence. Yet all the while conscience is gnawing at us, to such an extent that we are simply one wound. (*Stories* 142)

Beneath the verbiage Spinell is confessing his voyeurism to its object.

Previously (ch1n10) notice is taken of how Bergler describes the manner by which "a [writing] person makes out of the *duality* (mother-child) a *unity*" (1949: 187). Thus the writer "denies the oral-masochistic attachment to mother by intrapsychically *denying her mere existence*" (1949: 187). But when Spinell's exhibitionism reverts to voyeurism, he no longer has a sense of unity—his fellow residents sense his condition, for he is known as "the dissipated baby" (*Stories* 138). Now he is frantic to regain unity by attaching himself to Gabriele. He is so desperate to experience the "boundless, unquenchable exultation of union" (*Stories* 154) evoked by Wagner's *Tristan und Isolde* that he urges Gabriele to play the score on the piano, even though he knows that her doctors have forbidden her playing (*Stories* 151).

When her husband is called back to the sanatorium by the doctors, "[o]ur author from the window of his chamber had seen him arrive" (*Stories* 157); Klöterjahn's reappearance so infuriates the voyeuristic Spinell that he writes a long letter of condemnation, saying, "I feel an impulse to clarify for you your own thoughts and actions; because it is my inevitable task on this earth to call things by their right names, to make them speak, to illuminate the unconscious. The world is full of what I call the unconscious type, and I cannot endure it; I cannot endure all these unconscious types!" (*Stories* 160). Indeed, he asserts that the sexual demands produced by Klöterjahn's unconscious have driven his wife into a moribund condition. At least, Spinell concludes, he has seen to it that Gabriele will not die as an unconscious type, for he (with a little help from Herr Wagner) has introduced her to the "gentle glow of longing, soothing and kind, ah, yielding sweet-sublime, ah, raptured sinking into the twilight of eternity" (*Stories* 155). Upon receiving the letter, Klöterjahn visits Spinell, finding him reading his own novel. Calling the letter "a scrawl full of idiotic abuse" (*Stories* 163), Klöterjahn describes Spinell's voyeurism by contrast: "I don't leer at women out of the corner of my eye; I look at them square, and if I like their looks I go for them" (*Stories* 164). Then he is called to the bed of his wife, who is dying. Spinell flees the scene, only to be confronted in the garden by "Gabriele Eckhof's fat son" sitting in his perambulator, "plump-cheeked, well cared for, and magnificent" (*Stories* 166), in short, the baby that Spinell never was, and that has made all the difference.

Question: Did Mann's unconscious prompt him to write a story about a man suffering "writer's block" in order to warn him to treat that reservoir with great respect?

[18]Kirchberger writes: "were it not for the fact that Thomas Mann's crucial experience of Sigmund Freud belongs to a later date, one could also talk of an Oedipus complex and make Gabriele Klöterjahn the imago of Spinell whose infantility Mann maliciously asserts in the term 'verwester Säugling' and at the same time ironically denies by noting the inappropriateness of this epithet applied to Spinell by a facetious sanatorium guest" (1960: 295).

[19]The "sword lily" is the gladiolus. With *"Gladius Dei"* fresh in his mind, Mann seems to be offering another hint that Detlev sees Gabriele as the Madonna.

[20]In *The Incest Theme in Literature and Legend,* Otto Rank sees *Don Carlos* as a key representative of one of the types of drama that manifest the Œdipus complex:

> The incest fantasy is realized in *Oedipus,* and the son lovingly embraces the mother (though he does not know it). In *Hamlet,* owing to greater repression, only the reverse side of love for the mother appears—jealous hatred. In *Don Carlos* the rejection of the incest wish has gone so far that it is no longer even the actual mother the son desires, but rather the stepmother—a woman who only bears the name Mother; she is no blood relative, but is nevertheless the father's wife. In *Oedipus,* that the son considers his mother a stranger makes a sexual relationship possible. In *Don Carlos* this remains impossible even though the mother is not a blood relative—even though the obstacle is no longer present— since the internal mechanisms against incest have become too powerful within the playwright. (1992: 36)

In like manner Tonio's repression of his incest fantasy is so severe that he cannot face its stark representation (as in *Oedipus),* yet he unconsciously acknowledges its existence by esteeming its disguised representation (as in *Don Carlos*). Further, he unconsciously recognizes that his blocked desire for his mother has been deflected into desire for the son-figure whom his mother would love.

[21]In "Tonio Kröger", alluding to two of his recent stories, "The Dilettante" and "Tristan", Mann has Tonio engage in self-mockery: "Take the most miraculous case of all, take the most typical and therefore the most powerful of artists, take such a morbid and profoundly equivocal work as *Tristan and Isolde,* and look at the effect it has on a healthy young man of thoroughly normal feelings. Exaltation, encouragement, warm, downright enthusiasm, perhaps incitement to 'artistic' creation of his own. Poor young dilettante!" (*Stories* 105).

[22]Heilbut identifies the model for Daniel as "Ludwig Derleth,[...] a Catholic reactionary who traipsed around in a monkish outfit, excoriating the vices of Schwabing bohemia" (1996: 178). It is highly likely that Derleth was also one of the models for Hieronymus, in *"Gladius Dei",* especially since Daniel has a reproduction of Savonarola in his room, along with "Napoleon" (*Stories* 285), "Luther, Nietzsche, Moltke, [Pope] Alexander VI, Robespierre" (*Stories* 286), all absolutists in one field or another. Mann's appellation of "Daniel", 'my judge is God' (Saydon 1953: 621), for the "prophet" modeled on Derleth indicates his estimate of Derleth as an absolutist. Perhaps hoping to foster his religious mystique by his absence, Daniel delegates one of his "young men", as his sister calls them (*Stories* 285), a "young man from Switzerland" (*Stories* 286) to serve as his priest, by reading his Sacred Word

and taking "a swallow from the beaker of red wine" (*Stories* 288). From this parody of the Last Supper, it can be concluded that in both *"Gladius Dei"* and "At the Prophet's" Mann was harshly critical of Ludwig Derleth's religious activities.

[23]In his stage directions, Mann says of Fiore:

> The impression she gives is of height, slenderness, symmetry, poise; she is almost masklike.[...]The brows above her rather long eyes have been artificially removed or made invisible, so that the hairless part above the drooping lids seems drawn upwards with a searching expression. The skin of her face is taut and as it were polished, her delicately chiselled lips are closed in an ambiguous smile". (*Stories*216)

Emphasizing her masklike and reptilian features, Mann comes close to suggesting that she is a Gorgon.

[24]The goddess Diana mentioned in Acts 19 is now identified as the Anatolian goddess whose name was Hellenized as Artemis, the goddess of many breasts (Willoughby 1963: 58). Given Savonarola's oral neediness (revealed by his reference to "poison" and to "wolf's milk"), this is surely the goddess to whom he refers.

[25]Winston argues that Mann's introduction of the "warring brothers" (*feindliche Brüder*) idea alludes to the artistic differences that existed between Thomas and Heinrich: "Lorenzo is no portrait of Heinrich, any more than Savonarola is a portrait of the author. But the sensitive reader will detect, in the speeches of each, aspects of the two brothers, the characteristic timbres of their different voices" (1981: 200). The phrase *feindlich Brüder*, according to Winston, "harkens back to the title of Schiller's tragedy *Die Braut von Messina oder Die feindlichen Brüder*". Rank traces the fraternal animosity in that play back to an "infantile origin" (1992: 468), adding that Schiller had written an early play concerning the conspiracy of the Pazzis against the Medicis, *Kosmos von Medicis*, in which two brothers struggle over the same woman, but that he destroyed it (1992: 470). Perhaps the dramatic struggle between Lorenzo and Savonarola for Fiore and Fiorenzi had its origin in the struggle between Thomas and Heinrich to claim the fantasy mother?

[26]Mann's early and persistent identification of himself as a prince makes a powerful argument that he was under the sway of the "Nobel Prize Complex", identified by Helen H. Tartakoff and then developed more fully by Michael A. Sperber (see bibliography for references). By the time Tartakoff and Sperber described the complex that they had discovered, the attainment of royal status had long since lost its allure, except in England. Since the Nobel Prize Awards were instituted in 1901, though, their description is an apt caption for the mentality so overwhelmed by ambition that it becomes neurotic. His mind formed in an earlier age, Mann continued to liken the great writer to the prince, but he was surely aware of the prestige of the Award, especially after Gerhard Hauptmann won it for literature in 1912.

Boys, rather than girls, usually the first-born and often the only child, are likely to develop this complex. While Mann was not the first-born and had four siblings, his behavior toward his older brother often betrays his resentment of his brother's seniority, his pretense that the brother did not exist, his rivalry with his brother until he had surpassed him, and his subsequent condescension. The complex stimulates a precocious ego development that often contains two abiding fantasies, (1), an active, omnipotent, grandiose conviction of being the "powerful one", and (2) a passive confidence in being destined to be the "special one". Inspired by these two fantasies, the ego of the newly alienated child comes to believe that a singular feat must be accomplished in order to reclaim mother's favor. In time the feat takes the form of winning some great award, for example the Nobel Prize. Mann's conviction that he was the "powerful one", evinced by his regal posturings in childhood, must have been the source of his drive and discipline in his vocation and of his defiance of Hitler and of the understanding of Hitler that he displayed in "This Man is my Brother". Mann's confidence that he was the "special one" inspires his assertion that he had been his mother's favorite child and a Sunday child. His confidence is also evident in his comment shortly after receiving the Nobel Prize for Literature in 1929:

> The famous award of the Swedish Academy, which once more, after a space of seventeen years, fell to Germany's lot, had, I knew, hovered over me more than once before and found me not unprepared. It lay, I suppose, upon my path in life—I say this without presumption, with calm if not uninterested insight into *the special character of my destiny*, of my "role" on this earth which has now been gilded with the equivocal brilliance of success; and which I regard entirely in a human spirit, without any great mental excitement. And just so, in such a spirit of reflective and receptive calm, I have accepted as my lot in life the resounding episode, with all its festal and friendly accompaniments, and gone through it with the best grace I could muster—even inwardly, which is a harder matter. (qtd. in Heilbut 1996: 498-99; my italics)

The persistence of the incestuous mother complex and the Nobel Prize complex testifies to the failure to resolve the original oral conflict. The time had to come, of course, when these fantasies were threatened by lack of recognition, stymied projects, loss of a romantic object. That time came in the sexual crisis Mann experienced when he was twenty years of age. Then—if the clinicians are correct—the person so served develops psychosomatic symptoms, experiences depression, and threatens or even commits suicide. All of these reactions were characteristic of Mann's behavior at the time, yet they never became severe enough to doom him to ineffectuality.

[27]Mann's reconstruction of his mental state as an infant shifts attention away from the manifest behavior that accompanied it: he was transforming his face into a mask, a Gorgoneion, a response, no doubt, to the look that he thought he saw when his mother looked at him.

[28]According to Peter de Mendelsson Mann had begun his "Tiergarten-Novelle" before he ever visited a house in that section of Berlin (Schneider 1995: 20). Then Katja, six months pregnant, took her husband to meet her relatives the Rosenbergs, who lived in the Tiergarten (Heilbut 1996: 191). Mann finished the story in October (Wysling 1998: 72).

[29]Blissett uses the phrase "cannibalistic summons" to characterize the Aarenholds as "carnivorous" and as "highly civilized beasts of prey" (1960: 55).

[30]In her chapter "Narcissism and Sibling Incest" Schneider uses "narcissism" several times (1995: 25, 51, 53) to refer to the relationship between Siegmund and Sieglinde. Her concluding statement:

> I concentrated mostly on one of the major themes in *Wälsungenblut*: the sibling incest that is committed at the end of the novella. There are several reasons for the incest to have developed. Among them is an act of imitation. The Aarenhold twins intensely enjoy and identify with the incestuous stage meeting of Siegmund and Sieglinde in Wagner's *Walküre*. Another cause for the incest is revenge. Siegmund feels threatened by von Beckerath who, by becoming engaged to his twin sister, takes away Siegmund's most prized possession. Yet an even more important incentive for engaging in incest than revenge is narcissism and a lack of identity. Siegmund, who has artistic ambitions, mirrors himself in his sister in whose large eyes, dark curls, slender hands and pleasantly scented skin, he recognizes himself. Instinctive recognition and a naive delight in his own beauty, which he sees reflected in his sister, lead to incest. Incest exists here as "Ebenbürtigkeitswonne", a self-coined word by Mann, whose meaning consists in a kind of "narcissism à deux", the self-centered joy of the siblings in each other at the expense of any outsider. (1995: 53)

Schneider does not cite Freud's conclusion that the male homosexual becomes narcissistic in consequence of his mother fixation. Thus she sees the twins as equally culpable for their climactic act. Yet there is nothing in the text to suggest that Sieglinde is even vaguely aware of what Siegmund has in mind.

[31]Monika Mann recalls her experience as a child being welcomed to her mother's bedroom: "She wished us a good morning in a deep, husky, caressing voice. It was very pleasant first to stand barefoot on the thick bearskin rug, or sometimes to kneel, before creeping in under the cornflower-blue comforter and to breathe in the peculiarly astringent fragrance of the bedclothes—smelling, as it seemed, of the very scent of security" (1960: 7-8). Could Katja's rug have been borrowed for Siegmund's bedroom? It came, after all, from a room in which virtual incest occurred.

[32]The revised version of the sentence, in *Stories of Three Decades,* is "he ought to be grateful to us. His existence will be a little less trivial, from now on". Beckerath's existence would only be affected if he learned of his betrayal from one or both of the twins, a revelation that, at the least, would subject them to humiliation, at the most to imprisonment. But in the privacy of Mann's mind, his Sigmund (unconscious) part could communicate with his Beckerath (conscious) part via fantasy, a common method of reducing life's triviality.

[33]Bade notes that in "From Childhood Play to *Death in Venice*" Mann is "echoing Freud's *Der Dichter und das Phantasieren*" (1978: 23fn1), but he does not specifically indicate that Mann had read Freud's piece. Nor does Bade offer an interpretation of any of Mann's fiction based on the Freud article. From Mann's statement about childhood games and fantasy in his 1940 lecture "On Myself" Cullander speculates that "Mann had read Freud's 1908 essay" (1999: 33), but he does not use his speculation for textual interpretation.

[34]Freud concludes his treatment of phantasy and creativity by offering an explanation of the popularity of "egocentric" fiction and its benefit. While people are ordinarily ashamed of having day-dreams and are repulsed by learning of another's day-dreams, the creative writer uses the tools of his craft, altering and disguising his day-dream, the purely subjective, and objectifying it through his mastery of form. We read his work with the experience of *"fore-pleasure"*, which results from the reduction of our own tensions, thus making "possible the release of still greater pleasure arising from deeper psychical sources" (153). Indeed, the experience may enable us "thenceforward to enjoy our own day-dreams without self-reproach or shame".

[35]Even so, Heilbut argues that "Mann must have known that 'left-handed' and 'shriveled' were almost clichéd signs of homosexuality and impotence" (1996: 213-14). Whether or not Mann intended to make such a suggestion cannot be verified, but it is worth noting that, according to Rank, a person victimized by the sibling incest complex probably has homosexual proclivities.

[36]According to Izenberg, Mann, in a letter to Agnes Meyer written many years later,

> noted his mother's "sensuous, pre-artistic nature" and her "inclination to the Bohemian", but also her characteristic coldness, and the vanity that had made her suffer greatly as she aged; he had memorialized those sufferings, he added, in the portrait of Grand Duchess Dorothea, mother of the autobiographical Prince Klaus Heinrich, in his novel *Royal Highness*. (2000: 109)

In conformity to his thesis, Izenberg continues:

> the idea of a biographical origin for the attraction to and fear of narcissistic women evident in Mann's early work, however plausible, must remain speculative, and even more so any insinuation of its relevance for his homosexuality. What in any case is most significant about the representation of women and of men's feelings toward them in the stories is not that it might supply a possible explanation for the sexual preference of their author, but that it renders a particular image of desire; it is a heterosexual counterpart to the passive homosexual longing Mann later described and admitted to. (2000: 109)

[37]Page references to the segment of "Felix Krull" being studied at the present time are to the Denver Lindley translation published in 1955.

[38]Mrs. Lowe-Porter's translation in *Stories of Three Decades* is much more discreet about Krull at the breast, crediting him with "certain feelings" ("Felix" 371).

[39]This passage, especially "either a fairytale or a dream", could easily suggest that Mann had read "Creative Writers and Day-Dreaming", especially the following paragraph:

> We must not neglect, however, to go back to the kind of imaginative works which we have to recognize, not as original

creations, but as the re-fashioning of ready-made and familiar
material.[...]Even here, the writer keeps a certain amount of
independence, which can express itself in the choice of material
and in changes in it which are often quite extensive. In so far as
the material is already at hand, however, it is derived from the
popular treasure-house of myths, legends and fairy tales. The
study of constructions of folk-psychology such as these is far
from being complete, but it is extremely probable that myths, for
instance, are distorted vestiges of the wishful phantasies of whole
nations, the *secular dreams* of youthful humanity. (152; ital. in
orig.)

[40]The episode in the delicatessen did not appear in the Krull fragment that
Mann wrote in 1910. Hayman says that it was inserted when Mann returned to the
Krull story in 1951, though he does not say when it was written (1995: 580).

[41]Heinz Kohut's analysis of "Death in Venice" supports mine:

the mother symbol seems to be represented first of all by the sick
city itself from which Aschenbach cannot extricate himself; it is
not only a city, but also the sea, and death—the whole atmosphere
of Venice, death, and the sea together—toward which
Aschenbach's deepest wishes are directed. As death is overtaking
him, Aschenbach sees Tadzio, beckoning him outward into the
open sea, "into an immensity of richest expectation". This picture,
then establishes clearly not only the symbolic identity of death
and the sea but also the connection between the boy, Tadzio, and
the sea-death-mother motif. (1957: 226)

[42]Summarizing his discussion of doubleness as a provocation of the
experience of the uncanny, Freud writes: "When all is said and done, the quality of
uncanniness can only come from the fact of the 'double' being a creation dating back
to a very early mental stage, long since surmounted—a stage, incidentally, at which it
wore a more friendly aspect" ("Uncanny" 236). Mann's fascination with twins and
doubles indicates his capacity to regress to a very early mental stage through artistic
creativity.

III

The Magic Mountain

I. Hans Castorp

The view that Mann's artistic imagination is fundamentally ironic has been popular ever since Erich Heller published *The Ironic German: A Study of Thomas Mann* in 1958. Ten years later James R. McWilliams completed a dissertation entitled *Brother Artist: A Psychological Study of Thomas Mann's Fiction* (published in 1983). In effect, McWilliams, accepting Heller's contention that Mann's irony is pervasive, sees Hans's derision of psychoanalysis as Mann's contrary hint that the reader should give respectful attention to it as a tool for assessing Hans's thoughts and behaviors. Thus McWilliams summarizes his theme:

> Mannian protagonists seek continual atonement for guilt feelings that have their origin in infantile sexuality based on parricidal hatred and on a desire for incestuous union with the mother.[...]Each story from the author's pen is, almost without exception, concerned with the protagonist's search for a solution to sexual drives in terms of a classic Oedipus complex. (1983: 8)

But McWilliams' reliance on the "classic Oedipus complex" fails to provide him with a thesis sufficiently explanatory for *The Magic Mountain*. He seems to realize the inadequacy of his thesis when he writes:

> If Hans Castorp's threatening involvements in an affair of the heart constitute a dangerous journey for him, then the nature of the danger must be a recollection from childhood—for nothing really happens in the whole scope and sequence of *The Magic Mountain* which can possibly be interpreted as a major crisis or justification for suicide on the battlefield. Castorp was soured on life even before his arrival on the Mountain, and now the fairly harmless replay of the Oedipal situation [the Castorp-Chauchat-

> Peeperkorn triangle] is enough to tilt the scales in favor of
> punishment and death. In Berghof, Hans Castorp finds nothing
> new—he merely confronts an old specter and acts out the
> subconscious phantasmagoria that he has brought up to the
> sanatorium with him! (1983: 228)

McWilliams apparently senses that *something* happened in Hans's early childhood, but, faithful to his reliance on the Oedipal situation—and finding no evidence thereof—he is at a loss to identify the *something*. That *something* is to be found in a phase of mental development that precedes the Oedipal situation, a phase that Freud never adequately examined.

In *An Outline of Psycho-Analysis* Freud thus introduces the Oedipus complex: "When a boy (from the age of two or three) has entered the phallic phase of his libidinal development, is feeling pleasurable sensations in his sexual organ and has learnt to procure these at will by manual stimulation, he becomes his mother's lover" (189). This description accounts for the innate drive that causes the subsequent triadic ("Oedipal") complexity— son's guilt over desiring mother and hating father—that McWilliams describes above and finds at the core of *The Magic Mountain*. But immediately before his introduction to the "phallic phase" Freud writes:

> A child's first erotic object is the mother's breast that nourishes it;
> love has its origin in attachment to the satisfied need for
> nourishment.[...] And for however long it is fed at its mother's
> breast, it will always be left with a conviction after it has been
> weaned that its feeding was too short and too little. (*Outline* 188-
> 89)

Because he was so absorbed with investigating and stressing the significance of the Oedipal situation, Freud never materially explored the dyadic relationship between infant and mother as the first phase in the development of "mental life" (*Outline* 188). It was not until the 1960s that a third era of psychoanalytic theory formation, that of object-relations psychology, was developed to guide the investigation of "the earliest object relationships, primarily the mother-infant relationship, in the developmental process of self-object differentiation and primary structure formation" (Settage 1980: 524).

Thus an inquiry into Hans's "primary structure formation" must begin at an earlier phase of development than that investigated by McWilliams. I am not saying, of course, that my inquiry rejects all of his analysis of Hans's thoughts and behaviors. Rather, I argue that use of the insights of post-Freudian psychoanalysis enables a reader to marvel at the brilliant intuitions that Mann reveals in his characterization of Hans Castorp.

Even before Hans ridicules psychoanalysis, he has already exhibited behaviors suggesting that his relation with his "first and strongest love-object", his "first seducer" (Freud *Outline* 188), was frustrated. On the train from Hamburg to Davos Hans has been reading *Ocean Steamships* (3). His choice of reading matter seems an obvious, even clumsy, authorial clue: the book pertains to the career upon which he is embarking, and his reading it even on vacation testifies to his dedication to his career—or to his stultifying lack of other interests. But subsequent information reveals that what is not obvious is the psychic origin of his career choice. Later we learn "that he had always liked ships" (33):

> As a small boy he had filled the pages of his note-books with drawings of fishing-barks, five-masters and vegetable-barges. When he was fifteen, he had had a front seat at the christening ceremony of the new double-screw steamer *Hansa*. He had watched her leave the ways at Blohm and Voss's, and afterwards made quite a happy water-colour of the graceful ship, done with a good deal of attention to detail, and a loving and not unskilful treatment of the glassy green, rolling waves. [His uncle and guardian] Consul Tienappel hung it in his private office, and somebody told him that it showed talent, that the artist might develop into a good marine painter—a remark which the Consul could safely repeat to his ward, for Hans Castorp only laughed good-humouredly, and not for a moment considered letting himself in for a career of being eccentric *and not getting enough to eat*. (my italics)

Hans's fear of "not getting enough to eat" is an indication of oral neediness that his behavior subsequently reveals.[1] The name of the ship being christened, while it publicly celebrates the Hanseatic League (c. 1157-1669) that Hamburg had dominated, also intimates that Hans thinks that he was born to be a *Bürger* in Hamburg. But the scene of the launching of the *Hansa* unconsciously reminds Hans of his first and strongest private movie, his image of himself as a ship sliding from the amniotic sea into the universal ocean.

Much, much later, Hans tells the chief physician at International Sanatorium Berghof, Hofrat Behrens, that in his youth he "never painted anything but ships and water, of course", adding, "But not withstanding, in my eyes the most interesting branch of painting is and remains portraiture, because it has man for its immediate object" (260). Hans seems oblivious to the notion that the subject freely chosen by a painter would reveal anything about his subjectivity. And he would scoff at the notion that the book title *Ocean Steamships* betrayed his fantasy of re-experiencing the mental state of infantile fusion with the mother which Romain Rolland termed the "oceanic feeling" (Lawson 1996b).

Already the narrator has explained in full—or fulsome—detail Hans's identification with Hamburg and its maritime commerce, avowing that

> you would swear that this young Castorp was a legitimate and genuine product of the soil in which he flourished, and strikingly at home in his environment. Nor would he, had he ever put such a question to himself, have been for a single second doubtful of the answer.

Hans especially loves being harborside in the presence of the "mammoth bodies of great ships" (30):

> All these were familiar sights to Hans Castorp from his youth upwards, awaking in him only the agreeable, homely sensations of "belonging," which were the prerogative of his years. Such sensations would reach their height when he sat of a Sunday forenoon with James Tienappel or his cousin Ziemssen—Joachim Ziemssen—in the pavilion at Alster, breakfasting on hot cuts and smoked meat, with a glass of old port; or when, having eaten, he would lean back in his chair and give himself up to his cigar. For therein especially was he true to type, that he liked good living, and notwithstanding his thin-bloodedness and look of over-refinement clung to the grosser pleasures of life as *a greedy suckling to its mother's breast.* (my italics)

Mann continues with his description of Hans: "[c]omfortably, not without dignity, he carried the weight of culture with which the governing upper class of the commerical city endowed its children. He was as clean as a well-cared-for baby". Indeed, he looks something like a baby: "[s]tanding and walking, he rather stuck out his abdomen". But there is a hint that in babyhood he had suffered calcium deprivation, for "[h]is teeth were rather soft and defective and he had a number of gold fillings" (31). The deprivation probably resulted from an interference with calcium's earliest source, breast milk. Whether it was denied him or it was spurned by him, he now says that he "could never abide [milk]", requesting porter instead (68). His liking for the substitute originated in childhood, when his physician recommended that he drink "a good glass of porter after third breakfast every day", for he had always been "a little anæmic" (29). Since Hans was so young when his anemia was diagnosed, it was very likely brought on by the absence or curtailment of breast-feeding (Stuart-Macadam 1998: 57). The porter regimen daily left his mind temporarily stupefied and his teeth prone to caries, for porter contains four percent alcohol by volume and a rich concentration of saccharine matter. Hans did love to eat, though, and since the servant Schalleen served the rich food upon which Hans gorged, "she it was who, so far as in her lay, took the place of a mother to little Hans Castorp" (29).

David Blumberg offers a valuable insight when he quotes (from the Woods translation) an early description of Hans's psychology:

> Hans Castorp loved music with all his heart, its effect being much like that of the porter he drank with his morning snack— profoundly calming, numbing, and "doze"-inducing—and he listened now with pleasure, his head tilted to one side, mouth open, eyes slightly bloodshot. (Woods 36-37)

Later in his essay Blumberg cites the great influence on Mann of Richard Wagner, who "illustrates music's universality by comparing it to the prelinguistic utterance, to 'the cry for help, the wail, the shout of joy'" (1990: 90). Blumberg convinces me that Hans's love of music had its grounding in his oral neediness, though I question his diagnosis of Hans's bloodshot eyes, for, depending on a quotation from Wagner, he thinks that the condition is caused by Hans's listening to music (1990: 90, 94n18). I would argue that Hans's bloodshot eyes betray his lack of the "Sleep, Sweet Sleep" that Mann praises in his essay of the same title. This mother-induced insomnia drives him to seek the kind of reverie that music, as an oral substitute, offers.

When he was five years of age, Hans's mother had died

> quite suddenly, on the eve of a confinement, of an arterial obstruction following neuritis—an embolus, Dr. Heidekind had called it—which caused instantaneous cardiac arrest. She had just been laughing, sitting up in bed, and it looked as though she had fallen back with laughter, but really it was because she had died. (19)

In this case, the condition of neuritis, inflammation of a nerve or nerves, probably resulted from a metabolic factor, specifically a toxemia of pregnancy (Thomas 1981: 949). One type of embolism, "[b]lockage of an artery by a clump of material traveling in the blood stream", occurs "when some of the [amniotic] fluid that surrounds the baby in the uterus is forced into the mother's circulation toward the end of a normal pregnancy" (Clayman 1989: vol. I 396). In this case, the embolus caused a fatal heart attack which instantly killed Hans's mother and the fetus that she was about to deliver. Supposedly she had been laughing when she died, but that may be a five-year-old's interpretation; it is likely that she suffered a convulsion brought on by eclampsia, a convulsion that begins with "fixation of the eyeballs, rolling of the eyes, twitchings of the face" (Thomas 1981: 448). The appearance of his mother's face during her death throes will be repressed, but it will affect Hans eighteen years later when he first lays eyes on Clavdia.

Hans was old enough to comprehend his mother's dying, but not to understand that her death resulted from the process of giving life. It seems unlikely that he was old enough to comprehend that his mother, in the process of giving life, instead gave death to her fetus. It seems certain that, even if he could comprehend both the dying and the birthing phenomena, he could not have comprehended any relation between them, likeness or differences or cause-and-effect, ironic or otherwise. Hans never consciously thinks of his mother during the seven years that his mental life is exposed at the Berghof; or rather, it should be said that he thinks incessantly during those seven years that he must not think about his mother. Such repression means that his exposed unconscious psychic activity and his manifested behavior must be all the more closely plumbed for meaning.

In his attempt to substitute bodily well-being for psychological well-being, the child Hans languishes in the oral phase and does not evolve from it as he grows older. On his first evening at the Berghof, Hans eats "heartily, though his appetite did not turn out quite so stout as he had thought. But he always ate a good meal, out of pure self-respect, even when he was not hungry" (13). In childhood his daily glass of porter leaves him "sitting staring into space, with his jaw dropped and his thoughts fixed on just nothing at all" (29), as satiated as a slack-jawed nursling. And, in adolescence, since he never had enough of the maternal teat, the mucous membranes of his oral cavity demand the cigar. The name of his favorite brand, *Maria Mancini* (he brings two hundred with him to the Berghof [11]), indicates, however, that the cigar will be superseded as a substitute for the teat. Glenway Westcott notes that the actual brand was named after one of the mistresses of a French king (176). As a paramour, Maria was a substitute for an unsatisfying consort. Her family name duplicates the hint of illegitimacy: the

Italian *mancina/mancino* means 'left-handed, dirty, treacherous, underhanded'. This Maria is not Santa Maria, the apotheosis of motherhood.

Although the daily porter that the child Hans drank was supposed to be "a blood maker" (29), he still experiences anemia at twenty-three. That is to say, despite all the attention that he pays to himself as body, there is still some biological factor missing, something that transmutes to the psychological right before our very eyes. He certainly is not hot-blooded, for as Weisinger writes, "so far as we know, Hans[...]has had no sexual experience" (1990: 192), noting that in

> one of the few fragments of the *Zauberberg* manuscript which survive, we can see that Mann originally made allusion to Hans Castorp's earlier sexual experience (and that experience was cautiously left without a specifically gendered partner); but in the final version Mann carefully deleted this passage. (1990: 216fn41; parenthesis in orig.)

Weisinger does not mention a revelation offered late in the novel, when Hans apprehensively attends a seance: "he was reminded of the peculiar and unforgettable mixture of feelings—nervousness, pridefulness, curiosity, disgust, and awe—with which, years ago, he had gone with some fellow students, a little tipsy, to a brothel in Sankt-Pauli" (671). But this scene is inconclusive—given everything else known about Hans, it could be inferred that his visit to the brothel was motivated by curiosity about the female genital, that he was overcome by his maternal awe of it, and that he was left impotent by his awe, even if he still felt desire. Support for this inference will be offered when Clavdia Chauchat is introduced. Hans's unconscious repression of his loss of the original object has forced his unconscious repression of his sex drive. In effect, Hans Castorp is *ein Kastrat.*

Another Freudian critic writes: "Mann devotes but twenty-five pages to tell of Castorp's life previous to his arrival and seventy pages to describe his experiences on his first day at Haus Berghof. This proportion indicates their relative psychological impressions on Castorp" (Slochower 1937: 59n1). Slochower, too, stands loyally by the "classic Oedipus complex". And, too, he must be seduced by Mann's artful arrangement of the early chapters: luggage in hand, Hans arrives in Davos in Chapter 1, which closes as he goes to bed exhausted; Chapter 2, which presumably takes place while Hans sleeps/dreams, reveals the past and hints at the psychological luggage that Hans carries; Chapter 3, which begins the next morning as Hans, now apparently refreshed, begins to unpack his luggage, psychological and otherwise. In effect, the remainder of the book is a commentary on those "twenty-five pages".

When Hans ascends the Alps to recover from anemia, he is unwittingly returning to the magic mountain of the maternal breast, from which he must separate if he is ever to realize his heterosexuality. That Hans has returned to the locality of the maternal is made clear by Joachim's question, "You are looking at the landscape?" (7), as he and his cousin drive from the station to the sanatorium. The road goes "straight up the axis of the valley", across a water course, then up "toward the wooded slopes" (7-8). "Magnificent!" claims Hans; "Think so?" slyly asks Joachim (7). When they reach the point "where the valley narrowed to its entrance, the more distant ranges [above *mons veneris*] showed a cold, slaty blue[,] [a] wind had sprung up, and made perceptible the chill of evening" (8), Hans, in bravado, says that, after all, he does not find the view "so overpowering": "Where are the glaciers, and the snow peaks, and the gigantic heights you hear about? These things aren't very high, it seems to me". Joachim disagrees, saying that they are nearly to the tree line, beyond which there is "snow all the year round" (8). Remember that in *The Interpretation of Dreams* Freud interpreted *déjà vus* of landscape and localities as symbols of the genitals of the mother (*SE* 4 399).

Hans is immediately presented with radically different responses that are available to him, being placed in room 34, with his cousin Joachim rooming on his right and a "bad Russian" couple rooming on his left. Joachim has never smoked, "out of sheer doggedness" Hans opines (48), nor, apparently, has he ever allowed himself to use his own cigar. Joachim is attracted to a "good Russian" girl, the big-breasted Marusja—Russian for "Marie" he informs Hans—and she is attracted to him. But Joachim the officer candidate finds Marusja "too undisciplined" (72), so that, though her name and figure promise that she would be a perfect mother-mate, he never allows himself to court her. Unintentionally, then, Joachim exemplifies for Hans the renunciation of sexuality—appropriately, Joachim proclaims that he puts no stock in Dr. Krokowski's theory that impediment of the sex drive causes disease (17).[2] Hans's "bad Russian" neighbors provide the polarity, disturbing Hans's sense of decorum by indulging themselves sexually every evening and again as the sun also rises, thus personifying the popular belief that sanatoria were dens of leaping salacity (40). The number 34 offers a clue to the mind set of the new inhabitant of the room. Since Erich Heller's Questioner stresses that "the superstitious number seven" is related "to almost any arrangement on the Magic Mountain" (1961: 192-93), that seven is "the magic number of *The Magic Mountain*"

(201), a little creative mathematics seems warranted here, $3 + 4 = 7$.
(In his extensive psychoanalytic comment on the use of the number
seven in the novel, Neider uses the same equation, but does not link it
to the mother figure, even after he notes that Clavdia occupies room
number seven [1968: 342].) The room number ($3 + 4 = 7$) becomes a
revelation when viewed through a comment by Katja Mann:

> Thomas Mann believed that he would die at seventy like his
> mother; he even wrote about it and was also interviewed on the
> subject, but I can't imagine that he actually believed it. He wasn't
> really supersititious. He was devoted to the number 7, and he was
> devoted to his mother too, but I doubt that he was seriously
> convinced that he would in fact die at the age of seventy. (1975:
> 131)

Given the context, her fusing of number devotion with mother
devotion is significant. Indeed, Agnes Meyer makes the same point: "It
is interesting to remember that Thomas Mann's mother fixation and his Dantesque
belief in numerology once led him to prophesy that his death would probably take
place in[...]his seventieth year" (1968: 326).[3]

Since Hans is haunted by the "oceanic feeling", nostalgia for
Eden before the Fall, he is frequently situated in a garden locale. The
first such scene occurs on his first morning at the Berghof, when he
observes "an elderly lady, of melancholy, even tragic aspect" (39), veiled and
dressed all in black, this sight occurring even as Hans is scandalized
by the rushing Russians' early "nooner". When Joachim is asked about
"that dark woman down in the garden" (41), he tells Hans that she is known
as "Tous-les-deux"[sic]. Five weeks before she had brought her eldest son,
"a hopeless case", to the sanatorium; then, three weeks later, a second son
arrived, "to see his brother before the end". Both handsome, the brothers
"fluttered the dovecots". But, soon enough, the second son manifested the
virulent stage of tuberculosis, thus condemning the mother, who
speaks only Spanish, to wander the garden, uttering the only phrase by
which she can communicate her wretchedness to others. Although the
brothers are apparently not guilty of the offence that allegedly brought
about the Fall, sexual knowledge, yet they are condemned to death.
Although Hans understands the French she utters (42), he is too naïve
to understand the pathos it conveys, making the joke to Joachim that
they, *"tous le deux"* (41; sic), should now go to breakfast. Not only are
there two shadows in the garden, but also two foreshadowings.

Having a care to fill his cigar case (41), Hans looks forward to
breakfast, for he still relies on compensatory pleasures to satisfy his

infantile need. He begins his meal with rice (43), the food that twenty-year-old Mann had contemplated as a libido-suppressant. But he is quickly disturbed by the slamming of a glass door: "[w]hether from his upbringing, or out of a natural idiosyncrasy, he loathed the slamming of doors, and could have struck the guilty person" (45). This first time, Hans does not glimpse the "guilty person". After breakfast Joachim introduces Hans to the senior physician, Hofrat Behrens, who, observing Hans Castorp's greenish complexion, immediately declares that he is "[t]otally anæmic, of course" (47). Although the physician does not use the term *chlorosis*, he knows that a greenish complexion justifies the immediate and unequivocal diagnosis of that severe form of iron-deficiency anemia. This disorder was first noticed in modern medicine in 1554 and soon became popularly known as the "green-sickness" (Stuart-Macadam 1998: 50). Since it commonly affected teenage girls, it was also known as the "virgin's disease" or the "maiden's sickness"; physicians—males all—diagnosed the melancholy female teenagers as pining away for physical "love", rather than considering that their patients' condition of iron deficiency was exacerbated by the onset of menstruation. Despite the popular conception of chlorosis as a condition gender-specific to the female, Hofrat Behrens' diagnosis is accurate, for Stuart-Macadam notes that the three studies of iron deficiency anemia in young children that differentiated the sexes have all found the condition more common in young boys (1998: 53). Something of a psychoanalyst himself, Hofrat Behren may be silently concurring with his oldtime medical brethren, concluding that Hans Castorp needs a penis. As a medical materialist, though, he recommends that Hans behave as if he "had a slight *tuberculosis pulmonum*" (47) during his stay. But, of course, he would have known that tuberculosis, like chlorosis, had long been linked with love-frustration.

Still completely repressed, Hans takes notice that he is in a garden, an emotional environment that induces him to light up a Maria Mancini and offer the praise of smoking already cited. He does add, "when a man has a good cigar in his mouth[...]a man is perfectly safe, nothing can touch him—literally. It's just like lying on the beach" (48), revealing the connection between homosexual desire and infantile desire for the mother. During the walk that follows, Hans, in conversation with a new acquaintance, Herr Settembrini, complains that early breakfast had left him feeling oppressed and that, for some reason, his morning cigar "hasn't the right taste, something that as good as never happens to me, or only when I am seriously upset" (60), and that he had finally thrown it away. When second breakfast is served, every place is provided with a half-litre glass of milk, but Hans requests porter, receiving instead Kulmbacher beer, "a capital substitute" (68) as a 'summit stream' would be, especially for one who is a "come-backer", a regressor. The beer leaves Hans "stupefied and befuddled", so that, when once again the door is slammed, "for the second time, he was unable to fix upon the person who was guilty of behaving in that reckless way about a door". To emphasize that Hans has had the equivalent of a breast-feeding or an oral orgasm, Mann further describes him: "His eyelids were heavy as lead; his tongue would not shape his simple thoughts when out of politeness he tried to talk" (69). As if to repay Hans for his earlier scoffing at psychoanalysis, Dr. Krowkowski, as in a dream Hans thinks, takes a seat directly across from him, "repeatedly looking him sharply in the eye" (70).

After the meal, as the two cousins walk down to Davos-Platz, Hans once again flings away "his familiar and wonted indulgence" (71), his after-breakfast cigar. Finding that all of his "brilliant ideas" had fled his mind, so that he can only talk of "concerns of the body—what he said sounded odd enough in his mouth". The only thing that would not be odd for him to have in his mouth would be a thermometer; he talks of one (71). Soon enough it is back to the table, for the midday meal, at which all gossip is about sanatorium sexual shenanigans. The glass door once again slams, just as they are having the fish course--appropriately for something is fishy here. This time Hans Castorp is determined to see the slammer:

> a woman, or rather girl, of middle height, in a white sweater and coloured skirt, her reddish-blond hair wound in braids about her head. Hans Castorp had only a glimpse of her profile. She moved, in singular contrast to the noise of her entrance, almost without sound, passing with a peculiarly gliding step, her head a little thrust forward. (76)

Snake in the grass!

Hans is accustomed to looking at hands:

> It was not particularly lady-like, this hand that was putting the braids to rights; not so refined and well kept as the hands of ladies in Hans Castorp's own social sphere. Rather broad, with stumpy fingers, it had about it something primitive and childish, something indeed of the schoolgirl. The nails, it was plain, knew nothing of the manicurist's art; they were cut in rough-and-ready schoolgirl fashion, and the skin at the side looked almost as though someone were subject to the childish vice of finger biting.

Just as Johannes Friedemann fixes on Gerda's arm as a substitute
breast, so Hans fixes on Clavdia's fingers as substitute teats, noting,
perhaps jealously, that they are already being used for oral purposes.
The woman takes her place beside Dr. Krokowski:

> As she did so, she turned her head, with the hand still raised to it,
> toward the dining-room and surveyed the public; Hans Castorp
> had opportunity for the fleeting observation that her cheek-bones
> were broad and her eyes narrow.—A vague memory of
> something, of somebody, stirred him slightly and fleetingly as he
> looked. (77)

Hans is told that the woman is Madame Chauchat, said to be a
Russian, said to be married to a Frenchman. Does he think of the other
woman to whom he had spoken in French, "Tous-les-deux"? Does he
think of a more distant woman, whose fixed eyes he had observed as
she died? The fleeting glance of Madame Chauchat is sufficient to
disturb Hans's attempt to sleep during afternoon rest-cure (82). At the
evening meal Hans makes a concerted attempt to conquer his disquiet
by relying on the customary maternal substitutes, plenty of food and "a
bottle of Kulmbacher" . These oral pleasures do their job, making him
"unmistakably aware that bed was the best place for him" (83). But before he
can get to bed, he sees "Frau Chauchat's full face, with its narrow eyes and
broad cheek-bones. 'What is it, what or whom in all the world does she remind me
of?' But his weary brain, despite the effort he made, refused an answer" (87). His
brain may refuse, but his unconscious knows that the stare of the
Mother-Medusa is upon him.[4] Going to his room, Hans tries his
formerly fail-safe substitute, Maria Mancini, but it tastes "like glue, like
coal, like anything but what it should taste like" (88). That leaves only the
ultimate security, sleep: "He had thought to fall asleep at once, but he was
wrong. His eyelids, which he scarcely been able to hold up, now declined to close;
they twitched rebelliously open whenever he shut them" (89). When, finally, he
does sleep he is beset by dreams of Clavdia, in one of which he
dreams of borrowing from her a lead pencil (91) and in another, which
occurs twice, he dreams of Clavdia, after crashing through the glass
door, confronting him in the dining-hall with the invitation to kiss the
palm of her hand (92). His eyes, like those of Herr Friedemann, have
been turned to stone.

II. Clavdia Chauchat

In the extensive critical exploration of *The Magic Mountain* there have been many sightings of Clavdia Chauchat as the avatar of a goddess. Several have discerned Venus (Slochower 1937: 70, Thirlwall 1950: 293, Meletinsky 1998: 288-89). Several, too, have accepted Settembrini's designation of Clavdia as Circe (Slochower 1937: 71, Campbell 1968: 488, Meletinsky 1998: 288-89). Ezergailis thinks that Clavdia is suggestive of a cat goddess (1975: 32) and that her capacity to intoxicate Hans links her to Dionysus (1975: 45). Meletinsky argues that Clavdia's "fling" with Hans during Carnival indicates that she is Earth Mother (1998: 288-89). But Weisinger disagrees: Clavdia may be the "spectral Mother", as Lubich (1993: 729-763) has written, but she "displays far too many traits of gender ambiguity to be considered a serious candidate for the role of a Magna Mother" (1990: 216n40). Since this obviously is a mountain upon which polytheism is preached, I propose Medusa as Clavdia's tutelary goddess. It is true that Mann does not mention Medusa in *The Magic Mountain*, but he is only honoring tradition, for his illustrious predecessor Homer does not mention Medusa, so notes Barnes, adding that both the *Iliad* and the *Odyssey* show that he is respectfully aware of the power of the Gorgon (1974: 3).

In proposing that Clavdia is an avatar of Medusa, though, I must add a stipulation. Kerényi offers an essential observation about myth:

> A divinity with a number of aspects is very apt to appear only in the *one* aspect under which he or she is being regarded at the moment.[...] Those of us who are inclined to regard the Greek divinities as unmixed types must, in this case, accustom themselves to a duality of fundamentally different goddesses. (1963: 120)

The case to which he refers is that of the goddess whose aspects include Medusa as well as Demeter, Persephone, and Hecate (1963: 120, 126). All are aspects of the Great Mother, even as Edelman describes Medusa as an aspect of the Terrible Mother and Pallas Athena as her counterpart aspect, the Good Mother, and even as Neumann sees Hecate as the Gorgon, as the Terrible Mother aspect, and Demeter as the Good Mother (1955: 170). In *The Magic Mountain* the Medusa aspect dominates the mother figure who fascinates Hans Castorp, but in the "Snow" chapter other aspects appear. This change is not a whimsy, mere textual embellishment, but rather a proof of

Mann's unconscious dedication to the complexity of the mother-theme.

There is a tradition that the story of Medusa entered the Greek world from much farther east. Dumoulié suggests that it originated in the Indian story of "the demon Humbaba who was decapitated by Gilgamesh" (1995: 779), while Elworthy notes that "[n]ot only were the Greek and Etruscan Gorgons common in Europe, representing a widely-received myth, but in the East, Bhavani, the Destructive Female Principle, is still represented with a head exactly agreeing with the most ancient type of the Medusa[...]" (1970: 161). Both Behrens and Settembrini must give credence to the tradition, for they identify Chauchat as a member of one or another of the eastern tribes which migrated to the area north of the Black Sea. Behrens' identification is both mythological and medical. Chauchat is described as having "hyperborean cheekbones" (257), thus linking her with that mythic people living above the north wind (Rose 1959: 135); since she is often described as having high cheekbones, Behrens might be implying that at least part of her heritage is Oriental. She also exhibits the "epicanthus" (257), a small fold of skin around the inner corner of the eye, a common characteristic of the yellow race, but rare in other races except in infants (Clayman 1989: vol. I 410), so Behrens must detect a racial mixture in her heritage.

Since Settembrini despises the East as the birthplace of all values contrary to his Western humanism, he scorns all Eastern ethnic groups. He simply lumps Chauchat in with the other convalescent Russians, who are, he says, "nothing but Parthians and Scythians" (223, 228). On another occasion Settembrini complains, "Asia surrounds us—wherever one's glance rests, a Tartar physiognomy". He continues, as the mail is distributed, "They ought to set up an altar to Pallas Athen[a], here in the vestibule—to ward off the evil spell". Then the evil eye of Medusa on Athena's aegis could stare down the evil eyes of Chauchat's/Medusa's Tartar cohorts. Observing a squabble between a Russian and Lawyer Paravant, Settembrini sides with the latter: "for my part, Lawyer Paravant fights under the ægis of the goddess" (241). Then, pedant that he is, he explains to Hans what he is talking about. Settembrini has, in addition to an ideological antipathy for Chauchat, a personal score against her, for her tutelary deity Medusa had, according to Dante, "seriously frightened" his beloved Virgil, just outside of Dis (Barnes 1974: 32).

Probably Settembrini's learning is lost on Hans, anyway. Hans does, however, apply a tribal epithet to Chauchat. His early sightings of her stir his unconscious until a memory of an early adolescent infatuation with a male schoolmate pops out. This lad was Pribislav Hippe, the

> grafting of Germanic stock with Slavic, or the reverse. True, his close-shorn round pate was blond; but the eyes were a grey-blue, or a blue-grey—an indefinite, ambiguous colour, like the hue of far-distant mountain ranges—and of an odd, narrow shape, were even, to be precise, a little slanting, with strongly marked prominent cheek-bones directly under them.

He is called "the Kirghiz" (120). With his eyes evoking the Caucasus and his family name evoking the horse, his nickname appropriately connects him with a one of the tribes, like the Scythians and Parthians, who were famed horsemen in the land north of the Black Sea--*pace* Weisinger, who asserts that "[y]oung Hippe is by no means of Kirghiz extraction" (1990: 209). Since Chauchat possesses the same facial traits as Hippe, Hans, when he finally looks directly at her, readily applies the same tribal epithet to her eyes (142, 160, 205). It is appropriate, then, that Chauchat originally comes from and returns to the ancient home of her tutelary goddess, after she has fulfilled her mission of breaking down Hans's defense. That the goddess Medusa had other adherents in Scythia is established by artifacts found there by excavation (Anon. s.d.: 112-113n85; Napier 1986: 100, 102, 105).

Clavdia's physical features disturb Hans in both his personal and his collective unconscious. In the former mentality her upper facial characteristics nearly call forth to consciousness two faces from his past, those of his mother and of Hippe. In the latter mentality— she, as a marionette of Medusa, evokes an unconscious response, according to Carl Jung's conception of the archetypes (Wolman 1973: 398).

Appropriately, Clavdia claims Hans's attention during the fish course, for her inspiration, Medusa, was the daughter of Keto, whose name proclaims that she is 'sea-monster-woman' (Rose 1959: 27). Since Hans's mind has never emerged from its original aquarian environment, he would be especially susceptible to the wiles of the archetype *sea-goddess* (who was eventually divested of her divinity— so that she could be decapitated by Perseus, who gave her head to Pallas Athena for use as a prophylactic).

Before Medusa became anthropomorphized, she "had golden wings, but hands of brass, mighty tusks like a boar's, and [a body] girdled with serpents" (Kerényi 1951: 49). Indeed, in her earliest body Medusa seems to have been the Snake Goddess (Pollack 1997: 131).

Herodotus tells us that some Greeks over around the Pontus told him that the original Scythes (first sovereign of Scythia) was the son of Hercules and "a strange being, between a maiden and a serpent, whose form from the buttocks upwards was like that of a woman, while all below was like a snake" (Anon. s.d.: 130-31). If this is not just a snake tale, then Medusa was there before Scythia was. Over time Medusa underwent beautification, until the only vestigial remnant of her reptilian origin was her serpentine tresses, a "recognized symbol of divine female wisdom, and equally of the 'wise blood' that supposedly gave women their divine powers" (Walker 1983: 629). A psychoanalytic interpretation of the curious coiffure is that it represents "female (that is, maternal) sexuality as something dangerous and frightening" (Caldwell 1989: 46), a restatement of Freud's original assertion that terror is caused by the spectacle of Medusa's snaky head, cut off and held aloft by Perseus, which, to the primitive mind, resembles the female genitals that, since they have no penis appending, must have been cropped ("Medusa's" 273).

Clavdia's fidgeting with her hair—she has an eternal bad hair day—is the first hint that she is incorrigibly Medusan. But she habitually displays a "gliding step" (76 et seq.) with "her head a little thrust forward" (76), a locomotion that would arouse sneaking suspicion. Perhaps her characteristic slow scan of the audience, ready to lithify those driven by voyeurism (Caldwell 1989: 68), even as she still tips her hand with her fingers, is the best tip-off to her identity. Yet even though Hans Castorp is under Clavdia's stare for two lengthy periods—"dead, immobilized, impotent, but at the same time[...] fixed forever in the act of looking, frozen in fascination and fixation before a scene from which he literally can never turn away", as Caldwell describes Medusa's victim (1989: 68)--he never inquires about her genealogy.

There is a second event at this meal that Hans Castorp notices. Another patient, Dr. Blumenkohl, is forced to leave the dining hall, observed by the ill-bred Frau Stöhr, who, as Hirschbach points out, is the spokeswoman for aggressive sexual curiosity among the female patients (59). Stöhr comments, "Poor creature,[...] He'll soon be at his last gasp. He had to go out to talk with his 'Blue Peter'" (78), the nickname for "a flat, curving bottle of bluish glass, with a metal cap", used by a patient with an active case to collect his sputum (7), which can be analyzed to detect the stage of his disease (Thomas 1981: 1354). Hearing the "grotesque phrase[...], Hans Castorp felt a mixture of repugnance and desire to laugh" (78), the former reaction to the mention of a body fluid and a morbid one at that, the latter in nervous embarrassment over her insertion of the phallus into polite company.

That Clavdia has thus been associated by proximity with Dr. Krokowski suggests that her mysterious effect on Hans Castorp may be interpreted by psychoanalysis. That her arrival prompts Dr. Blumenkohl's talk with his "Blue Peter"—*post hoc, ergo propter hoc* being perfectly permissible in neurotic thinking—suggests that because of Hans Castorp's infatuation with Clavdia, he too will soon have to have a talk with his "Blue Peter". After the meal, Hans lies on his loggia between the glass walls—of repression that Clavdia keeps bursting through—that separate him from his chaste cousin and from the randy Russians. "On using his handkerchief he discovered it to be red with blood, but had not enough energy to think about the fact, though he was given to worrying over himself and by nature inclined to hypochondria" (78). Realistically, the blood may indicate that his tuberculosis has reached the stage of hemorrhage; surrealistically, it may indicate that he, a victim of the "virgin's disease", is experiencing menstruation, the onset of sexual maturity. "Two or three times his breast was shaken by inward laughter at the horrid expression which that ignorant creature, Frau Stöhr, had used" (78). By name a disturber of the peace, *Friedensstörerin,* Frau Stöhr has caused quite a stir in Hans's cabinet of love and love-disease.

No sooner had Hans arrived at the sanatorium than he had begun to complain of exhaustion and a red face (10, 12, 17, 40). Rycroft writes,

> After repression of unacceptable feelings or recollections has occurred, the process of neurosis-formation may—apparently at least—stop. The result is a person who is stable and free of neurotic anxiety but inhibited, and whose health is contingent on his remaining limited and incapable of realizing his full potentialities—and on his successfully avoiding situations which might upset his equilibrium. (1968: 60-61)

Such an inhibited life Hans had led in Hamburg, but eventually he began to display the chronic fatigue that is a common symptom of inhibition (Rycroft 1968: 62). His removal to the highly allusive maternal landscape "has upset his equilibrium", demanding more and more of his energy to maintain repression. Then Hans experiences, in Rycroft's formulation, the "return of the the repressed":

> neurotic symptom-formation is essentially a process by which the repressed achieves its way back, usually either in disguise or by establishing some link with a part of the repressing self which enables a compromise between the repressed and the repressing forces to occur—the sudden irruption of an undisguised,

> unmodified repressed impulse, or the sudden total recall of a
> traumatic memory usually only occurs in psychosis or nightmares
> and constitutes a complete failure of signal-anxiety. The forms of
> disguise and compromise which are used depend on the precise
> repressed and repressing forces at war in any particular case, and
> on the types of defence habitually used by him[...]. (1968: 62-63)

That Hans's unconscious awareness of the cause of his exhaustion is a source of shame to him can be seen in the description of blushing everytime he mentions his tiredness, for, as Gershen Kaufman puts it, "[b]lushing[...]only compounds shame, causing one even to feel ashamed of shame" (1989: 18). Hans thus has a secret that lies at the core of his being, a secret that, in disguise, begins to invade his dreams.

    Clavdia's characteristic door-slamming invasion of the place in which Hans eats and drinks to satisfy his nursing need announces the "irruption" of the repressed. On her third appearance, there is no mention that Hans is drinking his milk-substitute, so he is able to see the agent of his milk-deprivation, albeit with an infant's eyes. First he sees her in profile, as he would view her if his head were being cradled below one of her breasts. Later he sees that her cheek-bones are broad and her eyes narrow, as both features would appear if he were gazing up at her. Responding to her only as a part-object, he concentrates on her stumpy fingers, "primitive and childish", teat-like, then further concentrating on them as objects associated with the mouth. Little wonder that Clavdia evokes a "vague memory".

    In the next chapter Hans takes in garden goings-on below his loggia, just as if he were a moviegoer. Appropriately, since it is adjacent to a sanatorium, the garden boasts a defiant banner: "the caduceus lifted itself now and again in a breath of wind" (78). Consisting of two serpents twined around a winged staff, the caduceus, now thought to represent the attribute of Asklepios, the Greek god of medicine and of healing, is an honorable symbol of the medical profession (Evans 1981: 14), but its original meaning in the East caused it to be associated with Hermes, the god of the phallus, when it entered the Greek imagination (Rose 1959: 145). Both meanings hover over the scene as Herr Albin thrills a flock of "silly geese" (79) with *double-entendre* about his "knife" and "revolver". In so doing, he reveals that the garden is infused with a phallic atmosphere, but then the honorific "caduceus" is revealed, ironically, when he announces that his case is hopeless and that when the time comes he will use his revolver on himself (80-81). Thus Herr Albin, like "Tous-les-doux" before him, reveals that the garden is home for fatality as well as fertility. But

Hans is far from ready to see that his movie will end exactly as Herr Albin's, thinking only that Herr Albin must be "finally relieved of the burden of a respectable life and made free of the infinite realms of shame" (81). Now, everytime he sees Clavdia, Hans is reminded of something or someone, but he cannot remember what or whom (84, 87). At the same time, he discovers that his post-meal cigar has lost its savor (88).

Thus he is out of sorts at bedtime, all the more so for having to listen to the wrestling Russians (90). When sleep comes, he dreams of borrowing a lead pencil from Clavdia—and is jarred into wakefulness because he immediately realizes the significance of his dream and wants to fix it in his memory. Then he dozes off, to dream again, of fleeing from Dr. Krokowski, who wants to psychoanalyze him. Continuing his dream, Hans is so terrified that he runs into the garden, there attempts to climb "the red-brown flagstaff" (21). Whether the pole suggests a papilla or a penis makes no difference, for to Hans they are the same. After a succession of other dreams, he ends his midnight movie by twice dreaming that in the dining-hall Clavdia "glides noiselessly" over to him, extends the palm of her hand not occupied by teasing her hair, which he kisses, all the while aware of its stumpy fingers, feeling "himself free of the burden of a good name, and tast[ing] the boundless joys of shame" (92). To a heterosexual male the extending of the female palm could be taken as an invitation to paddle it, but to Hans the palm-up extension probably only intensifies his awareness of the projecting fingers, his need of them, hence his shame.

On his fifth day at the sanatorium, Hans once again notices Clavdia's glide into the dining-hall (110), but even though she is all dressed up for Sunday, he is not noticeably distracted by her appearance. The reason becomes apparent:

> Hans Castorp was smoking with his dark beer, which he had brought out from breakfast. From time to time his cigar gave him a little pleasure. Rendered torpid, as often, by the beer and the music [a band is playing on the terrace], he sat with his head on one side and his mouth slightly open. (111-12)

In his satiated condition Hans cannot follow Settembrini's argument that while music "quickens us to the finest enjoyment of time" it, as a private indulgence, "dulls us, sends us to sleep, works against action and progress" (114). Predictably, Hans is drowsy the remainder of the day, his condition aggravated by Clavdia's absence on an outing and by Sunday-sumptuous meals and beer.

The next day Dr. Krokowski is to deliver his semimonthly lecture on the "general title: 'Love as a force contributory to disease'" (116). But before the lecture, feeling the need for fresh air, Hans goes for a solitary walk. As he walks, he sings until he is thoroughly exhausted (118). He comes to a "small enclosed landscape before him, a scene composed of elements both peaceful and sublime", featuring a mountain waterfall. Outstanding is a mighty fir, which "thrust[s] itself aslant into the picture, with bizarre effect". Hans crosses a footbridge, with a mind to rest on a bench and listen to the rushing waterfall, a music that he loves perhaps even more than music itself (119). Now under the influence of the Medusa archetype, Hans responds to the scene as an archaic Greek, who, according to Motte, associated "gardens, meadows, and fields" with "female sexuality or the maternal genitals" (qtd. in Caldwell 1989:158). "The Greek word *pedion*, as in *Elysion pedion* (Homer's 'Elysian field'), means both 'plain, field' and '(sexually mature, i.e., maternal) feminine genitals'" (Caldwell 1989: 158). Given the total picture and certain of its parts, *slanting fir, rushing waterfall*, and *footbridge*, Hans is in both a genital and a transitional environment. A sudden, persistent nosebleed, forcing him to lie supine on the bench for thirty minutes, indicates a change of state as absolute as a deflowering. Suddenly he recalls his dream of borrowing a pencil from Clavdia, then an even earlier memory, of an event which occurred when he was thirteen. Hans had become infatuated with a boy of his own age, but a year advanced in their school, Pribislav Hippe (120). Struck by his "Kirghiz" eyes, "prominent cheek-bones", and "pleasantly husky voice", Hans had silently watched Hippe from afar, until one day he asked to borrow a pencil; keeping it only for a period, Hans sharpened "the pencil a little, and cherished three of the red shavings nearly a year, in an inner drawer of his desk—no one seeing them would have guessed what significance they possessed" (123). Hans returned the pencil, and Hippe soon moved away, and after a while Hans repressed the incident. At that early age Hans was already under Medusa's domination, for Hippe's name echoes *hippos,* Greek for 'horse', and "the earliest stratum [of the Medusa myth] connects her with the horse" (Baring 1993: 342). Blood will tell, if that observation may be applied to mythic creatures: Chauchat as Medusa is the mother of Hippe as Pegasus. When Hans responds unconsciously to the Hippe facial features that Clavdia displays, therefore, he is subjected to a second irruption of the repressed. The facial features of both unconsciously remind Hans of his mother (and Mann of his mother: Heilbut notes that Mann's brother Heinrich remembered that their mother had "deep, emotive eyes and imposing cheekbones" [1996:10]). Hans "was penerated by the unconscious conviction that an inward good of this sort [i.e., his borrowing of the pencil] was above all to be guarded from definition and classification" (121). Probably his act of censorship is explained by Freud:

> No one will feel inclined to dispute, I think, that the mucous membrane of the lips and mouth is to be regarded as a primary 'erotogenic zone', since it preserves this earlier significance in the act of kissing, which is looked upon as normal. An intense activity of this erotogenic zone at an early age thus determines the subsequent presence of a somatic compliance on the part of the tract of mucous membrane which begins at the lips. Thus, at a time when the sexual object proper, that is, the male organ, has already become known, circumstances may arise which once more increase the excitation of the oral zone, whose erotogenic character has, as we have seen, been retained. It then needs very little creative power to substitute the sexual object of the moment (the penis) for the original object (the nipple) or for the finger which does duty for it, and to place the current sexual object in the situation in which gratification was originally obtained. So we see that this excessively repulsive and perverted phantasy of sucking at a penis has the most innocent origin. It is a new version of what may be described as a prehistoric impression of sucking at the mother's or nurse's breast. ("Fragment" 52)

Hans had thus requested from Hippe a pencil in place of a penis, which, in turn, would have been in place of a nipple. Then, his "phantasy of sucking" failing to give him relief, he had, as Freud puts it, "a powerful motive for drinking and smoking" (*Three* 182). Those substitutes served him well until, leaving Hamburg to return to the breast of the magic mountain, the locus of both oral regression and the new psychoanalysis which forefronted its significance, he saw Clavdia's stumpy Medusan fingers and lost his taste for cigars.

Hans barely makes it back before the lecture begins, is annoyed to find that he is sitting behind Clavdia, especial so when she turns to stare at the blood on his coat (125). At first Hans is so offended by Clavdia's bad posture— "drooping shoulders and round back; she even thrust her head forward until the vertebra at the back of the neck showed prominently"—that he does not pay attention to the lecture. When he does begin to listen, he is annoyed at what he hears:

> In particular the speaker employed the word love in a somewhat ambiguous sense, so that you were never quite sure where you were with it, or whether he had reference to its sacred or its passionate and fleshly aspect—and this doubt gave one a slightly seasick feeling. Never in his life had Hans Castorp heard the word

uttered so many times on end as he was hearing it now. When he reflected, it seemed to him he had never taken it in his own mouth, nor ever heard it from a stranger's. That might not be the case, but whether it were or no, the word did not seem to him to repay such frequent repetition. The slippery monosyllable, with its lingual and labial, and the bleating vowel between [*Liebe, leeb^e*]--it came to sound positively offensive; it suggested watered milk, or anything else that was pale and insipid; the more so considering the meat for strong men Dr. Krokowski was in fact serving up. For it was plain that when one set about it like that, one could go pretty far without shocking anybody. He was not content to allude, with exquisite tact, to certain matters which are known to everybody, but which most people are content to pass over in silence. He demolished illusions, he was ruthlessly enlightened, he relentlessly destroyed all faith in the dignity of silver hairs and the innocence of the suckling babe. (126-27)

Hans's silent rumination clearly reveals that his conception of love is solely that of a private oral activity, nursing the breast (though the idea of fellatio threatens to break into consciousness). Indeed, for Hans, the difference between the mucous experience of love and the mouthing of the word *love* is the difference between whole milk and watered milk. While he obviously understands that human beings are copulating animals, he is so bound up in the dyadic relation with the original object that his very limited view of what goes on in the outer world is seen merely as a reflection of his inner world. How can he retain "the innocence of a suckling babe" in the presence of such psychoanalytic twaddle?

For all his alleged ambiguity in the early part of his lecture, Dr. Krokowski develops his thesis with admirable precision:

the two opposing groups of instincts—the compulsive force of love, and the sum of the impulses urging in the other direction, among which he would particularly mention shame and disgust— both exhibited an extraordinary and abnormal height and intensity when measured by the ordinary bourgeois standards; and the conflict between them which took place in the abysses of the soul prevented the erring instinct from attaining to that safe, sheltered, and civilized state which alone could resolve its difficulties in the prescribed harmonies of the love-life as experienced by the average human being. This conflict between the powers of love and chastity—for that was what it really amounted to—what was its issue? It ended, apparently, in the triumph of chastity. Love was suppressed, held in darkness and chains, by fear, conventionality, aversion, or a tremulous yearning to be pure. Her confused and tumultuous claims were never allowed to rise to consciousness or to come to proof in anything like their entire strength or multiformity. But this triumph of chastity was only an apparent, a pyrrhic victory; for the claims of love could not be crippled or enforced by any such means. The love thus suppressed was not dead; it lived, it laboured after fulfilment in the darkest and secretest depths of the being. It would break through the ban of chastity, it would emerge—if in a form so altered as to be unrecognizable. But what then was this form, this mask, in which suppressed, unchartered love would reappear?[...] And Dr. Krokowski answered his own question, and said: "In the form of illness. Symptoms of disease are nothing but a disguised manifestation of the power of love; and all disease is only love transformed." (127-28)

Dr. Krokowski then concludes with a fervent invitation to all assembled to make a commitment to the new faith. Tired from his walk and incapable of understanding much of the lecture because of naïveté (128-29) or repression, Hans dismisses it by concluding, "Thank God I am healthy, that business has nothing to do with me" (130). When he joins his cousin Joachim—whose condition has just been thoroughly diagnosed by the lecture—they silently agree to "let the subject rest, both then and thereafter" (131).

With the start of his second week, Hans is aware that his nerves are being affected by Clavdia's presence (135). Yet he cannot keep his eyes off her, and, aware of his weakness, she seems to take pleasure in staring him down (142-43). He is thrilled to hear her speaking his "mother-tongue" (144), even though she does not speak German well. In addition, he comes to realize that her face "had been familiar to him as long as he could remember, and spoke to his very soul as nothing else could in all the world" (146). But since he has not made her acquaintance, he is happy to notice, in his third and—supposedly—final week, that his post-meal cigar has "regained a little of its savour" (152), perhaps in anticipation of Hans's return to total dependence on his Maria for buccal stimulation.

Unfortunately, Hans still gets an occasional nosebleed and a flushed face, and now a cold. A newly-purchased thermometer indicates that he is running a temperature (168), so that he is examined by Hofrat Behrens—called by the humanist Settembrini "Rhadamanthus" (195), presumably because in Greek myth he, as the lord of the Elysian field, judges the dead, newly arrived from points above (Rose 1959: 84). The examination reveals that Hans has long had tuberculosis (181); Hofrat Behrens tells Hans that he had "made a pretty shrewd guess that you were one of us" (180). As Hans departs to begin "a couple of week's" absolute bed rest, a smiling Dr. Krokowski shakes him "warmly by the hand" (182) for, according to the psychoanalyst's belief, Hans's tuberculosis is proof that he suffers from "love transformed" (128). If the psychological disease is cured by "the redeeming power of the analytic" therapy (130), then its physiological corollary will disappear.

After three weeks of bed rest have sped by, Hans returns to ambulatory status. During those three weeks Hans convinces himself that he is "in love" with Clavdia (205), so that when he returns to the dining-room he is even more her fascinated observer than before. Love-sick, he learns of rivals: there is a "male visitor" from down at the Platz whom Clavdia is said to entertain in the afternoon (207); there is an ethereal young patient—a Mannheimer (210), his "home-sickness" diagnosed by the name of his home town—who plays on the piano "the wedding march from *Midsummer Night's Dream"* every evening as he moons over Clavdia (209); and there is Hofrat Behrens, for whom Clavdia exhibits her body daily as he paints her portrait (208).

When Hans finally goes for his x-ray examination, he is surprised by Clavdia's sudden appearance: "Hans Castorp recognized her, staring-eyed, and distinctly felt the blood leave his cheeks. His jaw relaxed, his mouth was on the point of falling open" (211). Thus he reveals her effect on him both as Medusa-archetype and as mother figure. His veiled observation unwittingly reveals certain serpentine features that he had not before noticed:

> Frau Chauchat had crossed one leg over the other again, and her knee, even the whole slender line of the thigh, showed beneath the blue skirt. She was only of middle height[...]but relatively long-legged and narrow in the hips. She sat leaning forward, with her crossed forearms supported on her knee, her shoulders drooping, and her back rounded, so that the neck-bone stuck out prominently, and nearly the whole spine was marked out under the close-fitting sweater. (213)

Hans and Joachim are called into the examination room-underworld, where Behrens-Rhadamanthus calls the former "Castor" and the latter "Pollux" (214), linking them with the myth of the Dioscouri, "the striplings of Zeus" (E. Hamilton 1942: 41). As such they mythically appear riding white horses, serving the sea-god Poseidon (E. Hamilton 1942: 42). Although the devoted twin brothers were divine, they were also mortal, so that when Castor was killed, Pollux pleaded with their father Zeus to let his brother and himself continue to share existence. Zeus satisfied the plea by the ruling that they would alternate days

between "upper air, and under the earth" (Graves 1957: vol. 1, 248). As
expected, the examinations confirm that the cousins have active cases,
but the effect of seeing the skeleton and organs beneath the skin has a
memorable impact on Hans: "for the first time in his life he understood that he
would die. At the thought there came over his face the expression it usually wore
when he listened to music: a little dull, sleepy, and pious, his mouth half open, his
head inclined toward the shoulder" (219). His reaction to death, as to music,
is identical to his reaction to oral satiation.

Clavdia's x-ray examination following Hans's offers him an
opportunity to think *post hoc, ergo propter hoc*. Her naked breast will
press the same glass as his naked breast; thus their naked breasts will
be joined. Further, since the plates produced by the x-rays reveal their
interior bodies, they will be joined subcutaneously. Thus Hans can
indulge in the fantasy that he and Clavdia share a common skin
containing a fused body, the skin-ego fantasy described earlier by
Anzieu (cf. ch1n7).

One beautiful October afternoon, Hans and Joachim sit
silently in the garden, Hans with his cigar "between his lips, precisely in the
centre of his mouth, and drooping a little" (252). They are joined by Hofrat
Behrens, also enjoying his postprandial puff. Each displaying a cigar
taken from his case, the smokers compare: Hans's "brown beauty" (253)
and Behrens' "very black one" (252). Hans praises Maria Mancini,
"medium mixture, very fragrant, but cool on the tongue", while Behrens praises,
"St. Felix, Brazil",

> [t]emperament, you know, juicy, got some guts to it[...,]burns like
> brandy, has something fulminating toward the end. But you need
> to exercise a little caution—can't light one from the other, you
> know—more than a fellow can stand. However, better one good
> mouthful than any amount of nibbles.

Then

> [t]hey twirled their respective offerings between their fingers, felt
> connoisseur-like the slender shapes that possessed, or so one
> might think, some organic quality of life, with their ribs formed
> by the diagonal parallel edges of the raised, here and there porous
> wrapper, the exposed veins that seemed to pulsate, the small
> inequalities of the skin, the play of light on planes and edges.

But it becomes obvious that each cigar-lover is unconsciously
reminded of a different slender shape. Hans remembers putting "Maria
in an air-tight tin box, to protect her from damp. Would you believe it, she died!
Inside of a week she perished—nothing but leathery corpses left" (253). Like the

shavings of Hippe's pencil that Hans had forgotten, Maria in a box, another nipple replacement, loses her vitality if hermetically sealed (as he wants everything to be). But Behrens, in discussing the sensation of smoking, likens it—and male orgasm—to "simply dissolving with felicity" (254). Since St. *Felix* and *felicity* arc cognate, Behrens is reminded of his postcoital penis by his cigar stub, neither of which can be lighted "one from the other".

Since Hans is, at that moment, experiencing *Sehnsucht*, he suddenly asks Behrens if he and Joachim might see his paintings some time. So flattered is Behrens that he invites them at once to take coffee in his quarters. There, Hans pretends an interest in the collection, but discreetly searches for Clavdia's portrait. It is not a skillful painting, as Behrens himself admits; he thinks that he tried so hard on every detail that he "botch[ed] the ensemble" (257). Behrens is proud of his rendering of the "epicanthus, a racial variation" (257)--which gives Clavdia's eyes their distinctive appearance—and of her skin. Hans is indifferent to the "ensemble", thrilled to study the skin closely:

> The pale shimmer of this tender, though not emaciated, bosom, losing itself in the bluish shadows of the drapery, was very like life. It was obviously painted with feeling; a sort of sweetness emanated from it, yet the artist had been successful in giving it a scientific realism and precision as well. The roughness of the canvas texture, showing through the paint, had been dexterously employed to suggest the natural unevennesses of the skin—this especially in the neighbourhood of the delicate collar-bones. A tiny mole, at the point where the breasts began to divide, had been done with care, and on their rounding surfaces one thought to trace the delicate blue veins. It was as though a scarcely perceptible shiver of sensibility beneath the eye of the beholder were passing over this nude flesh, as though one might see the perspiration, the invisible vapour which the life beneath threw off; as though, were one to press one's lips upon this surface, one might perceive, not the smell of paint and fixative, but the odour of the human body.

These impressions the narrator attributes to Hans, adding that "he, of course, was in a peculiarly susceptible state" (258). The impressions indicate the associated sensations of an infant at breast—or of a voyeur. When Behrens dilates upon the subdermal properties of Clavdia's "birthday suit" (259), Hans reponds with a delirious "harangue" (260). Then he abruptly confesses that as a youth he painted nothing but pictures of ships and water, revealing his association of the nursing environment with the "oceanic feeling". All the while, without being conscious of his action, he carries the painting with him, prompting Behrens' question, "Hullo, where are you going with the ham?" (261). Behrens' rude description of Clavdia could be inspired by his Rhadamanthus knowledge that she, as Medusa, was the daughter of Phorkys and his sister Keto, a sea-monster (Rose 1959: 27, 29) and therefore one of the Gorgons, who were known as the Phorcids, 'sow's children' (Graves 1957: vol. 1, 127). Medusa was, in her earliest appearance, a goddess, in Joseph Campbell's words, of "the lunar-serpent-pig context" (qtd. in Baring 1993: 341). Or Behrens may simply have insulted Clavdia because he was at the moment discussing the significance of fat, "the upholstering, you know, full of oil ducts, the underpinning of the lovely female form" (259). Dimly, Hans responds, "And the plasticity of the female form—so that is fat, is it?" Behrens may conclude that Hans is making a goddess out of Clavdia, for he rather snappishly replies, "That is fat[...]. Did you think it was ambrosia?" (261).

All the while Behrens has been brewing the coffee. As Hans idly looks at the coffee mill and service, "Indian or Persian", he suddenly perceives that all pieces have a pornographic design and blushes "unawares" (262). In the face of such rampant genitality, Hans seeks security by gazing at Clavdia's portrait and asking Behrens to tell him more about skin. Undeterred from his project of dragging Hans from the oral to the genital phase, Behrens discusses the contractions and expansions of the sensory sheath, especially the latter: "How the cock really swells his comb, or any of the other well-known instances come about, is still a mystery, particularly where it is a question of emotional influences in play" (263). Obviously, this is pre-Viagra medicine. Remaining an immovable object, Hans wants to hear more about the lymphatic system (264). Behrens cannot resist lecturing:

> People talk about the blood, and the mysteries of its composition, and what an extraordinary fluid it is. But it is the lymph that is the juice of juices, the very essence, you understand, ichor, blood-milk, *crème de la crème*; as a matter of fact, after a fatty diet it does look like milk.

Behrens describes the entire system; what Hans notes is one detail, "[t]he flow of the breast milk". Back at the beginning of things, Hans wants to know an ultimate answer: "What is the flesh? What is the physical being of man?" (265) Again, Behrens cannot resist explaining—in this case, that both living and dying are processes of oxidation—but in so doing, becomes "melancholy" (267), absolutely devoid of the felicity that he had earlier praised, perhaps melancholy with the knowledge that art transcends reality when it depicts eternal tumescence. As he excuses himself (267), it is obvious that a would-be father figure has utterly failed to convince Hans to switch from the Maria Mancini to the St. Felix. Indeed, the St. Felix appears to have burned out—with no fulmination toward the end.

Hans spends the next several months trying to learn the secret of life from textbooks, while around him other patients are participating in the secret of dying. Although he seldom thinks of Clavdia, she must always be on his mind, for he seems to realize that her person somehow encompasses both great secrets. His long-desired introduction to her occurs at the carnival on Shrove Tuesday, *Fasching*. The situating of the meeting on the holiday we know as *Mardi Gras* is a clue to the substance of the meeting, but the meaning of the clue is not that the meeting will be characterized by release from the rules of the flesh, but by its contrary: *carnival* derives from "the Old Italian *carne,* meaning 'flesh', and *levare*, 'to take away'" (Bethel 1951: 89). In other words Hans does not evolve to the genital phase with Clavdia, but deepens his fixation to the maternal-Medusa figure.

The chapter that culminates in the *tête-à-tête* between Hans and Clavdia is entitled "Walpurgis-Night". By his reference to Goethe's scene "Walpurgis-Night", in *Faust*, Part One, Mann all but announces that Hans is to consort with witches. Settembrini, the humanist, Hans's would-be Virgil (59, 62), had soon advised Hans, his could-be Dante, to leave the Berghof immediately (86-87). Since, however, Hans will not turn back, Settembrini hopes to educate him to an awareness of his danger. A few days before *Mardi Gras*, then, he begins his campaign to warn Hans of the upcoming revelry. When Hans asks "what it would be like", Settembrini replies, "Every bit as lively as it is in the Prater", quoting from *Faust* (Goethe 1932: line 4211). The saliency of his reference to the park in Vienna is that it immediately follows Mephistopheles' warning to Faust about the girl who looks like Gretchen:

> It is a magic image, lifeless eidolon.
> It is not well to meet that anywhere;
> Man's blood grows frigid from that rigid stare;
> And he is turned almost to stone.
> The story of Medusa you of course have known.
> (Goethe 1932: lines 4190-94)

In like manner, Settembrini implies the Chauchat who reminds Hans's unconscious of mother is really Medusa.

On Shrove Tuesday, the presence of Medusa is announced by midday, when paper snakes are launched in the dining-hall (323). By the evening meal paper snakes hang down from the chandeliers (324). Offered champagne mixed with burgundy by devilish Lawyer Einhuf—'one-hoof'—Hans swallows that devil of a drink. Settembrini counters the offer by another advisory quote from *Faust* (Goethe 1932: lines 3868-70):

> But mind, the mountain's magic-mad to-night,
> And if you choose a will-o'-the-wisp to light
> Your path, take care, 'twill lead you all astray.
> (324)

Hans would have essayed a reply, but found that he had no pencil. Nor, indeed, do his tablemates, so he looks toward Clavdia, only to be distracted from his purpose by her "special toilet" (325), which Ezergailis describes as a "serpentlike gown" (1975: 35). At this point Mann borrows from "Little Herr Friedemann". Chauchat's gown shows no Rinnlingen cleavage, but "it left free to the shoulder Clavdia's arms, so tender and yet so full, so cool, so amazingly white, set off against the dark silk of her frock, with such ravishing effect that it made Hans Castorp close his eyes, and murmur within himself: 'O my God!'" Like Friedemann a fetisher of arms, Hans is ready to nurse: "The utter, accentuated, blinding nudity of these arms, these splendid members of an infected organism, was an experience so intoxicating[...]as to leave our young man no other recourse than again, with drooping head, to whisper, soundlessly: 'O my God!'" (325).

The devilish drink is having its effect on the assembly, so the coffee-drinking Settembrini moves over to sit beside Hans. There he attempts once again to educate Hans by referring to Goethe's "Walpurgis-Night": "'The Harz,'[...]'Near Schierke and Elend'. Did I exaggerate, Engineer? Here's a bedlam for you!" (326) Many of the revelers have disappeared, to return in cross-dressing masquerade. When Frau Stöhr reappears "as a charwoman, with skirt looped up" the sight prompts Settembrini to think of mythic, skirt-looping Baubo, "the old woman who consoled Demeter after the abduction of Persephone, by showing her genitalia on which was drawn the laughing face of the child Iacchus" (Dumoulié 1995: 786). Then Settembrini recalls that *Faust* offers a different description of Baubo, for he quotes its first line: "See beldam Baubo riding now" (Goethe 1932: line 3962). Settembrini also gives "the next line too, in his clear and 'plastic' delivery", but Mann does not quote it: "She's riding upon a farrow-sow" (Goethe 1932: line 3963). Nor does Mann allow Settembrini to quote Goethe's follow-up lines:

> So honour to whom honour is due!
> Dame Baubo 'fore! to lead the crew!
> A sturdy sow with mother astride,
> All witches follow in a tide.
> (Goethe 1932: lines 3964-67)

As Lubell notes, there are two distinct representations of Baubo, the "scandalous old crone" found in the myth and the scandalously nude sow-riding young woman with exposed "sacred vulva" found on terra cotta statuettes (1994: 105). Taking note of "the ancient, acknowledged kinship of Baubo to Medusa" (1994: 35), Lubell sees Medusa as an intermediary representation in the progression from the earlier literary Baubo to the later Baubo dolls, nymphet legs surmounted only by a head whose facial features are vulviform (1994: 105). While Goethe would have learned Baubo's connection with Demeter from mythic sources, he discovered Baubo's connection with a pig in an Italian museum during his journey of 1786-1788, so Lubell speculates (1994: 122). The plausibility of Lubell's speculation is greatly increased by the fact that Goethe developed a lasting attraction to the Medusa mask in that same period (Trevelyan 1981: 140). (Mann probably got his information on Baubo from Nietzsche [Dumoulié 1995: 786], as well as from Goethe.)

Frau Stöhr is certainly no seductive feminine principle, so Settembrini is using her as an example to warn Hans of the snaky charms of Frau Chauchat. Even so, Frau Stöhr is sufficiently literary to know that she has been insulted, and she retaliates by calling Settembrini a "turkey-cock", addressing him "with the thou"! This violation of convention, more than her retort, gets Settembrini's goat, and he is about to reply when Chauchat returns, having added only "a simple cocked hat of white paper" (327) in tribute to the occasion. Immediately Settembrini warns Hans that Clavdia is "Lilith", but that citation from *Faust* (Goethe 1932: line 4117) is lost on Hans, who replies, "Dear me, you're full of poetry to-night. What Lily do you mean? Did Adam marry more than once? I didn't know it". Settembrini identifies her as "Adam's first wife", adding: "According to the Hebraic mythus, Lilith became a night-tripping fairy, a 'belle dame sans merci,' dangerous to young men especially, on account of her beautiful tresses" (327). Here he cribs Mephistopheles' warning to Faust:

> That lovely hair of hers, that ornament
> With which she shines preëminent!
> When by that means she can a youth obtain,

She does not soon let him go free again.
(Goethe 1932: lines 4119-23)

Settembrini could have added that Lilith was the personification of the snake as the "feminine principle" (Cirlot 1962: 273).

When Settembrini continues his pedagogy, Hans, who is getting tipsy, lets him know that he will no longer be his "delicate child of life" (329). Then he coolly suggests that they join the others. Perhaps Hans thus precludes Settembrini's use of Mephistopheles' reference to Medusa in *Faust,* previously mentioned, when he warns Faust that the image of woman that he sees "seems to each as though his love were she" (Goethe 1932: line 4200). Faust thinks that the image is Gretchen, but he is really looking at a witch; Hans looks at the image of Clavdia, but what he sees as Mother is really Medusa.

Hofrat Behrens is serving punch. Incapable of resisting a commentary, Settembrini calls him "Herr Urian" (330), thus identifying him as "Sir Urian", the Devil in "Walpurgis Night" (Goethe 1932: line 3959). In *Faust* "Sir Urian" presides over the appearance of Baubo on the farrow-sow. Thus Behrens presides over a new diversion; with eyes closed and head thrown back he sketches a pig on the back of a visiting-card. As another would-be father, Behrens, like Settembrini, is warning Hans of the threat from Baubo-Medusa. Behrens has been to Italy, for he later shouts to Hans, "I'm not a pimp. I'm no Signor Amoroso on the Toledo, in *Napoli bella*" (419). But this pig signifies not; all the audience wants to do is to imitate Behrens' feat. All the while mindful that his present action is a repetition of his past action with Hippe, Hans, since he has no pencil, boldly walks up to Clavdia, using the second person singular to ask if he might use her pencil (332):

> *"Voilà,"* she said [as if performing magic], and held the toy by its end before his eyes, between thumb and forefinger, and lightly turned it to and fro.
> Since she thus both gave and withheld it, he took it, so to speak, without receiving it: that is, he held out his hand, with the fingers ready to grasp the delicate thing, but not actually touching it. His eyes—in their leaden sockets—went from the little object to Clavdia's Tartar physiognomy. His bloodless lips were open, and so remained,[...] (333)

Clavdia's behavior is suggestively maternal: she holds her pencil-nipple between thumb and forefinger, prepared to caress her infant's lips to initiate his sucking reflex. Hans's behavior is instinctively infantile: with mouth open, he waits for the nipple, at the same time shifting his gaze to his mother's face. Clavdia's face declares her Medusan threat; Hans's leaden eyes declare that the threat has had its impact.

Hans and Clavdia sit down facing one another, talking quietly as they watch the dancers (334). To Hans the whole scene is as a dream. Having succeeded in causing Hans's awakening to his need for the nipple, Clavdia tells Hans that she is to leave the magic mountain the next day (337). Hans asks if she is going home to Daghestan, in the Caucasus, where, it is rumored, she has a husband. Perhaps for a while, she replies. Her imminent departure causes him to become frantic. Eventually he declares himself: "'*Je t'aime*,' he babbled, '*je t'ai aimée de tout temps, car tu es le Toi de ma vie, mon rêve, mon sort, mon envie, mon éternel désir—*'". The verb *babbled* indicates the infantile inspiration of Hans's use of the verb "*aimer*". The noun "*envie*" confesses that he suffers from *Sehnsucht*. He is rewarded by a caress on the back of his head. "[B]eside himself at her touch, now on both his knees, with bowed head and closed eye", Hans makes his plea. Acknowledging the inseparability of the body, love, and death, he celebrates the body, which offers a home for love and death. He praises the "*symétrie merveilleuse de l'edifice humain*"(342), but, in his ardent condition, features those parts of the female body that receive erotic attention and provide life and nurture: "*les épaules et les hanches et les mamelons fleurissants de part et d'autre sur la poitrine, et les côtes arrangées par paires, et le nombril au milieu dans la mollesse du ventre, et le sexe obscur entre les cuisses!*" (342-43) Hans reveals his oral fixation by his positive description of the breast and by the ambiguous adjective that he attaches to the "*sexe*". That fixation is further revealed by his plea, "*Laisse-moi toucher dévotement de ma bouche l'Arteria femoralis*"[...] (343), the artery whose branches supply the external genitals (Thomas 1981: 1678). "He did not stir, or open his eyes; on his knees with bowed head, his hands holding the silver pencil outstretched before him, he remained, swaying and quivering".

With good reason, Clavdia replies, "*Tu es en effet un galant qui sait solliciter d'une manière profonde, à l'allemande*", implying, perhaps, that, given the widespread allegation about the lingual love-making of Frenchmen, Hans knows more French than he professes. She puts on his head the paper cap that she had had been wearing, "the kind one makes for children, a simple cocked hat of white paper" (326), "with its reddish braid wound round it like a wreath" (340-41)--a cavity guarded by a snake. Her action crowns him a child; her final words constitute a follow-up invitation:

> She slipped from her chair, and glided over the carpet to the door,
> where she paused an instant, framed in the doorway; half turned
> toward him, with one bare arm lifted high, her hand upon the
> hinge. Over her shoulder she said softly: *"N'oubliez pas de me
> rendre mon crayon"*. (343)

Ezergailis points out that Hans has associated Clavdia with a doorway
from his first breakfast (1975: 36-37), first as the intruder who came
crashing through it and then as its usher. Surely she knows what she
doing by lifting her fetishable arm as she issues her Mae West
invitation to Room Number 7.

     We do not know Hans's state of mind, but we may assume
that he does not toddle as he follows Clavdia to her room. There he
returns her pencil, receiving in return a

> keepsake, his treasure, that consisted, this time, not of a few
> reddish-brown shavings [from Hippe's pencil], but a thin glass
> plate, which must be held toward the light to see anything on it. It
> was Clavdia's x-ray portrait, showing not her face, but the
> delicate bony structure of the upper half of her body, and the
> organs of the thoracic cavity, surrounded by the pale, ghostlike
> envelope of flesh. (348)

The narrator reports that Clavdia had given Hans assurances that she
would return, "not during that reported conversation in the French tongue, but in a
later interval, wordless to our ears" (347). In the "later interval" the French
tongue may also have been used, for Hans later remembers, stimulated
by one of his numerous studies of Clavdia's x-ray, "that flesh which once,
in Carnival week, [he] had so madly tasted" (389). It is possible that the
rendition of his memory is not a euphemism for genital-to-genital
activity, but a factual description of cunnilingus or even nursing
activity. Tasting flesh during the period when "flesh is taken away" hardly
supports a genital interpretation.[5]

     With Clavdia gone from the Berghof, Hans becomes "very
dependent" upon his "Maria", but that cigar is so expensive that he asks
Behren to recommend a "domestic product". The request is really a ploy
to use his tongue with Behrens to talk about Clavdia. In response to
Hans's hints, Behrens assumes that he had had an ordinary genital
affair with Clavdia: "Pretty nice, what?" (352). Apparently his other
father figure, Settembrini, makes the same assumption, asking Hans:
"Well, Engineer, and how have you enjoyed the pomegranate?" Hans understands
neither the ancient likening of the pomegranate hemisphere to the

vulva nor the mythological account of the pomegranate's effect on Persephone (Rose 1959: 92) or Eurydice (Walker 1983: 806), a description explained by Settembrini: "Gods and mortals have been known to visit the nether world and find their way back again. But in that kingdom they know that he who tastes even once of its fruits belongs to them" (354). Settembrini is so convinced of Hans's copulation that he even imagines him condemned to "the second circle of the Inferno", the locus of those caught in carnality. But then, having reflected that his exaggeration is comical, Settembrini burlesques himself by saying that he swoons "out of sheer pity" and falls "'as a dead body falls'" (357), as Dante did after seeing the perforated pair Paola and Francesca (*Inferno* Canto 5 1950: 34).

   The "affair" with Clavdia has in no sense given Hans any peace, and, since he had once scoffed at psychoanalysis, it must be desperation that drives him to "Dr. Krokowski's analytic lair" (367). He is not, however, purged of his irrational thought processes. Pursuing a wide-angled education, he studies botany, but when he focuses on the ranunculus family of flowers, he is reminded by the columbine or aquilegia of the bench above the bridge where he had had his nosebleed a year before, a locale that he has since frequented many times. He is again drawn to the little stream that runs down from the Schatzalp, where he had "seen the apparition of Pribislav Hippe" (387) and where he now takes out the x-ray of another 'snowy-treasure-mountain' that he carries next to his breast, even as he remembers the flesh that he "had so madly tasted":

> What wonder his unstable heart stood still or wildly throbbed when he gazed at it, and then, to the sound of the rushing waters, leaning with crossed arms against the smooth back of his bench, his head inclined upon one shoulder, among the blossoming aquilegias, began to turn over everything in his mind! (389)

Hans remains on the magic mountain in the nursing position, awaiting the return of Clavdia (421), even though Behrens informs him that he is cured of tuberculosis, albeit he still runs a slight fever (419).

   When Joachim decides to forgo further treatment in order to join his regiment, Hans loses his confidant. But there remain two tablemates with whom he walks, the Anton Karlowitsch Ferge, "good-natured" as befitting one born in St. Petersburg, and the forlorn Mannheimer, Ferdinand Wehsal, whose pain is plainly in his name (Curme 1960: 412). Like Hans, Ferdinand has "poor teeth" and a passion for Clavdia and "since that carnival night" has "sought Hans Castorp's company" (427). Indeed Ferdinand even implores Hans to tell him what had taken place after the *mardi gras* festivities, and Hans Castorp had good-naturedly complied, without, as the reader may imagine, introducing any wanton or flippant element into his recital. Still, there seems every reason, on our part and on his, not to go into it very much, and we will only add that thereafter Wehsal carried his friend's overcoat with even more self-abnegation than before. (428)

Since Wehsal has the same oral desires as Hans, it may be concluded that his deference to Hans is an acknowledgement that at least Hans has an x-ray trophy, perhaps even had a taste of maternal *trophia*.

Although there are further diversions for Hans—the abruptly-curtailed visit of his uncle James Tienappel and the incessant wrangling between Leo Naphta and Ludivico Settembrini—he is preoccupied by his anticipation of Clavdia's return. With the onset of the snow season, his anticipation rises, for the white peaks of the Alps have always reminded his unconscious of the maternal breasts. Lying on his loggia, Hans loves the spectacle of the snow, likening it to the spectacle of the "sea-shore". But "walking in the snow was as toilsome as on the dunes"; so Hans decides to purchase skis, especially because he is "irresistibly drawn" to the mountains, before which, he thinks, his thinking and "stock-taking" will be clearer (473).

When Hans becomes skilled enough to reach the closest towering peak, "[t]here was no thunder of surf, a deathly stillness reigned, but roused similar feelings of awe" (475). The awe that Hans experiences is maternal awe, aroused by natural or constructed objects that evoke the memory of the mother, especially the mother's breasts (I. Harrison 1975: 181-95). So emboldened is Hans by this experience that he "went up on the funicular to the Schatzalp". In such an environment Hans feels a "religious awe" (476), a "pious awe": such scenes were "a fitting theatre" for the experience of the uncanny (477).

On a certain day Hans climbs higher and higher, "thrust[ing] the end of his stick in the snow and watching the blue light follow it out of the hole it made". The color emanating from the hole reminds him of the eyes of Hippe and Clavdia. As he proceeds, "his spirit heard behind him words of warning in a mellifluous tongue", such as Settembrini had used on carnival night. The snowy landscape is as beautiful as a breast. He is drawn to a "grove", whose trees stand "in a wedge-shaped group", the delta of Venus. He rests there to smoke a cigarette, proud of having reached "surroundings such as these" (479). But then, as he pushes on through dune-like scenery (480), passing a hut, he is caught in a snowstorm

(482), which must impress him as a dream screen . (Regressing to the breast and beyond is dangerous, perhaps even fatal.) Hans knows that if he simply goes downhill he will reach the Berghof, but he decides to press forward. Then, getting lost, he wastes what seems an hour going in a circle, for he again comes upon the hut in the gathering darkness. Significantly the hut, seemingly a shelter, is "barred, the door locked fast, no entrance possible" (487). (Although Hans has reached the pubic region in fantasy, he finds that it is unassailable, in reality. But frustration by reality only drives Hans once again into fantasy.) Hans decides to rest under its projecting roof and to take several swallows of port that he had brought with him—the fortified wine so-called because it is shipped from Oporto, Portugal—but surely he is soothed by the homonym of *port* derived from the Latin, 'a haven'. It has "an effect much like that of the Kulmbacher beer on the evening of his arrival at the Berghof" (488)--and like that, of course, of the *port*er that he had drunk in childhood, when he first felt the need of a haven. His nursing immediately fuddles him, so that he imagines that, on carnival night, he had returned to Clavdia *"son crayon",* not her pencil, but his, Hippe's. (That is to say, that he had relinquished his temptation to fantasize fellatio as a nursing activity, so to remain true to the nipple that he dreamed of receiving from her.) His acknowledgement, "That was the wrong way to go to work", may refer to his language activity or to his lingual activity. He corrects himself: "*'Son crayon!'* That means her pencil, not his pencil, in this case; you only say *son* because *crayon* is masculine. The rest is just a pretty feeble play on words" (489). But the play on words does not stop there: Hans had returned the son's *crayon* to his mother.

Leaning his head in the nursing position, he thinks he feels warmth from the hut's log wall, falling asleep to dream of a "park", "the homeland" (490). The scene changes to that of the strand of a southern sea—which he had never known, and "yet—he *remembered*"—behind which are mountains. The Arcadian scene is populated by boys active with the mastery of archery and horses and girls active with the mastery of music and dancing—most of both sexes are occupied in activities free of sexual connotation, but there are exceptions: "Pairs strolled along the beach, close and confiding, at the maiden's ear the lips of the youth".

The whole scene appears to be rendered pastoral by a "young goatherd, wearing perched on his brown curls a little hat with the brim turned up behind,[...]watching them from a height, one hand on his hip, the other holding the long staff on which he leaned" (492). But his environment and accouterments suggest otherwise. The "young goatherd" seems to owe his existence to a cluster of stones, as did the pre-Greek god Hermes (Suhr 1967: 70); then in Greek times the god was represented in the form of a Herma, a rectangular stone column, tapered at the bottom, sporting, about halfway up, his protruding phallus, and, above that, his bust (Rose 1959: 146). Two comparisons are significant: the "young goatherd" wears "a little hat with the brim turned up behind", just as Hermes wears a *petasos,* a broad-brimmed covering favored by travelers (Rose 1959: 145); and the "young goatherd" carries "a long staff on which he leaned", just as Hermes carries a herald's long *kerykeion,* now better known as a *caduceus* (Suhr 1967: 59). A contrast points to another Hermes-hint. The whole scene of "these children of the sun", as the narrator calls them (492), has left Hans thrilled; if anything, his emotions are heightened by the culmination of the scene. All the boys and girls pay homage to a young mother who sits

> pressing her breast with her forefinger to ease the flow of milk to her babe, glancing up from it to acknowledge with a smile the reverence paid her—this sight thrilled Hans Castorp's heart with something very close to ecstasy. He could not get his fill of looking, yet asked himself in concern whether he had a right, whether it was not punishable, for him, an outsider, to be a party to the sunshine and gracious loveliness of all these happy folk.

He is mindful of the *"theatophilia"* that is so prominent an aspect of his character. Thus "[h]e felt common, clumsy-booted. It seemed unscrupulous" (493). He is "clumsy-booted", while Hermes, the god of fertility, who inspired the whole scene, has "straps" on his boots (and often wings as well), "straps" that are the leafy remnants, Suhr believes, of his origin as a god of " tree and plant life in general" (1967: 61). In any event, Hans—all too mortal, too "common"—has been an observer of a prohibited, divine scene, and he feels guilt.

There is another, less exalted source of Hans's guilt. He is engaging in voyeurism: his desire to watch originates in his oral nostalgia, but it becomes contaminated by the genital drive, hence it becomes an activity that inspires a vague sense of guilt (Wurmser 1981: 147). Heilbut notes that Mann "found a postcard reproduction of Praxiteles' Hermes 'adorable'" (1996: 556) and asserts that he created "fictional Hermeses from Felix Krull and Tadzio to young Joseph" (1996: 557). Heilbut also notes that Mann kept Ludwig von Hofmann's oil painting *Die Quelle* in his successive studies from 1914 until his death, saying that, in Heilbut's words, "he was 'charmed' by the youthful physicality, and by Hofmann's 'arcadian fantasy of beauty'" (1996: 419, 419n). Heilbut convincingly asserts that Hofmann's painting "inspired the Arcadian scene in the chapter 'Snow'" (1996: 419), but he does not identify the "young goatherd" as a Hermes-figure or offer any other details in support of his assertion. The painting, "The Spring", or, figuratively, 'The Source', poses three naked young men, one of whom rests on his knees as he drinks from a spring, while the second, reclining above him, intently watches him drink—and watches the drinker watch him, and while the third, his torso bent forward nearly horizontal with his left thigh rampant because his left foot rests on a boulder, seems to be surreptitiously watching the drinker's buttocks. If the drinker has returned to the maternal source, then his buttocks have become the source of homosexual desire in the youth with the rampant thigh over the big stone.

In the "Snow" dream, Hans sees part of what is posed in the painting--a Peeping Tom becomes a peep show:

> A lovely boy, with full hair drawn sideways across his brow and falling on his temples, sat directly beneath him, apart from his companions, with arms folded on his breast—not sadly, not ill-naturedly, quite tranquilly on one side. This lad looked up, turned his gaze upward and looked at him, Hans Castorp, and his eyes went between the watcher and the scenes upon the strand, watching his watching, to and fro. But suddenly he looked past Hans Castorp into space, and that smile, common to them all, of polite and brotherly regard, disappeared in a moment from his lovely, purely cut, half-childish face. His brows did not darken, but in his gaze there came a solemnity that looked as though carven out of stone, inexpressive, unfathomable, a deathlike reserve, which gave the scarcely reassured Hans Castorp a thorough fright, not unaccompanied by a vague apprehension of its meaning. (493)

The "lovely boy" seems suddenly to have become a servant of Hermes the herald, directing a stare at Hans, in effect indicating that there will be no third boy with rampant thigh. This Hermes-figure has yet another aspect of Hermes, that of escort for those entering the underworld (as Naphta is to tell Hans [524]), which is where he is immediately headed. Here Mann follows Goethe, who pictures Faust's descent into the realm of the Mothers, where he experiences the "central Eleusinian mystery of death and resurrection" (Jantz 1969: 57). Looking past Hans, the boy reveals a new facial expression that frightens Hans, who looks in the same direction, to find an ancient architectural complex. What Hans sees is described in great detail:

Behind him rose towering columns, built of cylindrical blocks without bases, in the joinings of which moss had grown. They formed the façade of a temple gate, on whose foundations he was sitting, at the top of a double flight of steps with space between. Heavy of heart he rose, and, descending the stair on one side, passed through the high gate below, and along a flagged street, which soon brought him before other propylæa. He passed through these as well, and now stood facing the temple that lay before him, massy, weathered to a grey-green tone, on a foundation reached by a steep flight of steps. The broad brow of the temple rested on the capitals of powerful, almost stunted columns, tapered toward the top—sometimes a fluted block had been shoved out of line and projected a little in profile. Painfully, helping himself on with his hands and sighing for the growing oppression of his heart, Hans Castorp mounted the high steps and gained the grove of columns. It was very deep, he in it as among the trunks in a forest of beeches by the pale northern sea. He purposely avoided the centre, yet for all that slanted back again, and presently stood before a group of statuary, two female figures carved in stone, on a high base: mother and daughter, it seemed; one of them sitting, older than the other, more dignified, right goddesslike and mild, yet with mourning brows above the lightless eye-sockets; clad in a flowing tunic and a mantle of many folds, her matronly brow with its waves of hair covered with a veil. The other figure stood in the protecting embrace of the first, with round, youthful face, and arms and hands wound and hidden in the folds of the mantle. (493-94)

As Hans is led into a deeper stratum of his unconscious, he turns from maternal landscape imagery to specific imagery of the Good Mother. The mention of propylæa argues that Hans is envisioning Eleusis, whose complex of temples for the worship of the goddesses Demeter and Kore-Persephone was known throughout the ancient Mediterranean world for its porticos. Here I follow Lubich, who—himself following Wedekind-Schwertner—notes that "[d]ie Thomas-Mann Forschung hat wiederholt Castorps Schneevision mit der Demeter-Persephone Konfiguration in Verbindung gebracht[...]" (1993: 741). In a subsequent article Lubich also cites Mann's use of the Eleusinian Mysteries (1994: 113).

Mann would have, of course, been familiar with the myth of Demeter and Persephone from his childhood introduction to mythology, an introduction that he always associated with his mother. Perhaps his introduction to the Eleusian Mysteries which that myth inspired came from *Archäologische Beiträge zur Geschichte des eleusinischen Kults,* a 1904 doctoral thesis published by Heinz

Gerhard Pringsheim, a Bonn D. phil. in archaeology (Degener 1935: 1243). Pringsheim became his brother-in-law when Mann married his sister Katja in 1905. Katja later recorded that her brother's book had an honored place in the Pringsheim family mansion on Arcisstrasse (G. Mann 1990: 8-9). Mann also read Erwin Rohde's *Psyche*, in 1907, if not before (Lehnert 1964: 299), which treats the Mysteries and mentions the statue of Demeter and Persephone several times (Lehnert 1964: 303). It will be assumed here that Mann's knowledge of the Eleusian Mysteries was principally dependent on Rohde's interpretation of them, although much later scholarship by Karényi and Mylonas will be cited to identify the archeological phenomena in Mann's narrative.

Situated on a mount overlooking the sea, ancient Eleusis was connected with Athens, twelve miles east, by the Sacred Road. The Temple of Artemis of the Portals and of Father Poseidon—"in Arcadia , Artemis was the sister and Poseidon the father of Persephone" (Kerényi 1967: 70)--provides the entrance to the sacred precincts. Hans apparently begins his trek at that edifice, at the side of which gifts were left for the goddess of the underworld, Persephone (Kerényi 1967: 70). Then he walks up the flagged street to the Great Propylaia, passes through them to enter the Lesser Propylaia, walks through them to reach the interior rear wall. There, in ancient times, was a majestic doorway, ten feet wide and twenty feet high, on each side of which there stood the statue of a priestess bearing on her head the *cista mystica*, the "basket concealing the sacred utensils" of the Eleusinian rites (Keréyi 1967: 75). For the priestesses Mann substitutes "two female figures carved in stone, on a high base: mother and daughter, it seemed". Mylonas writes that

> [y]ears ago Otto Kern very ingeniously figured out that the cult statues of Eleusis represented a Demeter seated on her cylindrical kiste with Persephone standing by her side. He based his conclusion on reliefs from Eleusis on which the Goddesses are so represented, suggesting that they reflected the monumental cult group. Very important among the examples cited by him is the fragment illustrated in Figure 63. It is exhibited now against the east wall of the hall of the Museum of Eleusis. Demeter is seated on her kiste, dressed in chiton and peplos, with Persephone similarly clothed standing beside her. (1961: 190)

Mann's placement of the figures and description of their clothing argues that he is alluding to the statuary pictured in Mylonas' Figure 63, but if so, he takes artistic license in describing the statuary, for, lacking the heads of both goddesses, it is only a fragment of the original. Appropriately, Hans's vision has taken him back to Eleusis before it was destroyed by Alaric, king of the Goths, in 396 C. E. There can be no doubt that this "mother and daughter" are the divine Demeter and Kore, "the Maiden" (Kerényi 1967: 28) or, as she was later named when she was kidnapped to the Underworld, Persephone. The myth of these two goddesses was the story celebrated by the rites at Eleusis for nearly two thousand years. The ancient Greeks thought that Demeter and Kore-Persephone and the cult that they inspired came from Crete in Mycenaean times (1500 to 1100 B. C. E.). When her daughter Kore disappeared while gathering flowers, a grieving Demeter sought her all over the world. Since her personal concern caused her to neglect her cosmic concern—her divine matronage caused plant germination and maturation—all life was in danger of perishing by famine. After nine days, the Sun told Demeter that Hades was forcing her daughter to remain in the underworld as his wife. Since Hades, like Poseidon, is a brother of and cosmic co-regent with Zeus, Demeter suspected a royal conspiracy—especially since her daughter was sired by Zeus (Rose 1959: 91), whom Hades must have consulted beforehand. Looking for an entrance to the underworld, Demeter came to Eleusis. According to Kerényi,

> The name Eleusis[...]refers to the underworld in the favorable sense and may be translated as "the place of happy arrival." Grammatically, it is differentiated by accent and inflection from *eleusis,* "arrival," but, like it, is related, according to the rules of Greek vowel gradation, to Elysion, the realm of the blessed. (1967: 23).

It is worth repeating Caldwell's gloss offered earlier: "The Greek word *pedion*, as in *Elysion pedion* (Homer's 'Elysian field'), means both 'plain, field' and '(sexually mature, i.e., maternal) feminine genitals'" (1989: 158).

That the landscape was given a name evoking feminine genitality sheds light on the next incident in the story. Disguised as an old woman, Demeter sat down beside the Parthenion well, the 'virgin's well' (Kerényi 1967: 36), which lies immediately east of the Great Propylaia. While Demeter was resting there, the daughters of the local king, happening by, invited her to their home. Demeter was welcomed by their mother, Metaneira— 'she who lives among maidens' (Graves 1957: vol. 2,   400)--with her infant son at her breast (Kerényi 1967: 38). Metaneira offered Demcter a beaker of wine, which she declined, saying that if she drank it she would offend "the order of nature". Kerényi explains that she knew that the rape and abduction of her daughter had been perpetrated not by Hades but by Dionysos, the wine god; if she drank the wine she might appear to be countenancing his treatment of her daughter (1967: 40). Rather she requested *kykeon,* barley water flavored with mint; this drink would be true to the order of nature, for, according to Graves, Demeter means 'barley-mother' (1957:   vol. 2, 388). Because of this request, the drinking of the *kykeon* became an essential commemorative stage in the initiation of a follower of the Eleusinian cult, who had to avow: "I fasted: I drank the *kykeon*: I took from the chest: having performed (or 'handled' or 'dealt with'; the object is not specified) I put away into the basket and from the basket into the chest" (qtd. by Guthrie1951: xiii; parenthesis in orig.).

The sight of a mother nursing her baby must have deepened Demeter's grief, for the sadness of her expression struck the others present. Whereupon the serving maid Baubo—not upon her pig this time—heisted her skirt to parade her private parts, spraddled her legs and talked trash, and then humped around on the floor. She was being true to the order of her nature, for her name means 'belly' (Kerényi 1967: 40). Even a proper lady like Demeter could not help cracking up at such a promise that such actions insure the replacement of a lost child (Motz 1997: 131).

Perhaps it was Demeter's sudden lightness of mien that prompted Metaneira's proposal that her visitor become the nurse of her son, the infant Demophoön. Kerényi notes that the queen did not nurse her son (1967: 41), though he does not, like Rose (1959: 92), imply that Demeter became Demophoön's wet nurse. Rose records that Demeter, intending to immortalize him, salved the infant with ambrosia, but surely that action must be a mythic euphemism for breast-feeding him with ambrosia, the food of divinities and immortals, for an unguent containing ragweed, genus *Ambrosia,* would be allergenic. The description of Demeter's next action also seems euphemistic—each night she laid the infant in the fire to burn away his mortality (Rose 1959: 92)--but supports the speculation that she intended to immortalize him by giving him the divine breast. One does not have to be a Freud or a goddess to know that a well-nursed infant is confident of immortality. Metaneira was maternal, not mythic, for when she saw Demeter's bedtime routine she was horrified. Outraged by her immediate protest, Demeter pitched Demophoön to the ground (Rose 1959: 92), all the while informing the mother just whom she was dealing with: "Unknowing are ye mortals and thoughtless: ye know not whether good or evil approaches" (qtd. in Kerényi 1967: 41).

Still in divine dudgeon, Demeter demanded that a temple be built over the Parthenion well and that annual rites be conducted there to honor her intentions toward Demophoön. These rites were, presumably, the original Eleusinian Mysteries. The temple was built— very quickly—and Demeter took occupancy, vowing to continue the famine until Kore was returned to her. Zeus knew that something had to be done, so like any CEO he sent various underlings to Demeter to see if something might be worked out. To every argument or blandishment she was immune, insisting on her mother's right to talk with her daughter. Faced with an implacable parent, Zeus knew that his brother Hades had no choice but to release Kore, so he sent Hermes to Hades to fetch her. But before that speedster could get Kore into his chariot for the trip back, Hades got her to swallow a pomegranate seed. Demeter's joy at the return of her daughter was shadowed when she was told of Hades' trickery, for she suspected that some kind of deal had been struck. Her fear was borne out when Zeus sent his mother, Rhea, to tell her that each winter Kore would have to die for four months, before escaping Hades to revive in the spring (E Hamilton 1942: 52-53).

By this sequence of mythic events the simple ancient worship of the grain goddess developed into the mysterious religion celebrating the death and rebirth of her daughter. Presumably the statuary of the goddess and her daughter seen by Hans Castorp catches the moment when Demeter's jubilation at the return of her daughter is shaken by her realization that the life process is a lot more tortuous than she may have thought. Somehow Hans Castorp senses the same premonition; perhaps he remembers warning allusions offered him by Behrens and Settembrini. When Hans and Joachim had visited the Berghof clinic for an x-ray examination, Behrens had saluted them as "our Dioscuri, Castor and Pollux" (214), the twin brothers who, in one version of their myth, arranged to switch places daily, one in heaven and the other in the underworld (Rose 1959: 231). The privilege of living, Behrens could be saying, is inextricably linked to the fate of dying. He might even be saying more: since the Dioscuri were famous initiates to the Eleusian cult (Guthrie 1951: 286; Kerényi 1967: 257-59), Behrens might be prophesying the future of Hans and Joachim. And when Hans had viewed the portrait of Clavdia in Behrens' apartment, he had taken great interest in the "plasticity of the female form" resulting from the higher ratio of fat to total body mass in that sex.

The materialist Behrens provides a chemical analysis, "[p]almitin, stearin, olein", then asks, "Did you think it was ambrosia?" (261). He seems to be warning Hans that ingesting or getting smeared by Clavdia's ambrosia will not confer immortality upon him. Weeks after Walpurgis-Night, Settembrini, assuming that Hans Castorp had had carnal relations with Clavdia and had therefore entered *Elysion pedion* (and gotten involved with death), asks, "Well, Engineer, and how have you enjoyed the pomegranate?" (354). Given Settembrini's low opinion of Clavdia, he must think that her seduction of Hans, like Hades' trick with the pomegranate seed, confirms his fate.

Like a movie director, Mann, having used a process shot to follow Hans through the temple to the statuary, now uses a reaction shot: "Hans Castorp stood looking at the group, and from some dark cause his laden heart grew heavier still, and more oppressed with its weight of dread and anguish" (494). Assuming that Rohde's exhaustive interpretation provides the source of Mann's information about the Eleusinian Mysteries, then Hans's "dread and anguish" might result from his *intuition* that the Truth revealed through the agency of Demeter and Persephone offers little comfort. According to Rohde:

> many of our modern mythologists and historians of religion have been all the more eager to assert that the performances at the Eleusinian mysteries were in reality the true and mystic celebration of the Greek "Religion of Nature" as discovered by themselves. Demeter, in this view, would be the earth; Korê-Persephone, her daughter, the seed of corn; the Rape and Return of Korê would mean the sowing of the seed in the earth and rise of the young grain from beneath the soil; or, in a more general sense, "the yearly decay and renewal of vegetation." In some way or other the Mystai must have had revealed to them the real meaning of the "nature symbolism" hidden in the mystical performances. Witnessing these performances they are supposed to have learnt that the fate of the seed of corn, represented by Persephone, its disappearance beneath the earth and eventual rebirth, is an image of the fate of the human soul, which also disappears that it may live again. This, then, must be the real content of the holy Mystery. (1972: 223-24)

Offering several arguments to discredit the assertion of "our modern mythologists and historians of religion", Rohde concludes:

> we must not look to the Eleusinian mysteries for the ecstatic exaltation of the soul to the recognition of its own godhead— though such exaltation was the motive force and the essential core of Greek *mysticism,* as of all mysticism and mystic religion. From

the mysteries of Eleusis, however, it remained far removed; the belief there fostered, with its absolute division and distinction between the divine and the human, never transgressed the bounds of popular Greek religion, over whose portals stood the universally prescriptive words:[...] "the race of men is one, and the race of gods is another." Nor was Eleusis any exception to this rule: the mysteries did not point the way to mysticism. (1972: 225)

The cult statuary of Demeter and Persephone, then, does not evoke the promise of salvation for the soul that Hans seeks:

Scarcely daring to venture, but following an inner compulsion, he passed behind the statuary, and through the double row of columns beyond. The bronze door of the sanctuary stood open, and the poor soul's knees all but gave way beneath him at the sight within. Two grey old women, witchlike, with hanging breasts and dugs of finger-length, were busy there, between flaming braziers, most horribly. They were dismembering a child. In dreadful silence they tore it apart with their bare hands—Hans Castorp saw the bright hair blood-smeared—and cracked the tender bones between their jaws, their dreadful lips dripped blood. An icy coldness held him. He would have covered his eyes and fled, but could not. They at their gory business had already seen him, they shook their reeking fists and uttered curses— soundlessly, most vilely, with the last obscenity, and in the dialect of Hans Castorp's native Hamburg. (494)

Presumably this horrible sight occurs in the Telesterion, "so called because here the goal, the *telos,* was attained. *Teleo,* 'to initiate,' is derived from this noun, and *telete,* a general term for the celebration of mysteries or similar rites, is related to the same root" (Kerényi 1967: 47). Hans proceeds through a "double row of columns"—there were six rows of seven columns to support the roof (Kerényi 1967: 87). Thus he approaches the sanctuary, the Anaktoron, at whose single door is the throne of the Hierophant, "he who makes [the holy things] *appear*" (Kerényi 1967: 90; ital. in orig.).

There is no indisputable account of what the holy things were or of the impact their appearance had on the *mystai,* the initiates of Eleusian mysteries, for they were sworn to secrecy. But it is known that the "appearance" in the sanctuary occurred in absolute silence accompanied by very bright illumination (Papachadzis 1971: 93-94; Kerényi 1967: 91-92). These two phenomena accompany the "appearance" that Hans sees in the "sanctuary".

The universal message signified by the two witches would seem to be the exact opposite to that signified by Demeter and Persephone, child destruction as opposed to child protection. Seemingly, Hans has been forced to descend to yet a lower stratum of the unconscious, occupied by the Terrible Mother. And the vision is not only mythological but also deeply personal.[6] The longing that has always possessed Hans Castorp's unconscious has been of his infant self lying satiated on his mother's breast—paradise unlost. The vision that he now sees is of "hanging breasts and dugs of finger-length"—the paradise that never was. Moreover, rather than his active vision of consuming his mother, there is his passive vision of being consumed by the mother figure, the former a world-creation fantasy, the latter a world-destruction fantasy, each a product of the oral phase (Lewin 1946: 426-29). Lest there be any misunderstanding about the identity of this mother figure, doubled for emphasis and for ironic association with the Goddesses, she speaks the dialect of Hans Castorp's mother. And those "dugs of finger-length" ought to remind him of the warnings by Behrens and Settembrini about the Gorgon nature that Clavdia Chauchat dangles right down to her digits.

Now that he "sees" as an initiate, he would rather not: "He would have covered his eyes and fled, but could not". In consequence of his fixation at the oral phase, Hans has also revealed his fantasy of returning to the womb (Lewin 1946: 428). His very progress through the Eleusinian topography, *Elysion pedion*, must have awakened that fantasy. Now that he has reached the womb, though, he discovers that it is not a hermetic refuge, but a trap: "It made him sick, sick as never before" (494). Hans

> tried desperately to escape; knocked into a column with his shoulder—and found himself, with the sound of that dreadful whispered brawling still in his ears, still wrapped in the cold horror of it, lying by his hut, in the snow, learning against one arm, with his head upon it, his legs in their skis stretched out before him. (494)

In his struggle to escape the horrible womb, Hans nearly lodges against the pubic bone, but finally emerges into consciousness, his head having the whole time been inclined against the imagined warmth of the hut wall that reminded his unconscious of a bosom.

The only escape is to awaken, not only from his immediate dream but also the dream that has been his life. But "[i]t was no true awakening" (494). He continues to dream, "no longer in pictures, but in thoughts hardly less involved and fantastic". He reflects that the dream-vision has, paradoxically, given him "bliss and terror both at once":

> Now I know that it is not out of our single souls we dream. We dream anonymously and communally, if each after his fashion. The great soul of which we are a part may dream through us, in our manner of dreaming, its own secret dreams, of its youth, its hope, its joy and peace—and its blood-sacrifice. (495)

As Thirlwall points out, Hans here gives voice to the idea of the collective unconscious "which Freud suggested and which Jung developed" (1950: 292).

The "terror" that Hans has just experienced is understandable, especially since it is so personal. But if the "bliss" had been aroused by his earlier response to the statuary of the loving mother and reclaimed daughter, would it not have been dissipated by the vision of the dismembered child? The scene of "terror" caused Hans's experience of "bliss", even though Hans, typically, does not delve into his ambiguous reaction. Observations by Lehnert (1964: 301) and by Wedekind-Schwertner (1984: 332) that Mann studied closely the account of the "Dionysos cult" in Rohde's *Psyche* may point to a reason for Hans's "bliss".

Rohde's description of "The Eleusinian Mysteries", Chapter VI, is followed by a extended treatment of the "Dionysus cult", requiring. three chapters: "Origins of the Belief in Immortality", Chapter VIII, "Dionysiac Religion in Greece", Chapter IX, and "The Orphics", Chapter X. In Chapter VIII Rohde examines the origin of the worship of Dionysos Bakcheios among the Thracian tribes (1972: 256). These people learned that by frenzied dancing and ingestion of intoxicating drinks and fumes they could reach a state of "ekstasis" (1972: 259):

> There can be no doubt that the experiences and visions that their "ekstasis" gave them were regarded by them as the plainest and most literally real of facts. The belief in the existence and life of a second self distinct from the body and separable from it was already encouraged by the "experiences" and independent behaviour of that self in dreams and fainting fits. (1972: 264)

The cultists, mostly women, "raged wildly until every sense was wrought to the highest pitch of excitement, and in the 'sacred frenzy' they fell upon the beast selected as their victim and tore their captured prey limb from limb. Then with their teeth they seized the bleeding flesh and devoured it raw" (1972: 257). By such means the soul could temporarily escape the body to communicate directly with the god whose presence is in the victim beast (1972: 259).

According to Rohde the Thracians only planted the seed of "a mystical form of religion" (1972: 265). This seed grew to fruition when the Dionysos cult was transplanted to Greek culture, Rohde's subject in Chapter IX. There the frenetic behavior inspired by Dionysos-Bakcheios, "the Lord of Spirits and of the Souls of the dead", was submerged into the mellow rituals inspired by the native Dionysos, "the tender and delicate Wine-God" (1972: 285). Thus "the old Thracian Dionysos" became "Hellenized and humanized":

> Cities and states celebrated him in yearly festivals as the giver of the vine's inspiring fruit, as the daimonic patron of vegetation, and the whole of Nature's rich and flourishing growth. He was worshipped as the incarnation of all natural life and vigour in the fullest and widest sense[...]. (1972: 284-85)

But there were times when all the features of Bacchic frenzy, including human sacrifice, still intruded (1972: 285-86). And, through the influence of Thracian mysticism, a new phenomenon appeared, the "ecstatic prophet", the Sibyls and the Bakides (1972: 292):

> they resembled the Homeric omen-interpreters, and continued their work; but they differed from them profoundly in the mode of their prophesying. They were "seized by the god" and in ecstatic clairvoyance saw and proclaimed unseen things. It was no academic skill that they possessed, enabling them to interpret the meanings of signs and omens that anyone could see—they saw what was visible only to God and to the soul of man filled with God. (1972: 293)

In Chapter X, "The Orphics", Rohde traces the further evolution of Dionysos-worship: "A secondary wave of influence thus broke upon the long-since-Hellenized god, the Thracian Dionysos in Greece, and *this* wave the official worship either had not the power or lacked the will to assimilate" (1972: 336). Those devoted to the new influence participated in what Herodotos called "the 'Orphic and Bacchic' mysteries" (1972: 335). The story that was the heart of these mysteries concerned Dionysos-Zagreus, the son of Zeus and Persephone. As an infant Dionysos-Zagreus was attacked by the Titans, enemies of his father. He tried to escape by transforming himself into different animals, but he was finally caught in the form of a bull, was torn to pieces, was devoured. All but his heart, which was saved by Athena, who brought it to Zeus, who himself swallowed it. With bolts of lightning Zeus incinerated the Titans, the embodiment of evil. But from their ashes came the human race, a mixture of evil Titan qualities and the Dionysian qualities which they had ingested. When Zeus and Semele then produced a baby, it was Dionysos-Zagreus returned to life (1972: 340-41).

For the Orphic believer, then, the goal of life is to "free himself from the Titanic element and, thus purified, return to the god, a fragment of whom is living in him" (1972: 341). "When a man dies, Hermes leads the 'deathless soul' into the underworld" (1972: 343). But the soul, freed of its body by death, soon inhabits another body. Such a transmigration may simply be one in an endless and hopeless cycle of repetitions, but for the believer in Dionysos and the follower of the Orphic "ordinances of salvation" (1972: 342), a new life is an opportunity for increased happiness (1972: 344). The ordinances emphasize asceticism, a dissociation from all worldly things in an absolute effort to achieve pure communion with the divinity (1972: 343). But that communion is not reached until the soul experiences the "final death": "now it is free and will no more suffer death; it lives for ever like God, for it comes from God and is itself divine" (1972: 354). Hans's "bliss" comes, therefore, from his epiphany of the infant-god in torment, whose body dies but whose soul, soon re-embodied, will live on. He acknowledges that since he came to the magic mountain "the breath almost left my poor body":

Yet now from the base of my column I have no meagre view. I have dreamed of man's state, of his courteous and enlightened social state; behind which, in the temple, the horrible blood-sacrifice was consummated. Were they, those children of the sun, so sweetly courteous to each other, in silent recognition of that horror? It would be a fine and right conclusion they drew. I will hold to them, in my soul, I will hold with them and not with Naphta, neither with Settembrini. They are both talkers; the one luxurious and spiteful, the other for ever blowing on his penny pipe of reason, even vainly imagining he can bring the mad to their senses. It is all Philistinism and morality, most certainly it is irreligious. Nor am I for little Naphta either, or his religion, that is only a *guazzabuglio* of God and the Devil, good and evil, to the end that the individual soul shall plump into it head first, for the sake of mystic immersion in the universal. Pedagogues both! Their quarrels and counter-positions are just a *guazzabuglio* too, and a confused noise of battle, which need trouble nobody who keeps a little clear in his head and pious in his heart. Their aristocratic question! Disease, health! Spirit, nature! Are those contradictions? I ask, are they problems? No, they are no problems, neither is the problem of their aristocracy. The recklessness of death is in life, it would not be life without it—

and in the center is the position of the *Homo Dei*, between
recklessness and reason, as his state is between mystic community
and windy individualism. (495-96)

Acknowledging that he has a soul, he vows,*"For the sake of
goodness and love, man shall let death have no sovereignty over his thoughts.—And*
with this—I awake". He continues by proclaiming: "For I have dreamed it out
to the end, I have come to my goal" (496-97). (He had indeed entered the
Telesterion.) Filled with happiness, he further proclaims:

> Long, long have I sought after this word, in the place where
> Hippe appeared to me, in my loggia, everywhere. Deep into the
> snow mountains my search has led me. Now I have it fast. My
> dream has given it me, in utter clearness, that I may know it for
> ever. Yes, I am in simple raptures, my body is warm, my heart
> beats high and knows why. It beats not solely on physical
> grounds, as finger-nails grow on a corpse; but humanly, on
> grounds of my joyful spirits. My dream word was a draught,
> better than port or ale, it streams through my veins like love and
> life, I tear myself from my dream and sleep, knowing as I do,
> perfectly well, that they are highly dangerous to my young life.
> (497)

From the time when Hans was led into the temple complex by a
Hermes figure, then, he was descending toward his confrontation with
death in the underworld of regression to the maternal and his salvation
through conversion to the "Orphic and Bacchic mysteries" of the
compassionate mother and the sacrificial son. (Mann follows Rohde,
who asserts that the Eleusinian mysteries eventually incorporated the
worship of Dionysos [1972: 220], although Rohde never offers a
detailed examination.) By the end of the evening, back at the Berghof,
Hans appears to have forgotten his experience: "What he had dreamed was
already fading from his mind. What he had thought—even that selfsame evening it
was no longer so clear as it had been at first" (498). But his subsequent actions
argue that his conversion is sincere and active.

Hans's new faith is soon tested, for he receives word that his
cousin Joachim has had a relapse in his battle with tuberculosis and
must return to the Berghof (499). When Joachim arrives, he is
accompanied by his mother Louisa Ziemssen, who

> had the same gentle and beautiful dark eyes as Joachim. Her hair,
> that was quite as black, but mingled now with many threads of
> grey, was confined by a nearly invisible net; an arrangement
> characteristic of the mild and measured composure of her

personality, which was simple, and at the same time dignified and
pleasing. (503)

It is likely that her appearance with her hair covered prompts two
memories for Hans.The first is of Hans's first glimmer of death in his
garden when he meets the veiled woman called, he learns, "Tous-les-
deux". Later, continuing to wear his veil of repressed knowledge, he
meets the woman, with "a black veil wound about her disordered silver hair and
tied under her chin", for whom he offers the commiseration that he has
rehearsed. Very pleased with himself, he then tells Joachim that,
really, too much is made of death on the mountain (309). His facile
thinking is jeopardized when he and Joachim visit the veiled Mexican
woman at the bedside where her surviving son lies near death. The
cousins draw the veil over this visit, even to each other, preferring to
visit their friend Ferge, who tells them of an awful operation that had
been attempted on him as he lay conscious with a cloth over his face
(310). Since he had somehow survived, Ferge still has a figurative
cloth over his face, a veil of sorts, enabling the cousins to continue
their denial of the body's mortality. Presumably Hans remains in the
state of willed ignorance until he envisions the statuary in the temple:

> mother and daughter, it seemed; one them sitting, older than the
> other, more dignified, right goddesslike and mild, yet with
> mourning brows above the lightless empty eye-sockets; clad in a
> flowing tunic and a mantle of many folds, her matronly brow with
> its waves of hair covered with a veil. (494)

As Jane Harrison notes, the symbolism of the veil is rapidly
fading from human memory. There must be, in some rites, brides who
"lift the veil" at their wedding. There must still be novices who "take the
veil" when they become nuns. Perhaps somewhere there are still
women who veil themselves when they are widowed. And there might
even be those eulogists who speak of the deceased as "beyond the veil".
Even so, according to Jane Harrison, the veil is "almost emptied[...]of its
solemn ancient content" (1959: 521). Yet each of the above usages retains
some connection with that content. Plutarch asked, "Why do men veil their
heads when they worship the gods and uncover them when they wish to do honour to
men", then noted that veiling was prominent in Orphic ritual. From this
clue Jane Harrison deduces that wearing the veil originally
symbolized devotion, a consecration to the divinity that involved the
sacrifice of innocent children (1959: 521-22). Hans's second memory,
that of Demeter's veil, provides him with a sight that will, when he

needs it, inform him of the right attitude that one must take toward the mystery of death.

Joachim resumes therapy, and his mother returns to Hamburg (505). When Joachim is once again ambulatory, he, Hans, and their friends Ferge and Wehsal, resume their visits to "those two devoted opponents" Settembrini and Naphta (507). On one of these visits Naphta, in his effort to discredit Settembrini's humanism, accuses the Italian of being a Freemason. Then, to discredit Freemasonry, he charges that it had incorporated "feasts of Eleusinian mysteries and aphrodistic rites"—though now "it is a god-forsaken bourgeoisiedom, in the form of a club" (513). With equal derision Settembrini attacks Naphta's beliefs. Both argue eternally about ideas, but neither pays any attention to the body. They exemplify the polar positions that Hans had rejected after his snow vision.

In a short time, Joachim's body fails him, so that he suffers the shame of being a *"moribundus"* (533-34). When Joachim's mother returns, Hans is prepared to look for the right attitude: "Louisa Ziemssen was a brave soul. She did not dissolve in grief at sight of her dear son. The almost invisible net that confined and kept in order her hair was symbolic of her composed and self-controlled bearing" (535). One afternoon Joachim begins floccilation, dying within the hour. At the very end Mrs. Ziemssen, like Demeter, has her arm around his shoulders, as he, in delirium, says that "he must write out an application for an extension of his leave" (538). One of the Dioscuri departs for the House of Hades, while the other remains above. Hans's gravity at this time occurs not just from his personal loss of his cousin but also from the deepened insight that he had gained in his descent to the underworld in the snow.

III. Pieter Peeperkorn

When Clavdia does return to the Berghof, she is accompanied by her lover Mynheer Pieter Peeperkorn, an elderly Dutchman who had made his fortune as a coffee planter in Java. Like Clavdia, Peeperkorn is under divine influence. It is only fitting that he is first an avatar of Poseidon, the brother of Zeus, for that sea god imposed his regnant libidinity on both the goddesses who have claimed our attention, Bad Mother Medusa and Good Mother Demeter. By Poseidon Medusa produced Pegasos and Chrysaor (Rose 1959: 30); by Poseidon Demeter bore Arion and Persephone ("or a goddess equated with her") (Rose 1959: 66-67). The first child in both cases was a horse, the spit and image of his father. Pribislav Hippe is, figuratively speaking, Clavdia's love child by Peeperkorn. Peeperkorn is introduced ordering a drink (548)--an action indicating fluid as his element that he continually performs throughout his presence in the novel. Later, he asks Hans, "Will you take a glass of red wine with me? I will drink, for I am thirsty. I have given out a considerable amount of water to-day"—a confession certainly to be expected from a storm-god. Then, filling a water-glass, "[h]e poured out the wine, with Hans Castorp's help, as his hand trembled slightly, and drank thirstily, as though it had been water" (602). His introductory drink is ordered in the third person, as befitting royalty, and the epithets that Mann applies to him also attest to his exalted origin: "regal" (551) and "kingly" (556) are routinely repeated. Peeperkorn habitually uses a gesture: "the lifted hand, whose thumb and forefinger were joined in an O, while the other three with their lanceolate nails stood stiffly up" (552). Thirlwall interprets this gesture as a "Trinitarian symbol" (1950: 296) used to emphasize Peeperkorn's Christ-aspect, soon to be discussed. But Peeperkorn repeatedly uses this gesture, associated with his "sea-captain's hand" (563), soon after his arrival, long before he is invested with any Christ-like attributes. Thus the gesture points to the Poseidon trident that Peeperkorn carries with him at all times, perhaps signifying by the thumb and forefinger 0 that he encircles the universe and so deserves the Poseidonian epithets 'Earth-holder' and 'Earth-shaker' (Caldwell 1989: 166-67). Mann's other recurrent epithet for Peeperkorn, "sea-captain" (560), continually reminds us that he dominates the watery dimension and all those who fall under the spell of his "personality" (563):

> He had a way of lifting that little circlet formed by thumb and forefinger to a poise above his ear, and coyly twisting his head away from it—one watched him as one might an elderly priest of some oriental cult, with the skirts of his robe snatched up, doing a dance before the sacrificial altar. Again, flung back in Olympian repose, with one arm stretched out on the back of his neighbour's chair, he beguiled them all to their confusion,[...] He made love to every female within reach, without discrimination or respect of person[...]. (572)

It is likely, too, that the "sea-captain" epithet links Peeperkorn with Mann's father, who, when Mann was eight, bought a steamship (Hayman 1995: 92), and who was remembered by his son Heinrich as striding about confidently, in Hayman's words, "like a captain on his ship" (85). Psychoanalytically interpreted, then, Poseidon "primarily represents the procreative sexuality of the father" (Caldwell 1989: 166), and Peeperkorn carries that symbolic burden when he arrives at the Berghof. When Hans first comes to the magic mountain, content with his substitute bottle and cigar, the mother whose memory he has repressed bursts through the glass door of his consciousness until he transfers his childish desire to her. Confident that Hans will remain in thrall to her, Clavdia goes off to work her Medusan mischief from Baku to Castile (559). When she returns, she seems subdued; she no longer gets to slam the door to announce the return of the repressed. Rather Peeperkorn gently closes the door, then puts her in her place, as if to indicate that male potency has superseded female enticement (554). Hans waits for "some three or four weeks" (556) to be recognized by Clavdia, then becoming bitter one night, he decides to "escape by the hall door and exchange the empty gaieties of the salon for the frosty solitude of his balcony, and the society of his Maria". That old succuba Clavdia can read his thoughts, for she immediately appears, her voice reminding him of the pencil she had lent him: "Slowly he let his newspaper fall, and turned his face up a little, so that the crown of his head came against the straight back of his chair. He even closed his eyes, but quickly opened them, and gazed somewhere into space" (557). Once again, Hans is primed to abandon his cigar for the real thing.

But her first words are an inquiry about Joachim. When Hans tells her that his cousin is dead, she replies, "Did I not tell you your cousin would die if he went down to be a soldier?" He replies *"Tu l'as su"* (558), a near echo of *"tous les deux",* reminding himself that when he had spoken French to a woman, he had opened his heart not only to love but also to death. That Chauchat voices her awareness of his sudden pensiveness suggests the deepening effect of his snow vision on his sensibility.

Understandably Hans prefers to talk about the x-rays that they had exchanged, but at that moment Peeperkorn appears. He

> stood like a tower, so close to Hans Castorp as to rouse the latter from his trance, and make him realize that it was in place to get up and be mannerly. But they were so close he had to slide sidewise from his seat, and then the three stood in a triangle, the center of which was the chair. (560)

The triangle could indicate that Hans is experiencing an Oedipal moment; if Thirlwall is correct, it could also introduce the Orphic motif that is associated with Peeperkorn's Dionysos-aspect (1950: 293), soon to be discussed. Peeperkorn seems genuinely taken with Hans, for Clavdia intuits from his characteristic circumlocution that he wishes to make an occasion of his introduction to Hans. She proposes that others be invited to join them for a party. Although Clavdia proposes the party, it is dominated by Peeperkorn, who, starting to drink himself into a stupor, insists that his guests follow his example. Thus, as an enthusiast of Dionysius, he introduces the Orphic belief that "the life of the blessed in the other world" will be "a banquet of the holy or, literally translated,[...] a 'carousal'" (Nilsson 1980: 218). At the banquet Hans is seated between "his kingly host and Clavdia" (561), but in a group that now totals twelve the struggle for his allegiance will not be so naked.

At this point an explanation by Kerényi again becomes useful: "A divinity with a number of aspects is very apt to appear only in the *one* aspect under which he or she is being regarded at the moment" (1963: 120). Peeperkorn's Poseidon-aspect gives way to a double aspect: Bacchus/Dionysos and Jesus Christ. (But the transmutation is neither totally complete nor totally different: the Poseidon-aspect still occasionally appears; and the Poseidon-aspect and the Dionysos-aspect share a notable feature, for Dionysos, like Poseidon, as Otto writes, "comes out of the water and returns to it" [1965: 162]). At the party Hans himself links Peeperkorn with "Bacchus himself" (566), and all assembled, saving Hans and Clavdia, take their cue from Peeperkorn to get orgiastic. But Peeperkorn is not entirely caught up in the Bacchic instant; his words and mannerisms indicate that the aspect of Dionysos, the suffering god, now inhabits him, revealing to him his future. Although his body seems powerful, he implies that he is now impotent before the "sprawling female" (566) both in the body of Clavdia and in the feminine body of life itself, which early on entices all humanity to sexuality and sooner or later rules that death must occur. His supporting cast again takes its cue from his growing spiritual torpor, as Clavdia informs him. Roused, Peeperkorn makes his face "masklike" (569). To reclaim his worshipers he uses the mask, for by it, as Otto notes, Dionysos "was known as the god of confrontation" (1965: 90):

> He held them all, he pressed them afresh into service of his personality, sinking the tip of his forefinger till it met the tip of his thumb, and erecting the three others straight and stiff with their long nails. He stretched out his sea-captain's hand, checking them, warning them, and words issued from his cracked lips—words utterly irrelevant and indistinct, yet exerting on their spirits a resistless power, thanks to the reserves of personality behind them. (569)

Peeperkorn's effect on them seems like the effect that Otto attributes
to Dionysos:

> Thus the mask tells us that the theophany of Dionysus, which is
> different from that of the other gods because of its stunning
> assault on the senses and its urgency, is linked with the eternal
> enigmas of duality and paradox. This theophany thrusts Dionysus
> violently and unavoidably into the here and now—and sweeps
> him away at the same time into the inexpressible distance. It
> excites with a nearness which is at the same time a remoteness.
> The final secrets of existence and non-existence transfix mankind
> with monstrous eyes. (1965: 91)

How fitting that the female body which seals Peeperkorn's fate bears
the face of Medusa, whose eyes overpower his eyes.

Peeperkorn's incoherence reveals that his mad-Bacchus-
aspect is once more dominant. But the aftertaste of his Dionysian
moment encourages sentimentality, for he drunkenly lapses into a
mood in which he compares himself to Jesus Christ on the night of His
betrayal in the Garden of Gethsemane (569). Again his "disciples"
respond to his prompting, feeling that they had betrayed him by their
drowsiness (570). Thus pleased, Peeperkorn reverts to his Bacchic-
aspect for a "Bacchanalian rout" (571). Finally, helplessly drunk, he
allows Clavdia and Hans to take him to his apartment, at the door of
which he orders Hans to kiss Clavdia on her brow. Compliance to his
order would show deference to his person, Peeperkorn explains. But
even though Hans acknowledges Peeperkorn as "Your Majesty", he
refuses, regarding the command as "sheerest nonsense" (574).

Thus begins a protracted struggle between Peeperkorn and
Clavdia to possess Hans, though, to appearances, they continue to live
together. Hans, for his part, is still drawn to Clavdia even as he
becomes drawn to Peeperkorn. Hans places himself so to be
approached by Clavdia one night when Peeperkorn is too sick to take
his dinner in the dining-room. In a deliberate repetition of his original
approach to her, Clavdia glides up to ask him for a postage stamp for
the letter that she has written. When he says that he has none, she
engages in *double-entendre*:

> "Well, then, lost soul, at least give me a *papiros*" said she, and sat
> down opposite him on a bench with a linen cushion, one leg over
> the other. She stretched out her hand. "With those, at least, you
> are provided." She took a cigarette, negligently, from the silver
> case he held out to her, and availed herself of his little pocket-

device, the flame of which lighted up her face. The indolent "Give me a cigarette," the taking it without thanks, bespoke the spoiled, luxurious female; yet even more it betokened a human companionship and mutual "belonging," an unspoken give and take which came both thrilling and tender to his love-lorn sense. (593-94)

Does Hans realize that she is attempting to reignite his fascination for her? By requesting a pencil-like cigarette she intends to recall the time when she had allowed him to use her pencil. Clavdia's calling the solicited cigarette a *papiros*, a reed, emphasizes her sexual implication. She soon makes another move: "She had taken his hand, and played absently with the fingers[...]" (597). When even that gets no rise out of him, Clavdia redoubles her effort: she says that she brought Peeperkorn to the Berghof because she knew that there was already one there upon whom she could depend, and she kisses that one on the mouth. Mann refuses to comment on the nature of the kiss: "To try to make a clean-cut distinction between the passionate and the soulful—that would, no doubt, be analytical. But we feel that it would also be inept—to borrow Hans Castorp's useful word—and certainly not in the least 'genial'" (599). Mann's polarities do not explore all possible meanings of Clavdia's kiss. Clavdia must know the etymology of the verb *kiss*, 'to suck', which acknowledges an instinct that must be stroked soon after birth: a neonate's lips or cheeks must be stimulated to activate the nursing reflex. That such stimulation activates another reflex is discovered by Felix Krull, if not by Hans Castorp.

Moviegoer Mann "cuts" to a scene featuring Hans at the bedside of Peeperkorn. As he drinks, Peeperkorn, rather coherent for once, instructs Hans on his masculine role:

> I repeat, that therein lies our duty, our sacred duty to feel. Feeling, you understand, is the masculine force that rouses life. Life slumbers. It needs to be roused, to be awakened to a drunken marriage with divine feeling. For feeling, young man, is godlike. Man is godlike, in that he feels. He is the feeling of God. God created him in order to feel through him. Man is nothing but the organ through which God consummates his marriage with roused and intoxicated life. If man fails in feeling, it is blasphemy; it is the surrender of His masculinity, a cosmic catastrophe, an irreconcilable horror. (603)

Peeperkorn the Dionysiast thus urges Hans to transfer his desire from the oral satisfactions to the genital, to become God's organ, at the same time hinting at his own impotence.

As the afternoon wears on, Peeperkorn begins to tax Hans about his relationship with Clavdia, noting that Hans carefully avoids saying *"Sie* to Madame" (605). He also recalls that Hans had refused to kiss Clavdia on the brow. Hans begins to fear "an exhibition of royal rage", thinking, "Perhaps I'd best keep an eye on his fist, he may be holding it over me already. Certainly I am in a fine position—between the devil and the deep blue sea, as it were"—hardly a Homeric simile but adequate to describe Hans's status between Clavdia-Medusa and Peeperkorn-Poseidon.

Peeperkorn gently concludes: "You were Clavdia's lover when she was here before" (606). Hans honestly replies, "I should be boasting if I say yes, lying if I say no" (607), then enters into a long explanation of his feelings for Clavdia, eventually coming as close as he ever does to an admission of his unconscious motivation:

> I had a profession, as you may have heard, a good, two-fisted job, which is even supposed to do its share in drawing together the nations of the earth—but somehow it did not draw me. I admit this freely; but the reasons for it I cannot describe otherwise than to say that they are veiled in obscurity, the same obscurity that envelops the origin of my feeling for Madame your mistress. (610)

In *Ocean Steamships* he had sought the "oceanic feeling" that would "draw" him together, reverse the feeling of dissipation felt since infancy.

Perhaps Peeperkorn thinks that Hans has reached sufficient understanding of himself that he is now poised to transcend his oral orientation, thus to assume the genital orientation. For he proposes that they drink once again and begin, as brothers, to use the Thou (611). Hans confesses,

> I might better say that I am immensely happy, and can hardly grasp how this has all come about, it is like a dream. What an immense honour for me! How I have deserved it I scarcely know, certainly in no active sense. It is not surprising that at first it seems entirely too bold, and I doubt if I shall be able to fetch it out—especially in Clavdia's presence, who is not quite so likely to be pleased with the new arrangement, all at once.

Peeperkorn responds, "Leave that to me,[...]the rest is a matter of practice and habit. Go, now, young man. Leave me, my son. The night has fallen, our loved one may return any moment, and a meeting between you just now would perhaps not be quite well-advised" (612). Perhaps "Papa" fears that his "son" will succumb once more to "Mama's" charm?

Peeperkorn's health declines from malaria, which has damaged his liver and spleen, but in May he feels strong enough to take a party—his usual retainers, Clavdia, Hans, Ferge, Wehsal, Settembrini, Naphta, all to be served by his Malay valet—to visit a waterfall in Fluela Valley (613). It is possible that the site and its name were chosen for Hans, who has a "native love of falling water" (612). The new order of things is announced when Peeperkorn lays "his left hand on Hans Castorp's shoulder, saying: 'Well, young man, and how goes it, my son?'" (614). By the ancient ritual of the laying on of hands, the divine power can be transmitted (Gen. 48: 14).

The party is large enough to require two landaus, each drawn by two magnificent horses, "sturdy, glossy, well-fed beasts, with a blaze on each forehead" (618). It is only fitting that Poseidon be conveyed in such royal style, for his theriomorphic appearance was as a horse (Suhr 1967: 25, 27), an appearance commemorated when he became anthropomorphic by his "standing title Hippios, 'He of the Horse(s)'" (Rose 1959: 63).

Very likely Peeperkorn has an additional reason for selecting the site of the outing. Graves points out that the source of Poseidon's name was *"potidan*, he who gives to drink from the wooded mountain" (1957: 406) long before he became god of the sea (Suhr 1967: 28). If Peeperkorn, acting under Poseidon's inspiration, intends to declare Hans his heir, what better place than one which testifies to his longevity and majesty?

There are indications, though, that the ritual of succession will not proceed smoothly, even if the site lies at the source of fluid. Indeed, the landscape in "Flowing Valley" has a pubic aspect:

> the route was bordered here and there by crumbling rock tufted with grass and flowers. Telegraph-poles flew past. Their way wound along the mountain forests in pleasant curves that invited the interest and led it on; in the sunny distance glimmered mountain heights still partly covered with snow.

The landscape becomes even more evocative when they walk through the wood to reach the falls, so evocative that "[t]hey all talked about the wood":

> the wood was not quite usual, it had a peculiarity which made it picturesque, exotic, even uncanny. It abounded in a hanging moss that draped and wreathed and wrapped the trees: the matted web of this parasitic plant hung and dangled in long, pallid beards from the branches, so that scarcely any pine-needles were visible

> for the shrouding veil. A complete, a bizarre transformation, a
> bewitched and morbid scene. For the trees were sick of this rank
> growth, it threatened to choke them to death—so all the visitors
> felt, as the little train wound along the path toward the sound, and
> the hissing and splashing swelled. (618)

Now that the uncanny overwhelms the scene, banishing the Good
Mother, her attribute, the veil, becomes a shroud, a transformation that
will recur with the introduction of Senhora Kuckuck in *Confessions of
Felix Krull*. It is as if the woods have become the Gorgon's head, so
that the visitors are justified in fearing that they will be choked,
especially when the hissing sound reinforces the serpentine sight of
the hanging moss. Their sense of the uncanny is provoked by maternal
awe, or fear of maternal sexuality, Caldwell calls it (1989: 46).[7] Little
wonder that Peeperkorn is so weak that he must lean on Clavdia as he
walks.

     After allowing some time for contemplation of the spectacle
of the falls, Peeperkorn indicates that tea—or communion—will now
be served, not at some distance that would allow conversation—as
Settembrini would have wanted—but immediately adjacent to the
falls. Suddenly Peeperkorn begins to speak: "[...]with the winecup in his
right hand, he raised his forefinger, stretching his left arm palm outwards toward the
water". From his facial expressions and his gestures, it is clear that his
speech is full of sound and fury, but it signifies nothing to the
audience deafened by the roar:

> He even stood up! There, in his crumpled ulster, that reached
> nearly to his heels, the collar turned up; bare-headed, cup in the
> hand, the high brow creased with folds like some heathen idol's in
> a shrine, and crowned by the aureole of white hair like flickering
> flames; there he stood by the rocks and spoke, holding the circle
> of thumb and forefinger, with the lancelike others above it, before
> his face, and sealing his mute and incomprehensible toast with the
> compelling sign of precision. (620-21)

Dramatic though his placement is, though, the fact remains that he
cannot triumph over his own element. Much moved, his audience

> saw his head sink sideways, the broken bitterness of the lips, they
> saw the man of sorrows in his guise. But then quite suddenly
> flashed the dimple, the sybaritic roguishness, the garment
> snatched up dancewise, the ritual impropriety of the heathen
> priest. He lifted his beaker, waved it half-circle before the
> assembled guests, and drank it out in three gulps, so that it stood

bottom upwards. Then he handed it with outstretched arm to the
Malay, who received it with an obeisance, and gave the sign to
break up the feast. (621)

Once again Peeperkorn alternates his Dionysian-aspect with his
Bacchus-aspect, before employing gestures that imply his Christ-
aspect. For the ritual that follows his inaudible "sermon" suggests the
solemnity of the Mass, in which a sacrifice occurs as the wine is
drunk. More than anything, the scene evokes Sir James Fraser's
descriptions of the divine king who must be killed when his strength
fails (1958: 309-19), epitomized by Fraser's description of the King of
the Wood at Nemi (1958: 1-3).

There is yet another meaning for the visit to the waterfall that
the ironic Mann may be implying, a meaning both personal and
mythical. Earlier was cited Heilbut's contention that the inspirational
painting "The Spring" may be glimpsed in the "Snow Vision" , in which
Hans is pictured descending into the underworld to confront Death. It
would be fitting, as well, that the painting also be glimpsed in the
waterfall scene, in which, though it is parodied, Peeperkorn's
performance is a ritualistic avowal of intention to sacrifice himself for
Hans. Inspired by Poseidon, Peeperkorn the father means to defeat
Chauchat, who is possessed by Medusa the mother, thus freeing their
son Pegasus from his mother. Since the winged horse gets his name
from his birthplace "near the springs of Ocean" (Barnes 1974: 36),
Peeperkorn's choice of a place of sacrifice is significant. In effect,
Peeperkorn offers Hans the opportunity to become "the favored pet of the
Muses" (Barnes 1974: 37). Just as Medusa's death brings about
Pegasus' birth, so Chauchat must "die" before Hans can be "reborn", so
Mann must disavow his yearning for stasis by gazing every morning
at "The Spring" before he picks up his pen to transform the personal into
the mythical. Barnes's quotation from Erich Neumann's *Origins and
History of Consciousness* is appropriate: "What the winged horse symbolizes
is the freeing of libido from the Great Mother and its soaring flight, in other words, its
spiritualization" (1974: 21). Stripped of its Jungian glitter, Neumann's
statement presents the idea central to Bergler's thesis that creativity
begins in defiance.

Hans does not sleep well that night, nor is he surprised when,
at two o'clock, he is called to Peeperkorn's quarters. Peeperkorn has
committed suicide, using a mechanical contraption that has the action
and effect of a snake bite (623). Mindful of his kingly status, he
probably had had it made during his years in the East, its use to await

his decline. But its use at a time when he has been warring with Clavdia, who in her earliest appearance was a snake, certainly could suggest that his method of self-destruction is dictated by his recognition that, alive but impotent, he can rescue Hans from Clavdia's control only by sacrificing himself. Hofrat Behrens' opinion that Peeperkorn died from "quick suffocation, probably easy and painless", and Hans's response to "the uncanny toy" (624)[8] should recall for Hans the walk through the "uncanny" woods the day before, when the men felt that the "parasitic plant" "threatened to choke them to death" (618). By his suicide Peeperkorn succeeds in loosening Clavdia's control over Hans, for when Hans speaks to her he uses the formal *Sie*. Hans speaks obliquely of Peeperkorn: "He was built on such a grand scale[...]that he considered it a blasphemy, a cosmic catastrophe, to be found wanting in feeling. For you must know, he regarded himself as the instrument of God's marriage".

Hans refers to his conversation with Peeperkorn which had ended with Peeperkorn's recognition of Hans as his son (612), during which Peeperkorn declared:

> feeling, young man, is godlike. Man is godlike, in that he feels. He is the feeling of God. God created him in order to feel through him. Man is nothing but the organ through which God consummates his marriage with roused and intoxicated life. If man fails in feeling, it is blasphemy; it is the surrender of His masculinity, a cosmic catastrophe, an irreconcilable horror. (603)

Thus Peeperkorn knew that he could only save Hans by effecting a "'heightening,' enhancement *(Steigerung)*" of feeling, a process that Mann asserts is present in the novel both formally and thematically ("The Making" 723).

Clavdia seems to accept the reason that Hans offers for the suicide, for she replies, *"C'est une abdication"*. But she immediately follows up, "He knew of our folly?" Hans replies that Peeperkorn had guessed of their relationship, by Hans's refusal to kiss her on the forehead, then asks if he might now fulfill Peeperkorn's request, to which Clavdia assents (624). By his use of the *Sie* and of the honorific kiss he acknowledges that his infatuation with Clavdia is over, but his nostalgia for the spectral mother is not completely vanquished.

IV. "The Thunderbolt"

Although Clavdia has apparently defeated Peeperkorn the man, she may realize that his Dionysian sacerdotal efficacy will enable Hans eventually to believe that he is the son whom Peeperkorn, in his divine aspect, acknowledged. Peeperkorn is the godhead Dionysos (like Dionysos in Euripides' *The Bacchic Women* he appears among humans impersonating himself). With divine paternity, Hans will come to realize that he need not look backward in maternal longing at his first and only birth but rather may look forward in anticipation of the rebirth which follows death. But this transformation in Hans does not occur immediately. Although Clavdia leaves the magic mountain in defeat, she leaves Hans once again to experience maternal awe in the form of the uncanny (627). With no one on whom to project the fantasy of reunification that his maternal awe induces, Hans falls prey to "The Great God Dumps," boredom. But his experience of boredom must be viewed in light of Phillips' analysis of boredom as a defense mechanism:

> Boredom, I think, protects the individual, makes tolerable for him the impossible experience of waiting for something without knowing what it could be. So the paradox of the waiting that goes on in boredom is that the individual does not know what he was waiting for until he finds it, and that often he does not know that he is waiting. (1993: 77)

That "something" is a gramophone that Behrens installs in the reception room. The gramophone is an example of the "transformational object", Bollas' term for those objects that individuals seek as substitutes for the lost mother-environment (Phillips 1993: 76-77). The psychoanalyst Pinchas Noy offers confirmation that "longings for the lost paradise of oral infancy" frequently spur a recurrently pressing need for music (Storr 1992: 89-95). The very first record that Hans plays signals that in his boredom induced by nostalgia lies the potential for his salvation: *Orpheus in the Underworld,* entrances Hans, who, after years on the magic mountain, must be sensitized to the charms of mythology, especially to the story of one who wishes to rescue his beloved from the abode of the dead or, alternatively, one who dreams of being rescued from the abode of the dead. Very early Settembrini had recognized that desire with his allusions to Persephone (354), and more recently Hans must have learned of Orpheus' descent to the underworld through his introduction to the Orphic/Bacchic rites. Inspired by the Thracian Orpheus and Dionysos, Hans loves music as much as the proverbial Thracian (J Harrison 1959: 456). As if that were not enough, when the waltz melody is reached, the words

attached to it would have awakened Hans's unconscious yearnings, his
Sehnsucht, "Ach, ich habe sie verloren" (637).

When Behrens must attend to other duties, Hans asserts that
he will be the gramophone operator: "He was filled with the surest
foreknowledge of a new passion, a new enchantment, a new burden of love" (639).
Although Behrens' gift of the gramophone was for the good of all and
certainly not for the detriment of Hans, even so it is the medium
through which the mother fantasy, defeated in her guise as Clavdia,
can continue the struggle for control of Hans's soul. Hans spends
hours organizing the record library; that night,

> from two to seven he dreamed of the wonder-box. He saw in his
> sleep the disk circling about the peg, with a swiftness that made it
> almost invisible and quite soundless. Its motion was not only
> circular, but also a peculiar, sidling undulation. (640-41)

Not only does the spectacle of the sidling movement tug at his
repressed memory of Clavdia, but also the circular motion tugs at an
even earlier memory, that of the maternal "peg". Mann here describes a
phenomenon much discussed in psychoanalytic literature, dreams of
objects representing the breast (Lawson 1996a).

Quite appropriately, Hans had, before sleeping, paused, when
arranging the library, at the sight of a record containing a *Lied* that he
had known from childhood, one that he now "began to attach to it a quite
special love and clothe it with many associations" (640). Heilbut argues that
"when Hans Castorp selects a series of operatic arias, each one contains an erotic
subtext—evident to him alone—and refers to his beloved, now dead cousin, Joachim"
(1996: 37), but he overlooks a large amount of evidence to the
contrary. If Hans feels any desire at all for his cousin, it, like his
infatuation for Hippe, is merely an secondary form of the oral
nostalgia that dominates his unconscious.

Soon enough Hans exerts a monopoly over the gramophone,
keeping its key in his pocket. His action suggests that Clavdia is the
clavette to his love of music. After the last daily public concert, he
remains for *la solitude à deux*:

> Hans Castorp was alone among four walls with his wonder-box;
> with the florid performance of this truncated little coffin of violin-
> wood, this small dull-black temple, before the open double doors
> of which he sat with his hands folded in his lap, his head on one
> side, his mouth open, and let the harmonies flow over him. (642)

If Hans only had his Maria Mancini and his Kulmbacher, he would be having a full night-nursing. (But this temple, this vulvar coffin, is but a parody of the temple of the snow vision, for in its miniature precincts death, not rebirth, is worshiped.)

Other favorite musical compositions reflect Hans's unconscious. He is enthralled by the opera *Aida,* especially the ending: Radames refuses to betray his love for Aida, is condemned to be buried alive, then discovers that Aida has contrived to share his fate (645). Thus she joins him in the hermetically-sealed chamber of love (and death) for which Hans has always yearned. Surely, Hans must think, he is being true to Clavdia-mother by remaining on the magic mountain, believing that, somehow, his constancy will be rewarded. Dubussy's *Afternoon of a Faun* offers him a rendition of his ancient garden fantasy:

> Here is the dream Hans Castorp dreamed: he lay on his back in a sunny, flower-starred meadow, with his head on a little knoll, one leg drawn up, the other flung over—and those were goat's legs crossed there before him. His fingers touched the stops of a little wooden pipe, which he played for the pure joy of it, his solitude on the meadow being complete. (646)

Additional details of "his head on a little knoll" and his playing with his "little wooden pipe" merely underscore the orality/infantile sexuality of the dream scene.

Similarly, Hans is overwhelmed by *Carmen,* in which José is torn between his love for Carmen and his duty to the army. When José confesses to Carmen, "Sometimes I cursed the hour I met thee, and tried all vainly to forget thee" (648), he registers a thought that must have often tried to penetrate Hans's consciousness. Hans is also moved by the lover's use of "thee" in Gounod's *Faust* (650), celebrating for him a memorable moment in his past.

For the fifth of Hans's favorite pieces the narrator turns not to a foreign composition but to a German piece, not an opera but Schubert's *Lied* "Linden-tree" (650).[9] Hans is never more the autobiographical character than in his obsession with the *Lied.* Nigel Hamilton offers full documentation:

> The one thing that really aroused Thomas' enthusiasm[...], apart from Schiller and his books, was music. From infancy he had listened to his mother at the piano, to her playing the Etudes and Nocturnes of Chopin, but even more to her singing. From Mozart and Beethoven, from Schubert, Schumann, Robert Franz, Brahms

> and Liszt to Wagner she commanded a range of *Lieder* which
> Thomas would never forget, arrangements of Eichendorff and
> Heine's poems which became part of his being, his property.
> (1979: 44)

Since Mann first heard "Linden-tree" from his mother's lips, he must
have associated it, both as form and as content, with his earliest
impressions of his mother, some of which he may have remembered
but some of which were repressed.

The narrator then offers a lengthy technical analysis of the
male voice to which Hans is listening, all the while knowing full well
that, for Hans, the male voice is drowned out by the female voice
which first conveyed the emotion of the song to him. Then, claiming
success in interpreting "Hans Castorp's intimate emotional participation in the
[other] chosen numbers of his nightly programme" (651), the narrator
acknowledges that "great delicacy" will be required to describe Hans's
response to the *Lied*. Here, as throughout the "Linden-tree" episode, the
narrator uses a wall of verbiage to obscure his meaning:

> May we take it that our simple hero, after so many years of
> hermetic-pedagogic discipline, of ascent from one stage of being
> to another, has now reached a point where he is conscious of the
> "meaningfulness" of his love and the object of it? We assert, we
> record, that he has. To him the song meant a whole world, a world
> which he must have loved, else he could not have so desperately
> loved that which it represented and symbolized to him. (651)

The narrator *does not* identify the world represented by
"Linden-tree", except to say that it seemed to Hans that, because of "the
motions of his conscience", he loved his "world of forbidden love" (652). But
before there was "a world of forbidden love" there had to have been a
world of abundant love, either actual or imagined, for how can one
conceive of an absence but in relation to a prior presence? The world
of abundant love is the world of infancy—when fingers and lips rest
on the breast and eyes rest on eyes expressing love. Thus, for Hans,
the mother's song "Linden-tree" is a Siren song, always awakening
Sehnsucht, for, while promising a return to original unity, it takes its
victim back only to original awareness of forbidden love, of relentless
longing. Out of such awareness of futility comes the temptation to
self-obliteration, either psychological or physical. Thus, without
acknowledging the temptation's source—"The Spring"—the narrator can
conclude that, for Hans, "the world behind the song" is "death" (652).

Apparently Dr. Krokowski's psychoanalytic therapy—for
which Hans first had disdain and to which he later made a furtive

appeal—has not enabled Hans to penetrate his repressed past. Yet the analytic approach would seem to offer the only alleviation for Hans's burden, so it seems inevitable that Hans would once again enter Dr. Krokowski's orbit. Gradually Dr. Krokowski's lectures had turned to aspects of parapsychology, and his enthusiasts had begun to explore spiritualism. Hans would have been succeptible to spiritualistic experiments because of his recent submersion in Orphic/Bacchic ritual, for according to Rohde, the Thracian worship of Dionysos led to a new phase of Greek thought, "belief in the independent, indestructible life of the soul, a life not confined to the period of its sojourn in the body which at present envelops it". Rohde adds: "The belief in the existence and life of a second self distinct from the body and separable from it was already encouraged by the 'experiences' of the separate existence and independent behaviour of that self in dreams and fainting fits" (1972: 264).

Such a "second self" Hans glimpsed in his "snow vision". That brief out-of-body experience constitutes his introduction first to the Eleusinian Mystery and then to the Orphic/Bacchic rites. From this introduction he unconsciously experiences a revaluation of values: because of the trauma that attended his "birth"—witnessing the death of his mother and of the child whom she takes with her to the underworld—Hans has experienced his life, both at home and on the magic mountain, as a shadowy existence among all the others who are shades because they died uninitiated. If he has achieved a complete Orphic conversion, he realizes that only physical death can free his soul, so to experience the rebirth that would mitigate, perhaps even completely remove, the trauma of his first birth. Thus he desires death, which is freedom, but must wait for it to claim him, for in Orphism suicide is sternly forbidden (Rohde 1972: 342).

Enter a new patient, Ellen Brand, who confesses that she has a "familiar" (658), Holger, who gives her information that permits her to perform seemingly occult feats. Ellen is for the Berghof community what the Sibyl was for the Bacchic/Orphic community, for, according to Rohde, "In hoarse tones and wild words the Sibyl gave utterance to what the divine impelling power within her and not her own arbitrary fancy suggested; possessed by the god, she spoke in a divine distraction" (1972: 293). Although Ellen is a nineteen-year-old "flaxen-haired Dane" from Odense-on-Fünen (655), she, like such mythic predecessors as Persephone, spends a portion of her time in the underworld. But she must spend enough time in Odense to maintain a sterling reputation, for her "Holger" may be "Holger Dansk", the national hero (Evans 1981: 804). Behind Dr. Krokowski's back, Hans and the other enthusiasts plan a "spiritualistic sitting, a table-tipping, glass-moving game" (660). With Ellen Brand as his medium, Holger makes his presence known by performing several actions that have personal significance to Hans. There is the extemporaneous creation of a long poem, beginning with the description of a northern seascape, then shifting to a hermit's hut and expanding into the celestial vastness which was the object of the hermit's contemplation (663-64), a intinerary describing Hans's hermetic-pedagogic development. When Hans asks how long his stay at the Berghof will be, beyond the initial three weeks, Holger makes "the word, or the syllable Go, and then the word Slanting and then something about Hans Castorp's room" (665). Apparently Holger is indicating that he will make a beeline for Hans's room, for, after the occurrence of mysterious auditory and visual phenomena, Hans finds his x-ray of Clavdia in his lap, an item that Holger had apparently fetched from number 34 (=7), somehow knowing its significance (666). Is Holger implying that Hans must remain in the underworld of the magic mountain as long as he remains enthralled by the spectral mother, a period that will be seven years? Hans, benefiting from the clue provided by Ellen Brand's name, "Hell Fire", decides that the "futility and vulgarity of the scene as a whole had been so unmistakable that he felt quite willing to let it go at these few vagrant sparks of hell-fire" (666).

As expected, Settembrini chides Hans for his credulity in having attended the sitting, and Hans does for a while abstain from further experiments, now conducted by Dr. Krokowski. Perhaps the revelation that Ellen's hypnotic trances are facilitated by the use of the gramophone provides sufficient promise of regression to bring Hans once again to the meetings. In honor of his return, he is designated as "the control of the medium" for the evening: he is to sit facing Ellen, clasping her legs together with his knees, surely aware of her "maidenly breasts" just beneath "a night-gownlike garment of white *crêpe*" (672). According to his previous commitment, Holger is requested to make visible the spirit of a deceased patient—when no one else suggests a name, Hans volunteers "Joachim Ziemssen" (675). Ellen, now possessed by her familiar, goes into a labor that lasts more than two hours. As the second hour comes to a close, Ellen reaches "that dangerous and unavailing stage obstetricians call eclampsia" (679), presumably marked by those facial features characteristic of convulsion, though they are not noted. Although unconscious of the fact, Hans is viewing a scene that recalls the death of his mother.

Hans ventures an idea that he had had from the beginning, that "a certain song, from Gounod's *Faust,* Valentine's Prayer" (679), might be played. Hans had earlier associated "Valentine's Prayer" with Joachim (650) and must feel that playing a record of it would especially beckon Joachim's appearance. The record can be sent for, Hans says, but the attendant to the gramophone, Herr Wenzel, announces that, miraculously, the record is already in his possession. Stimulated by its playing, Ellen "started up convulsively, pumped, carried the slippery hands to her brow", presumably still bearing the Medusa-features of eclampsia, while "[s]he raised herself, drew in a straggling breath, sighed a long, long, outward sigh, sank down and was still" (680). In effect, Ellen has gone to the underworld to retrieve a soul, then given birth to it, for Joachim materializes, appearing as he had at the time of his death, except that he is dressed as a combat soldier, with his head enclosed in the *Stahlhelm* that would not be introduced until the last year of the war to come. The *Stahlhelm* is a crystal ball in which Hans divines that his deliverance from the captive life would come from the war that is prophesied. If Ellen's features had been Medusan, her action indicates she has become a Persephone, a Good Mother. Thus Hans is finally free of the trauma suffered so early in life.

Hans is understandably overcome. As he maintains his hold on Ellen, he looks "through the red darkness at the guest in the chair", then struggles for breath as if being born, whispers "Forgive me!" Apparently mindful that he is one of the Dioscuri, Hans must conclude that he is alive because Joachim took his place in the underworld. Then Hans releases Ellen, stands up, and, overwrought, demands the key so that he can leave the room (681).

If Ellen's convulsed face awakens the terror that he had felt when he thus saw his mother's face, then the spectacle of Ellen "giving birth" to a dead man would also awaken his understanding that his mother had also given birth to a dead child. The Medusa-stare to which he has always been sensitive, then, terrorizes him because he associates it with the death that was caused—*post hoc, ergo propter hoc*—by hetereosexual genital consummation. Such terror has crippled his genital development, created his longing for the earlier oral phase (manifested in his oral excitement for female breasts and genitals and for penises), required such repression that his life has been experienced as a dream. Even though one may attempt to suppress love by denial, as did Joachim, yet the love becomes a disease that kills. Even though one may attempt to suppress love by turning to such substitute objects as music, yet love becomes a (psychic) disease that entices one to embrace death-in-life or to escape from it in actual death. Understandably, Hans no longer wants to remain in a (hermetically) sealed room, now demanding a key that releases him instead of a key that binds him.

As time goes by, growing nationalistic, racial, and ideological animosities bedevil the inhabitants of the International Sanatorium Berghof. In Hans's immediate group the outbreak of *bellum*-fever leads to a *duellum* when Settembrini is challenged by Naphta. Although he rationally abhors the institution of duello, Settembrini accepts. As the duelist challenged, Settembrini fires his weapon first— into the air, not at Naphta. When he will not fire again, by his refusal ridiculing the code, Naphta honors it by killing himself (704-05).

But there is no record that even such an event as the duel disturbs the dreaminess of Hans's existence, now in its seventh year on the magic mountain. He is no longer a concern of the doctors, for his body is cured. But his cured body is apparently a body devoid of desire, in keeping with the "Orphic life" of asceticism (Rohde 1972: 342-43). Hans's triumph over desire is implied by the reference to another male patient. As a boy, Teddy had been the pet of the maternal ladies, who took him on their laps. Then, becoming a youth, he "shot up": "he took them on his instead, and both sides were as well, or even better pleased". "The shooting-up, however, did not suit the lad Teddy; the temporal became him not. In his twenty-first year he departed this life; dying of the disease for which he had proved receptive; and they cleansed and fumigated after him" (707). Sex destroys hermetic security, thus invites death. Hans lives; *ipso facto,* he has not shot up. He no longer smokes "his old-time charmer" Maria Mancini, instead has switched to a brand just as suggestively named, "Light of Asia": "armed with which, and no other solace, Hans Castorp could lie and bear it out indefinitely, as one does at the sea-shore". His cigar burns

> so evenly and regularly that it might have served the smoker for an hour-glass, and did so, at need, for he no longer carried a timepiece. His watch had fallen from his night-table; it did not go, and he had neglected to have it regulated, perhaps on the same grounds as had made him long since give up using a calendar, whether to keep track of the day, or to look out an approaching feast: the grounds, namely, of his "freedom." Thus he did honour to his abiding-everlasting, his walk by the ocean of time, the hermetic enchantment to which he had proved so extraordinarily susceptible that it had become the fundamental adventure of his life. (708)

Thus the Orphic Hans nourishes his soul, which can experience bodily life only as death.

Then the war starts. The man in room $3 + 4 = 7$ has lived on the magic mountain for seven years. The tension between the absolutes of sexual indulgence and celibacy and the identification of mother love with death has kept him in a dream state. But the first days of the war arouse him from his dream:

> These were the moments when the "Seven-Sleeper," not knowing what had happened, was slowly stirring himself in the grass, before he sat up, rubbed his eyes—yes, let us carry the figure to the end, in order to do justice to the movement of our hero's mind: he drew up his legs, stood up, looked about him. He saw himself released, freed from enchantment—not of his own motion, he was fain to confess, but by the operation of exterior powers, of whose activities his own liberation was a minor incident indeed! Yet though his tiny destiny fainted to nothing in the face of the general, was there not some hint of a personal mercy and grace for him, a manifestation of divine goodness and justice? (208)

Like Siegfried under the linden tree (the second time), Hans Castorp is awakening to an unfamiliar emotion, Love. Like the Seven Sleepers, Hans had awakened once, in the Snow Scene, then had fallen asleep again, not to awaken until the resurrection (Evans 1981: 1117-18).

The conventional incitements to volunteering do not seem present in Hans. Rather he reveals a Thracian motivation: "The cheerfulness with which the Thracians faced death in battle was explained by the persuasion which they held that death was only an entrance into a higher life for the soul. They were even credited with a real desire for death, for to them 'dying seemed so fair'" (Rohde 1972: 265). Imprisoned by death-in-life and forbidden to use the "cheap and easy slipping back" of suicide (Rohde 1972: 342), Hans believes that "divine goodness and justice" offer him a return to Life, that is, the eternal life of the soul freed of the body.

Soon he is a member of "a volunteer regiment, fresh young blood and mostly students, not long in the field" (713), which is ordered to make a suicide attack. In the extended description of the charge of the German troops across plowed fields, the naturalistic detail of muddiness is cited. Perhaps the mud is only mud to the other soldiers, but to the Orphic Hans it is the mud into which the uninitiated corpse is plunged upon his arrival in the underworld (Rohde 1972: 344; J. Harrison 1959: 473; Mylonas 1961:265-67). Even when he is hit on the shin by a "great clod" he "smiles at it", for he knows that he will persevere to the place where mud does not exist. As Hans staggers forward, he sings, half-soundlessly, snatches of *"Lindenbaum"* (715), the song of love that leads to death, which is Life.

At this point the narrator says to Hans, "Farewell, honest Hans Castorp, farewell. Life's delicate child! Your tale is told. We have told it to the end, and it was neither short nor long, but hermetic" (715). When Hans first heard the word *hermetic* (511), he thought of hermetically-sealed jars of food in Schalleen's pantry, certainly a plausible image of prenatal containment. Now we see that his life had been hermetically sealed back in Hamburg by his fixation on an infant's desire. The unconscious memory of that pleasure had given rise to the vision of the southern sea that he had experienced in the snow (490). Only through his initiation has he come to realize the transcendent signficance of the hermetic as the doctrine that teaches the right conduct toward Death. The narrator refers to that revelatory vision here at the end:

> Ah, this young blood, with its knapsacks and bayonets, its mud-befouled boots and clothing! We look at it, our humanistic-æsthetic eye pictures it among scenes far other than these: we see these youths watering horses on a sunny arm of the sea; roving with the beloved one along the strand, the lover's lips to the ear of the yielding bride; in happiest rivalry bending the bow. (714)

Now, though, he does not need any longer to fantasize about Paradise Lost, secure in his faith that by dying he enters Paradise Regained.

Notes to *The Magic Mountain*

[1] Heilbut writes, "It's safe to characterize Hans Castorp, with his love of marzipan and cigars, as contentedly oral" (1996: 425). Is an adult trapped in the oral phase ever content?

[2] In 1944 the American literary critic Frederick J. Hoffman attempted to elicit a statement from Mann dating and detailing his introduction to Freud's published work, but received little help from Mann's reply: "One could be influenced in this sphere[...]without any direct contact with his work, because for a long time the air had been filled with the thoughts and results of the psychoanalytic school" (qtd. in Hoffman 1957: 209). Hoffman thinks that Mann accepts Krokowski's ideas, even though he satirizes the man himself. Here, as elsewhere in his study, Hoffman focuses on Mann's conscious use of Freudian ideas, not on manifestations of his unconscious that lend themselves to psychoanalytic interpretation.

[3] Heinz Kohut writes:

> Beyond the portrayal of problems posed by the mother identification and by the ambivalently passive attitude toward the

father, the trend toward union with the mother can also be discerned in Mann's writings. This wish, however, is more strongly repressed and seems to evoke even deeper guilt than the ambivalent attitude toward the father. Rarely does it, therefore, reveal itself in a sublimated, egosyntonic form of object love and, if instances of this type occur, they are by no means unambiguous. One might speculate that perhaps the Slavic features of Tadzio (or of Hippe and Claudia Chauchat in The Magic Mountain) contain a hint of effectively sublimated love for the mother who, in real life, was an "exotic type". Yet almost always when we encounter the wish for the mother we find it presented either in vague, deeply symbolic terms or in the regressive form of "identification" rather than as object love. In addition some kind of punishment, mostly in the form of death or disease, is expressed or implied. This holds true not only for Thomas Mann's literary productions but also for his actual beliefs, as can be inferred from his superstitious prediction that his life would come to an end in 1945, when he should have reached the age at which his mother had died. (1957: 225)

[4]Recalling her stay at *Waldsanatorium* in Davos in 1912 (during which her husband conceived the idea of *The Magic Mountain*), Katja Mann said that there actually "was a Madame Chauchat, who always slammed the door. At first, she really did get on my husband's nerves a great deal, but later he became very sensitive to her charm" (1975: 70-71). Her name, 'hot cat', is a happy accident if it is remembered that, according to Feldman (1965: 492), one of the original attributes of Medusa was a "menacing, shaggy, feline head".

[5]For a survey of critical clairvoyance into Clavdia's room, see Ridley (1994: 11-12).

[6]Bergler offers the "children-eating witch of Grimm's fairy tale" as the prototype of the *"pre-œdipal mother"*, the mother whom the child blames for depriving him of the breast (1949: 9). For nearly fifty years that image in Mann's unconscious had lain in wait.

[7]See ch2n4

[8]An observation by Freud explains why Hans regards the "toy" as "uncanny":

> It often happens that neurotic men declare that they feel there is something uncanny about the female genital organs. This *unheimlich* place, however, is the entrance to the former *Heim* [home] of all human beings, to the place where each one of us lived once upon a time and in the beginning. ("Uncanny" 245, interpolation in orig.)

Sight of the "toy" arouses Hans' fear of the "dentate vagina".

[9]Although Blumberg infers that the narrator seems embarrassed when he admits that Hans has no German operas among his favorites (89), I would argue that the lack of a German opera, specifically one by Wagner, indicates that Hans is unaware (through unfamiliarity or incomprehension or repression) of the

meaningfulness of love that Mann discerns in Wagner's work and later analyzes in "The Sufferings and Greatness of Richard Wagner".

IV

Mann meets Freud

Freud points out that, in mourning,

> people never willingly abandon a libidinal position, not even, indeed, when a substitute is already beckoning to them. This opposition can be so intense that a turning away from reality takes place and a clinging to the object through the medium of a hallucinatory wishful psychosis. Normally, respect for reality gains the day. Nevertheless its orders cannot be obeyed at once. ("Mourning" 244-45)

Thus Mann, even after "[r]eality-testing", completed *The Magic Mountain* without revising the Good/Bad Mother characterization of Madame Chauchat. And such a "turning away" continued until 1930 when Mann published *"Das Bild der Mutter"* (*GW* 420-23). Objecting to the statements by critics that the characterization of Tonio Kroger's mother is based on his mother, Mann presented what he thought was an objective portrait. But his daughter Erika, who should know, rejects the accuracy of his portrait, saying that his description "describes his mother the way he saw her as a boy, a stylized portrait, not really very lifelike, stereotyped, not at all detailed, a little romanticized" (qtd. in K. Mann 1975: 82).

Erika's statement holds a very useful clue. As a boy in Lübeck, Mann saw a different mother from the one whom he, as a late adolescent, saw when he rejoined her in Munich, after she had abandoned him and was receiving male visitors. Mann's recollections of being his mother's favorite child, his statements to Katja (K. Mann 1975: 24) and to Erika (K. Mann 1975: 82) revealing his strong attachment to his mother, his portrait of her in "A Vision", as well as his portrait of her in *"Das Bild"*, are all conditioned by his Lübeck picture of her. The picture that appears in his drawing in *Bilderbuch für artige Kinder* and in fiction from "Little Herr Friedemann" on is conditioned by the return of the repressed, which caused him to create a mother image apparently attractive, but essentially destructive. In their "Portrait of our Father" Erika and Klaus Mann write, "Not until *Joseph and His Brothers* does the autobiographical and confessional element seem quite to fade into the background" (E & K Mann 1939: 91). First and foremost that "element" concerns the mother figure. Granted that their observation was made in 1938, when their father still had seventeen years of writing before him, and that their next sentence acknowledges some "familiar traits" in *Joseph*, even so, their original point has some validity. While all Mann's post-*Magic Mountain* fiction contains an occasional "autographical and confessional element"—mostly alluding to the mother-theme—there is a decided change of tone in treatment, for every mother-element is presented not in the tragic mode, but in the grotesque and/or comic mode. That mode is present even in the "realistic" depiction of Frau Senator Rodde in *Doctor Faustus*.

In terms of Mann's creative evolution, a three-step process may be observed. In the period from "A Vision" through *The Magic Mountain*, Mann's creativity was dominated by the unconscious mother fantasy attempting to force its way into consciousness. Realizing that his future as a creative writer depended on an unconscious in which exhibitionism continued to supplant voyeurism—if Bergler's argument is valid—Mann struggled to remain ignorant of Freud's excavation of the unconscious. Even so, he had no choice but to acknowledge Freud's penetration of his awareness by 1929. Then in the Thirties, further shocked into reality by his mother's death, he was able to speak, if only indirectly, about the mother complex that had previously dominated his fiction, and to allow himself to identify the trait of his mother's that had prompted his portrait of the Bad Mother. (Two such identifications are known. In 1935 his own distant behavior toward an old friend, Ida Herz, forced him to recall, "The stiffness and coolness with which I reacted made me think of Mama, who used to treat unwelcome demonstrations of love in the same way" [qtd. in Heilbut 1996: 14]. And in a 1939 letter to Agnes Meyer, he

> noted his mother's "sensuous, pre-artistic nature" and her "inclination to the Bohemian," but also her characteristic coldness, and the vanity that made her suffer greatly as she aged; he had memorialized those sufferings, he added, in the portrait of Grand Duchess Dorothea, mother of the autobiographical Prince Klaus Heinrich, in his novel *Royal Highness*. (Izenberg 2000: 109)

His final phase was his ever increasing denial of the threat of the return of the repressed by treating the mother figure as a comic character. In the end, though, he succumbed to writer's block, a sure sign, if Bergler is correct, that he was finally forced by his *"inner conscience,"* as Bergler calls it (1949:187), to acknowledge his basic flaw, oral dependency.

Although the history of Mann's introduction to Freud's writing will probably never be traced with absolute precision, there can be little doubt that it caused an ever-widening fissure in his unconscious, through which repressed memories, which had provided the energy for creativity, escaped into consciousness.[2] Earlier I suggested that Mann probably read "Creative Writers and Day-Dreaming" in March 1908. Beharriell believes that the narrator's description of infantile sexuality in the early version of "Felix Krull" (1911) reveals Mann's knowledge of *Three Essays on the Theory of Sexuality* (1962: 150). Manfried Dierks has offered a strong argument that "Death in Venice" (1912) reveals Mann's knowledge of Wilhelm Jensen's novel *Gradiva* and Freud's "Delusions and Dreams in Jensen's *Gradiva*", Freud's "first published literary analysis" (Berlin 1992: 109). Brennan states that, sometime during the writing of *The Magic Mountain* (1913-1924), "Mann had experience with psychoanalytic treatment" (qtd. in Lehmann 1970: 204). Mann did not contradict the statement when he read Brennan's manuscript prior to its publication.

In a 1925 interview in an Italian newspaper, without citing a specific psychoanalytic text, Mann acknowledged Freud's influence on "Death in Venice" and his reservations about such influence:

> As regards myself, at least one of my works, the novella *Death in Venice*, came into being under the direct influence of Freud. Without Freud I would never have thought of treating this erotic motif, or I would surely have handled it differently. If I may use a military expression, I would say that Sigmund Freud's thesis constitutes a sort of general offensive against the unconscious with the aim of conquering it. To be sure, as an artist I must confess that I am not at all satisfied with Freudian ideas; rather, I feel perturbed and diminished by them. After all, an artist is probed by Freud's ideas as by X-rays to the point of violating the secret of his creative act. (qtd. by Berlin 1972: 111, from Michael, "Mann auf dem Wege zu Freud"; tr. Berlin)

Joyce Crick sees a connection between the 1925 interview and *The Magic Mountain*, noting that the "X-ray metaphor is a significant indication of [Mann's] distaste, for it recalls the consulting room of Krokowski the analyst in *Der Zauberberg*, the psychical counterpart to Behrens' X-ray chamber"

(1966: 175). More recently, Berlin has argued that Mann used Freud's *Three Essays* when in 1915 he wrote the "Analysis" chapter of *The Magic Mountain*, adding that he "parodies the psychoanalyst in the figure of Dr. Krokowski" (1972: 111).

Berlin notes that the "first mention of Freud in Mann's notebooks is dated 1916" (1972: 111). Presumably that mention is connected with his pondering during the composition of the essays that were collectively published as *Die Betrachtungen eines Unpolitischen* in 1918. Crick is convincing when she argues that, although he does not specifically mention Freud in that book or in "Friedrich und die grosse Koalition" (1914), Mann reveals in both that his thinking has been affected by the new psychology, however much he might dislike it or fear it (1966: 179-84).

By 1925 Mann must have felt that psychoanalysis was a dog that would not let go of his pants leg. Answering a request from "the Freudian circle itself" (Crick 1966: 173) he wrote "Mein Verhältnis zur Psychoanalyse" for the *Almanach der Psycho-Analyse, 1926.*[3] In the same year "Thomas Mann und die Psychoanalyse" appeared in *Internationale Zeitschrift für Psychoanalyse*. Perhaps it is a reprint of the interview in *La Stampa*, for it contains a nearly identical segment: "As an artist I must confess that I am not wholly satisfied with Freud's ideas; rather, I feel myself disturbed and belittled by them. After all, Freud's ideas penetrate the artist like X-rays, right down to destroying the secret of his creativity" (qtd. in Crick 1966: 174).

Satisfied with Freud's ideas or not, Mann was coming to see that they were valuable. In his 1926 article "Über die Todesstrafe", he quoted Freud to support his argument against capital punishment:

> A little psychoanalysis! In his great treatise on *Totem and Taboo*, Freud says, "If one member of the community has succeeded in satisfying the repressed desire [to commit homicide, in this instance], then the same desire must be alive in all his fellows. In order to control this temptation, the one who is actually envied must be destroyed and deprived of the fruit of his daring, and not infrequently the punishment gives its executors the opportunity to commit the same sinful deed themselves, justified as retribution. (qtd. in Crick 1966: 186)

Thus Mann credits psychoanalysis for converting him into an opponent of capital punishment. The passage that Mann quotes is buried deep in *Totem and Taboo*, in Chapter 2, Section 4, 72 (in a translation which differs slightly from Crick's), indicating that Mann was a very close reader. But it is not likely that his initial interest in the book was inspired by such a specific topic. Rather it was probably the first chapter, "The Horror of Incest", which concludes with a passage that could, in Bergler's phrase, "open the literary safe" (1949: 190):

> Psycho-analysis has taught us that a boy's earliest choice of objects for his love is incestuous and that those objects are forbidden ones—his mother and his sister. We have learnt, too, the manner in which, as he grows up, he liberates himself from this incestuous attraction. A neurotic, on the other hand, invariably exhibits some degree of psychical infantilism. He has either failed to get free from the psychosexual conditions that prevailed in his childhood or he has returned to them—two possibilities which may be summed up as developmental inhibition and regression. Thus incestuous fixations of libido continue to play (or begin once more to play) the principal part in his unconscious mental life. We have arrived at the point of regarding a child's relation to his parents, dominated as it is by incestuous longings, as the nuclear complex of neurosis. This revelation of the importance of incest in neurosis is naturally received with universal scepticism by adults and normal people. Similar expressions of disbelief, for instance, inevitably greet the writings of Otto Rank [e.g. 1907 and 1912], which have brought more and more evidence to show the extent to which the interest of creative writers centres round the theme of incest and how the same theme, in countless variations and distortions, provides the subject-matter of poetry. (*Totem and Taboo* 17; interpolation in orig.)

Here is Freud the X-ray operator whom Mann has feared. Insisting that incestuous longings constitute the "nuclear complex of neurosis", which, in his scheme, originates in the Oedipal stage, Freud anticipates the argument of Edmund Bergler used elsewhere in this study. (It should be remembered, however, that Bergler finds the origin of the complex in the oral stage.) And, too, Freud conscientiously cites Rank's contention in *The Incest Theme*, also used in this study, that literary creativity has its origin in incestuous longing.

The same year Mann was philosophic, if nostalgic, when he spoke of "Lübeck as a Way of Life and Thought":

> What I did in *Buddenbrooks* in my youth, I did unconsciously. But I would be very much mistaken if I concluded I had done it by chance. Nowadays we know something about the forces of the

unconscious and to what extent everything that is really decisive springs from this essential realm which philosophy once called 'the will' and which is only poorly and belatedly controlled by the intellect. (xiv)

If Bergler's theory is valid, Mann at this point was unconsciously fearful that exposure to Freudian ideas would cost him his creativity, since it is stoked by energy provided by the unconscious. Accordingly, Mann had to "convince his inner conscience that he is *not interested in his original wish, but only in the defense*" (Bergler 1949: 189; ital. in orig.). That is to say, he reveals his "spiteful desire for *oral* independence" (Bergler 1949: 187; ital. in orig.), rather than his "greediness or a wish 'to receive' in repetition of the child-mother situation" (Bergler 1949: 187):

> The writer's alibi before his conscience, is peculiar and specific for him. He denies the oral-masochistic attachment to mother by intrapsychically *denying her mere existence*. His unconscious argument runs something like this: "How can I be accused of masochistic attachment to mother, when mother doesn't even exist? How can I be accused of the wish to be refused, when my wish is to get?" In his giving to himself, the defensive alibi-wish is dramatized! (187; ital. in orig.)

If Mann could convince his "superego" (Bergler 1949: 189) that he was displaying his defense against the original oral fantasy by writing and therefore feeding himself, then he would be, in effect, rejecting as invalid Freud's theory that creative writing simply reveals the original oral fantasy. Yet more research by Freud and the growing acceptance of his theory could still be a danger to Mann's creativity, by weakening the censor and thus allowing repressed material to escape, so he had to erect yet another defense:

> Enlisting of the reader as "*accomplice in crime*" must be successful. Every work of art contains implicitly an invitation to the reader or spectator to partake in the writer's inner guilt. The writer unconsciously reasons: "If people approve of my work, they accept its unconscious contents, too; my guilt is therefore shared by them and lightened." This mechanism of expiation, first stressed by Rank and Sachs, must be modified insofar as the reader is invited to share the writer's inner defenses and not his inner wishes directly. (Bergler 1949: 189; ital. in orig.)

A desperate Mann must have decided that if he gave Freud a friendly reading, he might receive one in return. It may not have been a coincidence that in May 1929 Mann gave a lecture to the Munich Democratic Students Club, "Freud's Position in the History of Modern Thought" (Prater 1995: 176). Since he had publicized his reservations about analysis, why would he be given the invitation and why would he accept it—unless he had let his availability and conversion be known? In keeping with his title, Mann discusses Nietzsche and Schopenhauer as forerunners of Freud for the first six pages of his speech before introducing him by citing *Totem and Taboo* (171), in which, he said, Freud

> treats of the totem feast and the very realistic conception of blood communion as identity of substance on which it rests—that earliest feast of mankind, that commemoration of the primeval crime of parricide "in which so many things—social organisations, ethical prohibitions, religion—had their beginning." And he traces back through the ages the identity of the totem feast with animal sacrifice, theanthropic human sacrifice and the Christian Eucharist, probing with careful, inexorable surgeon's probe this whole horrifying and culturally highly fecund morbid world of incest dread (*Inzestangst*) and murder remorse (*Mordreue*), and yearning for salvation (*Erlösungsdrang*); analysing and illuminating, until the mind passes at length from consideration of these primitive abominations from which religious feeling takes its rise, from reflections upon the deeply conservative nature of all reforms, to dwell upon the author himself, his position and affiliations in the history of thought. (qtd. in Prater 1995: 171-72; parentheses and ital. in orig.)

Despite once again betraying his disquietude about psychoanalytic "probing", Mann has come to praise Freud, offering a lengthy, though highly generalized, summary of his theory, without mentioning any other text by name (though Lehmann points out that he quotes from *Beyond The Pleasure Principle* [1970: 205]) or any aspect of his treatment of creativity. Even so, a hint of criticism creeps into Mann's concluding description of Freud's "teaching":

> It might be called anti-rational, since it deals, in the interests of research, with the night, the dream, impulse, the pre-rational; and the concept of the unconscious presides at its beginnings. But it is far from letting those interests make it a tool of the obscurantist, fanatic, backward-shaping spirit. It is that manifestation of modern irrationalism which stands unequivocally firm against all reactionary misuse. It is, in my sincere conviction, one of the great foundation-stones to a structure of the future which shall be the dwelling-place of a free and conscious humanity. (198)

Freud used his X-ray machine on the essay when Mann sent it to him, for he wrote Lou Andreas-Salomé,

> Thomas Mann's essay is no doubt quite an honour. He gives me the impression of having just completed an essay on romanticism when he was asked to write about me, and so he applied a veneer, as the cabinetmaker says, of psychoanalysis to the front and the back of this essay: the bulk of it is of a different wood. (qtd. in Lehmann 1970: 207)

Even so, he was seduced, for he continued, "Nevertheless, whenever Mann says something it is pretty sound". By 1935 Freud, in a letter to Mann, was calling "himself one of Mann's 'oldest' readers and admirers" (Lehmann 1970: 208).

Mann next spoke of Freud in 1933, when he put aside work on his Joseph narrative to write a lecture that the Goethe Society had requested, "The Sufferings and Greatness of Richard Wagner", delivered on 10 February (N. Hamilton 1979: 265). No one knows what Mann actually said, for his lecture was excerpted from the essay that was subsequently published, but Prater notes that Mann later said that he omitted much of the psychological material (1995: 202).

In his introductory paragraph Mann proclaims his love for the nineteenth century and for Richard Wagner, who is its "complete expression" (15). Twelve pages later, Mann expands on his love of Wagner:

> My passion for the Wagnerian enchantment began with me so soon as I knew of it, and began to make it my own and to penetrate it with my understanding. All that I owe to him, of enjoyment and instruction, I can never forget: the hours of deep and single bliss in the midst of the theatre crowds, hours of nervous and intellectual transport and rapture, of insights of great and moving import such as only this art vouchsafes. My zeal is never weary, I am never satiated, with watching, listening, admiring—not, I confess, without misgivings. (27-28)[4]

It is singularly appropriate that Mann confesses never being satiated by Wagner's opera: all music evoked Mann's yearnings for his mother, but the music of Wagner more than that of any other composer. His mother was enraptured by the "radical modern composer" (Winston 1981: 10), so that her infant at the breast associated her music with her milk. When he was deprived of the milk, music became all the more precious to him, especially the Wagnerian promises that somewhere, sometime, if only in death, his fantasy of reunion with the Good Mother would be realized.   In the twelve pages separating his avowal of love and his description of it he first considers the century as a "perfect forest of giants" (17), notably in the belletristic neck of the woods, in which reside Balzac, Tolstoi, Zola, Nietzsche, Ibsen, each of whom expressing a genius that links him to Wagner. Then he focuses on Wagner, who, he implies, is greater than all the others, for he is the gem which captures all their remarkable facets.

Mann celebrates two "forces and gifts of genius" (22), usually thought incompatible, that vitalize Wagner's work, psychology and myth cultured in music. He acknowledges that "psychology does seem too much a matter of reason to admit of our seeing in it anything but an obstacle on the path into the land of myth", yet

> precisely this complex, of psychology, myth and music, is what confronts us, an organic reality, in two great cases, Nietzsche and Wagner. A book might be written on Wagner the psychologist, on the psychology of his art as musician not less than as poet—in so far as the two are to be separated in him. (22)[5]

Perhaps Mann is exhibiting his famous irony when he calls Wagner a psychologist. Speaking on the fiftieth anniversary of Wagner's death, Mann must be ruefully aware of how fortunate Wagner was to create before the advent of the X-ray operator. Whom Mann now imitates:

> From the beginning Wagner's poetry goes beyond the bounds of suitability for his libretto—though not so much in the language as precisely in the psychology displayed. "The sombre glow" sings the Dutchman in the fine duet with Senta in the second act:
>
> > "The sombre glow I feel within me burning—
> > Shall I, O wretch, confess it for love's
> > yearning?
> > Ah, no, it is salvation that I crave—
> > Might such an angel come my soul to save!"
>
> The lines are singable; but never before had such a complex thought been sung or been written for singing. The devoted man loves this maid at first sight; but tells himself that his emotion has nothing to do with her. Instead it has to do with his redemption and release. Then confronting her again as the embodiment of his hopes for salvation, he neither can nor will distinguish between the two longings he feels. For his hope has

taken on her shape and he can no longer wish it to have another. In plain words, he sees and loves redemption in this maiden— what interweaving of alternatives is here, what a glimpse into the painful abysses of emotion! This is analysis—and the word comes up in an even bolder and more modern sense when we think of the youthful Siegfried, and the way Wagner vitalises, in his verse and against the significant background of the music, the spring-like germination, the budding and shooting up of that young life and love. It is a pregnant complex, gleaming up from the unconscious, of mother-fixation, sexual desire and fear—the fairy-story fear, I mean, that Siegfried wanted so to feel; a complex which displays Wagner the psychologist in remarkable intuitive agreement with another typical son of the nineteenth century, the psychoanalyst Sigmund Freud. When Siegfried dreams under the linden tree and the mother-idea flows into the erotic; when Mime teaches his pupil the nature of fear, while the orchestra down below darkly and afar off introduces the fire-motif: all that is Freud, that is analysis, nothing else. (22-24)

Surely, by using Freud to analyze Wagner's work, Mann is tacitly confessing that he now sees the "complex[...]of mother-fixation, sexual desire and fear" that has inspired his own work? Not if he expects to continue his work.

Mann is not yet done with analysis, for he then cites the "erotic mother-complex[...]in *Parsifal*, in the seduction-scene in the second act[...]" (24).[6] That complex emanates from Kundry, "the dual personality" (25), who is beautiful when she is bad, but sad and sullen 'twixt times. In penance for mocking Jesus as He carried His cross, she now serves the Grail, whenever Klingsor has no work for her. Like many a girl gone wrong, she cannot help herself, for her act threw her under the control of an evil magician. Already he has used her to snare King Amfortas, who was so smitten by her beauty when he encountered her in Klingsor's garden that he dropped his Sacred Spear. Whereupon Klingsor snatched it up, giving Amfortas a wound that has not healed—and will not be healed until it is again touched by the Sacred Spear. According to a mysterious voice, only a "guileless fool" will be suitable to perform that act.

Enter Parsifal, who has just shot a swan on Grail grounds, thus unwittingly committing a sacrilegious act. When questioned by Gurnemanz, the top knight, Parsifal reveals such an ingenuous nature that he is accepted as the "guileless fool". When he is taken to see an unveiling of the Grail, Parsifal acknowledges, by mutely shaking his head, that he has no idea of what he has seen. Appalled by Parsifal's utter uncultivation, Gurnemanz directs him to get out of Graildom.

Meanwhile, Klingsor has seen the whole happening in his magic mirror. When he sees Parsifal heading his way, he commands Kundry to appear, stripped for action. Knowing that Parsifal is the only chance for salvation for King Amfortas—and herself—she struggles to escape Klingsor's control, but in vain. Like Hugh Hefner, Klingsor fills his garden with entranced and much enhanced maidens, but Parsifal, when he comes, is not uplifted by the sight. Then he hears a voice call his name, a vocable that he last heard from the mouth of his mother Herzeleide ('Heart's Sorrow'). From her flower bower, Kundry enjoins Parsifal to enjoy her, then plants a passionate maternal kiss on his uncultivated lips. Will he fall prey to the "complex of mother-fixation, sexual desire and fear"? While her wile has worked on numerous knights, this time it backfires, for it "transforms the 'guileless fool' into a conscious man, and that man conscious of a mission" (Harewood 1976: 329). Still compelled to cling to Klingsor, Kundry begs him to do something. He hurls the Sacred Spear, but it only hovers over Parsifal's head. Grabbing it, the newly conscious Parsifal uses it to make the sign of the Cross, leveling Klingsor's props sundry, also Kundry.

It takes an eternity for Parsifal to get back to Grail country. Kundry, now revived and chastened, knowing that she has been a Magdalene, washes Parsifal's feet and dries them with her hair. Fulfilling his mission, Parsifal baptises her and cures Amfortas with the Sacred Spear. Then he elevates the Grail, as all the knights acknowledge his leadership and as Kundry welcomes the death so long denied her. Mann praises Kundry as "the boldest, most powerful creation among Wagner's figures—he himself probably felt how extraordinary she was" (24-25). Her extraordinary nature Mann finds in "her tortured and distracted duality, now as *instrumentum diaboli*, now as salvation-seeking penitent, [which] is portrayed with clinical ruthlessness and realism, with a naturalistic boldness of perception and depiction in the morbid realm" (ital. in orig.).

That "duality" Mann had always experienced, when, in responding to his mother, he conceived of her as Good Mother (the faceless breast in "A Vision") or Bad Mother (the Gorgon in *Bilderbuch für artige Kinder* and elsewhere). He had long been aware of the strange effect *Parsifal* had upon him, for he noted in his diary for 19 September 1919:

> Five o'clock at the Prinzregenten-Theater: *Parsifal* with Bertram and Glöckner. Center seats. Extremely powerful impression: emotion, admiration, and the usual intrigued mistrust. Never was a work of art so naively contrived a product, a compound of

religious impulse, sheer lasciviousness, and sure-handed
competence that comes across as wisdom. The aura of sickness: I
feel "hopelessly at home" in it, I said to Bertram. Whereupon
both of us, as if speaking with one voice, exclaimed: "Why of
course, it's *The Magic Mountain*". (66-67)

If , as I have suggested, the theme of *The Magic Mountain* is
Sehnsucht for the lost breast, and if *Parsifal* is its inspiration, is not
Mann, by using the phrase "hopelessly at home", unwittingly
confessing that the "uncanny" lurks in both works? There is a
mysterious transition, as Freud tells us, from the *heimlich* to the
unheimlich. The likeness of *The Magic Mountain* to *Parsifal* Mann
again realized when he read Howard Nemerov's dissertation, *The
Quester Hero. Myth as Universal Symbol in the Works of Thomas
Mann*, for in his 1940 Princeton lecture, "On my own Work", he
wrote:

> Hans Castorp, as one sees, has a mystical-knightly ancestry. He is
> the typical, in the highest sense, curious neophyte who willingly,
> only too willingly, embraces sickness and death because
> immediately his first contact with them gives him promise of
> extraordinary understanding, of adventurous advancement. Hans
> Castorp as a seeker for the Grail—I had no such notion when I
> wrote about him; I myself was the guileless fool. ("On" 65)

In "The Sufferings and Greatness of Richard Wagner", then, Mann
confesses that he had been profoundly attracted to Wagner's work
because it gave form to his unconscious fantasy and that he now
credits Freud's work for breaching his unconscious.

　　　　Having praised Wagner's psychoanalytic insights, Mann turns
to Wagner's use of myth. His judgment is that Wagner is the "discoverer
of the myth for purposes of the opera, as saviour of the opera through the myth"
(26). That he might also be talking about his own use of myth—in a
different genre—is borne out when he adds: "When [Wagner] forsook the
historical opera for the myth he found himself; and listening to him one is fain to
believe that music was made for nothing else, nor could have any other mission but to
serve mythology" (26). He is, in so many words, implying the admission
that he later made explicit in "The Making of *The Magic Mountain*",
that by the time he wrote that novel he was employing Wagner's
complex combination of psychoanalysis, mythic allusion, and musical
structure to heighten the effect of his fiction (725). Such additions
enable his prose, like Wagner's opera, to be imbued with "the density of
the mythological atmosphere" ("Sufferings" 26). His characters, in addition

to embodying the psychological singularity provided by nature and nurture, become "all more to the reader than they seem; in effect they are nothing but exponents, representatives, emissaries from worlds, principalities, domains of the spirit" ("On" 63). Wagner could use "the density of mythological atmosphere" to imply that Siegfried and Parsifal are evocative of "Tammuz, Adonis whom the boar slew, Osiris, Dionysius, the dismembered ones, who are to return as the Crucified whose side a Roman spear must pierce that men may know him" ("Sufferings" 27). Similarly, Mann could imply that Hans Castorp is evocative of Siegfried and Parsifal and the dismembered ones by whom they are possessed. As Heilbut puts it, Mann's "Sufferings" essay transforms Wagner "into an avatar" of its author (1996: 517).

Notes to Mann meets Freud

[1] Five days after his mother's death Mann wrote a friend, "I do not believe I have ever in my life felt so sad" (qtd. in Hayman 1995: 341). It was an experience that time did not heal. Nearly twenty years later, he offered his condolescences to an American friend, Caroline Newton:

> Now your mother too has departed from you—with my whole heart I can enter into the anguish of sudden loneliness that must fill you, with both your parents gone. I can still vividly remember how I felt when my mother died at the age of seventy: what an unexpectedly bitter grief the rending of this bond was. (Winston 1971: 353)

Ten years later, his letter to Erich Kahler reveals the ache that he still felt: "above all, our sympathy for your grief over your mother. 'You know, 'tis common[...]'. And you were expecting the inevitable. Nevertheless, it is a totally unique shock and wrench, as I very well remember from my own experience" (Winston 1975: 156).

[2] In 1951 Mann wrote Joyce Morgan (later Joyce Crick):

> [S]ince *The Little Herr Friedemann* [sic] [...]psychoanalytic writers have been interested in my problems, and evidently I have always had an affinity with this sphere. Besides, very soon the atmosphere was rife with psychoanalytic theories, and people absorbed them without expressly studying them. I cannot swear that even before writing *Death in Venice* I had not read some psychoanalytic writings that derived from Freud and had been sent to me by their authors. (qtd. in, and presumably tr. by, Berlin 1992: 107)

[3] Lehmann provides a paraphrase of "Mein Verhältnis":

> It is a brief article by Mann entitled My Relation to Psychoanalysis[...]. He calls this relationship "unsimple". Mann says one can see in psychoanalysis something great, admirable, a

bold discovery, a profound advance of insight, a surprising even
sensational increase of the knowledge of man. One can find on
the other hand that it can—improperly introduced to people—
grow into an instrument for malicious enlightenment, for an
uncivilized mania for disclosure and discreditation. Its concern is
insight, melancholic insight, especially where art and artist are
concerned at whom it is aimed in particular. Mann says this was
nothing new to him when he first encountered it. He had
experienced it essentially with Nietzsche, especially in his
Wagner critique, and it had become, in the form of irony, an
element of his intellectual make-up and production. This is a
circumstance to which he undoubtedly owes the fact that
psychoanalytic scholars have shown a predilection for critical
attention to his writings. Mann quotes a passage from Death in
Venice which he calls "strongly anti-analytic" but which he says
has been interpreted as a characteristic example of "repression".
Somewhat crisply he states that indeed what may lend the artist-
neurotic the impudence to do what is *his*, despite all analytic
uncovering, will have to be marked not only as repression but—
more aptly, even if more unscientifically—as "letting a thing be".
With this somewhat angry reproach out of the way, Mann begins
to   concede—perhaps   begrudgingly—the   usefulness   of
psychoanalysis and the incontrovertible fact that it can no longer
be eliminated. He says that his preceding remarks mean in no way
simply hostility, because insight, in principle unproductive, may
yet, as the phenomenon of Nietzsche demonstrates, have much to
do with art, and the artist can be on excellent terms with it. It also
means nothing less than the delusion that the world can never
again get around the discoveries of Freud and his group by
closing its eyes. The world cannot get around them at all and
neither will art. Psychoanalysis plays into the fiction of our whole
sphere of culture, has colored it, and will possibly influence it to
an increasing degree. Mann mentions that psychoanalysis plays a
role in the just published novel, The Magic Mountain. "Dr.
Krokowski, as its agent is named in the novel, is admittedly a
little   comical.   But   perhaps   his   funniness   is   only   an
indemnification for the deeper concessions which the author
makes to psychoanalysis in the core of his works" (1970: 202-
204).

[4]What was Wagner's hold on Mann? Bryan Magee's generalization
forcefully explains it:

> Wagner gives expression to things that in the rest of us, and in the
> rest of art, are unconscious because they are repressed. Modern
> psychology has familiarized us with the idea—and convinced
> most of us of its truth—that in the process of growing up and
> developing independent personalities, and learning to live in
> society, we have to subordinate some of our most powerful

instinctual desires, especially erotic and aggressive ones—for instance passionate sexual feelings toward parents and siblings, or the urge to attack and destroy those on whom we are emotionally dependent—so that these are driven underground, below the level of consciousness, and kept there at the cost of some strain, as a result of which they remain charged with a high emotional voltage. Most of the really important taboos in our society, such as the incest taboo, relate to them. This repression, this inner conflict, is inseparable from living, and is part of the personality of each one of us. I believe that it is from, and to, this level of the personality that Wagner's music speaks. (1988: 34)

[5]On 20 January 1933, three weeks before he delivered his lecture, Mann wrote Walter Opitz, an old friend, "You will understand that for me to have let myself in for the theme of Wagner was dangerous from the beginning, for there is quite a bit to say, especially for me, and it is something of a feat not to write a book" (Winston 1971: 193). He seems to have failed in his attempt to restrain himself.

[6]My summary of *Parsifal* depends--in the letter, if not in the spirit--upon *The New Kobbé's Complete Opera*, ed. and rev. by the Earl of Harwood. New York: Putnam, 1976. 316-32.

V

Joseph and His Brothers, The Beloved Returns: Lotte in Weimar, The Transposed Heads, Joseph the Provider

Joseph and His Brothers

Late in 1923 or early in 1924 Hermann Ebers, a Munich painter, asked Mann to write an introduction for his "folio of pictures" capturing the high lights of the life of the Patriarch Joseph ("On my own Work" 70). Ebers' "graphic representation of the fate of Joseph" induced Mann to reread the story in his "old family Bible". As he was reading it, Mann thought of Goethe's judgment in *Dichtung und Wahrheit*: "This natural tale is most gracious—only it appears too brief, and one feels called upon to fill out all the details" (qtd. in "On my own Work" 70).

Reacquaintance with the Joseph story awakened Mann's "first impressions of childhood", when Bible stories and fairy-tales served as mirrors that introduced him to himself in space, time, and relation. He soon felt the urge to create a fiction, for, as he acknowledged nearly twenty years later in "The Theme of the Joseph Novels",

> A work must have long roots in my life, secret connections must lead from it to earliest childhood dreams, if I am to consider myself entitled to it, if I am to believe in the legitimacy of what I am doing. The arbitrary reaching for a subject to which one does not have traditional claims of sympathy and knowledge, seems senseless and amateurish to me. (9)

Mann contemplated "a one-volume narrative as a wing-piece of a historical triptych, the other pictures of which were to treat Spanish and German subjects" ("On my own Work" 74). As a "wing-piece", not the central panel of an altar-piece, the Joseph story did not, presumably, manifest the "principal subject" that Mann envisioned for the book (Runes 1946: 29). But, as he grew increasingly involved in research for the Joseph manuscript, he abandoned his plan to write the other two works. Even with that decision made, though, he did not begin writing, for he had several unfulfilled commitments.

While his consciousness was occupied by his ongoing projects, his unconscious occupied itself thematizing the Joseph story. As he later realized, "What is my Joseph other than once again an artist's variation on his own problems" ("On my own Work" 72). One of the ways that Mann conceived of himself as an artist was as a confidence man; he admitted his identity at a celebration of his fiftieth birthday when he prefaced a public reading from the *Krull* fragment with a confession, "My kind of artist is a con-man" (qtd. in Reed 1996: 416).[1] During the same period he was coming to see Joseph as *"eine Art von mythischem Hochstapler"*, as he wrote his daughter Erika (*Briefe* 1961: I 261) and his friend Bertram (*Briefe* 1961: I 262).

Since Mann calls both himself and his creation Joseph (and his earlier creation Krull) a *Hochstapler*, Bergler's "clinical picture" of the type ought to shed light on both the creator and his creation. Although *The New Cassell's German Dictionary* defines *Hochstapler* simply as a 'swindler' (Betteridge 1958: 237), Bergler prefers the definition 'impostor' as the description of a general type, one frequent activity of which is swindling. Mann's translators, by using 'confidence man' for *Hochstapler*, understand that Mann also intended the word to convey a personality type whose commanding trait is imposture.

Bergler discerns "specific *descriptive* characteristics" in the type "impostor" (1949: 266): as a "high-stepper" (*hoch* + *stapfen*) he passes himself off as a member of the social class higher than his origin in order to prey upon its members (1949: 267); he charms both men and women by his "firmness and self-assurance", often attracting women because of "feminine trends" in his personality that appeal to them; as a dissimulator he is always armed with an ironic outlook; he is an actor, always conscious of his technique as he manipulates his dupe (1949: 268); although he gives "the impression of being an everlasting optimist", he suffers from "deep depression" (1949: 268-69); even when he is most successful, he becomes easily bored and "unconsciously provokes his own downfall" (1949: 269).[2]

The literature on Mann's personality provided by his own introspection, by his family members and other observers, and by critical inferences from his creations confirms that it manifested Bergler's several characteristics. Mann himself revealed his early pretense to royal status; that he never relinquished his attraction to it may be assumed by his comment to Erich Kahler, 10 September 1949: "It is really curious that a life of playing games and dreaming can—if only you go on with it for long enough—lead to your being treated like royalty" (qtd. in Hayman 1995: 564).[3] The characteristic of charm has its origin in narcissism, a condition attributed to Mann by critics and biographers; a review of the relevant literature is included in McDonald's treatment of the subject (1999: 142-43). Much has been written about Mann's irony. Mann the actor has been examined by McDonald in his treatment of the theme of "performativity":

> it seems plausible that Mann derived real psychological benefits from his performances. His journals and notes from as early as 1897 show his preoccupation with what he terms "nervous strength" and its constant companion, nervous exhaustion. He often felt himself on the edge of collapse, worn down not simply by effort but by the complex, unstable, irony-laced territory in which an artist must reside. Comparatively brief, complete, and unambiguous, public performance offered temporary respite from the high-wire act of suspended convictions and the nervous toll of irony's endless reflections and rebounds. It wasn't only the applause or the eagerness of upturned young faces, though both were important; performance also offered relief from, counterpoint to, the exhausting craft of the writing desk. The sheer performance of the equivocal text was, when compared to its production, blessedly unequivocal. (1999: 34)

McDonald's thoughtful analysis also demonstrates that while Bergler's characteristics seem to be discrete verbal entities in a list, they are both symbiotic and competitive forces within the individual personality. Ronald Peacock uses the neglected subject of Mann's utilization of comedy to argue that Mann "works from the golden mean of reason" and that he has a "humanist faith" (1988: 190-91). To the public Mann thus gives "the impression of being an everlasting optimist", even though, according to his wife, the private Mann was "nervous and sensitive and tended to depression" (K. Mann 1975: 149). Finally, acknowledging in both *A Sketch of My Life* (71) and "On my own Work" (74) that he quickly became bored if he was not creating, Mann managed to maintain the psychological defense that enabled him to avoid "writer's block", which would have constituted for him the most hideous kind of downfall (cf. ch2n9).

For Bergler the "*descriptive* characteristics" of the "impostor" are signs pointing back to a "*genetic*" cause (1949: 270). That cause is "pre-oedipal disappointment in the mother" (1949: 271), a condition which leads the sufferer to "*take revenge upon people whom* [he identifies] *with the mother of the pre-oedipal period*" (1949: 272; ital. in orig.).[4] With that we return to the theme of the present study.

When Mann reread the Joseph story, thus being reminded of Goethe's comment about it, he must have intuited that its basic plot and the sketchiness of its presentation challenged him to infuse it with his life-theme, the mother-problem. Mann's intuition recalled another influence provided by Goethe, a "secret reference to[...]Faust which my work dared to take while it grew" ("Theme" 17). *The Magic Mountain* had dared to use the same secret reference, Faust's descent into the underworld realm of the Mothers, there to experience what Jantz calls "the central mystery of the Mothers scene", "the central Eleusinian mystery of death and resurrection" (1969: 57). In the "snow" chapter of *The Magic Mountain* Hans Castorp had dreamed of the Eleusinian ritual, a process thus described by Goethe: "Formation, transformation, / Eternal mind's eternal recreation" (qtd. in Jantz 1969: 59). Mann now uses the same "Mothers scene" to set the tone for "the anthropological prelude" to the entire Joseph story: "Entitled 'Descent into Hell' it is a fantastical essay which seems like the cumbersome preparation for a risky expedition—a journey down into the depths of the past, a trip to the 'mothers'" ("Theme" 8). Mann knew that the cult of Demeter at Eleusis was the oldest mystery religion in the Greek world, but he also knew that it was similar to and probably derivative of several Levantine mystery cults—e.g., Osiris, Adonis, Tammuz—of earlier origin (Chadwick 1963: 683) to which he must refer in the Joseph story. Inspired by the Mothers scene, the "Descent into Hell" tells us that the Joseph story will, like the mystery religions, reveal death being vanquished by resurrection. Hence it is, as Mann often said (Koopmann 1988: 240-42), a comedy—in the sense that Dante used the term.

In the "Descent" the narrator primarily describes the anthropology—chiefly the religious beliefs—of the tribe into which Joseph was born. This tribe was neighbored by many other tribes with similar anthropologies, even though tribal names for the divine mother and sacrificed son might differ. Underlying the widespread basic religious system was the taboo of incest, which is revealed, Rank argues, when "the first prohibitions on sibling marriage" inspired people to project their incestuous desire onto brother sun and sister moon (though in some instances sun was sister and moon was brother):

> The tendency for this projection is a justification in a double
> sense. It is at once an expression of defense placing these rejected
> impulses of human psychic life into the farthest possible external
> realm and an expression of comparison (identification) through

reference to divine (celestial) right, held to be an example for
mankind. (1992: 366; parentheses in orig.)

The chief evidence of the narrator's intention to emphasize
astral religion is his frequent association of Abram with the moon. We
are quickly told that Abram's legendary place of origin was Ur, whose
populace worshipped the moon in the person of the god Sin (Power
1953b: 85) and that Abram did "as the moon did" (4), wandering and
roving. Thereafter Abram is referred to with such epithets as "moon-
man" (5, 19) and "moon-wanderer" (6, 7). The narrator acknowledges that
it is more likely that Abram was born in Harran (8), also a center of
the moon-cult (Bright 1963: 5). There he must have met his bride
Sarai ('princess'), a name which corresponds with Sarratu, the name
of the Harran "moon-goddess, the consort of Sin" (Hooke 1963b: 887). She
might have been the moon-goddess or merely a mortal dedicated to
the moon-goddess. Either of the possibilities would explain why the
God of Abram renamed her "Sarah" (Gen. 17:15)--as, indeed, God
renamed her husband "Abraham" (Gen. 17:5). Beyond hinting that
Abram and Sarai might have become anthropomorphized over time
(more about Abraham and Sarah below), the narrator offers copious
reference to the prevalence of astral religion: e.g., "the sun's very son"
(3), "Ishtar's star" (4), "the divine lights of the firmament" (4), "the towering house
of the sun, E-sagila" (5), "the star-worshippers and astrologers at Shinar: (9), the
"image of the sun-god" (11), and "the worshipped planet" (20).

Another revelation of incest taboo is implied in "Descent", if
Freud's account of god-formation is accepted:

> The son's efforts to put himself in the place of the father-god
> became ever more obvious. The introduction of agriculture
> increased the son's importance in the patriarchal family. He
> ventured upon new demonstrations of his incestuous libido, which
> found symbolic satisfaction in his cultivation of Mother Earth.
> Divine figures such as Attis, Adonis and Tammuz emerged,
> spirits of vegetation and at the same time youthful divinities
> enjoying the favours of mother goddesses and committing incest
> with their mother in defiance of their father. (*Totem* 152-53)

In "Descent" the narrator mentions these incestuous divinities
frequently (11, 12, 13, 14, 19). Thereafter, frequent references to the
dying and resurrected son-gods emphasize that Jewish—and later
Christian—belief and ritual was profoundly influenced by the
Levantine mystery cults (Chadwick 1963: 683).

Then, too, many of the major figures in the religious history of Joseph's tribe were associated with incest. The narrator mentions Abram, the first Hebrew recorded as a monotheist, who called his wife "sister", "probably out of tenderness" (4). If Abram is to be trusted, though, the relationship between his wife Sarai and himself was incestuous, for he tells King Abimelech: "She is my sister; she *is* the daughter of my father, but not the daughter of my mother; and she became my wife" (Gen. 20:12; ital. in orig.). The narrator also remembers Lot--traditionally known as Abraham's nephew, who, made drunk on wine by his two daughters, impregnated the older the first night, the younger the second night (Gen. 19:32-38)--but excuses the daughters, saying that they acted as they did, "being under the delusion that save themselves there were none left upon the earth, and out of womanly carefulness for the continuance of the race" (8). The narrator also mentions Abraham's son Isaac (10), who married Rebekah, his first cousin once removed (she was the granddaughter of Abram's brother Nahor [Gen. 24:15]). Later the narrator tolerantly observes:

> Marriage between relatives was at that time, for excellent reasons, quite the usual thing. It was the only proper, sensible and respectable arrangement—we know how poor Esau damaged his postion by his eccentric marriages. It was no personal crotchet of Abram's which caused him to insist that Yitzchak "the true son" should take a wife only from his race and his father's house, that is from Nahor's house at Harran, in order that one might know what one was getting. (166-67)

There will be more instances of incest (and first-cousin marriage), both of gods and of men, to confront Joseph as he enters the story.[5]

Chapter I of *The Tales of Jacob* opens with seventeen-year-old Joseph sitting by a well,[6] a locus that is to be a multifaceted recurrent image throughout the tetralogy, as McDonald notes (1999: 118). The narrator anticipates the significance of the object *well* with the first sentence of the "Prelude": "Very deep is the well of the past" (3). But the well is also the medium of the present and the future:

> In Christian symbolism the well falls within the group of ideas associated with the concept of life as a pilgrimage, and signifies salvation[....]The well of refreshing and purifying water is symbolic of sublime aspirations, or of the "silver cord" which attaches man to the function of the Centre. Demeter and other deities were shown standing beside a well. (Cirlot 1962: 350)

Mann intended the well to suggest that life for Joseph would be a pilgrimage leading down to the underworld but then up to salvation, for he later spoke of the "risky expedition—a journey down into the depths of the past, a trip to the "mothers"" ("Theme" 8). And with his research into the Eleusinian mystery, he must have known of the association of the well with Demeter, hence of the association of the underworld with the mother-goddesses. The common association in dreams of a well with the womb and the nourishing breast suggests a universal unconscious meaning (Gutheil 1951: 153): Joseph's presence beside the well indicates his susceptibility to oral regression. And, finally, Mann would have known the story of the virgin Rebekah (Gen. 24), the source of the Hebrew tradition that "the first step to a marriage is often a meeting at a well" (Power 1953a: 209).

Although all of these meanings eventually attach themselves to the image of the well as it recurs, in the first scene the well as womb and breast best serves to introduce my particular concern, the mother-problem. A vestige of the old astral worship is manifested in Joseph's divinization of the moon as he sits by the well, for he salutes it with "Babylonian pet names for the moon, as Abu (father) and Hammu (uncle)", even thinks of it as "Abram, the name of his own supposed ancestor" (39). Even so, it soon becomes evident that for Joseph the moon is ultimately feminine and inextricably related to the mother goddess of the mystery cults, especially in her guise as Ishtar, whom he calls by her familiar name "Mami" (64).[7] Following his father's example, he had called his mother by the same name (256). When Jacob observes Joseph at the well, he accuses him of kissing his hand like a Babylonian (61-63), that is, actually elevating the moon to the godhead (Sutcliffe 1953b: 436). Even though Joseph is described experiencing a "seizure" (40), "moon-struck", as people thought at the time (Hooke 1963a: 674), he denies worshipping the moon by avowing his veneration for "the God of Abraham" (62). Thus he tells the truth as he knows it, but not the whole truth, for he is unaware of his unconscious motives. His purpose is not to worship the moon, but to expose his naked flesh for admiration by the moon and the mother for whom she stands. Removing neither "the light myrtle wreath from his hair nor the amulet that hung round his neck" (37), he strips to the waist to wash and then oil his torso with hands whose finger nails are dyed "brick-red". As an exhibitionist, he loses no opportunity to display his beauty. Jacob's stern order, "Cover thy nakedness" (42), suggests that he is well aware that his favorite son is a narcissist.

In the first paragraph of his impressive study McDonald anticipates one of the major themes of Mann's Joseph story: "Its dramatic narrative begins with an adolescent's narcissism and a father's loyal love, and ends with a father's mythic narcissism and a son's loving loyalty" (1999: 2). In time McDonald discusses the origin of the "adolescent's narcissism":

> Both Genesis and *Joseph and his Brothers* maintain a silence about the psychic beginnings and the childhood development of Joseph's narcissism. The tetralogy devotes itself to filling in the numerous gaps in Genesis's narrative, but not that one. The God of Genesis shows little interest in infancy and childhood, but we may well expect the author of *Buddenbrooks* and "Tonio Kröger" to do so. The opening phrase of *Young Joseph*—"Now it is said that Joseph, being seventeen years"[...]—slyly uses Biblical authority to set aside the question. Eliezer has been Joseph's teacher from the beginning, but the narrator dramatizes only the lessons at age seventeen and summarizes the rest in the parodic conservatism of the mentor's "grand style"[....]The narrator claims that our actions arise from our "fundamental tastes and sympathies," but the example he cites for the thirty-year-old Joseph comes not from early childhood but his seventeenth year [....]He gives us no cameos of the child in Laban's house, no tales of him composing sagas for elders' entertainment, managing the Canaanite equivalent of a puppet theater, or even grieving for his dead mother. When they brought him to Rachel at the end, "she did not know him." We know that he looked on her, but his reaction is not recorded[....] We know that he stopped and poured oblations at her grave on his way to Shechem, but he is too caught up in his "childish foolishness" to feel anything [....]Of his emotion at the moment of her death the text is silent. Put figuratively, he cannot behold her face. (1999: 156-57; page references omitted)

McDonald soon caps his argument:

> Mann gives us virtually no trace of the intervening stages of Freudian devlopment: no permanent tainting of infant love with the loss and pain of maternal withdrawal; no decisive Oedipal opposition and rivalry that disrupt the loving gaze. The mother does not play a central role; Rachel's love for Joseph hardly figures in Mann's retelling. In Joseph's case the psyche begins not with maternal care nor early trauma, but with sustaining fatherly love intercalated between narcissim's fluctuations; the gaze of Jacob fell upon the infant Joseph, and for good and ill he loved him. (1999: 159)

McDonald then introduces his explanation of Mann's "silence":

> I am of course not suggesting that Mann has somehow failed his
> readers here, or missed some splendid narrative opportunity. His
> reasons for silence were deliberate. As we shall see, it continued
> his strategy of containment of Freud, and yielded yet another way
> to highlight the central features of Joseph's narcissism. (1999:
> 157)

In pursuing a different analysis of Joseph's narcissism I will return to Mann's conception of Joseph and of himself as a confidence man, in light of Bergler's analysis of the "basic neurosis" and its particular manifestations in the impostor and in the creative writer (cf. ch1n10).[8] Mann does not tell us about the relationship between Rachel and the infant Joseph, any more than he could tell us about the relationship between Julia and his infant self. (And, even if he could, he would not dare to tell himself, much less us, for fear the revelation would, according to Bergler [1949: 186-93], destroy his creativity.) But, patterning Joseph's psychological development on his own experience—as far as he is aware of it—Mann offers us a Joseph whose behavior contains enough early outcroppings of regressive behavior to make us suspect that there was, in McDonald's words, "early trauma".

It is exactly appropriate that, having discussed the well of the past in the Prelude, the narrator begins his narrative by alluding to what Bergler calls the "'geologically' deepest and historically oldest layers of the unconscious: those of oral regression" (1949: 1). Joseph's initial haunting of the well and solicitation of the moon argue that he had suffered, in Bergler's words, a "deep narcissistic wound" (1949: 3) when he felt that he was deprived of Rachel's breast. According to Bergler, the infant first lives in a "fantasy of magic omnipotence", fantasizing that he and his mother are one, that therefore he feeds himself (1949: 2). When, inevitably, he realizes that he does not feed himself, he projects his aggression onto his mother, conceiving of her as "cruel, malicious, refusing, devouring" (1949: 9), the pre-oedipal Bad Mother. The Good Mother would be the idealized feminine image of the pre-trauma paradise who always immediately offers a bountiful breast. Like many of Mann's protagonists, Joseph suffers from *Sehnsucht*, even if it remains almost undetected under his narcissism. The "wound", the cause of the basic neurosis, causes Joseph to develop the behaviors that Bergler attributes to "psychic masochists" . To these behaviors are joined two significant behaviors which Bergler attributes to the creative writer: he "is a *voyeur* who utilizes his exhibitionistic tendencies as a defense against these scopophiliac impulses" (1949: 188; ital. in orig.) and his

> type of neurotic orality is not greediness or a wish "to receive" in repetition of the child-mother situation, but rather a spiteful desire for *oral* independence. By this, the artist *identifies* himself with the "giving" mother out of defensive pseudo-aggression toward her, and thus eliminates her. He achieves oral pleasure for himself through "beautiful" words and ideas. In its deepest sense, it is a desire to refute the "bad" pre-oedipal mother and the masochistic "disappointments" experienced through her, by establishing an "autarchy," *acting a magic gesture* (1949: 187; ital. in orig.)

When Joseph was nine-years-old his mother died. As McDonald notes (1999: 156-57), Mann creates scenes in which Rachel does not recognize Joseph and Joseph does not display filial mourning. The inclusion of these details hints at the true nature of the relationship that had existed between the pair. Beyond the tower of Eder, soon after Rachel's death, "it came to pass, when Israel [Jacob] dwelt in that land, that Reuben went and lay with Bilhah his father's concubine: and Israel heard *it*" (Gen. 35:22). In Mann's amplification of the scene, Joseph informs his father of the transgression:

> Joseph, lounging idly about the camp, if not precisely with intent to spy, had learned enough of this scene of passion to make simple and zealous report to the father that Reuben had "sported" and "laughed" with Bilhah. The words conveyed less than he really knew, yet in the local parlance they insinuated everything. (52)

In the first sentence, the narrator's feeble exoneration of Joseph only emphasizes that he truly is a voyeur. In the second sentence, the narrator coolly convicts Joseph of deviousness. Then he explains Jacob's reaction:

> Bilhah, because he himself slept with her, was really Reuben's mother; his words of thunder rumbled the sinister old idea that Reuben, by lying with his mother, had betrayed his wish to be lord over all—and Jacob met the assumption by making him lord over nothing. He stretched forth his arm and took away from the groaning sinner his firstborn rights—took them indeed only unto himself, without for the moment bestowing the title further; so that from then on the matter was undecided, save as the majestic partiality of the father's heart took the place for the time being of legal fact. (53)

Like his father before him, nine-year-old Joseph has stripped the firstborn of his rights. Beyond that, he has seen to it that paternal punishment is delivered to the perpetrator of maternal incest, an act whose attraction lingers in his unconscious.

The narrator then asserts that Joseph's talebearing against Reuben is indicative of his emerging character:

> the simpleton learned nothing from the early and serious occurrences with Reuben; made no amendment through the latter's magnanimity and as he grew up became a more dangerous eavesdropper and talebearer than he had been as a child. Dangerous to himself too, and in particular, for the rôle he had taught himself to play daily heightened both his observation and his isolated state; prejudiced his happiness, drew down upon him a hatred which it was not in the power of his nature to bear and gave him every ground to fear his brothers—the which then supplied fresh temptation to flatter the father and secure himself against them[...]. (53-54)

Indeed, Joseph even slanders his brothers, his action all the more glaring because of the narrator's absurd attempt to excuse it (54).

Having accounted for the origin and development of Joseph's personality, the narrator then leaves Joseph sitting by the well in the moonlight, as it were, while he traces the history of the tribe into which the "confidence man" had been born. But the final paragraph of *Tales of Jacob* returns us to the event which revealed Joseph's "basic neurosis": "When the earth had closed above the beloved [Rachel], on the spot where God had taken her, by the wayside, Israel passed on, and made a stage at Migdal Eder, an ancient tower. There Reuben sinned with Bilhah, the concubine, and was cursed" (258).[9] Since we know that Reuben's downfall resulted from Joseph's neurosis-driven tattling, we expect that he will continue such behavior until, like the typical confidence man (Bergler 1949: 271-72), he achieves his own downfall.

The stage for Joseph's fall is set in "The Coat of Many Colours". The Biblical source is Genesis 37:3, "Now Israel loved Joseph more that all his children, because he *was* the son of his old age: and he made him a coat of *many* colours". Mann's departures from the source continue his creation of Joseph as a victim of what Bergler calls the "basic neurosis". In Mann's version, Rachel's father Laban, having purchased the veiled coat from a traveler years before (192), tells Jacob that Rachel is to wear it at her wedding. He describes the garment:

> It may have belonged to a king's daughter in times past, being the maiden garment of a daughter of princes, so artfully is it

embroidered throughout with manifold symbols of Ishtar and
Tammuz, but she, the spotless one, shall veil her head in it. For
immaculate is she and shall be like one of the *enitu*, like to the
bride of heaven, whom each year at the feast of Ishtar, the priests
of Babel lead up to God before all the people up the steps of the
stairs and through the seven gates, and take from her some piece
of her garment and her ornaments at every gate, and at the last
gate her shame, and they lead the holy maid naked into the
uppermost bedchamber of the tower E-temenanki. There she
receives the god upon the bed in the darkness of the night and
exceedingly great is the mystery. (192-93)

Rachel will wear it when she marries Jacob—just as her sister
Leah before her (320). Understandably, Rachel must be greatly down
in the mouth as she gazes at the veiled coat that Leah will put on and
take off first. The narrator describes what she sees: "Here was Ishtar-
Mami, in various shapes, a tiny nude figure, pressing milk out of her breast with both
hands, the sun and moon on either side" (195). And, after an elaborate
analysis of the coat's other depictions, the narrator quotes one of the
sayings "woven into the veil": "I have put off my coat, how shall I put it on?" This
sentence, thought to be part of an ancient Hebrew liturgy celebrating
"the marriage of the Sun God with the Mother Goddess" (Wevers 1963: 931), is
embedded in *The Song of Solomon* (5:3).

After the songs of the wedding ceremony—also embedded in
The Song of Solomon—are sung, Jacob marries the Ishtar figure,
receives his bride in a darkened wedding chamber, and at dawn
discovers Leah in the bridal bed. Jacob accuses Laban of the old bait-
and-switch game, but seems somewhat mollified when Laban says that
just as soon as Leah's week-long wedding festivities are over
(Sutcliffe 1953a: 198), Jacob can marry Rachel (Gen. 29:28), provided
that he serve him seven more years. Just for good measure, Laban
throws in two concubines, Zilpah and Bilhah (207).

The veiled garment returns to the story when Joseph, now
seventeen, inveigles his father in the manner of his mother (316),
displaying the impostor's "*[p]seudo-identification mimicry*" (Bergler 1949:
268). Joseph claims that, at their meeting by the well, his father had
promised to give him a present (319). Charmed into helplessness,
Jacob confesses that the gift is Mami's wedding garment (320).
Sinuously, Joseph entices his father with all the eloquence of a born
con man and succeeds, despite his father's plea: "Be quiet, tempter. Leave
me, and coax me not, that thy folly may not overflow and fall upon my head" (321).
Helplessly, Jacob brings out the coat, which Joseph rapturously

describes down to the last detail, even the ancient saying: "I have put off my coat; how shall I put it on?" (322).

Describing a significant characteristic of the impostor, *"[c]harming, disarming behavior"*, Bergler writes, "Women, especially, are charmed by the occasional feminine trends in these men, finding narcissistically some unconscious similarity to themselves" (1949: 267). Bergler's observation serves as an apt introduction to the narrator's description of Joseph in the climax of the scene:

> He looked, of course, like a young god. The effect he produced was only to be expected, and his eagerness to bring it about did anything but strengthen Jacob's resistance. We shall do well to recognize at once the irrestible guile by which he had finessed the garment out of Jacob's hands into his own. And this was scarcely done when the thing was on his back—put there by two or three deft and assured motions which themselves evinced great skill in the art of dressing. How well it set him off! It covered his head and wrapped his shoulders, the silver doves glittered and the gay embroideries glowed, it fell in folds about his youthful form and made him look taller than he really was. But not only so. For the festal garment became his face to such an extent that nobody who saw him could have disputed the popular verdict upon his charms. It made him so lovely and so well-favoured that the phenomenon was actually no longer quite earthly; in fact it bordered on the supernatural. Worst of all, the likeness to his mother—her look, her forehead and brows, the shape of her mouth—had never stood out so clearly as in this dress; poor Jacob was so smitten by it that his eyes overflowed, and he thought nothing else than that he was beholding Rachel in Laban's house, on the day of the fulfilment.
>
> It was the mother-goddess who stood there before him smiling, in the boy's lovely guise, and asked: "I have put on my coat—shall I take it off?"
>
> "No, no, keep it, keep it!" the father said. The young god rushed away. Jacob lifted his brow and his hands, and his lips moved in prayer. (322-23)

Jacob knows that Joseph's capture and display of the coat will announce to his other sons that Joseph has enticed the blessing from him. And, certainly, that was Joseph's conscious motive for his behavior. But the narrator also means to imply an unconscious motive for Joseph by his description of Joseph's triumphant use of the legend on the coat. By putting himself within his Mami's coat, he has—at least to the satisfaction of his unconscious—re-entered his mother's body, cured himself of his "basic neurosis". He finds himself back in command of "magic omnipotence" (Bergler 1949: 2), having regressed to the experience of being inseparable from his mother, who seems to be regarded as an avatar of Ishtar. Little wonder that Joseph loses no time in telling his disfavored brother Reuben:

> I and my mother are one,[...]Knowest thou not that Mami's garment is likewise her son's and that they wear it by turns, one in the other's place? Name her and thou namest me. Name what belonged to her and thou namest what is mine. (335)

Thereafter Joseph insists on telling his brothers his dreams of preferment and flaunts his mother's coat, infuriating them. His behavior is characterized by Bergler: "The impostor[...]overdoes his triumph, seems to get 'bored' with it, and unconsciously provokes his own downfall" (1949: 269). Joseph is also the impostor when he insinuates that he is of divine origin, which is "social climbing" of the highest order (Bergler 1949: 266). Ultimately his brothers attack him, throw him into a dry well, and send Jacob the coat (stained by blood from "a beast of the flock" [418]) as a sign that Joseph has been killed by a beast of the wild. Naked and trussed in the well, Joseph must acknowledge that he and his mother are not one, for he calls out, "Mother! Save thy son!" (394) That he implores "Mother" rather than "Father" argues that he remains on the pre-Oedipal level of psychological development and that, despite his assurance to his father that he worships the "God of Abraham" (62), he remains on the pre-paternal level of religious development.

But it is a fatherly Ishmaelite (396) who orders Joseph lifted from the well, gives him milk to drink and a mantle to wear (397), and comments upon his rescue: "he came naked and foul out of the depth as from the body of his mother and is as it were twice born". Immediately charmed by Joseph, the Ishmaelite quickly proposes buying him when his caravan stops at the tents of Joseph's brothers (408). Now a slave, Joseph is bound for Egypt.

One night, on the way, the Ishmaelite tells Joseph that his "second birth and resurrection" reminds him of the story of Osiris, "the mangled one", "the First of the West, king and judge of the dead" (464), "the most popular of all Egyptian deities" (Frazer 1958: 420). Prompted by Joseph, the Ishmaelite discusses the Egyptian belief that all who believe in Osiris' resurrection will themselves be resurrected. Thus, at death, a believer becomes Osiris, even taking his name as a praenomen (465). Earlier Joseph had told the Ishmaelite that he could not remember his name (454). Now, in appreciation for the discourse on Osiris, Joseph volunteers his name, "Usarsiph" (466). The impostor who had formerly claimed that his mother Ishtar and he were one will now claim that Osiris and he are one. On "the Street of the Son" (522), before "Usarsiph" reaches the place where he will be offered for sale, he has become "Osarsiph" (523).

The Ishmaelite enters the estate of Petepre ("Potiphar" in the Bible), a high official in Pharaoh's government, for he wishes to persuade Mont-Kaw, Petepre's overseer, to buy Osarsiph. Before Mont-Kaw appears, though, the foreign traders are greeted by two minor functionaries of the estate, Dudu and "sa'ankh-Wen-nofer-Neteruhotep-em-per-Amun" (530), better known as "Bes". Both are dwarfs, but they stand poles apart. Dudu is a reactionary creature of "phallic strutting", as McDonald notes (1999: 182), inordinately proud of his marriage to a woman of normal size, upon whom he has sired two sons of normal size. The emptiness of his vanity is suggested by his function: he is overseer of Petepre's wardrobe (540), including Petepre's jewels (625). But, alas, Petepre has no family jewels, for his parents had him castrated as an infant, so that, according to his father, he might not be contaminated by sex and so that, according to his mother, he might better pursue advancement as a courtier (582). Bes is described by his bitter enemy Dudu as a "clown and court fool" (541), not much superior to the red monkey always perching on his shoulder (548). Bes spends most of his time being an *amusant* for the occupants of "Amun's southern house of women" (515, 528)--whom he probably mocks by his grotesque cross-dressing. Seemingly a "simpleton" (527), Bes is mocked by the other slaves of the house with the title "vizier", but, in the tradition of court fools, he provides wisdom for one who seeks it.

Because of his worship of Amun, the totalitarian divinity of Egyptian fundamentalism (McDonald 1999: 192), Dudu instantly hates Osarsiph the Canaanite pagan. Bes, on the other hand, immediately thinks that Osarsiph is "[g]ood, wise, and beautiful" (531), that he is, in other words, charismatic. He immediately confesses his true name to Osarsiph, translating it as "May the Favouring Essence (in other words, Osiris) preserve the beautified of the gods in the house of Amun" (530; parenthesis in orig.). Dedicated at birth to Osiris, Bes now dedicates himself to Osarsiph: "Are you born from the reeds?[...]Are you an Usir in the rushes? Did the mother search and find you in the water?" (531)

When Mont-Kaw deliberates whether or not to purchase Osarsip, the dwarfs boisterously shout contrary recommendations. Seeking to incline Mont-Kaw to make the purchase, the Ishmaelite offers seven gifts, the seventh of which is Osarsiph himself, describing him as "eloquent of tongue" (537). Mont-Kaw has already been struck by Osarsiph's beauty and by his speech (536), and when the scoffing Dudu questions the origin of Osarsiph's "gift of tongues" (537), the overseer deciphers the dwarf's raillery as unintended verification of the slave's charisma. In response to the overseer's question, the slave says that his name is Osarsiph, arousing the overseer's comment: "Osarsiph?[...]I know not the name. It is not foreign; indeed, it is comprehensible, since he from Abodu occurs in it, the lord of the eternal silence" (539). Sensing the presence of Osiris in Osarsiph, Mont-Kaw purchases him.

Mann concludes the scene with a *tableau vivant*:

> The two little men stood, hands on knees, on Joseph's either side as though he were a tree, scolding and spitting at each other round him. The crowd, Egyptian and Ishmaelites together, and the overseer with them, roared with laughter at this petty war going on at the level of their knees. (541)

As a figurative tree Joseph towers over the "two little men", but also as a symbolic tree he presents an erect penis (Gutheil 1951: 138). In the Biblical tradition, he is the forerunner of the father of David, Jesse, whose erect "Tree" documenting Jesus' genealogy graces many a stained-glass church window (Evans 1981: 610). Granted that the apocryphal direct lineage passes through Judah, Joseph's brother (Gilmour 1963: 496), but certainly Joseph ought to be a branch on the Jesse's Tree for his preservation of Judah in Egypt.

True to his impostor nature, Joseph had become "Usarsiph/Osarsiph" when he was sold to the Ishmaelite, for he, like Osiris, had "died" (in the dry well) and been resurrected. Thus he would imply that his physical and mental attributes testify to his god-likeness. Consciously standing there "as though he were a tree" Osarsiph represents what Frazer calls perhaps the earliest characterization of Osiris in the Egyptian mind, a tree spirit (1958: 441-42). But maybe Osarsiph has not been sufficiently aware of Osiris' salient behavior as a god of fertility. Even after suffering death at the hands of his brother Set, Osiris is yet capable of siring a son with his sister-bride Isis, who, in the form of a hawk, settles herself upon his erection (Frazer 1958: 422). Later, Set cuts the corpse into fourteen pieces and scatters them across Egypt. Isis was able to find thirteen pieces, donating them to temples as relics to be worshipped, but the *pièce de résistance*, having been gobbled by a fish, was not recovered, so Isis had a sycamore replacement member fitted to Osiris' image (Frazer 1958: 424).

In the annual fertility festival women carried the Osiris image, dramatically jerking a string to levitate the divine prosthesis, according to the narrator (641) "as long as an ell" (a measurement from twenty-seven to forty-five inches, depending upon the country). Standing there "as though he were a tree", Osarsiph first of all reminds Petepre's household of Osiris the phenomenal phallus. The impression would be reinforced by the bracketing pair of dwarfs, who are themselves penis symbols (Freud *Interpretation* 357; Gutheil 1951: 136); such doubling is dream insurance against the threat of castration (Freud *Interpretation* 357), a theme integral to the Osiris myth, according to Rank (1992: 248). Of course, the penis would be very little without the testicles, so the dwarfs play another symbolic role as they cluster at the base of the tree, although they interpret that role in much different ways. Dudu's immediate hostility—later focused on an obsession to see Joseph castrated (790)--seems to be fueled by a superabundance of testosterone, while Bes's immediate alignment with him may result from his intuition that Joseph is threatened by the same fate that he suffered, castration (779) if Dudu's word can be trusted.[10]

Bes immediately initiates his protection of Osarsiph, when he urgently instructs him to throw himself flat on the ground at the approach of a "gilded carrying-chair":

> Leaning among the cushions, with crossed feet, was an Egyptian lady, exquisitely got up, glittering ornaments in her curling locks, gold about her neck, with beringed fingers, and arms like lilies, one of which—very white and lovely—hung idly down at the side of the chair. Beneath the wrought-gold garland on her head Joseph saw her profile: that peculiar and personal, despite all adherence to the fashion quite unique and individual profile, with its eyes lengthened toward the temples by cosmetics, its flattened nose, its shadowy cheeks, its mouth at once thin and soft and sinuous as a snake between its two deep corners.
>
> It was Mut-em-enet being borne to her evening meal; the lady of the house, consort of Petepre—a personality big with fate. (549)[11]

While Bes averts his eyes, his monkey and Joseph do not. What the monkey sees only the monkey knows; what Joseph sees is the return of the repressed. Like Little Herr Friedemann he focuses on the naked arm of a female, a sight that awakens his unconscious breast hunger. Sight of that "lily arm" (556, 568) will be mentioned from time to time as testimony to its lodgement in Joseph's unconscious.

Although Joseph has been purchased, he is not given a task for at least three months and therefore has no opportunity to impress Petepre. Then, through the good offices of Bes, he serves as dumb waiter for Petepre's doddering parents, the twins Huia and Tuia (572-86), learning from their conversation of their fear that their daughter-in-law might someday rebel against the unfructified condition imposed on her by their tinkering with their tot (584). Here it must have occurred to Joseph that it was his divine destiny to be a coy boy toy.

Again Bes gains Joseph a task (590). The crafty narrator avers that it is not mentioned in any of the other "accounts, Oriental or Occidental, in prose or verse" (589), thus all but shouting that the incident is designed to further his mother-theme. Joseph begins work in Petepre's orchards, is soon assigned responsibility for pollinating the date palms, an activity he recalls seeing depicted on the fateful coat once worn by his mother (591). He is taught to climb the male palms to gather the seed fronds, then climb the female palms to hang a seed frond inside each "ovary-bearing flower-stalk" (592). Thus, when Petepre enters the palm grove, Joseph is embodying two essential aspects of Osiris, inhabiting the tree and initiating fertilization. When he is questioned, Joseph unleashes such a stream of deferential eloquence that Petepre is swept off his feet. Told to identify himself, Joseph says that his name is "Osarsiph" (602), inclining his owner to imagine that his new slave is very much like Osiris himself.

The next day Joseph is appointed body servant to Petepre, attending him at meals and reading to him afterwards. Serving his first meal Joseph is very much aware of Mut, now adorned with a wig "shaped rather like the head-cloth of a sphinx", still flashing those "bare white arms" (608). At the same time, Mont-kaw begins to train Joseph to be his successor as Petepre's overseer. These signs of Joseph's success infuriate Dudu, who schemes to use Mut to cut him down a notch or two (649).

With the death of Mont-kaw (663), Joseph becomes Petepre's overseer, thus is often in Mut's presence. The prevenient Bes, noticing the increasing eye-contact between mistress and slave, warns Joseph that he is playing with fire, but Joseph affects "not to understand" (677). Desperately ambivalent that she will be undone by Joseph's extended presence, Mut pleads with Petepre to send him away, but is secretly pleased when her husband refuses her request (705). Enter, then, the priapic Dudu with hoisted expectation, for he senses that he can use her infatuation with Joseph to prune the pagan's growth.

Dudu shifts tack toward Joseph, now professing his loyalty
(712). Joseph does not trust the dwarf, but, as an eavesdropper and
clever rogue himself, says that he "needs eavesdroppers and clever rogues and
must prize their services" (714). At Dudu's departure, the eavesdropping
Bes warns Joseph of his peril, but Joseph, in recalling the time when
he first saw Mut's "lily-white arm" (715), betrays his desire to play with
fire. Thus Joseph disregards the warning of a friendly eavesdropper.
His professions to the contrary not withstanding, Joseph is again
motivated by the vanity that landed him in the pit, determined to
compel Mut to love him more than herself. He is so confident that his
soul will be protected by the living God that he ignores the salient
evidence that his body is possessed by Osiris, "the god in deathly readiness,
rigidly awaiting the vulture-woman" (718).

Thus begins the strange three-year relationship between the
older Mut and the now-twenty-seven-year-old Joseph. In the first year
Joseph, perhaps sensing that Mut becomes blue once a month, refers
to Ishtar and to his mother while reporting to her (726), an action that
increases her "maternal longing" (730). In the second year Mut is now
desperate enough to "let Joseph see her love" (737). Dressing in "Asiatic
dress" (740), she tries to awaken his longing for his mother, whose
absence she can then fill. To this visual appeal she joins her frequent
verbal appeals (744). She, "the smitten one, was the cause of Joseph's increased
masculinity" (746), of which he is painfully aware, for he thinks of "the
awakening of the dead Osiris by the female vulture which hovered over him and
received from him the god Horus".

In the third year both dwarfs become aware that Joseph walks
around "in the state of the god when his wrappings were rent" (758); reacting to
this emerging development, both act quickly. First Dudu solicits a
note from Mut to Joseph proposing that they sleep together, then
delivers it (762). Then Bes advises Joseph to refuse further notes,
indeed to forgo further appearances before Mut (764).

Yet Joseph must finally assent to her request for his presence.
The narrator announces that Mut now possesses a different kind of
beauty,

> a suspect, an uncanny kind, which may even approach the ugly
> and wield for evil the power over the emotions which it is the gift
> of beauty to wield; by virtue, that is, of sex, which has usurped
> beauty's place and takes its name. Then it is no longer a spiritual
> beauty revealed in the feminine, but a beauty in which the
> feminine reveals itself, an eruption of sex, the beauty of a witch.
> (765)

As well as hinting that Mut awakens Joseph's maternal awe, Mann's sly insertion of "uncanny" anticipates the transformation that is to occur. Mut's breasts have "developed in voluptuous splendour" (766); her thighs have become "large and vigorous," giving "the impression that they gripped a broomstick between them, over which the creature bent, with shrunken back and swelling breasts, and rode to the mountains"[12]. The other parts of her body, including her hitherto fetching arms, have withered, and her face, "with its frame of black curls" now reveals a "morbid, mask-like tension". Her nose, noted in her initial appearance as "flattened" (549), is now described as "saddle-nosed". Mut has become a Gorgon, with snaky locks (and mouth) and porcine proboscis, resembling the "*Mvtter Natvr*" whom the twenty-year-old Mann drew for *Bilderbuch für artige Kinder*, a "Picture Book for Well-Behaved Children".[13]

There is one very significant departure in appearance in Mann's description of Mut as Gorgon, Gorgoneion, Medusa. Whereas in *Bilderbuch für artige Kinder* "*Mvtter Natvr*" displays a lolling tongue (read "penis") that she had chopped off with her "dentate vagina" teeth, Mut has nearly bitten her own tongue off "because it so overpoweringly craved to say to her husband's young steward that which she had already written to him in a rebus" (764). When Joseph does appear before her, they begin to play a game of chess, whose maneuvers, both understand, mimic the game of sexual strategy in which they are engaged (767-68). When Joseph comments that they have "checkmated" each other, she collapses and, "in her abandonment" (768), lisps the words that she does not want to say, "Thleep—with me!" (769) By using humor Mann has transformed the mother-image from the grotesque threat of his early fiction into a comic foil (cf. ch1n5).

Although reader tension is defused by the intrusion of comedy in the scene, still some physical activity to separate Joseph from Mut seems warranted. Yet Mann keeps them together, talking. Mut claims that she is "Isis", implying that he, as Osiris, owes her (769). As "Isis" she announces that her "evil son" (770) has a duty to perform:

> Hearken to what I whisper: for you, Osarsiph, my body has changed and been transformed to a vessel of love from tip to toe; when you come to me and yield me the glory of your youth, you will not believe that you lie next a human woman, but will satisfy the lust of a god with mother, wife, and sister, for lo, I am she! (772)

She even proposes the murder of Petepre: "We could kill him and put him out of the way, what ith there to that, my falcon? It ith nothing" (774). Just to let him know that she is familiar with the Oedipal theory that she has just vocalized, she declares, "With his mother each man sleeps—the woman is the mother of the world, her son is her husband, and every man begets upon his mother— do you not know, must I teach you these simple things?" (776).

Joseph's response to Mut's importunity reveals Mann's reason for stretching out the scene. Prefacing his strategy, Joseph informs Mut that he will "speak and choose consoling words" (772) with her, for he is genuinely concerned for her welfare. That is likely true, but Joseph has an ulterior motive for acting "literary" which he soon reveals:

> Hearken, Eni, and in God's name recall your understanding for that which I would say, for my words will stand, and when our story comes into the mouths of the people, so will it sound. For all that happens can become history and literature, and it may easily be that we are the stuff of history. (773-74)

To her proposal that they commit incest and kill Petepre, he, also knowing his Freud, responds, "remember that we are perhaps, yes, very likely, in a saga; then pull yourself together![...] it is my case and concern that it shall remain but a thought and that we shall make no such history as that!" (775). Then he does leave, as Mut cries after him:

> Do you think to escape me? Do you think we shall escape each other? I know, I know already of your zealot god to whom you are sealed and whose wreath you wear. But I fear no stranger god and I will tear your wreath, of whatever it is made, and give you to wear a wreath of ivy and vine for the mother-feast of our love! Stay, beloved! Stay, loveliest of the lovely! Stay, Osarsiph, stay! (776)

What has been happening here? Mann would no doubt say that he had only felt, in Goethe's words, "called upon to fill out all the details". But beneath the erotic histrionics Mann has written a drama that is explicated by Bergler's analysis of "writer's block". Joseph is, by the time we meet him, an impostor in that he "*identifies* himself with the 'giving' mother out of defensive pseudo-aggression toward her, and thus eliminates her" (Bergler 1949: 187). Never betraying his authentic feelings for his mother, he transforms his voyeurism into exhibitionism, thus develops a "plot" for his life (188).[14] He is then capable of living a life made meaningful by ordered movement. "The writer's productivity [and

Joseph's success] denotes that his alibi of 'overcoming' the oral-masochistic conflict has been accepted by the superego—temporarily at least" (Bergler 1949: 188). "In cases in which the superego does not accept the alibi and accuses the writer of infantile sexual connotation (of being an infantile Peeping-Tom), the alibi is 'lack of imagination,' hence sterility results" (Bergler 1949: 189; parenthesis in orig.). Mut, animated by the archetype Great Mother, represents the "return of the repressed", threatening to destroy Joseph's imposture that he is immune to mother-longing. Thus Mann has Joseph use the terms of narrative to explain to Mut that he cannot allow her to destroy his "plot". And thus Mann, like Joseph an impostor, can assert that his work does not "express his unconscious wishes and fantasies", but rather "his unconscious *defense against these wishes and fantasies*" (Bergler 1949: 187; ital. in orig.).

Mann continues to "fill out all the details" provided by Genesis 39:7-21. Since the treatment of Mut's failure to seduce Joseph is sufficiently detailed in its original version, Mann is free to develop his subtext, Mut's transmogrification. This he does openly in the chapter "The Bitch", in which she is described as "witchlike" (809) and as a "hag" (810). In this condition she enlists her black servant Tabubu in the worship of the "arch-hag", "the gracious mistress bitch", hoping to conjure Joseph into submitting to her wish to be fructified. When the "arch-hag" refuses to co-operate, Mut's face once more reveals her identity as a Gorgon: "the corners of her half-open, masklike mouth had sagged more and more bitterly, as though weighted down; it was piteous to see, this mouth, with its stiff, tragic lips" (814).

Defeated in her attempt to capture Joseph's spirit, Mut makes one last attempt to claim his body. Joseph is commanded by Mut to enter her room in the otherwise empty house. True to his nature as an impostor, Joseph "talked very volubly, almost breathlessly, bringing to bear all his wit and charm against the woman's desire, in the attempt to talk her out of it" (829). At the same time, again true to his oral nature, Joseph displays "the state and condition of the dead god" (830), exhibitionism *in extenso*, for Mut begins to chant, "*Me' eni nachdtef!* I have seen his strength!" Joseph certainly feels no victory, for he is revealing that he is still susceptible to the enticement of the mother figure. All he had wanted to do, according to Bergler's analysis of the impostor, was to say: "I wanted only to prove to you that I could get your love—but I don't care to have it" (272).

The narrator states that it was appearance of the face of his father that "enabled Joseph, in that uttermost extremity, to tear himself away and flee" (830). Jacob's face also contained the features of Potiphar, Mont-Kaw, "and over and above all these were other, mightier traits", presumably those of Abraham, even his God? Egged on by the sly narrator, critics have variously interpreted the Freudian implications of this scene (McWilliams 1983: 253-55, McDonald 1999: 207-11, Hartwich 2002: 160-62). But then the narrator describes Joseph's escape from Mut's clutches, shucking his "jacket—the garment," "his outer raiment", as frantic as a man with a lizard in his drawers. The narrator's list of synonyms for "coat" is meant to recall Joseph's donning of "the many coloured-coat" (322), just at the onset of his narcissistic career; sounding like a burlesque queen, he had seductively questioned his father, "I have put on my coat—shall I take it off?" (323). Gaining his mother's garment was an act of pride, losing his "wreath" to Mut's clutches is the fall that proverbially follows. The comic context of the story of the impostor son who would get back at his mother, but instead gets his comeupance, makes any Oedipal interpretation superfluous.[15] Mann protested—too loudly, methinks—to his brother Heinrich (Wysling 1998: 194) and to Agnes Meyer (Winston 1971: 301), that his presentation of "the fruitlessly desiring Mut-em-enet" ("Theme" 11) was a "vindication" of a woman whose passion for Joseph, traditionally seen as sheer licentiousness, originates in her desire to be a mother. For con man Joseph she already is one, a Bad One.

Notes to *Joseph and His Brothers*

[1]Even as he had begun work on *The Confessions of Felix Krull*, back on 10 January 1910, he had confessed to Heinrich, "Working on it surprises me sometimes at the things that I'm finding in myself" (Wysling 1998: 102). The next sentence in the letter is significant: "But it is unhealthy work and not good for the nerves". Thereafter, his letters to Heinrich confess that the Krull manuscript is parasitic: on 20 March 1910, "The secret truth is that I couldn't get going on *The Confidence Man*; the torment of idleness caused me to lash out, of that I'm quite conscious myself, only further exhausting my energy" (Wysling 1998: 105); on 18 September 1910, "The Confidence Man inches slowly forward" (Wysling 1998: 108); on 24 March 1911, "I haven't accomplished anything of note in the last few months. My indisposition, which dragged on longer than usual and really got me down, was supposedly an irritation of the appendix, but ultimately was probably just the expression of a momentary exhaustion of the central nervous system. The aftereffects are still with me and my progress on the *Confidence Man* is wretchedly slow" (Wysling 1998: 111). His 1930 *Sketch of My Life* looks back on his relationship with the Krull manuscript. First he professes: "The idea has really great comic possibilities; and I so enjoyed writing the first chapters—this torso was later published by the Deutsche Verlags-Anstalt—that I was not surprised to hear from people well qualified to judge that the fragment as it stands is the happiest and best thing I have done. In a way it may be the most personal, representing as it does my attitude toward tradition, which is at once kindly and destructive, and which determines my 'mission' as a writer"

(43). Then he confesses: "It proved to be hard to sustain the right tone for the Krull memoirs over any great length of time; and probably my need for rest favoured the growth of the new idea by which they were presently—in the spring of 1911-- interrupted" (43-44). In the 1940 *On Myself* Mann says the same thing in so many words (48-49). Reed notes that *"Krull*, for whatever reason, remained Mann's performance favourite: his own reading from it was the last item at his last birthday celebration" (1996: 416). Since *Krull*—to which he had returned in 1951 and which he completed in 1954--was his last published fiction, it could be said that confession finally depleted him.

[2]I am ignoring several of Bergler's *"descriptive* characteristics" of impostors who are incorrigible career criminals, since I see no evidence that Mann was or regarded himself or his creation Joseph as a career criminal.

[3]The translation by the Winstons is subdued: "it is really curious to see to what regal situations such a life of play and dream finally leads, when you keep it up long enough" (Winston 1975: 150).

[4]In "The Relation of the Impostor to the Artist" (1958), Phyllis Greenacre, an Oedipally-oriented analyst, devotes ten pages to Thomas Mann, but ignores Bergler's *Basic Neurosis* (1949).

[5]Medical science is finally acknowledging the acceptability of the ancient custom of marriage between first cousins. See "Cousins: A New Theory of Relativity." *Time* 15 Apr. 2002: 60.

[6]Joseph was nine years old when his mother died (249-50). Eight years have passed since his mother died (50). Thus Joseph is seventeen years of age, the age as when his story is taken up in Genesis (37:2).

[7]Recall that in *"Die Einheit des Menschengeistes"* (1932), quoted on p. 46 and in "The Sufferings and Greatness of Richard Wagner" (1933), quoted on pp. 133-34n2, Mann had linked infant nursing behavior, adult sexual behavior, and the worship of the mother-goddess, Ninmah, Ishtar, Astarte, Mami, Nana.

[8]Hatfield notes that critics have equated "Joseph with the confidence man Felix Krull" (1979: 83), and he himself equates Joseph with Hermes, "a gifted, charming rogue" (1979: 71), but he does not stress the significance of these attributions.

[9]Mann's text follows the precedent of Genesis, which returns to Reuben's offense, 49:3-4.

[10]If "Bes" has been castrated, then those who nicknamed him are capable of a cruel irony, for Bes was the divine dwarf "with a disproportionately large member" whose figurines pilgrims placed in the "temple of Hathor, goddess of love" (Manniche 1987: 12).

[11]It is another divine irony that Mut is named after the goddess Mut, "mother", consort of the king of the gods Amun. Perhaps the assocation of goddess Mut with dwarfs (Armour 2001: 119-20) explains namesake Mut's association with Dudu.

[12]Discussing this scene, Heilbut terms Mut "an obscene caricature of two stereotypes, Madonna and whore" and "a parody of the Great Mother of Bachofen's anthropology" (1996: 552).

[13]McDonald observes that Mut "becomes over time not only a Cleopatra but a sphinx and dragon-woman" (1999: 197). The added attributions of "sphinx" and "dragon-woman" to Mut's person strengthen my contention that Mann unconsciously conceives of her as a Gorgon-figure. In his discussion of regression to "the

preconscious, prenatal phase", Jung speaks of "archetypal images" of "'divine' beings, part animal, part human", which, if positive, "appear as 'helpful animals' of fairytale and legend". But "if the attitude towards the parents is too affectionate and too dependent, it is compensated in dreams by frightening animals, who represent the parents just as much as the helpful animals did. The Sphinx is a fear-animal of this kind and still shows clear traces of a mother derivative" (1967: 181).

After discussing the role of the Sphinx in the Oedipus legend, Jung traces her genealogy. The Sphinx "was a daughter of Echidna, a monster with the top half of a beautiful maiden, and a hideous serpent below. This double being corresponds to the mother-imago: above, the lovely and attractive human half; below, the horrible animal half, changed into a fear-animal by the incest prohibition" (1967: 182). Jung footnotes this last sentence: "In Hellenistic syncretism, the Echidna became a cult-symbol of mother Isis". Born "of the All-Mother, Mother Earth, Gaia,[...]Echidna herself was the mother of all terrors, of the Chimera, Scylla, the Gorgon .[...] She also gave birth to a number of dragons".

[14]McWilliams notes:

> Joseph's relationship with Mut represents the culmination of a theme which began very early in the creations of Thomas Mann: passive feasting of the forbidden and passionate enjoyment without fulfillment. Voyeuristic teasing and repression bordering on the perverse sustain themselves in this prolonged account of three years of emotional intensity. (1983: 255)

What McWilliams does not note is that Joseph has always transformed his voyeurism into exhibitionism and that he does again spectacularly when he allows Mut to grab his garment, thus provoking her to repeat "over and over again": "*Me"eni nachtef!* I have seen his strength!" (830)

[15]My interpretation is supported by McWilliams:

> a study of the genesis of the *Joseph* tetralogy is not complete until we examine its scheme of composition. The first three volumes appeared successively in 1933, 1934, and 1936[...]. But *Joseph the Provider*, the last volume and the one which treats, supposedly, the concept of humanity, was not published until 1943, during which time two other major works, *The Beloved Returns* and *The Transposed Heads*, came into being. The intrusion of these works suggests that the final volume of the Joseph tetralogy was exposed to the danger of not being written at all; at least it shows that Mann had lost an all-consuming interest in it. In the middle of his labor on *Joseph the Provider* Mann complained of exhaustion and weariness with the theme of antiquity,[...]a feeling he undoubtedly did not possess while engaged in work on *Joseph in Egypt*, the story of Mut and her impact on the hero[...]. With the termination of that story, the author's interest flagged and the basic motive for the entire conception was satisfied. (1983: 271-72)

The Beloved Returns: Lotte in Weimar

Mann completed *Joseph in Egypt* on 23 August 1936. Well before that, though, he had begun to think about his next work of fiction. Since he had completed three-fourths of a project that Goethe had begun but never finished, Mann had his predecessor very much on his mind. As early as 1912, he thought of writing a fictional account of "Goethe's last love" (Winston 1971: 76), when, at age seventy, Goethe met at Marienbad a young girl, Ulrike von Levetzow, whom he wanted to marry. Mann's wife recalled that the fictional account "was supposed to take the Master down a peg or two in a humorous way. But at that time he simply didn't have the nerve to portray Goethe" (K. Mann 1975: 60). In a 1930 letter to his friend Bertram, Mann provided a preliminary sketch of the Goethe whom he would word-paint: "the only thing left will be for me to speak from *experience*,--on Goethe from experience: a mythical confidence trickster's identification with which perhaps the gap between 'Joseph' and 'Goethe' would be bridged" (Reed 1996: 340; Reed's translation).

Goethe, then, will be like Joseph. Mann himself later said of *Lotte in Weimar*: "It is a Joseph play[...]this novel. My 'imitatio' of Goethe corresponds to the 'imitatio dei'[...]in which the son of Rachael takes his pleasure: an identification and unio mystica with the father" ("On my own Work" 78). In his later "Fantasy on Goethe" (1948), giving evidence that he thought Goethe likened himself to Joseph, Mann wrote that Goethe, in his relationship to the Duke of Weimar, "did work his head off as minister, favorite, and 'second in the Realm,' as he once called himself—surely making some allusion to Joseph" (109). Although Eissler does not cite Mann's belief that Goethe thought himself like Joseph, he does cite Paul Piper's *Joseph, Goethes erste grosse Jugenddichtung* (1920) and Manuel Schnitzer's *Goethes Josephbilder. Joseph Josephdichtung* (1921), then relies on *Dichtung und Wahrheit* to establish Goethe's "Joseph Identification" (1963: 1099-1105).

Eissler also records another incident that he could have used to strengthen his "Joseph Identification":

> [Twenty-four-year-old Goethe] invited his mother and her guests to come and see him skating on the [frozen] Main river. That day she wore her "crimson fur which had a long train and was fastened in front with gold buckles." His mother and her guests reached the skating rink when Goethe was in full swing of skating. As soon as he saw the beautiful piece of female attire, he approached his mother and asked her for the fur. She reported decades later:

"You're not going to wear it?"—"Of course I'm going
to wear it." So I take off my magnificent warm coat, he puts it
on, winds the train around his arm, and he glides away like a son
of the gods on the ice. (1963: 104-05)[1]

A diary entry in 1933 indicates that Mann's interest in a
Goethe novel remained high (Elsaghe 2002: 191). The diary entry for
23 March 1935 records the defining moment for his fictional treatment
of Goethe: "In the evening got back to my Goethe-Lotte Kestner project, and after
some peripheral reading came across the story in Felix Theilhaber's book of their
slightly grotesque encounter late in life in Weimar. Stirred" (Kesten 1984: 237).
Identifying Theilhaber's *Goethe, Sexus und Eros* (1929) as the "first
ever psychoanalytical study of Goethe" (2002: 188), Elsaghe discusses its
impact on Mann:

> Even for so early a commentator as Theilhaber, Goethe's genius
> was no longer simply a superhuman culmination of vitality and
> inspiration, but, on the contrary, an expression of deep-seated
> psychic problems. According to Theilhaber, Goethe had a
> profoundly troubled relationship to the purely physical aspect of
> sexuality ("sexus"), which his artistic productivity enabled him to
> sublimate all too comprehensively in "eros". (2002: 189)

Small wonder that Mann was "stirred", for, at least unconsciously, he
felt a very close identification with Goethe.
    The first six chapters illustrate what Weigand calls the
"bewilderingly manifold aspects of Goethe and his milieu" (1988: 15). Chapter 1
immediately establishes the circumstances: shortly after eight o'clock,
on a late September morning in 1816 (3), sixty-three-year-old
Charlotte Kestner, "widow, née Buff", arrives in Weimar, accompanied
"by daughter and maid" (7). Intending to lodge at the "inn Zum Elefanten"
(3), she is greeted by the head waiter, who, glimpsing her name on the
guest register, realizes that she is the model for "Lotte" in the world-
famous *Sorrows of Young Werther* (1774), by Wolfgang von Goethe,
now a universal genius long resident in Weimar. His words presuming
that she has come to visit the man who made her a celebrity, the head
waiter, Herr Mager, is disabused by Charlotte, who tells him that her
purpose is to visit her sister (16). When he is dismissed, he spreads the
news, so that celebrity-seekers soon swarm in front of the inn.
Sending her daughter off to inform her sister of their arrival, Charlotte
reveals the validity of the head waiter's presumption by dispatching a
note to Goethe:

> My honoured friend:
> With my daughter Charlotte, I am paying a visit to my sister and
> shall spend a few days in Weimar. It is my wish to present my
> daughter to you; and I myself should rejoice if I might look once
> more upon a face which, while each of us has been pursuing his
> appointed lot in life, has become so well known to all the world.
> (24)

Does her misdating of the note "October 6" and her frequent involuntary nodding betray her excited state, her physical exhaustion, her cerebral deterioration, or a combination thereof?

Charlotte decides to rest, so the first part of Chapter 2 recounts her recollections--as she drifts off into regression, to sleep-- of the impression that the "mad youth" Goethe had left upon her when she was a nineteen-year-old engaged to be married (28). Primarily she thinks of Goethe's single snatched kiss that he had in his novel magnified into a "storm of kisses" that were returned, opened, to the sender. Not above exaggeration, herself, Charlotte fantasizes that Goethe, having actually received a ribbon from her frock as a "consolation", had "bestowed upon the warm-hearted souvenir a thousand rapturous kisses" (30). Thus Mann brazenly announces that his project is to be a meditation on Goethe's kisses.

After a two-hour nap Charlotte is pounced upon by an Irish autograph-hound, Rose Cuzzle, by whom she is "[e]ngaged and diverted" for forty-five minutes (39). Just as Miss Cuzzle finishes a sketch of Charlotte and gains the signature that will authenticate it, Mager announces Herr Doctor Friedrich Wilhelm Riemer, Goethe's secretary and companion (42). His lengthy visit is described in Chapter 3. Charlotte soon senses that Riemer is using "her as an opportunity to speak of the master and so to reach nearer the heart of a long-standing riddle which, it might be, dominated his whole life" (53). Ever more frustrated by his inability to resolve the opposed traits that Goethe presents, Riemer turns to Scripture: "I will say I am often reminded of the Bible story of Jacob, at the end of Genesis, where, you may recall, it says of Joseph that he was blessed by the Almighty 'with blessings of heaven above, blessings of the deep that lieth under'" (83). Goethe—who once told him, "Irony is the grain of salt without which nothing we eat would have any savour" (85)--simply defies his understanding, inspiring both adoration and abhorence.

Above all, Riemer is fascinated by Goethe's creativity, wondering, for example, how long before he used it in *Faust*, Goethe had retained the "picture" of an infant whose mother's breasts are dry and who must be fed watered cow's milk (73). (So early Mann brazenly hints at Goethe's image of himself.) Charlotte, who nursed nine infants and would have nursed two more if they had survived birth, does not make a response to Reimer's question, but her lack of response does not mean that she disregards the question. Soon enough Riemer reveals that he is appalled at Goethe's "consummate scepticism" (89) about the product of his creativity: "'A poem,' I have heard him say, 'is nothing at all. A poem, you see, is a kiss which one gives all the world. But no children come of kisses.' Then he would say no more" (90).

Riemer has become emotional, so "Charlotte essayed to relieve the tension by laughing at the joke about the kiss" (91). But it is likely that the narrator guilefully misconstrues Charlotte's laugh, for the words following her laugh reveal it as a bitter rejection of Goethe's equation of a poem to a kiss. She begins "somewhat at random":

> "But what would you have, my dear Herr Doctor? No harm or injustice is done to poetry, to liken it to a kiss. On the contrary, it is a pretty simile, and renders poetry to poetry, as is its due, setting it in proper and worthy contrast to life and reality[....]Would you like to know," she asked abruptly, as though she had thought of a way to calm the distracted man and put his thoughts in a more tranquil train, "how many children I have brought into the world? Eleven, if I count the two whom God took again unto Himself. Forgive me for boasting. I was passionately maternal, and I am one of those who like to let their light shine and boast of their blessings".

Although she professes to accept the "simile", a "poem[...]is a kiss which one gives all the world", she would not accept its reverse, a kiss is not a poem which one gives all the world. A kiss is bestowed upon an individual, even if the kisser is fool enough to think that he is kissing all the world. Moreover, children do come of kisses. Charlotte's passionate maternality has given her the insight to sense that Goethe has used kisses in order to make poems, but also that Goethe's habit of kissing and renouncing hints at a kink in his infantile development of which he is unaware.

The epitome of Riemer's sense of mystification is reached when he reveals his consternation at the fact that Goethe, even when he was young, rarely visited or communicated with his mother, father, and sister, that he did not even visit his mother during the last eleven years of her life, "the little mother from whom he got the joyous nature and love of spinning tales" (96). Spurning Riemer's parroting of the received opinion of Goethe's loving regard for his mother, Charlotte scornfully asserts that if one of her sons had so shamefully treated her, she "would show him what was what!" (98). Then she halfway acknowledges that Goethe had treated her that way--and that could cause her to wonder if his act of kissing and then leaving her and all the other beloveds represents a repetition of his renunciation of his mother, which originally occurred in his first eleven months, not in his mother's last eleven years.

She makes herself clear:

> For forty-four years, since the time I was nineteen, these things have remained a riddle to me, a tormenting riddle--why should I conceal it? The being content with poetry and silhouettes, content with kisses, and from them, as he well says, no children come. No they come from elsewhere: from Kestner's and my true and honourable love--eleven of them, if I count the two that died. Consider all that, else you cannot understand how it is that in all my life I have never got free of it. (100)

Charlotte has come to Weimar for Goethe's explanation.

In Chapter 4 Dr. Riemer defers to a new caller, Adele Schopenhauer, whom he describes as a "devoted friend of the master" (122). Adele soon proves her predecessor's description, for she acknowledges that, of all Weimar society, only her mother and she were hospitable to Goethe after he married his lower-class mistress of eighteen years, Christiane Vulpius (130). Adele has her reason for introducing that name, for the recent death of Goethe's wife gravely affects the future of Ottilie von Pogwisch, her best friend.

In Chapter 5 Adele recites the story of how her friend became ensnared in Goethe's plans. Dominated by his father's wishes, August von Goethe had become the suitor of Ottilie von Pogwisch, who felt that she could save him from his dissolute drinking and womanizing. Fate appears to save Ottile twice, once when she falls in love with Ferdinand Heinke and again when August spurns Ottilie out of jealousy, unaware that Ferdinand has already told Ottilie that he is betrothed to another. But as Adele sadly observes,

> August was a son—that was the distinguishing characteristic of life. In him one was dealing with his great father. And the father certainly had not approved the breach with the "little person"; the son had simply brought it about himself without Goethe's consent. Just as certainly the father would use all his authority to heal it. (206)

Ottilie will be a gracious hostess for Goethe's house, and now that his scandalous wife is dead and her son has been legitimized, Weimar's polite society will not dare object to the marriage.

At the beginning of Chapter 6, when August von Goethe's presence is announced, Adele must come to the point. She hopes that Charlotte can perform the miracle of persuading Goethe to change his mind. Although Adele's story has been about Ottilie's sad past and even sadder prospects, surely Charlotte has been most attentive to the revelations of Goethe's neglect of and domination of his wife and son, an attentiveness that Adele must have solicited. Now she hopes to evoke Charlotte's horror, for she declares:

> In a few minutes you will see the son, and in a few hours, I suppose, his august father. You might use your influence, might warn, might presume to do so. You might be August's mother. You are not, because the course of your life was otherwise decreed, because you would have it otherwise. Bring here in play that power of reason, that clear and sober sense of what is right and fitting, that actuated you in that earlier time. Save my Ottilie! She might be your daughter, she looks as though she were; and just because of that, she is today in the same danger you once escaped by opposing to it a deliberate and dignified rational sense. Be a mother to this image of your own youth, for that she is, and as such is she beloved, by and through a son. Protect this "little person" as the father calls her; on the ground of what you once were to the father, save her from being sacrificed to a fascination that makes me so inexpressibly afraid! The man whom in your wisdom you chose is gone, the woman who became August's mother is now no more. You are alone with the father, with him who might be your son, and with the dear child who might be your own daughter. Your voice would be like a mother's voice—lift it, then, against this wrong, this destructive course! This is my prayer, my invocation-- (218-19; pause in the orig.)

Adele stealthily suggests that Charlotte is right to return as the beloved to claim her rightful place beside Goethe. They will be married, if only in a figurative sense. The marriage of August and Ottilie would therefore constitute incest, again if only in a figurative sense, but with enough force to arouse Charlotte's feeling that a taboo would be violated.

When August enters the room, Charlotte is instantly maternal, thinking of the eleven times that she was a Good Mother, when her breast "had been heavy with milk" (220). August has come in place of his father to acknowledge receipt of Charlotte's note, a mission typical of the many intermediations for his father that he reveals. Charlotte avidly listens to August's worshipful talk of his father, but her first impression of August haunts her mind. She soon voices her emotional state: "I myself am a mother, I even might, as a matter of age, be yours" (233). Then she acknowledges "something like jealousy" when she discovers that he already has a "second or substitute mother", the widow of the dramatist Schiller (264). She invites him to speak to her without reservation, "as a son to his mother" (267). When he does not immediately take the bait, she jiggles her line: "let me ask you a maternal question: your story had to do with a thwarted friendship. Then you have never loved?" (272)

August states that he loves and intends to marry Ottilie. Yet the conversation that develops from this revelation suggests that August realizes that his feelings for Ottilie are subordinate to his father's determination to have yet another Lotte-type in his life, a "little person", to inspire his creativity (274). Deciding to capitalize on his realization that he and Ottilie are pawns in Goethe's game of unfinished monkey business, Charlotte rehearses Adele's argument that the marriage would violate a taboo:

> Pray do not think I have no appreciation of the advantages of a marriage wherein, if I may put it thus, youth would realize and make good what its elders had neglected and sacrificed. And still I must insist upon the doubtful side of an affair which, so to speak, is one between brothers and sisters—. (278; pause in the orig.)

Then Charlotte loses her nerve, pleading that she is "actually giddy" (279). Actually, she had become half-hearted in her effort to dissuade August when he stated that he was in love with Ottile and intended to marry her, thus acting quite unlike his father. Charlotte's collapse shocks August back to his assignment, to extend her an invitation to dine with his father. Accepting the invitation and the fact that August and Ottilie will play the roles that Goethe has written for them, Charlotte offers her blessing:

> Go now, my son. In three days I will come and dine with you— why not? How many times did he not eat bread and milk with us, in the House of the Teutonic Order? If you like each other, you young ones, then marry, for his sake, and be happy in your upstairs rooms. (280)

By encouraging the "young ones" to take the place designated by Goethe, Charlotte in effect confesses that she accepts the place into which Goethe put her forty-four years before, a place in his fiction, not in his bed.

Chapter 7 begins as Goethe wakes up, responding to his "seven-o'clock will" (284). Thus his awakening occurs before all of the events depicted in the previous chapters, as, indeed, his personality had been set long before he displays the behaviors that now mystify and dominate both Charlotte and her visitors. Just as Goethe awakened, he had been dreaming, for he is able to recall what he had last seen: "the goddess' bosom, fine resilient flesh, lay pressed into the shoulder of her handsome huntsman" (281). Goethe immediately traces "that splendid picture" back to a painting that he had once seen in the Dresden Academy, Alessandro Turchi's "Venus and Adonis". Concurrently, he observes that he has awakened with an erection: "What, what? Here's a brave showing, forsooth! Good for you, old man! Be not dismayed, blithe oldster that thou art!" (281)[2]

Still abed, Goethe muses about other projects that have too long remained unfinished, noting shortly thereafter that his creative symbol, his "unquenchable friend" (284), is now unobtrusive. As it will to a man of a certain age, that falling off reminds him of other body parts that are subject to wreck. When his servant Carl enters, Goethe is ready for his coffee and zweiback, while he reviews the urgent matters that threaten his benefactor, the Duke of Weimar. After dictating to Carl his advice to the Duke (306-07), he gives himself a sponge bath (309), all the while thinking of the past, perhaps even unconsciously reminded of his earliest baths.

His mind drifts away from the technicalities of a past scientific expedition to an encounter that occurred therein, his bold bussing of a young waitress in a country inn. All of a sudden, he imagines that he smells raspberries:

> Lovely fragrance, beautiful berries, swollen with juice under their dry velvety skin, warm with living fire, like women's lips. Love is the best of life, and of love the best the kiss: poetry of love, seal of ardent desire, sensual and platonic, sacrament midway between spiritual beginning and fleshly end, sweet commerce, held in a higher sphere than the other and with the purer organs of breath and speech—spiritual because still discriminating, still individual.... Bent back between thy hands that one and only head, beneath the lashes that serious, smiling gaze dissolving in thine; thy kiss says to it: I love thee, and I mean thee, precious particular of the divine All, expressly thee in all creation. For the other, procreation, is something else, anonymous, animal, at bottom without choice, shrouded in darkness. The kiss is joy,

> procreation is lust—God gave it to the worm. Well, in my time I have wormed it enough too; but after all the kiss is more my line, and the joy of the kiss, that fleeting visitation of conscious desire to fugitive beauty. There is the very same distinction between art and life. For the consummation of life for the human being, the making of children, is no affair of poetry's, or of the spirit-kiss on the world's raspberry lips.... Lotte's lip-play with the canary-bird—the sweet way the little creature pressed its bill to her sweet lips and then made contact from one mouth to the other with its pretty picking—how daintily depraved, how shatteringly innocent! Well set-up, gifted young fool, already knew as much about art as about love and privately meant one when he made the other! A mere young cockerel and already quite prepared to betray love and life and human beings to his art! (317-18, ellipses in orig.)

From the waitress he had once kissed to the raspberries that he and Charlotte were picking when he kissed her (28) to Charlotte kissing the canary to Goethe kissing her: it is as if Goethe's unconscious is anticipating the news that he will soon receive.

Then Goethe rings for Carl to dress his hair and his body, betraying his Joseph-identification by casting his eyes about for the dressing gown that he always wears as a signature when entertaining the ladies (320-21). In this domestic milieu he begins to think of his deceased family, his mother, father, and sister Cornelia. Then he requests his copyist, Herr John, whom, he confesses to himself—after an eternity of palaver with him—he cannot "abide" (351).

Saved by the arrival of his breakfast, Goethe once again ruminates on the demands of the day, then his unfinished work, until, inevitably, he turns once again to self-analysis:

> In the whole moral and sensual world the thing whereon my whole life long I have most dwelt with horror and desire is seduction—inflicted or borne, active or passive, sweet and terrible, like a command laid on us by a god; the sin we sinlessly commit, guilty as tool and victim both; for to withstand it does not mean we cease to be seduced. (357-58)

Goethe understands that his kissing and bolting has always been seduction, not of the body but of the spirit, but that he is unconscious of the motive of his seduction is proved by his attributing it to a transcendent agent.

As Goethe vows to undertake a work that will "proclaim and celebrate seduction", he must repeat the prayer to "Good Mother[...]kind, slow-moving Mother Nature" to give him time, just as he had previously pleaded for time to write a "history of nature" (296). Then Goethe is joined by his son, who hands him the note sent by Charlotte. Skimming the note, Goethe begins a lengthy tutorial on mineralogy, to the effect that while crystals do not change, humans do, then discourses on several responsibilities that he has delegated to August. Finally, August is able to return his father to the matter of a response to the note. Goethe directs his son to call upon Charlotte with an invitation to a formal dinner in three days (372).

In Chapter 8 that dinner takes place. Certainly the fullness of the description of the dinner testifies to the accuracy of Mann's prediction, at the novel's inception, that he was embarking upon "a project whose mastery will require much reading" (qtd. in Bürgin 1969: 124). Certainly, too, Mann accurately captured the tone of the dinner scene when he wrote his French translator that, after Chapter 7, Chapter 8 was to be a return to the "social comedy" of the first six chapters (Winston 1971: 311). Although the chapter is replete with observations of the celebrity Goethe dominating every aspect of the dinner, the focus is on Charlotte, who has, after all, come to Weimar after forty-four years to get some kind of explanation, first, for the kiss that Goethe snatched from her lips and, second, for his subsequent snatching of her privacy by including her in his novel.

Charlotte must feel that the moment of recognition has come at the end of the meal, when, not by coincidence but by Goethe's conscious choice, but unconscious design, the "sweet was a raspberry crème, mixed with whipped cream, with a delicious bouquet, and served with sponge fingers" (423-24). The raspberry points to the kiss that Goethe had snatched from Charlotte in an oral frenzy. That the memory intensifies his orality is indicated by what happens next: having "partaken copiously of the earlier wines", Goethe now drinks "two beakers of champagne in quick succession, as though he were thirsty, holding the emptied glass over his shoulder to the servant for the second filling" (424). "He seemed for a brief moment to be contemplating another diverting reminiscence, gazing diagonally upward into space with his close-lying eyes". His "thirstiness" and the direction of his unfocused vision suggest that in his mind's eye he looks at a scene in his most distant past. His lapsing into Frankfurtese (432)--dropping the final consonant--locates the place and earliest period of the past: "The slip, or whatever it was—sounded very odd after the precise and deliberate eloquence" to which the audience was accustomed (424). Charlotte must think that he is to welcome the return of the beloved, but at that moment Goethe, unconsciously reminded that behind Charlotte lies the mother figure, realizes that recognition of the return of the beloved would acknowledge the return of the repressed. Such acknowledgement would, according to Bergler (1949: 188-89), terminate his creativity. Goethe then shifts to an "amusing old anecdote" known by "most of the resident guests", but "new to the strangers present". The story tells of a young man in a frigid Weimar museum who surreptitiously kisses a copy of "Leonardo da Vinci's head of Charitas", but in so doing fogs the pane of glass covering it, so that his lip prints are discovered and his identity is exposed (425). Charlotte knows that the moral of the story—art is absolutely separated from reality—is for her benefit, for she blushes "as deeply, up to the roots of her crown of grey hair, as her delicate colouring would allow" (426). Artists kiss lips, then create art; sentimentalists confuse lips with art. Having been put in her place, she can hardly wait for the visit to be over.

Mann reserves the ninth and final chapter of the novel for Goethe to proclaim that, sure enough, the theme, the overt theme, of his life has been renunciation. Historically, Goethe, after the dinner he gave for Charlotte, invited her to use his equipage to attend the theater one evening (Elsaghe 2002: 187). Fictionally, Mann pictures Charlotte suddenly aware that Goethe is in the enclosed carriage when she is being returned to her hotel. Their conversation allows Goethe to use the defense that Mann had prepared for him, in "Goethe and Tolstoy", published in English in 1929 (*Essays of Three Decades*).[18]

The word *renounce* is introduced when Charlotte says that Goethe's pattern of jilting young women began with Friederike Brion, in 1771, the year before he first visited the Buff home (448). Soon Charlotte acknowledges that Goethe's reputation as a pedagogical author, his "actual" life, "is the effect of renunciation, and in consequence of impairment and loss; for renunciation and loss lie close together" (449). Given her core identification of herself as a nursing mother, she must intuit that Goethe's characteristic renunciation of the young women whom he has courted had its origin in the sense of loss that he experienced in his earliest relationship with his mother, against which memory he has defended himself by repressing it. Bitterly, she observes that, because of his celebrity, he escapes the judgment to which ordinary people are held: "Your reality looks different; not like renunciation, or unfaithfulness; but like purer fulfilment and a higher faith" (450). Speaking of herself and all the other young women, Charlotte asks Goethe: "what are they all but sacrifices to your greatness? Ah, it is wonderful to make a sacrifice—but a bitter, bitter lot to be one!" (451)

Then Goethe responds:

> Dear soul, let me answer you from my heart, in expiation and
> farewell. You speak of sacrifice. But it is a mystery, indivisible,
> like all else in the world and one's person, one's life, and one's
> work. Conversion, transformation, is all. They sacrificed to the
> god, and in the end the sacrifice was God. You used a figure dear
> and familiar to me; long since, it took possession of my soul. I
> mean the parable of the moth and the fatal, luring flame. Say, if
> you will, that I am the flame, and into me the poor moth flings
> itself. Yet in the chance and change of things I am the candle too,
> giving my body that the light may burn. And finally, I am the
> drunken butterfly that falls to the flame—figures of the eternal
> sacrifice, body transmuted into soul, and life to spirit. Dear soul,
> dear child, dear childlike old soul, I, first and last, am the
> sacrifice, and he that offers it. (451)

Mann had known his culmination point when he first
undertook *Lotte in Weimar*. In a letter to Heinrich, 3 March 1940, he
admitted as much:

> I don't know whether it is my most beautiful [novel], but it is
> dearest to me, because it contains the most about love and erotic
> union, in spite of all the mocking and ironically veristic aspects in
> which this love is clothed. Hence I see its weaknesses and
> pedantries with particular clarity. It would not be a novel at all,
> but something like a monograph in dialogue, were it not for an
> element of excitement in the initial conception that seems to have
> been retained in the execution. (qtd. in Wysling 1998: 232-33)

In justice to Mann's thought, I must acknowledge that he
introduces Goethe's habit of romantic renunciation within the larger
context of "the Spinozan motif of renunciation ('*Entsagung*'), which becomes the
general motif of Goethe's life and work, like the idea of freedom for Schiller and the
idea of redemption for Wagner" ("Goethe" 139; parenthesis in orig.). Then,
after the paragraph quoted immediately above, Mann clarifies his
intention:

> Goethe's pathos of renunciation—or, since we are speaking of
> permanent forces dominating the whole of existence, his ethos of
> renunciation—is of a more personal kind. It is his destiny, it is the
> instinctive mandate of his especially national gift, which was
> essentially civilizing in its mission. Or, rather, might this destiny
> and mission, this bond, this conditioning limitation and pedagogic
> duty of renunciation, be after all something less personal to him
> than it just now appeared? Might it perhaps be the law of his
> destiny, innate and inviolable save at the expense of heavy

spiritual penalties; the imperative which is the essence of the German spirit, destined always, as it is, somehow and in some degree, to feel itself called to a cultural task?--I spoke of the consciousness of a community of feeling, which Goethe must, at moments, have felt with Christianity. What did it consist in, and to what had it reference? Goethe pays homage to the "moral culture" of Christianity—that is, to its humanity, its civilizing, anti-barbarian influence. It was the same as his; and the occasional homage he paid it undoubtedly springs from his recognition that the mission of Christianity within the confines of the Germanic peoples bore a likeness to his own. And here, in the fact that he conceived his task, his duty to his nation, as essentially a civilizing mission, lies the deepest and most German significance of his renunciation. ("Goethe" 140)

Mann argues that Goethe's pursuit-and-abandonment of maidens must be regarded not as a isolated eccentricity but as a part of the pattern of self-sacrifice which dominated his personality. If that aspect of his total personality is regarded in isolation, he seems a cad; if regarded within the compass of his conduct, he is seen to be as much a victim as the young women. Pathos created his personal desire; ethos ruled his impersonal destiny. He realized that his purely personal feelings must be sacrificed to his duty to be Germany's teacher.

So much for the overt theme that is revealed in the final chapter of *Lotte in Weimar*, "the monograph in dialogue". But what of the covert theme that was inspired by Felix Theilhaber's *Sexus und Eros*? It implies the exact opposite, that Goethe's renunciation of the female (first mother, then all her surrogates) initiated his renunciation of everything which interfered with his career. Despite knowing the overt goal of his project—Goethe's "expiation and farewell" to Charlotte— Mann had difficulty finding the novelistic elements that would carry him to it. Soon after he began work on the novel, he wrote Gottfried Bermann Fischer, in late October, 1936:

> I am working on the Goethe story, *The Beloved Returns*, in the mornings, but I stalk it day and night without finding its form clearly in my mind. In any case, it will be something special—so much I feel already—it will be a handsome little book. (qtd. in Bürgin 1969: 124)

Fourteen months later, 11 January 1938, he confessed to his diary, "Tinkered with the August dialogue [Chapter 6], uncertainly. Perhaps I would do better to turn to the Schopenhauer essay and let *The Beloved* rest for the present" (qtd. in Kesten 1984: 291). The next day he wrote Fritz Strich that he was "now writing about [Arthur] Schopenhauer" (qtd. in Bürgin 1969: 131), not to return to the "Goethe story" for nearly a year (Bürgin 1969: 138). Throughout the first six chapters, Mann had depended almost entirely upon dialogue between Charlotte and her succession of visitors, almost all of it devoted to the enigma that Goethe's personality presents. But, at some point, he decided that in Chapter 7 he would rely primarily on Goethe's interior monologue to give his reader, in his words, "the illusion of learning exactly what *he* [Goethe] was really like" (Wysling 1998: 233; his interpolation). In mid-December 1938 an obviously jubilant Mann wrote Ferdinand Lion of the response of Erich von Kahler, who "was so impressed with the first twenty-five pages, which I recently read to him, that he went so far as to use the word 'magnificent'[....]I am writing very slowly on the chapter and enjoying the intimateness, not to mention the *unio mystica*, which is indescribable" (qtd. in Bürgin 1969: 138-39).[4]

To find out what Goethe "was really like"—according to Mann—we must return to his awakening from his dream (281): "Alas, that it should vanish! That my bright vision of the depths must so soon be gone again—as though the whim of a genie gave it and as suddenly snatched it away—it fades into nothing, I emerge" (281). Under the influence of *unio mystica* Mann introduces Goethe having the same experience that he himself must have had before describing it in "A Vision" so long ago, the experience of the "dream screen", the disappearing breast, symptomatic of oral deprivation . Here Mann presents Goethe regressing to the source of what Bergler terms the "basic neurosis", the actual or imagined deprivation of the breast, an action so destructive to the infant's sense of self-sufficiency that his principal psychological effort becomes the attempt to deny that the deprivation ever occurred.

There is evidence to support the speculation that the infant Goethe fantasized his mother depriving him of her breast. In 1809, a year after his mother's death, Goethe, at the age of sixty, began his autobiography; nearly a year later, to supplement his own recollections, he asked Bettina von Arnim to send him information about his childhood related to her by his mother shortly before her death (Eissler 1963: 1468). According to von Arnim, Goethe's mother had been very voluble about his birth and infancy:

> She [the mother] laid you to her breast, yet you could not be induced to suck; thereupon a wet-nurse was given you. "From her he drank with great appetite and pleasure; since it was now discovered," she said, "that I had no milk, so we soon noticed that he had been more intelligent that all of us in not wanting to drink from me." (qtd. in Eissler 1963: 267; his interpolation)

Goethe's doting mother might see the scene of his "refusal" as the first sign of his genius, but her explanation of his transference from her breast to that of a wet nurse threatened the infantile fantasy of deprivation upon which he had constructed his character.[5] Goethe therefore excluded this information from *Dichtung und Wahrheit,* saying of his perinatal period only that, "through the unskilfulness of the midwife, I came into the world as dead; and only after various efforts was I enabled to see the light" (Goethe 1974: 3). Indeed, in the same place, he excludes his mother's role from the scene of his birth, saying that the time and date when he "came into the world" depended upon the moon's opposition to the sun. Another von Arnim statement offers evidence of the onset of Goethe's fantasy formation:

> how he had already at the age of nine weeks anxiety dreams, how grandmother and grandfather, mother and father and the wet-nurse, stood around his cradle and listened, what violent movements were revealed in his features, how, when he woke up, he broke out into very distressed crying; often also he screamed so vehemently that he lost his breath and his parents feared for his life; they arranged for a bell; when they noticed that he became restless in his sleep, they rang and rattled it vigorously, so as to make him forget the dream immediately upon awakening. (qtd. in Eissler 1963: 1356)

If, within weeks of his birth, Goethe formed the fantasy of the Bad Mother because of his wakeful frustrations, he also experienced regression in drifting into sleep, then dreaming of the Good Mother. Thus, saying "I emerge" as his dream screen vanishes, Goethe, remembering the breast of Venus, so bountiful that its product created the Milky Way, fantasizes that the Good Mother has given rebirth to him. His reference to the dream "depths" anticipates his creation, in *Faust II*, of Faust's descent to the "Mothers" in order to return Helena (classical beauty) to the upper world.[6] In this manner the aged Goethe reveals that his mysterious relationship with the "Mothers" had been responsible for his creativity.[7]

Then Goethe turns to his tumescence—though there is no indication he realizes that it was stimulated by his dream of the breast or that its fading was caused by the dissipation of the dream. Undoubtedly Goethe would accept Eissler's dictum that "[i]n mythology, folklore, and art it is the erected penis that is taken as the symbol of creativity" (1963: 1282). By his erection Goethe is convinced that his posture—

Bergler might say "imposture"—as a *Dichter* is still a viable defense against writer's block, the admission of triumphant oral regression.

Thus Mann envisions Goethe maturing into a man who, because of his innate genius and his cultured family environment, chose writing as his way of defending himself against his "basic neurosis", his oral regression. Continuing the tactic of denying his mother's existence that had originated early in infancy, he became, in Bergler's phrase, a "one-person show" (1949: 187). When he became infatuated with the fairy-tales that his mother told in the evening before bedtime, he soon usurped her role as story-teller (characteristically, he omitted in *Dichtung und Wahrheit* the lavish account of the impact of her story-telling on him that his mother had given to von Arnim [Eissler 1963: 76].) Goethe's reaction to Cornelia, a sister sixteen months younger than he, is another evidence of his usurpation of his mother's role. From Goethe's mother von Arnim transmitted the following:

> He had the most affectionate attachment to his little sister Cornelia from the time when she still lay in the cradle; he carried everything to her and wanted to feed her and take care of her all by himself, and was jealous when anyone took her out of the cradle, in which he lorded it over her; then his fury could not be checked. He was in general far likelier to be infuriated than to cry. (qtd. in Eissler 1963: 71)

Eissler interprets Goethe's behavior toward his sister:

> Oral greed and envy, the inescapable reactions in a sibling to the arrival of a competitor, are turned into their opposites. Envy becomes charity. The impulse to appropriate is converted into the desire to give. The selfish origin of this early altruism can be seen in his attempt at considering the infant as his baby. Nobody must touch it. He is the only possessor—indeed, one might say, the creator—of the baby. It must be assumed that this conflict lies at the bottom of the whole behavior pattern: the denial of female superiority in regard to the capacity for bearing children[...]. (1963: 72)

What Eissler sees as "early altruism" Bergler could see as "early renunciation" and a desire to supplant the mother.

From von Arnim's transmission Goethe made the following draft for *Dichtung und Wahrheit*:

> He already loved his little sister Cornelia affectionately from the time when she still lay in the cradle, and he used to carry bread privily in his pocket which he would push into the child's mouth when she cried. If anyone wanted to pick her up, he became furious, as he was in general likelier to be infuriated than to cry. (qtd. in Eissler 1963: 71-2)

But it was eventually deleted (Eissler 1963: 71).

As Goethe entered adolescence he must have thought that his ability to produce beautiful words and ideas supplanted all of the maternal functions that he associated with his mother, so that, in his eyes, his mother vanished. He therefore created "oral pleasure" for himself without assistance. Awakening to an adolescent sex drive, he also learned another type of "oral pleasure", but with it some assembly would be required.

Regarding Goethe's kissing, Freud's followers do not see lip to lip. In *Fragments of a Great Confession* Theodor Reik reprints a two hundred seventy-eight page analysis of Goethe's relationship with Friederike Brion that he had first published in Freud's *Imago* in 1929 (1965: 28-29). Relying on the story Goethe himself tells in the Tenth and Eleventh Books of *Dichtung und Wahrheit* (1811), Reik announces his intention: while previous scholars have either condemned or justified Goethe's treatment of Friederike, he seeks only to understand it psychologically (1965: 57).

As the sixty-two-year-old Goethe tells the story, he, then a twenty-one-year-old, presents himself to Pastor Brion, his wife, and their two maiden daughters, at the manse in Sesenheim, displaying the dependence on disguises that a confidence man would employ. He appears as a poor theology student on the day of his arrival and the next day, after fleeing the manse but then returning, he appears as the son of a local innkeeper. Despite Goethe's outlandish behavior, Friederike, the younger daughter, is receptive to his attention, which soon becomes ardent. But he determines not to kiss her, reminding his reader that another girl, Lucinda, had recently placed a kiss and then a curse on his lips, saying that the kiss that he next gave a girl would kill her (see *DuW* 1974: I 425-32):

> Since that impassioned girl had cursed and sanctified my lips (for every consecration involves both), I had, superstitiously enough, taken care not to kiss any girl, because I feared that I might injure her in some unheard-of manner. I therefore subdued every desire by which a youth feels impelled to win from a charming girl this favour, which says much or little. But even in the most decorous

company a heavy trial awaited me. Those little games, as they are called, which are more or less ingenious, and by which a joyous young circle is collected and combined, depended in a great measure upon forfeits, in the calling in of which kisses have no small value. I had resolved, once for all, not to kiss; and, as every want or impediment stimulates us to an activity to which we should otherwise not feel inclined, I exerted all the talent and humour I possessed to help myself through, and thus to win rather than lose, before the company and for the company. (*DuW* 1974: II 68-69)

Passion will have its way, though, so that Goethe and Friederike are soon rendering and receiving, though nothing suggests that they are paddling palms. Goethe writes that, waking that night in a fright, he saw a horrible scene, but surely what he reports is the frightening dream which awakened him:

> I saw Lucinda, how, after the most ardent kiss, she passionately receded from me, and, with glowing cheek and sparkling eyes, uttered that curse, by which she intended to menace her sister only, but by which she also unconsciously menaced innocent persons, who were unknown to her. I saw Frederica standing opposite to her, paralysed at the sight, pale, and feeling the consequences of the curse, of which she knew nothing. (*DuW* 1974: II 75-76)

The name Goethe bestowed upon the female and his complementary description of her fury suggest that she was the light that railed. The scene offers the opposite of the standard "dream screen"; rather than seeing the receding bountiful breast of the Good Mother, Goethe sees the receding Bad Mother whose lips convey poison to his lips and thence to her rival. Thus the scene represents not the loss of the original oral pleasure but the prohibition of the pleasure that is so often its replacement. Goethe is horrified, wishing himself "at the other side of the world". He acknowledges that the curse is only a superstition, but he confesses that he had been willing to honor it:

> A certain conceit kept that superstition alive in me; my lips, whether consecrated or cursed, appeared to me more important than usual; and with no little complacency was I aware of my self-denying conduct, in renouncing many an innocent pleasure, partly to preserve my magical advantage, partly to avoid injuring a harmless being by giving it up.
> But now all was lost and irrevocable: I had returned into a mere common position; and I thought that I had harmed, irretrievably injured, the dearest of beings. Thus, far from my

being freed from the curse, it was flung back from my lips into
my own heart. (*DuW* 1974: II 76)

Reading this confession, Mann could have seen the origin of what he
regarded as Goethe's signature act, renunciation. In the morning, at
the sight of Frederike, Goethe avers, he renounced the superstition and
was pleased to be kissed by her as he left to return to his studies in
Strassburg (*DuW* 1974: II 76-77). While Goethe kept company with
Friederike for ten months, he ultimately jilted her (*DuW* 1974: II 120).

Reik asserts that Goethe's story of Lucinda's curse and its
consequences--which may be fictitious--is Goethe's confession that, at
that time, he had suffered from superstitious fear, "a syndrome which falls
under the general heading of fear of touch, and is very common in obsessional
neurotics" (1965: 89). Asserting that the Lucinda episode was not the
precipitating cause of Goethe's obsessional neurosis, but rather a vivid
illustration of many earlier experiences contributing to such fear, Reik
quotes Goethe, on "his superstitious fear of kissing: 'It was, indeed, based upon
early impressions'" (1965: 90). Among the "early impressions" influencing
Goethe that Reik discusses is Goethe's fear of touching Friederike
because he associates her with his sister Cornelia, for whom, he had
incestuous feelings, according to Otto Rank (1992: 184). Reik also
infers that another source of Goethe's fear of kissing was "an early
childhood fear of a pedantic and stern father" (1965: 172), which led to
Goethe's fear of "castration or death" (1965:168, 183, 203). Reik
concludes that Goethe's obsessional neurosis, displayed in the
extreme in his fear of kissing the next girl, but having its origin in his
early childhood experiences, rendered him "psychically impotent" with
Friederike (1965:168, 216, 377-78) and kept him in that condition
until he was nearly thirty-nine, when he met the Roman woman
Faustina (1965: 171, 378), in early 1788 (Eissler 1963: 1033). In a
parenthesis inserted in the 1965 reissue of *Fragment*, Reik claims that
his thesis that Goethe suffered from psychic impotence has been
"approved by Thomas Mann since [the original publication of his study]"
(1965: 216), but his claim must be based on inference, for he gives no
citation to a specific statement by Mann. Certainly the inference is not
based upon *Lotte in Weimar*, for Mann there pictures Goethe gloating
over the many times that he "wormed it" (298).

In *Goethe: A Psychoanalytic Study, 1775-1786*, a tome of
over fifteen hundred pages, Kurt R. Eissler also pays close attention to
Goethe's relationship with Friederike. Following Reik, Eissler
believes that Goethe's account of Lucinda's curse contains a highly

significant clue to the mystery of what Mann calls Goethe's pattern of "bolting". Early on, Eissler accepts Reik's conclusion: "What had kept [Goethe] from Friederike was, in all probability, actual impotence or fear of impotence. She, apparently, was still directly tied to his sister's image" (1963: 118). But nine hundred pages later, he thinks better of his acceptance, even though he still thinks "Reik's assumptions as to the contents of Goethe's unconscious may be correct" (1963: 1062). Eissler argues that these contents--"castration fears, death wishes, fears of retaliation"--would not be so powerful that Goethe could not consciously overrule them. There has to be another reason for Goethe's retreat: "It is far more probable that the unconscious fears, combined with the ego's tendency towards maximal emotional upsurge, once excited, led to a premature ejaculation, provoked through kissing".

Quoting Goethe's resolution to kiss kissing good-by, Eissler offers a reconstruction:

> Goethe let us know that he was struggling against a gratification that he could easily have achieved by simply kissing a girl. The fear of the "mental damage" he might bring upon the girl by his kissing her was only too much rooted in reality. In accordance with Lucinda's curse ("unhappiness upon unhappiness") one would rather have expected in Goethe fear of a damage more conspicuous than we associate with a mental damage. However, in view of the reaction he may on one occasion have noticed in a girl following his sexual peculiarity [i.e., premature ejaculation], he may easily have begun to fear lest his sexual weakness poison the girl's mind. From the great effect that the Friederike episode had upon Goethe and from the fact of his taking flight from her, I should surmise that it was in the relationship with her that Goethe was forced to take cognizance that his premature ejaculations were symptoms, and that he was suffering here from a real defect. Friederike, in her loveliest innocence--it can well be imagined--succumbed to his charms. Whereas Goethe for a while reached gratification while dancing and kissing, the situation finally came about when the girl wanted to surrender herself to him, and Goethe himself, being twenty-two years old, felt driven to perform the act, but discovered to his horror and humiliation that he was prevented by a premature ejaculation. Thereupon he turned in flight. (1963: 1064)

Eissler does not address the question of why it took Goethe at least nine months to get on his horse and go.

After a few pages, Eissler accounts for the origin of Goethe's behavior by citing his confession that his lips "whether consecrated or cursed" "seemed more important than usual":

> This passage describes the hypercathexis of the oral zone, which
> is indispensable for the kind of sexual disturbance I have assumed
> Goethe to have suffered from prior to his journey to Italy. It also
> describes the futility of voluntary effort in combating the
> symptom. (1963: 1068)

After a few more pages, Eissler writes that "a few remarks must be added
regarding Goethe's orality":

> The oral zone--always under the supposition that my hypothesis is
> correct--was the leading zone, which set the mechanism of
> ejaculation into motion, and therefore it is reasonable to expect
> signs in Goethe of intense orality in other respects. (1963: 1073)

Eissler treats such "signs"--Goethe's heavy consumption of alcoholic
drink and of food, his loquacity, his frequent use of food metaphors.
But he then insists

> that the great role which the oral erogenic zone played must not
> lead to the conclusion that the clinical picture presented
> constituted an oral character. The mouth functioned as a trigger to
> activate the genital mechanism, and also, in the situation of
> unrelieved frustration, as an organ substitute for the genital.
> (1963: 1075)

Eissler's recurrences to Goethe's orality suggest he is nagged by an
intuition that it might, if properly understood, undercut his grand
theory of premature ejaculation.

Edmund Bergler begins *The Basic Neurosis* with a highly
significant clarification:

> Freud started his discoveries of the dynamics of the unconscious
> on hysteric (phallic) neurotics and discovered first the libidinous
> drives which propelled these sick people: the Oedipus complex.
> Viewing that fact from the aspect of "analytic
> geology," Freud first came across the most superficial layers of
> the unconscious, and, to complicate matters, focused his attention
> exclusively on libidinous drives. True, you cannot prescribe to a
> genius the sequence of his discoveries.
> Imagine for a short moment the hypothetical possibility
> that Freud had discovered first the "geologically" deepest, and
> historically oldest, in the life of the individual, layers of the
> unconscious: those of oral regression. The result would have been
> the avoidance of a fantastically amorphous mass confusion. The
> "geologic" layers would have been presented in their "proper"
> order.

Things did not, of course, happen that way. The real development of the child starts with the oral level, and progresses to the "anal" and "phallic" phases. Freud discovered the phallic phase first, progressed later to the anal phase, and had very little to say about the oral phase.

Historic sequence of analytical *discovery*, and historic sequence of individual *development*, are thus reversed. Many people never clearly understood that confusing fact. (1949: 1; ital. in orig.)

Reik and Eissler, if their treatment of Goethe is representative of their psychoanalysis, are among those people who do not appreciate the primacy of the oral phase in psychological development. In Goethe's case, they helpfully discuss many of the neurotic behaviors that Bergler regards as signs of oral regression, but they regard them only incidentally as they theorize about the mystery of Goethe's sexual behavior before Faustina.

Relying upon *unio mystica*, Mann finds the *Anlage* of Goethe's consciousness/unconsciousness in the oral phase. This he does directly in Chapter Seven when he imagines both the conscious and unconscious contents of Goethe's mind and indirectly in the other chapters, especially in Chapter Three, when he supplies words for other characters describing actual behaviors of Goethe that are indicative either of oral regression or of defense against it. The analysis of Goethe that Mann implies in *The Beloved Returns* conforms to the general manifestations of "psychic masochism" and to the specific manifestations of several of its "clinical pictures" presented in Edmund Bergler's *Basic Neurosis*. Presumably the infant Goethe experienced enough frustration threatening his sense of "autarchy" that he created the fantasy that his mother denied him her breast. Thus he became fixated to the oral phase of development, even though he constructed an elaborate defense against feelings of dependence upon his mother and, in time, her surrogates. Beginning in adolescence, his unconscious wish to reclaim the oral pleasure lost in infancy stimulated his desire to kiss every girl in sight. But then, in each case, he was reminded that each such beloved threatened the return of the repressed. The pleasure of kissing threatened his adopted posture of independence through renunciation, so that he felt guilt, not for his seductions but for his betrayals of his defense system. He would renounce the girl he was then kissing, to return to his writing, the creative work which was the keystone of his defense system.[8] But that creativity, culminating in *Faust II*, continued to smuggle into publication his nostalgia for the breast and his search for the Good Mother.

Notes to *The Beloved Returns: Lotte in Weimar*

[1]This charming scene of wrapping himself in fur also suggests that Goethe was at the time under the influence of the "Marsyas Complex" (cf. ch1n7).

[2]In "Goethe and Tolstoy" Mann anticipates the ancient Goethe saluting his penis:

> Alter, hörst du noch nicht auf?
> Immer, Mädchen! (154)

[3]Entitled *"Die Idee der Erziehung bei Goethe und Tolstoi"*, the paper was first read in Lübeck on 4 September 1921, then published in *Deutsche Rundshau* in March 1922 (Reed 1996: 286). Revised, expanded, and entitled "Goethe and Tolstoy", the essay was included in *Bemühungen,* published in 1925 (Bürgin 1969: 65). Reed terms this essay "Mann's most balanced treatment of large cultural themes and his richest essay on Goethe" (1996: 337).

[4]From Rohde, *Psyche*, Mann could have learned that the "mystics find the basis of their method not in logic but in life: in the existence of a discoverable 'real', a spark of true being, within the seeking subject, which can, in that ineffable experience which they call the 'act of union', fuse itself with and thus apprehend the reality of the sought Object" (Underhill 1955: 24). Rohde finds the "first definite appearance" of such an experience in "the Orphic Mysteries in Greece and Southern Italy in the sixth century B.C." (Underhill 1955: 24fn1).

[5]Mann uses this information from von Arnim in *Confessions of Felix Krull* to describe the protagonist's response to his wet nurse (8), one instance of his parody of Goethe's autobiography (Prater 1995: 86). In "Fantasy on Goethe", first published in 1948, Mann also shows his dependence on von Arnim's transmission to Goethe of his mother's recollection of his birth: "Three days you hesitated before you came to the light of the world, and you caused your mother painful hours. You came black and without signs of life out of anger that you had been thrust forth perforce from the nature-given dwelling place". Von Arnim's transmission also records that Goethe's grandmother, who was attending her daughter, announced "Elisabeth, he lives" (quoted in Eissler 1963: 76). Mann's version:

> The child whom an eighteen-year-old mother brought into the world with great travail on August 28, 1749, just as the clock struck noon, was blue and looked lifeless. It seemed not to respond to the light that flooded into the Frankfurt burgher's home, and seemed prepared to go directly from the maternal womb to a little grave, as if it were unwilling to set out upon a path which was to carry it so far, to be so richly fruitful, so blessed with fulfillments, so glorious an example. Some time passed before the grandmother, standing behind the bed, could call out to the sighing mother: "Elisabeth, he is living!" (96)

[6]That Mann had this allusion in mind is confirmed by his letter of 6 December 1938 to Karl Kerényi: "I can not guarantee that the reading of your essay will not make itself felt in the Goethe novel [*The Beloved Returns*] as well, since in the end it will not get along entirely without Helen" (qtd. in Kerényi 1975: 83, interpolation in orig.)

[7]Eissler offers a psychoanalytic interpretation of the "Mothers":

> It is difficult to describe the mystery and greatness that surrounds these mythological figures, but here it is not a matter of conveying poetical values. They symbolize the primeval beginnings of life, and everything living returns to them. They too, like granite, are beyond life and death; they are beyond conflicts; everything that exists finds its place in their vicinity. That they are not beyond the erotic sphere is indicated by the symbolism of the key that grows in Faust's hand and leads to them. I believe they are not only called The Mothers, but they *are* the mothers, the mothers of an early time that, in individual development, can also be called primeval. Freud has called that period the preoedipal one. Mother alone existed for the child at that time; father, if perceived separately at all, was nothing but an intruder. I believe that Goethe's conception of the granite and his creation of The Mothers both go back to experiences pertaining to the preoedipal phase, which is viewed in both instances as a conflict-free resting in mother. It is in keeping with fantasies about this early phase, as well as with early modes of experience, that it is pictured as timeless and not subject to change. (1963: 872)

[8] Mann had first written about the mystery in his 1922 essay "Goethe and Tolstoy":

> Consider even his love-life, which likewise the popular mind tends to think of as sunlit and blissful, divinely favoured and without a cross. Certainly he was much loved and rich in love; certainly to him much enjoyment was given. In the realm of the erotic he had his spells of coarseness, when he behaved a little like a garden god [i.e., Priapus]: when, ingenuous and unsentimental as the antique world, he would enjoy without stint and indulge without a qualm. His marriage, a misalliance, socially and intellectually, was a result of this attitude of mind. But where he loved so that lofty poesy was the result, and not merely a Venetian epigram ticked out in hexameters on a maiden's back; where it was serious, the romance regularly ended in renunciation. He never actually possessed Lotte or Friederike, nor Lilli, nor the Herzlieb, nor Marianne, nor even Ulrike—and not even Frau von Stein. He never loved unrequited—unless in the immensely painful, absurdly shattering affair with little Levetzow. Yet in all these cases resignation was the order of the

day: either on moral grounds, or for the sake of his freedom. Mostly he bolted. (139-40)

The Transposed Heads

In October 1939 Mann wrote Agnes Meyer, "Now I am writing the last pages of *The Beloved Returns*. The day is near when I shall again write the words, "The End," and on the following morning, if I know myself, the first lines of Joseph IV will be put down on paper" (qtd. in Bürgin 1969: 145). But while his conscious intention was to conclude the Joseph story, his unconscious need was to continue his mother story. A glimmer of another such story had appeared in Chapter Seven of *The Beloved Returns*, when Goethe's interior monologue turns to seduction:

> In the whole moral and sensual world the thing whereon my whole life long I have most dwelt with horror and desire is seduction--inflicted or borne, active or passive, sweet and terrible, like a command laid on us by a god; the sin we sinlessly commit, guilty as tool and victim both; for to withstand it does not mean we cease to be seduced. It is the test no one withstands, it is so sweet, even to endure it spells defeat. It pleases the gods to send us sweet temptation, to make us suffer it, as its instruments, as patterns of all temptation and guilt, for the one is already the other. Never heard of a crime I could not have committed. Not committing it, you escape the earthly judge but not the heavenly. For in your heart you have committed it. Seduction by one's own sex--that might be a revenge, a mocking retribution for seduction practised by oneself--Narcissus, for ever deluded by his own image. Revenge for ever bound up with seduction, trial not overcome by victory--that is the will of Brahma. (357-58)[1]

Notice that Goethe admits that he has experienced seduction his "whole life long"; indeed he might say that it was the agent of seduction--that is, the other who first made him aware of his sexual self--who awakened him to his "whole life long". In other words, his mother or her substitute. This is not to say that the agent of original seduction actually touches the body or even attempts to; rather the agent actively or passively presents itself as body, seduces the mind by awakening desire. Thereafter, the seduced, like every other awakened human being, is unable to escape the "command laid on us by a god", to be seduced and to seduce. But, given the taboo against approaching the first agent of seduction (or the females in her line), Goethe retaliated by denying her existence, then, in adolescence, began his project of seducing the innocent female, awakening her desire, only to frustrate its consummation by his flight. Although he is "guilty as tool and victim both", yet he is innocent of "the sin we sinlessly

commit": "Revenge for ever bound up with seduction, trial not overcome by victory--
that is the will of Brahma". Mann's Goethe knows that his serial seduction
is a serial revenge against the Mother--a revenge that never satisfies.

Thinking for the third time of "a command laid on us by a god",
Goethe is reminded of a story that he had read many years before, in
"the Journey to East India and China", "Sonnerat's *Reise nach Ostindien und China*"
(Kerényi 1975: 219). When his response to the story has ripened in his
unconscious, he intends to write "the poem of the Brahman's wife, the Pariah-
goddess": "There in all the accents of horror I mean to proclaim and celebrate
seduction" (*Lotte* 358). He remembers the story:

> A picture of women, holy, noble, pure, walking down to the river
> daily for fresh water, needing nor jar nor ewer for the task, for in
> their pious hands the water rounds into a splendid crystal ball.
> How I love this crystal ball, carried by the pure wife of the pure
> Brahman in daily joyful ritual to her home: clear concrete symbol
> of untroubled clarity, untouched innocence, and its simple power.
> In the poet's sinless hand Water shapes a ball--yes, I am bent
> upon it, my crystal ball shall be this poem of seduction: the poet,
> much seduced, the tempting-greatly-tempted, he has the power
> and the gift, the pure hand that shall shape the crystal ball. But not
> so the woman. The river mirrored for her the image of the divine
> youth, she lost herself in gazing, the unique divine apparition
> seized upon her soul and shook it. Then the water denied her,
> would not form the ball. She stumbles homeward, her high lord
> sees her guilt and cries out for revenge. Drags the stricken guilty
> innocent to the sacrificial mound, strikes off her head. But the son
> threatens the avenging father to follow his mother to death, as
> widows do their husbands. It shall not be! Lo, truly the blood has
> not dried on the sword, it still flows fresh. Quick, join again head
> to body, say the prayer, bless the union with the sword, she will
> arise. So said, so done. Alas, alas! For on that mound of sacrifice
> two bodies are confused, the mother's noble form and the corpse
> of a condemned woman of the pariah caste. In his haste the son
> placed his mother's head on the outcast's body and healed it with
> the sword of judgment. A giant goddess arises, the goddess of the
> impure.--Make a poem of this, round and compress it to a crystal
> ball of words, pellucid, resilient. What more pregnant task? She
> became a goddess, but among gods, wild her 'haviour, wise her
> willing. Before the eyes of the pure woman the vision blissful of
> the youth will hover, heavenly tender; but sinking down into her
> impure heart it kindles lust and madness and despair. Ever
> endures temptation. Ever will it be repeated, the divine distracting
> vision, brush her garment as it passes, ever rising, ever sinking,
> ever brightening, ever fading--so hath Brahma willed. She stands
> before Brahma, the terrible goddess; warns him gently, rages at

him, from her racked and heavy-laden, sore-bewildered heart--
and in the mercy of the Highest all suffering creatures share.

I think Brahma fears the woman, for I fear her, fear her
as my own conscience when she stands before me, wishing
wisely, doing wildly--just so I dream the poem, put it off through
the decades, knowing some day I must write it[...]. (359-60)

Goethe eventually wrote the poem in 1824. Eissler describes *The Pariah* as a trilogy: "The first part of the trilogy is the pariah's prayer to Brahma that he too should have a god. The concluding part is the pariah's thanks for the great gift of having received a goddess. The middle part is a gruesome report of the miracle that gave the pariahs their goddess" (1963: 561).

Having just used the middle section of *The Pariah*, *"Legende",* as a vehicle for his depiction of Goethe's obsession with seduction, Mann must have thought it more than coincidence when, on 12 November 1938, he came across Heinrich Zimmer's *"Die indische Weltmutter"* in the just-published *Eranos-Jahrbuch* (Kesten 1984: 385). In "The Indian World Mother" Zimmer recounts another version of the tale of the transposed heads[2], *"Die vertauschten Köpfe"*, found "in Vetalapantschavimshati, tr. into German by H. Uhle *(Meisterwerke orientalischer Literaturen*, vol. 9, Munich, 1924)" (Zimmer 1968: 72fn3). Zimmer's paraphrase of *"Die vertauschten Köpfe"* provides the basic narrative for Mann's *Die vertauschten Köpfe*, dedicated to "Heinrich Zimmer, the Great Indian Scholar". By 9 December 1939 Mann had begun to plan his novella (Kesten 1984: 385). On 5 January 1940 he reported to Agnes Meyer,

> Just imagine. I am now writing something Indian, a Maya-grotesque concerning the cult of the magna mater, for whose sake the people cut off their heads--a game of separation and identity, not very serious. At the most, it will be a curiosity, and I do not know at all whether I shall finish it. (qtd. in Bürgin 1969: 146)

In the beginning of "The Indian World Mother" Zimmer stresses the importance of the goddess Kali, the "hideous aspect" (1968: 74)--as opposed to the "charming" aspect (1968: 95)--of the World Mother, "the Great Goddess" (1968: 75). Then he enters into an extended discussion of the "multiple manifestations" of her "one all-conquering form" (1968: 78), noting the different names by which she has been known to Hindus scattered across the Indian subcontinent:

> The Mother is as mercilesss as she is merciful, since she is life itself, and life remains as it is, whether man raises the plaintive cry of "Mother!" or clenches his teeth to withstand the aspect of

its Gorgon's head. It allows itself to be called "mother," and for one moment the sound of the word may relieve our heart of its boundless fear of the silent horror of life, unceasingly grinding its blossom in its jaws; but our cry does not change the Mother. She remains the dark figure adorned with the severed hands and heads of countless victims, raising the blood-filled goblet to her lips, quaffing the steaming sap of life with her broad, tigerlike tongue. (1968: 98-99)

Zimmer begins his essay by summarizing two tales in which Kali, the most widely known manifestation of the "hideous" aspect of the Indian World Mother, incites mortals to behead themselves. Then he alludes to her iconic appearance several times (1968: 74, 79, 81) before giving the amplified depiction above, in which he likens her to the Gorgon. He focuses on Kali because his project in the essay is to account for the existence of death-dealing intermingled with life-giving in the actions of the Indian World Mother toward her creatures. That account is eloquent and will be introduced in the summary statement about Mann's novella.

It was not merely Zimmer's summary of *"Die vertauschten Köpfe"* that challenged Mann's creativity; much more so it was Zimmer's examination of the role that Kali plays in the cult of the Indian World Mother. Zimmer's likening Kali's appearance to that of the Gorgon makes explicit the image that stirred Mann's unconscious to draw the picture of *"Mvtter Natvr"* that he had inserted in *Bilderbuch für artige Kinder* in 1897. Kali, then, represents for Mann the "return of the repressed". He was compelled to allow Kali into consciousness, but he would destroy her capacity to terrify him by employing the grotesque-comic sublimation, counteracting her threat by treating her as a caricature (cf. ch1n5).

Mann's use of the word *grotesque* in his letter to Agnes Meyer betrays the emotion that prompted him to undertake his exposé of Kali. Noting that Mann frequently used the word, Wolfgang Kayser concludes "that for him the grotesque entails a distortion and exaggeration of reality which reveals the true nature of a phenomenon" (1963: 158-59). Surely Mann was justified in using the word to describe the world that he intended to create in *The Transposed Heads*. But another of Mann's uses of the word, not cited by Kayser, conveys Mann's subjective response to the return of the repressed. In his essay "Conrad's 'The Secret Agent'" (1926) Mann says:

> I feel that, broadly and essentially, the striking feature of modern
> art is that it has ceased to recognise the categories of tragic and
> comic, or the dramatic classifications, tragedy and comedy. It
> sees life as tragi-comedy, with the result that the grotesque is its
> most genuine style--to the extent, indeed, that to-day that is the
> only guise in which the sublime may appear. (240-41)

In his letter to Agnes Meyer, Mann indicates that the "Maya-grotesque"
concerns "the cult of the magna mater"; in his Conrad essay, he indicates
that, for the modern sensibility, only the grotesque is capable of
evoking the experience of awe that the sublime once evoked. He will
overtly treat the experience of awe that Kali evokes, so that he can
covertly confess his experience of "maternal awe" (all previous
discussions of the "uncanny" in this study treat instances of such awe
in his fiction). But he indicates in his letter to Agnes Meyer his
intention to defend himself against Kali's (Mother's) attempt to
overwhelm him by denying any seriousness to her story. Thereafter he
described it as assuming "the character of a pastime" (Kesten 1984: 345),
as "no important work or major political undertaking--only a divertissement and
intermezzo" (qtd. in Bürgin 1969: 150), as "an improvisation with a few droll
moments, indifferently carried to its conclusion" (Winston 1971: 346), as an
"Indian jest" (Winston 1975: 38), and as "a metaphysical jest" (Kerényi
1975: 101), as "metaphysical pleasantry" ("Foreword" vi). Why, then, did he
waste his time on it?

  Thus the narrator introduces *The Transposed Heads*:

> The story of Sita of the beautiful hips, daughter of the cattle-
> breeder Sumantra of the warrior caste, and of her two husbands (if
> one may put it like that) is so sanguinary, so amazing to the
> senses, that it makes the greatest demands on the hearer's strength
> of mind and his power to resist the gruesome guiles of Maya. It
> would be well for the listener to take pattern from the fortitude of
> the teller, for it requires, if anything, more courage to tell such a
> tale than to hear it. (3)

Whereas Zimmer's version begins, "Two friends undertook a pilgrimage to a
bathing place sacred to Kali and there saw a beautiful girl" (72), the narrator's
version at once shifts the focus of his tale from the "friends" to the
inciting feminine presence, "daughter of the cattle-breeder". And since
Zimmer's paraphrase does not name the possessor of the "beautiful hips",
the narrator's revelation of her name indicates that it signifies: "The
word *sita* means "furrow," "the line made by the plow," (Kinsley 1986: 65), and
the word became the name "of a goddess of the plowed fields, [...]a goddess of

fertility" (Kinsley 1986: 67). Her "beautiful hips" framing her "furrow", the earthly Sita evokes man's image of the divine Sita and incites man's desire to enter/re-enter her body. The divine Sita was later revealed to be "the wife of Rama, the hero of the epic *Ramayana*", "revered as the model Hindu wife, who, although the victim of injustices, always remains loyal and steadfast to her husband" (Kinsley 1986: 65).

Then, rather than getting on with the story, the narrator ostentatiously intrudes into his text, flattering himself by saying that it takes more courage to tell this story than to hear it. Thus the narrator implies that the "listener" or reader must attend not only to the unfolding of the story but also to the narrator's involvement with its unfolding if its full significance is to be realized. Mann himself revealed a deep personal response to the story in another letter to Agnes Meyer:

> I can tell you that the day before yesterday I read my family and a few friends a new chapter from *The Transposed Heads* (a chapter involving an ascetic in the Indian jungle), and we all laughed until the tears came--not excepting the reader and author. Unfortunately I cannot read it aloud to you to prove my high spirits. It's somewhat indecent--the saint's fault. (Winston 1971: 338; parenthesis in orig.)

Laughing is frequently explained as the accompaniment of a spontaneous refusal to accept as real something suddenly perceived, just as crying is explained as the spontaneous acceptance of the loss of part of reality.

Then the narrator provides the exposition for his narrative:

> At the time when memory mounted in the mind of man, as the vessel of sacrifice slowly fills up from the bottom with drink or with blood; when the womb of stern patriarchal piety opened to the seed of the primeval past, nostalgia for the Mother reinvested with new shudderings the ancient images and swelled the number of pilgrims thronging in the spring to the shrines of the great World-Nurse; at such a time it was that two youths, little different in age and caste, but very unlike in body, were vowed to friendship. (4)

Using very ironic language--e.g., "the womb of stern patriarchal piety"--the narrator refers to what Zimmer termed the "late revival of an early matriarchal age" (1968: 96). Accepting Bachofen's thesis that the earlier worship of the Mother Goddess was supplanted by that of the Father God (Zeus, Jupiter, El, et al.), Zimmer distinguishes between Western and Eastern religious evolution: "In Hellas the maternal principle is overcome, while in India it is appeased, conciliated, and included among the sacred forces. And the mothers lose none of their stature and power in the process" (1968: 82). Zimmer sees dire consequences for Hinduism from its revival of the "cult of the World Mother and Mother Earth" (1968: 97): "The cry for the mother is regression to the elementary form of subordination and dependence; it is the suckling reflex of the baby, the return to infancy" (1968:97). Again linking "nostalgia for the Mother" with maternal awe, "shudderings", the narrator alludes to Zimmer's phrase "the suckling reflex of the baby" by describing the "pilgrims thronging in the spring to the shrines of the great World-Nurse" (4).

The two youths, Nanda and Shridaman, who now appear in the scene, are faithful Hindus, accepting subjugation by the World Mother. Although the narrator demonstrates that they are contrasts by caste, temperament, physique, mentality, yet they are fundamentally identical in being unawakened to sexual desire, although Shridaman is twenty-one and Nanda is eighteen. On a trip, "each on his own occasions" (11), they reach "a bathing place, sacred to Kali, the All-Embracing" (12): "Then they descended, cupping their hands, into the green river-bed; drank, poured the ritual water, dipped, and gave thanks" (15). As devotees of Kali, they believe that the river is the womb of the goddess, in which they must bathe and from which they must drink, in order to be in communion with her (Zimmer 1968: 89-90). Then, "like brothers" (15)--for they are both sons of Kali--they share their meal and their thoughts. As they rest, they seem to coalesce into one body, Shridaman representing its spirit and Nanda its flesh.

After a while, unobserved, they watch a young girl, beautiful in phiz (161) and figure (34), who, walking to the river bank, bares all in order to enter Kali's womb. After a while, Nanda recognizes her as Sita, having "swung her up to the sun" in a ritual (35), enabling the girl, as symbol of the spring sun, to rise higher--thus providing Mother Nature the human cooperation that she must have to be enable growth (Zimmer 1968: 75). After Sita's departure, the conversation between the two youths reveals that while Nanda is content to behold her "behind" (39) Shridaman yearns to "go behind it to reach the knowledge to which every phenomenon can lay claim, for it is more than phenomenon, and one must find the being, the soul, behind it" (41). The "certain quiver" (43) that appears in Shridaman's speech and the fieriness that appears on his "cheeks and forehead" (44) testify that he has been overwhelmed by maternal awe. His words soon reveal as much:

> Do you not know, then, that in every female shape--child, maid, mother, or grey-haired woman--*she*, the All-Mother, hides herself,

> the all-nourisher, Sakti, the great goddess; of whose womb all
> things come, into whose womb all things go; whom we honour
> and praise in every manifestation that bears her sign? (43-44)

To Nanda, "utterly ravished by these metaphysical words" (48),
Shridaman expands upon the World Mother:

> In her twofold shape we recognize her greatness; for she is the
> wrathful one, black and terrifying, drinking the blood of creatures
> out of steaming vessels; but at the same time is she the white and
> gracious one, source of all being, cherishing all forms of life at
> her nourishing breast. (46-47)

As it often happens, Shridaman dilates upon the metaphysical until he
gets physical:

> Lo, we came to a place where our life-dream flowed into the
> sacred bathing-place, and there appeared to us the All-Mother, the
> All-Consumer, in whose womb we bathed, in her sweetest shape,
> to amaze and exalt us--very likely as a reward, because we
> honoured her procreative emblem and poured water to it. Linga
> and Yoni--there is no greater sign and no greater hour in life than
> when the man is summoned with his Sakti to circle round the
> bridal fire, their hands are united with the flowery bond and he
> speaks the words: "I have received her!" (47)

At the moment when the human couple join Linga to Yoni, they
become "no longer human beings more, not he and she, one male, one female, but
the great pair, he Siva, she Durga, the high and awful goddess" (48). Pointedly,
Shridaman has an awful need to get deified.

After separating for several days to attend to "their respective
errands" (50), the two youths are reunited. Shridaman confesses "in a
strangled voice" that he has an incurable illness, "a sickness unto death": "It
was of such a nature, he said, that he not only must but would die, the must and the
will being entirely interwoven and indistinguishable, so that they formed a single
compelling desire, each issuing inevitably from the other" (52). Shridaman
concludes with a plea: "do me love's last service and build me the funeral hut
that I may go into it and burn in the fire". His "strangled, wildly agitated voice"
reveals that, still in the throes of maternal awe, he is now pricked to
pain by desire for Sita. Although he wishes to marry the mortal, who
evokes "the spirit of the white and gracious one, source of all being, cherishing all
forms of life at her nourishing breast", pious Shridaman is always aware that
the World Goddess is bi-polar, hence his piety demands a sacrifice of
himself to her dark aspect.

Himself unawakened by desire, the literal Nanda assumes that Shridaman is sure enough terminal and says that he will not only lay the pyre but also join his friend in lying on it (53). Then Shridaman has to confess to his obtuse friend: "If a man were afflicted by desire for a happiness of which no mortal but only a god might dream, and if he could not live without this happiness, then it was clear the man must die" (55-56). Relieved, Nanda cries: "Lovesick, lovesick! That is all there is to it. That is the mortal illness. What fun, what a joke!" Then, explaining that "Sita of Bisonbull is no goddess" (58), Nanda tells his afflicted friend,

> Take it not unfriendly, but only as cooling counsel to your overheated sense, when I say that you are mistaken if you think only gods have a right to the goal of your desires. That is exaggerated; indeed, nothing is more human and natural than that you are driven to sow in this furrow.

The narrator adds: "(He put it like this because the word Sita means a furrow.)" Nanda volunteers to negotiate Shridaman's suit for Sita, and, when the suit is successful, accompanies the newly wed but as yet uncoupled couple to the threshold of the marital chamber.

At this point, the narrator once again intrudes:

> Here we warn the listener, perhaps misled by the so far pleasing course of the tale, not to fall prey to a misconception of its real character. For a little space there was silence, it turned its face away; when it turns back it is no more the same, but changed to a frightful mask, a face of horror, distracting, Medusalike, turning the beholder to stone, or maddening him to wild acts of abnegation--for so Shridaman, Nanda, and Sita saw it, on the journey which they--but everything in its turn. (66)

By referring to the "real character" of "the tale" as "Medusalike", the Gorgon, not "the white and gracious one, source of all being, cherishing all forms of life at her nourishing breast", the narrator alludes to its "real character", the goddess Kali. Thus he warns "the listener" that the significance of what is to follow is not merely the grotesquerie of the human actions, but the revelation of what Zimmer calls a "passionate impetus toward the mother" that "may arouse all that is childlike in the worshiper of Kali and raise it to formative dominance" (1968: 101). About that "passionate impetus" the teller of the tale knows whereof he speaks.

Following the specifications of the tale in Zimmer's version (1968: 72), the narrator describes Nanda chauffeuring Shridaman and a slightly pregnant Sita on a visit to her native village. Disquiet rules all three, and their getting lost in the woods only emphasizes their feeling that they are in a muddle. After a night in the woods, they find that their only path is through a vaginal "stone gulley" (71) that leads to "a shrine of Devi, Durga the terrible and unapproachable, Kali the dark Mother".

"Obeying an impuse of his heart", Shridaman is drawn through yet another vaginal entrance:

> The entrance seemed to crouch beneath the wild mountain itself, supported by columns flanked by snarling leopards. There were painted pictures to right and left, also at the sides of the inner entrance, carven out of the rock; visions of life in the flesh, all jumbled together, just as life is, out of skin and bones, marrow and sinews, sperm and sweat and tears and ropy rheum, filth and urine and gall; thick with passions, anger, lust, envy, and despair; lovers' partings and bonds unloved; with hunger, thirst, old age, sorrow, and death; all this for ever fed by the sweet, hot streaming blood-stream, suffering and enjoying in a thousand shapes, teeming, devouring, turning into one another. And in that all-encompassing labyrinthine flux of the animal, human, and divine, there would be an elephant's trunk that ended in a man's hand, or a boar's head seemed to take the place of a woman's. (72)

The entire description--described by McWilliams as being "of questionable necessity" (1983: 298)--contributes to the grotesque effect evoked by the passageway. The "snarling leopards" provide a Gorgonian overture; all that follows reveals that the passageway is *grottesco*, grotesque in the Renaissance sense of the word, a cave "in which the dissolution of reality and the participation in a different kind of existence" occur (Kayser 1963: 22). The full effect, according to Mann, is, in contemporary life, the "only guise in which the sublime may appear".

Evoking awe, the passageway prepares Shridaman "for the beholding of the Mother" (73). After a two-page description of the idol of Kali, her ritual objects--swords and such--and the heads of animals recently sacrificed to her, the narrator records Shridaman's reaction to the scene:

> This was She, the Deathbringer-Lifegiver, Compeller of sacrifice--her whirling arms made his own senses go round in drunken circles. He pressed his clenched fists against his mightily throbbing breast; uncanny shudderings, cold and hot, surged over his frame in successive floods. In the back of his head, in the very pit of his stomach, in the woeful excitation of his organs of sex, he felt one single urge, driving on to the extremity of a deed against his own life in the service of the eternal womb. (75)

Overwhelmed by "uncanny shudderings", maternal awe, Shridaman prays, "Beginningless, that wast before all created! Mother without man, whose garment none lifteth!" and so forth.[3] Then he reaches his plea: "But let me enter again into thee through the door of the womb that I may be free of this self; let me no more be Shridaman, to whom all desire is but bewilderment, since it is not he who gives it!" (76) Instantly seizing the convenient sacrificial sword he beheads himself.[4]

Meanwhile, Nanda and Sita are getting restless, so Nanda, at Sita's request, enters the shrine, to find Shridaman, his head singularly distant from his body. Nanda glimpses the future: if he lives, it will be said that, lusting for Sita, he murdered his friend.[5] Since Nanda had previously declared that he would lie down on the pyre with Shridaman, he promptly beheads himself.

"Meanwhile, Sita, the furrow" (88), losing what is left of her patience, enters the shrine, discovers the unattached heads, and promptly faints. Regaining consciousness, she concludes that, however the deaths came about, she will be accused as the murderess of both men. Thus she runs from the shrine, intent upon killing herself, even if her act will destroy another life within her.

But just as she puts a noose braided of vine around her neck, she is upbraided by the voice of Kali, "with a maternal firmness about it" (97):

> "Will you just let that be for a minute, you silly ape!" it said. "Is it not enough to have let the blood of my sons, so that it flows in the runnels, but you will also mutilate my tree, and make your body--which is not a half-bad image of me--carrion for crows, together with the dear sweet warm little seed of life growing inside it?"
>
> "Perhaps you have not noticed, you goose, that you have missed your times and are in expectation from my son? If you cannot add two and two in women's matters, then hang yourself, do! But not here in my bailiwick, to make it look as though dear life should all at once perish and go out of the world, just on account of your silliness. My ears are full as it is of these quack philosophers who say that human existence is a disease, communicating itself through lust from one generation to the next--and now you, you ninny, start playing games like this with me! Take your neck out of the noose, or you'll get your ears boxed!" (97-98)

Up until the narrator's warning that "the so far pleasing course of the tale" (66) is now to change, the tone of the narrative is sprightly, broadly

humorous. Trusting the narrator, we anticipate a change from what
Käte Hamburger calls "the gaily parodistic narrative style" (1988: 63). But
even as the narrator spares no gruesome detail in dealing with
Shridaman's being driven to self-sacrifice by his fear and trembling
before the idol of the goddess, he never changes his tone. It is as if the
narrator cannot subdue his belief that the tale he tells is inherently
unworthy of serious consideration.

Now, with Kali condescending to descend into earthly affairs,
the narrator descends into the burlesque. Instead of being presented as
the Death-bringer, Kali is pictured as a tough old madam, having to
deal with a passion-provider in her establishment who has brought two
clients not the little death but the big one. After a lengthy
confabulation with "the furrow", Kali decides to employ divine
intervention, ordering Sita to rejoin the body parts, using the
sacrificial sword to bless and heal each point of severance in her
name, "Durga or Kali or simply Devi" (112), whatever. Mindful of Sita's
silliness, Kali reminds her to be sure to put the heads on face-forward
(113).

Sita gets the heads headed ahead, but crisscrossed: the
Brahman head on the hunk's body, the "goat-nosed" head on the
endomorphic somatotype (8).[6] To whom, then, does Sita now belong?
It is a marital-muddle worthy of the wisdom of King Solomon or
Queen Oprah. In the version of the tale that Zimmer follows, the king
opines that the new construction "bearing her husband's head was her
husband, for just as woman is the highest of delights, so is the head the highest part of
the body" (1968: 73). Then Zimmer concludes his treatment of the tale:

> Thus she was wedded to the friend's body, beneath the visible
> sign of the husband. Was the young woman guided by a secret
> desire in transposing the heads? Was the marriage unhappy; was
> it this that made the husband so ready for death, so eager for
> salvation? The story says not a word to indicate the answer but
> merely tells what happened. The strange mistake with its
> underlying motives stands unexplained.

In Mann's extension of the tale, the two men contend over
who shall be Sita's husband; in stalemate, they defer to her choice, but
alas she is incapable of coming to a decision. The three then appeal to
the ascetic hermit Kamadamana, the "vanquisher of desire" (137), but, like
many a vanquisher, he always has it on his mind:

Yes, yes, I know, I know it all: the body of love, with bitter lust bedewed--limb-play neath satin skin, unguent-imbrued--the graceful vault the shoulder makes--the sniffing nose, loose mouth that seeks--sweet breasts adorned with tender stars--the armpits' hollows with sweat-drenchèd beards--oh, pasturage for hands to rove, fair hips, fine loins, back supple, belly breathing love--the bliss-embrace of arms, the bloomy thighs, cool twin delight of hillocks that behind them lies--till all agog with lust at pitch they work at coupling play in hot and reeking dark, each urging other on more bliss to capture, they flute each other to a heaven of rapture--and this and that and here and there--I know it all, of all I am aware! (147-48)

(This is the segment that Mann dared not reveal to Agnes Meyer.) The naked ascetic's fervent description has jerked him into the Osiris condition, for he excuses himself to put on "a sort of apron made out of thin bark" (149) before rendering his decision, which is the same as that in the Zimmer version. Nanda-head heads off to a vacant lot in the forest, there to be a hermit, while Sita and Shridaman-head settle down in Welfare of Cows, closely studying Kamadamana's training manual.

All too soon, though, desire flees paradise. Shridaman's Nanda-body, dominated by the mind that we conventionally locate in the head, loses its Nandaness; his head's appearance, though, grows coarser, in sympathy with the body. Seeing these changes, Sita is no longer titillated to participate, even though participation provides *frisson* , being as it is an adulterous affair. Speculating that Nanda's head has endowed its Shridaman-body with mesomorphic measurements, she longs to see him at length.

Her longing is intensified each day when she looks at her son Samadhi, who was sired by Shridaman's body, now supporting Nanda's head. When Samadhi reaches his fourth year, Sita takes advantage of Shridaman's absence to take her son to see his father. After a long trip filled with peril, Sita rejoices to see the realization of her speculation that Nanda's Shridaman-body is Nandaized. Nor has the hermit life vanquished Nanda's desire for Sita. Giving little Samadhi, who is conveniently short-sighted, some "flowers and nuts to play with" (181), they head for the shed to play with the same.

Shridaman shows up the next morning, bearing two swords and a solution. In their bower of bliss Nanda and Sita have been awaiting him, for they defer to his Brahmanic wisdom. It is unthinkable that one man kill the other in order to live with Sita, for that act would dishonor their lifelong friendship. Polyandry forbidden, Sita cannot live with both men. But if she chooses one, she will inevitably pine for the other. The only satisfactory outcome is that the two kill each other, rather than kill themselves. Then they can, as friends, be burned on the same pyre, on which Sita joins them, honoring the practice of suttee or the virtuous wife. The bones not consumed by the fire are honored and enclosed in "an earthen pot which was thrown into the holy Ganges" (195), "Mother Ganges", whose water offers "immediate liberation" and "a safe journey to the realm of the ancestors" (Kinsley 1986: 192-93).

Although Kali has played no obvious role since she directed Sita to reattach the heads, she has not disappeared from the tale. As "the energy of the world, taking form in all things" (Zimmer 1968: 95), "the Great Goddess"--as Shridaman, Nanda, and Sita must realize--drives her children to seek the fulfillment of desire in life, only to find that that attainment is impossible. For them there is only one course:

> the true adept of the mother-goddess[...], since he seeks consciously and with all his strength to penetrate her secret, must renounce every gesture of maternal love and care on the part of the mother to whose worship he has dedicated his life, if he is to effect the dark balance of renunciation and yearning in the melancholy, inexorable knowledge which, through contemplating the hour of his death, he feels ready to accept. (Zimmer 1968: 101)

To illustrate the true adept's acceptance of death, Zimmer quotes Maharaja Ramkrishna, who "sings to Kali and Siva, in his preoccupation with his last hour":"When my mind is failing, then the name of Kali whisper in my ears, as I lie on my bed of sand. This body is not mine, the passions sweep it along. O Forgetful One [Siva], bring my rosary when I float in Ganges" (1968: 73).

In his continuation of the tale of the transposed heads, Thomas Mann answers the questions about its meaning raised by Zimmer (1968: 73). Mann clearly realizes that implicit in the tale Zimmer tells is the theme of maternal awe; thus he designs his continuation to emphasize Kali's person as "the inexorable actuality of life, the flowing circle of its forces and forms, racing headlong, changing and merging with one another" (95), like a river. Although Kali inspires fear and trembling, yet is she the source of all human energy, of life itself. She is, therefore, the source and substance of all tales, so Mann celebrates her mystery with defiant distortion. Since he completes the tale in which he reduces the Bad Mother to good comedy, he continues to vanquish writer's block. But, as a great artist, he knows that she is the end of all tales, and that what a tale, like Kali, can teach us is to accept the inevitability of our transience.

Notes to *The Transposed Heads*

[1]Karl Stern points out that "Goethe, like Kierkegaard, was obsessed throughout his life by the person of the seducer as a mystical key figure" (1965: 227).

[2]A translation in English of "Die indische Weltmutter" appears as "The Indian World Mother" in *The Mystic Vision: Papers from the Eranos Yearbook*, ed. Joseph Campbell and tr. Ralph Manheim, Princeton, NJ: Princeton UP, 1968, pp. 70-102. The tale of the transposed heads appears on pp. 72-73.

[3]Here Mann paraphrases Zimmer, who writes:

> The myth cannot actually reveal the genesis of the great mother-goddess, but only the manner in which she makes her appearance, for the myth knows of her beginninglessness, which is implicit in the term "mother": it knows that as mother she existed prior to any of the things to which she has given life. In the conception of the myth, any inquiry into her origins seems as childish and presumptuous as the act of that reckless adept who undertook to lift the veil of the goddess at Saïs and was stricken everlastingly dumb with horror and fear. For the statue at Saïs is the image of the mother-goddess who says[...] 'No one has raised my veil" [...] meaning the dress that cloaks her feminine nakedness; the term "veil" is a product of the prudery of later tradition. (1968: 78)

[4]Zimmer explains that "the goddess desires only the blood of the offerings, hence beheading is the form of sacrifice, since the blood drains quickly from the beheaded beasts. That is why the characters in the tales of the *Hitopadesa* [one of which, through Zimmer, is Mann's source] and the *Katha-sarit-sagara* cut off their heads, though it is also true that the head signifies the whole, the total sacrifice" (1968: 74; my interpolation).

[5]In his Oedipal reading McWilliams has this to say:

> The plot of *The Transposed Heads* revolves, therefore, around two apparently unmotivated suicides. But if there is madness in the method, the opposite is also true. By means of his friendship pact with Nanda, Shridaman succeeds in ridding himself of the person who seems to plague and threaten his entire existence, this person whose continual presence robs him of all his peace and spontaneity. His wish that the world be rid of him "who swung Sita" is granted. Symbolically, and in this story, actually, the protagonist Shridaman in his self-murder succeeds in killing the introjected father, the physical representative of life. Kali, the goddess herself, proves the timeless nature of the Oedipal wound by sanctioning the deep-rooted disaffection in the soul of Shridaman, whose self-sacrifice was carried out first to remove

the threatening father figure, but finally to appease and possess the eternal
mother. (1983: 299)

[6]Loyal to his thesis Heilbut sees the botched reconstruction in a lurid light: "Mann frequently gave heterosexual rivalry a homosexual spin: in *The Transposed Heads,* he even let two passionate rivals switch body parts, thereby achieving a union beyond intercourse" (1996: 139).

Joseph the Provider

Completing *The Transposed Heads* in August 1940, Mann resumed work on the completion of "the Joseph" (qtd. in Winston 1971: 345), published as *Joseph the Provider* (1943). Although in October 1939 Mann had written Agnes Meyer that he would turn to the Joseph story the day after he finished *The Beloved Returns*, he had, instead, written *The Transposed Heads*. Thereafter, he did return to the Joseph story, but his first segment, "a theological chapter", as he described it to Agnes Meyer (Winston 1971: 345), reveals his continued reluctance to return to his task. McWilliams concludes "that the subsequent adventures of his protagonist [Joseph] after the showdown with Mut were simply not vital to his artistic endeavors" (1983: 272).

Only after nine pages of "theology" does Mann reintroduce "the figure standing, arms bound behind his back, in a sailboat propelled by oars over the river of Egypt and down to his prison" (851). Even then, Mann quickly shifts his focus from Joseph to the Egyptian governor of the prison, like Mut unworthy of being named in Genesis but here identified as Mai-Sachme. Opining that new characters "do not come out of the void", Kurzke speculates that Mai-Sachme was modeled on Mann's friend Martin Gumpert, who was visiting him on 20 September 1940, when he began work on the prison chapter (2002: 396). According to Kurzke, Mai-Sachme has Gumpert's physical features, "sedate manner", and similar inclinations to writing and to doctoring. But Kurzke offers no reason for Mai-Sachme's emergence from the "void".

Indeed, on 25 October 1940, just days after introducing Mai-Sachme, Mann himself indirectly acknowledged that he had had no significant role in mind for the new character. Thanking Karl Kerényi for a copy of his recent essay *"Das Ägäische Fest"*, Mann wrote:

> It is remarkable how our thoughts sometimes run along the same lines. I was almost astounded when I read the passage in your study dealing with that mystical idea of antiquity, the identity of mother and daughter (Demeter-Persephone). For that same morning, in working on one of the chapters of the new Joseph volume[...], I had included an anecdote about someone who, without knowing who she is, falls in love with the daughter of a woman whom he had loved as a young girl twenty years earlier. I found that the little story somehow *fitted*, without knowing why. When I read you, I became aware of the reason. (Kerényi 1975: 96; ital. in orig.)

While experiencing a creative moment is wondrous, it is sometimes unsettling to be mystified by what the moment has produced. Mann was relieved to discover a reason for "the little story": it is somehow connected with the Demeter-Persephone material that he had used in the "snow" chapter of *The Magic Mountain* and in the "Descent into Hell" chapter of *Joseph and His Brothers*. Particularly, a pleasing symmetry is established between Joseph's initial appearance in the first volume and his initial appearance in the final volume. The mystery of why his unconscious had led him to include the anecdote is solved! Or is it?

Before Joseph is formally imprisoned, he is presented to Mai-Sachme, the governor of the prison, who is delighted to discover that Joseph is charged not with one of the common crimes--which are always boring--but with seduction--which is always interesting (867). Glancing up from Joseph's rap sheet, the governor asks, "Do you know the story of the Two Brothers?" (866), a popular Egyptian story featuring the same plot as the Mut and Joseph story (Thacker 1963: 783). Catering to Mai-Sachme's desire to wax literary, Joseph replies: "I know it well, my lord,[...] For I had often to read it aloud to my master, Pharaoh's friend, and I also had to copy it out fair for him, with black and red ink" (866). Not only had Osarsiph read the story to Potiphar but he also knew that he was playing out its plot with Mut, for he had told her,

> Believe me, woman, I have had the thought of putting an end to your agony and mine by making of myself what you impute to me, like the youth in one of your legends, who took a sharp leaf of the sword plant and cut himself and threw the offending member into the river for fish to devour, to witness his innocence. (795)

Pleased with Joseph's response, the governor of the imprisoned abruptly confesses to the new prisoner a fantasy that, in effect, imprisons him. Before telling his story, though, Mai-Sachme twice acknowledges his state of mind, saying, "Here utter boredom reigns" (863), and commenting on "the monotony of this settled place where a man already settled by nature is in danger of falling asleep" (867). The description of Mai-Sachme's person as he makes his confession is also noteworthy:

> Mai-Sachme stood there, his expression relaxed, not to say sleepy, his arms folded, the roll tucked under one of them; his head on one side, the heavy brows somewhat lifted under the

brown bullet-eyes. His rounded lips moved with measured gravity
and he began to narrate. (867)

His relaxed, "even sleepy" expression (862), his tilted head, his lifted
brows, and his rounded lips suggest that the fantasy had its origin in
his nursing experience.

Fittingly, the original fantasy is reawakened in a dream that he
had had when he was twelve years old, inspired by a girl whom he had
seen the day before (867). Then, as he studied in "the house of instruction
in the riding-school of the royal stables", he saw the girl, "who was probably three
years older" (868) than he, bringing a fellow pupil his lunch, "three pieces
of bread and two jugs of beer" (867). Unconscious of the effect that the
providing of sustenance--especially in the two jugs--had had on him,
Mai-Sachme innocently recalls that of all her parts he was most taken
with her arms, "which were bare and of that slender fullness that is so lovely"
(867)--a fetish that Joseph must have recognized, having himself, back
up the river, often ogled an arm. Mai-Sachme questions his fellow
pupil, Imesib, who tells him that the girl is his sister, Nekhbet.

That night, using his bag of books as his pillow, Mai-Sachme
had dreamed that he and Nekhbet were betrothed (thus Mann implies
the close tie between the unconscious and creativity). The dream was
"so vivid and beautiful" (868) that he awakened to believe it real until it
faded with the passage of time.Twenty years later, at an Egyptian
outpost in Syria, he was once again so entranced by seeing a young
girl that he remembered the dream. When he inquired her name, he
learned that she was Nofrure, daughter of Nekhbet (869). He admits to
Joseph that she did not resemble her mother in facial features,
complexion, or hair; "only her charming figure was like Nekhbet's--but how
many girls have figures like that!" This admission suggests that there is in
his unconscious the *Gestalt* of mother so vivid that the distinctive
features of a young girl seen virtually disappear. Now, he says, he
lives in hope that in twenty years he will meet the daughter of
Nofrure, so as to recapture once again the feeling. Mai-Sachme's
experience recalls Adam Phillips' analysis of boredom and paraphrase
of Christopher Bollas' concept of the "transformational object".

Initially the mother, [the transformational object] is "an object
that is experientially identified by the infant with the process of the alteration of self
experience." This earliest relationship becomes the precursor of, the
paradigm for, "the person's search for an object (a person, place, event, ideology)
that promises to transform the self." At the first stage

> the mother is not yet identified as an object but is experienced as
> a process of transformation, and this feature remains in the trace
> of this object-seeking in adult life, where I believe the object is
> sought for its function as signifier of the process of transformation
> of being. Thus, in adult life, the quest is not to possess the object;
> it is sought in order to surrender to it as a process that alters the
> self. (Phillips 1993: 76-77)

Phillips then discusses boredom as a defensive state that protects the person awaiting the transformative event from suffering severe stress arising from his *Sehnsucht*.

Mai-Sachme's friend the chaplain wonders "over the extraordinary fact that the captain had chosen to relate the tale at this moment, in however composed and level a tone"--Mann's indication of his awareness that many of his readers might agree with the chaplain. But Mai-Sachme has a reason for telling the tale, admitting that he has written several drafts of his experience, but none to his satisfaction:

> the principal trouble is that I doubt whether by temperament I am
> not too steady-going to give to my tale the thrilling character it
> should have, as for instance in the model story of the Two
> Brothers. The subject is too dear to me that I should want to take
> the chance of botching it. (870)

The narrator continues: "He broke off with a guilty air and said: 'But at the moment what I am doing is to induct the prisoner'". Having immediately intuited from his first glance at "the prisoner" that Joseph does not suffer from the weakness that, according to Bergler, results in writer's block, Mai-Sachme is inducing Joseph to help him write his story or, if that does not work, to write the story himself. That weakness, the inability to repress a still dominant oral neediness, Mai-Sachme shares with Detlev Spinell (cf. ch4n9).

Thus Mann's unconscious is offering Mann a cautionary tale: if he does not maintain the defense against the mother figure that Joseph had mounted against Mut, then he will not be able to complete Joseph's story or, for that matter, any other fiction. Having already confessed his pleasure in stories of seduction, Mai-Sachme has already confessed that he has been seduced by the mother figure. Rather than fear the return of the repressed, he solicits the return of the beloved.

As he had been up the river, Joseph is quickly entrusted with heavy managerial responsibilities. Performing them with consummate skill, he earns the respect of Mai-Sachme, who then employs him to inscribe "a de luxe edition" of the Tale of the Two Brothers (877).[1] By this pretext, he can seek advice about how to compose his own tale, "a tale of expectancy" (878), which would have to be written from the point of view of "an old man of at least sixty; and that, they feared, would detract from the thrillingness, which, even as it was, was bound to suffer from the governor's natural temperament".

The real reason that Mai-Sachme fails to finish his tale lies in his "natural temperament", his passivity before the mother figure, which leads, in Bergler's scheme, to "writer's block". As for the lack of "thrillingness" because of the age of the author, it is worth remembering that Mann was then sixty-five. Given Mai-Sachme's attraction to tales of seduction, particularly to the Tale of the Two Brothers, Joseph tells him of Mut's attempted seduction. Mai-Sachme attempts to write a tale of it, but the finished draft reveals that he had not rendered the tale as Joseph had told it, a seduction rebuffed, but instead had imposed the "pattern of the Two Brothers and he presently left off where he began" (878).

Having warned himself, Mann is able to persevere with the continuation of the Joseph story. Joseph's interpretation of the dreams of the butler and the baker eventually gains him Pharoah's notice. His interpretation of Pharoah's dreams gains him Pharoah's directive to prepare for the season of plenty and the season of drought to follow. When Joseph is named chief of staff, he calls Mai-Sachme up from his prison to be his major-domo, proving that he is capable of irony by saying:

> do not call yourself my servant, for we shall be friends as we were before, when I was beneath your feet; and together shall we meet the good and bad hours of life, the exciting and the unexciting. There will certainly be both, and I need you most for the exciting ones. For your careful oversight I thank you in advance. But it must not consume you to the extent that you have no leisure to guide the reed in your study as you love to do, to find the right and fitting form for the story of the three love-affairs. Great is the writer's art! (998)

The story that Mai-Sachme would write is never again mentioned, for Joseph, as he then tells his friend, has "brought" him into his story as his faithful side-kick.

Mai-Sachme's first large responsibility is to produce Joseph's wedding. For, at the bidding of the Pharaoh (977), Joseph, with no apparent guilt or even embarrassment, agrees to marry an Egyptian

virgin, Asenath, the daughter of the sun priest, no less (1000). The fact
that the marriage has more public significance than pubic is confirmed
by the absence of any description of Osarsiph stiffly walking around
in the Osiris condition. Joseph has apparently forgotten the
tribulations visited upon him by the virgin Mut, even if the narrator
has not. The latter still describes her as Medusa:

> How can we help thinking sadly of the poor serpent now, at the
> moment when the sun-dial points to the hour of Joseph's
> marriage, which he made with another woman and put heads and
> feet together with her instead of with the serpent? I have sought to
> forestall that natural sadness by speaking first of her, how that by
> now she had become once more a cool moon-nut, to whom the
> whole affair no longer mattered. It is easier to think of her thus;
> our faint remaining bitterness is quenched in the picture of her as
> the bigoted priestess she had now become. (999)

Although Mai-Sachme receives credit for producing the
wedding (1005), Mann carefully manages every detail to insure that it
is a retelling of the Demeter and Kore-Persephone story as it was
enacted in the Eleusinian rites (Kerényi 1975: 102-03). He even
begins the wedding chapter, "Well then, Asenath the maiden" (1004),
knowing full well that Kore's name means 'maiden' (E. Hamilton 1942:
330). Then he has the nerve to pretend to be offended by the presence
at the wedding "of a pregnant sow, actually with a rider in the shape of a fat, half-
naked old woman with an equivocal cast of countenance who gave out a stream of
bad jokes!" (1007). No doubt he would justify his allusion to "beldam
Baubo" by citing Goethe's precedent in *Faust*.

To characterize the wedding festivity, Mann uses the
Demeter-Kore Persephone allusion to link "a certain abandon and on the
other hand a savour of the grave" (1006). Thus he signifies what Joseph's
marriage means to the mother project of *Joseph and His Brothers*.
Having rebuffed Mut the Bitch Mother, Joseph must accept the
mysterious Good Mother who brings both desire and death into the
world as an inescapable part of the natural process. Thus Joseph weds,
joining the procession to the grave:

> Pharaoh walked between them when at last the feast ended and
> the procession re-formed. It now included all those present, who
> with jubilation and lamentation, with myrtle-strewing and the fist-
> shaking of the masked mothers, took their way to the bridal
> chamber, where the newly-wed pair were put to bed among
> flowers and fine linen. (1008)

The nuptial chamber is the funeral chamber. We experience death-in-life if we hanker after paradise lost; but if we accept death in the right spirit, faith teaches us, we experience paradise regained.

Again rising from the pit, Joseph once more becomes the man of destiny for both the Egyptians and the Hebrews. But the Joseph story is immediately interrupted by the Tamar story. There is precedent in Genesis for the interpolation of the Tamar story (Chap. 38) within the Joseph story, just after the Midianites sell Joseph to Potiphar. But Mann defers the Tamar story until after Joseph has withstood the blandishments of Mut and married Asenath. According to McDonald, "Mann liked to mention his "late discovery" of Tamar as the "right female character for the final volume" (1999: 231). His phrase "late discovery" is probably the literal truth. On 3 October 1941 he wrote to Agnes Meyer, "I have just finished the marriage of Joseph to Asenath" (qtd. in Bürgin 1969: 160). Soon after he began a lengthy lecture tour, which kept him away from his desk at home until about 27 November. When he again picked up his pen, he must have realized that all that lay ahead of him in the Joseph story was Joseph's unfettered triumph. He certainly realized, in recalling the three earlier novels, that he derived his pleasure not from the portrayal of Jacob and Joseph and his brothers but from the creation of "the Rachel of the first and second novels" and of "the Mut-em-enet of the third" ("Foreword" xi). All dressed up in Eleusinian allusion, the Asenath that he had just created is merely a name. It must have been then that Mann realized the possibilities of the episode that he had overlooked.

On 23 December Mann reported to Agnes Meyer: "I am now working on the Tamar episode, a short novel in itself, and a curious subject" (Winston 1971: 383). A letter to Kahler, on 31 December, reveals the theme that he would impose upon the story found in Genesis: "I have come to the story of Tamar, a big insert, practically a novella in itself. Do you recall? A remarkable female who shrank from nothing that would enable her to thrust her way into the sacred story" (Winston 1971: 385).

The only indication that Chapter 38 is connected to the Joseph story is that it features Judah, the fourth son of Jacob's wife Leah. Withdrawing from his brothers, Judah married a Canaanitess, who bore him three sons, in order of birth Er, Onan, and Shelah. When Er came of age, he was, by order of his father, married to Tamar. Something he did or, more likely, did not do, so angered the Lord that He slew him. Since Er died without issue, Judah ordered Onan, his second son, to marry Er's widow, for the custom was that the first son of the brother who married his widowed sister-in-law would be regarded as the heir of the deceased brother. Knowing that if he sired a son he would forfeit the inheritance of land that now devolved on him, Onan practiced coitus interruptus, so angering the Lord that He slew him also. Judah told Tamar to remain a widow in her father's house until such time as Shelah was old enough to marry her. In time Judah's wife died. When Shelah came of age, he was not ordered by his father to fulfill the custom. Realizing Judah's deceit, Tamar, apparently deciding to repay deceit with deceit, veiled herself as a prostitute, then waited along the road that Judah would travel from a sheep-shearing. Fooled by Tamar's disguise, Judah accosted her, offering to send her a "kid from the flock" for her services. Tamar required as a pledge his signet, his bracelets, and his staff. Judah went home happy, but Tamar went home happier. Later Judah sent the kid, but the prostitute could not be found. Later still, when Tamar's pregnancy had become obvious, Judah ruled that she should be burnt for her whoredom. Then Tamar displayed the pledges given her by the man who had lain with her. Judah acknowledged that he had given her the pledges, then said, 'she hath been more righteous than I; because that I gave her not to Shelah my son" (Gen.38:26). Read in its historical context, the story bears this interpretation: that Judah recognizes that his breach of the brother-marriage custom is far more serious than Tamar's fornication--even incest, some would say--the wickedness of which is mitigated by her determination to fulfill her role as childbearer (Sutcliffe 1953a: 196).

Mann greatly embellishes the basic story. In the first place he pictures Tamar as a convert to Jacob's teachings about the God he worships. The narrator says repeatedly that Jacob was "just a little in love with her" (1015), implying that there is something of both Rachel and Joseph in her demeanor. The narrator also asserts that Jacob had spoken to Tamar of Judah's line holding the scepter until Shiloh comes, whereas Genesis does not record his use of the word *Shiloh* until he tells his sons of what shall befall them "in the last days" (49:10). Mann also equates Shiloh with the Messiah, an interpretation not made in any ancient text (Gray 1963: 908).

Building upon these variations, Mann creates in Tamar a "seeker" (1024) who is determined to "be the foremother of Shiloh, no more and no less" (1030), thus to gain her place in history and in salvation. At first Tamar's strategic object is Judah, "for she knew him much too well as slave to the mistress [i.e., venery] not to be sure of success". But then she realizes that Judah's wife, having provided her husband with three sons, already is the foremother, barring three untimely deaths. Tamar then plans to enter Judah's line by being impregnated by his eldest son Er; to accomplish her marriage to Er, the narrator speculates, Tamar persuades Jacob to direct Judah to arrange the marriage (1032-33). In Mann's version Er soon dies of a hemorrhage while coupling with Tamar (1034)--capital proof that he is incapable of transmitting the blood of the line. Then Tamar demands that Onan be married to her. In Genesis 38 Judah quickly complies with Tamar's demand. In Mann's version Jacob objects that Onan may not wish to marry his sister-in-law, inciting the sister-in-law to lay down the law:

> "In that case," said Tamar firmly, "she shall stand forth before the people and say: 'My brother-in-law refuses to reawaken for his brother a name in Israel and will not marry me.' Then shall one require him and speak with him. But if he stand and speak: 'I like not to take her', then shall she stand to him before all the people and take one of his shoes from off his foot and spit upon it and answer and say: 'Thus shall one do to every man who will not build up his brother's house.' And his name shall be Barefooter!" (1034)

Spitting on Onan's shoe and calling him *"Barefooter"* would render him an object of humiliation (Evans 1981: 82). According to Mann, Jacob is so impressed with Tamar's argument that he proclaims "a general law" regarding Levirate marriage that directly quotes Tamar. It is recorded in Deuteronomy 25: 5-10.

In Mann's version Onan attempts to spill his seed, but is restrained by Tamar, who uses her "Astarte equipment" (1035) with such tortuosity that he dies of a cerebrovascular accident--yet more evidence of weakness in the blood line. Further embellishments will be treated below.

In *Judah and Tamar (Genesis 38) in Ancient Jewish Exegesis*, Esther Menn closely studies "three early Jewish interpretations" of the story (1):

> Early Jewish interpreters responded to the challenges of the story of Judah and Tamar with eagerness and creativity. The *Testament of Judah* presents Genesis 38 as the story of a warrior king's tragic weakness for women, which nearly results in his loss of royal status. By contrast, *Targum Neofiti* develops the characters of Tamar and Judah as positive exemplars of moral behavior under duress, who sanctify God's Name through their principled acceptance of death and ultimately gain divine reprieve. Finally, *Genesis Rabba* depicts Genesis 38 as a series of providential and

> miraculous events leading to the origin of the royal and messianic
> lineage from the union of two worthy ancestors. (1997: 2)

Given Mann's habit of thoroughly researching his writing projects, it is probable that he read German translations of all three of these books.

Of the three, the *Testament of Judah* offers the interpretation most congenial to Mann's intention. Almost certainly he relied on it or on a work influenced by it to establish Judah's character in *Young Joseph*:

> Jehudah, the next elder son, but three years younger than Reuben, was quite as tall, but walked with a stoop and showed traces of suffering about his nostrils and lips[...]. These last spoke of sensuality, but the nose, finely shaped and delicately arched, which drooped over them, suggested some gift of the spirit; while the eyes, large and prominent and heavy-lidded, like a stag's, had a melancholy cast. Like several of his brothers and half-brothers, Judah was already a married man[...]. It would not have been possible to compass marriages entirely irreproachable from the religious point of view; and in Judah's case Jacob had perforce to be satisfied with any which might bring the youth some tranquillizing and steadying influence, for his sex life had from the first been marked by disorder and suffering. His relations with the love-goddess kept him strained and unsatisfied, he writhed beneath her lash and was her unsubmissive slave--hence the deep conflict in his soul and the lack of unity in his character. His intercourse with the consecrate and the whores in the temples of Ishtar brought him into contact with the follies and abominations of the worship of Baal and the shamelessness of Canaan[...]. (329-30)

Relying on his earlier characterization of Judah, Mann describes a Tamar who knows that her strategic object is a "slave to the mistress" (1030) as she calculates how easy it would be to become pregnant by him.

Thus Mann sets in motion a theme upon which he had pictured Goethe meditating in *The Beloved Returns* (485-86). In that place Goethe speaks of seduction as "a command laid upon us by a god". Now he intends to picture Tamar practicing seduction in response to a command laid upon her not by a god but by the God. In *Joseph the Provider* he anticipates the theme: "There we have another key word; for it was by seduction that Tamar shoved herself into the great history of which this is an episode. She played the temptress and whored by the way, that she might not be shut out; she abased herself recklessly to be exalted..." (1016; ellipsis in orig.). As he looked back, in the "Foreword" to *Joseph and His Brothers*, written in 1948, Mann described his state of mind as he faced the task of beginning *Joseph the Provider*:

> The reason for my reluctance was simply this: that I feared an anticlimax, a falling off of the fourth volume from the third. The latter, *Joseph in Egypt*, seemed to me unquestionably the artistic zenith of the work, if only on account of the humane vindication that I had undertaken in it, the humanization of the figure of Potiphar's wife, the mournful story of her passionate love of the Canaanite major-domo of her *pro forma* husband. I had no female character in stock to balance the Rachel of the first and second novels, the Mut-em-enet of the third, and it took a long time before I became aware that I had one after all. It was Tamar, the daughter-in-law and seductress of Judah, whom I made into Jacob's pupil, an Astarte-like figure, endowed, at the same time, with features from the Book of Ruth; and in half-humorous style I developed her into the prototype of historical ambition. Through her, who eventually gave her name to an entire section of the novel, a short story in itself, I found the fulfilment of the charms of the remaining material and the final incentive to continue the narrative. Even today I see no exaggeration in the sentence of the text [on p.1036] that reads: "she might be called the most amazing figure in this whole story--few will be found to deny it". (xi-xii)

Mann may claim that he vindicated Mut by humanizing her, but he had, for a reason of which he must be unconscious, used comic distortion in describing her failed attempt at seduction--and in describing Joseph's escape from it more in panic than in piety. Now, the serious nature of both seduction and Joseph's character must be rehabilitated. Presenting Tamar's successful seduction of Judah as the fulfillment of God's plan, Mann offers a reinterpretation of the earlier seduction story. Mut's attempt at seduction for the fulfillment of her womanly desire--now regarded as pathetic--humanizes her, as are all human beings humanized when their desire is seen to be overruled by God's plan. Similarly, Joseph's protraction withers in significance when it is now understood that when he ran from Mut he was fulfilling God's plan. Thus our last glimpse of tumid Tamar, in *tableau vivant*:

> There she stands, tall and almost sinister, on the slope of her native hills; one hand on her body, the other shading her eyes, she looks out upon the fruitful plains where the light breaks from towering clouds to radiate in waves of glory across the land (1042).

She also looks to the chapter title on the next page, "The God-Story", in which Joseph wraps up God's plot.

Note to *Joseph the Provider*

[1]McDonald writes, "Potiphar has Joseph read the Egyptian 'Tale of the Two Brothers,' whose story of seduction gone wrong closely replicates his own. Plainly Joseph does not absorb the lesson, and Joseph's next mentor, Mai-Sachme, has him copy out the tale again--this time in a deluxe edition" (1999: 216n27). In the first place, in Mann's story the "Tale of the Two Brothers" predates Joseph's predicament. Although McDonald does not note it, Joseph tells Mut that he feels like replicating the action of the Brother who fed the fishes (795). But he does not, hence he plainly has learned the lesson, that he must rebuff Mut's seduction attempt rather than evade it by emasculating himself, which would be a replication of the Egyptian solution. Finally, Mai-Sachme's obsession for the Tale is not a warning to Joseph, but a revelation of Mai-Sachme's unconscious wish for emasculation, if only of the psychic variety. .

VI

Doctor Faustus

In the middle of March, 1943, Mann recalled a subject for fiction that he had first contemplated in 1901 (Bürgin 1969: 174). His recollection sent him looking for a "three-line outline of the Doctor Faust" written at that time. Later he found a longer note that he had written sometime between 1901 and 1905:

> Novella, or for "Maja." Figure of the syphilitic artist: as Dr. Faust, pledged to the devil. The poison works as intoxication, stimulant, inspiration; he is filled with ecstatic enthusiasm and creates works of genius; the devil guides his hand. But finally the devil fetches him: luetic paralysis. (qtd. in Bergsten 1969: 56)

Mann's identification of the infectious substance as the highly connotative "poison", instead of "spirochete" or some other denotative term, suggests that something is afoot here. In light of Mann's subsequent comments on the meaning that *Doctor Faustus* had for him and on the fictional strategies that he employed in it, one of Freud's comments should be kept in mind: "[t]he fear of being poisoned is[...]probably connected with the withdrawal of the breast" (*New* 122).

Mann hesitated before the challenge:

> The question was whether the hour had come for this task so long ago though so dimly sighted. Clearly, I felt certain instinctive scruples reinforced by the premonition that there was something uncanny about this subject and that it would cost heart's blood, a great deal of it to whip it into shape. (*The Story of a Novel* 20; hereafter *Story*)

Although, in this instance, Mann uses the German *"nicht geheuer"* (*Entstehung* 156) to convey the sense of the uncanny, there is another German word, *"unheimlich",* that is frequently used to convey that disconcerting experience. In that connection it is important to remember Freud's explanation for *"unheimlich"*. Citing Schelling's aphorism, *"'Unheimlich'   is the name for everything that ought to have remained...secret and hidden but has come to light"* ("Uncanny" 224; ellipsis and ital. in orig.), Freud offers his explanation of the *"unheimlich"*:

> an uncanny experience occurs either when infantile complexes which have been repressed are once more revived by some impression, or when primitive beliefs which have been surmounted seem once more to be confirmed. ("Uncanny" 249)[1]

Mann's reference to both "poison" and "the devil" includes both conditions Freud posits for the occurrence of the uncanny.

Three pages later Mann reveals two apparently unrelated features of the time when he was planning his novel:

> Incidentally, I was not feeling well. A throat and bronchial catarrh was giving me trouble in spite of the clear, warm weather, and I found myself "very dull in spirit," unsure of myself and pessimistic about my future creativity. (*Story* 23)

He must have been haunted by his prediction of 1930 that, like his mother, he would die at age seventy, in 1945 (*Story* 3), before he could finish his novel. Even so, he began the "biography" (*Story* 30) of Adrian Leverkühn, a German composer who, all the while suffering from syphilis, early realizes that his greatest challenge is to avert defeat by "writer's block"--Reed calls it "artistic sterility" (1996: 372), Fetzer calls it "a kind of compositional paralysis or creative impasse" (1996: 2).[2] The theme of *Doctor Faustus* is thus the contemporaneous theme of Dr. Mann, who, indeed, admitted in his diary in 1951 that the novel was "at least partially, 'my memoir'" (qtd. in Heilbut 1996: 137).

In commenting on Mann's intentions for and crafting of *Doctor Faustus*, I will rely on Edmund Bergler's *The Basic Neurosis*, whose analysis of "oral regression" and two clinical pictures of it, "the confidence man" and "writer's block", has been previously treated in this study. I realize that in forefronting the "mother theme" I will be neglecting those themes of the novel that many readers think more significant, the nature of fascism, musicology, the catastrophe for German culture in the twentieth century caused by its militaristic adventures, and others. But those themes have received voluminous treatment, whereas there is something yet to be said about the "mother theme".

Mann writes that he decided "to interpose the medium of the 'friend' [Professor Serenus Zeitblom] between myself and my subject [Adrian Leverkühn]"

(*Story* 30, my interpolation). His reason for the interposition is pertinent to my thesis:

> this strategy was a bitter necessity in order to achieve a certain humorous leavening of the somber material and to make its horrors bearable to myself as well as to the reader. To make the demonic strain pass through an undemonic medium, to entrust a harmless and simple soul, well meaning and timid, with the recital of the story, was in itself a comic idea. It removed some of the burden, for it enabled me to escape the turbulence of everything direct, personal, and confessional which underlay the baneful conception, to steer it into indirection and to travesty it as I depicted it through the eyes of this good, unheroic soul, who could only wring his hands and shake his head at these events. (*Story* 30-31)

If his strategy filters the demonic through an undemonic medium, it also filters the manifestations of Leverkühn's infantile complex through an uncomprehending medium, thus filters both provocations that awaken the sense of the uncanny. Mann's strategy, the "comic idea" (31), is to transform the unbearable into the bearable, by the process Annie Reich calls the "Grotesque-Comic Sublimation" (cf. ch1n5).

Beginning his novel on 23 May 1943, in Pacific Palisades, California, Mann has Zeitblom begin his biography on the same day, in Freising on the Isar, Bavaria. After a hesitant introduction of himself and his situation, Zeitblom gradually warms to his task. In Chapter IV he introduces his subject's mother:

> it is my purpose now to do honour to the image of the mistress of Buchel, Adrian's dear mother. Gratitude for a happy childhood, in which the good things she gave us to eat played no small part, may add lustre to my picture of her. But truly in all my life I have never seen a more attractive woman than Elsbeth Leverkühn. The reverence with which I speak of her simple, intellectually altogether unassuming person flows from my conviction that the genius of the son owed very much to his mother's vigour and bloom. (21)

Zeitblom is unwittingly warning us that his interpretation of Elsbeth's actions and his conjectures about her motives will be that of a man relying upon childhood impressions. So amply nourished in her kitchen, Zeitblom will never apprehend that Adrian feels that he was poisoned there. Indeed, Zeitblom's recourse to the word "uncanny" at least once in each of the first three chapters already suggests his

316   *Doctor Faustus*

nagging feeling that his rendition is revealing something that ought to remain hidden.

Zeitblom continues by describing Elsbeth's appearance:

> She was born near Apolda, and her type was that brunette one which is sometimes found among us, even in regions where there is no definite ground to suspect Roman blood. The darkness of her colouring, the black hair, the black eyes with their quiet friendly gaze, might have made me take her for an Italian were it not for a certain sturdiness in the facial structure. (21)[3]

Having dilated upon Elsbeth's appearance, Zeitblom turns to what he considers her salient feature:

> the finest thing about her was her voice, in register a warm mezzo-soprano, and in speaking, though with a slight Thuringian inflexion, quite extraordinarily winning. I do not say flattering, because the word seems to imply intention. The vocal charm was due to an inherently musical temperament, which, however, remained latent, for Elsbeth never troubled about music, never so to speak "professed" it. She might quite casually strum a few chords on the old guitar that decorated the living-room wall; she might hum this or that snatch of song. But she never committed herself, never actually sang, although I would wager that there was excellent raw material there. (22)

Zeitblom confesses, "I have never heard anyone speak more beautifully, though what she said was always of the simplest and most-matter-of-fact. And this native, instinctive taste, this harmony, was from the first hour Adrian's lullaby". While Zeitblom is at pains to praise, the inference to be taken is that Elsbeth never sang to baby Adrian, withholding that vital introduction to human communion.

In discussing Elsbeth as manager of domestic activities, Zeitblom unintentionally introduces her contrast: "the cowgirl Hanne, whose bosoms flapped as she walked and whose bare feet were always caked with dung. She and the boy Adrian had a close friendship, on grounds still to be gone into in detail" (23). When she milked a cow, "under her fingers there ran into our glasses the lukewarm foaming milk, smelling of the good and useful animal that gave it".

The contrast is not yet complete. After devoting a page or so to the landscape surrounding the Leverkühn farm, Zeitblom returns to a second feature that distinguished Hanne: she loved to sing, not only solo but in unison and in rounds with Adrian, his older brother George, and Zeitblom, intuitively possessing and introducing a "plane of musical culture already relatively very high, in a realm of imitative polyphony, which the fifteenth century had had to discover in order to give us pleasure" (28-29). A discordant note to her singing--though Zeitblom does not describe it as such--is Hanne's habit, when singing, of "stretch[ing] her mouth and laugh[ing] just like Suso the dog when we brought her her food" (27). Not his mother, then, but Hanne is the female who provides young Adrian with *mammae*, milk, and music and the fused image of the three.

Between the two descriptions of Hanne lies Zeitblom's description of the landscape of the farm and its environs:

> Buchel was a property of a size corresponding to the ownership of a team and cattle; it was a good fifty acres of meadow and ploughed land, with communal rights to the adjoining mixed woodland and a very comfortable wood and frame dwelling-house on a stone foundation. With lofts and stalls it formed an open square in the centre of which stood a never-to-be forgotten ancient linden tree of a mighty growth. It had a circular green bench round it and in June it was covered with gloriously fragrant blossoms. The beautiful tree may have been a little in the way of the traffic in the courtyard: I have heard that each heir in turn in his young years, on practical grounds, always maintained against his father's veto that it ought to be cut down; only one day, having succeeded to the property, to protect it in the same way from his own son. (11)

If it were simply an unidentified tree, it might be taken as an irenic symbol, that tree in the center of the Garden of Eden before the awful apple was eaten. But it is a linden tree, inspiration of the *Lied* of the same name, and as such, associated in Mann's mind from early childhood with his mother's beautiful singing voice. That linden tree would seem to be most *"heimlich"*. Yet Freud notes that *"heimlich"* has two separate meanings, first, "belonging to the house, not strange, familiar, tame, intimate, friendly, etc" ("Uncanny" 222), and second, "[c]oncealed, kept from sight, so that others do not get to know of or about it, withheld from others" ("Uncanny" 223). He concludes that "among its different shades of meaning the word '*heimlich*' exhibits one which is identical with its opposite, '*unheimlich*'. What is *heimlich* thus comes to be *unheimlich*" ("Uncanny" 224). The linden tree in the center of the courtyard is Adrian's mother in the center of his infantile universe. Thus Zeitblom's conclusion to his description of the tree carries more weight than he could possibly realize: "Very often must the linden tree have shaded the infant slumbers and childhood play of little Adrian, who was born, in the blossom-time of 1885, in the upper storey of the Buchel house" (11).

318   *Doctor Faustus*

To focus the Leverkühn farmstead Zeitblom positions two significant topographic features:

> I referred above to the pond which lay only ten minutes away from the house, surrounded by pasture. It was called the Cow Trough, probably because of its oblong shape and because the cows came there to drink. The water, why I do not know, was unusually cold, so that we could only bathe in it in the afternoon when the sun had stood on it a long time. As for the hill, it was a favourite walk of half an hour: a height called, certainly from old days and most inappropriately, Mount Zion. (25)[4]

Feeling "constrained to comment" (25), Zeitblom then reveals that

> the house and its surroundings in which Adrian later as a mature man settled down when he took up permanent quarters with the Schweigestills at Pfeiffering near Waldshut in Oberbayern-- indeed, the whole setting--were a most extraordinary likeness and reproduction of his childhood home; in other words, the scene of his later days bore a curious resemblance to that of his early ones. Not only did the environs of Pfeiffering[...]have a hill with a community bench, though it was not called Mount Zion, but the Rohmbühel; not only was there a pond, at somewhat the same distance from the house as the Cow Trough, here called the Klammer pond, the water of which was strikingly cold. No, for even the house, the courtyard, and the family itself were all very like the Buchel setting. In the yard was a tree, also rather in the way and preserved for sentimental reasons--not a lime tree, but an elm. (25-26)

There was a yard dog, Kaschperl, which after a while learned to come to Adrian when he called for "Suso", the name of the yard dog at Buchel. And there was a stable-girl, Waltpurgis, who "looked as much like Hanne of Buchel as one stable-girl does look like another" (27).[5]

Although Zeitblom "never spoke to Adrian about this whole singular and very obvious parallel" (26), he admits that he

> never cared for the phenomenon. This choice of a place to live, reproducing the earliest one, this burying oneself in one's earliest, outlived childhood, or at least in the outer circumstances of the same--it might indicate attachment, but in any case it is psychologically disturbing.

That it is Leverkühn who exhibits the phenomenon is all the more disturbing for Zeitblom, for he had "never observed that his ties with the parental home were particularly close or emotional" and had observed that his ties were severed "early without observable pain". Zeitblom regards Leverkühn's "return" as more than a whim, speculating that it was induced by a childhood trauma, but then falling silent, apparently unable to identify the trauma. Hence he does not realize that Adrian has not "outlived" his "childhood", that Adrian's "return" confesses his vulnerability to the "return of the repressed".

Zeitblom does not reveal what induced him to jump from the Buchel scene illustrating Adrian's pre-adolescence, in 1895 at the latest, to the Pfeiffering scene, which he visited once in 1910 (204) before moving there in 1912 (253). Nor does he acknowledge that, while "the house and its surroundings" at Pfeiffering "were a most extraordinary likeness and reproduction of his childhood home" (25), hidden within the "likeness and reproduction" were significant differences. Nor does he acknowledge that linking the two scenes so separated in time tends to minimize that span of time during which Adrian ages from ten to twenty-seven.

Zeitblom is hardly an objective biographer, but he is the only biographer of Adrian Leverkühn we have. Thus we must closely monitor what Zeitblom saw or thinks he saw, always being mindful that his admiration of Adrian and his mother precludes his being a reliable witness. From what he saw or thinks he saw, we must reconstruct the original relationship that existed between Adrian and his mother. Thus I follow a strategy directly opposed to that employed by Manfried Dierks, who announces:

> When in the following I sketch Adrian's personality in terms of self psychology (i.e. the theory of narcissism) my interest is not patho-psychology. Rather, I will use features of his personality clearly delineated by the text to construct a more complete image of a personality. This will form the background for a better understanding of Adrian's artistic creation. I will isolate the psychological argument following the statements of the novel whose text will not need to be supplemented to complement my findings. It is unnecessary to speculate about Adrian's early experiences, especially the ones with his mother. When Adrian appears in the novel he is sufficiently constituted as a psychological personality and represented as such. (1990: 39)

There is no direct evidence that contradicts Schoolfield's opinion that "Adrian Leverkühn[...]is the product of a happy home. He spends the greater part of his childhood sheltered from harm, at first on his father's prosperous farm, then at the home of his uncle, a maker of musical instruments" (1956: 172). But Schoolfield's view ignores the primary relationship, in which, it

may be inferred, the infant Adrian felt that his mother was
undemonstrative and distant toward him, a feeling that accounted for
his lifelong susceptibility to chills and his conception of himself as a
"cold" person. Even so, Schoolfield's speculation that the infant Adrian
experiences an incestuous desire for his mother is tenable, and not at
all atypical, if Freud is to be believed.[6] Adrian's early incestuous
desire, however, hardly has genital union as a goal. Could it not
merely give birth to the *Sehnsucht* that darkens the consciousness of
so many of Mann's mother-haunted males?

    Zeitblom records nothing that indicates that Adrian
experienced a revival of a repressed infantile complex before he
entered latency at about age six. Beginning when he is ten, Adrian
lives in Kaisersachern in his uncle's house, in order to attend the town
gymnasium. Zeitblom is largely silent about Adrian's first years there,
except to stress that he has a very quick mind. Only with the onset of
puberty, at age fourteen (32), does he manifest signs of a disturbing
psychosexuality. The migraine that first befalls him then is one of a
developing system of signs that betray his psychic stress. It is likely,
too, that his experimentation on the piano is accompanied by another
solitary practice, not masturbation but play. Rudnytsky's explanation
is convincing:

> it is necessary to abandon Freud's drive theory in favor of a
> theory of object relations, whose intellectual architect is W. R. D.
> Fairbairn and whose best-known proponent is D. W. Winnicott. In
> brief, the crucial point is that the greatest need of human beings is
> not for sex but for *attachment*, and hence Freud's essentially
> solipsistic model of behavior as motivated by the desire to reduce
> instinctual tensions must give way to one that places object-
> seeking in the forefront. The consequences of this recasting of
> psychoanalytic theory for the understanding of art are spelled out
> by Winnicott in *Playing and Reality* (1971). The nub of the matter
> is that the prototype for art is no longer masturbation but *play*.
> This play takes place in a *potential space* between child and
> mother that is neither purely internal nor external and becomes
> filled with *transitional objects* that are symbols of both separation
> and union. Play differs from masturbation precisely in that it
> entails a suspension of somatic urges, which terminate the activity
> if they become too insistent. Winnicott provides a psychoanalytic
> account of art that respects its integrity as an autonomous human
> activity and does not reduce it to a sublimation of sexual drives.
> (1992: xxxiii-xxxiv; ital. in orig.)

Zeitblom faithfully records the nine years that Adrian lived in Kaiseraschern before entering the university (38). Almost all of his commentary concerns Adrian's growing fascination for the properties of music. Notable is Zeitblom's account of finding fifteen-year-old Adrian arranging chords on "a little harmonium which stood rather unregarded in the corridor of the family rooms" (46). Asked what he is doing, Adrian "blushe[s] and laugh[s]", then replies: "Idleness[...]is the mother of all vice. I was bored. When I am bored I sometimes poke about down here". Describing what he has discovered about chords, he draws his conclusion: "Relationship is everything. And if you want to give it a more precise name, it is ambiguity" (47).

Zeitblom does not understand what he has seen. Adrian blushes, involuntarily acknowledging his shame over having been caught doing something, playing, that should be kept secret. Attempting to hide his shame by attributing his behavior to boredom, he unwittingly reveals his unconscious state of mind: he seeks what Christopher Bollas calls the "transformative experience". In such seeking, boredom, according to Adam Phillips, has the role to play that I have previously cited. Already Adrian has devised a secret code: when he talks about music as a transformative experience he is talking psychosexually, talking about a return to the bliss experienced at mother's breast. And he hints that he knows the source of his psychosexual distress. Ostensibly he talks about chords, but he talks about his mother-misery: "Relationship is everything. And if you want to give it a more precise name, it is ambiguity". The remainder of the scene (47-48) is high comedy, as first Zeitblom and then Adrian's "Uncle Niko" unwittingly perpetrate a string of *double-entendres* about music and masturbation.

With Uncle Niko's help, Adrian begins to take piano lessons from Wendell Kretchmar, the young town organist who has aspirations toward music composition and theory. Kretchmar also gives public lectures on music, even though his speech is often strangled by his stuttering. Zeitblom offers a full account of one lecture, "Why did Beethoven not write a third movement to the Piano Sonata Opus 111?" In his introductory remarks Kretschmar offers Beethoven's answer to the question why he did not conform to the conventional form of the sonata by providing a "third movement corresponding to the first" (51). Aging fast and rapidly losing his hearing, Beethoven merely said that he did not have time "and therefore had somewhat extended the second movement". Then Kretschmar plays the entire sonata, shouting his commentary all the while. Zeitblom indirectly quotes Kretschmar's final remarks:

> Much else happens before the end. But when it ends and while it
> ends, something comes, after so much rage, persistence,
> obstinacy, extravagance: something entirely unexpected and
> touching in its mildness and goodness. With the motif passed
> through many   vicissitudes, which takes leave and so doing
> becomes itself entirely leave-taking, a parting wave and call, with
> the D G G occurs a slight change, it experiences a small melodic
> expansion. After an introductory C, it puts a C sharp before the D,
> so that it no longer scans "heav-en's blue," "mead-owland," but
> "O-thou heaven's blue," "Green-est meadowland," "Fare-thee
> well for aye," and this added C sharp is the most moving,
> consolatory, pathetically reconciling thing in the world. It is like
> having one's hair or cheek stroked, lovingly, understandingly,
> like a deep and silent farewell look. It blesses the object, the
> frightfully harried formulation, with overpowering humanity, lies
> in parting so gently on the hearer's heart in eternal farewell that
> the eyes run over. "Now for-get the pain," it says. "Great was--
> God in us." "'Twas all--but a dream," "Friendly--be to me." Then
> it breaks off. Quick, hard triplets hasten to a conclusion with
> which any other piece might have ended. (55)

Zeitblom then quotes Kretschmar's coda:

> We had only needed, he said, to hear the piece to answer the
> question ourselves. A third movement? A new approach? A return
> after this parting--impossible! It had happened that the sonata had
> come, in the second, enormous movement, to an end, an end
> without any return.

Kretschmar, Adrian's teacher, could be speaking directly to his pupil, for just as the sonata, in the hands of a genius, needs no return, so Adrian's life, in the hands of a genius, needs no return. He should regard the stroke on the cheek, his mother's stroke on his cheek, as the tenderest accompaniment to her farewell look, rather than as the stimulus to activate his reflex to root for the breast.

Later Kretschmar gives another lecture, as Zeitblom tells us: "It was 'The Elemental in Music' or 'Music and the Elemental' or 'The Elements of Music' or something like that" (62). The lecture is devoted to "an ingenious and practical theory of melody" invented by Johann Conrad Beissel, who had migrated from the Palatinate to Pennsylvania (63). There he eventually became the leader of the Seventh-Day Anabaptists (64), for whom he devised a novel form of choral singing, strict in its theory but flexible in the theory's application: "The tones coming from the choir had resembled delicate instrumental music and evoked an impression of heavenly mildness and piety in the hearer" (66). After the lecture Zeitblom and

Adrian argue about Beissel's theory. Zeitblom regards the product of the theory as a "ridiculous and dogmatic arrangement" (68), while Adrian approves of the theory because it advocates rigid form:"Law, every law, has a chilling effect, and music has so much warmth anyhow, stable warmth, cow warmth, I'd like to say, that she can stand all sorts of regulated cooling off--she has even asked for it". Adrian continues by repeating that "the sounding breath of the human voice,[...]certainly the most stable-warm imaginable thing in the world of sound". When Zeitblom remonstrates, Adrian adds, "Abstract it may be, the human voice--the abstract human being, if you like. But that is a kind of abstraction more like that of the naked body--it is after all more a pudendum".

Zeitblom admits, "I was silent, confounded. My thoughts took me far back in our, in his past". Although he does not elaborate on his omission, he must have questioned his early belief that little Adrian had loved the singing of the stable-girl Hanne. Either he had wrongly interpreted Adrian's response to the girl or Adrian, he must consider, has developed such a repression of his love of her singing and of the milk which accompanied it that he now considers music as feminine sensuality personified, which always entices by flaunting its genitalia like a Baubo.

Kretschmar continues as Adrian's piano teacher, serving, as well, as his mentor in the study of *belles-lettres*. Graduating from the gymnasium, Adrian enters the university at Halle as a theology student. There is reason to think, though, that already he is aware that, sooner or later, he will be driven to commit himself totally to composition--and thereby arouse the hostility of the repressed mother. Zeitblom describes Adrian's work space in his new quarters:

> On the wall above the piano was an arithmetical diagram fastened with drawing-pins, something he had found in a second-hand shop: a so-called magic square, such as appears also in Dürer's *Melancolia*, along with the hour-glass, the circle, the scale, the polyhedron, and other symbols. Here as there, the figure was divided into sixteen Arabic-numbered fields, in such a way that number one was in the right-hand lower corner, sixteen in the upper left; and the magic, or the oddity, simply consisted in the fact that the sum of these numerals, however you added them, straight down, crosswise, or diagonally, always came to thirty-four. (92)

Many critics have noticed the magic square--Grimstad, perhaps the most recent critic, thus describes it: "This esoteric symbol points to a Pythagorean unity of horizontal and vertical dimensions, time and eternity, which Leverkühn seeks to achieve in a system of total composition that unifies harmony and melody, order and freedom, strict calculation and *expressivo*" (2002: 163). It may be, however, that for Adrian the inevitable sum, 34, rendered 3+4 = 7, constitues a powerful symbol of mother-attraction. Zeitblom himself sees the number as but one symbol among several, yet he neglects the focal symbol, the female figure, the only part of the drawing capable of experiencing *melancolia*, of whom Russell says, "most [critics] agree that the brooding, winged figure represents the artistic genius despairing of inspiration" (1967: 115). Yet it is exactly right that Zeitblom does not "see" the focal figure: only Adrian sees that figure, his future should he lose his will to repress his longing for his mother. The square will remain a *memento melancolia* above Adrian's writing table, for Zeitblom later notes that it was pinned above his "cottage piano" "the whole four and a half years he spent in Leipzig" (179).

Adrian knows that Kretschmar "would have liked [him] to give [himself] to Polyhymnia" (82), but he knows that he can placate his teacher by continuing to study music as a handmaiden to theology. A half-year afterward (86), Zeitblom joins him, attempting irony by saying, "I decided to draw my further nourishment from the breast of Alma Mater Hallensis" (86). He quickly observes with misgivings Adrian's immersion in his chosen subject:

> If I hesitate to describe those years by the epithet "happy"-- always a questionable word--it is because by association with him I was drawn much more effectively into his sphere of studies than he into mine, and the theological air did not suit me. It was not canny, it choked me. (87)

Then, if it was uncanny, the "theological air" must have incubated infantile complexes previously repressed and/or primitive beliefs previously discarded (cf. ch2n4)? In Zeitblom's case, given his psychological obtuseness, his feeling of uncanniness must have resulted only from revived primitive beliefs.

Given the nature of the faculty notables and their favorite subject-matter, Halle, it turns out, might as well be *Hölle*. As a Catholic humanist Zeitblom is opposed to the "liberal theology" that rules the theological faculty:

> Here one sees clearly the infiltration of theological thinking by irrational currents of philosophy, in whose realm, indeed, the non-theoretic, the vital, the will or instinct, in short the dæmonic, have long since become the chief theme of theory. At the same time one observes a revival of the study of Catholic mediæval philosophy, a turning to Neo-Thomism and Neo-Scholasticism. On these lines theology, grown sickly with liberalism, can take on

> deeper and stronger, yes, more glowing hues; it can once more do justice to the ancient æsthetic conceptions which are involuntarily associated with its name. But the civilized human spirit, whether one call it bourgeois or merely leave it at civilized, cannot get rid of a feeling of the uncanny. For theology, confronted with that spirit of life which is irrationalism, is in danger, by its very nature, of becoming dæmonology. (90)

Again, Zeitblom makes the Freudian connection between the uncanny and revived primitive beliefs. It is possible that he intuits the connection between revived primitive beliefs and revived infantile complexes, namely that either is a precondition of the uncanny, for he then analyzes the lectures of Doctor Eberhard Schleppfuss, Old Dragfoot himself, whose lectures on demons are mainly about Eve and her daughters as sexual temptresses. Zeitblom is not the first, nor will he be the last, to observe that when pious preachers pontificate on "the power of demons over human life, sex always play[s] a prominent role" (104).

Of the time that he observed Adrian at Halle Zeitblom makes no mention of Elsbeth. He does describe an event which reveals that Adrian's infantile complex is by no means vanquished. The student club to which he belongs and of which Zeitblom is an honorary member takes a hiking trip. Zeitblom captures the mood:

> a train conveys you in a few hours up the Saale into lovely Thuringia, and there, mostly at Naumburg or Apolda (the region where Adrian's mother was born), we left the train and set out with rucksacks and capes, on shanks's mare, in all-day marches, eating in village inns or sometimes camping at the edge of a wood and spending the night in the hayloft of a peasant's yard, waking in the grey dawn to wash and refresh ourselves at the long trough of a running spring. (114-15)

The topography suggests a return to the spring, the source, the Cow Trough. Zeitblom calls the trip an escape "into the primitive countryside and back to mother earth" (115). Yet almost all of his report on the trip concerns the debate about church, community, and state that the students carried on incessantly. He does eventually discuss the beauty of the land through which the group is passing, returning his focus to Adrian, noting that "nature lured from him no very enthusiastic cries and he looked at it with a certain musing aloofness" (125). But he immediately interprets Adrian's behavior:

> I do not doubt that its pictures, rhythms, the melodies of its upper airs, penetrated deeper into his soul than into those of his

companions. It has even happened that some passage of pure, free beauty standing out from the tense intellectuality of his work has later brought to my mind those days and the experiences we shared.

Certainly the landscape approaching Apolda "penetrated deeper into his soul than into those of his companions", for, if Freud is correct, he would experience the uncanny in the landscape of maternal genitality, an experience that would account for his aloofness. That Adrian ever permitted a "passage of pure, free beauty" in any of his compositions is to be doubted.

Zeitblom has reason to rejoice when Adrian decides to withdraw from his theological course after the third semester (126). Adrian is supported in his decision by Kretschmar, who has remained his mentor. To Zeitblom, Kretschmar gives his reason for encouraging Adrian to go another way:

> He has[...]the composer's eye; he bends on music the look of the initiate, not of the vaguely enjoying outsider. His way of discovering thematic connections that the other kind of man does not see; of perceiving the articulation of a short extract in the form of question and answer; altogether of seeing from the inside how it is made, confirms me in my judgment. That he shows no productive impulse, does not yet write or naïvely embark upon youthful productions, is only to his credit; it is a question of his pride, which prevents him from producing epigonal music. (128)

Zeitblom is delighted with Adrian's prospects, but, all the same, given his high regard for Adrian's mother, he sympathizes with what he calls her "protective concern".

Admitting a tension between Elsbeth and Kretschmar, Zeitblom offers an illustration:

> Never shall I forget a scene in the living-room at Buchel when we chanced to sit there together, the four of us: mother and son, Kretschmar and I. Elsbeth was in talk with the musician, who was puffing and blowing with his impediment; it was a mere chat, of which Adrian was certainly not the subject. She drew her son's head to her as he sat beside her, in the strangest way, putting her arm about him, not round his shoulders but round his head, her hand on his brow, and thus, with the gaze of her black eyes directed upon Kretschmar and her sweet voice speaking to him, she leaned Adrian's head upon her breast.

Despite his statement that the scene is unforgetable, Zeitblom is silent about its significance. His own words prove that he does not realize that Elsbeth is openly defying Kretschmar by demonstrating that she can still control her son by using her breast to stimulate his sucking reflex. In addition to seducing Adrian's sense of touch, his mother also captivates his sense of sight with her "black eyes" and his sense of sound with her "sweet voice", three of the five sensations active in a nursing.

Perhaps, then, Kretschmar's decision to relocate in Leipzig is a strategic withdrawal: better to fight and run away, then live to fight another day. Zeitblom learns of Kretschmar's decision on Michaelmas Day, the feast of the archangel Michael, who with his heavenly host defeated the angels who, rebelling, became demons (Rev. 12:7). Perhaps it is the celebration of Michael's victory that prompts Zeitblom to think "that since Kretschmar's move to Leipzig, his chances of getting his way were considerably improved" (129); at the same time Zeitblom predicts that Adrian is ready to "fling himself into the arms of music". In a letter to Kretschmar that Zeitblom perused, Adrian reveals his state of mind: since marrying himself to "one plot and profession" (130)--theology--he has suffered his worst bouts of migraine activated by "cold boredom". Now he anticipates experiencing music as if it were the "end pleasure", release from tension through orgasm:

> The brass does not start from the beginning as it did the first time, but as though its melody had already been there for a while; and it continues, solemnly, to that climax from which it wisely refrained the first time, in order that the surging feeling, the Ah-h-effect, might be the greater: now it gloriously bestrides its theme, mounting unchecked, with weighty support from the passing notes on the tuba, and then, looking back, as it were, with dignified satisfaction on the finished achievement, sings itself decorously to the end. (133)

With a quotation, Kretschmar replies in kind:

> Virginity is well, yet must to motherhood;
> Unear'd she is a soil unfructified for good. (135)

After a trip to Buchel to announce his decision to his parents, Adrian enters the university at Leipzig in the spring semester of 1905 (136). Although he had told his parents that he wanted to resume studying music with Kretschmar, he did not tell them that he was abandoning theology for philosophy. His biographer, although diagnosed with short-sightedness, a condition that could have been predicted by his earlier judgments, is required at this time to perform his year of military service in the field artillery, an assignment that could have been predicted by anyone familiar with military personnel placement.

Having, after two months, received a letter from Adrian, Zeitblom describes its impact on him: "I read it with feelings such as might move a mother at a communication of that kind from her son--only that of course one withholds that sort of thing from one's mother, out of propriety" (138). But does withholding the *"unheimlich"* preserve the *"heimlich"*? It seems that even on his first day in Leipzig Adrian had been led astray by his city cicerone, who must have thought that his charge wanted his introduction to climax at a red light (141-42). Before Adrian has a inkling, he finds himself in a reception room filled with *hetærae* for hire. He is so shaken that he rushes over to an open piano, striking a note, all the while collapsing onto the bench. Later Adrian writes Zeitblom what then happened:

> [a] brown wench puts herself nigh me, in a little Spanish jacket, with a big gam, snub nose, almond eyes, an Esmeralda, she brushed my cheek with her arm. I turn round, push the bench away with my knee, and fling myself back through the lust-hell, across the carpets, past the mincing madam, through the entry and down the steps without touching the brass railing. (142)[7]

Zeitblom prefaces his presentation of the letter "by saying that its antiquated style was of course intended as a parody of grotesque Halle experiences and the language idiosyncrasies of Ehrenfried Kumpf" (138). What specific "grotesque Halle experiences" Zeitblom has in mind are not made known-- leaving us to remember that, according to Zeitblom, the whole study of theology was pretty much about demonology and sex. Then Zeitblom reads the letter's heading:

> *Leipzig, Friday after*
> *Purificationis 1905*
> *In the Peterstrasse, house the 27th*

Adrian must have some reason to include in his heading a reference to the Feast of the Purification of the Virgin Mary, 2 February. Does his bent for parody require this heading for his account of an encounter with a prostitute?

According to his letter, Adrian was so green that he did not understand the meaning of the red lantern, hence was easily betrayed into the bordello by a porter resembling Schleppfuss, that is to say, a minion of Satan (141). Demonology is obviously on the loose. But when we recall that Kretschmar had told him that he had to lose his virginity in order to be creative, Adrian might have considered it his first order of business upon reaching Leipzig. After all, such a *rite de passage* would be a declaration of independence from mother. But the reality of "six or seven [prostitutes],[...]paps bare, thick-poudered, arms with bangles" looking at him "with expectant eyes"(142) was enough to scare the dickens out of him. Seeking refuge at the piano, Adrian is strangely solicited by "an Esmeralda", who brushes his cheek with her arm. Later Zeitblom speculates that her "caressing of his cheek with her bare arm, might have been the humble and tender expression of her receptivity for all that distinguished him from the usual clientèle" (154). But oftentimes in Mann's fiction an arm is not just an arm. Adrian's sucking reflex activated, hence arousing his conflicted feelings for his mother, he flies through the "lust-hell, across the carpets, past the mincing madam, through the entry and down the steps without touching the brass railing". Recall the sagacity of Polly Adler, "A house is not a home", and of Sigmund Freud, "What is *heimlich* thus comes to be *unheimlich*". Adrian has experienced the uncanny, aroused not by reawakened belief in demons, as he would imply, but by an infantile complex breaking through repression. Rather than repulsing the repressed he is routed by its return. Although he lives on "Peterstrasse", that street is "near the Collegium Beatæ Virginis" (179).

Zeitblom quotes the conclusion of the letter: "With the exclamation: "*Ecce epistola!*" the letter ends. Added is: "Goes without saying you destroy this at once." The signature is an initial, that of the family name: the *L*, not the *A*" (143). Adrian knows that "*Ecce epistola*", "behold the message", will remind Zeitblom of Nietzsche's *Ecce homo*, "behold the man", thus influence him to see Adrian as a Nietzsche-like character, for Nietzsche had also experienced consternation when he encountered a prostitute in a Cologne brothel (Bergsten 1969: 61).[8]

In Chapter XXI Zeitblom uses the one year in Leipzig that he shared with Adrian to sketch in "the other three of his stay there" (176). He asserts that what he tells us he heard from Adrian (155), but much of it is colored by his own conjectures and assumptions. He begins by telling us that while Adrian had run from Esmeralda, yet he was drawn to her, for, after a year, he went back to the brothel seeking her (154). That he sought her, not just any prostitute, indicates that he sought psychological, not sexual satisfaction. Learning that she was in Prozony, Hungary, Adrian invented a pretext for traveling near there: he wished to see the "first Austrian performance of *Salome*", at Graz (154). Reminding us that Adrian, with Kretschmar, had seen the opera's première six months earlier, Fetzer thinks it odd that he desired to see it again (1990: 48), concluding that it becomes an "opera-cipher" providing

> a fitting "objective correlative" for the kind of distorted, even perverted mode of Melos-Eros-Thanatos that suits twentieth-century (or at least post-Baudelairean) taste and temperament. Such an outlook is akin to, and apropos for, Leverkühn's own erotic adventure with Hetæra. (1990: 48-49).

It is likely that Adrian had a more specific "objective correlative" in choosing to return to an opera that he has seen: that work stresses Salome's obsession to kiss John the Baptist, even if John must die so that the consummation can occur. Perhaps, then, it is not odd that Adrian wished to see *Salome* again, for viewing its première had weakened his repression of his première with Esmeralda and inflamed his obsession to kiss her. Kissing, of the rendering and receiving type, revives the oral pleasure provided by nursing, so that Schoolfield's statement that "the prostitute answers the secret love for the mother" (1956: 184) has more significance than he intends.

Zeitblom writes that Esmeralda learned from Adrian's "own lips that he had made the journey thither on her account" (155). But from what other lips could she have learned his motive? If Zeitblom is employing indirect discourse, then Adrian could have been telling him that it was his kiss, not his words, that informed Esmeralda of the nature of his mission. At which time "she warned him against her body". It is the general assumption, no doubt influenced by the story of Nietzsche's willful contracting of venereal disease, that Adrian disregarded her warning, engaging in genital to genital contact. But syphilis can be transmitted by kissing (Clayman 1989: vol. II 961), and, given Adrian's arrest in the pregenital stage of psychosexual development, it is likely that he contracted syphilis through a kiss.

Zeitblom interprets the relationship between Adrian and Esmeralda as the

> embrace, in which the one staked his salvation, the other found it. Purifying, justifying, sublimating, it must have blessed the wretched one, that the other travelled from afar and refused

whatever the risk to give her up. It seems that she gave him all the sweetness of her womanhood, to repay him for what he risked. She might thus know that he never forgot her; but it is no less true that it was for her own sake he, who never saw her again, remembered; and her name--that which he gave her from the beginning--whispers magically, unheard by anyone but me, throughout his work.

Five weeks after Adrian's encounter with Esmeralda, his body displayed the initial lesion indicative of syphilis. Adrian became a patient of a Dr. Erasmi, but the good doctor died suddenly after treating him for three days (156). After two days, Adrian became a patient of a Dr. Zimbalist, but as he returned for his third treatment he met that good doctor being hauled off to jail (158). Zeitblom says that Adrian was "frightened off", so that "he never took up the cure again after that and went to no other doctor. He did so the less in that the local affection healed itself without further treatment and disappeared". It is likely, though, that Adrian forwent treatment not because of the disappearance of the chancre but because, experiencing the uncanny, he felt that the fate of the two doctors resulted from diabolic interference. Experiencing a reawakening of primitive beliefs, he also experienced a return of the repressed, for Zeitblom recalls that, soon after, Adrian suffered "'a two days' migraine, which except for its severity was not different from other earlier attacks of the same kind".

At this point Mann introduces a new character, Rüdiger Schildknapp, "whose name", Fetzer writes, "in its etymological components harks back to the age of medieval chivalry" (1990: 99). Knowledgeable early readers of *Doctor Faustus* quickly identified Schildknapp's model, Hans Reisiger; indeed his surname, an antique word for 'a knight on horseback', inspired the surname of his fictional counterpart. Reisiger, a poet, a writer of short fiction, an essayist, but primarily a translator, had been Mann's close friend and frequent visitor since 1906 or 1913 (accounts vary). On one of Reisiger's visits, 11 February 1934, Mann had involved him in the novel's conception:

> During my evening walk I thought again about the Faust novella, and also spoke about it to Reisiger. An abstract symbol of this sort for the character and fate of Europe might perhaps be not only more promising but also more accurate and more suitable than a literal accounting. (Kesten 1984: 195)

Ten years later, in July 1944, Mann devoted Chapter XX to "the portrait of Rüdiger Schildknapp", of which he later wrote: "It turned out an artistically successful bit, and at the time I was not even conscious of its recklessness in human terms--for it was a portrait, though a highly stylized one which differs in essential details from its model" (*Story* 87). Finishing the novel on 29 January 1947 (Bürgin 1969: 213), Mann soon decided to visit Europe, where, in Winterthur, Switzerland, he visited the publishing house in which *Doctor Faustus* was being printed (Bürgin 1969: 215). No evidence has been discovered that Mann communicated with Reisinger during his 1947 stay in Europe, though he must have learned of his survival of the war and of his present whereabouts.Mann read the galley proofs of the novel in Switzerland with Reisinger much on his mind. As Hayman puts it, Mann "was still worrying, and talking to Katia, about the risk of putting in so many undisguised portraits of friends and acquaintances" (1995: 544).   Aboard   ship returning to the United States he wrote, on 4 September 1947, "a letter to Hans Reisiger, which contains an explanation of *Doctor Faustus*. The letter is printed privately along with a note forbidding its publication" (Bürgin 1969: 218). It may be inferred that Mann said then what he said in a 1954

> birthday salute.[...]In the salute Mann describes him much as in the novel, and states in conclusion that Reisiger has forgiven Mann for turning him into "a humoristically engaging fantastical figure who, however, totally lacks a sense of responsibility toward life". (Bergsten 1969: 25)

Reed asserts that Mann included portrayals of "old acquaintances" to "support his imagination" (1996: 366), so that in the novel "[r]ealism operates alongside allegory" (367). His assertion is borne out in the case of Rüdiger Schildknapp, though the critics have been content to point to his origin in reality and to ignore his significance in allegory. An example in point: according to Heilbut, Reisiger was "gay" (1996: 492); yet Zeitblom offers no evidence that Schildknapp is a homosexual; therefore it is not Reisiger's actual existence but Schildknapp's allegorical function which counts. (Although there is a possibility, addressed in the next paragraph, that *Mann* conceived Schildknapp as a "gay" character.)

Unwittingly, Zeitblom soon provides the information necessary to decipher Mann's purpose in portraying Schildknapp as he does and introducing him when he does. Adrian had wanted Schildknapp, whose forte is translating English, to prepare the libretto for his opera based on *Love's Labour's Lost*, but Schildknapp, who, as Zeitblom tells it, habitually spurns any request made by his friends, rebuffs even Adrian (161). Then Zeitblom introduces a subject that violates the chronology of Adrian's life and thus obscures the pattern of his psychosexual development. For that reason the narrative of the "biography" will be violated in order to continue with the chronological development of Adrian's relationship with Schildknapp. Then that character's allegorical significance will be presented.

Despite Schildknapp's refusal to prepare the libretto, Adrian takes him on a beach excursion to Sylt on the North Sea (178). Sylt represents to Adrian what Travemünde represented to Mann, the fantasy of pregenital bliss. Knowing that Schildknapp is "gay"--and has thus, according to Bergler, suffered from "oral regression" in a way different from himself-- Adrian may have been satisfying his exquisite sense of irony by taking a fellow--but unwitting--victim of mother-alienation with him.

Adrian himself is aware of the falsity of the dream of paradise regained, for when he returned to Leipsig from Sylt he composed a mocking piece, *Meerleuchten* (178), *Ocean Lights*. Zeitblom calls it a "symphonic fantasy[...]. It is a piece of exquisite tone-painting, which gives evidence of an astonishing feeling for entrancing combinations of sound, at first hearing almost impossible for the ear to unravel". While the "cultured public saw in the young composer a highly gifted successor to the Debussy-Ravel line", Zeitblom is less that charitable about Adrian's composition:

> to be frank, this disillusioned masterpiece of orchestral brilliance already bore within itself the traits of parody and intellectual mockery of art, which in Leverkühn's later work so often emerged in a creative and uncanny way. Many found it chilling, even repellent and revolting, and these were the better, if not the best sort, who thus judged. All the superficial lot simply called it witty and amusing. In truth parody was here the proud expedient of a great gift threatened with sterility by a combination of scepticism, intellectual reserve, and a sense of the deadly extension of the kingdom of the banal. (151-52)

Zeitblom's detection of the appearance of the uncanny in Adrian's work hints at Adrian's being overcome by that feeling at Sylt, just as Mann had been at Travemünde. The feeling would have been evoked by the "oceanic feeling" experienced by Hanno Buddenbrook, Tonio Kröger, and Hans Castorp. If Hans Castorp carries *Ocean Steamships*, Adrian Leverkühn composes *Ocean Lights*. But while Hanno, Tonio, and Hans are unaware of the hold that the mother figure has over them, Adrian unconsciously intuits that he must triumph over it or succumb to writer's block. At this point, all he can do, as Zeitblom realizes, is to give his feeling form but disfigure it: "[i]n truth parody was here the proud expedient of a great gift threatened with sterility" (152). That

Ocean Lights had a "chilling" effect upon many who heard it is further testimony that the uncanny mother figure haunts it. There is an appropriateness in Rüdiger Schildknapp's association with Adrian at this time, as a later declaration by Zeitblom will demonstrate.

After composing *Ocean Lights* Adrian, Zeitblom tells us, began to be "more and more possessed" by the interconnectedness of word and music:

> Music and speech, he insisted, belonged together, they were at bottom one, language was music, music a language; separate, one always appealed to the other, imitated the other, used the other's tools, always the one gave itself to be understood as substitute of the other. (163)

To support his claim Adrian cites Beethoven, who often composed in words. Zeitblom remembers that Adrian then offered a generalization:

> The creative thought, he said, probably formed its own and unique intellectual category, but the first draft hardly ever amounted to a picture, a statue in words--which spoke for the fact that music and speech belonged together. It was very natural that music should take fire at the word, that the word should burst forth out of music, as it did towards the end of the Ninth Symphony. (163-64)

Zeitblom then discusses Adrian's early experiments with the interconnectedness of word and music during his Leipzig years. One composition, in particular, is memorable:

> the uncanny sixteen lines of "A Poison Tree," where the poet waters his wrath with his tears, suns it with smiles and soft deceitful wiles, so that an alluring apple ripens, with which the thievish friend poisons himself: to the hater's joy he lies dead in the morning beneath the tree. (165)

Zietblom's unwitting use of "uncanny" and "poisons" argues that Adrian is still expressing in his music his sense of breast-deprivation. Zeitblom's own purpose, musicological rather than psychological, is to convince his reader that Adrian was at this time already struggling to develop the form-breaking form that would give vent to his creative genius. Ever since first mentioning Schildknapp's name, Zeitblom, who admits to "a critical eye on the man" (166), has been setting him up as Adrian's foil. Adrian and Schildknapp share a "likeness in the colour of their eyes" (171), and Zeitblom obviously fears that there are more significant likenesses. Schildknapp tells them that his "father's social embitterment had poisoned" his life (167); could it be that Zeitblom intuitively fears that some parental influence will poison Adrian's career? Although he thinks that Adrian is taken in by Schildknapp's excuses for and rationalizations about his failure to produce anything significant, Zeitblom declares that Schildknapp suffers from a "lack of a genuine and telling creative impulse" (168). Hence, he invites the reader to realize that Adrian will be another Schildknapp unless he makes a breakthrough.[9] The very fact that Adrian envisions Schildknapp as his collaborator indicates how threatened he is by creative sterility, writer's block.

Out of Adrian's obsession with the interconnectedness of words and music, the "lyrical marrying of music with words" (182), comes his employment of the music cipher. Zeitblom proudly announces that he was the first to detect the cipher "in the probably most beautiful of the thirteen Brentano songs composed in Leipzig, the heart-piercing lied: "*O lieb Mädel wie schlecht bist du*"" (155), "O dear girl, how evil you are".[10] "The letters composing this note-cipher are: h, e, a, e, e-flat: hetæra esmeralda" (156), the name Adrian imposes on the poisonous prostitute, the mother substitute: "[t]hus in my friend's musical fabric a five- to six-note series, beginning with B [H] and ending on E flat, with a shifting E and A between, is found strikingly often, a basic figure of peculiarly nostalgic character" (155). Zeitblom ascribes Adrian's use of the cipher from this time forth to "the inborn tendency of music to superstitious rites and observances, the symbolism of numbers and letters" (155). For Adrian, then, music confesses the revival of primitive practices and of infantile complexes--Adrian's breakthrough music will be both an evocation of and denial of the uncanny.

After four and a half years in Leipzig (179), Adrian goes "home to Buchel to attend his sister's wedding" (185). Since Zeitblom is a guest, the two young men walk "to the Cow Trough and up Mount Zion" (186). As they walk, they talk about *Love's Labour's Lost*, for Zeitblom has now undertaken the task of writing the libretto that Schildknapp had rejected. Both Adrian and his father are that day suffering from migraine, so Zeitblom muses about heredity and the stress of the wedding as factors exacerbating that condition. As if aware of the particular source of his condition, Adrian speaks obliquely about the event of the day: "one has to admit that the domestication of sex, which is evil by nature, into Christian marriage was a clever makeshift" (187).

As always, when sex rears its ugly head, the Devil shows his ugly behind. Thus revived infantile complex accompanied by resurrected primitive belief drags in the uncanny. Adrian is haunted by migraine as he is haunted by his mother. He, who once proclaimed, "Relationship is everything. And if you want to give it a more precise name, it is ambiguity" (47), now announces a new credo, "Organization is everything. Without it there is nothing, least of all art" (190). He then discusses his "strict style", first accomplished by secreting the cipher in "*O lieb Mädel*" (191). Following the process described by Bergler (1949: 189), Adrian will deny the original relationship by denying the existence of the original object. Instead there is her surrogate, Esmeralda, whom he will confine in the coffin of his music. The "plot" of his music will stress his defense against *Sehnsucht* rather than his vulnerability to it; thus he will triumph over writer's block. But even at the moment that he implies what his strategy will be, as Adrian and Zeitblom pass the Cow Trough, there is an omen portending disaster for Adrian that Zeitblom records without understanding: "'Cold,' said Adrian, motioning with his head; 'much too cold to bathe.--Cold', he repeated a moment later, this time with a definite shiver, and turned away" (194). Having left Buchel that evening, sentimental Zeitblom can only imagine Adrian's leave-taking a few days later: "I see his mother kiss him and, perhaps in the same way as she had done that time with Kretschmar in the living-room, lean his head on her shoulder. He was not to return to her, he never did. She came to him".

In Chapter XXIII Mann introduces another new character, Frau Senator Rodde, who provides lodgings for Adrian, newly arrived in Munich. Once again, as Reed puts it, "[r]ealism operates alongside allegory" (1996: 367), for the model for the Frau Senator was Julia da Silva Bruhns Mann. Again the critics have treated the realism, but neglected the allegory. Perhaps they have relied too heavily upon Mann's comment to his brother Viktor, "You could not be more right about Frau Rodde. She is related to Mama only through the daughters and, at the most, through her position as an uprooted North German patrician in Munich" (qtd. in Bergsten 1969: 21). The Rodde daughters, Inez and Clarissa, are modeled on Mann's sisters, but, having no role to play in the allegory, they could not be the reason for the introduction of Frau Rodde. Rather she is introduced because she enables Mann to imply that, in Munich, he, at Adrian's age, had faced the same threat of blocked creativity that haunts Adrian, so much so that he had defended himself by caricaturing his mother as "*Mvtter Natvr*". That he presents her shorn of her caricature in *Doctor Faustus* only proves that he, unlike Adrian, did not succumb--at that time--to the cold, domineering mother. Erecting a defense against her in his fiction he thus defeated writer's block. Beneficiary of the grotesque-comic sublimation, she is no longer threatening, merely pathetic in her shallowness.

At one of Frau Rodde's soirees, yet another major character is introduced, Rudolf Schwerdtfeger, whose model was Paul Ehrenberg, with whom Mann had been so emotionally involved when he was twenty-five (Hayman 1995: 159-62). Again the reality of the model has led many critics to impose a significance upon the character that is not borne out by the text. What is significant about Schwerdtfeger is not the critical assumption about his homosexuality and bisexuality (the assumption of bisexuality based on the earlier assumption of homosexuality) but the role of the "gifted young violinist" (198) in Adrian's struggle to retain his creativity. Stock calls Schwerdtfeger a "seducer" (1994: 178); I would qualify that appellation by "would-be". That role develops over a lengthy period of time.

According to Zeitblom, Rudy from the first attempts to ingratiate himself with Adrian (119). In Zeitblom's view, an instance of his behavior is

> when Adrian, on account of a headache and utter distaste for society, had excused himself to the Frau Senator and remained in his room, Schwerdtfeger suddenly appeared, in his cut-away and black tie, to persuade him, ostensibly on behalf of several or all of the guests, to join them. (199-200)

Since Adrian's headaches have long been a sign of his repression of his "mother-problem", Rudi's effort to offer him respite is, arguably, an innocent attempt to alleviate Adrian's suffering. Soon enough, at "the artist festivals" (202), Rudi is taking Adrian by the arm and strolling with him, all the while addressing him "with the carnival *du*" and ignoring Adrian's lack of reciprocation of that language convention (203). Then Rudi comes to the point: he requests that Adrian write a violin concerto for him "with which he can be heard in the provinces". Yet, even though Rudi's motive is self-serving, he could still be seen as appreciating and fostering Adrian's creativity.

In the spring of 1911, on a bicycle outing, Adrian and Schildknapp visit the Schweigestill farm, outside Pfeiffering. Previously described, the farm and its residents impress Zeitblom as having a "singular correspondence" (205) to the Leverkühn farm and its residents, but he confesses that Adrian never spoke of his feelings upon first seeing it. Adrian's abrupt removal to Italy--accompanied by Schildknapp--by the first of June, 1911(210), is, however, eloquent testimony that he had experienced the return of the repressed, from which he had fled.

Adrian and Schildknapp remain in Italy until the autumn of 1912 (252), spending the two summers in Palestrina and the intervening winter in Rome (210). Zeitblom and his wife visit Adrian and Schildknapp in the summer of 1912; thus Zeitblom is able to describe Adrian's work at that time, an opera adapted from Shakespeare's early comedy *Love's Labour's Lost* (215). Having closely read the play, Zeitblom demonstrates his critical acumen by declaring:

> There can be no doubt that the strangely insistent and even unnecessary, dramatically little justified characterization of Rosaline as a faithless, wanton, dangerous piece of female flesh-- a description given to her only in Biron's speeches, whereas in the actual setting of the comedy she is no more than pert and witty-- there can be no doubt that this characterization springs from a compulsion, heedless of artistic indiscrepancies on the poet's part, an urge to bring in his own experiences and, whether it fits or not, to take poetic revenge for them. Rosaline, as the lover never tires of portraying her, is the dark lady of the second sonnet sequence, Elizabeth's maid of honour, Shakespeare's love, who betrayed him with the lovely youth. (216)

And yet, blinded by his admiration for Adrian's mother, Zeitblom does not suggest that Adrian is driven by his own compulsion to allude, perhaps to Esmeralda as the intermediary source of his betrayal, certainly to his mother as the principal. Zeitblom's blindness is especially glaring in light of his quotation of Act III, scene 1, lines 198-99: "whitely wanton with a velvet brow, with two pitch-balls stuck in her face for eyes" (215), which surely would remind him of Elsbeth Leverkühn's eyes (21).

Zeitblom then copies into his text "Adrian's secret record" (221), written during one of the summers that he spent in Palestrina. It is appropriately written on "music notepaper", for Adrian's subject in his record is identical to his subject in his music, his mother-problem. That the "record" is a fiction, Adrian hints at the beginning, when he contrasts himself and his creativity with his "old jester-fere" Schildknapp who, unthreatened by writer's block, "far away in the hall, travails and toils to turn the loved outlandish into the loathed mother tongue" (222).

Adrian records that all that day he had lain in the dark suffering a severe migraine, caused, apparently, by the strain of repressing his infantile complex. In the evening, though, he was able to sup the soup provided by his Palestrina proprietress "Mother" Menardi, to drink a glass of *rosso*, and to smoke a cigarette. With Schildknapp out for the evening, Adrian begins to "read Kirkegaard [sic] on Mozart's *Don Juan*" (223), soon becoming aware of someone else in the room. Adrian has probably read no further than Kierkegaard's declaration,

> our age does offer many horrible proofs of the daemonic power with which music may lay hold upon an individual, and this individual in turn, grip and capture a multitude, especially women, in the seductive snare of fear, by means of the all-disturbing power of voluptuousness (1959: vol. 2, 72),

before he lapses into a dreamlike state.

The mysterious someone, the essence of coldness (222, 223), is, Adrian writes, the Devil himself, come to offer a Faustian contract. Since coldness is the characteristic that he has always associated with his mother's nature, surely Adrian is confessing that, because of the impact of his reading upon his regressed state of mind, he has experienced an episode of extreme uncanniness. But he covers the true source of his sense of the uncanny, the revival of a repressed infantile complex, with the source hallowed by the Faust legend, visitation by the Devil, in other words, "primitive beliefs which have been surmounted seem[ing] once more to be confirmed" (Freud "Uncanny" 249). The lengthy dialogue with the Devil is an unconscious-generated fiction, whose import Adrian himself does not realize. What Adrian says the "Devil" proposes is that if he will forswear warm love he will be granted twenty-four years of musical creativity before being claimed by His Coldness (236, 237, 238-39, 249). Love in essence has its origin in the original relationship; thus Adrian must deny the existence of his mother, even renouncing the *Sehnsucht* motif and the parody of the "oceanic feeling" that have respectively crept into his previous compositions as defenses, however inadequate, against writer's block. The return of the untroubled, uninspired, and pleasantly bibulous writer Schildknapp interrupts the dialogue, so that Adrian does not indicate whether or not he signed the contract, but his subsequent actions reveal that he will honor it nevertheless.

In autumn 1912 Adrian returns briefly to Munich, not to his lodgings with Frau Rodde but to Pension Gisela. From there he engages with "Mother Else" (254) Schweigestill for room and board, remaining there until May, 1930 (492), not quite the nineteen years that Zeitblom calculates (257). Given a reconstruction of Adrian's life from early childhood to full manhood, his decision to remove himself to Pfeiffering is manifestly based not on "whim" but on crucial deliberation. He must subject himself to the landscape of his childhood (mother) in order to "convince his inner conscience that he is *not interested in his original wish, but only in the defense*" (Bergler 1949: 187; ital. in orig.)--the original wish, reunion with mother; the defense, rejection of mother.

Certain departures at Pfeiffering from the original setting at Buchel reveal that the irenic mother landscape has now become sinister in Adrian's eyes. To the "Herr Doctor ex-Theologus" (227), the change of the axial tree from the linden to the elm would be significant. Only once in the Bible is the elm mentioned, Hosea 4:13: "They sacrifice upon the tops of the mountains, and burn incense upon the hills, under oaks and poplars and elms, because the shadow thereof *is* good: therefore your daughters shall commit whoredom and your spouses shall commit adultery" (ital. in orig.), this out of the mouth of a prophet whose own wife Gomer had been "been pure and chaste before marriage" but in time fulfilled her "tendency to infidelity" (Paterson 1963: 398).

And there are other forms said to have darkened. Hatfield (1979: 115) is of the opinion that both the Buchel dog Suso and the Pfeiffering dog Kaschperl have names with sinister connotations, but it may be that he simply does not like Suso because she is "a rather mangy setter" bitch (23), for, otherwise, a dog named for a mystic seems definitely dexter. Kaschperl, on the other paw, is, as Bergsten notes, named for "the devil himself" (1969: 157). Now aware of his Faustian role, Adrian, who incidentally likes both dogs, would have noted two significant changes. The hill Rohmbühel, whose name is borrowed from the 1587 Faust chapbook, replaces "the city of David", Mount Zion. And Hanne, the Buchel stable-girl, is replaced by Waltpurgis, whose name alludes to the witches' carnival in Goethe's *Faust* (Hatfield 1979: 115). But there is more to Waltpurgis than just her name. Ezergailis notes that Hanne's face, when she sings, "contorts into a laughing grimace similar to that of the dog Suso at feeding time" (1975: 89), but she apparently does not see Hanne as an incipient Medusa or Gorgon. Being linked to Goethe's witches' carnival, Waltpurgis reminds us of Baubo riding on her farrow sow. Medusa (or the Gorgon) and Baubo are related. The image of the female that Adrian now sees is the one put in his head during his dialogue with the Devil. To explain his "involuntary changes of appearance" (Winston 1981: 99), the Devil blames the "[m]ummery and jugglery of mother Nature, who always has her tongue in her cheek" (228). Tying the Devil's description to Mann's caricature of

Mvtter Natvr in *Bilderbuch für artige Kinder*, Winston also revises Lowe-Porter's "tongue in her cheek" to "tongue in the corner of her mouth" (1981: 99fn). Well might Adrian blame all of the changes of appearance between Buchel and Pfeiffering on mother.

As Adrian settles in at Pfeiffering, his acquaintances from Munich pay him occasional visits. Zeitblom remembers that Rudy Schwerdtfeger at once resumed his effort to become Adrian's intimate friend (259-60). Having completed *Love's Labour's Lost* Adrian sends it to Kretschmar in Lübeck, who has it performed before an audience two-thirds of whom leave the theater before the final curtain (263). Perhaps the early departers sense that what they have so far seen is what Fetzer calls it, a "theatrical persiflage of love" (1990: 100). Adrian is by then composing songs and *Leider,* described by Stock as "cynical or heartbroken exposés of the inhuman reality[...]which refutes our dreams of meaning and value" (1994: 173). Zeitblom cites a typical rendition, music to accompany William Blake's "Silent, Silent Night", "the last stanza of which dismayingly enough runs" (263):

> But an honest joy
> Does itself destroy
> For a harlot coy.

Zeitblom continues:

> These darkly shocking verses the composer had set to very simple harmonies, which in relation to the tone-language of the whole had a "falser," more heart-rent, uncanny effect than the most daring harmonic tensions, and made one actually experience the common chord growing monstrous. (263-64)

As usual Zeitblom is sensitive to the presence of the uncanny without inquiring into its source.

Adrian then prepares for a major piece. Selecting the poem "Drop to the Bucket" from Friedrich Klopstock's *Spring Festival*, he writes a setting "for baritone, organ, and string orchestra" (265) to accompany it. In the poem the poet compares the earth to a drop in the ocean of the universe, but over the drop, in Zeitblom's words, "would he hover and adore" (266), favoring man over cosmos as the highest handiwork of God. Zeitblom admits that he was deeply moved "by this outburst of religious feeling" (265), but then later he realized "with shudders" that the outburst was prompted by "the threat of that visitor insisting that he was really visible" (266), the Devil. Once again the eruption of the uncanny, supposedly prompted only by the revival of primitive beliefs.

Then Zeitblom discovers that the *Spring Celebration*, whatever Adrian's motives, is but a "preparation" for another piece, *Marvels of the Universe*, a title that the biographer thinks flippant (274). For Zeitblom Adrian concocts an elaborate story of "an American scholar named Akercocke, in company with whom he was supposed to have set up a new deep-sea record" (267). For all of his linguistic study, Zeitblom does not know that "Akercocke" is a "nickname for the Devil" (Stock 1994: 173), thus misses another opportunity to shudder.

Zeitblom is fascinated by the tale so elaborately spun out:

> The mass curiosity with which these inconceivable creatures of the depths had crowded round the cabin [of the diving bell] had been indescribable--and quite indescribable too was everything that went whisking past the windows in a blur of motion: frantic caricatures of organic life; predatory mouths opening and shutting; obscene jaws, telescope eyes; the paper nautilus; silver- and gold-fish with goggling eyes on top of their heads; heteropods and pteropods, up to two or three yards long. Even those that floated passively in the flood, monsters compact of slime, yet with arms to catch their prey, polyps, acalephs, skyphomedusas-- they all seemed to have been seized by spasms of twitching excitement. (268)

To Zeitblom "these images of the monstrous and uncanny were grotesque in a solemn, formal, mathematical way" (274). These images Adrian transforms into a musical "mockery": "The piece has contributed not a little to the reproach levelled at the art of my friend, as a virtuosity antipathetic to the artist mind, a blasphemy, a nihilistic sacrilege" (275). Zeitblom simply fails to understand that Adrian's mockery is directed at those who foolishly believe that the "oceanic feeling" exists. We often say that the sea is the warm matrix from which we came, but Adrian can continue to compose only if he denies his need for that matrix, so he refashions the oceanic depths into an elaborate image of the *vagina dentata*.

With Adrian now lodged at the Schweigestills', Zeitblom turns his attention to his subject's social relations, 1912-1924. Thus Mann spotlights the realistic, though he always has the allegorical in the background. Zeitblom says little about Adrian's composing (and therefore his struggle against writer's block) until he mentions that his friend is working on a "vocal suite" (Fetzer 1990: 106) based on some stories found in the *Gesta Romanorum* (305). At the same time he is studying Kleist's essay on marionettes, in time deciding that the characters in his suite will be "puppets", not humans. Zeitblom is of the opinion (315) that the stories of the *Gesta* "were in the highest degree calculated to stimulate Adrian's penchant for parody, and the thought of dramatizing them musically in condensed form for the puppet theatre occupied him from the day he made their acquaintance" (316). But what do they parody? Since the stories that Zeitblom mentions Adrian using are about people enthused by Eros, it is safe to say that Adrian sees people who succumb to that savage god as puppets--even as he would be, were he to let down his guard. Since he has recently learned that Schwerdtfeger is about to be snared by Inez Rodde, he must consider the whistler a puppet (298). It is appropriate that, when learning of Schwerdtfeger's danger and replying, "Poor soul![...]But that's no joke for him.--He must see to it that he gets out of it whole" (298), Adrian is looking down on the chess game that he and Zeitblom are playing.

As he works on the *Suite for Puppets* (Schoolfield 1956: 174), Adrian often plays his latest additions for Zeitblom, Schildknapp, and, sometimes, Schwerdtfeger. One night, convinced that he possesses the self-sufficient duality that is, according to Bergler, essential for creativity (cf. ch1n10), Adrian is ebullient after playing. Zeitblom notices Schwerdtfeger's opportunism: "in abandoned familiarity, [he] availed himself of the licence of the moment: with a 'You've done it magnificently!' embraced Adrian and pressed him to his heart" (320). Schwerdtfeger's embrace is every bit as inimical to Adrian's creativity as his mother's. Relating the ensuing discussion of the possibilities of "the union of the advanced with the popular" in musical composition (320), Zeitblom describes the composer's rapture:

> Excited by the playing, he spoke with flushed cheeks and hot eyes, slightly feverish; not in a steady stream but more as just throwing out remarks, yet with so much animation that I felt I had never seen him, either in mine or in Rüdiger's presence, so eloquently taken out of himself. (321)

Schildknapp, ever the hack, argues against the "deromanticizing of music. Music was after all too deeply and essentially bound up with the romantic ever to reject it without serious natural damage to itself". Leverkühn tells Schildknapp, "I will gladly agree with you, if you mean by the romantic a warmth of feeling which music in the service of technical intellectuality today rejects". He then speaks of a "break-through from intellectual coldness into a touch-and-go world of new feeling", which would be the redemption of music "from a pompous isolation" (322): "We can only with difficulty imagine such a thing; and yet it will be, and be the natural thing: an art without anguish, psychologically healthy, not solemn, unsadly confiding, an art *per du* with humanity" .

Although Zeitblom doubts his sincerity, Adrian is confessing that he must continue to be the exhibitionist, in Bergler's sense of the term (cf. ch1n10), striving to make the "break-through". Schwerdtfeger has taken no part in the discussion, but he is still very much there, representing the temptation of the old romantic music that Adrian must continually denounce. Although Zeitblom does not recognize Schwerdtfeger's embrace as the Judas-act it is, he ends the scene by saying, "I kept an eye on Rudi Schwerdtgeger lest he again be moved to embrace him" (323).

In the spring of 1916, having married off her daughter Inez to Professor Dr. Helmut Institoris, Frau Senator Rodde moves from Munich out to Pfeiffering, across the road from the Schweigestills' (325), just as Frau Senator Mann had moved from Munich out to Polling (Bergsten 1969: 20). According to Zeitblom, Mother Schweigestill, gossiping with Adrian, dissects Frau Senator's fading beauty:

> she feels her age and she's singin' small, it takes different people different ways, I mean, eh, some don't care a hoot, they brazen it out and they look good too, they just get more restless and roguish, eh, and put on false fronts and make ringlets of their white hairs maybe and so on and so forth, real peart, and don't do any more like they used to, and act audacious and it often takes the men more than you'd think, eh, but with some that don't go, and don't do, so when their cheeks fall in and their necks get scrawny like a hen and nothin' to do for the teeth when you laugh, so they can't hold out, and grieve at their looks in the glass and act like a sick cat and hide away, and when 'taint the neck and the teeth, then it's the hair, eh, and with this one it's the hair's the worst, I could tell right off, otherways it's not so bad , none of it, but the hair, it's goin' on top, eh, so that part's gone to rack and ruin and she can't do an'thin' any more with the tongs, and so she's struck all of a heap, for it's a great pain, believe me, and so she just gives up the ghost eh, and moves out in the country, to Schweigestills', and that's all 'tis. (326)

Given the context of this study, such emphasis on unruly female hair hints that an aged Medusa lives across the road. Why did Thomas Mann, through the voice of Else Schweigestill, perpetrate such a cruel portrait of his mother in her old age? For the same reason that he abused the many other relations and friends, for his art. In the heat of raising them to allegorical significance, he lost sight of their reality. By this portrait of his mother he could prove to himself that he had maintained his creativity by defying his mother-obsession and thus contrast himself with his creation, Adrian, who struggles so hard toward the same end, only to lose in the end.

In 1918 Adrian is beset by stomach ailments, violent headaches, nausea, and sensitivity to light (341). Zeitblom is convinced that the condition is not "due to psychological causes" (342), but he limits such causes to contemporary events, "the national defeat with its desolating consequences". Adrian, if he can be trusted, says that he believes his condition is "merely an acute intensification of his father's migraine". Motherly Frau Schweigestill calls in Dr. Kürbis, but who can expect to receive soundness of body from a doctor named Gourd? The medico tries every remedy he knows, then recommends that Adrian turn to "a higher medical authority" (345). This recommendation Adrian rejects, saying the "he was convinced that he, more or less alone, out of his own nature and powers, would have to get rid of the evil". By likening himself to Andersen's "little sea-maid", with "eyes 'blue as the depths of sea'", who fell in love with "the dark-eyed prince", Adrian, if only unconsciously, has accurately diagnosed his condition.

In addition to Frau Schweigestill, others come to comfort Adrian. The motherly Nackedey and Rosenstiel come "by turns to Pfeiffering" (345). Schildknapp comes, but, seeing that his presence helps, ceases to come so often, citing his own poor health (346). Even Frau Senator Rodde comes across the road, visiting the sick bed to report on her daughters' doings. Schwerdtfeger comes often, very often. Zeitblom reports, apparently from information supplied later by Adrian, on one visit by Schwerdtfeger in January 1919 (348). Zeitblom supposes that it was because the day was "uncommonly brilliant" that Adrian "was seized with such severe head pains that he asked his guest to share with him at least for a while the well-tried remedy of darkness", but it is more likely that Adrian is reacting to the threat most akin to the threat of his mother, for it is soon revealed that he is in the first excruciating throes of composition. In the dark Schwerdtfeger puckers his lush labia to whistle for Adrian's entertainment, concluding with "the bourrée from *Love's Labour's Lost*" and then "the comic theme of the weeping little dog from the puppet play *Of the Godless Guile*" (349). Then he confesses to Adrian his affair with Inez Rodde Institoris. He excuses himself by saying that his relationship with her is merely physical, that, because of his "platonic nature" (350), he would prefer "having a serious, elevating, and worth-while talk with such a man" as Adrian.

Schwerdtfeger then pleads with Adrian to compose for him the violin concerto so often requested:

> I want to get it into myself so I could play it in my sleep, and brood over it and love every note like a mother, and you would be the father--it would be between us like a child, a platonic child--yes, *our* concerto, that would be so exactly the fulfilment of everything that I understand by platonic. (ital. in orig.)

For all of his mawkishness, Schwerdtfeger is a genuine threat to Adrian's continued creativity, for, despite his cold aloofness, Adrian has always yearned for a *per du* relationship, however inappropriate the partner.

Zeitblom calls it a "miracle" that Adrian, in the spring of 1919, recovered from his physical crisis (352). He now concludes that Adrian's illness was but prelude to an "almost breathless productivity":

> The conception of the apocalyptic oratorio, the secret preoccupation with it, then, went far back into a time of apparently complete exhaustion, and the vehemence and rapidity with which afterwards, in a few months, it was put on paper always gave me the idea that that period of prostration had been a sort of refuge and retreat, into which his nature withdrew, in order that, unspied on, unsuspected, in some hidden sanctuary, shut away by suffering from our healthy life, he might preserve and develop conceptions for which ordinary well-being would never summon the reckless courage. Indeed, they seemed to be as it were robbed from the depths, fetched up from there and brought to the light of day. That his purpose only revealed itself to me by degrees from visit to visit, I have already said. He wrote, sketched, collected, studied, combined; that could not be hidden from me, with inward satisfaction I realized it. Anticipatory announcements came out, from week to week, in a half-joking half-silence; in a repulse that out of fear or annoyance protected a not quite canny secret. (355)

Zeitblom's contention that Adrian's suffering inspired him to create must be countered with the contention that only by willing himself to create--therefore denying his need for his mother--could he survive his suffering. He therefore composes with "perfectly uncanny rapidity" (359), in Zeitblom's words, taking only six months of working time to complete the work (361). Unwittingly Zeitblom offers two clues to the course that Adrian's new work takes: the words "not quite canny" and "uncanny", suggest that Adrian had, during his illness, gone "down below" (355), as had Hans Castorp when he envisioned the two witches dismembering the child. In the "other world" (356) Adrian had been a witness to the uncanny, evoked by a resurgent infantile complex and/or by a revived primitive belief. Like many a witness before him, he returns feeling the call to be a "*testis*" (357) of his "journey into hell" (358). He therefore determines to compose an apocalypse or a revelation, the latter word derived from the Latin word for an unveiling or an uncovering (Barr 1963: 847). As a revelation of that which has been hidden, the apocalypse is perfectly suited to express and evoke the uncanny.

Honoring his *New Testament* predecessor, Adrian gives his "*testis*, the witness and narrator of the horrid happenings" (377), the name "'Johannes' the describer of the beasts of the abyss, with the heads of lions, calves, men and eagles". Zeitblom informs us that "this part, by tradition assigned to a tenor, is here given to a tenor indeed but one of almost castrato-like high register". Thus Adrian deprives his *testis* of *testes*. Through Zeitblom, Mann informs us that the *testis* is Adrian himself: Zeitblom reports that at the "first and so far its last performance" of *Apocalypsis* the role "was taken and sung in masterly fashion by a tenor with the voice of a eunuch, named Erbe", 'heir'. In this case the heir has been denied his estate by his mother. Although Adrian has not been physically denied mature sexual function, he surely knows that, because of psychological trauma, he is arrested in the pregenital phase. Adrian's preparations for composing an apocalypse are governed by the conventions of that genre. As a Doctor ex-Theologus (227), he would be cognizant of pseudepigrapha, "false or spurious writings", one form of which is the apocalypse, a work which purports to reveal that which is hidden (Metzger 1963: 820). There two broad forms of apocalypses, the historical and the mystical. The historical, a prototype of which is the Book of Daniel, divides history into periods and culminates with a great crisis followed by judgment and resurrection. In the mystical apocalypse "the visionary is typically taken on a tour of heaven or hell, guided by an angel. He is shown the mysteries of creation, including the abodes of the dead and places of judgment" (Collins 1987: 42). Adrian composes the latter form, adhering closely to its conventions: dependence upon borrowings from earlier apocalypses, especially *The Divine Comedy* (358), imagery, symbolism, and numerology (Kepler 1963: 849). Zeitblom summarizes Adrian's preparations (356-57) by writing

> that Leverkühn in the text for his incommensurable choral work by no means confined himself to the Revelation of St. John, but took in this whole prophetic tradition, so that his work amounts to

348 *Doctor Faustus*

the creation of a new and independent Apocalypse, a sort of résumé of the whole literature. (357)

Adding that the "title, *Apocalypsis cum figuris*, is in homage to Dürer", Zeitblom alludes to the fascination for numerology that Adrian has exhibited since his student days in Halle (92).

Unfortunately Zeitblom's comments about the *Apocalypsis* all but ignore its narrative while considering its musicology at length. Thus an adequate reconstruction of the plot is not possible. But surely Fetzer is correct in stating that "[o]ne of the central episodes[...]focuses on the 'great whore, the woman on the beast'" (1990: 68), a Biblical Baubo. Indeed, that episode must be the climax of the work. Zeitblom remarks that in his picture of the great whore of Babylon Dürer had depended upon the portrait of a "Venetian courtesan", one who exposes her private parts. She thus illustrates the form of revelation frequently referred to in the Old Testament (Barr 1963: 847), the type associated with sexual shamefulness/shamelessness. It is also the type most frequently noted by and most significant to psychoanalysis. Thus she reflects both a primitive belief and an infantile complex in Adrian, whose unconscious has for the first time dared to picture Hetæra Esmeralda and, behind her, mother Leverkühn.

Although the obvious "textual structure" (394) of the *Apocalypsis* concerns the descent into the Hell envisioned by those with primitive religious beliefs, the personal text expresses Adrian's awe for the "pudendum" (68) from which he came, whose enticement to return to it he must counter with every weapon he possesses. In the *Apocalypsis* Adrian defends himself with the weapon that he has trusted since childhood (28-29), laughter. Our only witness, Zeitblom, speaks of his

memory of that pandemonium of laughter, of hellish merriment which, brief but horrible, forms the end of the first part of the *Apocalypse*. I hate, love, and fear it; for--may I be pardoned for this all too personal excuse?--I have always feared Adrian's proneness to laughter, never been able, like Rüdiger Schildknapp, to play a good second to it; and the same fear, the same shrinking and misgiving awkwardness I feel at this gehennan gaudium, sweeping through fifty bars, beginning with the chuckle of a single voice and rapidly gaining ground, embracing choir and orchestra, frightfully swelling in rhythmic upheavals and contrary motions to a fortissimo tutti, an overwhelming, sardonically yelling, screeching, bawling, bleating, howling, piping, whinnying salvo, the mocking, exulting laughter of the Pit. (378)

Zeitblom senses that

> this hellish laughter at the end of the first part has its pendant in the truly extraordinary chorus of children which, accompanied by a chamber orchestra, opens the second part: a piece of cosmic music of the spheres, icily clear, glassily transparent, of brittle dissonances indeed, but withal of an--I would like to say--inaccessibly unearthly and alien beauty of sound, filling the heart with longing without hope.

But he does not perceive the significance of the contrast by which Adrian expresses his most intimate secret. Zeitblom calls the contrast "the profoundest mystery of this music, which is a mystery of identity", but if he has a clue about the mystery he remains silent about it. While in the first part (of his life) Adrian has defended himself with defiant laughter of rejection, yet he knows that he must live the second part ever tempted to yield to *Sehnsucht*.

Indeed, during the composition of *Apocalypsis* Adrian experiences a new aspect of the threat against his creativity. Zeitblom tells us that, when Adrian had nearly completed that oratorio, he suffered a relapse which "lasted for three weeks with pain and nausea, a condition in which, in his own words, he lost the memory of what it meant to compose, or even how it was done" (360). That is, Adrian had suffered a particularly violent recurrence of the repressed, although Zeitblom mentions nothing which might account for it. During the relapse Adrian has a visitor from out of the blue, the impish Dr. Edelmann, the noble editor of the Vienna publication "Universal Editions" (389). The visit was prompted by a recent article in *Anbruch*, "the advanced radical Vienna musical magazine" (390), praising Adrian's breakthrough creativity. The author, Desiderius Fehér, a "Hungarian musicologist and culture-philosopher",

> expressed himself with great warmth about the high intellectual level and religious content of the music; its pride and despair, its diabolic cleverness, amounting to afflatus; he invoked the attention of the world of culture, with ardour increased by the writer's confessed chagrin at not having himself discovered this most interesting and thrilling phenomenon. He had, as he put it, needed to be guided from outside, from above, from a sphere higher than all learning, the sphere of love and faith, in a word the eternal feminine. In short the article, which mingled the analytical with the lyrical in a way congenial to its theme, gave one a glimpse, even in very vague outline, of a female figure who was its real inspirer: a sensitive woman, wise and well-informed, actively at work for her faith.

Zeitblom reports that "Adrian was suffering almost to the point of collapse; but in the end was prevailed upon to play, in the Nike room, considerable portions from the manuscript", but he does not speculate about Adrian's willingness to play. Could it be that in the Victory room Adrian was, at least temporarily, overcome by the pride aroused by the *Anbruch* article, an emotion that would, if unchecked, entice him to rest on his laurels? Before leaving, Dr. Edelmann asks Adrian if he knows a Frau von Tolna.

Adrian can truthfully reply that he has never met her but that would not be the whole story. Zeitblom tells us that she had avidly followed Adrian's career, attending the performances of all his works and visiting all the places with which he was associated, including Kaisersaschern, Buchel, Palestrina, and Pfeiffering (392). At some point she had begun a correspondence with Adrian, in which she had told him of her devotion to his genius, mentioning two women who had nurtured it, Signora Menardi and Frau Schweigestill, calling both "Mère". This action causes Zeitblom to speculate: "Was it her idea to attach herself to all these maternal figures and call them sisters? What name fitted her in relation to Adrian Leverkühn? Which did she want or claim? A protecting deity, an Egeria, a soul-mate?"

The response to Zeitblom's question given here accepts Victor Oswald's 1948 assertion that "Frau von Tolna" is the name of Hetæra Esmeralda gained by marriage (249-53). But even if she is not the same woman, she has the same relationship to Adrian, as yet another mother-surrogate who would impersonate the Good Mother. Zeitblom informs us that her first letter to Adrian was accompanied by a gift, a ring mounted with "a splendid specimen of clear pale-green emerald from the Urals" (393). The geographic specificity of that description has a mythic precedent: when Prometheus was released from his punishment, he was forced to wear an iron ring mounted with a rock from the Caucasus "as a symbol of submission to his punishment" (Cirlot 1962: 261). The mythic *ambiance* of the ring is increased by another feature. On the upper facet of its stone is an engraving in Greek:

> What a trembling seized on the laurel-bush of Apollo!
> Trembles the entire frame! Flee, profane one! Depart! (393)

Zeitblom identifies the "lines as the beginning of a hymn to Apollo, by Callimachus. They describe with unearthly terror the sign of an epiphany of the god at his shrine".

He makes no attempt to apply the lines to Adrian, yet they constitute a message from the sender announcing an epiphany of the repressed. Since Apollo is the god of music and poetry, among other things, it is appropriate that the mysterious correspondent charge Adrian with profaning his "laurel-bush" by creating such radical music. Beneath the lines is a sign, "a winged snakelike monster whose tongue was clearly arrow-shaped". Zeitblom recalls that the "mythological fantasy made me think of the sting or shot-wound of the Chrysæan Philoctetes and the epithet Æschylus has for the arrow: 'hissing winged snake'", but he does not trace his reference to Philoctetes to its context in the Trojan Saga, in which the Greeks, on their way to Troy, land on the island of the goddess Chrysæ to offer a sacrifice to her. During the rite, Philoctetes, their guide, is bitten by a snake, causing an extremely painful wound that was not to heal for nearly ten years (Morford 1977: 314). With the ring Frau von Tolna is implying that she knows that Hatæra Esmerelda had "poisoned" him. Adrian must make a proper sacrifice to the goddess (in whatever avatar she appears), forswear his creativity.

Saying that Adrian "was childishly delighted" with the ring and wore it on his left hand "during the writing of the whole of the *Apocalypse*", Zeitblom firmly rejects the notion of the mystery woman as a baneful force:

> Did he think that a ring is the symbol of a bond, a fetter, yes, of possession? Obviously he thought no such thing; seeing in that precious link of an invisible chain, which he stuck on his finger while he composed, nothing more than a sort of bridge between his hermit state and the outside world; as a mere cloudy symbol of a personality, about whose features or individual traits he evidently inquired far less than I did.

Zeitblom simply does not understand that Adrian defies the injunction conveyed by the ring to cease his creative activity. His exertion is so exhausting that he suffers the relapse lasting three weeks (360). Hearing of his condition, Frau von Tolna must have rushed in her reinforcements, as it were, sending Dr. Edelmann to attack Adrian on the flank where his pride was exposed.

Persevering, Adrian completes the oratorio, but Frau von Tolna does not abandon her campaign. While Zeitblom believes her confession that she wishes "to lay on the altar of genius as much of" her wealth as possible (394-95), the contention here is that she continues to offer inducements to distract Adrian from his struggle. It is in connection with one of her inducements that Rudi Schwerdtfeger re-enters the story. By the spring of 1924, the fluting violinist performs the concerto that Adrian had finally finished, "the apotheosis of salon music", as even the ever-loyal Zeitblom calls it to Adrian's face (410). That the performance occurs in the highly reputable Ehrbar Hall in Vienna as "one of the so-called *Anbruch* evenings" suggests that Frau von Tolna is still using her vast resources and connections in pursuit of her goal. In fact, though Adrian is present at the performance, he declines to appear before the audience after its completion, pleading that he has a headache. A "headache" would be a convenient cover for the sense of shame that he feels for prostituting his genius, but in Adrian's case the headache is genuine, proof that he is being attacked by Frau von Tolna, who is aware that his defenses are now severely weakened by his succumbing to the temptation to be a *Dreck-Dichter*.

So far Adrian's story has featured his struggle against oral regression in order to forestall writer's block. But since the entry of Rudi Schwerdtfeger into the story, Adrian has also struggled against oral regression in its guise as the instigator of homosexual desire. Quoting Freud's connection "between homosexuality and sucking at the mother's breast", Bergler's view of the pregenital source of homosexuality (1949: 213-42) offers a means of seeing the direct connection between Hatæra Esmeralda's arm and Rudi's puckered lips. Adrian's completion of the violin concerto for Rudi betrays not only his waning resolve to create but his waxing desire to fellate. Frau von Tolna had sensed the latter inclination in Adrian, then offered Adrian the use of her Hungarian estate. Now in his weakened condition in Vienna, Adrian returns not to Pfeiffering but takes Rudi to spend "twelve days in stately domesticity in the dix-huitième salons and apartments of Castle Tolna" (396).

The widespread critical assumption that Adrian and Rudi engage in sexual activity while there is challenged here. Kurzke's rejection of the assumption takes precedence: stressing Adrian as an autobiographical character, he points out that Mann carefully avoided any textual statement that would lead "the reader to imagine homosexual practices between Rudi [Paul Ehrenberg] and Adrian [Thomas Mann]" (2002: 480). The rejection here added argues that the pregenital fixation of Adrian's ego simply precludes genital sexual activity--the gender-ambiguity of his first name suggests that he is frozen in incipience. Further, if Adrian had engaged in that form of oral regression, he would have subsequently suffered the other form of oral regression, victimization by writer's block. Adrian is able to repress his homosexual inclination in Hungary, but he knows that he must continue to repress it whenever Rudi is present.

In late 1924 the violin concerto is presented in Switzerland, first in Berne and then in Zürich (417). Now on a *per du* basis with Rudi, Adrian appears on stage hand in hand with him at both performances. After the second concert Adrian and Rudi are honored by a supper given by Herr and Frau Reiff in their home "in the Mythenstrasse, near the lake" (418), a location legendarily lovely. Although he was not present, Zeitblom learns from Jeanette Scheurl, a mutual friend, of an important development in Adrian's story, his introduction to the "still young" French Swiss, Mlle Marie Godeau (418):

> She had the loveliest black eyes in the world. I will begin with them: black as jet they were, as tar, as ripe blackberries; eyes not large indeed, but with a clear and open shine from their dark depths, under brows whose fine, even line had as little to do with cosmetics as had the temperate native red of the gentle lips. There was nothing artificial, no make-up about her, no accentuation by borrowed colour. Her native genuine sweetness--the way, for instance, in which the dark-brown hair was drawn back from her brow and sensitive temples, leaving the ears free and lying heavy at the back of her neck--set its stamp on the hands as well. They were sensible and beautiful, by no means small, but slender and small-boned, the wrists encircled by the cuffs of a white silk blouse. And just so too the throat rose out of a flat white collar, slender and round like a column, crowned by the piquantly pointed oval of the ivory-tinted face. The shapely little nose was remarkable for the animation of the open nostrils. Her not precisely frequent smile, her still less frequent laugh, which always caused a certain appealing look of strain round the almost translucent region of the temples, revealed the enamel of her even, close-set teeth. (419)

Discovered in Mythenstrasse Mlle Marie Godeau has the name and the looks to awaken Adrian's earliest and deepest yearnings for his mother. Clearly Adrian is taken with her, telling Zeitblom at their next meeting of "the likeness of her voice to his mother's" (421). At their next meeting Adrian hints that he is thinking of getting married and that Mlle Godeau would be "the woman of his choice" (422).

When Zeitblom next hears from Adrian, he discovers that his friend is suffering from "headache" (425), a sure sign that the repressed has returned, that if he is still in danger of succumbing to a secondary temptation, homosexuality, he is all the more in danger from the primary temptation, the mother. Adrian has called to ask Zeitblom to invite Marie and "her good Tantchen" (424) to take an excursion in the country with Rudi Schwerdtfeger, Rüdiger Schildknapp, Zeitblom and his wife, and himself. The invitation is made and accepted; the excursion is taken. Zeitblom thinks that Adrian makes a great effort to put Rudi in a good light, even as he makes no effort to indicate to Marie how he feels about her.

The next week Adrian calls Rudi to Pfeiffering. In a walk around the Klammerweiher Adrian asks Rudi to present to Marie his proposal for marriage (435-36):

> Would you, as my friend, want me to spend the rest of my life in this cloister? Consider me, I say, as a human being who suddenly realizes, with a sort of pang at the lateness of the hour, that he would like a real home, a companion congenial in the fullest sense of the word; in short, a warmer and more human atmosphere round him. Not only for the sake of comfort, to be better bedded down; but most of all because he hopes to get from it good and fine things for his working energy and enthusiasm, for the human content of his future work. (436)

That he makes this request in the environment of the Klammerweiher--which represents the coldness to which his creativity has responded--indicates the ironic deviousness of Adrian's request. Although his perception is dim, Rudy sees through the request. Through flattery, though, Adrian persuades Rudi to act as his "advocate for happiness" (437), even though Rudi confesses that he, too, is "not indifferent to [Marie]" (439).

All goes as Adrian had planned. Rudi presents Adrian's proposal, which is rejected; Rudy then presents his proposal, which is accepted. Zeitblom tries to persuade himself of the nobility of Adrian's machinations, but--aware of their results, he has to admit to a

> reality, harsher, colder, crueller than my good nature would have been capable of without stiffening in icy horror. That was a reality without witness or proof; I recognized it only by its staring gaze; and for all of me it shall remain dumb, for I am not the man to give it words. (442)

Unwittingly, Zeitblom, by his phrase "staring gaze", locates the origin of Adrian's plot, to forstall the mother's Medusan assault--through the avatar of Marie Godeau--upon his creativity. With the publication of

the engagement of Rudi and Marie, Rudi is murdered by Inez Rodde
Institoris, his cast-off mistress.

Zeitblom, present when the murder takes place on a streetcar,
picks up the telephone to break the news to Adrian, but puts it down,
realizing "that it was not necessary to tell Adrian now, that I should only in a way
be making myself ridiculous" (451). Realizing that the whole plot was
hatched by Adrian, Zeitblom, captive of his serene disposition, is
incapable of understanding that his friend had eliminated two
temptations to oral regression in order to maintain his artistic
creativity.

Given the stress that he has been through, Adrian lapses into
torpidity. Says Zeitblom: "He fell victim to a dearth of ideas, his mental
stagnation tormented, depressed, and alarmed him" (454). His physical
ailments indicate his realization that while he had disposed of
representatives of the repressed, the original repressed remained:
"severe attacks of migraine confined him to darkness; catarrh of the stomach,
bronchial tubes, and throat attacked him by turns" (454-55). Then in 1927 his
creativity returns, being manifested in a "high and miraculous harvest of
chamber music". Zeitblom later realizes that during that incredible period
of productivity Adrian was also conceiving a second oratorio, *The
Lamentation of Dr. Faustus* (483).

Enter Nepomuk Schneidewein, the five-year-old son of
Adrian's sister, who comes to stay with him while his mother
convalesces in a tuberculosis sanatorium (460). Nepomuk--"Echo" he
calls himself--is a most endearing little saint. Having his uncle's "blue
eyes" (461), he soon convinces his uncle that he is the fortunate child
who will escape the misery that he has endured. Adrian immediately
falls in love with his "Echo". But "Echo" soon dies in agony, a victim of
meningitis (474). That the signs he presents resemble those of paresis
(Clayman 1989: vol. II 961)--Adrian's fate--can only increase
Adrian's sense of the uncanny.

Attributing the death of "Echo" to the work of the Devil (477),
Adrian is spurred to create a work that will "take back" Beethoven's
Ninth Symphony (478). Restored to excellent health (and effectively
repressing his infantile complex), he grows a beard, so that Zeitblom
notes that he no longer shows "such a likeness to his mother" (483), looking
instead "Christlike". He resumes his composition of "the symphonic cantata
The Lamentation of Dr. Faustus", which, generally following the story of the original
Faust book (487), depends upon what Zeitblom calls the "echo-effect" for
its structure (486):

> The echo, the giving back of the human voice as nature-sound, and the revelation of it *as* nature-sound, is essentiallly a lament: Nature's melancholy "Alas!" in view of man, her effort to utter his solitary state. Conversely, the lament of the nymphs on its side is related to the echo. In Leverkühn's last and loftiest creation, echo, the favourite device of the baroque, is employed with unspeakably mournful effcct.

Since the death of "Echo" fatally crushes Adrian's hope of escaping the solitary state through love, it is perfectly apt that *The Lamentation* is, in effect, nothing but a wailing succession of echoes and "Ecce-homo[s]" (485), upon which is imposed the "strict style", the Hetæra Esmeralda note-sequence (486). Zeitblom describes the end:

> a symphonic adagio, in which the chorus of lament, opening powerfully after the inferno-galop, gradually passes over--it is, as it were, the reverse of the "Ode to Joy," the negative, equally a work of genius, of that transition of the symphony into vocal jubilation. It is the revocation. (489-90)

Yet Zeitblom finds at the end "the transcendence of despair" (491), for "expressiveness-expression as lament", creativity, has occurred. Zeitblom surely speaks for his creator here, for Mann wrote Kerényi about *The Lamentation*:

> Is it a singular frivolity or a blissful sense of confidence that allows us still to create *works*? For whom? For what future? And yet a work, though it be one of despair, must in its essence always be grounded in optimism, in a faith in life--and it is a strange thing about despair: it already carries in itself the transcendence to hope. (1975: 151)

In May of 1930 Adrian invites thirty or so people to attend his playing of some selections from the finished work. When all are assembled before the table at which he sits, he begins to speak:

> Now have I a friendly Christian request to you, that ye may not take and receive in evil part my homily, but that ye would rather construe it all to the best, inasmuch as I verily crave to make unto you, good and sely ones, which if not without sin are yet but ordinarily and tolerably sinful, wherefore I cordially despise yet fervidly envy you, a full confession from one human being to another, for now the houre-glasse standeth before my eyes, the finishing whereof I must carefully expect: when the last grain runs through the narrow neck and he will fetch me, to whom I have given myselfe so dearly with my proper blood that I shall

both body and soul everlastingly be his and fall in his hands and
his power when the glass is run and the time, which is his ware,
be fully expired. (497)

By his reference to the "houre-glass" Adrian indicates that in the scene
that he has set up he is parodying its precedent scene in "the old chapbook", the original Faust book (487). It is possible, then, that his
confession of having been "wedded to Satan" since his twenty-first year
is but a cover-story. But his reference to the "houre-glass" also connects
Adrian to "the winged Melencolia" (Bialstocki 1958: 522) in Dürer's
engraving, and this connection exhibits a sincere confession: that,
although he has fought valiantly, if at times inhumanely, to maintain
his creativity, he now accepts the triumphant return of the repressed.

In vague, indirect, allusive language Adrian returns to the
origin of his trauma:

it was but a butterfly, a bright cream-licker, Hetæra Esmeralda,
she charmed me with her touch, the milk-witch, and I followed
after her into the twilit shadowy foliage that her transparent
nakedness loveth, and where I caught her, who in flight is like a
wind-blown petal, caught her and caressed with her, defying her
warning, so did it befall. For as she charmed me, so she bewitched
me and forgave me in love--so I was initiate, and the promise
confirmed. (498)

Because of his repression, Adrian attributes his bewitchment not to his
mother but to her surrogate, the Leipsig prostitute. What he calls her,
though, "the milk-witch", points directly back to his infancy, when he, he
feels, he was denied the breast. According to Frazer, one of the
greatest fears of pre-agricultural humanity was the disruption or denial
of the milk supply; seeking a cause for these dire events, they blamed
the sisterhood of the milk-witch, who stole the milk or cast spells on
the cows. Thus fearful humanity created the religious rite of the
bonfire, celebrated on the Eve of May (of which Walpurgis Night was
a famous remnant) and/or the Eve of Midsummer, which concluded
with the domestic animals being led through the ashes to be "purified"
for the coming year (1958: 715-28). Seeking milk from Hetæra
Esmeralda, Adrian was bewitched by disease, but became an "initiate"
in creativity.

As he continues his wild confession, Adrian claims that long
before he "dallied with the poison butterfly" (499), he had dedicated himself
to the Devil, studying "nigromantia, carmina, incantation, veneficium" (500).
Then, in Palestrina, he made his pact with "the make-bate, the losel", who

procured "Hyphialta", presumably Hetæra in another guise, to his bed. From this union was born "a little son" (501) whom, he says, he loved--but since, according to the pact, he was not permitted to love any human being, the child died at the Devil's hand. He also confesses the scheme by which he disposed of Rudi Schwerdtfeger and Marie Godeau as threats:

> the magisterulus had marked that I was minded to marry me and was exceeding wroth, sith in the wedded state he saw apostasy from him, and a trick for atonement. So he forced me to use precisely this intent, that I coldly murdered the trusting one and will have confessed it today and here before you all, that I sit before you also as murtherer.

Finally, he implies that he is a child abuser, for he claims that there were times in his room when "most pretty children" (502) sang a "motet" to him.

Realizing that Adrian has gone completely mad, his audience trickles out of the room, until only a faithful few friends remain when he finally goes to the piano to play, as he says, "a little out of the construction which I heard from the lovely instrument of Satan and which in part the knowing children sang to me" (503). Striking the keys and wailing, he falls from the seat onto the floor. The similarity of this scene to the scene of his being brushed by the Leipzig prostitute's arm can only indicate a direct relationship between them--from poison to paresis.

When he awakens after twelve hours, he presents signs of paralytic stroke. Then he is moved to "a private hospital for nervous diseases, in Nymphenburg" (505), where a three-months observation determines that therapy will not halt the course of his condition (507). Then Adrian is returned to the care of Mother Schweigestill in Pfeiffering, whom he trusts more than anyone in the world. Having deferred informing Adrian's mother, in the hope that he would show improvement, Zeitblom and Schildknapp now inform him that they are writing her. An hour later Adrian is discovered trying to drown himself in the Klammerweiher, and, when rescued, "spoke repeatedly of the coldness of the water and added that it was very hard to drown oneself in a pond one had bathed and swum in often as a boy" (507-08), or even earlier as a fetus. Zeitblom feels obliged to add: "But that he had never done in the Klammer pool, only in its counterpart at Buchel, the Cow Trough".

Mother arrives. Fully realizing his fate, Adrian trembles as he lowers his head "on the breast of the woman he called *Mutter* and *Du*". But he does explode in "an outburst of rage" (508) on the train home, so that his mother must sit apart. Once there, though, Zeitblom assures us, Adrian passively accepts his mother's control during the last ten years of his life.

In *The Story of a Novel* Mann is obsessed with confession. Of Harry Levin's *James Joyce*, he writes, "There are sentences in Levin's book which touched me with a strange intensity. 'The best writing of our contemporaries is not an act of creation, but an act of evocation, peculiarly saturated with reminiscences'" (91). He quotes a 1946 diary entry: "How much *Faustus* contains of the atmosphere of my life! A radical confession, at bottom. From the very beginning that has been the shattering thing about the book" (Kesten 1984: 154). Of Adrian Leverkühn he wrote,

> Quite literally I shared good Serenus' feelings for him, was painfully in love with him from his days as an arrogant schoolboy, was infatuated with his "coldness," his remoteness from life, his lack of "soul"--that mediator and conciliator between spirit and instinct--with his "inhumanity" and his "despairing heart," with his conviction that he was damned. (89)

Many others who have been introduced to Adrian do not share Mann's love for him. But then only Mann knew how deep a shadow the linden tree cast on Adrian's life, only Mann knew, at the time of writing *The Story of a Novel*, how close he had come to sharing Adrian's fate.

Notes to *Doctor Faustus*

[1]During the time that he was at work on *Doctor Faustus*, Mann visited his friend Franz Werfel, who was bedridden with heart disease. Mann read the first three chapters to him:

> I shall not forget how struck he was--or shall I say premonitively disturbed--by Adrian's *laughter*, in which he instantly recognized something of the uncanny, an element of religious diabolism. He asked about it again and again. "The laughter!" he said. "What are you getting at there? Oh, I know, I know.[...]We will see." With insight and foresight, he thus picked out one of the small motifs of the book, the kind I most enjoy working with--like, say, the erotic motif of the blue and black eyes, the mother motif; the parallelism of the landscapes; or, more significant and essential, ranging through the whole book and appearing in many variations, the motif of cold, which is related to the motif of laughter. (*Story* 70-71)

Here again Mann uses *"nicht Geheueres"* (*GW* XI 191) to convey the experience of the uncanny. His further comments acknowledge both of the experiences that, Freud believes, incite the feeling of uncanniness, the revival of repressed infantile

complexes ("the blue and black eyes, the mother motif; the parallelism of the landscapes,[...] the cold") and the revival of primitive beliefs ("religious diabolism").
[2]According to Hayman, Mann, before starting to draft *Doctor Faustus*,

> discussed the project with Bruno Frank, who liked the idea of dealing with cultural crisis in terms of a pact with the Devil. As Thomas explained, the central character, the composer, Adrian Leverkühn, would be so desperate to find his way out of a creative block that he'd pay any price. (1995: 493)

While Mann consciously knew what his character's problem was, he would have depended upon his unconscious to work out the manifestation of the problem.
[3]Kurzke avers that "Adrian is not assigned the Julia Mann type of mother, rather an unbiographical, wished-for mother" (2002: 472); Stock avers that Adrian's

> mother seems[...]to resemble Mann's earlier artists' mothers (including his own). She, too, as a black-eyed brunette, calls up ideas of the south, and she is responsible for her son's artistic gifts, her inherently musical temperament being evident in her unusually pleasing voice. (1994: 156)

I stick with Stock, even though I put little stock in the significance he draws from this identification. Granted that Elsbeth Leverkühn is based on Julia Mann; that being the case, why does Elsbeth withhold her "inherently musical temperament", in contradistiction to Julia? Is not Elsbeth's refusal to sing a clue to her controlling, "cold" personality--and an implication that her inspiration, Julia, despite her "inherently musical temperament", was also a controlling, "cold" personality?
[4]Symbolically suggestive, the pond and the hill have been surveyed by the critics. Bergsten says of Adrian,

> His two favorite spots in Buchel and Pfeiffering are the hill and the pond, both Freudian symbols for the mother. The psychoanalyst would explain Adrian's attempt to drown himself in the pond [at Pfeiffering, as he, hopelessly invalid from a stroke, awaits his mother, who will take him home] as regression or infantilism. (1969: 148)

Although she does not climb the hill, Bergsten is good, so far as she goes, at the pond, but it must be added that both ponds are notable for their cold water. Adrian shivers from migraine as he stares into the Cow Pond, muttering, "Cold,[...]much too cold to bathe--Cold" (194); Zeitblom tautologizes that the water of "Klammer pond" at Pfeiffering is "strikingly cold" (25-26). And since the landscape at Pfeiffering is decidely more menacing than that at Buchel, it should be noted that "*Klammer*" hints at the clammy and choking nature of the cold mother.
Fetzer agrees with Bergsten that the hills "have phallic or perhaps even mammiform implications according to the psychoanalytic predisposition of the interpreter" (1990: 93). The psychoanalytic predisposition of the present interpreter is not to touch the mountain as phallus, rather to regard it as a mammiform magic mountain. As with Bergsten, a second order of identity would be useful to Fetzer. The

hill at Buchel is named, "most inappropriately", according to Zeitblom (25), "Mount Zion". Conventionally, "Mount Zion" is a figurative description of positive value, applied to "the chosen people, the Israelites; the church of God, the kingdom of HEAVEN" (Evans 1981: 1213; upper case in orig.). Since Zeitblom, obviously knowing that the figurative usage is traditionally positive, thinks it inappropriate here, he must be thinking of a specific Biblical citation, Lamentations 5:18, in which Mount Zion is said to "lie desolate". While Zeitblom may think the appellation inappropriate, the breast-hill of Buchel is ultimately revealed to have been a place of desolation for Adrian. After Adrian moves to Pfeiffering, uncanny in its resemblance to Buchel, he is drawn to *The Book of Lamentations* as a source for *Apocalypsis cum figuris* (357).

The five chapters of *Lamentations*, each a poem, lament the destruction of Jerusalem by the Neo-Babylonians in 592 B.C.E. The book is distinctive in form:

> Of the five poems, the first four are acrostics. The twenty-two strophes of chs. 1, 2, and 4 are introduced by the twenty-two letters of the Hebrew alphabet. Chs. 2-4 place the letter *Pê* before the letter `*Ayin*. The acrostic of ch. 3 is intensified with three lines beginning aaa, bbb, etc. The acrostic form was both an aid to memory and an expression of the totality of grief and hope, "from 'a' to 'z'". The last poem is alphabetic in that it contains as many lines as there are letters in the Hebrew alphabet. The dominant metric pattern in Lamentations is 3:2 (the so-called *kînah* or lament meter)[...]. (Gottwald 1963: 562; parenthesis in orig.)

Mann's early allusion to *Lamentations* thus invites attention to the acrostic style of his narrative and predicts Adrian's struggle to develop the acrostic "strict style" which he finally accomplishes in *Doctor Faustus' Lamentation*.

[5]Several critics have commented on Leverkühn's "return". Stock argues that in creating the correspondences between Buchel and Pfeiffering Mann violates "realism to emphasize a meaning,[...]that the artist clings to his childhood, not out of sentiment, but because the forms in which 'being' first appeared to him are his roots in the Whole, the Whole which tends toward the demonic" (157). Bergsten believes that "Adrian's inner development[...]follows rigidly deterministic lines. Here Mann seems to have made almost exclusive use of Freudian categories" (1969: 148). After that preface she writes that a "psychoanalytical search for childhood causes of [Adrian's] neurosis uncovers ample material. Thus Adrian's attachment to a certain kind of milieu can be seen as a bond with his mother[...]". But the "ample material" does not materialize. Dierks opines that the similarity of house, landscape, and persons between the Buchel and the Pfeiffering segments of the novel "give an image of a continuing postnatal symbiosis with the mother" (1990: 41). Prutti concludes:

> Our earlier question still awaits an answer. How are we to explain Adrian's re-creation of his early childhood environment? Is it a step-by-step regression or should we view him as progressng steadily by mastering the scenario of his childhood? I think that the ambiguity of this return cannot be resolved. Let me explain: in Adrian's re-creation of his past, we can discern yet a further mythical "walking in footsteps," as Thomas Mann has called it

somewhere else. Adrian retraces his own childhood, as it were, and thus he seems to remain completely within the mythical circle, i.e. in a regressive pattern. At the same time, however, this repetition can be seen as an act of liberation from childhood trauma. It is definitely not a mere "joke" or "game." The deliberate staging of the role of a "higher son" contains an element of playfulness, which allows for a temporary liberation from the maternal "embrace." To support my thesis of the essentially ambiguous nature of Adrian's liberation, it is of importance that the "game" that Adrian is playing can be taken as childlike behavior par excellence. In its childlike character, the *Lebenskindlichkeit* of the artist Adrian Leverkühn is revealed. The reproduction of his "earliest, outlived childhood"[...] must be seen and understood from this perspective. A comparison with Adrian's musical compositions and an adaptation of Nietzsche's formula "reaction as progress" come to mind at this juncture: the commitment to the self-imposed order of twelve-tone music results in a new freedom and subjectivity of the composer. The reestablishment of the childhood environment and relationships allows for a similar moment of liberation from the original, pre-existing "structures." Paradoxically, though, that the "bold" liberation goes hand in hand with an "archaic regression". (1990: 103-104)

None of these commentaries reconstructs Adrian's causative trauma--not even Prutti's stimulating advancement of the "return" problem, even though she had earlier said that "we can infer that substantial conflicts separated mother and son" (1990: 101).

[6]Schoofield makes a convincing argument that Mann's conception of Elsbeth Leverkühn is highly influenced by his response to Wagner's seductive mother figure:

The woman in *Doktor Faustus* serves both as musical inspiration and instrument of the devil. In *Leiden und Grösse Richard Wagners* Mann calls attention to the incestuous overtones in Kundry's relationship to Parsifal. During the opera's second act Kundry, attempting to seduce the young Parsifal, kisses him and states that he thus receives the first kiss of love from his mother. (Elsewhere in the essay Mann discusses the scene under the linden tree in *Siegfried*, where the "mother-thoughts" of the hero are slowly transformed into eroticism.) Beginning *Doktor Faustus* in earnest, Mann confesses that he had long called his old plan "Parsifal"; again, nearing the end of the novel, he mentions in his diary that the comparison with the opera *Parsifal* often occurs to him (*Entstehung*, 23, 193). Kundry, seductress and proxy mother, is the ancestress of the two women who direct the life of Parsifal-Leverkühn, his mother and the *hetaera esmeralda*. Frau Leverkühn and the prostitute are but two aspects of the same force--Leverkühn's feelings for his mother and those for his love will be seen upon closer investigation to be identical. (1956: 181-82)

Schoolfield's insight adds yet another allusive leaf to the linden tree in the center of the Leverkühn courtyard.

[7]Two aspects of the prostitute's description offer clues that Mann intends her to represent the deterioration of the "Good Mother" in his personal story. Regarding the "brown" complexion, Mann frequently commented that his mother inherited a creole cast from her Brazilian mother. By having Adrian refer to the prostitute as an "Esmeralda" Mann refers to a butterfly native to the Amazon basin (cf. Bergsten, 1969: 50-51, for a summary of the scholarship on this point).

[8]The present author offers another meaning for the allusion to "*Ecce homo*"-- "behold the Mann". In 1896, just when he was undergoing his sexual crisis, Mann wrote his friend Otto Grautoff that he had decided, in Hayman's words, "to burn all his diaries and some of his stories" (1995: 118).

[9]Bergler distinguishes between "the *typewriter-operator*" and "the *real writer*". Rüdiger Schildknapp is a "*typewriter-operator*" (1949: 190); he will never be threatened by writer's block, but he will never write anything of lasting significance, for he lacks the psychological imperative to develop a "plot" (1949: 188).

[10]Fetzer notes that the "Hetæra's theme" in the music is underscored not only by the words of the *Lied* but also by the sexual notoriety of its author, Clemens Brentano, which was well known to the German educated public (1990: 55-56).

VII

The Holy Sinner, Confessions of Felix Krull: Confidence Man, The Black Swan, Confessions of Felix Krull: Confidence Man. The Early Years

The Holy Sinner

Simply by completing *Doctor Faustus* while surviving a life-threatening disease, Mann demonstrated that he could do what his protagonist had not done: defeat writer's block caused by oral regression *and* withstand the terrible toll on his vitality caused by his successful struggle. Claiming victory, he could then exploit his unchecked creativity to present the orally-inspired incestuous fantasies that had always haunted, but never controlled him. That these fantasies were on a leash he would demonstrate by subjecting them not to grotesque but to comic treatment. On 10 October 1947 Mann wrote Mrs. Meyer,

> When I am feeling livelier I consider all sorts of writing projects: a medieval legend novella which, with *The Transposed Heads* and the Moses story, could form the third piece in my "Trois Contes"; working up the Felix Krull fragment into a modern picaresque novel set in the hansom-cab era. Comedy, laughter, humor seem to me more and more the soul's salvation; I long for them after the minimal portion of these in *Faustus*. (Winston 1971: 535)

While working on Chapter XXXI of *Doctor Faustus* in October 1945 Mann first encountered the story that was to be the source of his first post-*Faustus* novel. As he wrote Mrs. Meyer,

> Now I am on a grotesque opera suite for the marionette theater which Leverkühn is composing and the plot of which he takes from the old book of fables and legends, the *Gesta Romanorum*. There are stories there, at least one, which I should like best to

> take away from him and make an interesting novella from it
> myself. (qtd. in Bürgin 1969: 200)

Mann reported his encounter in his diary:

> In the evening read the *Gesta Romanorum* for a long time. The
> loveliest and most surprising of the stories is that concerning the
> birth of the sainted Pope Gregory. He is marked out for sanctity
> from birth, being the product of intercourse between brother and
> sister and then committing incest with his mother--all of which, to
> be sure, he atones for by an incredible seventeen-year span of
> asceticism on the solitary rock. Extreme sinfulness, extreme
> penitence; this alternation alone creates holiness. (qtd. in *Story*
> 147)

In *Doctor Faustus* Zeitblom offers a two-and-a-half-page summary of
the Gregory story, only one item of which will be cited here:

> The chain of complications is long, and I may as well relate in
> this place the history of the royal and orphaned brother-sister pair:
> the brother who loved the sister more than he should, so that he
> loses his head and puts her into a more than interesting condition,
> for he makes her the mother of a boy of extraordinary beauty.
> (317)

Having decided on 21 December 1947 to undertake the
project, Mann wrote the first lines exactly a month later (Bürgin 1969:
221). His narrative strategy was to be the same as that employed in
Doctor Faustus, the interposition of a "biographer" between himself
and the reader, in this case a Benedictine monk "called Clemens the
Irishman" (*Holy* 9), whose name-choice discloses his disposition.
Writing in the abbey of St. Gall, Clemens begins by referring to an
incident that occurs late in his story of Saint Gregory the Great, when
all the bells of Rome rang for three days, ceasing only when he
became Pope (302):

> Who is ringing the bells? Not the bell-ringers. They have run into
> the street like all the folk, to list the uncanny ringing. Convince
> yourselves: the bell-chambers are empty. Lax hang the ropes, and
> yet the bells rock and the clappers clang. Shall one say that
> *nobody* rings them?--No, only an ungrammatical head, without
> logic, would be capable of the utterance. "The bells are ringing":
> that means they are rung, and let the bell-chambers be never so
> empty.--So who is ringing the bells of Rome?--It is *the spirit of
> story-telling.* (4)

Clemens then emphasizes that "the spirit of story-telling" is incarnate in him (8). Inspired by a divine afflatus, he will "relate a tale, or[...]retell it (for it has already been told, even several times, if also inadequately), which abounds in bodily abomination and affords frightful evidence to what all the body gives itself" (9). Thus Clemens' writing, like the ringing bells, becomes an agent of the uncanny. While it would be immediately assumed that in both instances the sense of the uncanny is provoked by belief in the mysterious workings of the Holy Spirit (a primitive belief, according to Freud), there is good reason to consider that, in the case of Clemens' writing, the second provocation of the uncanny, the revival of an infantile complex, dictated his choice of subject-matter.

In the summary of his work on the incest theme, Rank writes:

> On our long path we have seen that incestuous impulses are by no means to be interpreted in a sexual-pathological manner, but that they belong, rather, to the most primitive expressions of human drives and emotional life. Real gratification becomes impossible to attain, and these impulses become more and more repressed in the individual. They are justified through myths; freedom from guilt is found in religion. Finally these impulses take refuge in literary production. For the individual gifted with stronger drives, literary production becomes the ultimate form of release from this psychic conflict produced by the demands of culture. Thus the creative artist is characterized especially by the strength and intensity of his drives. To dam them in the context of culture, so much repression work is required that abnormally high degrees of sublimation result. Give relatively minor disturbances, though, such sublimation fails to come to fruition. This can easily lead to neurosis, closely related in its conditioning factors and psychic mechanisms. The artist, given his need for more intensive repression, lives out his powerful drive impulses in his fantasy, just as primitive man abreacted these same impulses, when they were first repressed from reality, through myths and religions. Affectively speaking, both ontogenetically and phylogenetically, then, the artist, despite his highly intellectual achievements in sublimation, represents a regressive stage, a failure to pass beyond the infantile level. In his discussions of factors leading to psychoneurosis, Freud has described this as regression to infantilism. However, the study of neurosis and individual cultural-historical observations made from this point of view have revealed that the central problem of psychic (affective) infantilism is manifested in the incest complex. Supported by the results of our investigation, therefore, we can claim that the incest complex with all its diversity, opposing aspects, and derivatives represents the nuclear complex of neuroses and of the literary creative drive as well. (1992: 569-70)

Lengthy though it is, Rank's statement illuminates Mann's use of a "biographer": Clemens will be inspired by the incest fantasies that Mann must deny. It also becomes clear why the "biographer" is a member of a cloistered religious order "devoted primarily to contemplation and solemn liturgical observances" (Bethel 1951: 545): having early become anguished over the guilt originating in oral regression, Morhold (according to Stock 1994:191, 'place of death') becomes "Clemens", 'mild, forbearing', by becoming a Benedictine, finding a mother in the Church. But even the strictest observance of cenobitical exercises does not rid his mind of his fantasies, so, telling himself that he will further the faith by writing a hagiography, Clemens selects a subject saturated with sibling sexuality. While he vows to write in "a shapely prose" (11), not poetry in the manner of

> There was a prince by name Grimald,
> He had a stroke that laid him cold.
> He left behind twinn children fair--
> Aha, was that a sinful pair![1]

his "shapely prose" is obsessed with those shapely bodies.

Mann himself wrote to Mrs. Meyer that his main source, Hartmann von Aue's *Gregorius vom Stein*, was a "variation on the Oedipus myth" (Prater 1995: 405). It is possible, then, that he intended the sexual behavior in *The Holy Sinner* generally to conform with Freud's theories regarding the Oedipal phase. McWilliams' allusion to Mann's statement to Mrs. Meyer implies that he accepts the teller's intention and believes the Oedipal theme self-evident; he therefore slights the kind of psychoanalytic commentary often present in his treatment of other Mann fictions. The Oedipal aspect of the novel is a red herring, however, for the sexual motive in the novel originates in the earliest phase of development, which Anzieu characterizes as "the skin ego" (cf. ch1n7).

Enter Grimald, "Duke of Flaundres and Artoys" (12), who has weal, wealth, and wife. The only thing lacking is children, and, since he and his Baduhenna are both past forty, he fears that, at his childless death, the duchy will be devastated by contending claimants for his crown (16). Finally, though, the Duchess conceives, in due course bearing twins, a boy and a girl, but at the cost of her life. The boy is named Wiligis and the girl, Sibylla.

The twins' experience of the skin ego is rendered defective by their mother's death in childbirth, for they are deprived of the lips-to-breast contact that initiates the sense of oneness with the original object. Clemens's statement that the twins were fed "sweetened gruel and pap" (19) implies that they were not comforted by the breast that a wet nurse could have provided. That there is something enigmatic about the twins is suggested by the complexion of the skin they were born with, which resembles neither their mother's nor their father's, but is, in Clemens' judgment, "clearly an inheritance from distant forebears" (19).[2] As their irises darken, their eyes present an "uncanny" appearance (20), especially since both twins have "a way of looking sidelong out of one corner as though they were listening and waiting for something", indicating, in Bollas' formulation, a "person's search for an object (a person, place, event, ideology) that promises to transform the self". At seven both receive a scar from chicken-pox on their foreheads, "in exactly the same place and the same shape, namely like a sickle" (20).[3] Literally the pocks violate the skin surfaces, while their sickle shape symbolizes the fantasy of the defective skin ego that haunts the area just behind those foreheads.

Like the twins in "The Walsung Saga", Wiligis and Sibylla take up hand-holding (21), to gain a sibling skin ego in compensation for the lost maternal skin ego. Sharing the same bedchamber, they sleep in beds strapped with the skin of the salamander, a mythical monster; the salamander skins not only produce a fiery *ambiance* but also induce fantastic dreams. The beds also have phallic posts on which are carved entwined snakes, the caduceus, which has from time immemorial symbolized "balanced duality" (Cirlot 1962: 36). In those beds the twins may dream of restored duality-in-unity, their dreams inspired by the intuition that they had originally shared the same membrane-enclosed chamber.

At age eleven, sleeping nude in the same room, the twins become aware of certain differences in their anatomy when they take their morning bath (22-23). Clemens mentions the sickle scar on each sib's forehead as he describes their mutual gazing. The sickles on their skin make manifest their shared sense of a shredded skin ego and their dawning intuition that the salient anatomical difference possessed by one of them provides the tool for reunification. Having described the servant women rolling their eyes at the male twin's precocious pendulous part and excitedly declaring, "L'espoirs des dames", Clemens imagines the female twin's ripping retort: "I will--l'espoirs! Mine is the sweetheart. That damsel who has to do with him--j'arracherai les yeux"[...](23).

One day, after Wiligis has been practicing putting on "the knightly sword" (32), his sister lets him know that she, too, has plans for him. She subtly suggests her concavity by inviting him to sit with her in a window niche and share some skin:

> They did as she proposed, sat, with their arms in velvet and silk across each other's shoulders, on the bench in the niche and anon leaned their comely heads to each other. At their feet, head on his paws, lay their Anglo-Saxon hound, a pointer, Hanegiff by name, a very lovable creature, white, black only round one eye and both ear-flaps. He shared their sleeping-chamber and slept there always between their beds on a materas stuffed with horsehair. (27-28)

When she speaks of the latest seeker of her "hand in marriage" (28), he avails himself of that hand, fondles it, saying,

> For of us two no one is worthy, neither of you nor of me, worthy is one of the other, since we are wholly exceptional children, high of birth, that all the world must behave lovingly dévotement to us, and born together out of death, each of us with our graven sign on our brow. (29)

Thus he expresses the ancient claim that the highborn are exempt from the taboo of incest. When he becomes duke, he says, she will be his "sister-duchess" (30). His confirmation kiss elicits a reply: "I like it better[...]when you kiss me than when our dear and worthy lord scratches my neck and cheeks with his rust-coloured moustaches".

Enter the doughty duke, who has always favored his daughter, and as she approaches nubility his favoritism begins to hint of desire, as Stock notes (1994: 192). Replacing Wiligis in the niche, he threatens his son with a "couple of smacks" if he thinks "that such a precious child is closer to the brother than to her sound and sturdy father" (31), then sends him out to play. The next year, when the twins turn sixteen, Wiligis gets knighted and Sibylla gets a suite of supple suitors, all of whom her father rejects. It is at this time that Wiligis has the same nightmare two nights running: "He dreamed his father hovered over him with legs spread out behind in the air, copper-red in the face with rage, with bristling mustachios, and silently threatened him with both fists as though he would straightway take him by the throat" (33).

The onset of puberty merely intensifies the intimacy that has always existed between the twins, now made fiery by physical and hormonal changes. When they are seventeen (34) their father suffers a first, then a second--fatal--stroke. As his corpse lies in state in the castle chapel, the twins lie in their bedchamber:

They both lay naked under their covers of soft sable in the pale gleam of the swinging lamp and the scent of amber with which their beds were dusted--they stood, as fittingly, far apart, and between them coiled round like a snake, slumbered Hanegiff, their good hound. But they could not sleep, they lay with open eyes or only sometimes shut them perforce. How it was with the damsel I do not know, but Wiligis, o'erwrought by his father's death and his own life, groaned under the scourge of the flesh and under Valande's spur until at last he held out no longer and slipped out of his bed, went round Hanegiff on his bare foot soles, gently lifted Sibylla's cover and came, the godforsaken one, with a thousand forbidden kisses, to his sister. (38-39)

Sibylla reacts: "Lo, my Lord Duke, mickle honour you show me with your unexpected visit! What gives me the privilege of feeling your dear skin near mine" (39). She has other questions: "What means, my brother, this wrestling? How have I thy sweet shoulder at my lips? Why not"? Only a hound is Hanegiff, but even he knows that something uncanny is going on, so he "set himself on his haunches and gave lamentable tongue" (39). Wiligis hops out of bed, hops on Hanegiff to cut his throat, hops back in with Sibylla, who still has questions: "What have you done? I have not looked, but pulled the cover over my head. It is so still all at once and you are rather wet" (40). Coming closer, Wiligis addresses the undressed questioner--"Us may no one ask. Since Grimald is dead, no one, sister-Duchess, my sweet other-I, beloved"-- quite ready to reunite himself with his other-I under the soft skin of sable. Clemens' statement that Wiligis "babbled" reminds us of the deep infantile origin of the twin fantasy now coming into reality. Sibylla, so willing, has no more questions: "O Willo, quelle arme! Ouwe, mais tu me tues. Oh shame! a stallion, a buck, a cock! Oh, away and away! O angel boy! O heavenly friend!" (41). Here Mann takes considerable license with his source.

Having looked all their lives for the transformative object, the twins discover after some months of "the knightly sword" that it reposes in Sibylla's womb. In desperation they call upon Sieur Eisengrein, their father's grizzled vizier, to get them out of their fix. Like many a fixer before and after, he directs her to get to the country and him to get out of the county.

Wiligis starts off for the Holy Land, but dies of a broken heart before reaching Massilia (Marseilles) (74). Meanwhile, Sibylla spends her gravidity with "Mother Eisengrein" (61), to whom she tells her bad dream: "she dreamed she gave birth to a dragon who cruelly tore her womb. Then he flew away, which caused her great mental anguish, but came back again and gave her even greater pain by squeezing back into the torn womb" (62). For once, Sibylla lives up to her oracular name. After living six months cooped up "like a Strasbourg goose" (63), Sibylla bears a baby boy. His chances appear to be unpromising: "she held the child to her mother-breast and wailed aloud, so that the little one was feared, lost the nipple, and screwed up his face in bitter wailing" (66). But he soon gets the hang of it: "He had once more drunken his fill at the mother-breast and was swollen red for fullness" (69). On the seventeenth day of his life, he is placed in a cask with a "dowry of silken stuffs, gold-filled loaves, and written word [his mother's account of his conception and birth]" (69): "the plump little cask became his dwelling, a new mother-womb out of whose darkness if God pleased he should be born again". The cask is set afloat in the sea.

After two nights and a day (98), the cask is picked up by two fishermen who live on the island of St. Dunstan. The baby is discovered by "Gregorius, Abbot of the cloister Agonia Dei" (82), who, following the intent of the baby's dispatchers, gives him a christening and an education. For seventeen years (137) Gregorss gets ready to be a monk, then gets on a horse instead. Thus he follows his dream of "being one of Arthur's parfit gentil knights" (112):

> when he lay alone on the strand in his choir-boy's cassock, his head on a stone, he saw himself in far other wear, a scarlet mantle, hauberk and harsenière--and so coming on a spring in a thick wood where on a mighty tree hung a golden basin. If one took this, dipped water out of the spring, and poured it on the emerald platter beside the spring, there arose in the wood a mighty tempest which must undeniably have crushed foolhardy adventurers. But lightning and falling trees left him unscathed; calmly he awaited the coming of the armoured lord of the spring, who, quite as expected, demanded an accounting of him. The angry lord of the spring was twice as big and tall as he, but Gregorss knew better how to concentrate and therefore he struck down the giant, and in the sequel received the favours of the gracious widow of the fallen one. (112-13)

This is a "rescuing fantasy", involving the Oedipal situation as Freud and Rank point out (Gutheil 1951: 153), but the particularity of the "spring", a frequent symbol of the breast, from which Gregorss drinks, points to the pre-Oedipal origin of his dream.

At this point the Abbot gives him the tablet accounting for his begetting and the bequest that will enable him to quest. Like most teenagers, bewailing his fate as "the abominable fruit of sin", therefore "a horror, a monster, a dragon, a basilisk" (144), Gregorss is nevertheless excited by the prospect of the open road. Taking ship, he gets lost in a fog for seventeen days (151), then fetches up in Bruges, the capital city of the country ruled by Duchess Sibylla.

This lady has been besieged by King Roger the Goat-beard for the last twelve years; tiring of patient wooing, he turned, five years ago, to besieging Bruges. At once determined to be the Duchess' champion, Sir Gregorss the Fish obtains an audience with her. She is reminded of her "poor little mariner" (169); he thinks that he sees "the earthly image of the Queen of Heaven" (170). Soon he has captured the Goat's beard and the Duchess' heart (190-91). Sooner still she prays poetically: "Would he so hotly lust after my still unwearied breast, for only him I find of my bed worth, or grant of equal birth! Of his skin I'd fain be glad, yet hear no owlets' screams about my bed, nor Hanegiff up to the beams howl fearsomely and loud" (202). And so they marry. Clemens, speaking for universal maledom, blames the whole thing on Mother Nature (206-07).

Three years into marriage Sibylla has given birth to a daughter and is again pregnant (209). Gregorss has all that he could dream of: "In her arms, on her gentle breast he enjoyed perfect blessedness, the sweet security of the nursing babe, and no less mighty male delight" (211). Yet both are secretly plagued by a sense of guilt over the past. Gregorss' melancholy arouses the inquisitiveness of a servant, Jeschute, better named *Je scrute*, who is marked by that lolling tongue that Mann installs in his Gorgons (215). Discovering the place that Gregorss hides his tablet, she takes Sibylla to it (214). Then follows the inevitable scene in which the marital partners recognize their pre-existent relationship.

Their future is according to Gregorss' decree: his mother must descend from her position, then found an asylum in which to care for unfortunates; he must seek a hermitage appropriate for penance. In time he comes to the hut of a fisherman, who first turns him away with the charge that he only pretends to be a penitent beggar (235). But, after his wife pleads for Gregorss, the fisherman permits him to stay the night (236). Still suspicious of Gregorss, the fisherman makes an accusation that has a bearing on the theme of the skin ego:

> Thy arms and legs, they have not long been bare, don't tell me, they were well covered from wind and weather, and thy skin--I will tell you what kind of skin that is: it is the skin of a well-fattened feeder. Look what a lighter streak runs round thy finger: there was a ring there once. (238)

Will Gregorss be the type, like Wiligis his father, who was, when separated from the female with whom he shared the fantasy of a shared skin, overcome with the fantasy of a flayed skin? If so, will his quest, like his father's, quickly end in death?

The next morning the fisherman starts to leave Gregorss behind, so that Gregorss, in his haste to catch up, forgets to take his tablet with him, but carries a ladder like "the Lord Christ His Cross" (241), as the fisherman's wife piously proclaims. The fisherman rows Gregorss to the middle of a large lake, there to deposit him on a rock island--which has to be climbed by that ladder--and even to chain him to the rock with a lock, throwing the key into the lake.

The locale evokes the landscape of rebirth, as McWilliams notes (1983: 361). Indeed there is a superabundance of hints that Gregorss is undergoing regression to infantilism. On the second day he makes a vital discovery about his new environment:

> In the middle, almost exactly, there was a little trough in the stone, and a whitish cloudy wetness filled it up to the margin, probably yesterday's rain, he thought, only quite strikingly cloudy and milky--welcome to him in any case as a drink, however and whencever unclean it might be, he was the last to make conditions. So he bent over the little basin and sucked up with lips and tongue its contents, lapped it all out, little as it was, only a few spoonfuls, and even licked the bottom of the little hollow when it was empty. The drink tasted sugary and sticky, a little like starch, a little pungent like fennel and also metallic like iron. Gregorius had at once the feeling that not only his thirst but also his hunger had been satisfied by it, with surprising thoroughness. He was filled. He belched a bit and a little of what he had drunk ran out of his mouth again as though the little had already been too much. His face felt a little puffy, warmth rose in his cheeks and reddened them, and when he had got back by creeping to his first place at the edge of the stone, he fell asleep like a child, with his head resting on a small ledge of the rock. (246)

Clemens then spends over two pages exploring the ancient belief that humankind in its infancy was similarly nourished by "earth-milk" (249), arguing, in effect, that ontogeny recapitulates phylogeny. However diverting his remarks may be on this score, they offer no help in accounting for Gregorss' survival. That information, given unwittingly, he soon provides. Fettered as he is, Gregorss cannot escape the extremes of weather, hence he quickly learns to curl "in on himself" (249), even as his skin is activated to "the condition of pimply protection which we call gooseflesh". His "defensive skin" becomes "very horny and granular" (250) and his matted hair thickens to the consistency of felt: "in fifteen years he was not much bigger than a hedgehog, a prickly, bristly moss-grown nature-thing, whom no weather could affect, and whose shrunken members, the little arms and legs, even eye- and mouth-openings were hard to recognize" (251). However incredible the description of Gregorss' physical devolution may be, it offers an accurate description of his development of a thick-skinned ego, one which honors where it came from but harbors no fantasies about being inseparable from its source.

At this point in the story, the psychological is replaced by the theological. Although Clemens has been strangely silent about the agonies of penitence suffered by Gregorss, God is apparently satisfied that he has experienced perfect contrition after seventeen years on the rock. He divinely informs two Romans that Gregorss is to be the next pope, giving them the general location where he may be found. They find him, feed him bread and wine (297), an act of impanation which rather quickly--by a mystical transformation over water--restores him to his former appearance. Retrieving his tablet, he rides across "Christendom on his white, purple-draped beast" (303), sets the bells of Rome a-ringing, and receives the papal tiara (305). Becoming honored for the compassion he shows all sinners, he is requested of an audience by his mother/wife (333), accompanied by his two daughters/half-sisters. There is the inevitable recognition scene, in which both acknowledge that they had entered matrimony knowing the true identity of their spouse (330, 332). Thus they fullfill their incest fantasy, knowingly offering "God an entertainment", as Gregorss, now Pope Gregory, later puts it. In effect, then, Mann is fullfilling his incest fantasy, offering himself--and his audience--an entertainment.

Sibylla reverts to her earlier interrogative behavior: will the Pope, that is to say, her son-husband, annul their marriage? Leaving that decision up to God, the Pope says that it would be better if they appeared before the public with their relationship either as husband and wife or son and mother unknown. Again she asks, "But what, then, child, can we be to one another?" He replies, "Brother and sister,[...]in love and grief, in repentance and in grace". Since the whole story began with Wiligis having a hot head under the soft sable, it had better end with Gregorss keeping a cool head under the tiara.

Notes to *The Holy Sinner*

[1]Strangely enough, neither in the two letters previously cited nor in *The Story of a Novel* (147) does Mann note that the brother and sister are twins. Yet Mann did not, as Stock presumes (1994: 200n5), introduce this feature to the legend, for Rank cites a summary of it written in 1854 which so states their relationship (1992: 285).

[2]Here Clemens waxes doctrinal, implying that the twins' subsequent behavior is to be attributed to Original Sin. But their atavistic skin hints at a primeval

condition such as Rank attributes to incestual desire: "incestuous impulses are by no means to be interpreted in a sexual-pathological manner, but that they belong, rather, to the most primitive expressions of human drives and emotional life" (1992: 569).

[3]Here again Clemens, by alluding to the mark of Cain, pursues his didactic intention.

Confessions of Felix Krull: Confidence Man

Although he had put away the Krull manuscript by 24 July 1913 (Hayman 1995: 270), Mann continued to be haunted by the project. On 26 February 1919 he told himself, "How at home I always feel in the Goethean sphere, how it gladdens and stimulates me. If I manage to get to *The Confidence Man* I will be able to live and work entirely in that realm" (Heilbut 1996: 328). "Sometime before 31 May 31 1921, he composed a 'military examination scene'" (Heilbut 1996: 338) that, in 1951, he inserted in Book I. The part that he had earlier written was published as *Buch der Kindheit* in 1922; an article on it prompted Mann's letter of appreciation to its French author, Félix Bertaux:

> I am truly touched by today's letter from you which tells me so many beautiful and encouraging things about my *Felix Krull*. I do not know why I stopped then. Perhaps because I found the extremely individualistic, unsocial character of the book untimely. Perhaps also because it seemed to me that I had already given everything essential in this part. Still, I have never completely lost sight of the idea of a continuation and when I will have rid myself of the load that I now carry, I will perhaps find the chance to finish this peculiar thing. (qtd. in Cap 1993: 14-15)

In 1943 Mann considered returning to the Krull project before deciding to begin his Faust story (Prater 1995: 352). Even as he was immersed in that great project, he asked Hermann Hesse, "What would you feel[...]if I were to entertain myself in my old age by developing the Felix Krull fragment into a full-length picaresque novel" (Hayman 1995: 547). Upon his completion of the Faust project, Mann was confronted by competing appeals for his attention: the older Krull project and the younger Gregory project. It may have been that he chose to begin the latter merely because the legend provided him with a ready-made plot. But behind that practical reason lurked a personal reason. Unconsciouly jubilant at completing the Faust project, by which he proved that he had, unlike his character Adrian Leverkühn, withstood the return of the repressed, Mann must have feared taking up a manuscript that had already twice, or perhaps thrice, threatened to afflict him with writer's block.

In *The Holy Sinner* he had been able to play with the incest complex in both its forms, protected by the fact that the previous

378   *Confessions of Felix Krull: Confidence Man*

versions of the legend legitimized his obsession. On 26 October 1950 that novel was finished, and once again he was confronted by the challenge of the Krull project. His correspondence announcing his return to it betrays his ambivalent attitude toward it. To Otto Basler he wrote on 8 January 1951, "I have set myself to writing again on the *Confessions of Felix Krull*, a work which I deserted forty years ago" (qtd. in Bürgin 1969: 235). To Erich Kahler he wrote on 1 February 1951,

> I have taken up the ancient *Felix Krull* once again and am continuing it, letting him saunter on into the unknown without any real faith that I shall ever finish it. I suspended work on it in 1911 to write *Death in Venice*, and it is truly curious to take up the old fragment again after four decades and all I have done in between. I have actually resumed on the selfsame page of Munich manuscript paper (from Prantl on Odeonsplatz) where I stopped at that time, unable to go on. (Winston 1971: 607; parenthesis in orig.)

These statements differ markedly from a public statement Mann had made in 1923: "The novel[...]was begun twelve years ago, but had to be put on the shelf for the sake of other tasks, although the author never separated himself from it inwardly" (Berendsohn 1973: 173).

Resuming the story in Book Two, Chapter VII, Mann has Felix depart Frankfurt for Paris to take up the hotel position obtained for him by his godfather Schimmelpreester. His career in Paris is to be marked by the absolute success characteristic of a picaresque hero. In the customs shed at the border crossing, he avails himself of the opportunity to filch the jewelry case of a rich woman whose luggage lies open next to his small satchel (122). When he arrives at the Hotel Saint James and Albany, he proceeds to charm everyone whom he encounters, from scullion Stanko to director Stürzli (126). Indeed, it is through Stanko's good offices that he locates a fence for his stolen treasures. Predictably the fence is also charmed by Felix (160). Displaying his knack of carrying on conversation in French, English, and Italian though he really knows only a smattering of each, Felix so impresses director Stürzli that he is assigned a job as an elevator operator, rather than in one of the invisible jobs in the kitchen or in housekeeping. The director directs that Felix be called Armand, since he is taking the place of another Armand, who leaves immediately at the end of his shift.[1] Stürzli--called "the Rhinoceros" because of his *Stürzel*--also says, "It will be no misfortune[...]if in [your liftboy's uniform] you please the pretty women" (149). When director Stürzli advises that he learn to master the mechanism, Felix replies, "It will be handled with love". After all, anyone who can elevate his amatory anatomy at will will have no trouble lifting a lift.

Minutes later, entering the elevator, Felix spies the striking woman of a certain age whose jewels he had stolen. He must sense the irony of the situation: he is just on his way to fence them. As she exits the elevator, she says to the nearly departed liftboy, "*Merci, Armand*" (152). Thinking it "proof of her sociability" that she, "so recently arrived", had already learned the liftboy's name Felix quizzes him about the woman, but Armand's truculence forces Felix out of his customary character, for he says, "As a matter of fact, I'm Armand now. I'm following in your footsteps. I'm your successor and I'm going to try to cut a less boorish figure than you". For all his cleverness, Felix never gives voice to any suspicion that the Armand, *Arme mann*, whom he followed as liftboy may have preceded him in the rich woman's bed and, having quickly lost his head, has now therefore lost his job.

The next day, now in the uniform that pleases the pretty women, Felix sees the woman, who graces him with goo-goo eyes. She takes the adjacent elevator, but smiles back at Felix, once again indicating her receptivity by ogling her eyes (168). The next day she rides up in Felix's elevator, calling him "the new Armand", just as she had probably saluted a long line of liftboys. Properly menial he carries her shopping purchases into her room where she indicates her readiness for roughhouse.To emphasize the depth of her desire she plunges him speechless with a suctorial "pledge" (170). When he regains his breath he promises to come when his shift is over and hers is off.

Felix is somewhat put off by the woman's habit of "put[ting] everything into words" (173), even on the heights of the plateau stage. But his training by Rozsa stands him in good stead, so that he can concentrate on technique despite the talk. Thus they come to the ultimate, the simultaneous orgasm (174). Surely this is "The Best of All" or "The Great Joy" (46), the "pre-oedipal *unio mystica* with the maternal body" (Lubich 2002: 204), that Felix has sought since before memory. As they share the resolution phase, she talks of herself, Diane Philibert, married to the impotent Houpflé, who manufactures Strassburg toilets (179). She herself is a very successful novelist, modestly describing herself as "*d'une intelligence extrême*" (174). Like Tonio Kröger, she as an intellectual suffers severe alienation from those beautiful objects who simply live life unreflectively. As a girl of thirteen she had fixated on an early adolescent Hermes-type who personified beautiful blankness

(175); now that she is mature she seeks the same type who has taken some prizes. As she tells the latest Armand, she seeks "not you but the idea of you, the lovely instant you incarnate" (176).

The voluble voluptuary tells her bedmate that her mature passion is probably "transferred mother-love, the yearning for a son" she never had (176). Anticipating his reaction, she has a lecture ready:

> Perversity, do you say? And all of you? What do you want with our breasts that gave you suck, our womb that bore you? Isn't it your wish simply to go back to them, to become sucklings again? Isn't it the mother you illicitly love in the wife? Perversion! Love is perversion through and through, it can't be anything else. Probe it where you will, you will find perversion.

Then, waxing poetic, she offers, in alexandrines, an extended praise of "the enchantment of the youthful male" (177). By this literary display, she illustrates her belief that as long as she indulges her incestuous fantasy she will never cease to be creative. Thus she appears to stand on its end Bergler's theory that writer's block can be forestalled only by repressing the incestuous fantasy. But Bergler would counter that she is not a "*real writer*", only a "*typewriter-operator*" (190), a fount of formula fiction. Support for Bergler's rebuttal can be found in her claim that she has written "so many books" (174) and in her insistence that they are "*énormément intelligents*" (177).

Felix thinks that "so much praise and adulation" has pricked up his "manly state" again, but, more likely, it comes from hearing his own repressed incestuous desire expressed so forcefully. And by someone who could be his mother! His simple statement, "We were united again" (178), is a perfect presentation of the skin fantasy that will satisfy both of them until detumescence occurs.[2]

Diane's sexual excitement remains unslaked, for she pleads with her Armand to beat her: "There are your braces, take them, beloved, turn me over and whip me till I bleed!" *Ars amandi*, indeed! Given scruples by a certain enervation, Felix thinks to distract her by confessing to the theft of her jewelry. On the contrary, she is delighted: "*Mais ça c'est suprême*"! Such an activity only proves that he out-Hermes all her other Hermes hitherto. At her encouragement, Felix steals about the room gathering what she calls his "booty of love and theft" (180). Then he shakes his booty, accompanied by Diane's valedictory:

> *Adieu*, Armand! Farewell, farewell forever, my idol! Do not forget your Diane, for in her you will survive. After years and

years when--*il temps t"a détruit, ce cœur te gardera dans ton moment béni.* Yes, when the grave covers us, me and you too, Armand, *tu vivras dans mes vers et dans mes beaux romans,* every one of which--never breathe this to the world!--has been kissed by your lips. *Adieu, adieu, chéri*[...]. (181)[3]

The scene contains, as Heilbut notes (1996: 559), Mann's first description of an orgasm. With that scene--"completely isolated in its nakedness" from Mann's "total work", says Berendsohn (1973: 184)--he completed Book Two.

Book Three begins with a look back at his unforgettable night with Diane. Felix hastens to add there were later experiences with "ladies travelling alone, particularly older ladies" (185), but he feels compelled to say of those experiences:

> they fell far short of that significant and unique night, and at the risk of blunting my reader's interest in the further course of my confessions, I must announce that in the sequel, however high I rose in society [pun no doubt intended], I never again had the experience of being addressed in alexandrines.

But it is possible that what is "significant and unique" about that night is not what Diane said in poetry, but in prose. She accuses him of desiring to sleep with her because she is a substitute for his mother, and his failure to contradict her suggests that her charge has hit the mark. Inspired by her incestuous fantasy and the easily replaceable spark plug of the "instant you", she will sustain her writing, but will Mann retain his creativity, now that he has all but openly confessed his oral regression? Mann may have begun to realize, albeit unconsciously, that Diane's accusation might forecast doom not only for Felix but also for his creator's creativity.

Felix resumes his memoir with an accounting of "the treasure trove of love and theft" (185) that "the thieving god" , i.e. himself as Hermes, had gotten in Diane's room and of his lavish enjoyment of Paris, thanks to the theft part of the treasure trove. At first he is content to be an impostor on his evening off, remaining a liftboy by day, but by spring he has become bored (199). If Adam Phillips is correct when he asserts that the awareness of boredom indicates that one is waiting for something but does not know what, then it is likely that Felix's boredom reflects Mann's boredom, hinted at in his letter to Kahler dated 1 February 1951: "I have taken up the ancient *Felix Krull* once again and am continuing it, letting him saunter on into the unknown without any real faith that I shall ever finish it."

Feeling "imprisoned in [his] elevator cage", Felix eagerly accepts a new position in the hotel. Mann could have put Felix into several assignments in which he would have a greater opportunity to demonstrate his skills as an impostor. But he chose the one that matched his own mood: Felix becomes one who waits, that is to say, a waiter (200). Quickly his presence at service infatuates two shy guests, the first heterosexual, the second homosexual. The first is Eleanor Twentyman, a slender 'seventeen or eighteen" year-old blue-eyed blonde from Birmingham (207). Possibly she is only sixteen, for her immaturity suggests that has she never been kissed. The second is Nectan Lord Strathbogie, a fiftyish peer of the realm living with his mother in Aberdeen (213), who seems to share Eleanor's condition. Both subjects could be modeled after their creator: Mann often remembered his teenage self having the kind of "crush" on a boy that Eleanor has, and he could not forget his recent "crush", at age seventy-five, on the waiter Franz Westermeier (Hayman 1995: 573-75). Mann must have experienced a mixture of emotions in exposing those phases of his life that had given him such a thrill, but ultimately so much pain. It was probably his knowledge of the dashed hopes that Eleanor and Lord Strathbogie are enduring that induced him to picture Felix sympathetically rejecting both the heterosexual and the homosexual overture. Mann must have felt that Felix is waiting for the return of something that would transform his life, would transcend any pleasure that Eleanor or Lord Strathbogie could have provided.

Mann must have realized that if he was to continue the Krull manuscript he must re-emphasize Felix's role as an impostor, as well as engage him in an action that draws him toward a transformative event. Indeed, Mann anticipates these changes when he reveals Felix's thinking when Lord Strathbogie offers to adopt him:

> That was strong. Indeed, he certainly sprang all his mines at once. Ideas swirled through my mind, but they did not incline me to alter my decision. That would be a suspect lordship, the one he dangled before me because of his interest. Suspect in the eyes of the people and lacking the proper authority. But that was not the main thing. The main thing was that a confident instinct within me rebelled against a form of reality that was simply handed to me and was in addition sloppy--rebelled in favour of free play and dreams, self-created and self-sufficient, dependent, that is, only on imagination. When as a child I had waked up determined to be an eighteen-year-old prince named Karl and had then freely maintained this pure and enchanting conceit for as long as I

wished--that had been the right thing for me, not what this man
with his jutting nose offered me because of his interest. (221)

Proud of his career as an impostor, he will continue to make his way
on his own terms, confident that he will eventually be recognized for
his true nobility by the one who first betrayed him. Here Felix's
confidence reflects Mann's, for Mann wrote Kahler on 10 September
1949, "It's really curious that a life of playing games and dreaming can--if only you
go on with it for long enough--lead to your being treated like royalty" (qtd. in
Hayman 1995: 564).

In Book Three, Chapter III, Mann introduces the Marquis de
Venosta, christened Louis, a young man of about Felix's age (225).
Son of the chamberlain to the Grand Duke of Luxemburg, Venosta is
studying painting at the *Académie des Beaux Arts*. He dines at the
hotel once or twice a week, always choosing Felix's station. Like
everyone else charmed by Felix, Venosta soon establishes the
convention that their conversation will ignore their class differences.
That suits Felix just fine, for he believes that only the "accident of
wealth" determines who shall be master and who shall be servant (224).
Felix soon discerns that the Marquis de Venosta has no aim in life
other than to be catered to by everyone, including his mistress Zaza,
who sometimes accompanies him at dinner.

Felix has sublet a room to store the evening wear in which he
dresses on his nights off. It pleases him to be taken for a person of
prominence as he dines in an elegant restaurant before mingling with
high society at the theater (230). One evening he dines in "the attractive
roof garden of the Grand Hotel des Ambassadeurs on the boulevard Saint-Germain",
intending then to take in his favorite opera, *Faust* (231). Perhaps only
a Faust would serve as his role model? Having written of his
anticipation, Felix then adds: "That, however, was not to be. Fate had
something quite different and far more significant in store for me that evening". His
statement captures the idea that has always driven him, that he is
destined to experience the transformative moment.

Lifting his eyes to study the other diners, he spies Venosta,
who disbelieves his eyes until Felix smiles. Oblivious to Felix's
pretense, Venosta asks to join him and is cordially received; having
finished his meal Venosta talks and drinks while Felix has his. Thus
begins a conversation that consumes "four bottles of Lafite" (252). The
topic: Venosta's father and mother, a daughter of "German nobility"
(226), fearing that he will marry his mistress, have ordered him to take
a year-long world tour, hoping that a lengthy separation will wreck the

relationship. Gradually, Venosta unfolds his plan: Felix is to impersonate him on the tour, while he remains in Paris with his Zaza. Having anticipated the offer, Felix allows himself to be persuaded, then, ever the impostor, educates Venosta about the many tactics necessary to make the plan work. At the end of the evening Venosta drunkenly addresses Felix, *"Bonne nuit, à tanôt, monsieur le marquis"* (252). Felix writes, "I heard this style of address for the first time from his lips, and I shivered with joy at the thought of the equality of seeming and being which life was granting me, of the appearance it was now appropriately adding to the substance".

Mann had resumed work on the Krull manuscript at his home in Pacific Palisades, California, in January 1951. At first his subject matter, Felix's introduction to hotel life in Paris and his involvement with Diane Philibert, excited him, for he wrote on 22 March 1951, "The present erotic chapter apotheosizing the young man occupies me powerfully and urges me on" (qtd. in Heilbut 1996: 559). But within a month he was bored, for on 23 April 1951, Mann wrote Erich Kahler-- apropos of the recent death of Kahler's mother and of "the totally unique" shock he felt when his mother died--that he was continuing "the Krull memoirs, of which there is already a sizable heap of manuscript" then concluded, "But I doubt whether mood and strength will be sufficient under the present circumstances" (Winston 1975: 156, 158). The subject matter to which Mann referred was the waiter chapter. Nevertheless, in May he had, according to Prater (1995: 447), another chapter in mind. Presumably he wrote it before starting out for Europe on 4 July; presumably it was the chapter in which Felix becomes involved with Venosta. That he was not in the mood to push the story forward then is strongly suggested by the lack of any indication that he worked on any new material while in Europe. Instead, in September he rewrote the chapter involving Eleanor Twentyman and Lord Straithbogie (Hayman 1995: 588). He must have remained dissatisfied with it, for he afterwards deleted it from his manuscript, restoring it only at his daughter Erika's recommendation in January 1954 (Prater 1995: 482).[4]

On the return trip to California, Mann and Katja visited their youngest daughter Elisabeth Mann-Borgese in Chicago (Hayman 1995: 57). Subjected to one of those sight-seeing tours imposed upon visiting relatives, Mann was agreeably surprised. He wrote Hermann Hesse:

> Chicago has an outstanding museum of natural history, which we visited not once but, at my wish, twice. It contains quite graphic displays of the beginnings of organic life--in the sea, when the earth was still without form and void--the whole animal kingdom,

> the likeness and life of early man (reconstructed on the basis of discovered skeletons). I shall never forget the group of Neanderthal men (whose type marks the end of a line of development) in their caves and the devout, crouching, primeval artists who, using paints made from plants, cover the cliff walls with animal pictures, probably for magical purposes. I was completely fascinated. There is a peculiar sympathy that warms and enchants one on seeing these faces. (qtd. in Bürgin 1969: 239)

The cosmic view inspired by his visits to the Field Museum was to play a crucial role in the remainder of Mann's fiction.

In his introduction of the Venosta-Krull exchange of identities, Mann had had the Marquis inform Felix that his impersonation would take him first to Lisbon, there to board the *Cap Arcona* for Argentina (248). Around 5 November 1951 Mann began the chapter detailing Felix's trip by train to the Portuguese capital (Hayman 1995: 590). The train having left at six in the evening, Felix soon enters the dining car, to be seated across from a "middle-aged gentleman of fragile appearance" (259), whose most remarkable feature is his "starlike-eyes", which continually capture Felix's notice throughout the long quasi-lecture to which he is to be subjected. Nearly the first phrase that the man utters is a "description of the earth as a star" (261); that, "combined with the quality of his eyes," Felix confesses, "made a strange impression on me". Both the appearance and the utterance of the man introduce him as one who sees from the perspective of a star, that is to say, he studies the universe in its passage through eternity. Soon enough, the man introduces himself: Professor Antonio José Kuckuck, "Paleontologist and Director of the Museum of Natural History in Lisbon" (264). Felix simply introduces himself as "Venosta", but Kuckuck, polyhistor that he is, immediately places him as the Marquis, then places him on the Venosta family tree. Felix replies, "I feel free to say, *monsieur le professeur*,[...]that I have been fortunate in my place at table". Knowing that Venosta's mother came from Gotha, near his own German birthplace, Kuckuck assumes that Felix speaks German.

Changing languages prompts Kuckuck to introduce his background. Now fifty-seven, he has lived in Portugal for twenty-five years, having married "a child of the country--*née* da Cruz", of "ancient Portuguese stock" (265). Earlier he had spoken of the many racial groups, including the Negro, that have contributed to the formation of the Portuguese blood stock (262). In its racial characteristics, then, the Kuckuck marriage is similar to the marriage between Mann's father and mother, *née* da Silva-Bruhns. Kuckuck also mentions that he has a daughter, "Zouzou", a sound so similar to "Zaza" that Felix pricks up his ears. For if he is truly Venosta, then he should have a Zaza. His excitement is spurred on by the revelation that Kuckuck's daughter's Christian name is Susanna (265), Apocryphally-famed for her virtue.

Kuckuck then turns from the domestic to the cosmic. After he had written Kuckuck's expatiation on space and time, Mann wrote Paul Amann a précis on 23 December 1951:

> I have written all sorts of additions to the Krull memoirs, but I am always in peril of falling into a "Faustian" sprawl and losing control of the form. Thus I bring the hero, who is an amorist, into contact with the idea of Being itself, which perhaps is only an episode between Nothingness and Nothingness--as life on earth is only an incident with beginning and end, since the inhabitability of a planet is limited. At the same time all things pass imperceptibly into one another: Man into the animal realm, the latter into the vegetable realm, organic into inorganic being, the material into the immaterial, into scarcely-yet-being and into non-being, without space and time. Primal creation: How and when did the first vibration of being (electromagnetic or whatever) appear in the void? This is the true primal creation, the first newness. The second is that addition to the inorganic which we call life--something added without any addition of matter. A third addition in the realm of the organic and animal is the human element. Transition is conserved, something indefinable comes in, as when the turning point to "life" was reached. Love, understood as a sensual stirring in the face of the transitory quality of Being--not only of life, not only of man. And Being itself, then, perhaps an evocation by love out of the void?--But all this must strike you as incomprehensible gibberish. (Winston 1971: 634-35)

On 19 April 1953 Mann wrote Lavinia Mazzucchetti, "I am close to seventy-eight, feel my strength slowly ebbing away, and think about death a great deal. Though it has always been on my mind" (Winston 1971: 653). Surely the fascination for natural processes he reveals in these letters and in the Kuckuck chapters reveals a mind preparing itself for extinction. Facing the breakdown of his individual system, he sought an all-encompassing system to which his transitory presence had contributed. In other words, he yearned for original unity.

Yet even as Mann was desperately trying to push the Krull memoir forward, he was still expressing his fear of not being able to finish it. He wrote to Hermann Kesten on 20 November 1951, "The end is a great way off. I often doubt whether I shall be able to dredge up the necessary mood to carry through with the book" (qtd. in Bürgin 1969: 239). To Kahler, on 2 January 1952, he wrote,

> with the continuation of the *Krull* I have once more burdened myself with something whose demands, in whimsicality and inventiveness, go beyond my years, I fear. At the same time I am again being visited by the tendency to make everything I touch, even something so light, degenerate into the "Faustian" mode and turn into a pilgrimage through infinity. (Winston 1971: 164)

By 18 January 1952 the train chapter was finally finished, though Mann, in Hayman's words, "didn't feel proud as he usually did on completing a chapter" (592).

Even so, Mann continued with Krull's adventures among the Kuckucks, comprising Chapters VI and VII of Book Three. Chapter VI begins with Felix's description of his experience on the train after his conversation with Kuckuck. Attributing his jitteriness to both the excitement generated by Kuckuck's revelations and "six or eight demitasses of mocha" (278), Felix confesses that he did not enjoy his customary sound sleep, that regression to the oceanic feeling in which he had always exulted. Instead he has a lengthy dream, which presents the choice between existence and extinction that he must make. He dreams that he is riding on the skeleton of a tapir, his dreamwork depending on Kuckuck's citation of the tapir as the evolutionary ancestor of the horse (265). That he rides a skeleton acknowledges Kuckuck's theme that everything between Nothingness and Nothingness is transitory, first evolving, then devolving. The route that the tapir takes is "along the Milky Way" (278), which is really milk for it splashes upon his mount's hoofs. That is to say, that Felix, if only in his dreams, accepts the conventional view of Nature as Mother. Along the way people, apparently Portuguese, crowd both flanks. One young woman, apparently Zouzou or maybe Zaza, shouts, "*Voilà le voyageur curieux!*" (279). Felix tries to rein in his mount, so that he can talk to her about her own evolutionary ancestor (270). Instead, the tapir bucks him off into the milk, to "the derisive laughter" of all the crowd. Then, having prophesied the perils that Portugal will present for the dreamer, the dream ends. Felix must choose: Either accept Kuckuck's agnostic view of evolution-devolution or retain the view developed in infancy that drive satisfaction is the only goal, both of which amount to the same option. Or he must develop the view that the introduction of human self-awareness inaugurates a phase of cosmic development that supersedes the earlier views.

Felix interprets the dream merely "as a reminder that I had not yet learned to ride and must learn to without delay if I was to maintain my position as a young man of family", that is to say, of nobility. As a hedonistic impostor, he glories in his sumptuous suite in Lisbon's Savoy Palace Hotel (280). But he fails to ponder certain fixtures whose significance could awaken his self-awareness. There is on one wall "a tapestry representing a legendary rape" (281), and there is a

> cabinet with glass doors containing delightful porcelain figurines of cavaliers contorted into gallant postures, and ladies in crinolines, one of whom had suffered a tear in her dress so that the roundest part of her person was gleamingly revealed, to her great embarrassment as she looked back at it. (281-82)

These fixtures no doubt incite his behavior as an "amorist". But if he paused to ponder the "pendulum clock" (281) in another cabinet, he might be confronted with Kuckuck's starry view. Felix does seem to regard the fruit basket provided by the management as a cornucopia, for he freshens up from the skin out, eats a hearty dinner, and strides forth to see Lisbon. Where should his feet take him but to a café table adjacent to that of Senhora Kuckuck, Susanna (aka Zouzou), and Dom Miguel Hurtado, Professor Kuckuck's associate? A classic case of the accidental encounter. After contorting himself as a cavalier, Felix returns to the hotel with a luncheon invitation for the following day and with designs on both daughter and her "proud, ancient Iberian mother" (297).

In Chapter VII Felix decribes his visit to Kuckuck's museum, arranged to occur before the luncheon. The tour is basically a reprise of Mann's descriptions of his tour of the Field Museum, even including the tableau of the Neanderthalers (305). Felix does reveal that he still thinks of Kuckuck's evolution-devolution as the "forms that had poured uninterruptedly from Nature's womb" (300). And he says that, as he was impressed by the humanity displayed by the Neanderthalers, so is he equally thrilled by the cave man--the first artist?--making his figures of animals and men on the wall of the cave (305-06). But then the anticipation of luncheon impels him to address Professor Kuckuck with a period recalling his first impression on the train:

> Now[...]reluctant though I am to leave, we must not on any account keep Senhora Kuckuck and Mademoiselle Zouzou waiting. Mother and daughter--there is something thrilling about that, too. Very often great charm is to be found in brother and sister. But mother and daughter, I feel free to say, even though I

> may sound a trifle feverish, mother and daughter represent the
> most enchanting double image on this star. (307-08)[5]

Mann had hoped to complete Felix's adventures in Lisbon, follow them with his trip to Argentina, then publish the entire manuscript. At this point, though, he was in agony over his dilemma; he wrote in his daybook for 3 and 4 April 1952, "If I give up--and I must, I believe--what will take its place?" (qtd. in Hayman 1995: 592). The same month he sent Agnes Meyer a copy of the Venosta chapter, confessing, "I've burdened myself with something which is in no way[...] suitable to my age, and I often wonder whether I'd not do better to break off and leave it as an extended fragment" (qtd. in Prater 1995: 453). He was telling himself that his reluctance to go on with the Krull manuscript resulted from his feeling that its subject matter was too trivial to be his final work. But there may have been enough warning from his unconscious for him to intuit that the subject matter was so serious that he feared to confront its conclusion.

Notes to *Confessions of Felix Krull: Confidence Man.*

[1]Entitling her study *Ars amandi* Ursula W. Schneider studies "The Erotic of Extremes in Thomas Mann and Marguerite Duras". In her introduction she writes:

> If eroticism in Mann or Duras does not lead directly to the death
> of one of its victims, it is frequently accompanied by either
> narcissism, voyeurism, and incest, or by fetishism and sado-
> masochism. Homosexuality and lesbianism are included as well in
> the so-called darker sides of love, which are sometimes gathered
> under the more imposing title of "ars amandi". (1995: 5)

Could it be that Mann has Stürzli, who immediately classifies Felix as a boy-toy, create a portmanteau word from *"ars amandi"* for Felix's new name? Thus when Diane Philibert asks in the elevator, "The new Armand, if I am not mistaken" and Felix replies "At your service", she feels her incestuous desire aroused not only by his body but also by his name.

[2]On earlier occasions I have attributed the "oceanic feeling" to Mann's protagonist. In a recent article Lubich has discovered that experience in *The Confessions*: "Felix Krull, the *Glückskind*, repeatedly recaptures this pre-oedipal *unio mystica* with the maternal body in his exuberant embrace of *Frau Welt* cradling himself in her lap of sensuous mysteries and material luxuries" (2002: 204).

[3]Heilbut (1996: 558-65) argues that in Diane Philibert's voice Mann makes a full confession of his lifelong homoerotic attraction to the Hermes-type. He further asserts that Mann "remained enough of a bourgeois to find it 'incomprehensible' that something so tawdry should provide 'the foundation of artistic endeavor'" (1996: 558). This interpretation is not in conflict with Bergler's theory that the writer retains his creativity as long as he can "convince his inner conscience that he is *not interested*

in his original wish [to recapture the denied breast], *but only in the defense*" (1949: 189). Bergler writes: "Every analysis of homosexuals (the writer has analyzed dozens of them) confirms the fact that behind their frantic chase after the male organ the disappointing breast is hidden" (1949: 215). Since the male organ is a substitute, Mann, while confessing that "the temptation of manly youth[...]cannot be surpassed in the world" (qtd. in Heilbut 1996: 558), unconsciously knew that to succumb to the temptation would destroy his creativity. There is no unequivocal evidence that he ever did anything but look. On 14 July 1950 he wrote in his journal of his infatuation for the waiter Franzl, "Perhaps it is already over, and it will probably be a relief--the return to work as substitute for happiness. That is how it must be. It is the condition (and the origin?) of all genius" (qtd. in Hayman 1995: 574; parenthesis in orig.).

[4]At first Mann devoted a full chapter to the Twentyman family, but it was deleted from the novel at some point, being published separately in 1957 (Winston 1971: 662fn2). Mann not only deleted the Lord Straithbogie episode but also destroyed it. He wrote the Chapter 2 of Book Three that was published in *The Confessions* in March 1954 (Winston 1971: 663fn3).

[5]Mann had not exhausted his fascination for what he had glimpsed in the Field Museum. In July 1952, he interrupted his work on *The Black Swan* to write a five-minute presentation for the popular CBS television series *This I Believe*, *"Lob der Vergänglichkeit"* ("In Praise of the Transitory"). Prater provides its summary:

> Earth, insignificant and peripheral to the wider scheme of the universe, had witnessed a three-fold creation--first, that of cosmic existence from the original chaos, then the awakening of life from the inorganic, and finally the development of human life from the animal. All must be transitory, with a beginning and an inevitable end, and human life could be an episode only brief on the time-scale of aeons so far known; yet man's very awareness of this transitoriness gave him the restless energy and the power to transform the transient into the imperishable. Science might reduce it all to relative insignificance: for himself, he firmly believed that life on earth held a deep meaning, and that man was the ultimate purpose of the three-fold creation--"a great experiment...any failure of which, through the fault of man, would represent the failure of creation itself, its negation. This may or may not be so--but it would be well for man to conduct himself as if it were so". (1995: 452-53)

The Black Swan

Katja Mann said that one day--22 March 1952, Hayman says (1995: 592)--she and her husband were talking about a female friend who, though having reached a certain age, had not yet entered menopause. Katja said, "That worries me a little. It could be something pathological" (1975: 80). When Mann asked, "How do you mean," she replied, "I once knew a woman, Frau So-and-so. She was in love with a younger man. One day she came triumphantly to tell me her secret: 'Just imagine! I've begun menstruating again'. It turned out to be cancer of the uterus". Mann admitted being struck by the anecdote, saying, "You know, it's fascinating. It's so striking that I'm going to have to do something with it". He later described the anecdote as "an incident about which I heard and which gripped me through the horrible demonic nature which was expressed in it, and since it perplexed me, it stimulated me to productivity" (qtd. in Bürgin 1969: 249). Mann had the benefit of hindsight in the above statement, for he made it after he had finished *The Black Swan*. In a 16 May 1952 letter to Ida Herz, just as he was getting started on the novella, he was more deceptive and yet more revealing: "At the time I am quite tired but am working steadily, not just now on the Krull manuscript but rather on a novella, which, I think, will pleasantly interrupt the lengthy work. I should like to be finished with something again" (qtd. in Bürgin 1969: 240). Surely he feared the onset of writer's block if he attempted to continue with the Krull manuscript and needed to finish something to prove to himself that he could still fend it off?

There is a strong possibility that Mann was drawn to the anecdote because he sensed that it offered an opportunity to express something significant about his own life at the time. Heilbut (1996: 432-33) notes that, although Mann had been long and apparently faithfully married, he was still in his seventies getting crushes on young men that were consummated only by a feasting of the eyes. The story he would write, then, begins in a vein of classic humor, the depiction of an aged would-be lover who refuses to accept the restraints of age. As such, it contains self-mockery. But slowly, as any story inevitably must do, the story would return to the past, in this case to reveal that the protagonist's heterosexual yearning is motivated by an unconscious attempt to recapture the bliss of infancy. In the subtext Mann would imply that his homosexual yearning was motivated by the same attempt, yet he would offer this implication not to elicit sympathy from his reader but to express his inmost self. When

Mann speaks of "the horrible demonic nature", he is speaking of the lifelong feeling of being possessed that the original relationship imposes upon us. The nature of our relationship with mother determines the nature of our relationship with Mother Nature.

Mann finished *The Black Swan* on 18 March 1953 (Bürgin 1969: 246). It first appeared in serialized form in the "'Stuttgart journal *Merkur*" (Prater 1995: 471), then as a book in September 1953. His gift of the book to Karl Karényi with the dedication, "This small myth of Mother Nature" (Kerényi 1975: 23), stimulated his faithful correspondent to observe that Mann had once again taken up the "old skirmish with Mother Nature, of which we find an early trace in the caricature from 'Bilderbuch für artige Kinder'". Mann's dedication lays bare his intention; Karényi's observation provides the only suitable introduction for an analysis of Mann's accomplishment.

The German title *Die Betrogene*, 'The Deceived', gives the protagonist an unequivocal description, which is amplified by clues provided by her name, Rosalie von Tümmler. Although she is a Tümmler only by marriage, she merits the name, for she is a (tumbler)-pigeon, a dupe (Evans 1981: 864). Her given name is equally apt, for she has a rosy disposition. Two items offered on the first page by the narrator illustrate her propensity for seeing things through rose-colored glasses. At the beginning of the 1914-1918 war, her husband, a Lieutenant-Colonel, had been killed in "a perfectly senseless automobile accident" (3), yet the narrator reveals that his widow prefers to say that he died "on the field of honour". Apparently, too, she distorts her husband's actuality when she calls him her "cheerful husband, whose rather frequent strayings from the strict code of conjugal fidelity had been only the symptom of a superabundant vitality".

During her twenty years of marriage, Rosalie had lived in Duisburg where her husband was stationed. After her husband's death, Rosalie, "just turned forty", had moved to Düsseldorf "partly for the sake of the beautiful parks that are such a feature of the city (for Frau von Tümmler was a great lover of Nature)" (4; parenthesis in orig.). There, with her twenty-nine-year-old daughter Anna (6) and her seventeen-year-old son Eduard, Rosalie has lived for ten years in a "modest house[...]surrounded by a garden and equipped with rather outmoded but comfortable furniture". Her environment both outside and inside her house reflects the tenor of her thinking, *gemütlich* and *bourgeois*.

A "child of May" (6), Rosalie has just celebrated her fiftieth birthday around a "a flower-strewn table in an inn garden", where there had been many toasts, for Düsseldorf is a *Dusel-Dorf* (5). While she has retained her youthful figure and animation, her gray hair and age spots betray a body slightly past its prime. While she has many friends, she confides her most intimate thoughts only to her daughter, who, unmarried, still lives at home. Anna was born with a clubfoot, an accident of Nature which an operation in childhood failed to correct. Her disability barring her from physical activity with her peers, she turned, in compensation, to the solitary act of painting, using it to express her feeling that Nature did her an injustice. Her mother responds to one of her paintings entitled "Trees in Evening Wind":

> Are those cones and circles against the greyish-yellow background meant to represent trees--and that peculiar spiralling line the wind? Interesting, Anna, interesting. But, heavens above, child! adorable Nature--what you do to her! If only you would let your art offer something to the emotions just once[...]. (9)

In her effusion, Rosalie simply cannot understand that her daughter, by transforming Nature from the malleable to the mechanistic, is making a most emotional statement.

True to her name or, perhaps, to Saint Rosalie (Evans 1981: 964), Rosalie is fondest of "the Queen of Flowers" (18), swearing that the rose provides "the perfume of the gods". Such enthusiasm suggests that olfaction is the queen of her senses, hence that its sensitivity facilitates her recollection of earliest impressions. Accompanied by her reluctant daughter, Rosalie returns "time and again" (19) to a "declivity, a long depression in the ground, a shallow gorge, the bottom of which was thickly overgrown with jasmine and alder bushes, from which, on warm, humid days in June with a threat of thundershowers, fuming clouds of heated odour well up almost stupefyingly" (19). Led by her nose, Rosalie returns to the original declivity: "Child, child, how wonderful! It is the breath of Nature--it is!--her sweet, living breath, sun-warmed and drenched with moisture, deliciously wafted to us from her breast" (20). It seems incontrovertible that Rosalie's exuberance was born in the maternal environment.

Yet on another walk, in August, mother and daughter make a discovery of "something that had a suggestion of mockery" (22). Characteristically, Rosalie catches a whiff of the bad smell first. In two steps they come across excrement, perhaps animal, perhaps human, surrounded by swarming blowflies, rotting vegetation, and a decomposing small animal--in short, cell decomposition in a variety of forms. Following the scene in which the birth canal is celebrated as the location of life's origin, this scene offers the same location as the matrix of death. Thus it foreshadows Rosalie's fate.

As they return home, Anna confesses that she is suffering premenstrual tension (26), and Rosalie apologizes for being so out of tune with Nature that she has failed to remember her daughter's cycle. Admitting that she had never had menstrual pains, she characteristically elevates those pains and those of childbirth by viewing them as essential parts of Nature's perpetuation of life (27-30). Rosalie concludes by saying that she would gladly accept monthly pain if Nature would restore her capacity to conceive.

Rosalie has a specific reason for wishing her biological clock to be turned back. Her son Eduard is now learning English conversation from an American who tutors him at home and often remains for dinner. Ken Keaton, now about twenty-four, had taken his discharge from the U. S. Army in Europe, after recovering from a serious wound received in combat. His wound left him with one kidney and a small pension, but it did not damage his appearance of youthful vitality (43). Pretty soon, Rosalie's nose gets rosy when she anticipates Ken's entry into the room (46). As above, so below. But the nose may have been rosy all along because of menopause (Clayman 1989: vol. I 190).

In time the rosy nose becomes a full facial blush (63), giving Rosalie an appearance of "rejuvenescence" (76). The morning comes when Rosalie tells Anna that she is once again menstruating: "Kiss me, my darling child, call me blessed, as blessed I am, and, with me, praise the miraculous power of great, beneficent Nature!" (89). Then, with "her nose very red", she sinks back on her chaise longue, closing her eyes and smiling contentedly.

Since there is such a disparity in age between her beloved and herself, Rosalie spends a great deal of time discussing with her daughter the incestuous aspect of the affair of which she dreams (92-93). Such an aspect is all the more enticing for it strengthens her fantasy that the affair would constitute a return to the infant bliss of shared skin. To preclude Ken's thinking of her as a mother figure and therefore fending her off, she decides to use cosmetics (94), even toys with the idea of dyeing her hair (93). But bound by the conventions of her upbringing, she is so restrained in her flirting that poor Ken is utterly confused.[1]

A mild winter followed by an early spring convinces Rosalie that Nature is smiling on her endeavor (109), so she plans an outing to Holterhof Castle for her family, now augmented by Ken. Although the castle is a short trip south by street railway, Rosalie prefers to charter a motorboat, to go up the Rhine to the castle's park (116). She enjoys "the elemental charm of the journey by water" (119), no doubt having heard somewhere that mystical transformations are facilitated by a journey over water.

Once the tour of the castle begins, Rosalie and Ken, separated from Anna and Eduard, listen avidly to the guide as he lectures his party about its secret rooms. To illustrate his revelation the guide presses a hidden spring to slide aside a mirror, behind which is the entry to a "narrow circular staircase with latticed banisters":

> Immediately to the left, on a pedestal at its foot, stood an armless three-quarters torso of a man with a wreath of berries in his hair and kirtled with a spurious festoon of leaves; leaning back a little, he smiled down into space over his goat's beard, priapic and welcoming. (130)

The statue's stature portrays Priapus presenting. Ken and Rosalie dally until the other members of the tour move on, then press the spring to enter the forbidden space. Controlled by their passion, they become, in effect, diminutive, entering the forbidden space of the body. The fact that they are descending stairs furthers the illusion that they are entering the depths where transformations take place. Rosalie is instantly freed of all restraint and would sink down on the spot, while Ken leads her to an alcove presided over by "a carved Cupid" (133). Winged by the amorous archer, Ken would have shot his bolt right then and there, but Rosalie's nose intrudes:

> Ugh, it smells of death[...]. How sad, Ken my darling, that we have to be here amid this decay. It was in kind Nature's lap, fanned by her airs, in the sweet breath of jasmines and alders, that I dreamed it should be, it was there that I should have kissed you for the first time, and not in this grave! (133)

Here the original scene of the womb of jasmines and alders followed by the smelly scene of organic dissolution is repeated. Having descended to Cupid's cavern, they find it a "dead pleasure chamber". Through another door they re-enter the garden through a rusty gate.

That night Rosalie suffers severe hemorrhaging from the vagina. Summoned to her bed, her physician immediately hospitalizes her; sedated, she is subjected to an examination which confirms that she suffers from an inoperable cancer. The increased facial flushing that was taken as a sign of rejuvenescence may have been caused by the carcinoid syndrome (Clayman 1989: vol. I 234). The expert

diagnosis is that her tumor originated in the post-menopausal ovarian
cells that unaccountably become malignant in some women (139).
Awakening from sedation, Rosalie tells her daughter, "Anna, my child, he
hissed at me". To which Anna asks, "Who, dearest Mama?" Rosalie replies,
"The black swan". When the touring party had, the day before, debarked
at Holterhof, it had gone through the park to approach the castle,
surrounded by a moat. There appeared a pair of black swans,
celebrities because they were descendants of the original *rara avis*
(Evans 1981: 926), an exception to the natural order of things. Rosalie
had brought bread for them, but when Ken hands her the bread bag,
still warm from being in his pocket, she eats some of the bread (123),
angering one of the swans. Undoubtedly Rosalie's act has a sexual
significance, but it has a far more important analogical significance,
for like the swans Rosalie is, to her way of thinking, a rare bird, not
for her color, but for Nature's reactivation of her period, unheard of in
woman since the Biblical Sarah (Gen. 18:13-14), as Rosalie notes (80-
81). Awakening to the knowledge of her true situation, Rosalie now
understands why the swan hissed. Speaking for Mother Nature the
swan upbraids her for desiring the unnatural from Her. Rosalie tells
her daughter:

> Anna, never say that Nature deceived me, that she is sardonic and
> cruel. Do not rail at her, as I do not. I am loth to go away--from
> you all, from life with its spring. But how should there be spring
> without death? Indeed, death is a great instrument of life, and if
> for me it borrowed the guise of resurrection, of the joy of love,
> that was not a lie, but goodness and mercy. (140)

Rosalie's "failing whisper" is, "Nature--I have always loved her, and she--has been
loving to her child" (141). Here Mann is giving voice to his belief that the
introduction of love, "sensual stirring", represents the turning point in
cosmic evolution, a belief formulated after his visits to Chicago's
Field Museum and expressed in the letter to Paul Amann previously
cited. Completed when Mann was seventy-eight-years old, *The Black
Swan* reveals, as Kerényi writes, Mann's "old skirmish with Mother Nature"
(1975: 23), but its conclusion reveals Mann's honorable acceptance of
the terms set by the victress.

Note to *The Black Swan*

[1]Hayman complains that the "central conversation, which goes on for
eighteen pages, is between Rosalie and her clubfooted daughter, Anna, who tries to

discourage her mother from embarking on an affair, and the sequence reads rather like an exchange of letters in an epistolary novel" (1995: 601). Perhaps the conversation receives such prominence because it reflects the many conversations the conventional Mann had had with his impulsive self?

Confessions of Felix Krull: Confidence Man.
The Early Years.

By 11 April 1953 Mann was once again "seeking to find the specific 'tone of voice'" (qtd. in Bürgin 1969: 246) to resume the Krull manuscript. Chapter VIII begins with Felix's first visit to "Kuckuck Villa" (309). That it is enclosed in a garden perched on a rounded prominence overlooking Lisbon indicates that it will be the appropriate background for Felix's pastoral pursuit of Kuckuck's daughter Zouzou. Felix is also attracted to Kuckuck's wife Maria Pia, even, as he admits, he is terrified by the "animal quality" (310) that she projects. After lunch Felix and Dom Miguel, Kuckuck's assistant, escort the ladies through the public gardens "with their ponds and lakes, grottoes and open slopes" (315). In such a romantic setting, Felix attempts to convert tart-tongued Zouzou to an appreciation of eros. She finally becomes so agitated that her mother intervenes by substituting herself as Felix's promenading partner, a nice bit of foreshadowing by Mann. The exchange prompts Felix once more to become eloquent about "beauty in a double image, as childlike blossom and as regal maturity" (320).

The next chapter, IX, suggests that Mann's unconscious was not providing any ideas about Felix's further adventures with the "double image". The first eighteen pages contain a letter that Felix the impostor writes to Venosta's parents. Felix does mention the Kuckucks, but devotes almost all of the letter to the recital of his social successes: he had so impressed the Luxemberg diplomatic representative to Portugal that that worthy arranged for him an audience with the king, who was so impressed that he bestowed upon him "the Portuguese Order of the Red Lion, second class" (339). In the next six pages Felix describes his success in convincing Zouzou and her friends that he is an expert, albeit an awkward, tennis player, when he had never before picked up a racket. The last four pages contain a reply from Venosta's mother to the man posing as her son. It may be that Mann wrote the chapter merely in order to utilize his experience of a fifteen-minute "conversation *tête à tête*" with Pope Pius XII in April 1953 (qtd. in Burgin 1969: 246). Feeling himself a confidence man before the Pope, he must have enjoyed, if only briefly, describing Felix before the king.

When once again he took up the Krull task, Mann described a meeting between Felix and Zouzou every bit as sensual as that

between Felix and Diane Philibert. Chapter X does not take place in a
bedroom, as the Philibert scene had, but beside a tennis court--
excellent scene-setting, for the brisk serve-and-return on court has its
counterpart in the debate off court. The subject of the debate is
physical love; predictably, Felix holds for the affirmative. Yet Zouzou
holds her own against his eloquence, for, although she is not a
practitioner of love, she has apparently given a great deal of thought to
its anatomy. Consider this serve:

> What is the purpose of your melting words and melting glances.
> Something that is unspeakably laughable and absurd, both
> childish and repugnant. I say "unspeakably," but of course it is
> not at all unspeakable, and I shall put it into words. You want me
> to consent to our embracing, to agree that two creatures whom
> Nature has carefully and completely separated should embrace
> each other so that your mouth is pressed upon mine while our
> nostrils are crosswise and we breathe each other's breath. That's
> what you want, isn't it? A repulsive indecency and nothing else,
> but perverted into a pleasure by sensuality--that's the word for it,
> as I very well know; and the word means that swamp of
> impropriety into which all of you want to lure us so that we will
> go crazy and two civilized beings will behave like cannibals.
> (354)

Felix decides that the proper answer to the graphic is the
poetic:

> I beseech you, what a way to talk about love and its purpose!
> Love has no purpose, it neither wills nor thinks beyond itself, it is
> entirely itself and entirely inwoven in itself--don't scoff at
> "inwoven". I have already told you that I am intentionally using
> poetic words--and that simply means more seemly ones--in the
> name of love, for love is essentially seemly, and your harsh words
> far outdistance it in an area that remains alien to love, however
> familiar it may be with it. I ask you! What a way to talk of a kiss,
> the tenderest exchange in the world, silent and lovely as a flower!
> This unforeseen occurrence, happening quite by itself, the mutual
> discovery of two pairs of lips, beyond which emotion does not
> even dream of going, because it is in itself the incredibly blessed
> seal of union with another! (355)

Felix's echoing of St. Paul's tribute to caritas (1 Cor. 13) is probably
inadvertent, for his explanation of his use of the poetic implies his
profound unseriousness. He can aver that a kiss is just a kiss, for, as an

impostor, he cannot "woo Zouzou" with the aim of marriage. He might try to seduce her, but thinks the odds are against his success.

Although he desires her lips, he still fears her tongue. She serves again:

> Enwrapped and inwoven and the lovely flowery kiss! All sugar to catch flies, a way of talking us into small-boy nastiness! *Pfui*, the kiss--that tender exchange! It's the beginning, the proper beginning, *mais oui*, or rather, it is the whole thing, *toute la lyre*, and the very worst of it. And why? Because it is the skin that all of you have in mind when you say love, the bare skin of the body. The skin of the lips is tender, you're right there, so tender that the blood is right behind it, and that's the reason for this poetry about the mutual dscovery of pairs of lips: they in their tenderness want to go everywhere, and what you have in mind, all of you, is to lie naked with us, skin against skin, and teach us the absurd satisfaction that one miserable creature finds in savouring with lips and hands the moist surface of another. All of you do this without any feeling of shame at the pathetic ludicrousness of your behaviour and without giving thought--for it would spoil your game--to a couplet I once read in a book of spiritual instruction:
>
> However fair and smooth the skin,
>   Stench and corruption lie within. (356)

At the end of this occasion and during several later occasions, Felix is uncharacteristically dense, for, being victim of the Skin-Ego fantasy (cf. ch1n6,7), he cannot grasp that Zouzou is also its thrall.

Sometime before, Felix had "improved" some nude studies of Zaza done by Venosta by adding to them the ringlets of hair that Zouzou wears in front of her ears (317). Felix tells Zouzou that he has been inspired to sketch her, but refrains from telling her the character of his sketches. She must suspect their character, however, for on subsequent occasions she asks to see them. There comes an occasion when Felix has an exceptionally long opportunity to argue that eros and caritas are alike, in that in both, "one physically separate body ceases to be unpleasant to another" (364). Thus considered, a kiss and a handshake serve the same function, "the denial of the aversion of stranger for stranger, a secret sign of omnipresent love" (365). Out of pair-bonding evolve the other human bondings necessary for civilization.[1]

A moment later, Zouzou extends her hand and, when Felix lightly squeezes it, it squeezes back--then jerks away (366). That Zouzou has decided to equate handshaking with kissing is indicated by her heated request to see the drawings. When Felix protests that there has been no handy opportunity to present them, he receives a withering reply:

> Your lack of imagination in finding an opportunity[...]is pitiable. I see that I must help out your ineptitude. With a little more circumspection and better powers of observation you would know without my having to tell you that behind our house--in the little garden at the rear, you understand--there is a bench surrounded by oleander bushes, more of a bower really, where I like to sit after luncheon. By this time you might know that, but of course you don't, as I have occasionally said to myself while sitting there. With the slighest degree of imagination and enterprise you would long ago have found an opportunity when lunching with us, after coffee, to act as though you were going away and actually to go a little distance, and then to turn about and come to find me in the bower, so that you could deliver your handiwork to me. Astonishing, isn't it? An idea of genius? Or so it would seem to you. And so in the near future you will be kind enough to do this--will you? (366)

Felix fervently agrees, saying, "I give you my hand on it" (367). Zouzou replies, "Keep your hands to yourself! We can shake hands later on after we have returned home in your carriage. Meanwhile, there's no sense in pressing each other's hands all the time". Beginning with Zouzou's acknowledgement that lips and hands are partners in foreplay, the recurrent reference to hands underscores the "sensual stirring" that marks one of Mann's most adroit scenes.

Apparently Mann finished Chapter X in July 1953, but then experienced a creative slump "[d]espite Katja's encouragement" (Prater 1995: 476). A letter to Reisiger on 8 September describes the manuscript as moving "along only at a wearisome pace, interrupted by a hundred disturbances and spells of fatigue, basically by my no longer being in the mood to go on" (Winston 1971: 658). Mann must have had Chapter X in mind when he added, "Nevertheless, now and again I do manage to strike off some amusing things". That thought must have sustained him on those days in October when he could put down only twenty lines (Hayman 1995: 604).

Mann must have been desperate to end the Krull manuscript, however abrupt the conclusion might be. It is possible that his thoughts went back wistfully to the climactic scene in *The Magic Mountain*, the "Snow Vision", which directed that mammoth book toward a conclusion. At the start of Chapter XI Felix admits having second thoughts about seeking Zouzou in the bower. He attributes his reluctance to his fear of Zouzou's response to the drawings that purport to be of her, then offers another source of his reluctance,

> a distracting experience, a sombre celebration, that altered from one hour to the next my attitude toward the double image, reversing the emphasis by revealing one aspect, the mother, in the strongest light, blood-red in color, and putting the other, the enchanting daughter, a little in the shade. (368)

Mann had had Felix refer to mother and daughter as the double image before, but now the context of "the double image" invests mother with the persona of Demeter and daughter with that of Persephone.[2] These cult deities of the mystery religion located at Eleusis had been the subject of Mann's allusion in the "Snow Vision", in which Hans Castorp has a vision of going to the Underworld to confront death . The first hint that the two women have assumed a mythological dimension is when Felix perpetrates a pun, saying that Zouzou is now "a little in the shade". Literally, he means that the new context in which he sees Dona Kuckuck--the bull ring--inclines him to be more erotically aware of her than of her daughter. To refer to Zouzou as being in the shade, however, connects her with Persephone, who in myth became a shade living among the shades four months a year. Felix says,

> Very likely I use the metaphor of light and shade because the contrast between them plays so important a part in the bull ring-- the contrast, that is, between the sunny side and the shady side, with the shady side, where we people of distinction sat, having the preference, of course, while the small folk are banished into the sun. (368-69)

Felix is referring to the price distinction between *sol* seats and *sombra* seats, with the former the cheaper. But Mann, distinguishing between "sunny side" and "shady side", is alluding to those who see the *corrida* as a blood sport and those who see it as a ritual celebrating the inevitability of death, respectively. Mann, if not Felix, sits on the shady side between Kuckuck and Dona Maria Pia, who has announced her Demeter persona by wearing a "black *mantilha* over her high comb" (371), the veil being a signature accessory for that maternal divinity (374).[3]

In describing the first running of the program, Felix says of Dona Maria Pia,

> her bosom rose and fell faster and faster and, certain of being
> unobserved, I watched that face and the ill-controlled surging of
> that bosom more than I watched the sacrificial animal with the
> lance in his back, the ridiculously tiny wings, and the blood
> beginning to streak his sides. (375)

Now this is the first time that Felix has noticed the prominence of "that
bosom". It was absent from his description of her when he was
introduced to her at the café (289). His description of Dona Maria at
lunch the next day does not make a point about her breasts: "she had
chosen to appear in a different costume: a dress of very fine white moiré with a close-
fitting ruffled coat, narrow ruffled sleeves, and a black silk sash worn high under her
bosom" (309). Since he has always been proud of his keen observation
of women, why does he not consider that she has dressed to draw
global attention? Thereafter, his description of her on their several
walks is silent about her anatomy. But at the *corrida* Felix, once he
has noticed the tidal part of her anatomy, cannot keep his eyes off it:
"Back and forth I glanced, from her surging breast to the living statue of man and
animal, now rapidly dissolving, for more and more the stern and elemental person of
this woman seemed to me one with the game of blood below" (337).

After the *corrida* Felix must listen to Professor Kuckuck's
lecture on the rivalry between early Christianity and Roman
Mithraism, but he admits,

> I listened to all this with only half an ear, only in so far as it did
> not interfere with my absorption in the woman whose image and
> being had been so vastly enhanced by the folk festival, who had,
> as it were, been truly and completely herself for the first time,
> ripe for observation. Her bosom was now at rest. I longed to see it
> surge again. (379)

The following day, Felix has lunch with the Kuckucks, during
which Professor Kuckuck continues his lecture, drawing in passing a
connection between the Christian sacrament of communion and the
corrida, in that both have to do with "the god's blood" (379). Bored but
wondering about the effect of Professor Kuckuck's words on a certain
anatomy, Felix says, "I looked at the lady of the house, curious to see whether or
not her bosom was at rest" (379-80). Not a surge in sight.

After lunch Felix initiates his plan to visit Zouzou in her
bower. Taking care not to disturb Dona Kuckuck's siesta, he quietly
enters the rear garden. His attempt to make small talk is tartly rejected,
for Zouzou lets him know that she had watched him ogling her mother
at the *corrida*, then demands, "But to the point, marquis! Where are my
drawings?" (381). Felix hands them to her, sits down stiffly beside her

to observe her reaction. The instant that Zouzou looks at "her own sweet nakedness" (381) she blushes violently, then springs up, tearing the drawings to pieces, allowing them to flutter to the ground. Felix observes her next reaction closely: "she stared for an instant with a bewildered expression at the scraps of paper lying on the ground". While she had been deeply shamed by seeing herself stripped down to skin before the voyeur's eye, she is now terrified by the picture of a fragmented skin presented by the scattered scraps. No longer the tough-skinned individual (Anzieu's "narcissistic variant"), Zouzou feels the skin-neediness that she has always repressed. She wilts, sinks down, "burie[s] her glowing face on [Felix's] breast", regresses to infancy: "she gave little noiseless sighs that were nevertheless clearly perceptible, and at the same time-- and this was most touching of all--she kept up a rhythmic hammering against my shoulder with her little fist, the left one" (381-82). When Felix kisses her, she returns in kind. It was just such a regression that she had feared when she referred to kissing lovers as "cannibals" (354), intuiting what Freud was to state, that the first of the three stages of human development "is the oral or, as it might be called, cannibalistic" (*Three* 200).

Although Felix makes no interpretation of what he has just seen, surely he is convinced that it is his artistic creativity, his persistent eloquence, which has brought about "her conversion to love" (382). His next sentence reveals that the similarity between writing and wooing is on his mind, for he uses a literary term, "peripeteia", 'a reversal of fortune', to describe what happens next.

Before them stands Zouzou's mother, whose facial features Felix describes as he has so often: "we looked up at the august lady, at her large, pale countenance, jet earrings quivering on either side, at the severe mouth, widened nostrils, and stormy brows" (382). Felix makes an unexpected confession to his reader: "I ask you to believe that I was less cast down by this maternal apparition than one might have thought. However unexpected her appearance, it seemed fitting and necessary, as though she had been summoned, and in my natural confusion there was an element of joy". Literally understood, "maternal apparition" means Zouzou's mother's appearance, a phenomenon that both Felix and Zouzou see, but psychologically understood, the phrase means that Felix alone unconsciously sees in Zouzou's mother's "unexpected[...]appearance" the reappearance of the fantasy figure of the denying mother--the Return of the Repressed. Felix as much as admits that he has all his life both feared and longed for her return.

In Mann's fiction the Terrible Mother has always resembled Medusa, aka the Gorgon, and so Felix has frequently noted in Dona

Kuckuck's physiognomy the details that, in combination, reveal her archetypal identity. Felix's frequent references to Dona Kuckuck as "regal" (290, 319, 377), "royal" (310), "majesty" (310, 311), "queenly" (344), and "august" (358, 375, 382) and his impression that she towers over other people (310, 320) argue that from the start he unconsciously attributes a mythic magnitude to her. When she is with Zouzou he tends to think of her as Demeter. But when her given name, Maria Pia da Cruz, is mentioned he seems to regard her as the Madonna. Since Felix notes that her upper lip is "darkened by the faintest shadow of a moustache" (290), he may be reminded--as Lubich suggests (2002: 208)--of "the *Venus Barbata*, the 'bearded Venus',[...]the androgynous archetype of the Magna Mater", though probably her hirsuteness is the manifestation of a Gorgon gene. And no doubt when he is swayed by the surging bosom he sees her as Venus Genetrix. At any rate when Dona Kuckuck confronts Felix in the garden it becomes clear that the Gorgon has driven the other myths out of his mind.

When Felix attempts to talk his way out of his predicament, he is rebuffed: "'silence!' the lady commanded in her marvellously sonorous, slightly hoarse voice". From his first meeting with Dona Kuckuck Felix has been moved by her voice. At that time he refers to it as an "agreeable, husky contralto" (291); on subsequent occasions he applies to it the speech-tag "sonorous" (319, 320, 375). On other occasions he admits that Dona Kuckuck terrifies him (310, 323, 360), and it is likely that it is her voice that first inspires his terror. For if Feldman's argument is valid that the name *Gorgo* comes from the Sanskrit root denoting a "*gurg*ling, guttural sound, sometimes human, sometimes animal, perhaps closest to the *grrr* of a growling beast" (1965: 487; ital. in orig.), then Dona Kuckuck's voice hints at her true identity. Probably it is also her voice which causes Felix to attribute "an animal quality" to her person (310).

There are also aspects of Dona Kuckuck's physiogonomy that terrify Felix, some that he consciously registers and others that he does not. Her mien is somber (289), severe (289, 323, 374, 382), stern (289, 323, 360, 371), proud (297, 316 [twice], 360), and arrogant (310, 323). She has a "rather large face with its haughty, compressed lips, flaring nostrils, and two deep creases between her brows" (289). At the *corrida*, when Dona Kuckuck razzes a bull which prefers not to perform any more, Felix captures in one sentence many of the features he has noticed: "My august companion jumped up, whistled with startling shrillness, made a face at the coward, and emitted a sonorous thrill of disdainful laughter" (375). This is Medusa in fighting trim, putting on the stare that petrifies her enemy.

But where are her telltale snaky locks? From his first sight of Dona Kuckuck on, Felix is virtually mesmerized by her jet earrings, which sway (289), tremble (310), oscillate (372), and quiver (382). There is an ancient association between precious stones and snakes (Cirlot 1962: 155-56); given their proximity to Dona Kuckuck's hair, their color, and their constant motion (they do everything but hiss), the amber earrings (372) signify her snakiness.

Sending Susanna to her room, Dona Kuckuck orders Felix to follow her into the house. In the living-room, directing him to be silent, she upbraids him for acting like a child, even like an infant. Of his attempted seduction, she says:

> That was not choosing or acting like a man, but like an infant. Mature reason had to intervene before it was too late. Once when we were conversing you spoke to me about the graciousness of maturity and the graciousness with which it speaks of youth. To encounter it successfully requires, of course, a man's courage. If an agreeable youth only showed a man's courage instead of seeking satisfaction in childishness, he would not have run off like a drenched poodle, uncomforted, into the wide world. (383)

Sensing her invitation, Felix banishes the fearsome female form from his mind, intimately addresses her not as "Maria Pia" but simply as "Maria". He immediately finds himself in a "whirlwind of primordial forces [which] seized and bore me into the realm of ecstasy" (384). Maria exclaims "*Holé! Heho! Ahé!*" "in majestic jubliation" and in some apparently primordial language. Felix ends his story hinting at his triumph: "high and stormy, under my ardent caresses, stormier than at the Iberian game of blood, I saw the surging of that queenly bosom".

The last scene of *The Confessions* marks Mann's highest achievement as an ironist, if the description that Reed quotes from Plato's *Symposium* is used: the ironist "spends all his life in teasing mankind, and hiding his true intent" (1996: 8). The scene also proves that, to the very last, Mann maintained his mastery of narrative craft, for it leaves the reader asking the question, "What happens next?" So powerful is the human need for narrative closure that readers (and before them hearers) of stories have always been tempted to complete what appears to be a truncated tale.

Usually the conclusion supplied is adjudged plausible if it conforms to that which went before. But in Mann's fiction that which went before is often so fraught with irony that a conforming conclusion is impossible. Thus some critics, deliberately or unconsciously, supply a conclusion that conforms not with that which went before but with their own notions of probable human behavior. Heilman assumes, for example, that Senhora Kuckuck "will accept Felix as lover" (1964: 151). Stock seems to agree: asserting that Felix "does, after all, leave Zouzou unharmed" (1994: 215), he goes on to say that "the climactic experience of 'The Great Joy' which ends the tale of his 'early years' takes place in her mother's arms and does no harm at all".

Critics who rely on some version of psychoanalysis find that the last scene does conform to that which went before, on a subtextual level, so that the story, apparently truncated, is really complete. Detecting throughout Mann's canon of fiction an attraction sometimes to "spirit", sometimes to "nature", Kerényi sees Mann, in Krull's body, accepting the "jubilant cry--of Mother Nature!" (1975: 23). Pointing out that Mann, very early in his career, had, in *"Bilderbuch für artige Kinder"*, grotesquely caricatured Mother Nature, Kerényi sees the last scene of *The Confessions* as Mann's coming to terms with that pole of attraction. Kerényi's observation explains why Felix, having confessed his terror of Maria Kuckuck so often, so abruptly confesses his ardor for her. The transformation of the figure of Mother from hag to "queenly bosom" illustrates the type of grotesque-comic sublimation described by Annie Reich (cf. ch1n5).

Two subsequent psychoanalytic readings offer additional insights. McWilliams recognizes that although *The Confessions* ends abruptly the novel "represents the full circle of completeness" (1983: 378). Using Freud's Oedipal theory, he sees Professor Kuckuck as a father figure, who receives his patronymic in anticipation of his future as a cuckold (1983: 379). McWilliams sees the last scene as "the hero passionately clinging to the enormous bosom of the Portuguese-speaking mother" (1983: 379), thus realizing "a wish that was manifested in Mann's earliest works and one which, in no uncertain terms, threw its long shadow over all his writings". That is to say, Mann finally gives explicit voice to his incest fantasy. But beyond that fantasy lies the fantasy of returning to the breast, as the prominence of the "queenly bosom" in Felix's mind indicates. Of the last scene Lubich says, a little extravagantly:

> The mystical qualities of these panerotic emotions [experienced by Felix] have been compared to the "oceanic feeling" which psychoanalysis associates with the infant's blissful memories of intra- and extra-uterine union with the maternal body. Felix Krull, the *Glückskind*, repeatedly captures his pre-oedipal *unio mystica* with the maternal body in his exuberant embrace of *Frau Welt*,

cradling himself in her lap of sensuous mysteries and material
luxuries. (2002: 204)

There can be no doubt that the return to Mother/to the
Mother's return is the irony that haunts Mann's final scene. The
question is, why did it take so many years and so much agony to reach
that scene? From the very start of the Krull project, Mann realized that
if he wrote truthfully about himself he would place his career in peril.
His 1910 letter to Heinrich spelled out his apprehension: "I'm gathering,
noting, and studying for the confessions of the confidence man, which will probably
become my strangest work. Working on it surprises me sometimes at the things I'm
finding in myself" (Wysling 1998: 102). What he must have sensed, if
only as a glimmer, was that his orality and voyeurism, if
acknowledged, would cost him his creativity (Bergler 1949: 191).
Hence, he was compelled to continue the Krull project, in order to
"prove" to his superego again and again that he had overcome his "oral-
masochistic conflict" (Bergler 1949: 188). The next sentence in Mann's
letter to Heinrich acknowledges the strain of being an impostor: "it is
unhealthy work and not good for the nerves". Thus he fled the manuscript
several times, only to find himself compelled to resume his effort to
maintain the deception. The closer he came to the last scene of *The
Confessions* the more he experienced intimations of what its
completion would mean.

Courageously, regardless of the consequences, he continued.
In the Field Museum, having realized and accepted the looming event
of his physical extinction, he was driven to end his life's work in
fiction with a subtextual scene acknowledging his extinction as a
fictionist, his acquiescence to writer's block, even though the textual
scene can be read as merely a prelude to Krull's later adventures.
There is a detail in the last scene which, to my knowledge, has
escaped critical notice. When Maria leads him into the house, Felix is
surprisingly circumstantial, saying, "Thus we entered the living-room, from
which a door led into the dining-room. Behind the opposite door, which was not
entirely closed, there seemed to be a room of more intimate character. The austere
lady closed that door" (383). If the "room of more intimate character" is a
bedroom, would she not, if she intended seduction, open it competely
as an invitation? Alternatively, if it is a bedroom, her closing the door
would indicate that country matters are not to be contemplated. In
such case, "the surging of that queenly bosom" (384) must be caused not by
titillation, as Felix would have it, but by the spectacle of the death of
the "sacrificial animal", as it was "at the Iberian game of blood". It is more
likely that the mysterious room is a toilet, the place of cellular

extinction, whose door Mother Nature decorously closes for all of us-- at least for a while. The ambiguous floor plan brilliantly reveals that Mann remained the ironist to the end.

Notes to *Confessions of Felix Krull:*
Confidence Man. The Early Years.

[1] Mann wept as he worked out the role of love, "sensual stirring", in the evolution of life, for he believed it to be original (Hayman 1995: 604).

[2] Lubich has noted Mann's allusion to the Demeter-Persephone dyad in *Krull* (2002: 207-08). Lubich also notes that the characterization of Dona Maria Pia relies on aspects of the Great Mother and of Mary the Mother of God.

[3] Recall my many references to the veil in the chapter on *The Magic Mountain.*

VIII

Conclusion

By January 1954 Mann had decided to publish the existing Krull material as "Part One", telling Kahler (Winston 1975:171) and Kerényi (1975: 205) that his continuation of the story would depend upon a favorable response of its readers. Within a month he made a more candid admission:

> It is a volume of four hundred and forty-odd pages, "The First Part of the Memoirs," which is to appear in September--a fragment still, but a fragment the strange book will surely remain, even if time and mood might permit me to continue it for four hundred and forty pages further[...]. The most characteristic description which I can make of it is that it will be broken off, stopped, but never finished. (qtd. in Bürgin 1969: 251; ellipsis in orig.).

In mid-April he began correcting the proofs (Hayman 1995: 60), completing the job in May (Prater 1995: 484).

On 7 July he summed up his situation in a letter to his daughter Erika, who had, in early February checked the entire manuscript for discrepancies and needed revisions (Winston 1971: 662fn1):

> only recently I[...]was able to add a few amusing sidelights to the *Krull*, things that look as if they sprang from good humor, which was not the case--or at any rate, the good humor was extracted from ill humor. It is only too plain to me, I must admit, that after the "original" speech about love [Chapter X], nothing of any moment follows, and the end of the volume is rather slack and offhanded. My view of the whole thing is distinctly disgruntled, and I am steeling myself for its publication with some embarrassment. Certainly it's not a very dignified production. Is it right for a man to celebrate his eightieth birthday with such compromising jokes? What's wanted less than weary wantonness?--to put it in proverbial terms. Often I can't help thinking that it would have been better if I had departed from this

earth after the *Faustus*. That, after all, was a book of seriousness and a certain power, and would have been a neat finale to a life's labor, whereas now with *The Holy Sinner*, though I happen to love it, there begins an overhanging epilogue that probably would be better lacking. I have no impulse to go on spinning out the *Krull*, at least for the present, although it would be relatively easier than starting a new enterprise, as I am now trying to do[...]. But I don't really have any proper conception (as yet); I am studying a good many things, but know only vaguely what I want, and sometimes think I have completely forgotten how one goes about attacking and accomplishing a work. In other words, perhaps the talent, or the energy to work things out, has leaked away--a horrible feeling, for without work, that is, without active hope, I wouldn't know how to live. (Winston 1971: 667; my ellipses and interpolation)

On 12 August Mann admitted to Kahler that he had done "very little" since finishing "the Krull memoirs--as far as they go for the time being" (Winston 1971: 669). The report is cheery, compared to his attempt at self-analysis in a 6 September letter to Emil Preetorius:

my condition is not the best. A tormenting lack of energy has control of me, and my productive powers seem used up. After all, it is psychological, and I should give in to it as Hesse has done and settle myself to rest[...]. But I cannot understand this and do not know how to spend the day without working, struggling to accomplish something without being able to muster the vigor necessary to realize it. A tormenting situation[...]. And thus I am publishing the fragment grown into a novel, *Felix Krull*, as "The First Part of the Memoirs" and act as though the continuation of this jest were already under way, while not one word has been put on paper, and I know deep down that I shall never bring this absurdity to conclusion. (qtd. in Bürgin 1971: 254; ellipses in orig.)

On 16 March 1955 Mann wrote Agnes Meyer, "I cannot send you any news of *Krull*. On the continuation not one word has been put to paper" (Bürgin 1969:257).

In May 1955 Mann returned to Lübeck to accept honorary citizenship at the town hall and to give a reading in the opera house. That his visit was not just a return to a place but to a time is demonstrated by the fact that he requested "that the prelude to *Lohengrin* be played before the reading" (K. Mann 1975: 151). After a week in his hometown, he went for a rest to Travemünde, where he gave one of his last public utterances, an interview for *The New York Times*. In the place that was the cradle of his experience of the "oceanic feeling", he revealed that he was still conflicted about the mother whose presence/absence had inspired his entire career. Although he had confessed privately that he had succumbed to writer's block, he engaged in an elaborate subterfuge, telling the interviewer, "Well, in the second volume I shall put Krull through some matrimonial and penitentiary episodes ("Don't make the two sound so synonymous!" Frau Doktor warned him) and finally into a kind of retirement in London where he writes his memoirs" (Morton 1955: 33). His wife's collaboration in the subterfuge suggests that she intuited the true nature of his obstacle. Warming to the pretense, Mann volunteered his "most crucial reason for tackling 'Krull' again" : "As I'm getting on in age I've become more and more impatient for opportunities to make people laugh--to make them laugh constructively, if possible, that is to seduce them into amused self-recognition. My greatest joy now during a public reading is the sound of laughter". This statement manifests two of the defenses that he had learned to use against the return of the repressed. According to Bergler's thesis, he "fed" his audience when he read to them--if he was "mother", he did not need a mother (cf. ch1n10). According to Reich's thesis, he increasingly used the comic mode to diminish the threat that the return of the repressed presented (cf. ch1n5). Mann's defences had been breached--his return to Travemünde was to capitulate. The interview was aptly concluded by the arrival of an unidentified visitor who was to join the Manns for a promenade.

On 1 July 1955, in perhaps the last of his public utterances, Mann responded to an award given in the name of the Queen of the Netherlands. Praising the Dutch for their courage and condemning the Nazis for their inhumanity during the recent war, he thus concluded:

> The heroic, unbreakable resistance with which the people of Holland, in true union with their Royal House, withstood this evil was an inspiration to me and to all the world. It was a strong consolation to those of us Germans who at that time shunned our country because, in place of her former features, she wore a Gorgon's mask. (qtd. in E. Mann 1958: 78)

Having carried that mask in his soul all his life in an effort to understand his relationship with his mother, he must have thought it singularly appropriate to characterize his ambivalent relationship with his motherland.

Five weeks later, on 12 August 1955 Thomas Mann died of deep vein thrombosis, generally caused by sluggish blood flow, which occurs when a person has lain or sat still for long periods of time

(Clayman 1989: vol. II 981). His daughter Erika describes the death event:

> He had died in his sleep. The doctors had left him alone with my mother. He had not moved or altered the position of his body. Only, he had turned his head almost imperceptibly to one side and his expression had changed, as it might have done if he were dreaming. It was his "music face" that he now turned to my mother--the expression, absorbed and deeply attentive, with which he used to listen to his most familiar and beloved pieces. (1955: 114)

Perhaps Erika was alluding to her father's description of Hans Castorp's realization of the inevitablity of his death:

> At the thought there came over his face the expression it usually wore when he listened to music: a little dull, sleepy, and pious, his mouth half open, his head inclined toward the shoulder. (*The Magic Mountain* 219)

Perhaps she was not. She would be forgiven if she thought that he had turned his face only toward her mother.

Bibliography

Primary References

I. Thomas Mann

Original German titles are included in boldface.

Mann, Thomas. "Address at the Dedication of the Thomas Mann Collection at Yale University" (tr. H. T. Lowe-Porter). *Yale Review* 27 (1938): 702-11. **Rede bei der Eröffnung der Thomas Mann Library an der Yale University.**

--. "At the Prophet's". *Stories of Three Decades* (tr. H. T. Lowe-Porter). New York, NY: Knopf, 1936: 283-89. **Beim Propheten.**

--. *The Beloved Returns: Lotte in Weimar* (tr. H. T. Lowe-Porter). New York, NY: Knopf, 1940. **Lotte in Weimar.**

--. *"Das Bild der Mutter"*. Reprinted in *Gesammelte Werke* XI. Frankfurt: Fischer, 1974: 420-23. Hereafter referred to as *GW*.

--. *The Black Swan* (tr. Willard Trask). New York, NY: Knopf, 1954. **Die Betrogene.**

--. "The Blood of the Walsungs". *Stories of Three Decades* (tr. H. T. Lowe-Porter). New York, NY: Knopf, 1936: 297-319. **Wälsungenblut.**

--. *Buddenbrooks* (tr. H. T. Lowe-Porter). New York, NY: Knopf, 1964. **Buddenbrooks. Verfall einer Familie.**

--. *Confessions of Felix Krull: Confidence Man. The Early Years* (tr. Denver Lindley). New York, NY: Knopf, 1955. **Bekenntnisse des Hochstaplers Felix Krull. Der Memoiren erster Teil.**

--. "Conrad's 'The Secret Agent'". *Past Masters and Other Papers* (tr. H. T. Lowe-Porter). New York, NY: Knopf, 1933: 231-47. **Vorwort zu Joseph Conrads Roman Der Geheimagent.**

--. *Diaries, 1918-1939* (selected and foreword by Hermann Kesten; tr. Richard and Clara Winston). London: Clark, 1984. Selections from **Tagebücher, 1918-1921, 1933-1934, 1935-1936, 1937-1939** (ed. Peter de Mendelssohn). Frankfurt: Fischer, 1977-1980.

--. "The Dilettante". *Stories of Three Decades* (tr. H. T. Lowe-Porter). New York, NY: Knopf, 1936: 28-50. **Der Bajazzo.**

--. "Disillusionment". *Stories of Three Decades* (tr. H. T. Lowe-Porter). New York, NY: Knopf, 1936: 23-27. **Enttäuschung.**

--. *Doctor Faustus* (tr. H. T. Lowe-Porter). New York, NY: Knopf, 1948. **Doktor Faustus: Das Leben des Deutschen Tonsetzers Adrian Leverkühn, erzählt von einem Freunde.**

--. *"Die Einheit des Menschengeistes"* Reprinted in *GW*, X, 751-756.

--. *Die Entstehung des Doktor Faustus: Roman eines Romans*. Reprinted in *GW,* XI,
    145-301.

--. "Fantasy on Goethe". *Last Essays (*tr. Richard and Clara Winston and Tania and
    James Stern). New York, NY: Knopf, 1959: 97-140. **Phantasie über
    Goethe.**

--. "Felix Krull". *Stories of Three Decades* (tr. H. T. Lowe-Porter). New York, NY:
    Knopf, 1936. 340-77. **Bekenntnisse des Hochstaplers Felix Krull. Buch
    der Kindheit.**

--. *Fiorenza. Stories of Three Decades* (tr. H. T. Lowe-Porter). New York, NY:
    Knopf, 1936: 194-272. **Fiorenza.**

--. "Foreword". *Joseph and His Brothers* (tr. H. T. Lowe-Porter). New York, NY:
    Knopf, 1948: v-xiv. **Sechzehn Jahre. Zur amerikanischen Ausgabe von
    >Joseph und seine Brüder< in einem Bande.**

--. "Freud and the Future". *Essays of Three Decades (*tr. H. T. Lowe-Porter). New
    York, NY: Knopf, 1947: 411-28. **Freud und die Zukunft.**

--. "Freud's Position in the History of Modern Thought". *Past Masters and Other
    Papers* (tr. H. T. Lowe-Porter). New York, NY: Knopf, 1933: 165-98. **Die
    Stellung Freuds in der modernen Geistesgeschichte.**

--. "From Childhood Play to *Death in Venice". On Myself and other Princeton
    Lectures* (ed. James N. Bade). Frankfurt: Lang: 1997: 23-54. **Von
    Kinderspielen bis zum Tod in Venedig.**

--. "A Gleam". *Stories of Three Decades* (tr. H. T. Lowe-Porter). New York, NY:
    Knopf, 1936: 167-72. **Ein Glück.**

--. *"Gladius Dei". Stories of Three Decades* (tr. H. T. Lowe-Porter). New York, NY:
    Knopf, 1936: 181-93. **Gladius Dei.**

--. *The Holy Sinner.* (tr. H. T. Lowe-Porter). New York, NY: Knopf, 1951. **Der
    Erwählte.**

--."The Hungry". *Stories of Three Decades* (tr. H. T. Lowe-Porter). New York, NY:
    Knopf, 1936: 167-72. **Die Hungernden.**

--. "The Infant Prodigy". *Stories of Three Decades* (tr. H. T. Lowe-Porter). New
    York, NY: Knopf, 1936: 173-80. **Das Wunderkind.**

--. "Introduction". *Royal Highness*. London: Secker, 1940: v-x. **Vorwort zu einer
    amerikanischen Ausgabe von >Königliche Hoheit<.**

--. *Joseph and His Brothers* (tr. H. T. Lowe-Porter). New York, NY: Knopf, 1966.
    (References in the text are to the edition of 1948 containing all four
    volumes.) **Joseph und seine Brüder.**

--."Kinderspiele". *Das Spielzeug im Leben des Kindes* (ed. Paul Hildebrandt).

--. "Little Herr Friedemann". *Stories of Three Decades* (tr. H. T. Lowe-Porter). New
    York,NY: Knopf, 1936: 3-22. **Der kleine Herr Friedemann.**

--. *The Magic Mountain* (tr. H. T. Lowe-Porter). New York, NY: Knopf, 1965. **Der
    Zauberberg.**

--. *The Magic Mountain* (tr. John E.Woods). New York, NY: Knopf, 1995.

--. "The Making of *The Magic Mountain*", in *The Magic Mountain* (tr. H. T. Lowe-
    Porter). New York, NY: Vintage, 1969: 717-727. **Einführung in den
    >Zauberberg<. Für Studenten der Universität Princeton.**

--. "On Myself". *"On Myself" and Other Princeton Lectures: An Annotated Edition*
    (ed. James N. Bade; sec. rev. ed.). Frankfurt: Lang, 1997: 23-54. **Über mich
    selbst.** ("On Myself" consists of two lectures, "From Childhood Play to
    Death in Venice" and "On my own Work".)

--. "On my own Work". *On Myself" and Other Princeton Lectures: An Annotated Edition* (ed. James N. Bade; sec. rev. ed.). Frankfurt: Lang, 1997: 55-79. (The original text is without a title.) Reprinted in *GW*, XIII, 127-69.

--. "On Schiller". *Last Essays* (tr. Richard and Clara Winston and Tania and James Stern). New York, NY: Knopf, 1959: 3-96. **Versuch über Schiller. Zum 150. Todestag des Dichters--seinem Andenken in Liebe gewidmet.**

--. "Preface". *Stories of Three Decades* (tr. H. T. Lowe-Porter). New York,NY: Knopf, 1936: v-ix. The location of the German original is unknown (*GW*, XIII, 191 # 111).

--. *Royal Highness* (tr. A. Cecil Curtis). London: Secker, 1940. **Königliche Hoheit.**

--. *A Sketch of My Life* (tr. H. T. Lowe-Porter). New York, NY: Knopf, 1960. **Lebensabriss.**

--. "Sleep, Sweet Sleep". *Past Masters and other Papers* (tr. H. T. Lowe-Porter). New York: Knopf, 1933: 269-76. **Süsser Schlaf.**

--. *The Story of a Novel: The Genesis of Doctor Faustus* (tr. Richard and Clara Winston). New York, NY: Knopf, 1961. **Die Entstehung des Doktor Faust.**

--. "Sufferings and Greatness of Richard Wagner". *Essays of Three Decades* (tr. H. T. Lowe-Porter). New York, NY: Knopf, 1947: 307-352. **Leiden und Grosse Richard Wagners.**

--. "The Theme of the Joseph Novels". *Thomas Mann's Addresses Delivered at the Library of Congress, 1942-1949.* Washington, D.C.: Government Printing Office, 1963: 1-19. **Das Thema der Joseph-Romane.**

--. "Tobias Mindernickel'". *Stories of Three Decades* (tr. H. T. Lowe-Porter). New York, NY: Knopf., 1936: 51-57. **Tobias Mindernickel.**

--. "Tonio Kröger". *Stories of Three Decades* (tr. H. T. Lowe-Porter). New York, NY: Knopf, 1936: 85-132. **Tonio Kröger.**

--. *The Transposed Heads* (tr. H. T. Lowe-Porter). New York, NY: Knopf, 1941. **Die vertauschten Köpfe: Ein tragisches Reiseerlebnis.**

--. "Tristan". *Stories of Three Decades* (tr. H. T. Lowe-Porter). New York, NY: Knopf, 1936: 133-66. **Tristan.**

--. "A Vision". *Thomas Mann: Six Early Stories (*ed. Burton Pike; tr. Peter Constantine). Los Angeles, CA: Sun, 1997: 23-27. **Vision.**

--. "The Wardrobe". *Stories of Three Decades* (tr. H. T. Lowe-Porter). New York, NY: Knopf, 1936: 71-77. **Der Kleiderschrank.**

--. "A Weary Hour". *Stories of Three Decades* (tr. H. T. Lowe-Porter). New York, NY: Knopf, 1936: 290-96. **Schwere Stunde.**

--. "The Will to Happiness". *Thomas Mann: Six Early Stories (*ed. Burton Pike; tr. Peter Constantine). Los Angeles, CA: Sun, 1997: 73-97. **Der Wille zum Glück.**

--. "The Years of My Life". (tr. Heinz and Ruth Norden) *Harper's Magazine* 201 (1950): 250, 52, 54, 56, 58, 60, 62, 64. Excerpted from **Meine Zeit.**

II. Sigmund Freud

Freud, Sigmund. *Civilization and Its Discontents. The Standard Edition of the Complete Psychological Works of Sigmund Freud* (tr. and gen. ed. James

Strachey). Vol. 21. London: Hogarth, 1961: 59-145. Hereafter referred to as *SE*.

--. "Creative Writers and Day-Dreaming". *SE* Vol. 9: 142-53.

--. "Fragment of an Analysis of a Case of Hysteria". *SE* Vol. 7: 3-122.

--. *The Interpretation of Dreams*. *SE* Vol. 4: 1-338; Vol. 5: 339-565.

--. "Leonardo da Vinci and a Memory of his Childhood". *SE* Vol. 11: 59-137.

--. "Medusa's Head". *SE* Vol. 18: 273-74.

--. *Moses and Monotheism*. *SE*. Vol. 23. 3-137.

--. "Mourning and Melancholia". *SE* Vol. 14: 243-258.

--. *New Introductory Lectures on Psycho-analysis*. *SE* Vol. 22: 3-182.

--. *An Outline of Psycho-Analysis*. *SE* Vol. 23: 141-207.

--. "Screen Memories". *SE* Vol. 3: 303-23.

--. *Three Essays on the Theory of Sexuality*. *SE* Vol. 7: 125-245.

--. *Totem and Taboo*. *SE* Vol. 13: 1-161.

--. "The Uncanny". *SE* Vol. 17: 217-52.

Secondary References

Anon. 1975. *From the Land of the Scythians*. New York, NY: Graphic.

Anthony, E. James, and Therese Benedek. 1975. "Introduction" in Anthony, E. James, and Therese Benedek (eds). *Depression and Human Existence*. Boston, MA: Little.

Anzieu, Didier. 1989. *The Skin Ego* (tr. Chris Turner). New Haven, CT: Yale UP.

Armour, Robert A. 2001. *Gods and Myths of Ancient Egypt*. Sec. Ed. New York, NY: American U in Cairo P.

Bade, James N. 1978. *"Der Tod in Venedig* and *Felix Krull*: The Effect of the Interruption in the Composition of Thomas Mann's *Felix Krull* Caused by *Der Tod in Venedig"*. *Deutsche Vierteljahrsschrift für Literaturwissenschaft und Geistesgeschichte* 52: 271-78.

Baring, Anne, and Jules Cashford. 1993. *The Myth of the Goddess*. London: Penguin.

Barnes, Hazel E. 1974. "The Look of the Gorgon". *The Meddling Gods*. Lincoln, NE: U of Nebraska P: 3-51.

Barr, James. 1963. "Revelation" in Grant, Frederick C, and H. H. Rowley (eds) *Dictionary of the Bible*. Rev. Ed.. New York, NY: Scribner's: 847-49.

Beharriell, Frederick J. 1962. "Psychology in the Early Works of Thomas Mann" in *PMLA* 77: 149-55.

Berendsohn, Walter E. 1973. *Thomas Mann: Artist and Partisan in Troubled Times* (tr. and intro. George C. Buck). University, AL: U of Alabama P.

Bergler, Edmund. 1949. *The Basic Neurosis: Oral Regression and Psychic Masochism*. New York, NY: Grune.

Bergsten, Gunilla. 1969.*Thomas Mann's Doctor Faustus: The Sources and Structure of the Novel* (tr. Krishna Winston). Chicago, IL: U of Chicago P.

Berlin, Jeffrey B. 1992 . "Psychoanalysis, Freud, and Thomas Mann" in Berlin, Jeffrey B. (ed.) *Approaches to Teaching Mann's "Death in Venice"*. New York,NY: MLA: 105-18.

Bethel, John P. (ed.) 1951. *Webster's New Collegiate Dictionary*. Springfield, MA: Merriam.

Betteridge, Harold T. (ed.). 1958. *The New Cassell's German Dictionary*. New York, NY: Funk.

Bévenot, M., and Ralph Russell. 1953. "Christianity in Apostolic Times: Doctrine and Practice" in Orchard, Bernard (ed.) *A Catholic Commentary on Holy Scripture*. New York, NY: Nelson: 782-824.

Bialstocki, Jan. 1958. "Dürer, Albrecht" in Pallottino, Massimo (ed.) *Encyclopedia of World Art*, vol. 4. New York, NY: McGraw-Hill: 514-31.

Blissett, William. 1960. "Thomas Mann: The Last Wagnerite". *The Germanic Review* 35: 50-76.

Blumberg, David. 1990. "From Muted Chords to Maddening Cacophony: Music in *The Magic Mountain*" in Dowden, Stephen E. (ed.) *A Companion to Thomas Mann's The Magic Mountain*. Columbia, SC: Camden: 80-94.

Booth, Gotthard. 1979. *The Cancer Epidemic: Shadow of the Conquest of Nature*. New York: Mellen.

Brenner, Charles. 1974. *An Elementary Textbook of Psychoanalysis*. Garden City, NY: Anchor.

Bright, John. 1963. "Abraham" in Grant, Frederick and H. H. Rowley (eds) *Dictionary of the Bible*. Rev. Ed.. New York, NY: Scribner's: 5-6.

Brion, Marcel. 1960. *Pompeii and Hercvlanevm* (tr. John Rosenberg). New York, NY: Crown.

Bürgin, Hans, and Hans-Otto Mayer. 1969. *Thomas Mann: A Chronicle of His Life* (tr. Eugene Dobson). University, AL: U of Alabama P.

Caldwell, Richard. 1989. *The Origin of the Gods: A Psychoanalytic Study of Greek Theogonic Myth*. New York, NY: Oxford UP.

Campbell, Joseph. 1968. *The Masks of God: Creative Mythology*. vol. 4. New York, NY: Viking.

Cap, Biruta (ed.). 1993. *Thomas Mann-Félix Bertaux: Correspondence 1923-1948*. New York, NY: Lang.

Chadwick, Harold. 1963. "Mystery" in Grant, Frederick and H. H. Rowley (eds) *Dictionary of the Bible*. Rev. Ed.. New York, NY:Scribner's: 683.

Cirlot, J. E. 1962. *A Dictionary of Symbols* (tr. Jack Sage). New York, NY: Philosophical L.

Clayman, Charles B. (ed.). 1989. *The American Medical Association Home Medical Encyclopedia*. vols. I and II. New York, NY: Random,.

Collins, John J. 1987. "Apocalyptic" in Komonchak, Joseph A. et al (eds). *The New Dictionary of Theology*. Wilmington, DE: Glazier: 42-43.

Crick, Joyce. 1966. "Thomas Mann and Psychoanalysis: The Turning Point" in Manheim, Leonard, and Eleanor Manheim (eds) *Hidden Patterns: Studies in Psychoanalytic Literary Criticism*. New York, NY: MacMillan: 171-91.

Cullander, Cecil C. H. 1999. "Why Thomas Mann Wrote". *Virginia Quarterly Review* 75: 31-48.

Curme, George O.1960. *A Grammar of the German Language*. New York, NY: Ungar.

Dante Alighieri. 1950. *The Divine Comedy* (tr. John Carlyle, Thomas Okey, and Philip Wicksteed). New York, NY: Modern L.

De Caro, Stefano. 1994. *Il Museo Archeologico Nazionale di Napoli*. Naples: Electra.

Degener, Hermann A. L. 1935. *Wer ist's?* Tenth Edition. Berlin: Degener.

De Mendelssohn, Peter (ed.). 1974. *Briefe an Otto Grautoff, 1894-1901, und Ida Boy-Ed, 1903-1928*. Frankfurt: Fischer.

Deri, Susan. 1985. *Symbolism and Creativity*. New York, NY: International Universities P.

Dierks, Manfried. 1990. "Doctor Faustus and Recent Theories of Narcissism" in Lehnert, Herbert, and Peter C. Pfeiffer (eds) *Doctor Faustus: A Novel at the Margin of Modernism.* Columbia, SC: Camden: 33-54.

Dumoulié, Camille. 1995. "Medusa" in Brunel, Pierre (ed.) *Companion to Literary Myths, Heroes and Archetypes* (tr.Wendy Allatson, Judith Hayward, and Trista Selous). London: Routledge: 779-87.

Edelman, Sandra. 1998. *Turning the Gorgon.* Woodstock, CT: Spring,.

Ehrenzweig, Anton. 1967. *The Hidden Order of Art: A Study in the Psychology of Artistic Imagination.* Berkeley, CA: U of California P.

Eissler, Kurt Robert. 1963. *Goethe: A Psychoanalytic Study, 1785-1786.* Detroit, MI: Wayne State UP.

Elsaghe, Yahya. 2002. *"Lotte in Weimar"* in Robertson, Ritchie (ed.). *The Cambridge Companion to Thomas Mann.* Cambridge: Cambridge UP: 185-98.

Elworthy, Frederick T. 1970. *The Evil Eye: The Origins and Practices of Superstition.* New York, NY: Collier.

Evans, Ivor H. 1981. *Brewer's Dictionary of Phrase and Fable.* Centenary Ed., Rev. Ed. New York, NY: Harper.

Ezergailis, Inta Miske. 1975. *Male and Female: An Approach to Thomas Mann's Dialectic.* The Hague: Nijhoff.

Feldman, Thalia. 1965. "Gorgo and the Origins of Fear". *Arion* 4: 484-94.

Fellner, Rudolph. 1958. *Opera Themes and Plots.* New York, NY: Schuster.

Fetzer, John F. 1996. *Changing Perceptions of Thomas Mann's Doctor Faustus: Criticism 1947-1992.* Columbia, SC: Camden.

--. 1990. *Music, Love, Death and Mann's Doctor Faustus.* Columbia, SC: Camden.

Feuerlicht, Ignace. 1982. "Thomas Mann and Homoeroticism". *Germanic Review* 57: 89-97.

Frazer, Sir James George. 1958. *The Golden Bough: A Study in Magic and Religion.* Abridged Edition. New York, NY: Macmillan.

Fuller, B. A. G. 1945. *A History of Philosophy.* Rev. ed. vol. II. New York, NY: Holt.

Gilmour, S. MacLean. 1963. "Jesus Christ" in Grant, Frederick C. and H. H. Rowley (eds) *Dictionary of the Bible.* New York, NY: Scribner's: 477-96.

Goethe, Johann Wolfgang von. 1932. *Faust* (tr. George M. Priest*).* New York, NY: Covici.

--. 1974. *Dichtung und Wahrheit* (tr. John Oxenford and intro. Karl J.Weintraub). vols. 1 and 2. Chicago, IL: U of Chicago P.

Gottwald, Norman. 1963. "Lamentations, Book of" in Grant, Frederick C. and H. H. Rowley (eds) *Dictionary of the Bible.* New York, NY: Scribner's: 562.

Graves, Robert. 1957. *The Greek Myths.* vols. I and II. New York,NY: Braziller.

Gray, John. 1963. "Shiloh" in Grant, Frederick C. and H. H. Rowley (eds) *Dictionary of the Bible.* New York, NY: Scribner's: 907-08.

Greenacre, Phyllis. 1958. "The Relation of the Impostor to the Artist". *The Psychoanalytic Study of the Child* 13: 521-40.

Grimstad, Kirsten. 2002. *The Modern Revival of Gnosticism and Thomas Mann's Doktor Faustus.* Rochester, NY: Camden.

Gutheil, Emil A. 1951. *The Handbook of Dream Analysis.* New York, NY: Grove P.

Guthrie, W. K. C. 1951. *The Greeks and their Gods.* Boston, MA: Beacon.

Hamburger, Käte. 1988. "The Sense of Structure" in Ezergailis, Inta M (ed.) *Critical Essays on Thomas Mann.* Boston, MA: Hall: 58-77.

Hamilton, Edith. 1942. *Mythology: Timeless Tales of Gods and Heroes*. New York, NY: Mentor.

Hamilton, Nigel. 1979. *The Brothers Mann*. New Haven, CT: Yale UP.

Harewood, the Earl of. (ed.) 1976. *The New Kobbé's Complete Opera Book*. New York, NY: Putnam.

Harrison, Irving B. 1975. "On the Maternal Origins of Awe". *The Psychoanalytic Study of the Child* 30: 181-95.

Harrison, Jane. 1959. *Prolegomena to the Study of Greek Religion*. Cleveland, OH: World.

Hartwich, Wolf-Daniel. 2002. "Religion and Culture: *Joseph and his Brothers"* (tr. Ritchie Robertson) in Robertson, Ritchie (ed.) *The Cambridge Companion to Thomas Mann*. Cambridge: Cambridge UP: 151-67.

Hatfield, Henry. 1979. *From The Magic Mountain: Mann's Later Masterpieces*. Ithaca, NY: Cornell UP.

Hayman, Ronald. 1995. *Thomas Mann: A Biography*. New York, NY: Scribner's.

Heilbut, Anthony. 1996. *Thomas Mann: Eros and Literature*. New York, NY: Knopf.

Heilman, Robert B. 1964. "Variations on Picaresque (*Felix Krull*)" in Hatfield, Henry (ed.) *Thomas Mann: A Collection of Critical Essays*. Englewood Cliffs, NJ: Prentice: 133-54.

Heller, Erich. 1961. *Thomas Mann: The Ironic German*. New York, NY: World.

Hirschbach, Frank Donald. 1955. *The Arrow and the Lyre*. The Hague: Nijhoff.

Hoffman, Frederick J. 1957. *Freudianism and the Literary Mind*. Sec. Ed. Baton Rouge, LA: Louisiana State UP.

Hooke, S. H. 1963a. "Moon" in Grant, Frederick C. and H. H. Rowley (eds) *Dictionary of the Bible* (eds). New York, NY: Scribner's: 674.

--. 1963b. "Sarah" in Grant, Frederick C. and H. H. Rowley (eds) *Dictionary of the Bible*. New York, NY: Scribner's: 887.

Hutton, Edward. 1958. *Naples and Campania Revisited*. London: Hollis.

Izenberg, Gerald N. 2000. *Modernism and Masculinity: Mann, Wedekind, Kandinsky through World War I*. Chicago, IL: U of Chicago P.

Jantz, Harold. 1969. *The Mothers in Faust: The Myth of Time and Creativity*. Baltimore, MD: Johns Hopkins UP.

Jung, C. G. 1967. *Symbols of Transformation* (tr. R. F. C. Hull). Sec. Ed. Princeton, NJ: Princeton UP.

Johnson, Franklin P. 1968. *Lysippos*. New York, NY: Greenwood P.

Kaufman, Gershen. 1989. *The Psychology of Shame*. New York, NY: Springer.

Kaufmann, Fritz. 1973. *Thomas Mann: The World as Will and Representation*. New York, NY: Cooper.

Kayser, Wolfgang. 1963. *The Grotesque in Art and Literature* (tr. Ulrich Weisstein). Bloomington, IN: Indiana UP.

Kepler, T. S. 1963. "Book of Revelation" in Grant, Frederick C. and H. H. Rowley (eds) *Dictionary of the Bible*. New York, NY: Scribner's: 849-50.

Kerényi, Károly C. 1967. *Eleusis: Archetypal Image of Mother and Daughter* (tr. Ralph Manheim). New York, NY: Random.

--. 1951. *The Gods of the Greeks*. London: Thames.

--. 1963. "Kore". in Jung, C. G., and C. Kerényi .*Essays on a Science of Mythology* (tr. R. F. C. Hull. Rev. Ed. New York, NY: Harper.

--. (ed.). 1975. *Mythology and Humanism: The Correspondence of Thomas Mann and Karl Kerényi* (intro. Karl Kerényi and tr. Alexander Gelley). Ithaca, NY: Cornell UP.

Kesten, Hermann (ed.). 1984. *Thomas Mann Diaries 1918-1921, 1933-1939* (tr. Richard and Clara Winston). London: Clark.

Kierkegaard, Søren. *Either/Or* (tr. David F. Swenson and Lillian Marvin Swenson). Garden City, NY: Doubleday, 1959. Vols. 1 and 2.

Kinsley, David. 1986. *Hindu Goddesses: Visions of the Divine Feminine in the Hindu Religious Tradition*. Berkeley, CA: U of California P.

Kirchberger, Lida. 1960. "Thomas Mann's 'Tristan'". *Germanic Review* 35: 282-97.

Kirshner, Lewis A. 1990. Review of Anzieu (1989) in *International Journal of Psycho-Analysis* 71:543-46.

Kohut, Heinz. 1957. "'Death in Venice' by Thomas Mann: A Story about the Disintegration of Artistic Sublimation". *Psychoanalytic Quarterly* 26: 206-228.

Koopmann, Helmut. 1988. "The Decline of the West and the Ascent of the East: Thomas Mann, the Joseph Novels, and Spengler" in Ezergailis, Inta Miske (ed.). *Critical Essays on Thomas Mann*. Boston, MA: Hall: 238-65.

Kurzke, Hermann. 2002. *Thomas Mann: Life As A Work of Art* (tr. Leslie Willson). Princeton, NJ: Princeton UP.

Lawson, Lewis A. 1996a. "The Dream Screen in *The Moviegoer*" in *Still Following Percy*. Jackson, MS: UP of Mississippi: 29-55.

--. 1996b. "Will Barrett and the 'the fat rosy temple of Juno'" in *Still Following Percy*. Jackson, MS: UP of Mississippi: 161-79.

Lehmann, Herbert. 1970. "Sigmund Freud and Thomas Mann". *Psychoanalytic Quarterly* 39: 198-214.

Lehnert, Herbert. 1964. "Thomas Mann's Early Interest in Myth and Erwin Rohde's *Psyche*". *PMLA* 79: 297-304.

Lesér, Esther H. 1989. *Thomas Mann's Short Fiction: An Intellectual Biography*. Rutherford, NJ: Fairleigh Dickinson UP.

Lewin, Bertram D. 1953. "Reconsideration of the Dream Screen", *Psychoanalytic Quarterly* 22:174-99

--. 1946. "Sleep, the Mouth, and the Dream Screen". *Psychoanalytic Quarterly* 15: 419-35.

Lubell, Winifred Milius. 1994. *The Metamorphosis of Baubo*. Nashville, TN: Vanderbilt UP.

Lubich, Frederick A. 2002. "*The Confessions of Felix Krull, Confidence Man*" in Robertson, Ritchie (ed.) *The Cambridge Companion to Thomas Mann*. Cambridge: Cambridge UP: 199-212.

--. 1993. "*Thomas Manns Der Zauberberg: Spukschloss der Grossen Mutter oder Die Männerdämmerung des Abendlandes*". *Deutsche Vierteljahrsschrift für Literaturwissenschaft und Geistesgeschichte* 67: 729-63.

--. 1994. "Thomas Mann's Sexual Politics—Lost in Translation". *Comparative Literature Studies* 31: 107-27.

McDonald, William E. 1999. *Thomas Mann's Joseph and His Brothers: Writing, Performance, and the Politics of Loyalty*. Rochester, NY: Camden.

McDougall, Joyce. 1985. *Theaters of the Mind: Illusion and Truth on the Psychoanalytic Stage*. New York, NY: Basic.

McWilliams, James R. 1983. *Brother Artist: A Psychological Study of Thomas Mann's Fiction*. Lanham, MD: UP of America.

Magee, Bryan. 1988. *Aspects of Wagner*. Oxford: Oxford UP.

Mann, Erika. 1958. *The Last Year of Thomas Mann* (tr. Richard Graves). New York, NY: Farrar.

--. (ed.). 1961. *Thomas Mann Briefe*, vols. I-III. Frankfurt: S. Fischer.

Mann, Erika, and Klaus Mann. 1939. *Escape to Life*. Boston, MA: Houghton.

Mann, Golo. 1965. "Memories of my Father" in *Thomas Mann*. Bonn: Inter Nationes: 5-20.

--. 1990. *Reminiscences and Reflections* (tr. Krishna Winston). New York, NY: Norton.

Mann, Katja. 1975. *Unwritten Memories* (eds Elisabeth Plessen and Michael Mann, tr. Hunter and Hildegarde Hannum). New York, NY: Knopf.

Mann, Monika. 1960. *Past and Present* (tr. Frances F. Reid and Ruth Hein). New York, NY: St. Martin's P.

Mann, Viktor. 1964. *Wir waren fünf*. Sec. Ed. Konstanz: Südverlag.

Manniche, Lise. 1987. *Sexual Life in Ancient Egypt*. London: KPI.

Meletinsky, Eleazar M. 1998. *The Poetics of Myth* (tr. Guy Lanoue and Alexandre Sadetsky). New York, NY: Garland.

--. (ed.). 1982. *Tagebücher, 1940-1943*. Frankfurt: Fischer.

Menn, Esther. 1997. *Judith and Tamar (Genesis 38) in Ancient Jewish Exegesis*. New York, NY: Leiden.

Metzger, B. M. 1963. "Pseudepigrapha" in Grant, Frederick C. and H. H. Rowley (eds) *Dictionary of the Bible*. New York, NY: Scribner's: 820-21.

Meyer, Agnes E. 1968. "Thomas Mann in America" in Neider, Charles (ed.) *The Stature of Thomas Mann*. Freeport, NY: Books: 326-29.

Morford, Mark P. O., and Robert J. Lenardon. 1977. *Classical Mythology*. Sec. Ed. New York: Longman.

Morton, Frederic. 1955. "A Talk with Thomas Mann at Eighty" in *The New York Times Book Review* (5 June 1955): 6, 32-33.

Motz, Lotte. 1997. *The Faces of the Goddess*. Oxford: Oxford UP.

Murray, John. 1892. *A Handbook for Travellers in Southern Italy and Sicily*. Ninth Ed. London: Murray.

Mylonas, George E. 1961. *Eleusis and the Eleusinian Mysteries*. Princeton, NJ: Princeton UP.

Napier, A. David. 1986. *Masks, Transformation, and Paradox*. Berkeley, CA: U of California P.

Nathanson, Donald L. 1992. *Shame and Pride: Affect, Sex, and the Birth of the Self*. New York, NY: Norton.

Neider, Charles. 1968. "The Artist as Bourgeois".in Neider, Charles (ed.) *Stature of Thomas Mann*. Freeport, NY: Books. 330-57.

Nemerov, Howard. 1963. "Themes and Methods in the Early Stories of Thomas Mann" in *Poetry and Fiction: Essays*. New Brunswick, NJ: Rutgers UP: 288-302.

Neugroschel, Joachim (tr.). 1998. "Little Herr Friedemann" in Neugroschel, Joachim (ed.) *Death in Venice and Other Tales*. New York, NY: Viking: 21-50.

Neumann, Erich. 1955. *The Great Mother* (tr. Ralph Manheim). Princeton, NJ: Princeton UP, 1955.

Nilsson, Martin P. 1980. *A History of Greek Religion* (tr. F. J. Fielden). Westport, CT: Greenwood.

Oswald, Victor A. 1948. "Thomas Mann's *Doctor Faustus*: The Enigma of Frau von Tolna". *Germanic Review* 23: 249-53.

Otto, Walter F. 1965. *Dionysus: Myth and Cult* (tr. Robert B. Palmer). Bloomington: Indiana UP, 1965.

Papachadzis, N. D. 1971. "Religion in the Archaic Period" in Christopoulos, George A. (ed.) and Philip Sherrard (tr.) *History of the Hellenic Period: The Archaic Period*. London: Heinemann: 74-101.

Parkes-Perret, Ford B. 1996. "'Myth plus Psychology' in Thomas Mann's *'Der kleine Herr Friedemann'*". *Neophilologus* 80: 275-96.

Paterson, James. 1963. "Hosea" in Grant, Frederick C. and H. H. Rowley (eds) *Dictionary of the Bible*. New York, NY: Scribner's: 397-98.

Patterson, John. 1963. "Marriage" in Grant, Frederick C. and H. H. Rowley (eds) *Dictionary of the Bible*. New York, NY: Scribner's: 623-28.

Peacock, Ronald. 1988. "Much Is Comic in Thomas Mann" in Ezergailis, Inta Miske (ed.) *Critical Essays on Thomas Mann*. Boston, MA: Hall: 175-91.

Phillips, Adam. 1993. *On Kissing, Tickling, and Being Bored:Psychoanalytic Essays on the Unexamined Life*. Cambridge, MA: Harvard UP.

Pollack, Rachel. 1997. *The Body of the Goddess*. Shaftsbury: Element.

Power, E. 1953a. "Exodus" in Orchard, Bernard (ed.) *A Catholic Commentary on Holy Scripture*. New York, NY: Nelson: 206-28.

--. 1953b. "The History of Israel (to 130 B.C.)" in Orchard, Bernard (ed.) *A CatholicCommentary on Holy Scripture*. New York, NY: Nelson. 84-102.

Prater, Donald. 1995. *Mann: A Life*. Oxford: Oxford UP.

Pringsheim, Heinz Gerhard. 1905. *Archäologische Beiträge zur Geschichte des eleusinischen Kults*. Munich, Germany: C. Wolf.

Prutti, Brigitte. 1990. "Women Characters in Doctor Faustus" in Lehnert, Herbert, and Peter C. Pfeiffer (eds) *Thomas Mann's DoctorFaustus: A Novel at the Margin of Modernism*. Columbia, SC: Camden. 99-112.

Rank, Otto. 1932. *Art and the Artist: Creative Urge and Personality Development*. New York, NY: Tudor.

--. 1992. *The Incest Theme in Literature and Legend: Fundamentals of a Psychology of Literary Creation* (tr. Gregory C. Richter). Baltimore: Johns Hopkins UP.

Reed, T. J. 1996. *Thomas Mann: The Uses of Tradition*. Sec. Ed. Oxford: Clarendon P.

Reich, Annie. 1973. "The Structure of the Grotesque-Comic Sublimation" in *Psychoanalytic Contributions*. New York, NY: International UP: 99-120.

Reik, Theodor. 1965. *Fragments of a Great Confession*. New York, NY: Citadel.

Ridley, Hugh. 1994. *The Problematic Bourgeois: Twentieth-Century Criticism on Thomas Mann's Buddenbrooks and The Magic Mountain*. Columbia, SC: Camden.

Rohde, Erwin. 1972. *Psyche: The Cult of Souls and Belief in Immortality among the Greeks* (tr. W. B. Hillis from the eighth ed). Freeport, NY: Books.

Rose, H. J. 1959. *A Handbook of Greek Mythology*. New York, NY: Dutton.

Rudnytsky, Peter L. 1992. "Introductory Essay" (tr. Gregory C. Richter) in Rank, Otto *The Incest Theme in Literature and Legend: Fundamentals of a Psychology of Literary Creation*. Baltimore, MD: Johns Hopkins UP: xxi-xxxv.

Runes, Dagobert D., and Harry G. Schrickel (eds). 1946. *Encyclopedia of the Arts*. New York, NY: Philosophical L.

Russell, Francis. 1967. *The World of Dürer: 1471-1528*. New York, NY: Time.

Rycroft, Charles. 1968. *Anxiety and Neurosis*. Harmonsworth: Penguin.

--. 1951. "A Contribution to the Study of the Dream Screen". *International Journal of Psycho-Analysis* 32: 178-85.

Saydon, P. P. 1953. "Daniel" in Orchard, Bernard (ed.) *A Catholic Commentary on Holy Scripture*. New York, NY: Nelson: 494-513.

Scheffauer, Herman George (tr.). 1928. *Children and Fools.* (containing first English tr. of "Little Herr Friedemann"). New York: Knopf.

Schneider, Ursula W. 1995. *Ars amandi: The Erotic of Extremes in Thomas Mann and Marguerite Duras*. New York, NY: Lang.

Schoolfield, George C. 1956. *The Figure of The Musician in German Literature. University of North Caroline Studies in the Germanic Languages and Literature*, Number 19. Chapel Hill, NC: U of North Carolina P.

Settage, Calvin F. 1980. "The Psychoanalytic Theory and Understanding of Psychic Development During the Second and Third Years of Life" in Greenspan, S. I. and G. H. Pollock (eds) *The Course of Life: Psychoanalytic Contributions Toward Understanding Personality Development, Vol. I: Infancy and Early Childhood*. Adelphi, MD: NIMH: 523-39.

Share, Lynda. 1994. *If Someone Speaks, It Gets Lighter: Dreams and the Reconstruction of Infant Trauma*. Hillsdale, NJ: Analytic P.

Slochower, Harry. 1937. *Three Ways of Modern Man*. New York, NY: International .

Sperber, Michael A. 1972. "Freud, Tausk, and the Nobel Prize Complex". *Psychoanalytic Review* 59: 282-93.

--. 1972. "Symbiotic Psychosis and the Need for Fame". *Psychoanalytic Review* 61: 517-34.

Stern, Karl. 1965. *The Flight from Woman*. London: Unwin.

Stock, Irvin. 1994. *Ironic Out of Love: The Novels of Thomas Mann*. Jefferson, NC: McFarland.

Storr, Anthony.1992. *Music and the Mind*. New York, NY: Ballantine.

Stuart-Macadam, Patricia. 1998. "Iron deficiency anemia: exploring the difference" in Grauer, Anne L., and Patricia Stuart-Macadam (eds) *Sex and Gender in Paleopathological Perspective*. Cambridge: Cambridge UP: 45-64.

Suhr, Elmer G. 1967. *Before Olympos: A Study of the Aniconic Origins of Poseidon, Hermes and Eros*. New York, NY: Helios.

Sutcliffe, E. F. 1953a. "Genesis" in Orchard, Bernard (ed.) *A Catholic Commentary on Holy Scripture*. New York, NY: Nelson: 177-205.

--. 1953b. "Job" in Orchard, Bernard (ed.) *A Catholic Commentary on Holy Scripture*. New York, NY: Nelson: 417-41.

Tartakoff, Helen H. 1966. "The Normal Personality in Our Culture and the Nobel Prize Complex" in Loewenstein, Rudolph M. (ed.) *Psychoanalysis—A General Psychology*. New York: International UP: 222-52.

Thacker, T. W. 1963. "Potiphar" in Grant, Frederick C. and H. H. Rowley (eds) *Dictionary of the Bible*. New York, NY: Scribner's: 783.

Thirlwall, John C. 1950. "Orphic Influences in *The Magic Mountain*, or Plato, Christ, and Peeperkorn". *Germanic Review* 25: 290-98.

Thomas, Clayton L., (ed.). 1981. *Taber's Cyclopedic Medical Dictionary*. Fourteenth Ed. Philadelphia, PA: Davis.

Trevelyan, Humphry. 1981. *Goethe & the Greeks (*foreword by Hugh Lloyd-Jones). Cambridge: Cambridge UP.

Underhill, Evelyn. 1955. *Mysticism*. New York, NY: Noonday P.

Wagner, Nike. 1998. *The Wagners: The Dramas of a Musical Dynasty* (tr. Ewald Osers and Michael Downes). Princeton, NJ: Princeton UP.

Walker, Barbara G. 1983. *The Woman's Encyclopedia of Myths and Secrets*. San Francisco, CA: Harper.

Wangh, Martin. 1979. "Some Psychoanalytic Observations on Boredom". *International Journal of Psycho-Analysis* 60: 515-27.

Wedekind-Schwertner, Barbara. 1984. *"Dass ich eins und doppelt bin"*. *Studien zur Idee der Androgynie unter besonderer Berücksichtigung Thomas Manns*. Frankfurt: Lang.

Weigand, Hermann J. 1988. "Thoughts on the Passing of Thomas Mann" in Ezergailis, Inta Miske (ed.) *Critical Essays on Thomas Mann*.Boston, MA: Hall: 11-24.

Weisinger, Kenneth. 1990. "Distant Oil Rigs and Other Erections" in Dowden, Stephen E. (ed.) *A Companion to Thomas Mann's The Magic Mountain*. Columbia, SC: Camden: 177-220.

Westcott, Glenway. 1962. "Thomas Mann: Will Power and Fiction". *Images of Truth*. New York, NY: Harper: 164-241.

Wevers, John William. 1963. "Song of Songs (or Canticles)" in Grant, Frederick C. and H. H. Rowley (eds) *Dictionary of the Bible*. New York, NY: Scribner's: 930-31.

Willoughby, Harold R. 1963. "Artemis" in Grant, Frederick C. and H. H. Rowley (eds) *Dictionary of the Bible*. New York, NY: Scribner's: 57-58.

Winston, Richard. 1981.*Thomas Mann: The Making of an Artist, 1875-1911*. New York, NY: Knopf.

Winston, Richard, and Clara Winston (eds). 1975. *An Exceptional Friendship: The Correspondence of Thomas Mann and Erich Kahler* (tr. Richard and Clara Winston). Ithaca, NY: Cornell UP.

--. 1971 (eds). *Letters of Thomas Mann: 1889-1955*. (tr. Richard and Clara Winston, intro. Richard Winston). NY: Knopf.

Wolman, Benjamin B. (ed.). 1973. *Dictionary of Behavioral Science*. New York, NY: Van Nostrand.

Wurmser, Leon. 1981. *The Mask of Shame*. Baltimore, MD: Johns Hopkins UP.

Wysling, Hans (ed.). 1998. *Letters of Heinrich and Thomas Mann, 1900-1949* (tr. Don Reneau). Berkeley, CA: U of California P.

Zimmer, Heinrich. 1968. "The Indian World Mother" in Campbell, Joseph (ed.). *The Mystic Vision: Papers from the Eranos Yearbooks* (tr. Ralph Manheim). Princeton, NJ: Princeton UP: 70-102.

Index

Degener, Hermann A. L., 184
delophilia, 48, 49, 52
Demeter, 157, 173, 183-90, 195-96,
    238, 240, 301, 302, 306, 402,
    405, 409n2
Deri, Susan, 21
Derleth, Ludwig, 100, 138-39n22
Dierks, Manfried, 221, 319, 361n5
Dionysos (Dionysus), 142n6, 157,
    186, 191, 192, 193, 194, 198,
    199, 200, 201, 205, 206, 207,
    211
doubleness (duality, original unity),
    25, 131-32, 136-37n17, 143n42,
    157, 190, 200, 210, 229, 258-
    59n13, 343, 369, 386, 388-89,
    398, 402
dream screen, the, 16-19, 27n13, 78,
    180, 273, 274, 277
Dumoulié, Camille, 50, 51, 52, 158,
    173, 174
Edelman, Sandra, 37, 38, 157
Ehrenberg, Paul, 80, 95, 337, 352
Ehrenzweig, Anton, 47, 53
Eissler, Kurt Robert, 260, 274-81,
    282n5, 283n7, 287
Elsaghe, Yahya, 261, 270
Elworthy, Frederick T., 158
Evans, Ivor H., 41, 56, 69, 88, 102,
    162, 211, 215, 250, 309, 361n4,
    392, 393, 396
exhibition(ism, ist, istic), 12, 22n5,
    25n9, 48, 52, 136n17, 137n17,
    220, 241, 244, 255, 256, 259n14,
    344
Ezergailis, Inta Miske, 23n8, 46, 157,
    173, 177, 340
Feldman, Thalia, 37, 38, 217n4, 405
Fellner, Rudolph, 122
Fetzer, John F., 314, 330, 331, 341,
    342, 348, 360n4, 363n10
Feuerlicht, Ignace, 13
Fischer, Gottfried Berman, 272
Fischer, Samuel, 68
Frazer, James, 22n6, 248
Freud, Sigmund, on infantile
    sexuality, 8-9, 21n3, 145-46, 209,
    221; on the Oedipus (and "pre-
    oedipal") complex, 12, 13, 23-
25n9, 67, 138n18, 145-46, 151,
198, 217n6, 223, 237-38, 242-43,
244, 248, 255, 257, 258n4, 280-
81, 283n7, 299n5, 368, 372, 379,
389n2, 407; on the castration
complex, 12, 28n16, 251, 278,
279; on the oceanic feeling, 12,
14, 23n8, 61, 70, 93, 94, 148,
153, 170, 202, 333, 339, 342,
387, 389n2, 407, 413; on the fear
of being poisoned, 13, 34,
139n24, 277, 313-14, 315, 334,
335, 351, 357, 358; on the return
(or irruption) of the repressed, 7,
13, 18, 42, 44, 52, 54, 71, 73, 79,
84, 85, 90, 91, 92, 102, 108, 132,
134n4, 136-37n17, 150, 154, 161-
62, 164, 195, 198, 208, 210, 211,
216-17n3, 219-20, 221, 222, 224,
232-33n4, 251, 256, 269-70, 281,
288, 304, 314, 319, 320, 323,
324, 329, 331, 337-38, 339, 349,
351, 353, 355, 357, 359-60n1,
367, 377, 380, 404; on dreaming,
14-19, 27n13, 45, 76-79, 116-18,
142-43n39, 163, 180-91, 221,
236-37, 267, 274, 383, 414; on
the skin ego, 10-11, 23n7, 134-
35n6, 368, 368-69, 373; on artistic creativity, 21-22n5, 24-26n9,
116-18, 119, 142n34, 142n39,
143n42, 205, 220-21, 222, 223,
224, 225, 243, 262, 266, 270,
274, 281, 288, 303, 314, 336,
337, 338, 339, 343, 345, 346,
349, 351, 354, 355, 356, 357,
360, 363n9, 380, 381, 389-
40n3,404, 408; on homosexuality
("inversion"), 26-27n12, 28, 78,
82, 110, 116, 132, 134n3, 135n7,
142n35, 142n36, 337, 352-54,
382, 389n1, 389-90n3, 391; on
the loss of the original object,
28n16, 60, 81, 151, 165, 166,
336, 368-69; on screen memories,
48; on hysteria, 31; on railway
travel, 76-77; on the oral phase,
34, 150, 190, 213, 216, 281; on
the uncanny, 52, 59-60, 134n4,

143n42, 179, 203-04, 206, 207, 217n8, 230, 253, 254, 289, 295, 313-14, 315, 315-16, 17, 324, 325, 326, 328, 329, 331, 333, 334, 335, 336, 339, 341, 342, 346, 347, 355, 359-60n1, 360-61m4,366, 367, 369, 371; on the collective unconscious, 191; on mourning, 219; on Jensen's *Gradiva*, 221; on taboo, 97, 109, 222, 223, 225, 233n4, 238, 239, 265, 285, 370; on Thomas Mann, 226; on god-formation, 239-40; on regression to infantilism, 367; on the rescuing fantasy, 372

Fuller, B. A. G., 104

Gilmour, S. MacLean, 250

Goethe, von, Johann Wolfgang, 107, 174, 182, 260, 275, 282n2, 286, 287, 299n1, 310, 377; his *Faust,* 172, 173, 174, 175, 238, 241, 262, 274, 282n5, 283n7, 306, 340; his *Dichtung und Wahrheit*, 235, 238, 255, 275, 276, 278; in *The Beloved Returns*, 260-83; his *Sorrows of Young Werther*, 261-62

Gorgon (Gorgoneion), 37-39, 40, 41, 42, 47, 49, 51, 69, 75, 139n23, 140n27, 156, 157-60, 171, 190, 204, 229, 254, 256, 258-59n13, 287-88, 293, 294, 340, 373, 404-06, 413

Gottwald, Norman, 361n4,

Grautoff, Otto, 30, 31, 32, 33, 61, 76, 80, 135-36n15, 363n8

Graves, Robert, 39, 169, 171, 185, 203

Gray, John, 308

Greenacre, Phyllis, 258n4

Grimstad, Kirsten, 323

grotesque, the, 7, 21n4, 59, 160, 220, 249, 254, 261, 287, 288, 289, 293, 294, 328, 342, 365, 407

Gutheil, Emil A., 37, 45, 72, 77, 241, 250, 251, 372

Guthrie, W. K. C., 186, 187

Hamburger, Käte, 296

Hamilton, Edith, 168, 187, 306

Hamilton, Nigel, 8, 9, 10, 12, 26n11, 29, 30, 81, 104, 209, 226

Harewood, the Earl of, 229

Harrison, Irving B., 179

Harrison, Jane, 38, 195, 207

Hartwich, Wolf-Daniel, 257

Hatfield, Henry, 258n8, 340,

Hauptmann, Gerhard, 139n26

Hayman, Ronald, 8, 11, 14, 16, 20n1, 26n11, 29, 30, 31, 32, 41, 43, 45, 47, 61, 80, 81, 86, 104, 105, 106, 107, 115, 123, 129, 135n9, 143n40, 197, 231n1, 237, 332, 337, 360n2, 363n8, 377, 382, 383, 384, 385, 387, 389, 389-90n3, 391, 396-97n1, 401, 409n1, 411

Hecate, 157

Heilbut, Anthony, 8, 13, 14, 16, 20n1, 26n11, 30, 32, 35, 36, 39, 41, 42, 43, 52, 59, 95, 97, 98, 104, 107, 114, 124, 135n11, 135n12, 138n22, 140n26, 140n28, 142n35, 164, 181, 181-82, 205, 208, 216n1, 220, 231, 258n12, 300n6, 314, 332, 377, 381, 384, 389-90n3, 391

Heilman, Robert B., 407

Heller, Erich, 145, 152-53

Hera, 69

Hermes, 8, 11, 13, 27n12, 35-36, 37, 60, 127, 162, 181, 182, 187, 193, 194, 258n8, 379, 380, 381, 389n3

hermetic, the, 49, 170, 190, 209, 210, 212, 213-14, 216

Hildebrandt, Paul, 118

Hirschbach, Frank Donald, 43, 44, 160

Hitler, 140n26

Hochstapler, der, (the impostor, the confidence man), 8, 123, 124, 126, 236, 237, 243, 245, 247, 248, 250, 256, 257n1, 258n2, 258n4, 258n8, 276, 377, 398, 408

Hoffman, E.T.A., 136n16

Hoffman, Frederick J., 216n2

352, 363n9, 365, 377, 380, 391, 408, 413
Wurmser, Leon, 47, 48, 52, 88, 181
Wysling, Hans, 26, 30, 33, 81, 84, 96, 100, 101, 105, 108, 115, 116,

124, 140n28, 257, 271, 273, 408
Zimmer, Heinrich, 287-298, 299n2, n3
Zola, Émile, 227, 258; his *Nana*, 46, 133-34n